Marbles
Illustrated

Robert Block

4880 Lower Valley Road, Atglen, PA 19310 USA

Published by Schiffer Publishing Ltd.
4880 Lower Valley Road
Atglen, PA 19310
Phone: (610) 593-1777;
Fax: (610) 593-2002
E-mail: Schifferbk@aol.com
Please visit our web site catalog at
www.schifferbooks.com

In Europe, Schiffer books are distributed by Bushwood Books
6 Marksbury Avenue Kew Gardens
Surrey TW9 4JF England
Phone: 44 (0)181 392-8585;
Fax: 44 (0)181 392-9876
E-mail: Bushwd@aol.com

This book may be purchased from the publisher.
Include $3.95 for shipping. Please try your bookstore first.
We are interested in hearing from authors with book ideas on related subjects.
You may write for a free printed catalog.

CONTENTS

ACKNOWLEDGMENTS

No book is written by the author alone. First, I'd like to acknowledge the thousands of marble collectors who have consigned to the Chip Off The Old Block CyberAuctions and who have participated as bidders. You have made the CyberAuctions a great success and I thank you. Second, I'd be remiss if I didn't acknowledge the tremendous contribution made by the Marble Collectors Society of America and by my parents, Stan and Claire Block, to the hobby of marble collecting. Finally, considering the amount of aggravation that I caused Peter Schiffer and his staff, I have to acknowledge their superb level of professionalism and dedication.

INTRODUCTION

All marble books currently in print list the author's best estimate of the average value for average examples. They do not tell you the prices for which marbles have actually been sold. The actual price of a marble depends on a number of factors. In a perfect marketplace, the actual value of a marble would be determined by rarity, size and condition. Those factors are fairly objective and can be quantified with relative ease by any collector with a little practice. But, every marble is different (they are not a commodity item), and the antique and collectibles marketplace is an inherently imperfect market. The price of a marble at any particular point in time is determined by factors other than rarity, size and condition. That value is also determined by eye appeal and by the emotions of the person(s) trying to purchase and sell it. This book reports the actual prices realized for actual, individual marbles.

The actual realized auction price for over 6,900 lots of marbles are reported in this book. This is a price record of every lot sold in A Chip Off The Old Block CyberAuctions during 1998 (CyberAuctions #54 through #186). Almost 5,200 of those lots are individual marbles.

This book consists of two parts. Part One lists, for each major marble type, the ten to fifteen individual lots selling for the highest price. This is a total of about 250 marbles, each one individually illustrated. Part Two lists every lot sold during 1998 and reports the actual price realized. They are grouped by marble type and subtype, and then sorted in price order, for easy reference.

A CHIP OFF THE OLD BLOCK

A Chip Off The Old Block has been an innovator in the use of the Internet to conduct auctions. We conduct marble "CyberAuctions" three nights a week. These auctions are conducted live in an Internet chat room. The CyberAuctions are the oldest "live" auction on the Internet. In fact, only eBay™ has been conducting any type of auction on the Internet for a longer period of time, and that is a "proxy" auction, not a live auction. A Chip Off The Old Block was the first auctioneer to conduct auctions completely live on the Internet. They also conducted the first simultaneous live Internet/on-site auction at the Philadelphia MarbleFest in 1995. More information on A Chip Off The Old Block and the CyberAuctions may be found at www.blocksite.com and at www.auctionblocks.com

1998 ANALYSIS

The marble market really consists of several segments. The first segmentation of the total market is Handmade Marbles, Machine Made Marbles, and Non-Glass Marbles. Each of those sub-markets can be further subdivided into smaller markets. Generally, handmades are classified by type of construction (swirl, end of day, etc.) and machine mades are classified by manufacturer (Akro Agate Company, etc.).

For each lot in A Chip Off The Old Block auctions, a value estimate is published in the catalogue. Catalogue estimates are consistently applied across lots in an auction. And catalogue estimates tend to lag behind changes in overall pricing (since we do not know whether a change is a temporary increase or decrease, or if it is permanent). Measuring the realized prices against the catalogue estimates can give us a sense for which segments of the market are strong and which are soft. The 1998 results are as follows:

Segment	% of Estimate
Akro Agate Company	123%
Christensen Agate Company	117%
Contemporary Handmade	111%
End of Day	108%
Lutz	94%
M.F. Christensen and Company	126%
Marble King, Inc.	111%
Master Marble/Glass Company	116%
Non-Glass Handmade	114%
Other Handmade	114%
Other Machine Made	101%
Peltier Glass Company	115%
Sulphide	98%
Swirl	108%
Transitional	109%

On average in 1998, all lots sold for 111% of estimate. Based on that, we could say that lutzes · and sulphides were lagging the rest of the marble types in 1998. Additionally, Akro Agate, Christsensen Agate, M.F. Christensen, Master Marble and Peltier Glass marbles were performing better than the rest of the market. The remaining categories performed at about the market average.

Most collectors know that condition is an important determinant of value. During the past couple of years, we have seen Mint examples bring higher premiums, while non-Mint examples have continued to sell at a discount. This trend has continued during 1998. Mint (9.9-9.0) examples sold on average at 121% of catalogue estimate, Near Mint (8.9-8.0) examples at 98% on average and Good (7.9-7.0) examples at 76% on average.

The hobby continues to experience positive growth, both in terms of prices and in terms of the number of collectors active in the field. While the various Internet auctions and websites seem to be having some effect on the attendance at marble shows, we continue to see more marble shows being run around the country.

In addition, several books on marble playing were published during 1998. Marble playing continues to be a positive activity for kids and marble collecting continues to be a fun hobby.

Expanded Listings:

Handmade and Machine Made Marbles

HANDMADE MARBLES
SWIRL

Divided core. Superior colored glass divided core swirl in English colors from near an end of the cane. Transparent teal base glass. A white band and an yellow band in the center. Offset from that are two white strands and one yellow strand. Surface is pristine with just one melted spot of dirt on it from manufacturing. Stunning marble. Very rare. Germany, circa 1880-1915. 1-3/8". Mint (9.8). $650. (Auction #89, lot #50).

Joseph Coat. Stunning example. Transparent clear base. Subsurface layer of strands of white, green (with lots of aventurine), blues, reds, black, orange, and some clear spaces. There is a core of the same coloring. Surface is superb! Exceptional example!!! Germany, possibly English, circa 1880-1920. 1". Mint (9.9). $445. (Auction #184, lot #50).

Latticino core. Superior marble. Latticinio core of alternating white and yellow strands. There is an elongated teardrop air bubble inside the net. The outer layer has eight bands. Four are red on yellow, two are green on white, two are blue on white. The only defects I can find on the surface are two very tiny flat spots, and three small cloudy spots (one may possibly be a hit spot. Absolutely unbelievable for a swirl this size!!! I don't think you'd be able to find one in much better shape. Unbelievable! A swirl this size in this condition is about as rare as a Mint Guinea larger than 11/16" or a Mint 3/4" Golden Rebel, to give you some perspective. Germany, circa 1870-1915. 2" (perhaps just a hair under). Mint (9.4). $420. (Auction #71, lot #27).

Latticinio core. Superior marble!! Yellow latticinio core swirl. Six outer bands of transparent red and opaque white. The outstanding thing about this marble is that the surface is as perfect as the day it was made. Has a couple of tiny flat spots from being set down when it was hot. But, there is absolutely no damage on this marble. You will not find a latticinio core swirl anywhere near this size that is in better shape than this one. Absolutely outstanding!!!! Germany, circa 1870-1915. 1-3/4". Mint (9.9). $400. (Auction #76, lot #45).

Solid core. Superior first-off-cane "flower-type" end of cane solid core. Stunning marble. One of the finest examples I have ever seen. These are very rare. Transparent lightly blue tinted base. Core of opaque yellow with bands of transparent pink and two bands of transparent green on it. Outer layer has six evenly spaced white strands. There is no twist to the marble. The design just shoots right out of the top of the marble. Absolutely stunning!!! You will be hard pressed to find a better example. The marble surface has no damage; however, there are both melted glass and manufacturing rough spots, typical of this type. Germany, circa 1870-1915. 3/4". Mint (9.4). $400. (Auction #91, lot #38).

Solid core. A superb three layer caged solid core swirl. Very large marble. Opaque white solid core. The core consists of white bands packed close together. A couple of bands are missing. Middle layer has six transparent pink bands, three transparent green bands and three transparent blue bands. All evenly spaced. Outer layer has twelve yellow strands in a cage pattern. There are some pinpricks on the surface of the marble. One I would term a very tiny chip. The marble views very nicely and this size is very hard to find in anything approaching Mint condition. Unfortunately, I cannot grade this marble as Mint because of the pinpricks, but it is about as close as you can get. Germany, circa 1870-1915. A hair over 2-1/8". Near Mint(+) (8.9). $380. (Auction #147, lot #39).

Solid core. Lot of ten marbles. An unbelievable set of ten matched solid core swirls, all off the same cane. Opaque white core. Outer layer has four bands. Two are red and white. One is green and yellow. The last is blue on pink with yellow. Creates a lavender effect. Outstanding set!!!! Very rare. A couple have melt spots, one has some hits. 9/16" to 19/32". Mint (9.9) to Near Mint(+) (8.8) (only one not Mint). $350. (Auction #178, lot #50).

Ribbon core. Naked single ribbon core swirl. Outstanding design. Ribbon is thin. Opaque white, opaque yellow, transparent blue, transparent red and transparent green. A few small subsurface moons and sparkles. But, you just don't see them that often in these larger sizes. Super marble. It is stunning. The marble views much better than the condition indicates. Rare opportunity. Germany, circa 1870-1915. 1-5/16". Near Mint (8.4). $310. (Auction #150, lot #40).

Latticinio core. Huge first-off-cane white latticinio core swirl in superior condition. Teardrop air bubble inside the white latticinio core. Outer layer has four bands. Two are blue and pink on white, two are pink and green on yellow. All end before the bottom pontil. Base glass has a bottle-green tint to it. One very tiny sparkle near the bottom pontil, one very tiny pinprick. Unbelievable condition for a marble this size. Super opportunity to own a large end of cane swirl. I doubt you will find one in any better condition. Germany, circa 1870-1915. 2-1/8". Mint (9.7). $300. (Auction #150, lot #45).

Solid core. Very unusual marble. Transparent green/blue glass. Solid core of four panels, two different color schemes. Outer layer has a cage of white strands. Thick casing. Surface has a number of subsurface moons, a flake and a couple of small chips. Still, a huge marble and in colored glass. Germany, circa 1870-1915. 2-7/16" (over 2-3/8"), one of the largest swirls I have ever seen. Good (7.5). $295. (Auction #165, lot #21).

Latticinio core. Very interesting swirl, in remarkably Mint condition given the condition of almost every other big hand-made in this collection. White latticinio core. Four outer bands. Two are green, red, white and yellow. Two are blue, red, white and yellow. There are a number of flat, wide air bubbles in that layer. Very, very unusual. Surface has one tiny sparkle, which you don't really notice, as the sub-surface air bubbles sparkle too. Other than that, no damage on the surface. Excellent design and construction. Very unusual. Germany, circa 1870-1915. 2-1/16". Mint(-) (9.1). $290. (Auction #94, lot #51).

Latticinio core. Very rare, larger latticinio core swirl in emerald green glass. You occasionally find these in the smaller size. I can't remember seeing one this big in these larger sizes. Transparent emerald green base. White latticinio core. Outer layer has three narrow opaque white bands alternating with three sets of two white strands. Surface has a couple of tiny chips and a few small subsurface moons. Still, a beauty. Germany, circa 1870-1915. 31/32". Near Mint(-) (8.2). $290. (Auction #160, lot #24).

Solid core. Extremely rare, huge, three layer, solid core, from near the end of the cane. Huge only begins to describe the size of this marble. Opaque white core. Middle layer was to be our transparent pink band, two transparent green and two transparent blue. One pink and one green are only about twenty percent present. The outer layer was supposed to be a cage of sixteen yellow strands. Five are missing and one is partial. Absolutely remarkable!! Probably the second of the cane. One small moon near the top. Two areas of melt pits on the side. A few tiny areas of rough-ness. In spectacular shape for the size. I have to grade it NM+ cause of the moon, but that doesn't do the marble justice. Germany, circa 1870-1915. 2-1/16". Near Mint(+) (8.9). $275. (Auction #100, lot #49).

Latticinio core. Very rare core. Core consists of eighteen strands. Four sets of four white and one bright red. Almost impossible to find. Outer layer has three yellow bands, two transparent green bands and two bright red bands. There is a yellow band missing, air bubble in its place. Very rare marble. And large! Surface has a number of tiny, shallow chips and rough spots and a couple of small, shallow chips. Views remarkably well. Superb marble. Germany, circa 1870-1915. 1-5/8". Near Mint (8.5). $270. (Auction #100, lot #45).

Peppermint with mica. Very rare peppermint swirl with mica. Transparent clear base. Subsurface layer of opaque white, two transparent blue bands and four narrow transparent pink bands. There is mica in the blue on both sides. Two very, very tiny flakes, a couple of pinpricks and some very minor wear. Very difficult to find, and highly sought after. Germany, circa 1870-1915. 9/16". Near Mint(+) (8.8). $270. (Auction #85, lot #43).

Ribbon core. Outstanding example. Single ribbon. Razor thin. Wide. Transparent clear base. Ribbon is white, pink, yellow and green. Ribbon has an excellent twist. Great balance and symmetry. Exceptional example. Surface has three tiny to small pinpricks. In great shape. Super marble. Germany, circa 1870-1915. 13/16". Mint(-) (9.0). $260. (Auction #167, lot #48).

End of cane. Superior and very rare looped first-off-cane swirl. This was a solid core swirl with a white core with pink, blue and green bands, and an outer layer of yellow strands. The marble was folded over when it was made, resulting in the looping "tunnel" pattern. Stunning and very rare. One small chip and a few subsurface moons. Germany, circa 1870-1915. 7/8". Near Mint (8.6). $260. (Auction #85, lot #15).

Divided core. Outstanding example of a large swirl. Core is three bands, very closely space. Almost a solid core. Each band is the same complex pattern of pink, green, yellow and blue on white. Outer layer has three sets of four white strands. Set to mirror each band face. Very symmetrical. Exceptional balance. This one shows excellent design and workmanship. The best thing is that the surface is undamaged!!! Some minor melt and flat spots, as well as some bumpiness, all typical of these large ones. Excellent opportunity!!!! Germany, circa 1870-1915. 1-23/32". Mint (9.7). $250. (Auction #167, lot #44).

Solid core. Superior three layer solid core swirl. Outstanding example. Opaque white core. Middle layer has two bands of pink strands, one of blue strands, and one of green strands, floating above the core. Outer layer has a cage of yellow strands, with one missing. Stunning marble. In super shape. Two tiny pits. You won't find many examples that are bigger or in nicer shape. Germany, circa 1870-1915. 1-5/8". Mint(-) (9.2). $250. (Auction #172, lot #50).

Joseph Coat. Wow!!! Looks just like a Wald Beach Ball, but it's an antique handmade. Transparent clear base. Six panels consisting of strands. Light green, lavender, yellow, dark blue, red, white. Tiny annealing fracture in the lavender panel. Stunning marble. Very, very rare. Germany, circa 1870-1915. 11/16". Mint(-) (9.2). $230. (Auction #85, lot #12).

LUTZ

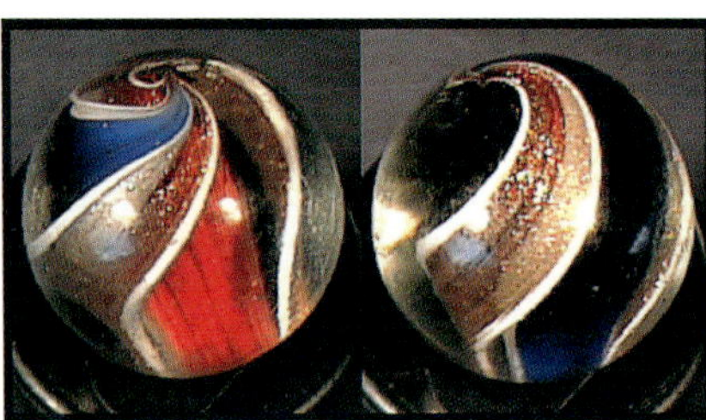

Ribbon. Shooter, in great shape. Transparent clear base. Opaque white core. One face has transparent blue on it, one has transparent red. The ribbon is edged by two wide lutz bands, edged in white. The marble is from somewhere near an end of the cane. The ribbon was shoved off to one side of the marble. However, the lutz bands are properly placed, indicating that the rod drooped after the ribbon was made and while the second layer of clear casing was being placed on it. Larger size. Has a sparkle on it. It is almost impossible to find these larger ones in anything near Mint shape. Germany, circa 1870-1915. 7/8". Mint(-) (9.1). $700. (Auction #168, lot #49).

Indian. One of the rarest types of lutz, if not the rarest. Stunning example of a swirl-type Indian Lutz. Opaque black base. Three bands of lutz on the surface, equidistantly space. One is edged by opaque white, one by opaque gray and one by opaque yellow. An absolute beauty!!! The surface is pristine, with just one very tiny piece of unmelted sand on the black. Almost impossible to find. This one is a superior example! Germany, circa 1870-1915. 19/32". Mint (9.8). This consignment came with the Indian Lutz in Lot 50 of CyberAuction 148. These two may very well have been a matched pair. $700. (Auction #173, lot #50).

Indian. One of the rarest types of lutz, if not the rarest. Stunning example of a swirl-type Indian Lutz. Opaque black base. Three bands of lutz on the surface, equidistantly spaced. One is edged by opaque white, one by opaque gray and one by opaque yellow. An absolute beauty!!! The surface is pristine, with just one very tiny piece of unmelted sand on the black. Almost impossible to find. This one is a superior example! Germany, circa 1870-1915. 19/32". Mint (9.8). $580. (Auction #148, lot #50).

Ribbon. Beautiful ribbon lutz, in outstanding condition. Superior example. Transparent clear base. One ribbon is translucent yellow, the other is translucent light blue. Small air bubble in the blue. The ribbons are edged by bands of lutz, edged in white. Surface is pristine. Superior example. Very hard to find ribbon lutzes (or any lutzes) in any nicer shape. Germany, circa 1870-1915. 9/16". Mint (9.9). $500. (Auction #93, lot #45).

Ribbon. Stunning lutz!!!! You won't find a ribbon much better. The ribbon fills almost the entire core. Fat opaque white ribbon. Transparent blue on one face and transparent pink on the other. Two wide lutz bands, edged in white. Super marble!! Slightly flattened at the top. Germany, circa 1870-1915. 21/32". Mint (9.8). $480. (Auction #113, lot #50).

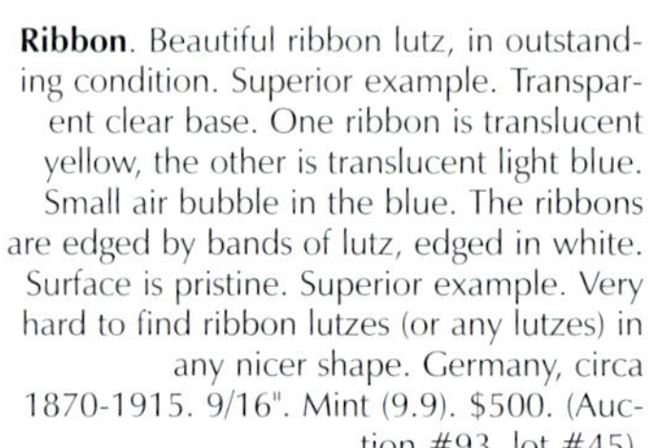

Opaque banded. Extremely rare, first off cane, opaque banded lutz. The first I have ever seen. Opaque black base. Three lutz bands (one is partial). Six light green band (several are partial). Small crease on one end, but the surface is pristine. Absolutely superior marble and extremely rare. Germany, circa 1870-1915. 21/32". Mint (9.9). $490. (Auction #125, lot #50).

Solid core mist. Opaque black core. Core is completely covered by lutz. Cased by transparent clear. One manufacturing melt spot. Several tiny pits. There are several tiny pieces of unmelted sand in the clear layer. Very hard type to find! Germany, circa 1870-1915. 21/32". Near Mint(+) (8.9). $475. (Auction #142, lot #47).

Ribbon. Stunning lutz!!!! You won't find a ribbon much better. The ribbon fills almost the entire core. Fat opaque white ribbon. Transparent green on one face and transparent pink on the other. Two wide lutz bands, edged in white. Super marble!! One small flat spot on the surface. Germany, circa 1870-1915. 21/32". Mint (9.6). $470. (Auction #55, lot #45).

Indian. Another superior example. Opaque black core. Two narrow bands of yellow and white. The two wide black bands are covered by lutz. There is no lutz on the yellow/white bands. Whole marble cased in clear. One tiny melt spot near the top pontil and one barely visible sparkle (partial subsurface moon). Super marble and a very hard type to find. Germany, circa 1870-1915. 19/32". Mint(-) (9.0). $435. (Auction #147, lot #48).

End of day onionskin. Superior end of day onionskin lutz. Core is white with transparent light blue, light pink and light green bands. A tremendous amount of lutz on the core. Completely covers one side of the marble and is fairly heavy on the other side. No twist to the marble. A great example. Germany, circa 1870-1915. 21/32". Mint (9.7). $435. (Auction #103, lot #50).

End of day onionskin. Stunning example of an onionskin lutz, in super shape. Opaque white core. Two wide panels of pink, two narrow panels of blue. Overall lutz on the core, with some heavy bands. Surface in great shape, with one small melt spot near the top. Excellent marble. Paneled onionskin lutzes are hard to find, and you won't find one in much better shape, or with this much lutz. Germany, circa 1870-1915. 3/4". Mint (9.5). $420. (Auction #149, lot #50).

Ribbon. Ribbon core lutz in colored glass. The base glass is blue. Ribbon is fat and opaque white. Edged in lutz. Surface has one flat spot, a minuscule flake and a tiny rough spot. Great coloring and these colored glass ones are very hard to find. One of several colored glass lutzes consigned by one person. Germany, circa 1870-1915. 21/32". Near Mint(+) (8.9). $410. (Auction #140, lot #50).

Mist. Shooter green mist lutz. Hard size to find. Transparent green core. Subsurface layer of lutz completely covering the marble. Superb lutz in this one. Has a large manufacturing dimple on one side with a small pit near it. Still, a stunning marble. Germany, circa 1870-1915. 25/32". Mint(-) (9.0). $405. (Auction #74, lot #45).

Banded. Transparent clear base. Four light green bands. Two white-edged lutz bands. This is an absolutely outstanding example. There are three very tiny very shallow flakes on one side. You simply do not find them this large with this kind of surface. No signs of wear what-soever. I have to classify it as less than Mint because of the three marks, but it seems a shame to do that. It certainly views much better than the condition grade indicates. Super marble. Rare. Germany, circa 1870-1915. 1-1/8". Near Mint(+) (8.9). $400. (Auction #182, lot #48).

Ribbon. Superior shooter ribbon lutz, which unfortunately has one moon. Transparent lavender base glass. Fat opaque white ribbon. Lutz on either ribbon edge. Surface is in pristine shape, except for one hit mark. The subsurface moon is 3/16". Rare color, very hard size to find. Marble is 7/8". Germany, circa 1870-1915. 7/8". Near Mint(+) (8.9). $400. (Auction #100, lot #44).

Ribbon. Ribbon core lutz in colored glass. The base glass is amber. Ribbon is fat and opaque white. Edged in lutz. Surface has one tiny melt spot. This is an exceptional marble. Germany, circa 1870-1915. 21/32". Mint (9.7). $385. (Auction #134, lot #50).

End of day onionskin. Opaque white core with lutz bands on it. Great sparkling and shimmering. The surface on this one is pristine!!! You won't find one in better shape. Definitive example. Germany, circa 1870-1915. 23/32". Mint (9.9). $375. (Auction #81, lot #42).

End of day onionskin. Absolutely outstanding example. One of the most colorful I have ever seen. Superior marble, in pristine shape. Core is opaque white, covered by pink, yellow, blue and green. This then has several bands of lutz on it and other lutz sprinkled on it. Outstanding!!! Germany, circa 1870-1915. 11/16". Mint (9.9). $375. (Auction #124, lot #48).

Ribbon. Ribbon core lutz in colored glass. The base glass is blue. Ribbon is fat and opaque white. Edged in lutz. Surface in great shape. Great coloring and these colored glass ones are very hard to find. One of several colored glass lutzes consigned by one person. Germany, circa 1870-1915. 21/32". Mint (9.7). $370. (Auction #161, lot #50).

END OF DAY

Paneled onionskin. Absolutely stunning four-panel onionskin with mica and slight lobing. Transparent clear glass. Fat opaque white core. Two panels of transparent pink, with a little blue in them. One panel of transparent blue with a little turquoise in it. One panel of transparent turquoise with a little blue in it. Nice sprinkling of mica on the core, not tons, but not incidental either. The two pink panels have a small lobe in them. The core is slightly shrunken on the blue side. One 1/16" scratch and one very tiny rub spot. This marble is huge. In absolutely phenomenal condition, given the size and age. You will be hard-pressed to find an onion with mica that is this large and in this nice a shape. Germany, circa 1870-1915. 2-3/16". Mint(-) (9.1). $1600. (Auction #183, lot #50).

Onionskin. This is one of the finest marbles that I have ever had at auction. Four-panel, four-lobe onionskin. Core is opaque white. Overall pink splotches. A panel of blue splotches and a panel of green splotches. Four very deep lobes. Equidistantly spaced. Almost no twist to the marble. It is absolutely gorgeous. Superlatives cannot begin describe how good looking this marble is. Terrific colors, style and balance. Great workmanship! The surface has one tiny sparkle and one slightly larger one. Both only show up under a very bright light. There is a small flake at the edge of the pontil. However, this occurred when the marble was broken off the rod. The pontil is ground and the grinding is on the flake too. Superior marble!!!! Germany, circa 1870-1915. 1-17/32". $1350. (Auction #167, lot #50).

Paneled onionskin. Absolutely stunning four-panel onionskin, in superior condition. Quite simply, you will be hard-pressed to find one better than this. Opaque white core. Two panels of transparent blue. Two are covered by transparent yellow, with transparent red on it. The core was then flattened on each side, before the outer casing of clear was added. That is, each panel was made flat, so that it was a rectangular rod, not a circular rod. Gives the illusion of slightly lobed panels. Almost no twist to the core, except at the top. The only defects I can find are a tiny pit at the top and a small sparkle on the equator. No scratches or other signs of wear. Outstanding, and very rare!!!! A hair over 2". Mint(-) (9.2). $725. (Auction #176, lot #50).

Onionskin with mica. Stunning marble. Very rare. Two-panel "blizzard mica" onionskin. Transparent clear base. Thin core of opaque white covered by transparent pink. Two subsurface panels of mica covering sixty percent of the marble. This type of mica is called "blizzard" because it is so dense. There is an annealing fracture covering a longitudinal plane, not through the center. Pontil is pointy, it has not been ground or melted. This is a stunning marble. It views perfectly from the side opposite the fracture and views very nicely from all other angles. It will be a great display piece. Surface is perfect. If this marble did not have the fracture, it would carry a low estimate of $1,500. Germany, circa 1870-1915. 1-7/16". $600. (Auction #89, lot #48).

Onionskin. Superior end of day onionskin with mica. Opaque white core with stretched splotches of blue and green. Finely ground mica sprinkled on the core. Super example!! Surface is superb with two tiny melt spots. Stunning!!! Germany, circa 1870-1915. 1-5/16". Mint (9.8). $600. (Auction #145, lot #50).

Cloud. Superior cloud end of day, in absolutely stunning condition!!! Transparent clear base. Core is opaque orange/yellow, almost looks very light mocha brown. Four panels. Two are red splotches and two are green splotches. Some stretching near the bottom pontil, but minimal stretching on the upper half. Three lobes!!! Surface is pristine!!!! Absolutely no signs of wear. The only defect that I can point out is that there is a small area of transparent white on the surface. Rare marble anyway, but you will never find this in better condition!!!! Stunning! Germany, circa 1870-1915. 1-7/16". Mint (9.9). $575. (Auction #159, lot #50).

Onionskin. A fantastic onion-skin. Very rare. Subsurface layer of stretched bands and splotches of white, pink, blue and yellow. Slight left hand twist. The surface shows no wear and is original. Both pontils are ground!!! Stunning marble. A jewel in any collection. Wow!!! Germany, circa 1870-1915. 25/32". Mint (9.8). $525. (Auction #142, lot #49).

Ribbon onionskin. Extremely rare ribbon onionskin. Transparent clear base. Two opposing subsurface panels, each covering about forty percent of the marble. One has transparent blue splotches on opaque white. The other has transparent pink splotches on opaque yellow. Slight left hand twist. The two narrow clear panels each have a narrow band of translucent white. Very, very unusual and rare. Very seldom seen. Surface has a small chip (1/8") near the bottom pontil and a few very tiny subsurface moons. Other than that, no damage. Outstanding example. Germany, circa 1870-1915. 27/32". Near Mint(+) (8.7). $460. (Auction #93, lot #42).

Onionskin cloud. And yet one more stunning marble. Transparent clear base. Core is stretched bands of translucent to opaque colors of white, pink, yellow and green. Lots of clear space in the core. On it are dots and splotches of blue. Very slight left hand twist. Surface is in great shape with a few tiny melted air holes. One tiny manufacturing pit. Bottom pontil is ground. Superior and very hard to find marble!!! Germany, circa 1870-1915. 21/32". Mint (9.7). $450. (Auction #124, lot #50).

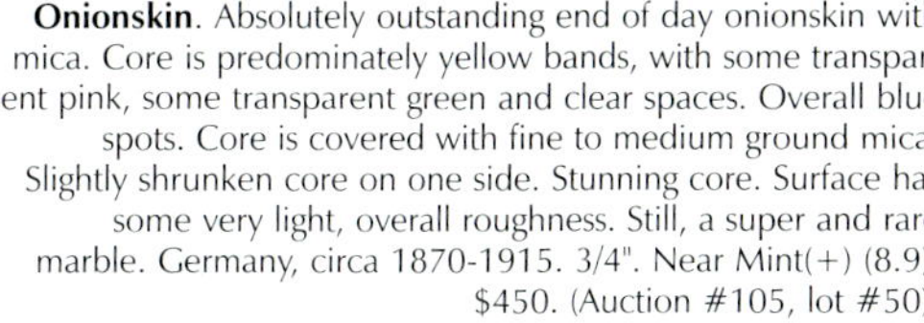

Onionskin. Absolutely outstanding end of day onionskin with mica. Core is predominately yellow bands, with some transparent pink, some transparent green and clear spaces. Overall blue spots. Core is covered with fine to medium ground mica. Slightly shrunken core on one side. Stunning core. Surface has some very light, overall roughness. Still, a super and rare marble. Germany, circa 1870-1915. 3/4". Near Mint(+) (8.9). $450. (Auction #105, lot #50).

Onionskin. Absolutely outstanding example!!! Stunning! Opaque white core. Skin of translucent dark green. Core and skin are close to the surface. In spectacular shape, given its size and age. One tiny sparkle, one very tiny pinprick, one very tiny scratch. I can find no other defect on the surface. This is a superior example! The dark shade of green is not often seen. Germany, circa 1870-1915. 1-9/16". Mint(-) (9.2). $400. (Auction #182, lot #50).

Paneled onionskin. Outstanding example. Four-panel onionskin. Opaque white core. Two panels of transparent green splotches and two of transparent pink. "Smeared" type of coloring. Superb!!! Core has a tiny annealing fracture on it. There are two tiny pits and a couple tiny sparkles. Exceptionally well looking example. Superior. I have not seen many better looking than this one. Germany, circa 1870-1915. 1-11/16". Mint(-) (9.0). $410. (Auction #169, lot #50).

Paneled onionskin. Wow!! This is one of the rarest onionskins I have ever seen. Three panel onionskin with mica!! Three panels of about the same width. One is blue on white, one is pink on white and the last is green and blue on yellow. Overall sprinkling of mica, heavier in two wide bands, almost like panels. Surface has two sparkles (one is a very small subsurface moon) and overall very light haze. You hardly notice the sparkles because of all the mica. Germany, circa 1870-1915. 7/8". Near Mint(+) (8.9). $390. (Auction #91, lot #44).

Paneled Cloud. Unbelievable and very rare four panel cloud. In super shape. A very rare find!!! Two panels of yellow and two of white. Clouds of pink and green on the panels. There are two splotches of white on the surface. Has one small annealing fracture in the core, near the top pontil that travels near the surface. But, the surface is pristine. This marble has seen no damage. The annealing fracture only reflects from one angle. Stunning marble. You will be hard pressed to find one of these in this condition any time soon. Germany, circa 1870-1915. 21/32". Mint(-) (9.2). $380. (Auction #113, lot #42).

Paneled onionskin. Superior and outstanding example of a four panel onionskin. Surface is pristine. Stunning example. You will be hard pressed to find a better one. Two panels of white with some blue, pink and turquoise splotches on it. The other two panels are yellow on the white, with lots of pink, and some blue and turquoise. Surface has two tiny scratches, but it is incredibly clear. Superb example. Germany, circa 1870-1915. 1-9/16". Mint (9.8). $365. (Auction #126, lot #50).

Onionskin. A very rare end of cane (first off cane) four panel onionskin. I could count on one hand the number of these that I have ever seen. And this may very well be the most perfectly formed one. Certainly, you would be hard pressed to find one much better. Transparent clear base. Opaque yellow core with two panels of transparent green and two panels of transparent red. The core ends two-thirds up the marble. The entire top of that core is open, so you can see down into it. Outstanding. About a half dozen very tiny chips and pits. Super marble. Germany, circa 1870-1915. 25/32". Near Mint(+) (8.8). $350. (Auction #80, lot #45).

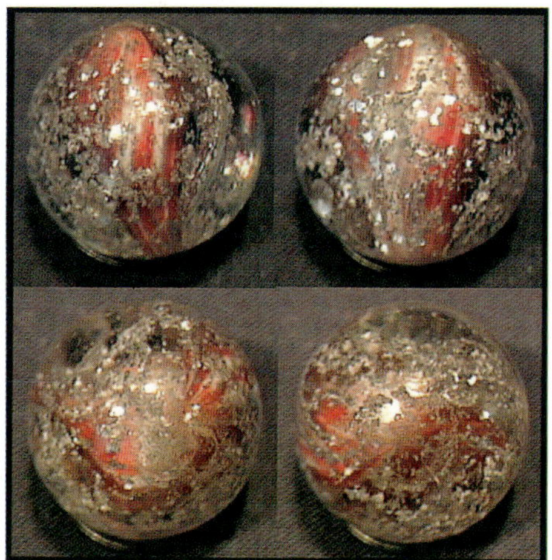

Blizzard. One of the finest looking examples of a blizzard onionskin that I have ever seen. Transparent clear glass. Inner core is an onionskin core in ribbon form. Pink on white. Subsurface layer is a blizzard of mica. Unfortunately, the marble has seen the lightest of buffs, probably to remove a surface haze. Pontils are completely intact. You can see the remnants of tiny hit marks. Only a few remnants visible to the naked eye under a bright light, more visible under a 10x loupe. The sparkle of the mica layer helps this one by hiding the imperfections. While it has been buffed, it is still a very hard type to find. Germany, circa 1870-1915. 3/4". $330. (Auction #154, lot #47).

Onionskin. Very rare onionskin. Larger size. Opaque white core. Stretched splotches of blue and red on it. Three very deep lobes, almost to the center of the marble. This type is very rare. I have shown a top-view of the marble so that you can see the depth of the lobes. Small chips and subsurface moons on the marble, as well as some pits and pinpricking. Nothing deep. I think you could do a very light polish and not take too much glass off, although you will probably lose the pontils. Still, very rare. Germany, circa 1870-1915. 1-1/2". Good (7.9). $330. (Auction #147, lot #26).

Cloud. Superior three-panel end-of-cane (first off) Cloud. Rare marble, excellent opportunity. Opaque white core. One panel each of blue, green and pink clouds. Top quarter of the core is open. Left-hand twist. Since this is the first off the cane, the core is very close to the surface. One tiny chip, just next to the bottom pontil. Outstanding looking marble!!! A stunner! Germany, circa 1870-1915. 13/16". Near Mint(+) (8.9). $300. (Auction #156, lot #46).

SULPHIDE

SULPHIDE. Very rare figure in colored glass. This figure has been called a leprechaun seated on a chair. The glass is emerald green. The figure is very large for the marble and well detailed. Well-centered too. Figure of a small man seated on a chair. Wearing a hat, dressed in a suit. Small body for the head size and short legs for the body size, leading most to conclude that it is a leprechaun or dwarf. One leg is askance. The right hand rests on the leg, the left is on the chest, possibly holding something. Chair back has a heart on it. Super figure. No air bubbling on the figure, although some floating near the surface. Several small and tiny pits, but none interfere with viewing the figure. Very rare opportunity. 1-7/16". (8.8). Pictured on page 71 of *Marble Mania*. $4300. (Auction #168, lot #50).

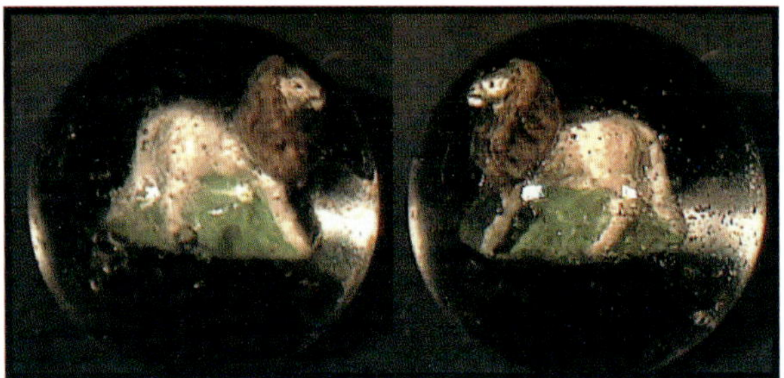

SULPHIDE. Rare hand-painted sulphide. Transparent clear glass. The figure is hand-painted. Standing male lion. Green grass. Brown mane. Black eyes, mouth and nose. Excellent detail to the figure and excellent painting. Set slightly off-center. The surface has some overall very light haze. Two tiny subsurface moons. The very lightest of buffs will reveal an absolute beauty. These hand-painted ones are very, very hard to find and this is one of the nicest figures that I have seen in quite some time. Superb marble. Great opportunity. Germany, circa 1870-1915. 1-3/8". Near Mint (8.6). $2125. (Auction #147, lot #50).

SULPHIDE. Extremely rare sulphide. Disk with image of a laughing boy on both sides. The image is from the shoulders up. Same image on both sides. Disk is set slightly high in the marble. No air bubbles on the image. A couple of small air bubbles between the surface and the disk on one side. Nothing on the other side. Surface has one very tiny pit. Stunning example. This is only the fourth one that I have ever seen. Extremely rare. And this one is in super shape!!! Very rare opportunity. Germany, circa 1870-1915. 1-3/8". Mint(-) (9.0). $1775. (Auction #160, lot #50).

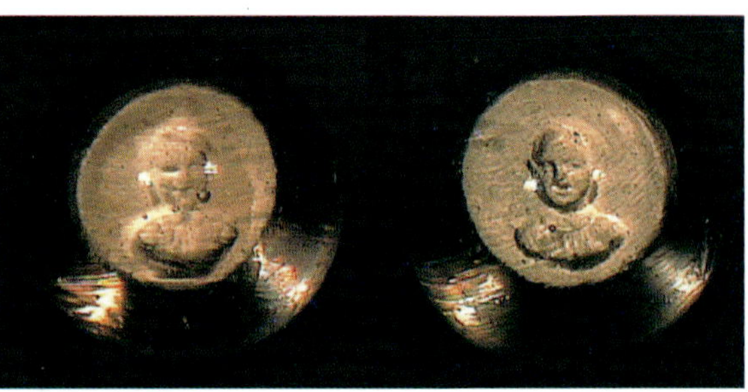

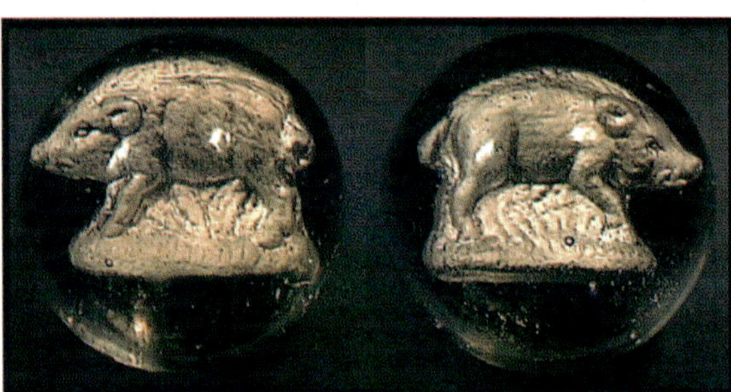

SULPHIDE. The only thing I can say about this marble is WOW! One of the finest sulphides that I have ever seen! Very large figure of a running wild boar. Incredible detail to the figure. You can make out the hooves on his feet, and the two protruding bottom teeth. Great curly tail. Running over some bushes or grass. Nice ridge on his back. Figure has no air bubbling at all. Excellent silvering, and yes, the marble is fluorescent. Figure is set a little high and back, but who cares. Surface is in great shape. Pontil is under the figure. There are some marks on one side that are from manufacturing. Stunning sulphide!! Germany, circa 1870-1915. 1-5/8". Mint (9.8). $550. (Auction #59, lot #45).

SULPHIDE. Hand-painted sulphide. Figure of a reclining ram. Black horns, eyes, eyebrows, nostril and mouth. Reclining on green grass. The unpainted surface of the sulphide figure has excellent silvering. Set slightly off to one side in the marble. No air bubbles! Surface has a small chip at the bottom (you don't even see it when viewing the figure) and several small and tiny subsurface moons and sparkles. A little scratching on the marble surface. Pontil is on the side and well-ground. You can view the figure very well from all angles. None of the wear interferes with viewing. Super marble. Very hard to find. Germany, circa 1870-1915. 1-1/4". Near Mint(-) (8.2). $1085. (Auction #179, lot #50).

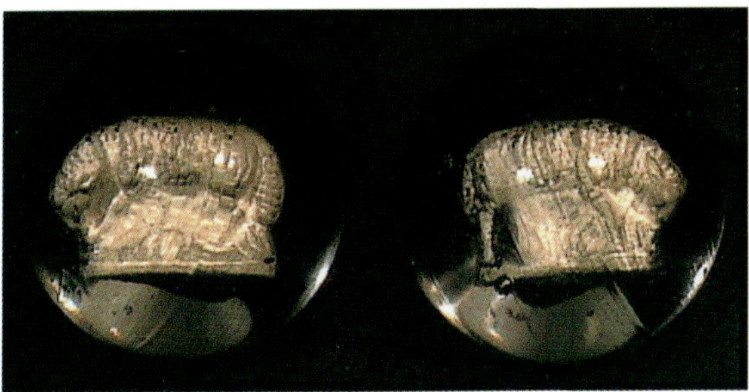

SULPHIDE. Superior, very large sulphide. Figure of a grazing sheep. Exceptional detail to the figure. A little bit of shallow air bubbling on either side, near the base. Small air bubble under the base. Well centered. Excellent silvering and great detail. Surface has one tiny abrasion spot near the bottom and one tiny spot on the back. Pontil is on the side and is ground. Exceptional sulphide, you'll be hard pressed to find one this big in better condition. Germany, circa 1870-1915. 2-1/8". Mint(-) (9.1). $355. (Auction #160, lot #22).

SULPHIDE. Figure of Kate Greenaway. Nice detail to the figure. This is the type with her arms at her side, not holding a purse in front of her. Figure is very slightly off-center. No air bubbles on or near the figure. Surface is real nice, except for a small subsurface moon on one side. You cannot see it when viewing the figure from the front or back. Actually, I missed it the first time I looked at the marble. Germany, circa 1870-1915. 1-3/8". Near Mint(+) (8.9). $350. (Auction #74, lot #38).

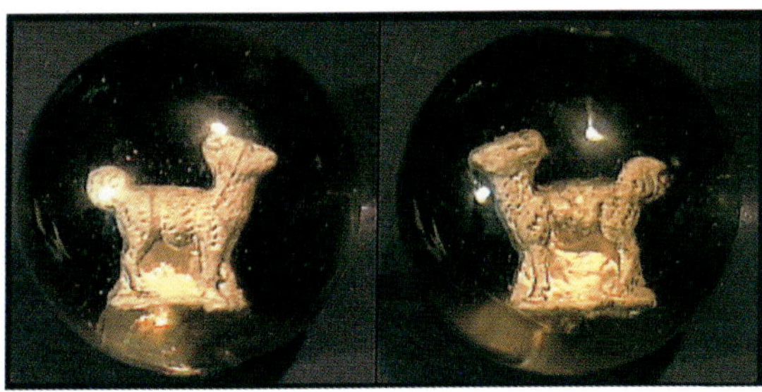

SULPHIDE. Huge marble. Figure is usually called a standing doe or deer. Exceptional detail to the figure. It is set slightly low in the marble, but there are absolutely no air bubbles. The marble is so large it has a slight bottle-glass green tint. Surface has two tiny subsurface moons, as well as several small melt and flat spots. I'm going to have to grade it less than Mint, although quite frankly on a marble this size, the hit marks are inconsequential. Super example, a centerpiece for any sulphide or handmade collection. Germany, circa 1870-1915. 2-5/16". Near Mint(+) (8.9). $340. (Auction #150, lot #48).

SULPHIDE. Figure of a floating angel. Male figure. Figure is floating, with slightly bent knees. Hands are clasped over lower abdomen (covering private parts). Outstretched wings. The wing tips and feet are intact, usually they break off on insertion. Minimal air bubbling on the front of the figure. A small air bubble on the reverse, covering the lower back and upper legs. Figure views very well. The figure is very slightly off to one side. Marble surface has been polished. No pontil. There is the small remnant of a chip on the bottom. Very hard figure to find. Especially with the figure intact and has nice detailing. Germany, circa 1870-1915. 1-9/16". $330. (Auction #58, lot #44).

SULPHIDE. Very nice sulphide in great shape. Figure is a seated dog, head cocked to one side. Excellent detail to the figure. No air bubbles. Set slightly high and slightly off-center. Has a couple of sparkles, but no missing glass. Very light red glass. Super marble. Red is very rare. Germany, circa 1870-1915. 1-1/4". Mint(-) (9.1). $310. (Auction #96, lot #43).

SULPHIDE. Very rare figure. Demonic figure seated on a rock. Naked. Crossed legs. Right hand is on resting on the right knee. It's left hand is clutching an object to its chest. The object appears to be an erection!! There is an air bubble on the figure on its left hand side. Also, there is a small air bubble on its chest and lower abdomen. You can see its left hand and the top of the object it is grasping. It is harder to make out what is below the left hand because of the air bubble. However, erotic sulphide figures are known to exist and it makes sense with this one, as it is definitely a demon. Set off center. Excellent detail. Some chips, but luckily none immediately in front of the figure. Very rare. Germany, circa 1870-1915. 1-1/4". Good (7.5). $280. (Auction #65, lot #42).

SULPHIDE. Figure of a standing horse, head turned slightly to one side, with a English saddle. Figures of horses with saddles are rare! Large figure for the marble. Excellent detail. No air bubbles. Excellent silvering. Set slightly off to one side. Surface has been polished. Beautiful marble. Germany, circa 1870-1915. 1-5/8". $295. (Auction #77, lot #45).

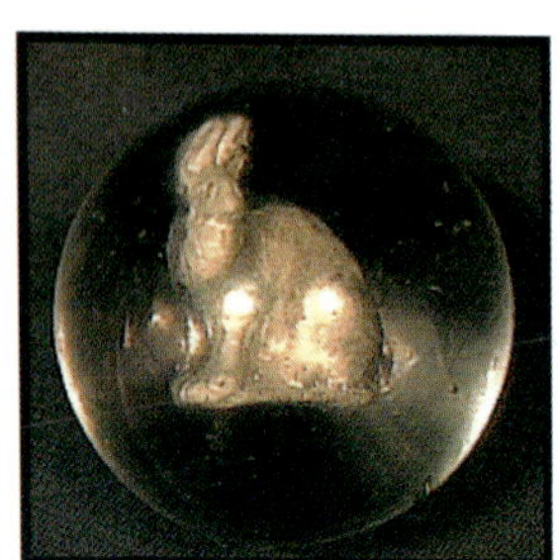

SULPHIDE. Superb figure of a crouched rabbit with its head turned to one side. Excellent three-dimensional figure with great depth. Not a trace of air bubble on or near the figure. It is almost impossible to find these without air bubbles in the cavities or with the ears intact (they usually break off). Set slightly off center. There are four very tiny subsurface moons on the surface. None is near the front or rear of the figure, so none detracts from viewing. An exceptional sulphide, very hard to find. Germany, circa 1870-1915. 1-1/2". Near Mint(+) (8.7). $270. (Auction #121, lot #46).

SULPHIDE. Very rare figure. Standing angel. Clothed figure, wearing a robe similar to a shepherd. Hands clasped in front of chest, in prayer. With wings. Excellent detail to the figure. It is set slightly high in the marble. About half of the right wing broke off and the top edge of the left wing broke off during insertion. However, absolutely no air bubbles on the figure. Just one floating air bubble in the marble near the bottom on the back side. One chip near the top, several subsurface moons. There are no subsurface moons in front of or behind the figure. Very rare figure, you almost never find angels!!! Germany, circa 1870-1915. 1-3/8". Near Mint(-) (8.1). $260. (Auction #173, lot #46).

SULPHIDE. Figure of a floating angel. Male angel. Hands clasped over his groin. Two outspread wings. The feet are broken off above the ankles. The wings are intact. Excellent detail to the face. There is a very shallow air bubble on the front chest and on the back. Neither hurts the viewing. Set slightly high in the marble. Fills almost the entire marble. Angels are very rare. This marble has been polished. Victorian mourning piece. 1-1/4". $240. (Auction #104, lot #47).

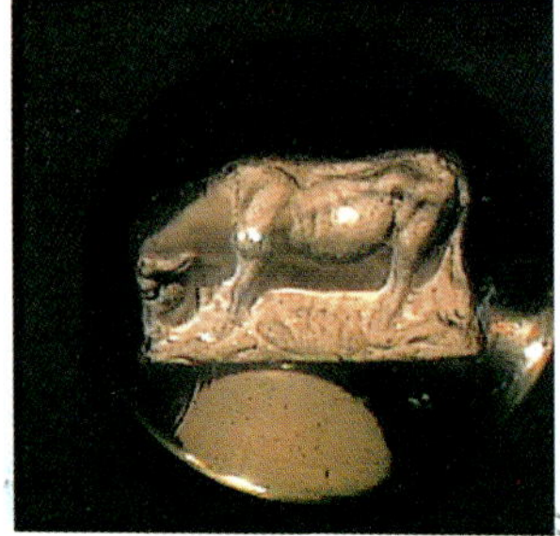

SULPHIDE. One of the largest sulphides I have ever seen. Figure is a feeding cow, with its ribs showing. Very minor air bubble on the neck. Nice silvering. Well-centered. Pontil is well placed, on one side. There are three or four tiny hit marks on the surface, so I can't grade it as Mint, but the marble is so huge you hardly notice. Very clear glass. Super example. Germany, circa 1870-1915. 2-1/8". Near Mint(+) (8.9). $235. (Auction #126, lot #48).

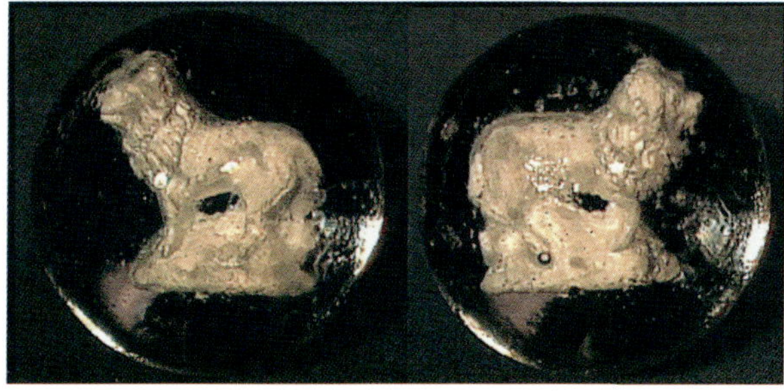

SULPHIDE. Rare type of sulphide. Roaring male lion with a "doughnut hole" between the body and the ground. "Doughnut hole" sulphides, especially without cracks or air bubbles, are very hard to find. Exceptional detail to the figure. Large, well-centered. No cracks or bubbles. Not even a bubble in the hole. Surface has one tiny moon and overall very light pitting. The marble needs a very light buff and you will have a beauty. Very rare. Germany, circa 1870-1915. 1-11/16". Near Mint (8.5). $235. (Auction #147, lot #38).

SULPHIDE. Outstanding figure. Razorback. Exceptional detail to the figure. Nice silvering. No air bubbles on the figure, although there is a small air bubble floating in the marble. Set slightly off center. One tiny flat spot on the top that looks like it may have been hit too. Exceptional example. Germany, circa 1870-1915. 1-11/16". Mint(-) (9.3). $220. (Auction #65, lot #19).

OTHER HANDMADE

Lightning Strike. Very rare marble. I've seen maybe a dozen of these in over ten years. And this one is exceptional. Translucent opalescent base. A translucent blue lightning bolt on one side and a translucent red lightning bolt on the other. The two bolts encircle the entire equator (unusual). Ground pontil. These are so rare that I don't even put a value on them in my Price Guide. There is a picture of one on page 76 of *Marble Mania*. This one has two small sparkles. Superior example and very, very hard to find. A centerpiece of any collection! German or English, circa 1870-1920. 1-5/8". Mint(-) (9.0). $2625. (Auction #154, lot #50).

Clambroth. Opaque white base with pink strands. One small, very shallow flake (not as deep as the pink strand), several subsurface moons. Still, in remarkably good shape. You don't find these big ones very often and usually they have large chips because the glass is so soft. Nice example. Probably American, possibly German, circa 1880-1915. 1-7/8". Good(+) (7.9). $725. (Auction #166, lot #50).

Clambroth. Unbelievable marble. Very rare coloring. Opaque black base. Thirteen light red bands. Very rare coloring. Surface is pristine. Superb marble. Germany, circa 1870-1915. 23/32". Mint (9.9). $700. (Auction #113, lot #46).

Indian. Superb and very rare four-panel three hundred and sixty degree Indian. Opaque black base. Four panels, all the same size. Two are pink on white and two are pink on mustard. Surface in superb shape. Very rare marble. 19/32". Mint (9.8). $625. (Auction #88, lot #13).

Mica. Very large mica!!!! Transparent green with a superior subsurface layer of mica. Four shallow lobes. Surface is almost pristine, except there are two subsurface moons where it was hit. These two moons created a fracture running from just off-center latitudinally through the entire marble. Superb view from one side. Definitely, a "what a shame marble." Still, stunning from the side without the fracture. And perhaps it can be "healed." You will rarely find one this big without major chips or damage. Without the fracture you would have been looking at a $1,500-$3,000 marble. Germany, circa 1870-1915. 1-7/8". Near Mint (8.5). $575. (Auction #121, lot #50).

Banded opaque. Superb example. Opaque white base. Two bands covering about ninety percent of the surface. The bands are bright yellow, bright red, blue, green and aqua. One tiny manufacturing rough spot. Stunning marble. Germany, circa 1870-1915. 21/32". Mint (9.4). $525. (Auction #98, lot #49).

Indian. Hard to find three hundred and sixty degree Indian. Absolutely outstanding example of this type!! Opaque black base. Completely covered by stretched splotches of opaque white, opaque mustard yellow, transparent green, transparent pink and transparent blue. Superb coloring. Surface is in pristine condition. You will not find one of these in better shape. Germany, circa 1870-1915. 11/16". Mint (9.9). $420. (Auction #81, lot #38).

Indian. Astounding three hundred sixty degree Indian! Opaque black base, completely covered by stretched mustard yellow, white, blue, green and pink bands. Surface is in superb shape. Germany, possibly American, circa 1870-1920. These are very hard to find. There were six of these, that I would term as either 360 Indians or uncased end of days, in one collection I received on consignment. This is the third. I have never seen this many in one collection. 23/32". Mint (9.9). $420. (Auction #64, lot #36).

Banded Opaque. Superb banded opaque. Opaque white base. Two bands covering about sixty percent of the marble. Both bands are green, pink, blue and yellow. Superb condition. Exceptional example. Germany, circa 1870-1915. 21/32". Mint (9.9). $390. (Auction #94, lot #48).

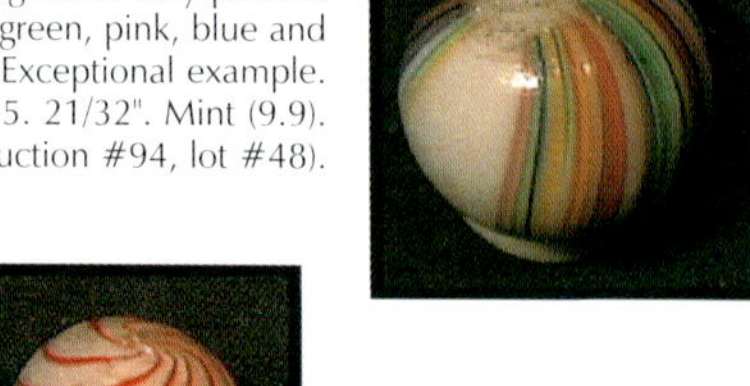

Clambroth. Rare clambroth. Opaque white base. Band pattern on the surface is: pink band, yellow strand, green band, yellow strand, pink band, yellow strand, blue band. Missing the last yellow strand. Surface is pristine!!! There is one manufacturing pit near the top pontil. Stunning marble. Very rare!!! Germany, possibly American, circa 1870-1915. 21/32". Mint (9.8). $385. (Auction #179, lot #47).

Cased clambroth. Popularly referred to as a "cased clambroth" by collectors, this is really a rare form of a banded swirl. Transparent clear base. Subsurface layer of opaque white with eight thin red bands. Surface in great shape. Very difficult to find, especially Mint. Probably German, circa 1870-1915. 9/16". Mint (9.7). $320. (Auction #83, lot #45).

Indian. Superior shooter size Indian. Opaque black base. Two bands covering about seventy five percent of the surface. The bands are both opaque mustard and transparent red. There are no hit marks on the marble. There are a couple of tiny air holes, typical of this type (on the bands). Stunning example. The condition on this one is almost impossible to find in this size. Germany, circa 1870-1915. 7/8". Mint (9.7). $310. (Auction #160, lot #36).

Indian. Three hundred and sixty degree Indian. Superb marble. Opaque black base. Surface is completely covered by white, pink, yellow, blue and green. One large subsurface moon. Still, a stunning marble. Germany, circa 1870-1915. 11/16". Near Mint(+) (8.9). $310. (Auction #74, lot #43).

Banded Translucent. Rare marble. Translucent white base. Filament core. Outer surface is covered by bands and loops of transparent pink. Superb marble!!! In great shape. German, possibly American, circa 1880-1920. 23/32". Mint (9.9). $300. (Auction #164, lot #46).

Indian. Three hundred sixty degree Indian. Super marble. Opaque black base. Completely covered by white, pink, green, blue, orange and yellow. An exceptional marble. Has a manufacturing dimple near one pontil and one spot where it was hit, although there appears be no damage except perhaps an extremely fine subsurface fracture. Germany, circa 1870-1915. 23/32". Mint(-) (9.2). $290. (Auction #78, lot #39).

Indian. What can I say but Wow! Shooter size Indian. Very hard to find these this large, and this one is in great shape, which is rare. Opaque black base. Two colored bands covering about sixty percent of the surface. One band is pink and mustard. The other is pink and white. There is a manufacturing flat spot at the edge of the pink/white and the black. There is also a tiny manufacturing flake on the pink/white. Superb marble!! Germany, circa 1870-1915. 29/32" (just over 7/8"). Mint(-) (9.2). $265. (Auction #60, lot #45).

Indian. Opaque black base. Two bands covering about forty percent of the marble. The bands are end of day type. One is stretched white with some transparent blue. The other is stretched white with some transparent green. One tiny sparkle. Otherwise, in super shape. And this one is a large shoot!!! Germany, circa 1870-1915. 7/8". Mint(-) (9.1). $250. (Auction #76, lot #42).

Clambroth. Opaque black base. Seventeen white strands. Very nicely made. Has a couple of tiny manufacturing marks on the surface. Super marble! Germany, circa 1870-1915. 11/16". Mint (9.6). $220. (Auction #68, lot #39).

Indian. Super shooter. Opaque black base. Stretched white, green and yellow covering about ninety percent of the marble. Only one small panel missing. Surface has some manufacturing roughness typical of this type. Hard to find. Germany, circa 1870-1915. 3/4". Mint (9.5). $220. (Auction #82, lot #41).

Clambroth. Translucent white base. Eleven blue bands. Well-spaced. Super looking marble!!! Has one small moon, but other than that, no damage. Unfortunately, I have to grade it below Mint because of the hit. Views much better than that. Translucent base is hard to find too. Germany, circa 1870-1915. 25/32". Near Mint(+) (8.9). $200. (Auction #97, lot #43).

NON-GLASS HANDMADE

Scenic china. Extremely rare glazed hand-painted china. Superb marble. Opaque white. The top and bottom have blue pinwheels. The equator has pink roses with green leaves. Two, diametrically opposed, spots on the equator have a black pinwheel on a yellow circle. Some rubbing of the paint, prior to glazing. This marble is extremely rare. This is only the third scenic rose china known to exist. One is in my father's collection (pictured in my book). One is in another New England collection. This is the only one with pinwheels on the equator. 1-1/4". Mint (9.4). $6925. (Auction #131, lot #50).

China. Very hard to find King's Rose china. Opaque white china. Painted on one side with a well formed red rose with four sprigs of green leaves. Superior example. These roses are very difficult to find. Germany, circa 1870-1915. 11/16". Mint (9.9). $400. (Auction #160, lot #46).

China. Exceptional china!!!! Three equidistantly spaced lines, encircling poles. One is light blue, one is light yellow, one is green leaves. No equatorial ribbon. Surface in great shape. This is a very rare marble!! Either German or English, circa 1850-1925. 13/16". Mint (9.5). $130. (Auction #64, lot #45).

China. Rare hand-painted china. Unglazed. Six-vane red pinwheel on each pole. Five green bands around the equator. In great shape. The pattern of the pinwheels is very unusual. Super marble!!! Germany, circa 1860-1920. 3/4". Mint (9.7). $195. (Auction #173, lot #49).

China. Large unglazed hand-painted china. Has six bulls eyes, perfectly spaced at the axis poles. Two green, two red, and two black. Several are faded, but I think they were rubbed off (you can see one of the black ones is smeared) before they dried. Surface in great shape. This is one of the largest I have ever seen. Excellent example. Germany, circa 1850-1920. 1-5/16". Mint (9.7). $130. (Auction #94, lot #17).

Crockery. Lined crockery. Blue and green lines swirled on opaque white. This is one of the largest that I have ever seen!! Superb marble. German or American, circa 1850-1920. 1-1/16". Mint (9.9). $120. (Auction #124, lot #42).

Bennington. Rare bennington. One side is brown, one side is blue. Half and half benningtons are hard to find. Large eye on the blue side. In great shape. Germany, circa 1860-1920. 25/32". Mint (9.9). $100. (Auction #160, lot #44).

China. Excellent unglazed hand-painted china. Four lines on each axis. Olive green, currant red and orange. Very unusual. Excellent example. Germany, circa 1850-1920. 25/32". Mint (9.8). $85. (Auction #141, lot #45).

Crockery. Lined crockery. Blue and green lines swirled on opaque white. Glazed, one salt spot. This is one of the largest that I have ever seen!! Superb marble. German or American, circa 1850-1920. 1-1/8". Mint (9.9). $80. (Auction #136, lot #48).

China. A hand-painted china. Super marble. Opaque white. Has four black lines on the equator. Each pole has a flower. The flower has a green stem and leaves, red flower and then two green leaves coming out of the top. Unusual flower. The marble is not glazed, but is in remarkably good shape for its age. Probably German, circa 1850-1915. 23/32". Mint (9.7). $80. (Auction #58, lot #37).

Bennington. Shooter size pink bennington. It is hard to find pink benningtons, but shooter sizes are even harder. Very nice example. Opaque pink base. Fancy colors of brown and blue. In nice shape. Two "salt" spots. One tiny hit spot. Probably Germany, circa 1860-1920. 25/32". Near Mint(+) (8.9). This was originally sold as Lot #4 in CyberAuction #51. $75. (Auction #137, lot #10).

Stoneware. Very nice stoneware with blue spatter splotches. Salt-glazed. In great shape. Origin unknown, circa 1850-1920. 1-1/2". Mint (9.9). $65. (Auction #138, lot #23).

China. Beautiful unglazed hand-painted china. Four intersecting lines on each axis. One is green, one red and one black. In super shape with nice bright, crisp colors. Germany, circa 1850-1920. 1-3/16". Mint (9.9). $65. (Auction #116, lot #41).

Bennington. One of the largest benningtons that I have ever seen. Blue bennington. In perfect shape. Superb example. Germany, circa 1860-1920. 1-7/16". Mint (9.9). $65. (Auction #104, lot #38).

TRANSITIONAL

Leighton. Outstanding and very rare ground pontil transitional. Transparent clear base. Perfect spiral of opaque bright yellow and semi-opaque white on the surface. Five rotations. Technically, this is a horizontal, but because of the two different colors, there is very little clear showing through, so it is hard to see. Two small air holes on the lower half of the marble, near each other. No damage to the surface!!!! An absolutely outstanding example, almost impossible to find, especially in this condition. Very rare opportunity! American, circa 1880-1910. 13/16". Mint(-) (9.1). $825. (Auction #156, lot #49).

Leighton. Rare Leighton ground pontil transitional. Transparent olive green base swirled with opaque lavender and opaque yellow. Super "9" pattern on one end, nice trailing tail and excellent ground pontil. There must have been a chip on one side, because that side has been polished, resulting a flat spot. The remainder of the marble is untouched. I can't really assign a grade to it because of that polished spot. There are two tiny flakes on the unpolished portion of the marble and no other damage. These are almost impossible to find in any condition. American, circa 1880-1910. 25/32". $230. (Auction #129, lot #33).

Ground pontil. Stunning example!!!!! Transparent blue base with wispy white swirling. Opaque white "9" right on the top. The tail ends abruptly. Nicely ground pontil. Surface is pristine! You will not find one in better condition. Superb marble!!!! American, circa 1880-1910. 25/32". Mint (9.9). $220. (Auction #183, lot #35).

Regular pontil. This is a single-pontil hand-gathered slag. Very early American marble. These are almost impossible to find, especially this large, and almost unplayed with. I have seen maybe five or six of these large ones in all my years of collecting. Opaque dark purple or purple/brown glass. Translucent white design covering one third of the marble (the end opposite the pontil). Excellent regular pontil. Has one moon hit mark. Very rare marble! Excellent addition to any collection. American, 1880-1910. 1-5/16". Near Mint(+) (8.9). $200. (Auction #150, lot #30).

Ground pontil. Very rare ground pontil transitional with oxblood. Transparent green base with opaque white and opaque oxblood swirl. Super pontil. Two tiny air holes near the pontil. Also, one tiny moon and two tiny pinpricks. Still, a superb marble and very hard to find. American, circa 1890-1910. 21/32". Near Mint(+) (8.8). $185. (Auction #88, lot #44).

Leighton. A beauty. Transparent green base with lots of unmelted sand in it. Swirl of translucent yellow in it. Excellent "9". Nicely ground pontil. There are two manufacturing pits on the top and a tiny very shallow chip on the bottom. Super example. American, circa 1880-1910. 13/16". Near Mint(+) (8.9). $160. (Auction #172, lot #46).

Pinpoint pontil. Stunning example of this rare type. Aqua slag with a nice white "9" on one end and a small pinpoint pontil on the other. In pristine shape!! Very difficult to find in any condition. American, circa 1910-1925. 3/4". Mint (9.9). $170. (Auction #110, lot #50).

Leighton. Rare marble. Transparent clear base. Swirled with opaque white, opaque yellow and oxblood. Loads of oxblood! The oxblood forms the wide "9". Ground pontil. The marble has seen usage. A few small chips and subsurface moons. Some haziness. American, circa 1880-1910. 13/16". Good(+) (7.8). $150. (Auction #179, lot #17).

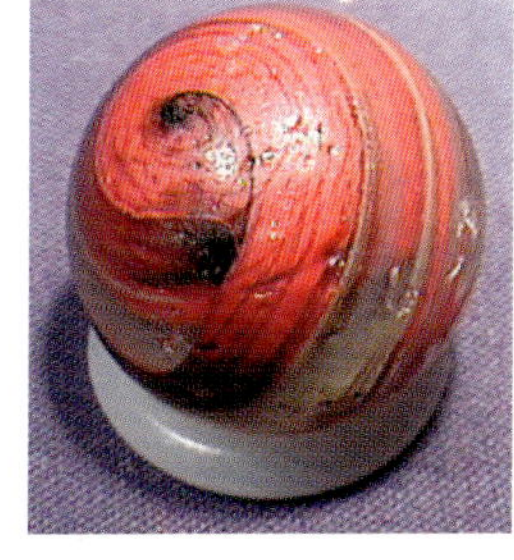

Ground pontil. Exceptional example. Light green slag. Superior "9" and excellent ground pontil. Surface is pristine!! You are not going to find a better example of this type. American, circa 1900-1915. 13/16". Mint (9.9). $145. (Auction #110, lot #47).

Pinpoint pontil. Super example of this rare type. Aqua slag with a nice white "9" on one end and a small pinpoint pontil on the other. In pristine shape!! Very difficult to find in any condition. American, circa 1910-1925. 25/32". Mint (9.9). Same consignor as Lot #50 in CyberAuction #110, this may be a match to that marble. $140. (Auction #134, lot #42).

Regular pontil. Outstanding example of this type. I believe that this marble is Navarre. Very dark purple with white looping. Exceptional regular pontil. One sparkle. This is a superior example, perhaps the best I have ever seen. American, circa 1880-1910. 15/16". Mint(-) (9.1). $140. (Auction #179, lot #48).

Ground pontil. Green slag. Gorgeous "9". Surface in great shape. Superb ground pontil on the bottom. Exceptional example of this type. Ohio, circa 1900-1915. 21/32". Mint (9.9). $140. (Auction #75, lot #42).

Ground pontil. Superb example. Blue and white slag. Excellent "9" on the top. Great pontil on the bottom. This has one of the best "9"s that I have ever seen! One sparkle. American, circa 1890-1910. 25/32". Mint (9.4). $135. (Auction #104, lot #44).

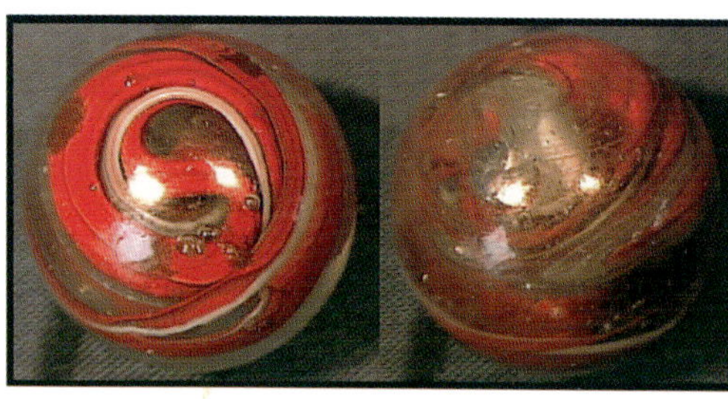

Leighton ground pontil. Extremely rare marble. This is a Leighton ground pontil transitional with an incredible amount of oxblood in it. Transparent clear base with wide swirls of oxblood and white. Nice "9" on one end and a nice ground pontil on the other. At the top, in the oxblood, just below the surface, there are five spots of brown. These are air holes that have been filled with a polymer. Still, a great looking marble and hard to find. American, circa 1890-1910. 27/32". Mint (9.5). $130. (Auction #63, lot #43).

Leighton. Nice Leighton transitional. Ground pontil. Swirled transparent teal, bright yellow and wispy white. There is also some burnt oxblood swirled in. The glass has cold roll marks on it, probably it was too cold when it was made. Several small chips, but one side is undamaged and the pontils are undamaged. Hard to find. American, circa 1880-1910. 7/8". Near Mint (8.4). $120. (Auction #181, lot #47).

Leighton. Super example. Transparent smoky gray base with a wispy white swirl in it. "9" on the top. Excellent ground pontil on the bottom. Super example. American, circa 1880-1910. 13/16". Mint (9.8). $110. (Auction #142, lot #44).

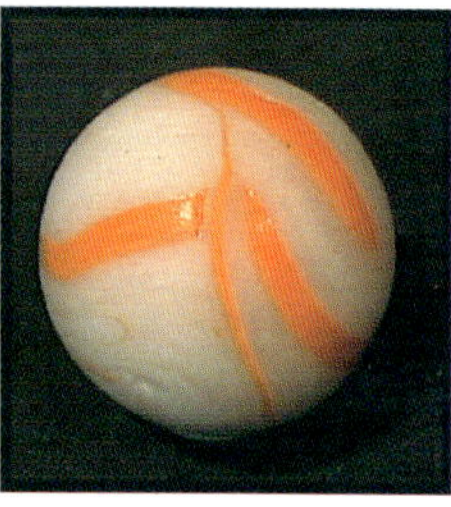

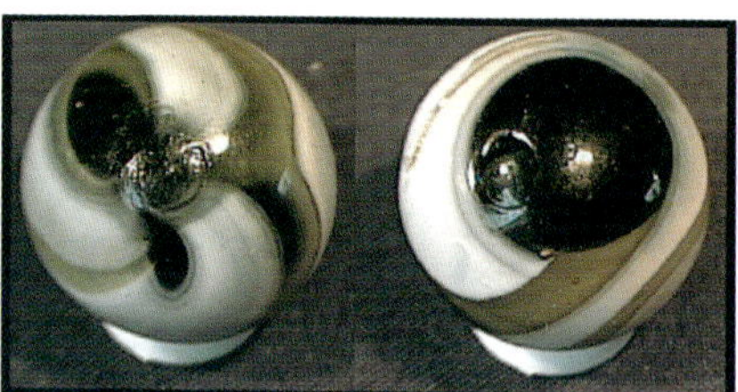

Melted Pontil. An exceptional example of a melted pontil transitional. Transparent light olive green base with translucent white swirling. Nice "9". Excellent melted pontil. Probably M.F. Christensen. There is a melted strand of glass on the surface and one very tiny demi-moon. No glass missing, barely visible. Provenance: ex-collection of Stanley Block. American, circa 1905-1915. 27/32". Mint(-) (9.0). $110. (Auction #64, lot #38).

Crease pontil. Rare example of a crease pontil. Opaque white base with bright yellow/orange swirls. This one is a shooter! It is very unusual to find the yellow on white combination, and this is one of the largest I have ever seen. Has several small flakes. It is not known if this is American or Japanese. Probably prior to 1935. I personally acquired this from an estate and none of the marbles that they had were later than about 1935. 1-1/16". Near Mint(+) (8.7). $100. (Auction #83, lot #2).

Ground pontil. Green slag. Super "9" on the top and an excellent ground pontil on the bottom. Surface in superb shape. An exceptional marble!!!! Ohio, circa 1900-1915. 13/16". Mint (9.9). $95. (Auction #76, lot #34).

M.F. CHRISTENSEN & SON COMPANY

Brick. Superior example. Oxblood red, white and black. Stunning marble. Excellent swirling, pattern and tail. Shooter size. You are not going to find one much better than this! Akron, Ohio, circa 1912-1917. 3/4". Mint (9.8). $250. (Auction #164, lot #47).

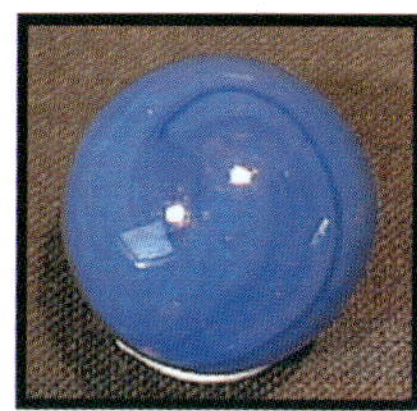

Opaque. Dark blue opaque. Has a "9" and tail pattern. This is the first dark blue M.F. Christensen opaque that I have ever seen. I believe they marketed this as "Royal Blue," but I can't put my hands on the copy of the ad to verify it. However, very rare, and in dead Mint condition. Superb marble. Akron, Ohio, circa 1912-1917. 21/32". Mint (9.9). $220. (Auction #87, lot #40).

Slag. Calling this marble a slag does not do it justice, although technically that is what it is. Transparent lavender glass with translucent opalescent white glass swirled inside it. Hand gathered. Faint "9" (because of the color combination) on the top. In superb shape. Rarely seen. Akron, Ohio, circa 1914-1917. 5/8". Mint (9.9). $180. (Auction #100, lot #43).

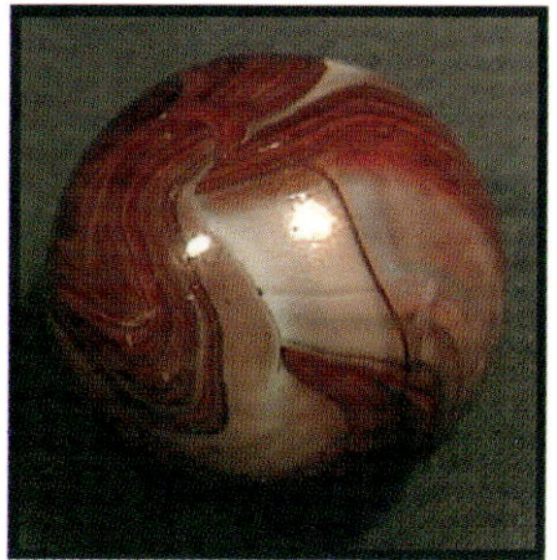
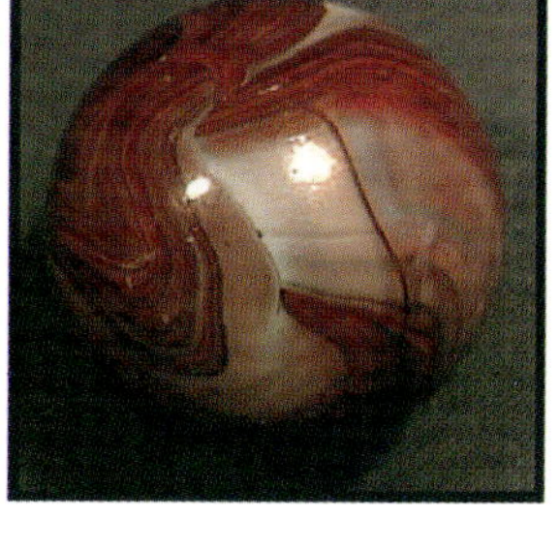

Brick. Large brick. Oxblood red with some white and a little black mixed in. A few small cold roll spots. Several tiny subsurface moons and a small annealing fracture. This marble looks Mint at first glance. You have to really inspect it under a light to see the damage. No glass missing. Super marble. Very hard to find them this large. Akron, Ohio, circa 1914-1917. 7/8". Near Mint(+) (8.8). $180. (Auction #137, lot #50).

Brick. Superior shooter green brick. One of the nicest I have ever seen. Almost all oxblood red with some transparent dark green mixed in. Superb detail. Has one melt spot and one sparkle. This is a fabulous marble. Akron, Ohio, circa 1914-1917. 25/32". Mint(-) (9.1). $170. (Auction #71, lot #20).

Oxblood slag. Very dark transparent green slag, with some swirls of oxblood in it. Surface in great shape. Very hard to find. Akron, Ohio, circa 1914-1917. 23/32". Mint (9.9). $165. (Auction #117, lot #46).

Brick. Shooter size marble. Lots of white. An absolute beauty. Two tiny melt pits. Nice cut-off line. Akron, Ohio, circa 1914-1917. 25/32". Mint(-) (9.1). $160. (Auction #94, lot #47).

Brick. Superb Brick. Predominately very rich oxblood with some white swirled in and a little black. "9" on top, and a bit of a tail. This one is gorgeous because the oxblood is so rich and textured. And a shooter! One tiny sparkle. Akron, Ohio, circa 1912-1917. 13/16". Mint(-) (9.2). $160. (Auction #140, lot #47).

Opaque. Very hard to find Imperial Jade. Opaque white. "9" on the top, spiraling to the bottom. M.F. Christensen cutoff line on the bottom. A tiny amount of white in the spiral, making it easier than usual to make out. Exceptional example! These are very hard to find. Akron, Ohio, circa 1914-1917. 11/16". Mint (9.8). $150. (Auction #167, lot #47).

Brick. Dark opaque oxblood-red, almost purple hued, with white blankets on it. Superb pattern. In great shape. Gorgeous marble. Akron, Ohio, circa 1914-1917. 19/32". Mint (9.9). $160. (Auction #67, lot #43).

Brick. Very hard to find large brick. Superior example. Excellent hand-gather. Could almost be a horizontal. Super "9" on the top. Oxblood red with white swirl and a little black. About five rotations. Nice M.F. Christensen cut-line on the bottom. Has two tiny subsurface moons and a couple of sparkles and pits. All on the lower half of the marble. Super example, and remarkably large for a brick. Akron, Ohio, circa 1912-1917. 27/32". Near Mint(+) (8.7). $130. (Auction #173, lot #22).

Brick. Super, shooter brick. Mostly oxblood red with a few wisps of black. Excellent, thin white "9" on the top. Nice M.F. Christensen seam on the bottom. A few very tiny pinpricks scattered on the marble. Akron, Ohio, circa 1912-1917. 27/32". Near Mint(+) (8.9). $120. (Auction #158, lot #39).

Brick. Super brick. Almost completely dark oxblood red, with some black and white mixed in. Small fold. Excellent pattern and surface. Akron, Ohio, circa 1914-1917. 11/16". Mint (9.7). $130. (Auction #87, lot #44).

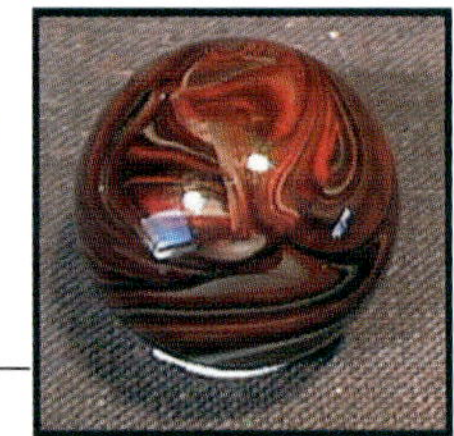

CHRISTENSEN AGATE COMPANY

Guinea/Cobra hybrid. Rare marble. I have to call this a Guinea/Cobra hybrid. Single seam example. The interior of the marble is completely filled with Guinea flecks, and the exterior is completely covered. Transparent clear base with flecks of yellow, orange, red, light green, light blue and lavender. There are some clear spaces on the exterior, allowing you to see the interior. There are no open panels. Cambridge, Ohio, circa 1927-1929. 9/16". Mint (9.7). $700. (Auction #85, lot #44).

Guinea. Authentic Guinea. Blue base. Transparent cobalt blue covered completely by colored flecks. Colors include lavender, yellow, green, orange, blue, white and black. Single seam. Superior example, one of the nicest that I have seen. This one is a little bigger than usual, coming in at 11/16". Super example. Cambridge, Ohio, circa 1927-1929. 11/16". Mint (9.9). $450. (Auction #91, lot #45).

Guinea. Super example. Transparent clear base. Single seam. Open panel opposite that seam covering about twenty percent of the marble. Yellow, green, blue, orange, black, lavender. Some color inside the marble, that you can see through the open panel. Surface in great shape. Superior example. Cambridge, Ohio, circa 1927-1929. 5/8". Mint (9.9). $440. (Auction #167, lot #49).

Guinea. Excellent Guinea. Transparent cobalt blue base with stretched light blue, green, white, orange, yellow and lavender flecks covering the whole surface. One seam. Exceptional example. Very hard to find. Cambridge, Ohio, circa 1927-1928. 9/16". Mint (9.7). $435. (Auction #56, lot #45).

Guinea. Transparent blue base. Completely covered by flecks of color. Includes light blue, orange, light green, yellow, black and lavender. Two seam example. Surface is pristine. Exceptional!! Cambridge, Ohio, circa 1927-1929. 17/32". Mint (9.9). $400. (Auction #112, lot #50).

Guinea. Blue base Guinea. Two seam. Has an open panel on about one-third of the marble. Lavender, orange, yellow and blue spots. In great shape. This is guaranteed authentic! Cambridge, Ohio, circa 1927-1928. Very rare size, it is a mere 1/64" over a peewee. 1/2"+. Mint (9.9). $390. (Auction #78, lot #42).

Guinea. Super Guinea. Transparent blue base. Single seam. Splotches of yellow, light green, orange, lavender and black. Open panel on about forty percent of the surface. In great shape. Harder to find. Cambridge, Ohio, circa 1927-1929. 5/8". Mint (9.9). $390. (Auction #128, lot #50).

Guinea. Transparent clear base Guinea. Two seam. Covered with tiny specks of lavender, orange, yellow and blue spots. A couple of sparkles. This is guaranteed authentic! Cambridge, Ohio, circa 1927-1928. 11/16". Mint(-) (9.1). $385. (Auction #185, lot #44).

Guinea. Gorgeous Guinea. Slightly larger size than typical. Transparent clear base. Stretched flecks of white, orange, yellow, lavender, light blue and black. There is a piece of unmelted sand on one side that has caused a small annealing fracture on that side. Still, a stunning marble to look at. Cambridge, Ohio, circa 1927-1929. 21/32". Mint(-) (9.0). $380. (Auction #81, lot #45).

Guinea. Beautiful Guinea. Two seam design. Transparent clear base. Overall coloring of yellow, lavender, light blue, orange, black, red. Hard to find. Cambridge, Ohio, circa 1927-1928. 21/32". Mint (9.8). $375. (Auction #183, lot #49).

Guinea. Transparent clear base. Two seam example. Colored splotches covering about ninety percent of the surface, with just one small open panel. Includes yellow, orange, light blue, light green, lavender and black. A real beauty!! Cambridge, Ohio, circa 1927-1928. 21/32". Mint (9.9). $370. (Auction #110, lot #44).

Guinea. Beautiful Guinea. Two seam design. Transparent clear base. Overall coloring, except for one small panel. Lots of Guinea flakes inside the marble too!!! Has one small, barely visible subsurface moon, else, no other damage. Hard to find. Cambridge, Ohio, circa 1927-1928. Near Mint(+) (8.9). $350. (Auction #65, lot #43).

Guinea. Beautiful Guinea. Two seam design. Transparent clear base. Covered with color. Predominately orange, with black, light blue, light green, white and lavender. Hard to find. Superb example. Cambridge, Ohio, circa 1927-1928. 9/16". Mint (9.9). $345. (Auction #104, lot #50).

Guinea. Transparent clear base. Single seam example. Open panel about ten percent of the surface. The coloring is light blue, light green, yellow, orange, black, lavender and white. Sparkle in the open panel. Beautiful example. Cambridge, Ohio, circa 1927-1929. 21/32. Mint(-) (9.0). $330. (Auction #169, lot #49).

Guinea. A beautiful Guinea. Guaranteed authentic. Transparent clear base. Yellow, light blue, orange, black, brown and lavender. Every Guinea color in this one. Open panel covering about thirty percent of the marble. Surface in great shape. Beautiful marble!!! Cambridge, Ohio, circa 1927-1928. 17/32". Mint (9.9). $330. (Auction #71, lot #45).

Guinea. Beautiful Guinea. Single seam design. Transparent clear base. Overall coloring, except for one small panel. One tiny spot that may be from manufacture. Hard to find! Cambridge, Ohio, circa 1927-1928. 5/8". Mint(-) (9.1). $325. (Auction #143, lot #48).

Flame swirl. Three color flame swirl. Outstanding example. Opaque light blue base. Dull red and gray/black swirls. Number of nice, tiny flame tips. Cambridge, Ohio, circa 1927-1929. 19/32". Mint (9.8). $320. (Auction #159, lot #48).

Swirl. Very rare hand gathered swirl. This one is stunning. Obviously hand gathered. It is a combination of a bright yellow and the bright red that you see in American Agates. Actually, if you look at some American Agates, you can see that they were hand gathered. Very early Christensen Agate marbles are hand gathered. This one has stunning colors and a super pattern. Ill-formed "9" pattern on one end with a trailing tail. Has one tiny melt/flat spot on it. Surface is pristine. A superb and very rare marble, certainly rarer than a Guinea or Flame. Cambridge, Ohio, circa 1927. 21/32". Mint (9.7). $320. (Auction #78, lot #45).

Flame Swirl. Outstanding example of a Flame Swirl. Brown/gray swirls on light blue. About a dozen flame tips. In exceptional shape. Great marble for any machine made collection. Cambridge, Ohio, circa 1927-1929. 19/32". Mint (9.9). $320. (Auction #164, lot #49).

Slag. Rare peach slag. Superior coloring. Gorgeous transparent peach color. Translucent and opaque white swirling. One tiny pinprick and a few tiny air holes. This is a great example of this type!!! Cambridge, Ohio, circa 1927-1929. 7/8". Mint(-) (9.2). $320. (Auction #149, lot #49).

MACHINE MADE MARBLES

AKRO AGATE COMPANY

Oxblood corkscrew. Very rare marble. Three-color corkscrew. Opaque yellow, transparent red and oxblood. Nice spiral of oxblood. This is an outstanding marble. Has one very tiny pinprick and a few tiny melted air bubbles (which is typical). Very rare! Clarksburg, West Virginia, circa 1928-1935. 25/32". Mint (9.6). $400. (Auction #183, lot #38).

Egg yolk/blue oxblood hybrid. Very rare marble. Translucent milky white base, opaque egg yolk yellow swirls and translucent blue swirls. Thin swirl of oxblood on the marble. Surface is pristine. This marble is almost impossible to find. Akro Agate, circa 1928-1938. 5/8". Mint (9.9). $300. (Auction #71, lot #39).

Carnelian oxblood. Semi-opaque white base. Lots of transparent brown swirling in the marble. Wide and rich oxblood swirl on the surface. Stunning!! In superb shape. Clarksburg, West Virginia, circa 1928-1935. 25/32". Mint (9.9). $280. (Auction #185, lot #49).

Popeye corkscrew. Very rare Popeye. Orange and green. The clear/white is mostly clear. There is a brown spiral between the orange and green. Extremely rare colors. Clarksburg, West Virginia, circa 1927-1935. 5/8". Mint (9.7). $260. (Auction #163, lot #41).

Orange oxblood. Translucent milky white base with translucent orange swirls and an oxblood swirl. In super shape. Hard to find. This one is a shooter. 3/4". Mint (9.9). $230. (Auction #111, lot #43).

Oxblood hybrid. Super orange/egg yolk oxblood hybrid. Translucent milky white base (one fluorescent spiral in it. On the surface is a spiral of egg yolk yellow, one of orange and one of oxblood. Two small manufacturing pits where the marble touched others as it was made and glass pulled off. Shooter. Hard to find. Clarksburg, West Virginia, circa 1927-1935. 3/4". Mint(-) (9.0). $200. (Auction #156, lot #47).

Hybrid oxblood. Very rare oxblood. The base is pale limeade. Very fluorescent. Has one very small opaque white swirl. More than half the surface is covered by oxblood. Small swirl at one side of the oxblood of transparent blue. Very wispy. Has one very tiny pinprick and one tiny melt spot. And a shooter too! Very rare. Clarksburg, West Virginia, circa 1927-1935. 25/32". Mint(-) (9.0). $195. (Auction #100, lot #32).

Cherryade. Very hard to find Cherryade shooter. Fluorescent "ade" base with opaque wispy white swirls and translucent red swirls on the surface. Absolutely outstanding example. This marble is pre-Freese Improvement. Very hard to find! Clarksburg, West Virginia, circa 1922-1927. 31/32". Mint (9.9). $185. (Auction #125, lot #49).

Egg yolk oxblood. Semi-opaque white base with a wide egg yolk yellow swirl and a narrower oxblood swirl. A real beauty. Shooter. Has two tiny manufacturing spots, but still gorgeous. Clarksburg, West Virginia, circa 1927-1935. 3/4". Mint(-) (9.1). $180. (Auction #169, lot #47).

Oxblood corkscrew. Transparent clear base. Ribbon of oxblood twisted 2-1/2 times. In great shape. Exceptional example!!!! Very hard to find. Clarksburg, West Virginia, circa 1928-1935. 5/8". Mint (9.9). $170. (Auction #167, lot #45).

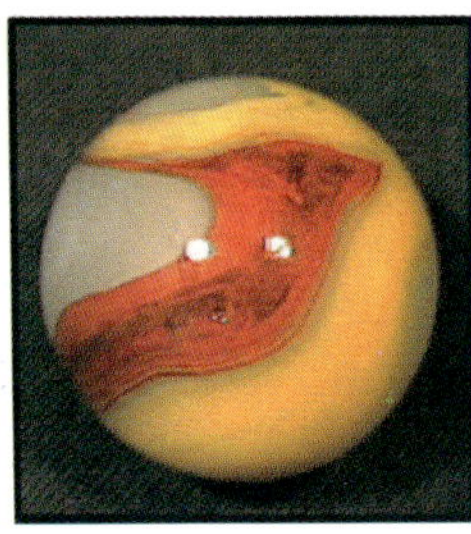

Egg yolk oxblood. Very nice swirl example. Translucent white base. Swirl of opaque egg yolk and swirl of rich oxblood. In great shape. Super shooter. Clarksburg, West Virginia, circa 1927-1935. 3/4". Mint (9.9). $170. (Auction #124, lot #45).

Egg yolk oxblood. Excellent example. Milky white base, opaque egg yolk yellow swirl, oxblood swirl. Surface is pristine. Superior. 19/32". Mint (9.9). $170. (Auction #142, lot #46).

Orange oxblood. Harder to find orange oxblood. Translucent milky white base. Swirl of translucent orange and swirl of thin oxblood on the surface. Several sparkles in one spot. Clarksburg, West Virginia, circa 1928-1935. 23/32". Mint(-) (9.0). $170. (Auction #173, lot #29).

Popeye corkscrew. Shooter size hybrid Popeye, in great shape. Wide spiral of translucent red. Narrow spirals of blue and green. A couple of very tiny pinpricks, one very tiny annealing fracture. Super. Clarksburg, West Virginia, circa 1927-1935. 3/4". Mint(-) (9.0). $165. (Auction #185, lot #34).

Cherryade. Very hard to find Cherryade shooter. Fluorescent "ade" base with a little bit of opaque wispy white swirls and with translucent red swirls on the surface. One tiny melt spot. Super example. Clarksburg, West Virginia, circa 1922-1927. 1". Mint (9.9). $160. (Auction #144, lot #50).

Popeye corkscrew. Purple and yellow shooter Popeye corkscrew. Hard to find. In super shape. Clarksburg, West Virginia, circa 1928-1938. 23/32". Mint (9.9). $150. (Auction #78, lot #30).

Egg yolk oxblood. Very nice corkscrew example. Translucent white base. Spiral of opaque egg yolk and spiral of rich oxblood. Two very tiny pits Clarksburg, West Virginia, circa 1927-1935. 23/32". Mint(-) (9.2). $150. (Auction #156, lot #38).

Cherryade. Super shooter size cherryade corkscrew. One of the nicest I have seen. Translucent fluorescent lemonade base. Opaque white swirls and a translucent red spiral. Has a small manufacturing melt chip and two tiny flat spots that have a little roughness. Super marble. Clarksburg, West Virginia, circa 1925-1935. 1". Mint(-) (9.0). $150. (Auction #92, lot #45).

Corkscrew. Experimental orange and blue corkscrew. These are very hard to find. Tiny partial moon at one end with a little roughness. Super marble. Clarksburg, West Virginia, circa 1925-1928. 1". Near Mint(+) (8.9). $150. (Auction #75, lot #44).

PELTIER GLASS COMPANY

Golden Rebel. Shooter size three color National Line Rainbo Golden Rebel. Very difficult size to find. This one is over 3/4"!!!! Opaque yellow base. Four red ribbons and two aventurine black ribbons. One of the black ribbons is very wide. Two small flakes and some roughness. Still, how many have you ever seen this big? Ottawa, Illinois, circa 1927-1937. 25/32". Near Mint(-) (8.2). $485. (Auction #71, lot #41).

Picture Marble - comic. Black transfer of Betty (Boop) on a mustard base, red patch marble. Average strike, a little light at the top of the head. Very well-centered. Marble in great shape. Betty is hard to find. Ottawa, Illinois, circa 1930-1935. 21/32". Mint (9.9). $410. (Auction #117, lot #49).

Superman. This is barely a Superman. Large shooter though and in great shape! Opaque light blue base. Four wide red ribbons. Two very narrow yellow ribbons with black bled near them. There is light aventurine in one of the yellow ribbons. Very large and Mint!!!! Ottawa, Illinois, circa 1927-1935. 27/32". Mint (9.9). $400. (Auction #103, lot #47).

Christmas Tree. Harder to find shooter, three color National Line Rainbo Christmas Tree. Reverse design. Opaque white base. Four translucent green ribbons and two opaque red ribbons. Usually it is two green and four red. Surface in superb shape. Rare marble!!! Ottawa, Illinois, circa 1928-1938. 13/16". Mint (9.9). $325. (Auction #65, lot #44).

Superman. Three-color National Line Rainbo Superman. This one is an exceptional example a Type II National Line Rainbo. Opaque light blue base. Four red ribbons and two yellow. Perfect spacing. Two red form a band around the equator. One red and one yellow form a ring near one pole, with the opposite effect at the other pole. You'll be hard pressed to find a better formed example of this type. In pristine shape! Ottawa, Illinois, circa 1927-1935. 11/16". Mint (9.9). $310. (Auction #110, lot #48).

Superman. What else can I say, but Wow!! A very rare three color National Line Rainbo Superman. This one is 25/32", halfway between 3/4" and 13/16". Light blue base with four red ribbons and two yellow. Two seams. Very nice example. Supermen over 11/16" are virtually impossible to find not beat up. This one has a small blown out air hole and three small subsurface moons on one side. It views very nicely. This marble is vintage, genuine and guaranteed authentic. There is a company in Mexico that has been producing large Supermen for a couple of years, but they are fairly easy to distinguish from original Supermen. Ottawa, Illinois, circa 1928-1938. 25/32". Near Mint(+) (8.8). $310. (Auction #58, lot #45).

Rainbo. Rare Rainbo, and this is an exceptional example. Bifurcated Rainbo. That is, each hemisphere is a different color. One side is two tan/brown ribbons on green, the other side is two red/brown ribbons on blue. Excellent example and very difficult to find. Ottawa, Illinois, circa 1930-1940. 21/32". Mint (9.9). $310. (Auction #92, lot #30).

Superman. Three color National Line Rainbo Superman. Light blue base. Three red ribbons, three yellow ribbons. The red ribbons are edged by brown. Surface in great shape! Ottawa, Illinois, circa 1928-1938. 5/8". Mint (9.9). $305. (Auction #55, lot #40).

Superman. Unusual four color National Line Rainbo Superman. Opaque light blue base. Six opaque red ribbons and two opaque yellow ribbons. There are brown ribbons edging the red. There is faint aventurine in the yellow ribbons! Surface is in great shape, with just one tiny manufacturing dimple. Superb example. You won't find many like this one!! Ottawa, Illinois, circa 1927-1937. 5/8". Mint (9.8). $290. (Auction #71, lot #43).

Liberty. Three color shooter, National Line Rainbo Liberty. Opaque white base. Six translucent red/orange ribbons (two are narrow) and two wide translucent blue ribbons. One very tiny pinprick. Super marble. Very large for the type, you rarely see them this large and Mint!!! Ottawa, Illinois, circa 1928-1935. 25/32". Mint(-) (9.2). $270. (Auction #184, lot #49).

Superman. Shooter size, three color, National Line Rainbo Superman. Opaque light blue base with two yellow ribbons and four red. Nice, large size. You won't find them much bigger. One small moon and three small subsurface moons. Cold roll spot at the top. Still, view very nicely from almost every angle. Rare. 27/32". Near Mint(+) (8.7). $260. (Auction #94, lot #49).

Picture Marble - comic. Black transfer of Betty on a white base/aventurine black patch marble. Excellent, very dark transfer. Well centered. It is rare to find Betty with an aventurine black patch. Ottawa, Illinois, circa 1930-1935. 11/16". Mint (9.9). $250. (Auction #134, lot #47).

Superman. Three color National Line Rainbo Superman. Opaque light blue base with four red ribbons and two yellow ribbons. The red ribbons are edged by translucent brown. Beautiful example. The surface is pristine. Another one where you are not going to find one in better condition. Ottawa, Illinois, circa 1928-1938. 21/32". Mint (9.9). $235. (Auction #81, lot #43).

Superman. Three color National Line Rainbo Superman. Very unusual example. Opaque light blue base. Six ribbons covering almost the entire surface. All are red on yellow. Two have very little red. Very unusual. There is a tiny subsurface moon and a couple of tiny pits. Still, views very nicely. Ottawa, Illinois, circa 1928-1938. 21/32". Near Mint(+) (8.9). $230. (Auction #96, lot #44).

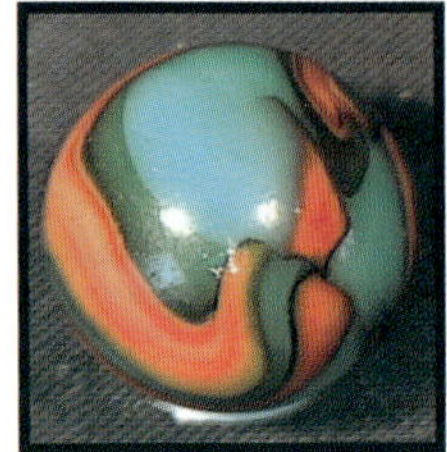

Blue Galaxy. Very hard to find four color National Line Rainbo. This is a type of Blue Galaxy. Opaque light blue base. Eight ribbons. Six of the ribbons are opaque yellow, covered by transparent red. Two of those are very short. The largest and widest ribbon has an edging ribbon on either side of it of translucent aventurine black. One tiny flake and two tiny pits. Very hard marble to find. Ottawa, Illinois, circa 1928-1938. 21/32". Near Mint(+) (8.8). $220. (Auction #63, lot #45).

Superman. Three color National Line Rainbo Superman. Light blue base. Three red ribbons and three yellow ribbons. The pattern is very unusual, because the red ribbons form a broken corkscrew design and the yellow ribbons form a complementary broken corkscrew. One tiny moon and some overall light haziness. Ottawa, Illinois, circa 1928-1938. 5/8". Near Mint(-) (8.2). $220. (Auction #54, lot #45).

Christmas Tree. Shooter, three color, National Line Rainbo Christmas Tree. Opaque white base. Four transparent red ribbons and two transparent green ribbons. An absolute beauty!! Hard to find shooter size marble. A cold roll spot and a tiny manufacturing spot on it. Ottawa, Illinois, circa 1927-1935. 3/4". Mint (9.5). $220. (Auction #131, lot #20).

Miller swirl. Superb example of a two color Miller swirl Zebra. One of the finest I have ever seen!! Opaque white base. Swirls of aventurine black. Very fiery aventurine. Superior design. Very rare and hard to find. Ottawa, Illinois, circa 1925-1930. 21/32". Mint (9.9). $220. (Auction #65, lot #41).

Christmas Tree. Three color National Line Rainbo Christmas Tree. Outstanding example of this type. Opaque white base. Three wide transparent red ribbons and three wide transparent green ribbons. The green is loaded with aventurine, the most I have ever seen in the green of a Peltier. Very little white showing. Excellent example. Ottawa, Illinois, circa 1927-1935. 19/32". Mint (9.9). $215. (Auction #129, lot #44).

Superman. Three color National Line Rainbo Superman. Opaque light blue base with three red ribbons and three yellow ribbons. Nice swirl to the marble. There are two wide ribbons of brown/gray, but those may just be blended colors. Surface in great shape. Super marble. Ottawa, Illinois, circa 1925-1935. 19/32". Mint (9.9). $210. (Auction #91, lot #43).

Graycoat. Three-color National Line Rainbo Graycoat. Opaque white base. Four thin ribbons of translucent red. Three thin ribbons of translucent gray. A couple of pinpricks. Ottawa, Illinois, circa 1927-1935. 21/32". Mint(-) (9.0). $210. (Auction #151, lot #47).

MARBLE KING, INC.

Watermelon. Rare marble!!! Very, very difficult to find! This is an excellent example with super symmetry. Opaque white base. A patch and ribbon of brushed green and a patch and ribbon of brushed red. Small "oxblood" patch on the green patch. There is some minor aventurine at one seam. Watermelons are almost impossible to find, I have seen less than a dozen in the past five years. Opportunities to add one to your collection are quite rare. This is a superb example. Paden City, West Virginia, circa 1950-1960. 19/32". Mint (9.9). $700. (Auction #129, lot #50).

Green Hornet. Rare two-color patch and ribbon Rainbow Green Hornet. It is very hard to find vintage examples of these. Opaque white base. A patch and ribbon of green and a patch and ribbon of black. The black ribbon is a little light, giving it a gray appearance. This marble is vintage. There were several of these in with a cloth Tournament Assortment bag. The bag was completely destroyed by mildew and water. But, I washed these up and they look great! This is one of the nicer ones of the group. I don't even have a Mint one in my collection! Circa 1950-1965. 5/8". Mint (9.9). $380. (Auction #150, lot #49).

Spiderman. A very hard to find Spiderman Rainbow. Blue and red patch and ribbon on opaque white. Has an oxblood band in the blue patch. Excellent example. These are very hard to find. 19/32". Mint (9.9). $200. (Auction #57, lot #45).

Spiderman. Superb example of a Spiderman. Vintage marble, not a reproduction. Alternating blue and red patch and ribbon on white. Some minor annealing crazing in one red ribbon. These are not that easy to find. Two very tiny pits. Paden City, West Virginia, circa 1950-1965.5/8". Mint (-) (9.1). $140. (Auction #67, lot #45).

Tiger. Two-color Rainbow Tiger shooter. Opaque white base. Black and orange patch and ribbon. White bands showing through. Paden City, West Virginia, circa 1950-1965. 7/8". Mint (9.9). $130. (Auction #178, lot #39).

Bengal Tiger. I have seen this color combination referred to as a Bengal Tiger or a Captain Marvel. This is a Bumblebee with red on top of the white. Outstanding, large example. One of the largest you will ever find, and the surface is pristine. Paden City, West Virginia, circa 1950-1965. 31/32". Mint (9.9). $120. (Auction #98, lot #50).

Rainbow. Two color Rainbow. Sometimes referred to as a "Poor Man's Watermelon." Opaque white base. Two wide ribbons of red and a patch of red. Two ribbons and a patch of very dark green. The red patch is light with the white showing underneath it. A dug marble, but only one tiny sparkle. Paden City, West Virginia, circa 1955-1965. 9/16". Mint(-) (9.1). $95. (Auction #172, lot #39).

Rainbow. Modern green hornet/bumblebee hybrid. Opaque white base. Black equatorial band. Yellow patches. One patch has green on top of it. Super example. Not sure of the age of this, but it is 1975 or later. This is not the more recent translucent type; this is the opaque type. Likely 1975-1985. Still, very hard to find this type of color combination. A nice shooter. 7/8". Mint (9.9). $85. (Auction #131, lot #48).

Dragonfly. Patch and ribbon Rainbow Dragonfly. Light green and light black veneered on white. This one has a very unusual design. Both the green and black are very light. There is a small spot of white showing at one end. The marble is heavily swirled. Very odd. One small sparkle. Paden City, West Virginia, circa 1950-1965. 5/8". Mint(-) (9.2). $70. (Auction #75, lot #3).

Spiderman. Two color patch and ribbon Rainbow Spiderman. A patch and ribbon of blue and a patch and ribbon of brown/red. Interesting colors. The blue is a little light on one of the blue ribbons, so you can see that there is white underneath. Not the bright red that you see on some Spidermen. Has one tiny pinprick. Paden City, West Virginia, circa 1955-1970. 19/32". Mint(-) (9.0). $70. (Auction #153, lot #47).

Blended. Blue and red blended Spiderman. Bands of red and blue on opaque white. Paden City, West Virginia, date unknown. 5/8". Mint (9.7). $55. (Auction #160, lot #6).

Rainbow. Lot of eighteen marbles. Eight Bumblebees, seven Cub Scouts, three Wasps. All about 5/8". Almost all Mint. $55. (Auction #174, lot #25).

VITRO AGATE COMPANY

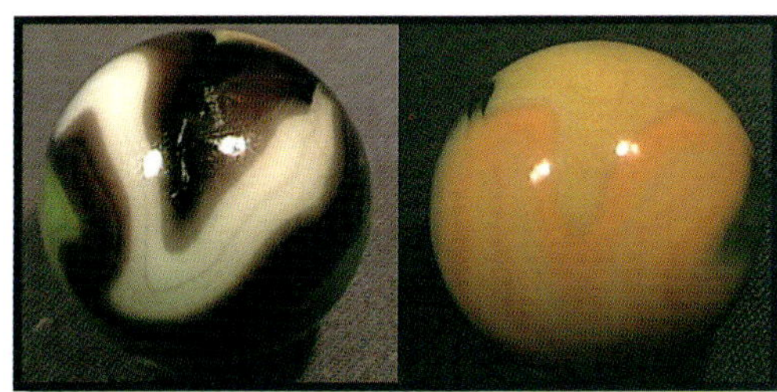

Parrot. Exceptional and definitive example of this type!! Opaque white base. Patches of black, aventurine green, yellow and light orange. There is an excellent "V" on one side formed by white showing through the black. There is a second exceptional "V" formed on the other side of the border of orange and yellow!! Superb example. One tiny pit on the black. Parkersburg, West Virginia, circa 1945-1955. 29/32". Mint(-) (9.0). $75. (Auction #59, lot #19).

Oxblood. Outstanding example of a Vitro oxblood. Semi-opaque white base. Band of wispy Vitro oxblood forming a nice "V". Outstanding marble. Parkersburg, West Virginia, circa 1945-1955. 9/16". Mint (9.9). $70. (Auction #98, lot #40).

Parrot. Nice Parrot. Opaque white base. Aventurine green, yellow, orange and black. Excellent white "V" outlined by black, with an orange one on the back. Surface in very nice shape. Parkersburg, West Virginia, circa 1945-1960. 29/32". Mint (9.9). $65. (Auction #126, lot #9).

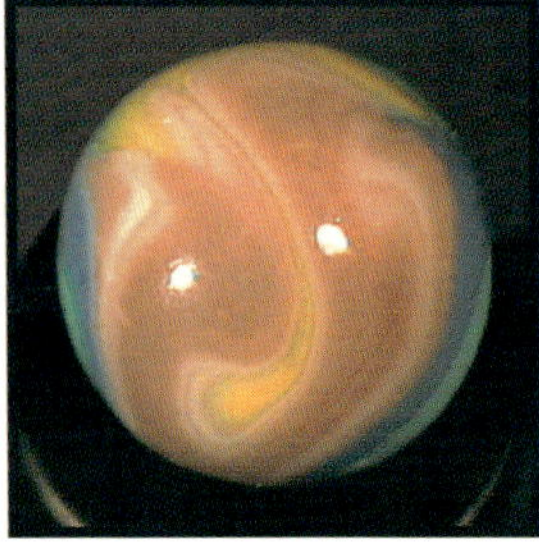

Parrot. Superb example. Opaque white base. Patches of light blue, blue, lavender and yellow. Stylized "V" in the lavender. No white showing. Excellent. Parkersburg, West Virginia, circa 1948-1958. 15/16". Mint (9.9). $65. (Auction #167, lot #38).

Parrot. Superb Parrot. Opaque white base. Black patch, yellow patch and aventurine green patch in between. There is a white "V" in the black patch and an orange "V" in the yellow patch. It is odd to have two well-formed Vs on the marble. Parkersburg, West Virginia, circa 1950-1965. 29/32". Mint (9.9). $65. (Auction #78, lot #32).

CONTEMPORARY HANDMADE

Salazar Art Glass. Experimental design, not put into production. Large, transparent cranberry red marble. On the top is a white bird, surrounded by iridescent clouds. Spiraling around the marble and framing the bird and clouds is an iridescent ribbon. Super design, but never put into production by Salazar. Signed on back "DP Salazar 4/90". 1-7/8". Mint (9.9). $385. (Auction #86, lot #33).

Beetem Glass. Globe marble. Stunning example of modern glasswork. Transparent clear base. Subsurface layer of opaque blue. Floating on the blue is an exact replica of the Earth's continents and land masses in dichroic silver. Floating above the ocean and land are opaque white clouds. Superior marble!!!! Each is individually numbered by Beetem. Signed on bottom "Geoffrey D Beetem 1998 570". Circa 1998. 2-1/16". Mint (9.9). $270. (Auction #86, lot #35).

Beetem Glass. A Beetem Globe marble. Very large. This is a replica of the planet Earth. Dichroic continents. Blue water. White puffy clouds floating above it. An absolute beauty. Signed on the bottom "Geoffrey D. Beetem 1998 654". Each is individually numbered. This is number 654. 3-1/4". Mint (9.9). $310. (Auction #135, lot #40).

Beetem Glass. Prototype Filigrana. Subsurface layer of alternating bands of aventurine green and aventurine green twisted with colored bands. No twist. Beetem produced 3 or 4 of 5 different color schemes as a prototype. These are not in production and Beetem says that even if he puts them into production in the future, they will be a much smaller size. Signed on bottom "Beetem 1998-P" (prototype). 2-1/2". Mint (9.9). $250. (Auction #135, lot #39).

Matthews Art Glass. Superior lobed onionskin. Transparent clear base. Opaque white subsurface layer. Seven loads. Loops of pastel transparent colors: pink, lavender, green, yellow. Superior marble. Handmade and signed "Matthews 1996". American, circa 1996. 1-15/16". Mint (9.9). $180. (Auction #99, lot #30).

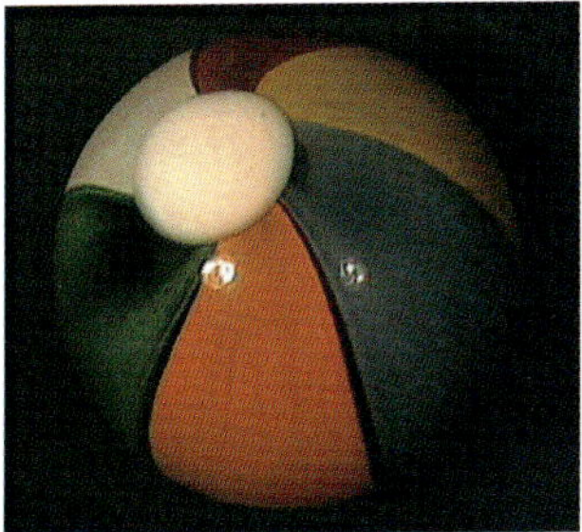

Matthews Art Glass. A Mark Matthews experimental Beach Ball. He never put this into production. Panels of blue, yellow, red, white, green and orange. With a white cap at either pole. Almost identical to a Wald Beach Ball. Very rare. I don't know if this is one of a kind, but it is close to it. The green panel is aventurine. Signed, between two panels, "Matthews 1991". 2-1/8". Mint (9.9). $175. (Auction #114, lot #31).

Salazar Art Glass. Prototype Moon and Stars. This marble has a blue moon and stars in white. Early Salazar prototype according to the consignor. Slightly flat on one side. Salazar abandoned using white as a base because it showed clear swirling (as you can see in this example). Rare marble. Signed on bottom "DP Salazar 4/93". Circa 1993. 1-7/16". Mint (9.9). $175. (Auction #86, lot #28).

T.C. Robertson. Very unusual marble. Called a Plated Marble. Transparent clear base. Latticinio core with bright primary colors surrounding a translucent yellow core. The surface is etched by copper metal, forming a number of flower-type open panels so that the interior can be viewed. Very odd. Handmade and signed "VM 92". American, circa 1992. 2-1/8". Mint (9.9). $170. (Auction #99, lot #22).

Fritz Glass. Limited Edition! These are called "Crazy Indians." Opaque black base with subsurface orange strands in a crazy swirl. Signature cane on the top pole!!! Fritz Lauenstein only made two of these, and individually numbered them. Handmade and signed "Fritz 1998 2-2" (#2 of 2 total). American, circa 1998. 1-9/16". Mint (9.9). $170. (Auction #99, lot #28).

Grablow Glass. Paperweight style of a rose flower in transparent clear glass. Aventurine green petals at the base of the marble. Red rose petals rising halfway up the marble. Signature cane "RG" set in the center of the petals on the bottom. Also, signed "R. Grablow". Grablow is a paperweight maker from southern New Jersey. He made a few marbles on a lark. He showed up at the first Philadelphia MarbleFest (1994). This is a beauty. And rare. American, circa 1990-1994. 2-1/4". Mint (9.8). $160. (Auction #142, lot #22).

Fritz Glass. Limited Edition prototype! This called a "Confetti." Transparent amber base. Surface layer of iridescent silver embedded with colored cane bits. Signature cane on the top pole!!! Fritz Lauenstein only made one! Handmade and signed "Fritz 1998 1-1" (#1 of 1 total). American, circa 1998. 1-9/16". Mint (9.9). $160. (Auction #99, lot #32).

Lundberg Studios. A Lundberg Studios "World Marble Classic." Excellent glass rendition of the Earth in a thick casing of transparent clear. This is an absolute beauty!!!!!! Signed on bottom "Lundberg Studios 1998 103071". Accompanied by a certificate numbered 103071. Lundberg Studios numbers all of their work sequentially regardless of what piece of glass they produce. Also, comes with a lucite display stand. 2-1/2". Mint (9.9). $160. (Auction #170, lot #49).

Salazar Art Glass. Very hard to find mid-1980s David Salazar marble. Transparent clear glass. Blue dichroic background. White chrysanthemum with green leaves and vines floating above the background. Signed on back "D P Salazar 2/85". This is part of a collection of seven mid-1980s Salazar marbles. Several, including this one, were designs I have not seen in a long time. According to David, once he retires a design he will not go back and make it again. This is a retired design. Rare opportunity!!! 2-1/4". Mint (9.9). $160. (Auction #173, lot #28).

Cape Cod Glass. Superb marble. White latticinio core. Outer layer has alternating bands of red or blue, on lutz. The bands are twisted so that they look like twisted ribbons of color and lutz. Beautiful effect. Handmade. Not signed, but made at Cape Cod Glass. 1-1/2". Mint (9.9). $160. (Auction #72, lot #35).

Matthews Art Glass. "King Tut". Very unusual. Opaque black base with a surface layer of Tiffany-favrille type iridescent swirling. Very nice. Signed "Matthews 1993". 1-7/8". Mint (9.9). $155. (Auction #135, lot #37).

Salazar Art Glass. Experimental aquarium scene. Paperweight type marble. Transparent clear base. Bottom layer is opaque dichroic white. Next layer has green anemone and kelp. Top layer has a sea horse, kelp and anemones. This is an experimental. Salazar abandoned the use of the white background because it made the foreground colors appear washed out. Very rare. Handmade and signed "DP Salazar". Undated. American, circa 1994. 1-5/8". Mint (9.9). $150. (Auction #99, lot #35).

Matthews Art Glass. Opaque banded lutz. Subsurface layer of opaque orange with six narrow pink bands and two wide white-edged lutz bands. Superb marble!! Signed on bottom "Matthews 1995". Circa 1995. 1-1/8". Mint (9.9). $150. (Auction #86, lot #34).

Salazar Art Glass. Very hard to find mid-1980s David Salazar marble. Transparent clear glass. Blue dichroic background. Hummingbird hovering next to two purple flowers. Signed on back "D P Salazar 1 86". This is part of a collection of seven mid-1980s Salazar marbles. Several, including this one, were designs I have not seen in a long time. According to David, once he retires a design he will not go back and make it again. This is a retired design. Rare!!! 1-1/2". Mint (9.9). $150. (Auction #181, lot #49).

Matthews Art Glass. Gorgeous onionskin. Transparent clear core. Subsurface layer of opaque white. Very satiny finish to it. Between the surface and the white layer is a layer of stretched thin color bands. Superb reverse twist, with the reversal occurring right at the marble equator. Superior workmanship. Signed "Matthews 1997". Handmade by Mark Matthews. Mark Matthews is arguably the finest marble artisan working today. 1-13/16". Mint (9.9). $135. (Auction #72, lot #32).

Salazar Art Glass. Super Iris marble. Paperweight style. Dichroic blue base. Two layer Iris with blue flowers and green stem and leaves. Creates an excellent three-dimensional effect. Much nicer depth than you usually see on Salazar marbles. Signed "D P Salazar 4/96". 1-3/4". Mint (9.9). $130. (Auction #156, lot #39).

Opposite page:
The color photographs from pages 49 to 96 illustrate the Complete Listing: Marbles by Type (pp. 97-223) chapter. Illustrations have been provided for as many marble descriptions as possible. The auction and lot numbers at the end of each description allow you to refer back to the marble illustrations presented here. As an example, Auction #55, Lot #2 is illustrated in photograph 55-2.

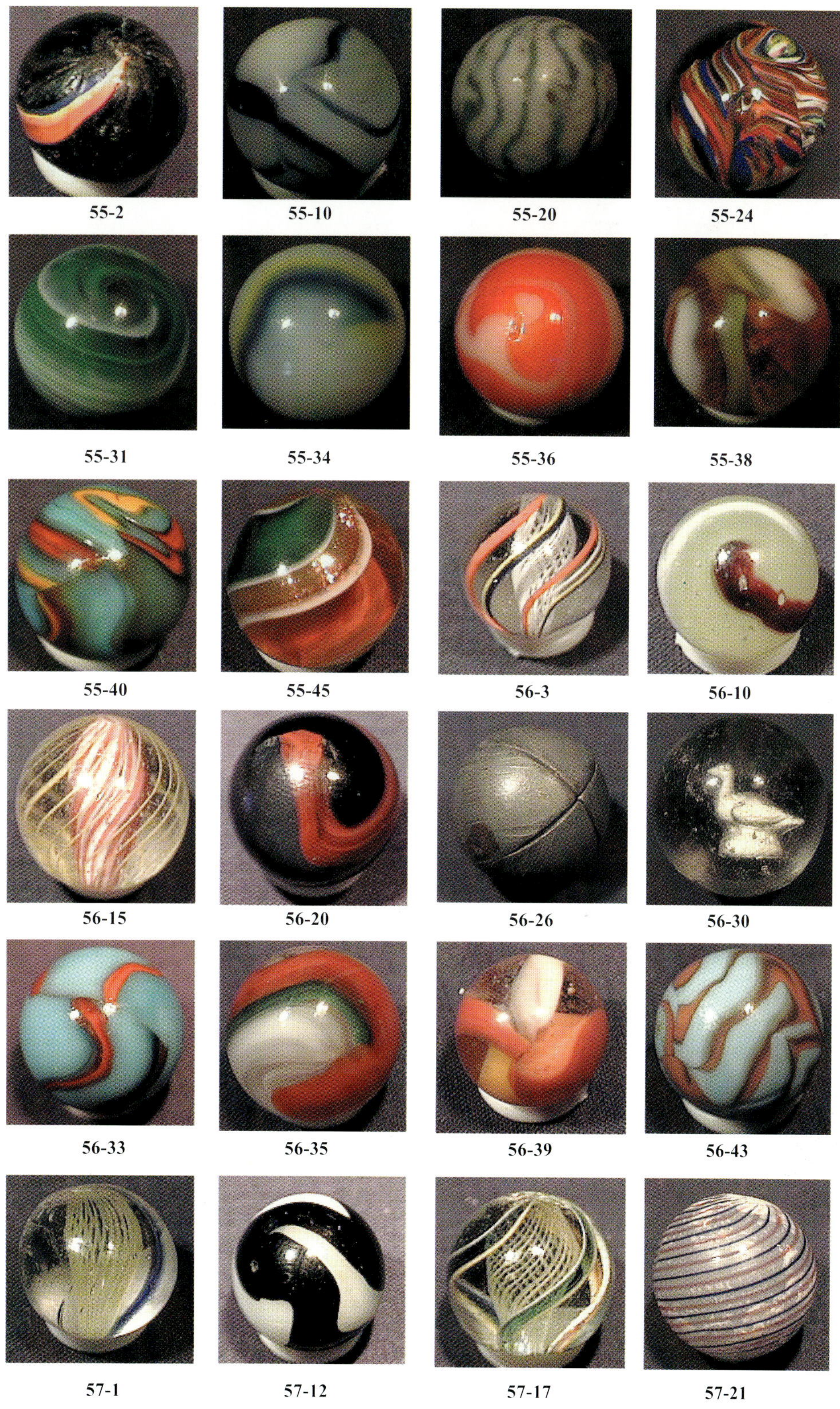

55-2
55-10
55-20
55-24
55-31
55-34
55-36
55-38
55-40
55-45
56-3
56-10
56-15
56-20
56-26
56-30
56-33
56-35
56-39
56-43
57-1
57-12
57-17
57-21

57-28   57-30   57-33   57-35

57-40   57-43   58-1   58-10

58-16   58-20   58-23   58-29

58-33   58-36   58-40   58-44

59-1   59-10   59-20   59-24

59-28   59-30   59-33   59-40

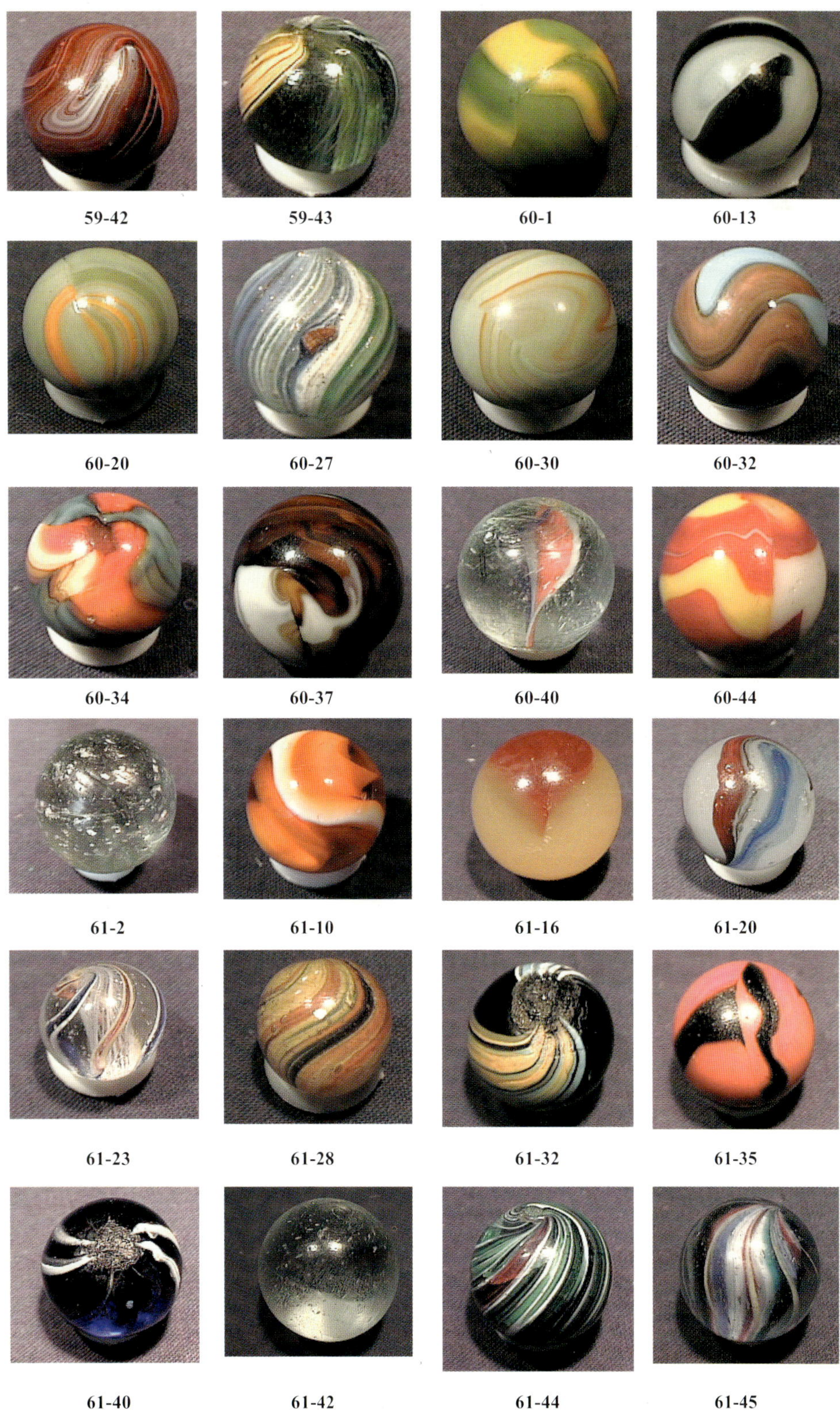

59-42
59-43
60-1
60-13
60-20
60-27
60-30
60-32
60-34
60-37
60-40
60-44
61-2
61-10
61-16
61-20
61-23
61-28
61-32
61-35
61-40
61-42
61-44
61-45

62-2	62-11	62-18	62-25
62-28	62-31	62-34	62-37
62-41	62-43	63-1	63-3
63-10	63-19	63-23	63-26
63-30	63-33	63-35	63-37
64-2	64-4	64-11	64-21

64-27

64-29

64-32

64-35

64-40

64-45

65-1

65-9

65-15

65-24

65-26

65-30

65-34

65-37

65-39

65-43

66-1

66-8

66-12

66-19

66-26

66-30

66-32

66-37

66-42	66-45	67-2	67-8
67-12	67-22	67-29	67-32
67-36	67-39	67-41	67-44
68-1	68-12	68-17	68-25
68-29	68-33	68-38	68-41
68-43	68-45	69-1	69-11

69-25   69-28   69-30   69-33

69-35   69-40   69-42   69-44

70-1   70-9   70-14   70-22

70-26   70-30   70-35   70-40

70-42   70-44   71-1   71-9

71-16   71-20   71-27   71-30

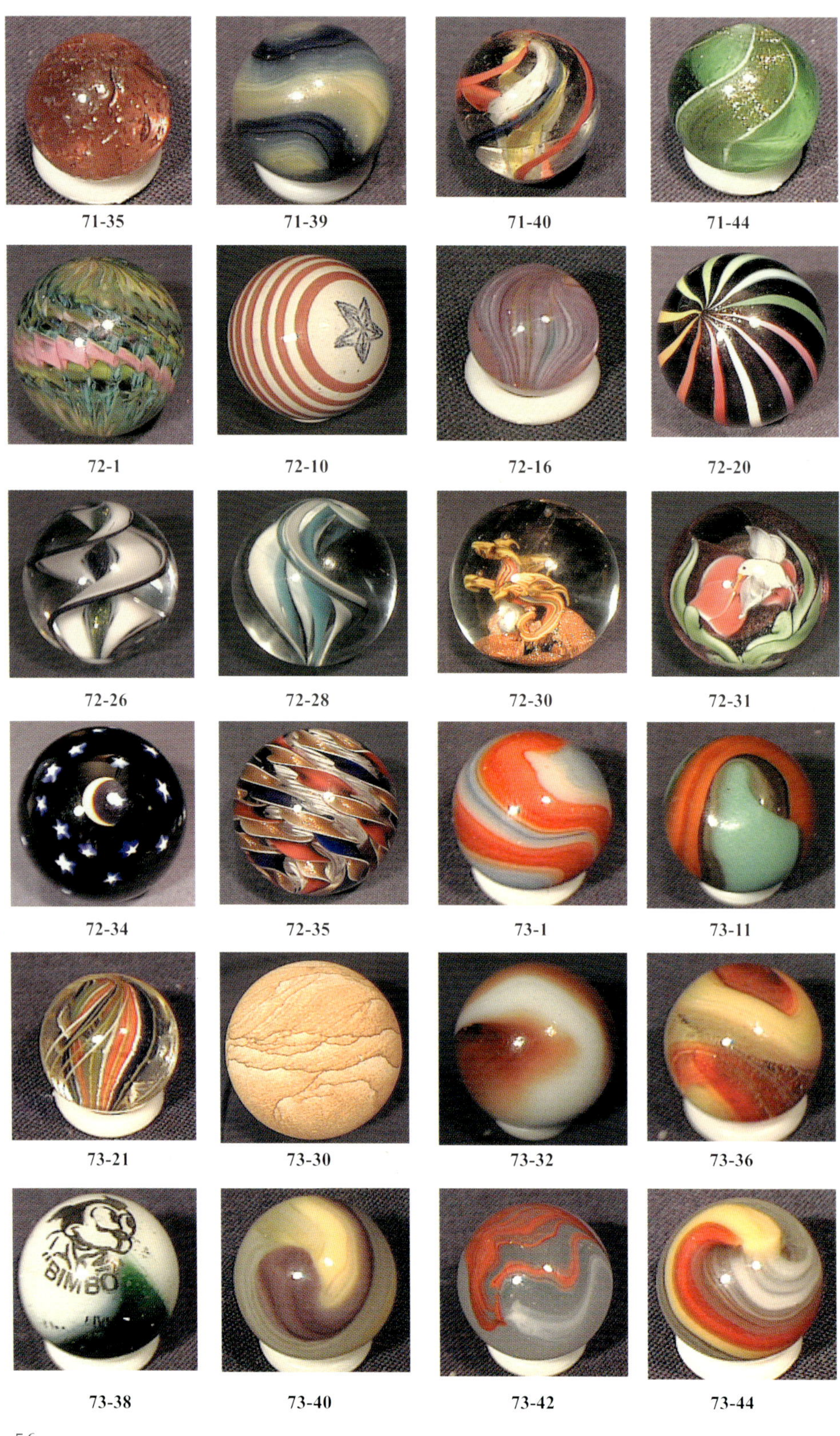

71-35	71-39	71-40	71-44
72-1	72-10	72-16	72-20
72-26	72-28	72-30	72-31
72-34	72-35	73-1	73-11
73-21	73-30	73-32	73-36
73-38	73-40	73-42	73-44

74-1	74-9	74-14	74-20
74-28	74-32	74-36	74-38
74-42	74-44	75-2	75-10
75-29	75-31	75-33	75-38
75-41	75-42	75-43	75-44
76-2	76-9	76-11	76-19

76-24	76-29	76-32	76-40
76-42	76-45	77-1	77-9
77-13	77-18	77-26	77-29
77-33	77-39	77-41	77-43
78-1	78-9	78-14	78-27
78-30	78-34	78-41	78-42

78-44	78-45	80-2	80-5
80-9	80-11	80-13	80-15
80-17	80-19	80-27	80-29
80-31	80-33	80-34	80-35
81-1	81-10	81-17	81-26
81-29	81-32	81-34	81-37

81-40	81-42	81-43	81-45
82-2	82-10	82-13	82-19
82-22	82-25	82-29	82-32
82-38	82-40	82-42	82-44
83-1	83-5	83-8	83-10
83-25	83-29	83-32	83-34

83-36   83-38   83-40   83-44

84-1   84-3   84-9   84-11

84-13   84-21   84-27   84-29

84-31   84-33   84-36   84-38

84-40   84-41   84-43   84-45

85-1   85-5   85-9   85-12

85-15	85-21	85-26	85-29
85-32	85-34	85-38	85-44
86-1	86-3	86-6	86-11
86-14	86-18	86-22	86-24
86-26	86-29	86-34	86-35
87-1	87-6	87-10	87-13

87-16	87-19	87-28	87-30
87-32	87-35	87-38	87-42
88-2	88-4	88-10	88-13
88-15	88-19	88-25	88-28
88-32	88-35	88-37	88-40
89-1	89-7	89-12	89-20

89-37	89-39	89-41	89-43
89-45	89-47	89-49	89-50
90-1	90-6	90-10	90-13
90-17	90-32	90-37	90-38
90-39	90-41	90-42	90-44
91-1	91-7	91-10	91-17

91-22	91-26	91-29	91-32
91-36	91-39	91-42	91-45
92-1	92-7	92-19	92-26
92-29	92-32	92-34	92-37
92-40	92-42	92-44	92-45
93-1	93-7	93-10	93-17

93-22   93-27   93-30   93-33

93-36   93-39   93-41   93-45

94-1   94-10   94-16   94-19

94-24   94-34   94-40   94-42

94-45   94-47   94-48   94-50

95-1   95-11   95-17   95-28

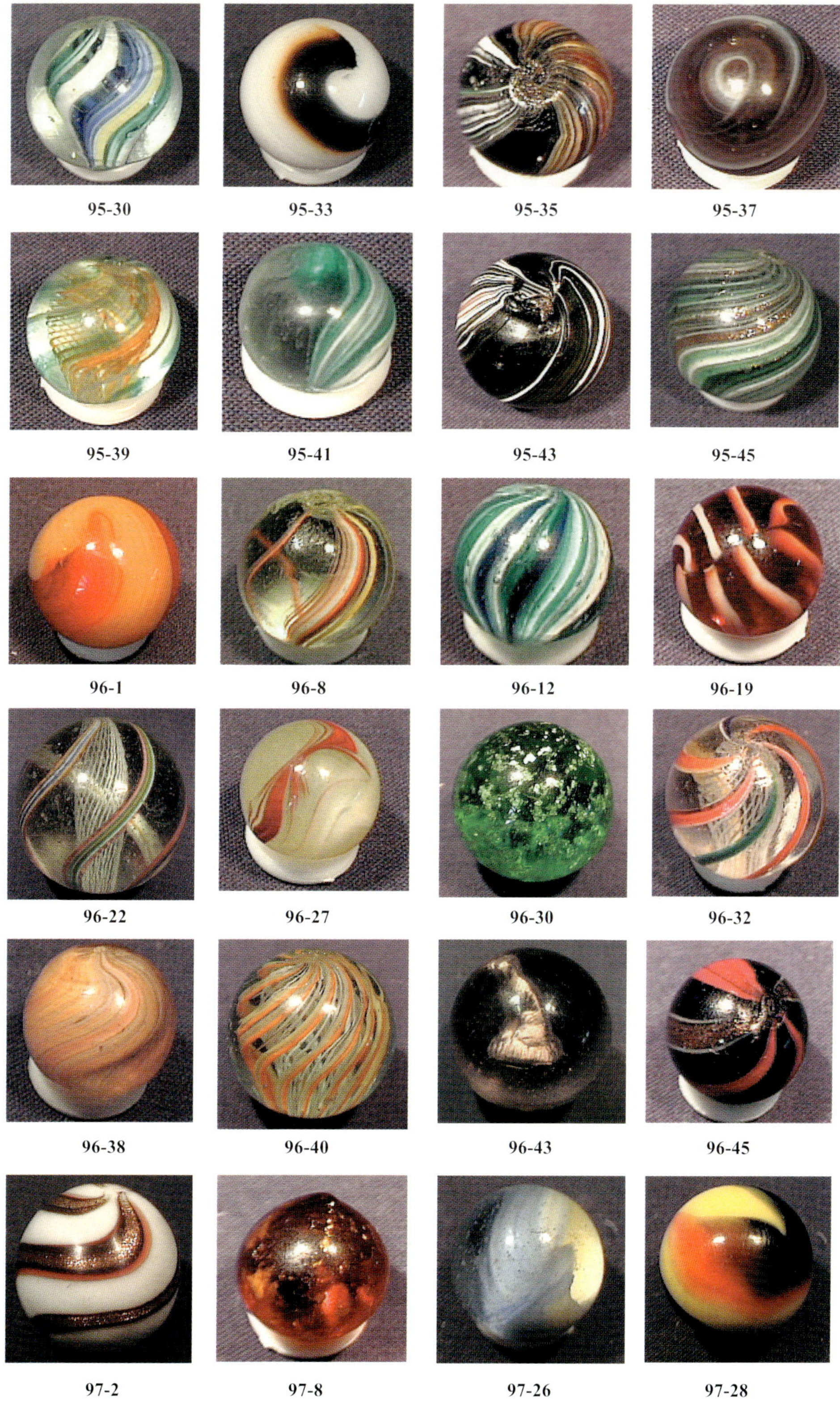

95-30	95-33	95-35	95-37
95-39	95-41	95-43	95-45
96-1	96-8	96-12	96-19
96-22	96-27	96-30	96-32
96-38	96-40	96-43	96-45
97-2	97-8	97-26	97-28

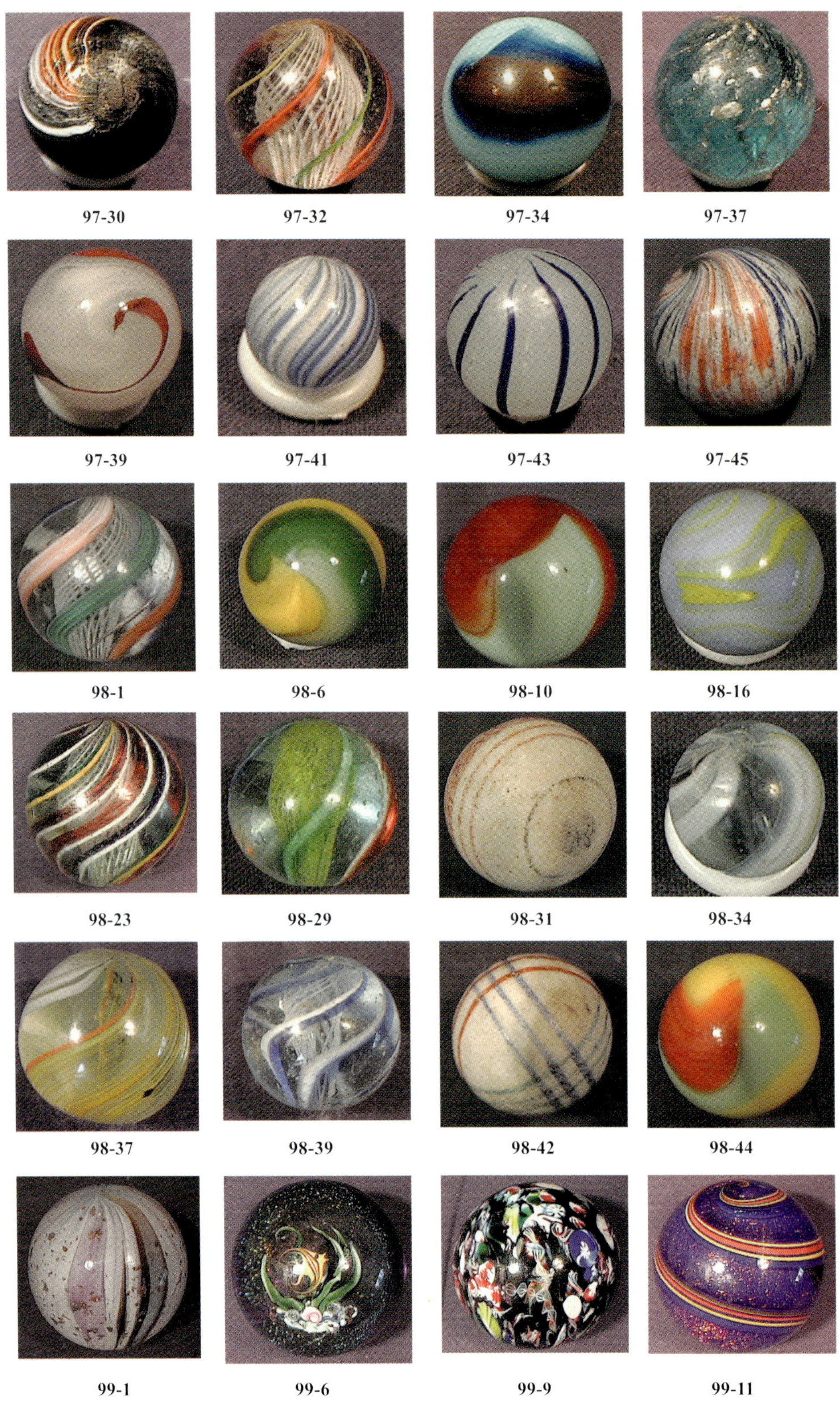

<table>
<tr><td>97-30</td><td>97-32</td><td>97-34</td><td>97-37</td></tr>
<tr><td>97-39</td><td>97-41</td><td>97-43</td><td>97-45</td></tr>
<tr><td>98-1</td><td>98-6</td><td>98-10</td><td>98-16</td></tr>
<tr><td>98-23</td><td>98-29</td><td>98-31</td><td>98-34</td></tr>
<tr><td>98-37</td><td>98-39</td><td>98-42</td><td>98-44</td></tr>
<tr><td>99-1</td><td>99-6</td><td>99-9</td><td>99-11</td></tr>
</table>

68

99-15   99-18   99-24   99-28

99-30   99-33   99-34   99-35

100-2   100-9   100-12   100-19

100-22   100-30   100-34   100-40

100-42   100-44   100-47   100-50

101-1   101-9   101-20   101-23

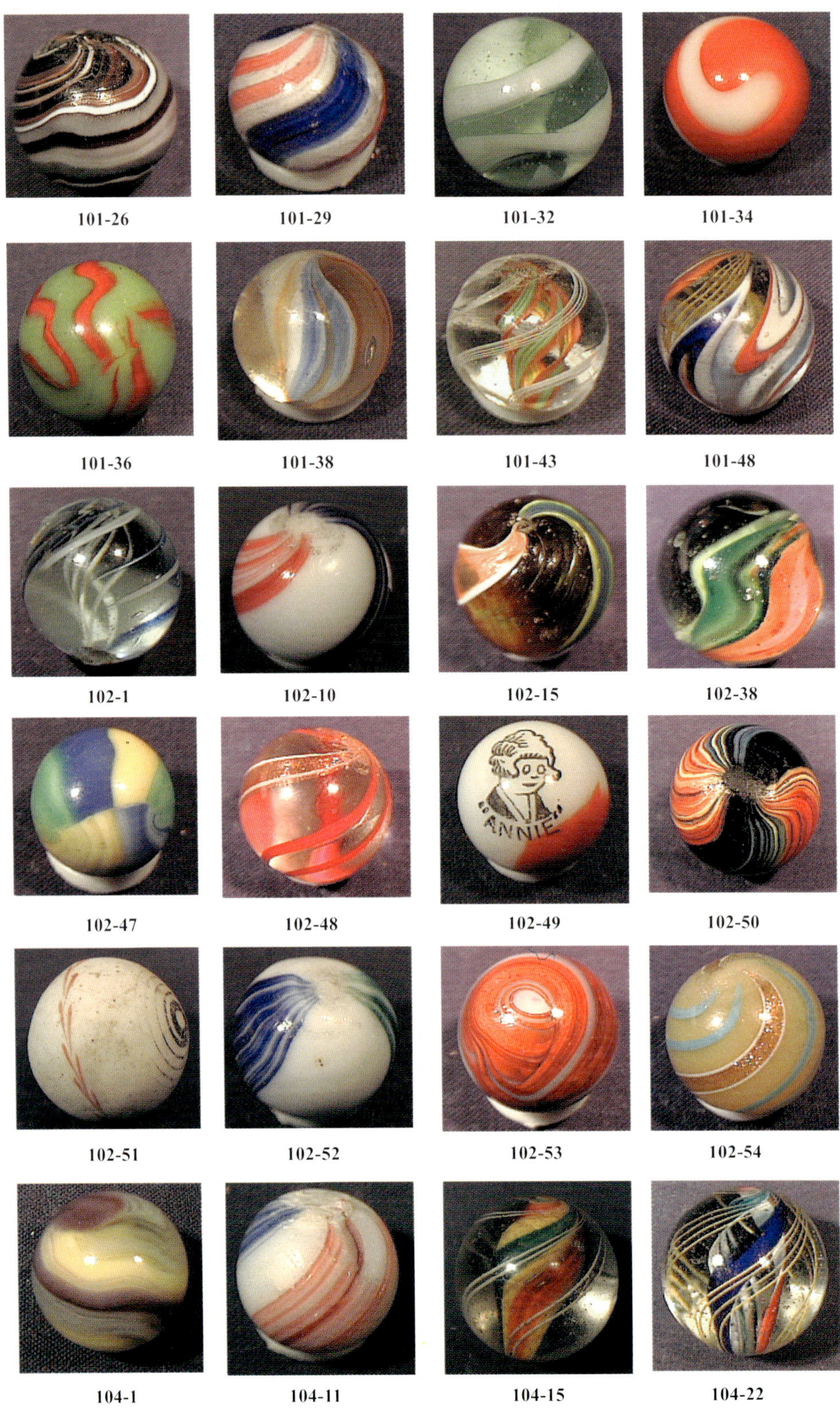

101-26	101-29	101-32	101-34
101-36	101-38	101-43	101-48
102-1	102-10	102-15	102-38
102-47	102-48	102-49	102-50
102-51	102-52	102-53	102-54
104-1	104-11	104-15	104-22

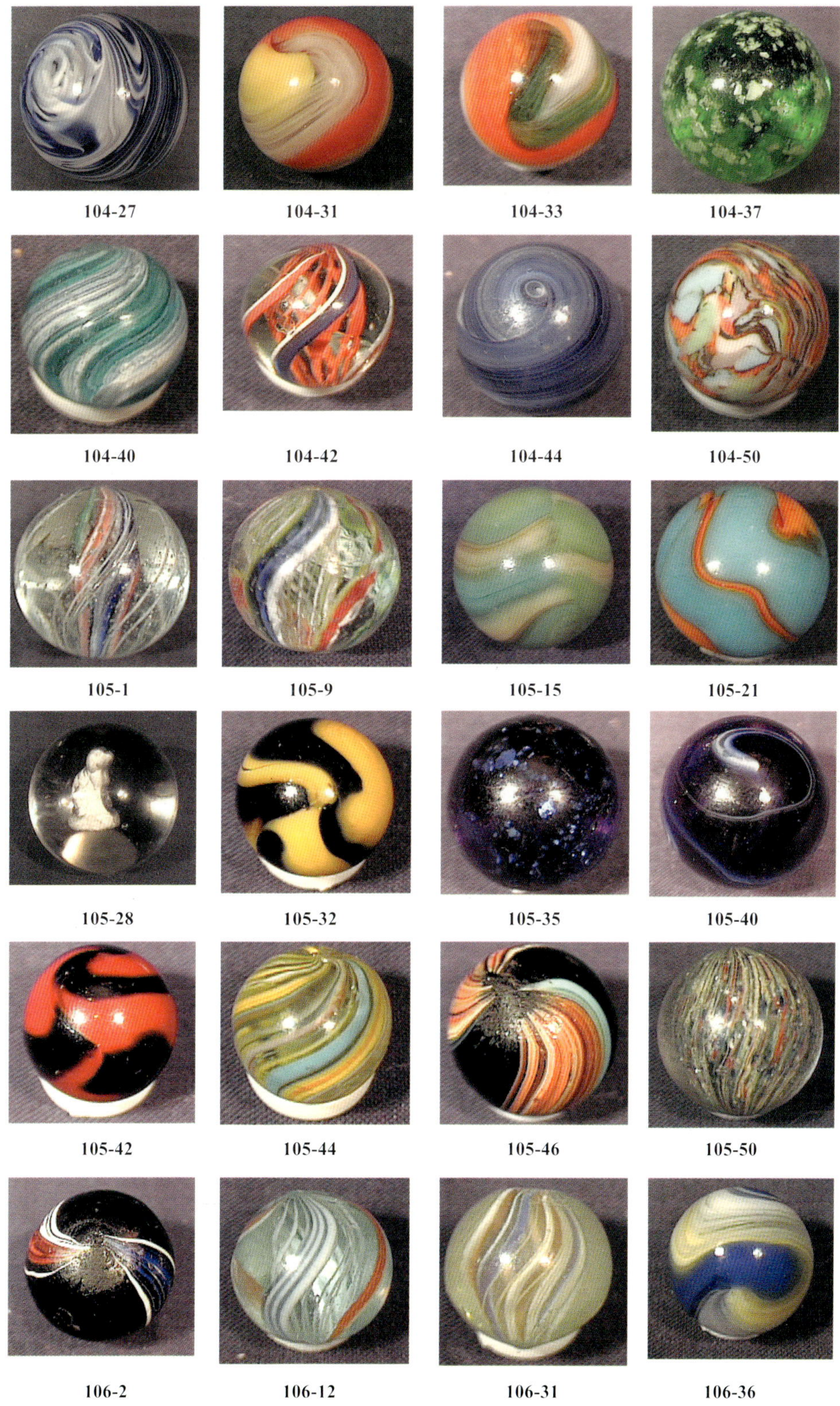

104-27	104-31	104-33	104-37
104-40	104-42	104-44	104-50
105-1	105-9	105-15	105-21
105-28	105-32	105-35	105-40
105-42	105-44	105-46	105-50
106-2	106-12	106-31	106-36

106-40
106-42
106-43
106-44
106-46
106-47
106-48
106-49
107-1
107-9
107-14
107-20
107-24
107-30
107-34
107-39
107-41
107-43
107-47
107-49
108-2
108-8
108-19
108-38

108-39	108-40	109-1	109-5
109-10	109-12	109-14	109-16
109-22	109-30	109-31	109-35
109-37	109-38	109-40	109-41
109-43	109-45	109-47	109-50
110-1	110-9	110-12	110-20

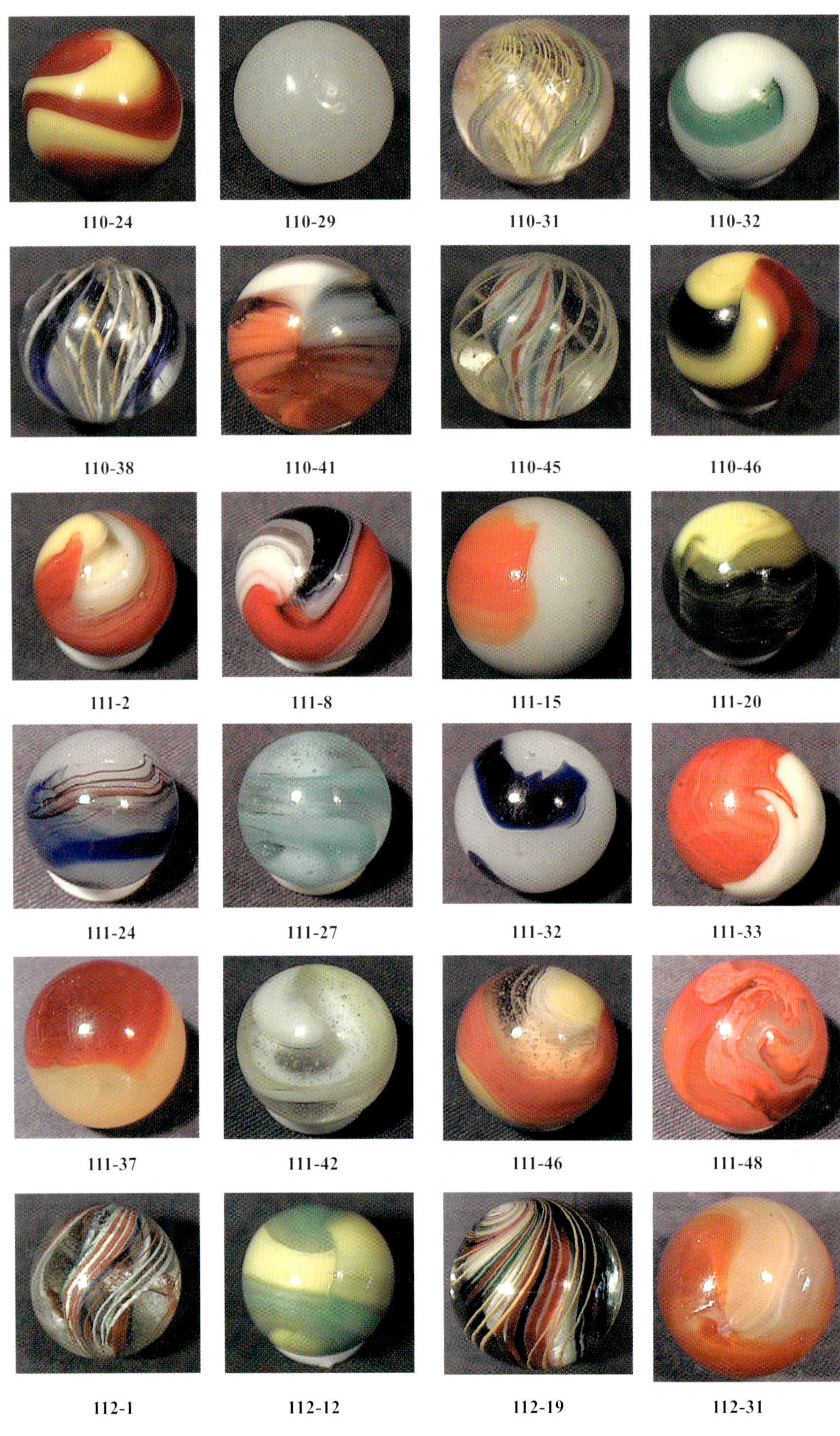

110-24 110-29 110-31 110-32

110-38 110-41 110-45 110-46

111-2 111-8 111-15 111-20

111-24 111-27 111-32 111-33

111-37 111-42 111-46 111-48

112-1 112-12 112-19 112-31

112-33	112-35	112-38	112-40
112-42	112-46	112-48	112-50
113-3	113-9	113-15	113-21
113-24	113-27	113-30	113-34
113-37	113-39	113-43	113-49
114-1	114-5	114-8	114-11

114-15	114-19	114-21	114-23
114-27	114-30	114-33	114-34
115-1	115-10	115-19	115-22
115-31	115-33	115-38	115-40
115-42	115-44	115-46	115-48
116-1	116-10	116-15	116-20

116-26   116-29   116-31   116-34

116-38   116-41   116-43   116-50

117-3   117-10   117-20   117-21

117-32   117-34   117-36   117-39

117-41   117-44   117-46   117-48

118-1   118-9   118-14   118-20

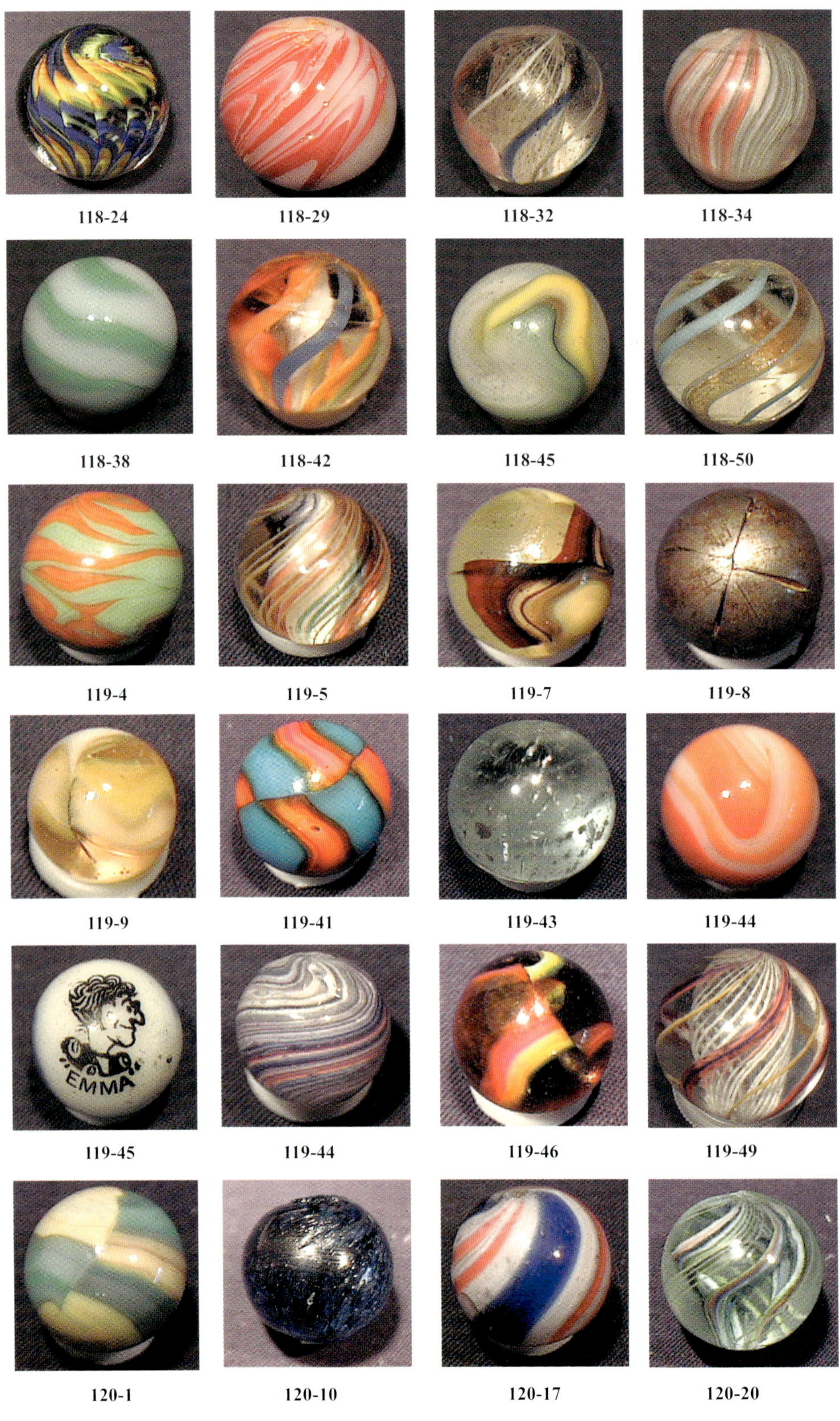

118-24	118-29	118-32	118-34
118-38	118-42	118-45	118-50
119-4	119-5	119-7	119-8
119-9	119-41	119-43	119-44
119-45	119-44	119-46	119-49
120-1	120-10	120-17	120-20

120-30
120-33
120-38
120-41
120-44
120-45
120-47
120-50
121-2
121-10
121-16
121-27
121-29
121-32
121-34
121-36
121-40
121-43
121-45
121-49
122-1
122-10
122-22
122-26

122-30	122-35	122-38	122-40
122-43	122-45	122-48	122-50
123-2	123-10	123-20	123-27
123-33	123-40	123-42	123-44
123-46	123-47	123-48	123-50
124-2	124-7	124-10	124-21

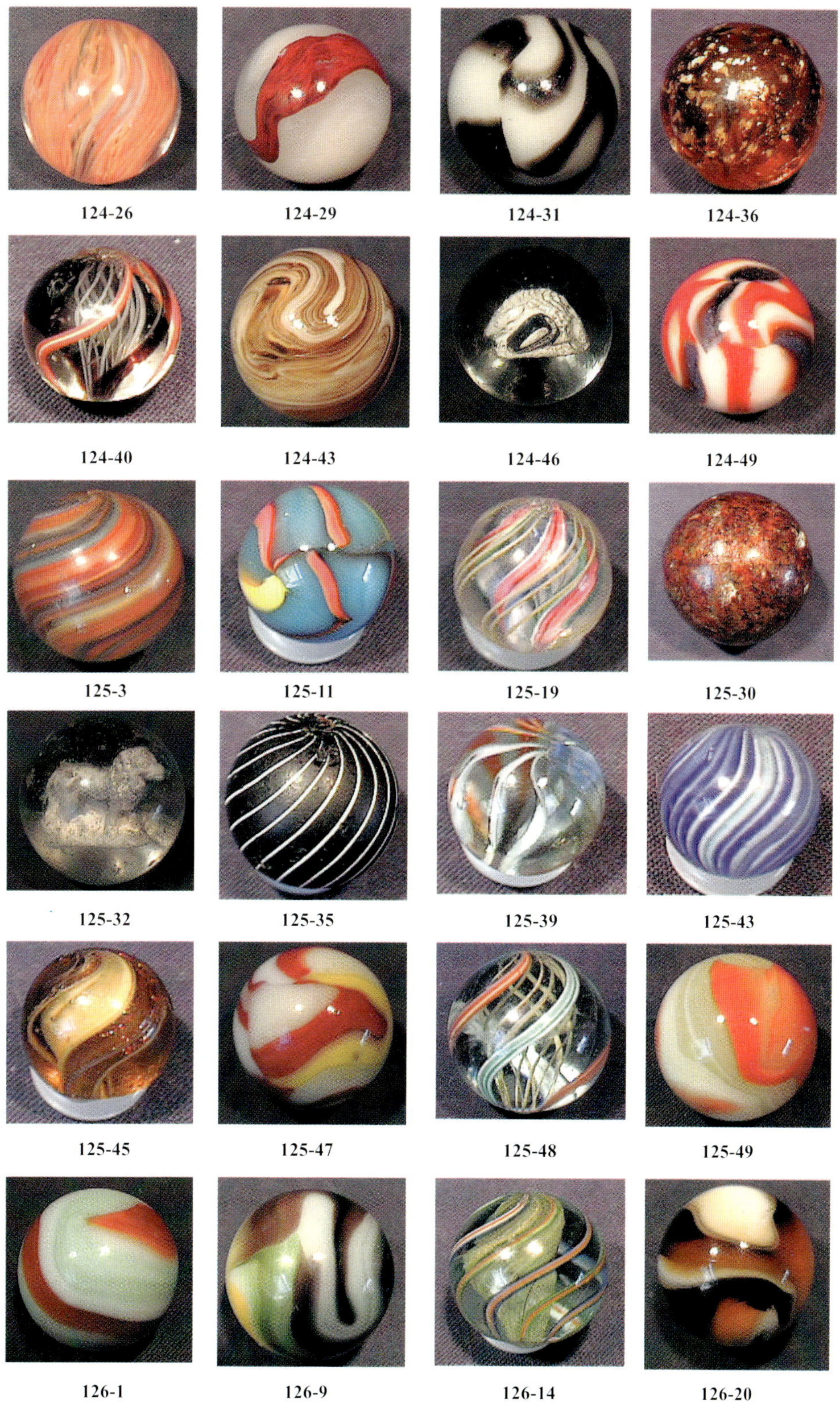

124-26	124-29	124-31	124-36
124-40	124-43	124-46	124-49
125-3	125-11	125-19	125-30
125-32	125-35	125-39	125-43
125-45	125-47	125-48	125-49
126-1	126-9	126-14	126-20

126-24	126-29	126-32	126-34
126-36	126-40	126-44	126-49
127-1	127-4	127-6	127-7
127-27	127-30	127-33	127-36
127-40	127-42	127-43	128-2
128-6	128-10	128-11	128-14

128-16	128-21	128-26	128-29
128-33	128-34	128-36	128-39
129-2	129-9	129-11	129-13
129-18	129-20	129-26	129-32
129-40	129-42	129-46	129-49
130-2	130-9	130-13	130-16

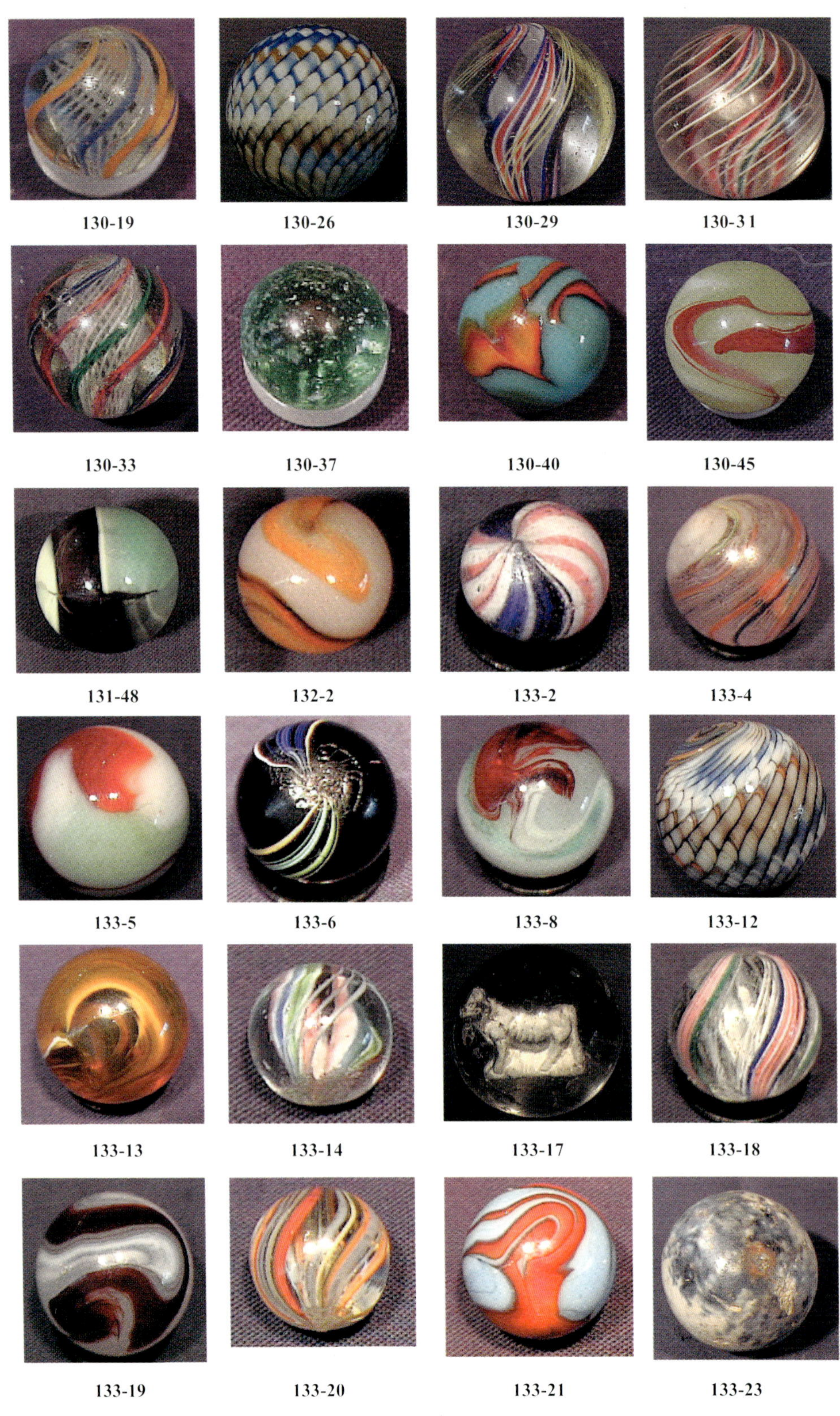

130-19	130-26	130-29	130-31
130-33	130-37	130-40	130-45
131-48	132-2	133-2	133-4
133-5	133-6	133-8	133-12
133-13	133-14	133-17	133-18
133-19	133-20	133-21	133-23

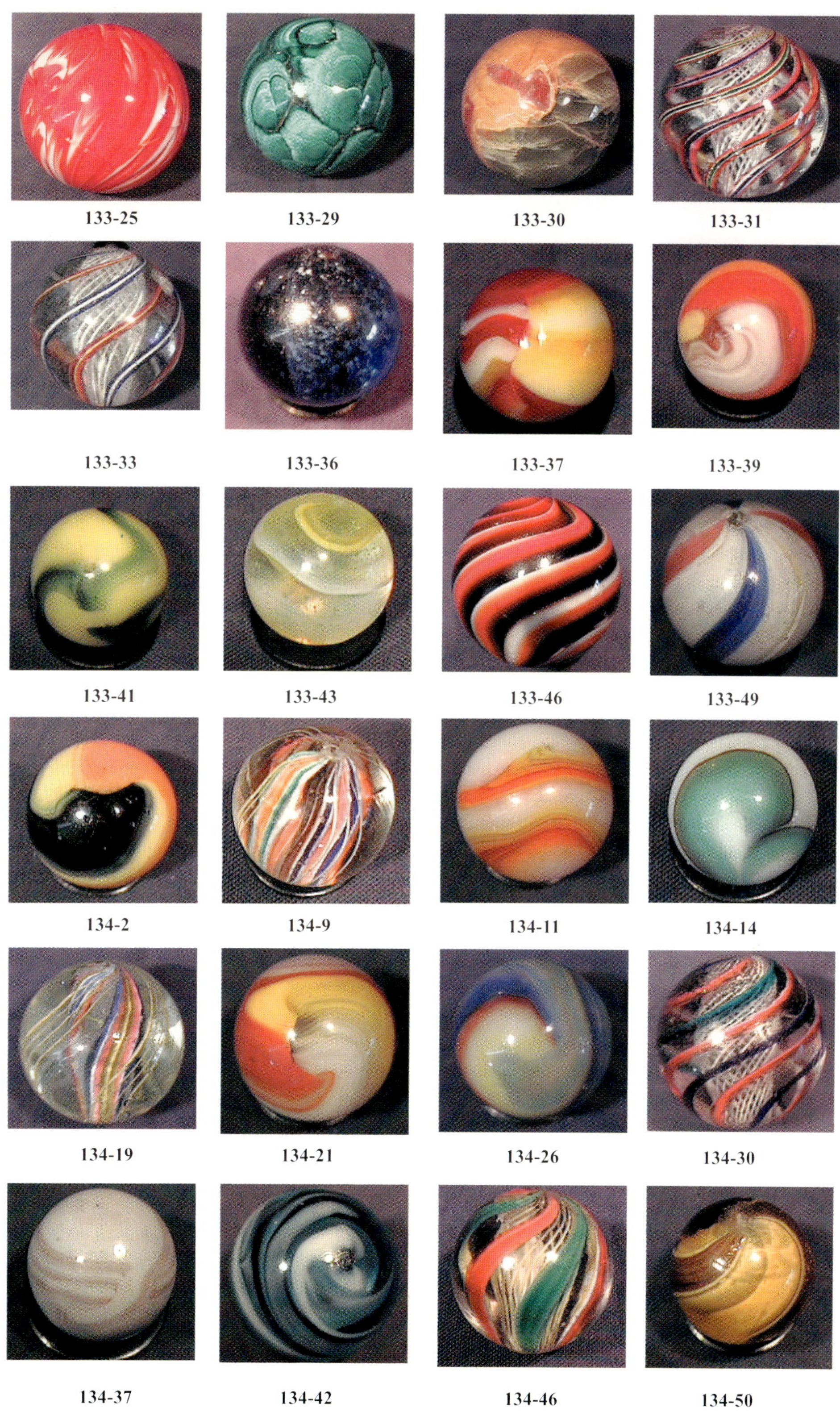

133-25	133-29	133-30	133-31
133-33	133-36	133-37	133-39
133-41	133-43	133-46	133-49
134-2	134-9	134-11	134-14
134-19	134-21	134-26	134-30
134-37	134-42	134-46	134-50

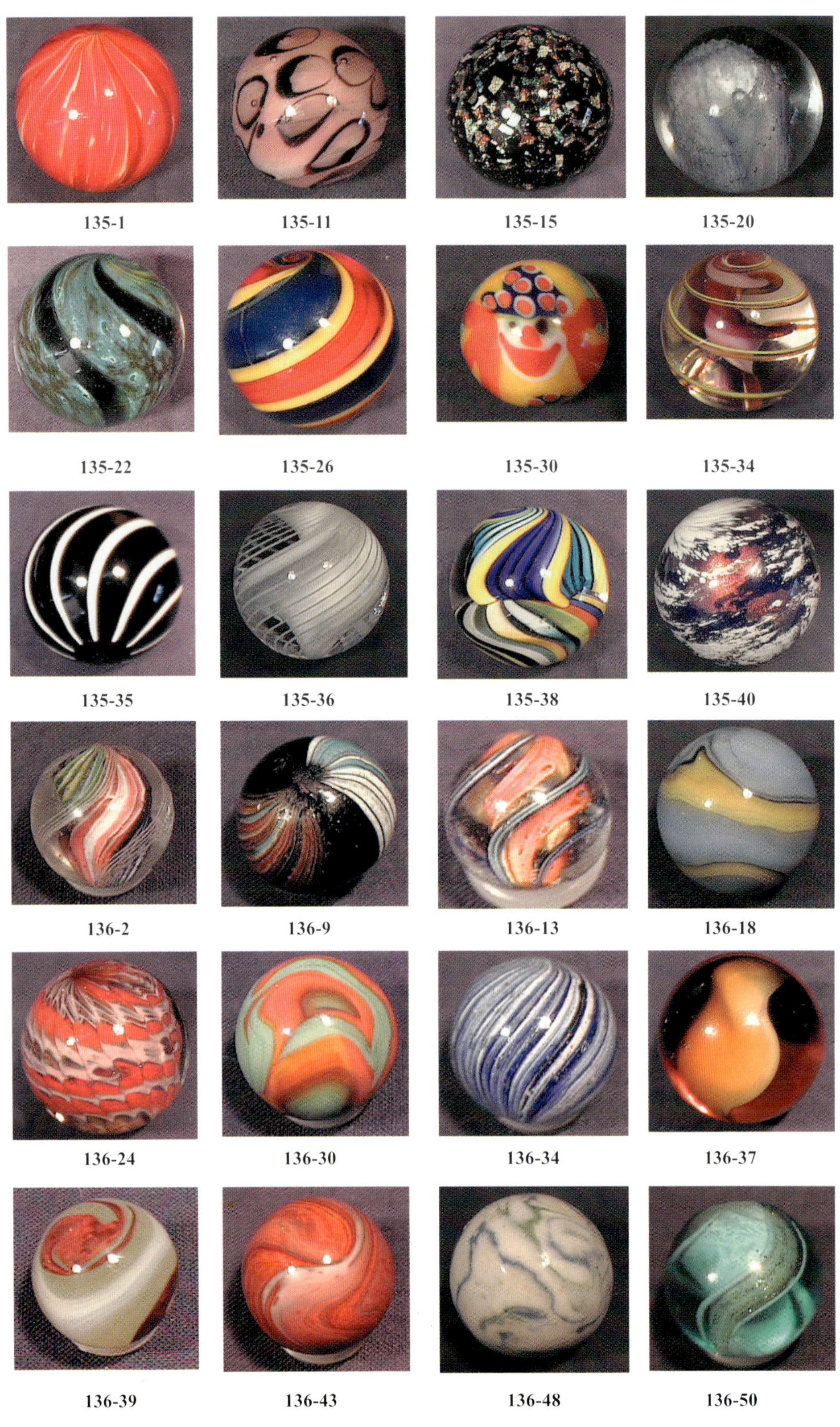

135-1	135-11	135-15	135-20
135-22	135-26	135-30	135-34
135-35	135-36	135-38	135-40
136-2	136-9	136-13	136-18
136-24	136-30	136-34	136-37
136-39	136-43	136-48	136-50

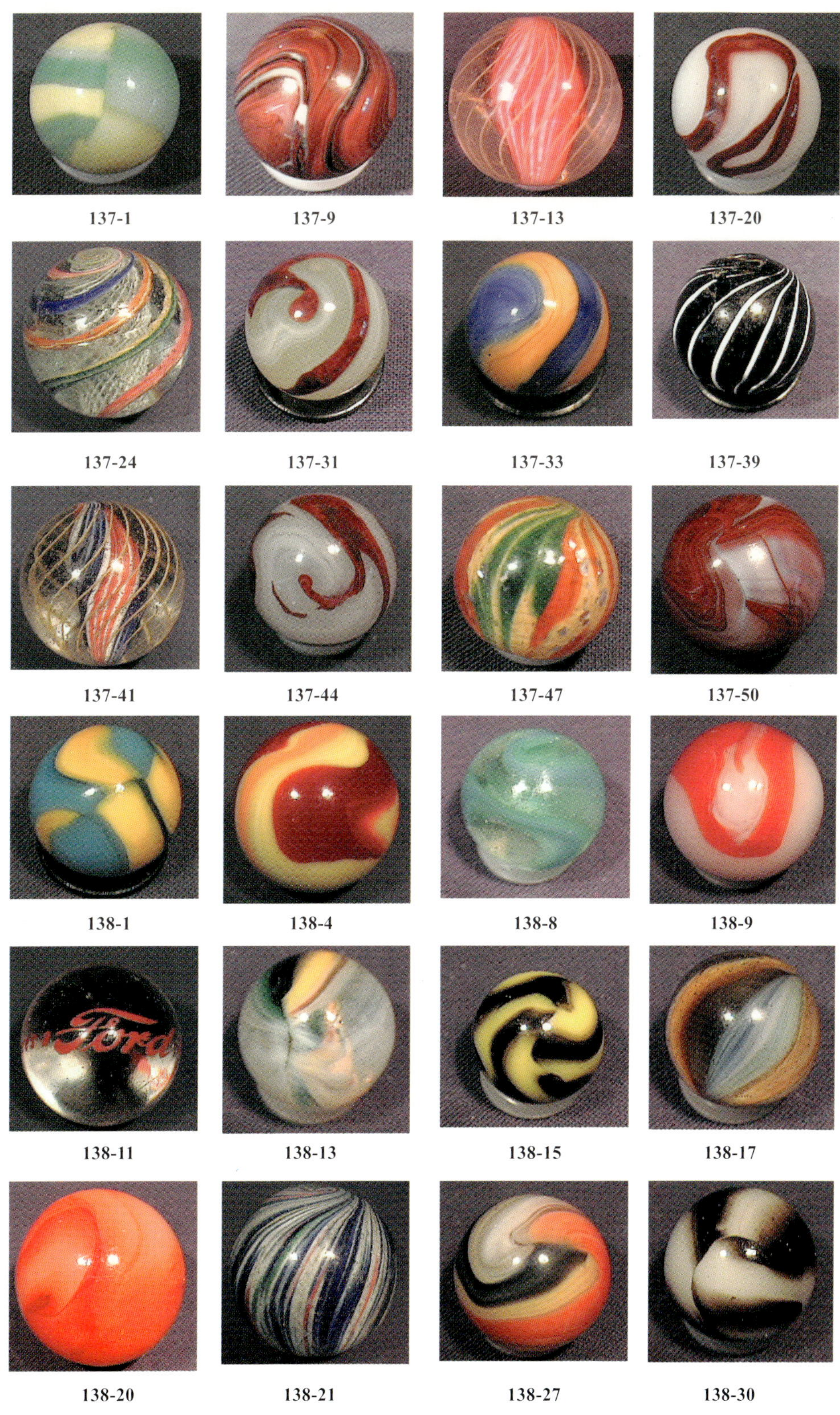

137-1	137-9	137-13	137-20
137-24	137-31	137-33	137-39
137-41	137-44	137-47	137-50
138-1	138-4	138-8	138-9
138-11	138-13	138-15	138-17
138-20	138-21	138-27	138-30

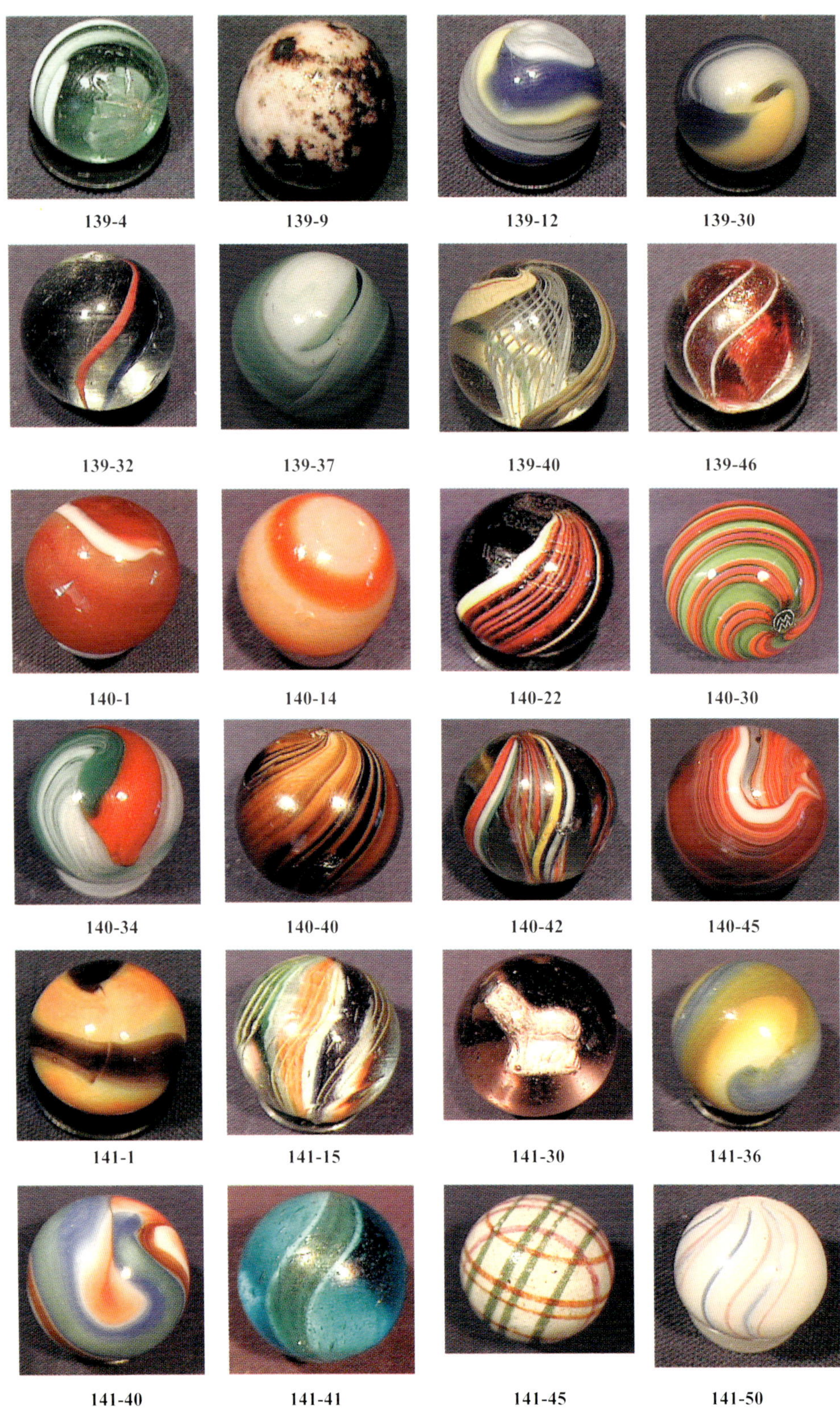

139-4
139-9
139-12
139-30
139-32
139-37
139-40
139-46
140-1
140-14
140-22
140-30
140-34
140-40
140-42
140-45
141-1
141-15
141-30
141-36
141-40
141-41
141-45
141-50

142-1	142-17	142-26	142-32
142-41	142-43	142-46	142-47
143-1	143-4	143-8	143-38
143-40	143-43	143-45	143-48
144-1	144-37	144-41	144-42
144-43	144-45	144-47	144-50

145-1   145-14   145-29   145-32

145-38   145-40   145-47   145-49

146-2   146-7   146-10   146-30

146-33   146-42   146-44   146-46

147-1   147-18   147-29   147-33

147-36   147-40   147-46   147-47

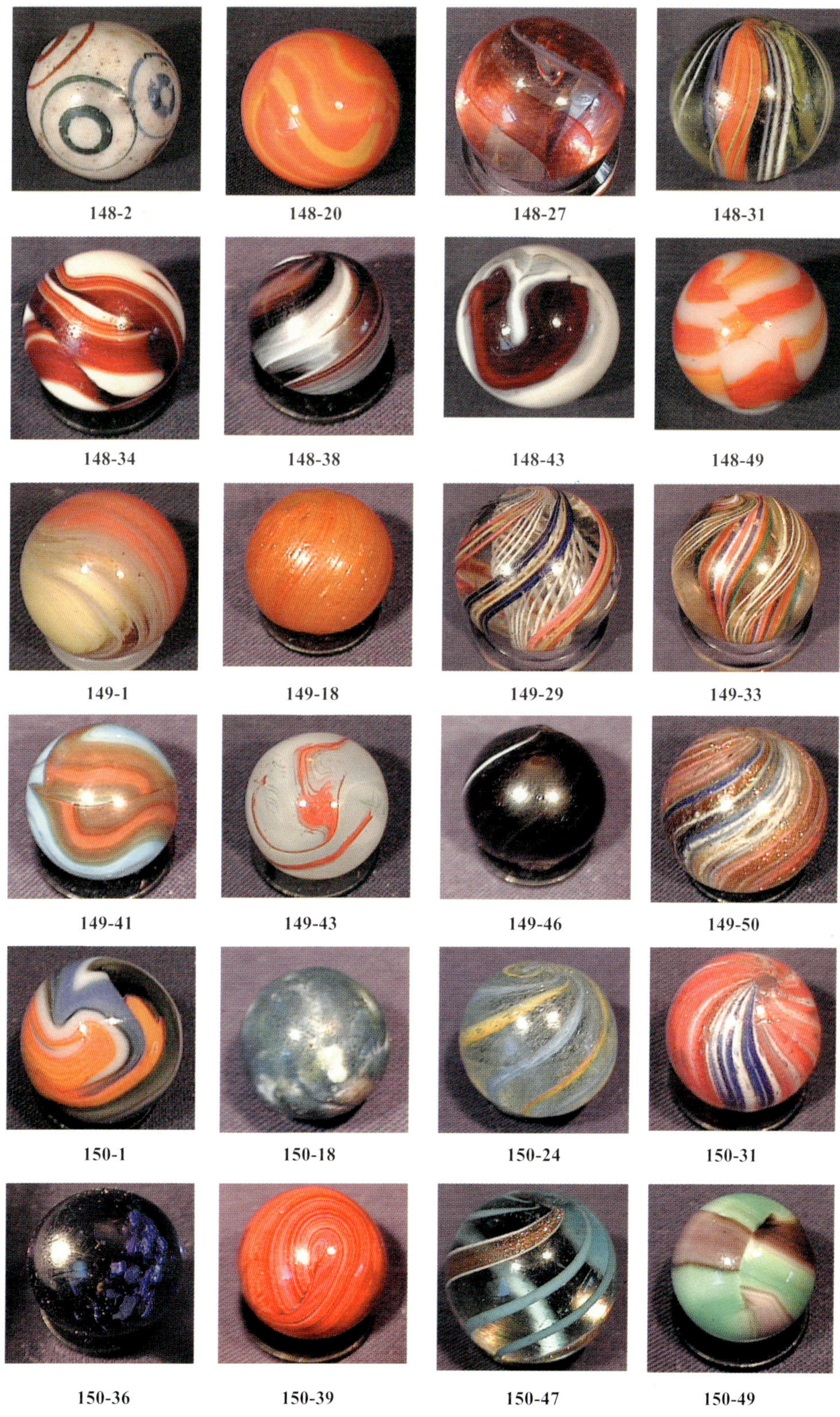

148-2	148-20	148-27	148-31
148-34	148-38	148-43	148-49
149-1	149-18	149-29	149-33
149-41	149-43	149-46	149-50
150-1	150-18	150-24	150-31
150-36	150-39	150-47	150-49

151-3	151-19	151-28	151-30
151-36	151-39	151-42	151-50
152-3	152-38	152-42	152-50
153-1	153-25	153-30	153-31
153-33	153-38	153-44	153-47
154-1	154-27	154-40	154-46

155-3	155-11	155-41	155-50
156-1	156-36	156-40	156-50
157-1	157-34	157-44	157-45
158-1	158-31	158-40	158-49
159-1	159-27	159-34	159-46
160-1	160-24	160-42	160-49

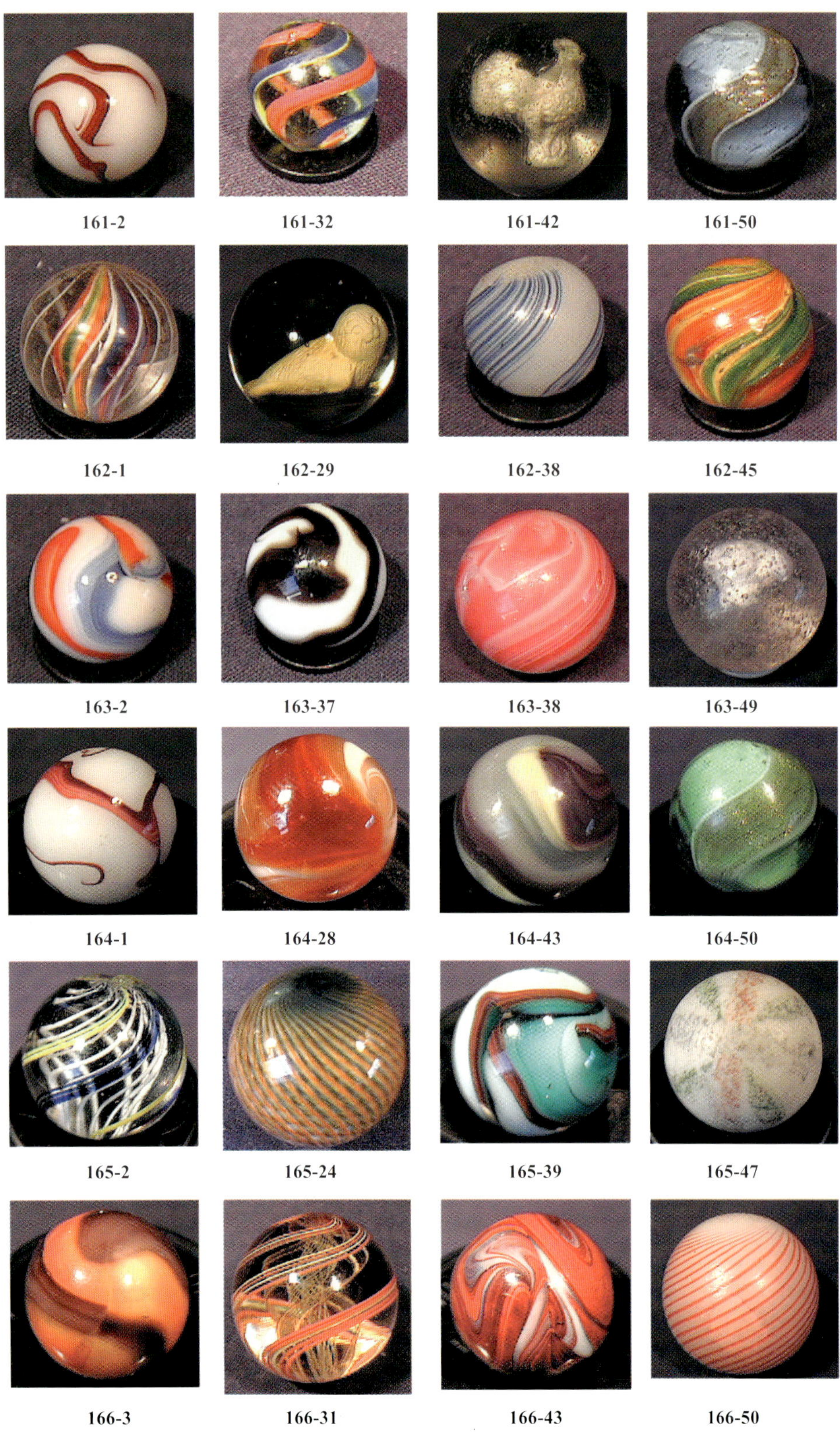

161-2	161-32	161-42	161-50
162-1	162-29	162-38	162-45
163-2	163-37	163-38	163-49
164-1	164-28	164-43	164-50
165-2	165-24	165-39	165-47
166-3	166-31	166-43	166-50

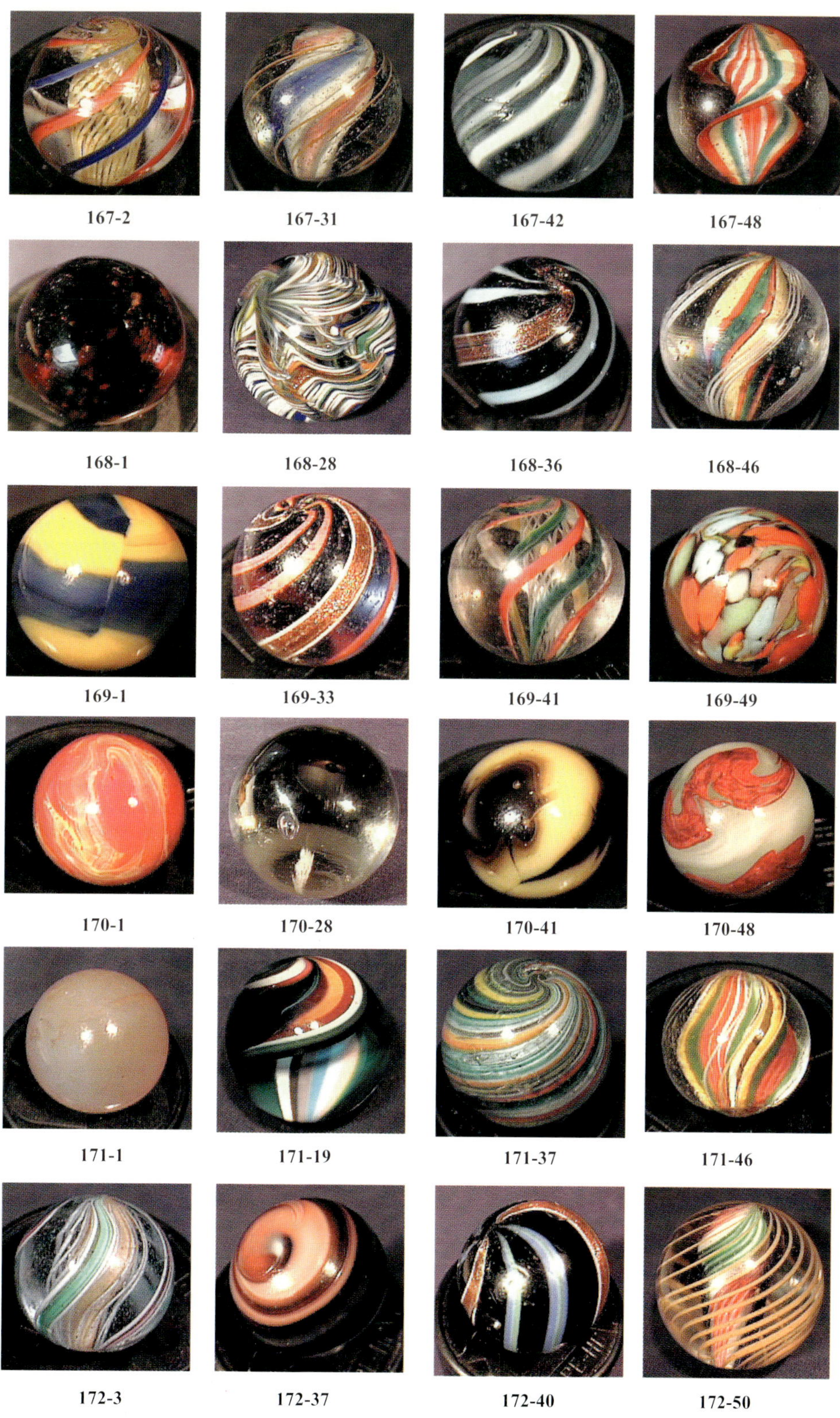

167-2   167-31   167-42   167-48

168-1   168-28   168-36   168-46

169-1   169-33   169-41   169-49

170-1   170-28   170-41   170-48

171-1   171-19   171-37   171-46

172-3   172-37   172-40   172-50

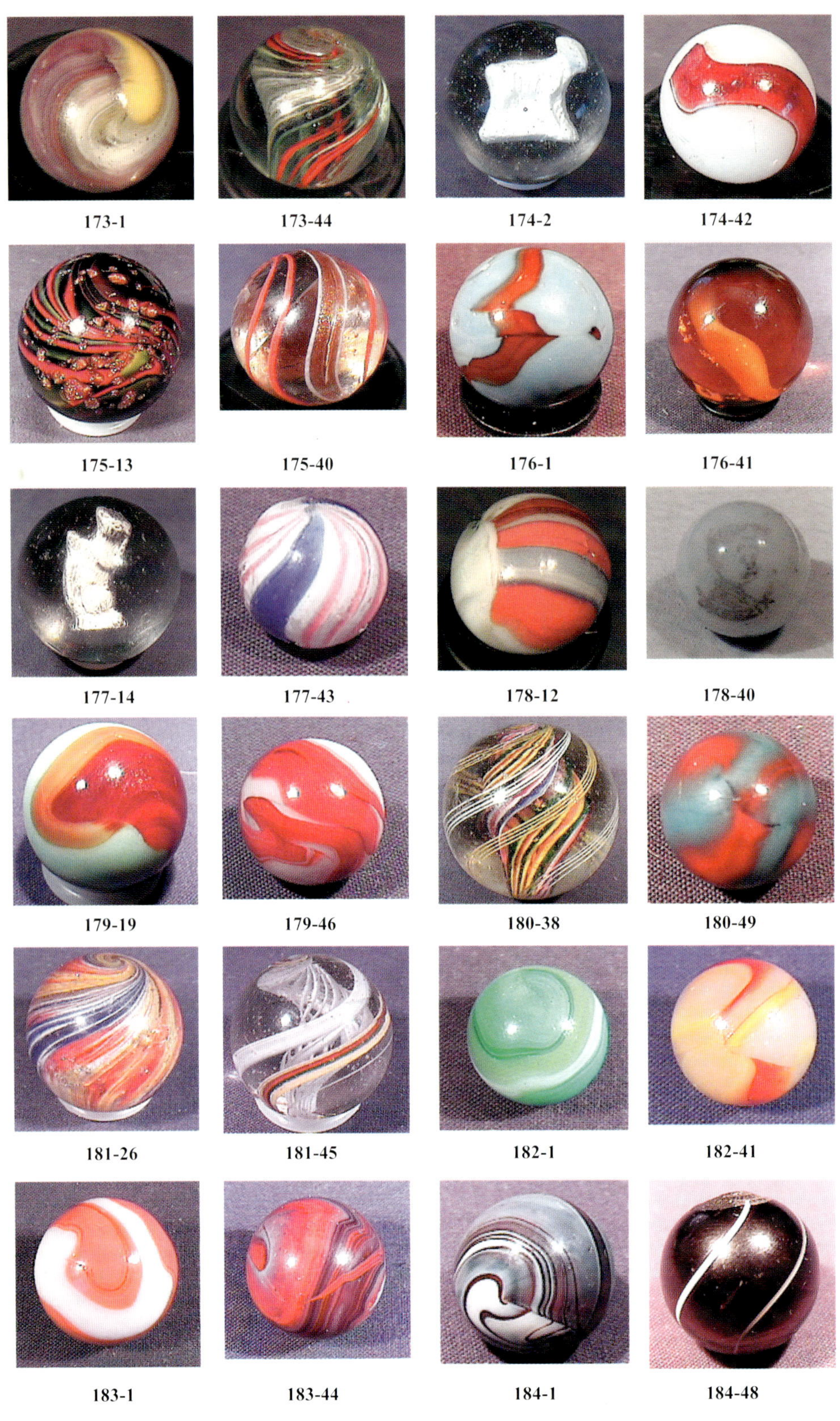

173-1	173-44	174-2	174-42
175-13	175-40	176-1	176-41
177-14	177-43	178-12	178-40
179-19	179-46	180-38	180-49
181-26	181-45	182-1	182-41
183-1	183-44	184-1	184-48

Complete Listing: Marbles by Type

AKRO AGATE COMPANY. Ace. Beautiful shooter Ace. Translucent milky white base. Translucent very dark blue spiral on the surface. 31/32". Mint(-) (9.2). $26. (Auction #78, Lot 12).

AKRO AGATE COMPANY. Ace. Translucent blue on translucent milky white. One small sparkle and one melt spot. Shooter. 1". Mint(-) (9). $22. (Auction #111, Lot 32).

AKRO AGATE COMPANY. Ace. Three color Ace. Translucent milky white base. Swirl of pale opaque egg yolk yellow and translucent. 21/32". Mint (9.9). $17. (Auction #113, Lot 27).

AKRO AGATE COMPANY. Ace corkscrew. Translucent milky white base with an orange/red semi-opaque spiral. Fantastic shooter! One tiny sparkle. 1". Mint(-) (9.2). $37. (Auction #115, Lot 12).

AKRO AGATE COMPANY. Ace corkscrew. Nice three color Ace. Hard to find. Translucent milky white base. Spiral of green and one of blue. 1". Near Mint(+) (8.9). $35. (Auction #156, Lot 42).

AKRO AGATE COMPANY. Ace hybrid. Hard to find corkscrew. Shooter size. Translucent milky white base. One spiral of opaque yellow. 31/32". Near Mint(+) (8.7). $26. (Auction #63, Lot 38).

AKRO AGATE COMPANY. Ade. Lot of two marbles. Lemonade corkscrew, 19/32", Mint (9.6). Limeade corkscrew, 5/8", Mint (9.9). $60. (Auction #175, Lot 43).

AKRO AGATE COMPANY. Ade. Lot of two marbles. Limeade. Corkscrew. Sparkles and surface wear. 19/32". Near Mint(+) (8.9). $25. (Auction #88, Lot 5).

AKRO AGATE COMPANY. Ade. Lemonade/orangeade hybrid. Lemonade swirl with orange mixed in with the opaque yellow. One chip. 5/8". Near Mint (8.6). $22. (Auction #130, Lot 38).

AKRO AGATE COMPANY. Ade hybrid. Lemonade/limeade hybrid swirl shooter. Fluorescent ade base. White swirling. Dark yellow swirling. 1". Near Mint (8.3). $55. (Auction #178, Lot 37).

AKRO AGATE COMPANY. Ade hybrid. Orangeade/lemonade hybrid. Unusual. Lemonade swirl. Orange on top of the yellow. Couple of tiny spar. 5/8". Near Mint(+) (8.8). $27. (Auction #141, Lot 44).

AKRO AGATE COMPANY. Ades. Lot of three marbles. Nice set of Ade shooters (only missing the orangeade). Lemonade corkscrew, tin. $70. (Auction #103, Lot 16).

AKRO AGATE COMPANY. Ades. Lot of three marbles. All are shooters. Lemonade, 31/32", Near Mint(+) (8.7). Limeade, 15/16", Near . $60. (Auction #84, Lot 18).

AKRO AGATE COMPANY. Ades. Lot of three marbles. A lemonade, limeade and orangeade. Lemonade is 5/8", Near Mint (8.6). Limeade. $48. (Auction #57, Lot 22).

AKRO AGATE COMPANY. Ades. Lot of three marbles. Two lemonades. 5/8" & Near Mint(+) (8.9), 21/32" & Near Mint(+) (8.7). Limeade. $28. (Auction #84, Lot 24).

AKRO AGATE COMPANY. Advertising marble. Translucent blue marble printed "Ing-Rich Beaver Falls PA". Some sparkles on the marble. 21/32". Ne. 21/32". Near Mint(+) (8.9). $60. (Auction #111, Lot 36).

AKRO AGATE COMPANY. Akroite. Rectangular Ashtray, Short Tab, No. 259. Oxblood, blue and opalescent white. Very fluorescent. Hard . $75. (Auction #150, Lot 29).

AKRO AGATE COMPANY. Akroite. Round Three-Rest Ashtray with Hole for Cigarette, on Holder. Hardy lists this in his book (#24). $50. (Auction #111, Lot 45).

AKRO AGATE COMPANY. Akroite. Mexicali Jar with Hat Lid, No. 803-B. This one is orange and white. Very fluorescent. 3" x 2-5/8". M. $40. (Auction #111, Lot 41).

AKRO AGATE COMPANY. Akroite. Cigarette cup. Octagonal. Oxblood and opalescent white. Hard to find. 2-3/4" x 2-3/8". Mint (9.9). $40. (Auction #150, Lot 23).

AKRO AGATE COMPANY. Akroite. Small Square Ashtray, No. 252. Oxblood and white. 2-7/8". Mint (9.9). Two ashtrays available. $30. (Auction #111, Lot 35.10).

AKRO AGATE COMPANY. Akroite. Rectangular Ashtray, Long Tab, No. 259. Oxblood and white. A beauty. 4" x 2-1/8". Mint (9.9). $30. (Auction #146, Lot 32).

AKRO AGATE COMPANY. Akroite. Small Square Ashtray, No. 252. Oxblood and white. 2-7/8". Mint (9.9). Two ashtrays available. $28. (Auction #111, Lot 35.20).

AKRO AGATE COMPANY. Akroite. Small Square Ashtray, No. 252. Oxblood and white. 2-7/8". Mint (9.9). Two ashtrays available. $25. (Auction #146, Lot 27).

AKRO AGATE COMPANY. Akroite. Cornucopia, No. 765. Plain foot style. White, clear and green. In great shape. 3-1/4". Mint (9.9). $22. (Auction #152, Lot 37).

AKRO AGATE COMPANY. Akroite. Cigarette cup. Octagonal. Opaque blue. 2-3/4" x 2-3/8". Mint (9.9). $22. (Auction #111, Lot 17).

AKRO AGATE COMPANY. Akroite. Oval Planter, No. 654. In great shape. Green and white. 6" x 3-1/4" x 2-3/8". Mint (9.9). $22. (Auction #152, Lot 31).

AKRO AGATE COMPANY. Akroite. Small Square Ashtray, No. 252. Oxblood and white. 2-7/8". Mint (9.9). Two ashtrays available. $20. (Auction #146, Lot 27.20).

AKRO AGATE COMPANY. Akroite. Rectangular Ashtray, Long Tab, No. 259. Orange and white. 4" x 2-1/8". Mint (9.9). $18. (Auction #111, Lot 39.20).

AKRO AGATE COMPANY. Akroite. Rectangular Ashtray, Long Tab, No. 259. Orange and white. 4" x 2-1/8". Mint (9.9). $18. (Auction #111, Lot 39).

AKRO AGATE COMPANY. Akroite. Rectangular Ashtray, Long Tab, No. 259. Green and white. 4" x 2-1/8". Mint (9.9). $18. (Auction #111, Lot 39.30).

AKRO AGATE COMPANY. Akroite. Lily Vase, No. 658. Orange and white. A couple of tiny rim chips. 4-1/4". Mint(-) (9.0). $17. (Auction #111, Lot 12.10).

AKRO AGATE COMPANY. Akroite. Oval Planter, No. 654. In great shape. Green and white. 6" x 3-1/4" x 2-3/8". Mint (9.9). $15. (Auction #111, Lot 22).

AKRO AGATE COMPANY. Akroite. Lily Vase, No. 658. Orange and white. 4-1/4". Mint (9.9). There are five available in assorted colors. $15. (Auction #111, Lot 12.20).

AKRO AGATE COMPANY. Akroite. Lily Vase, No. 658. Orange and white. 4-1/4". Mint (9.9). There are five available in assorted colors. $15. (Auction #111, Lot 12.30).

AKRO AGATE COMPANY. Akroite. Lily Vase, No. 658. Green and white. Tiny rim chips. 4-1/4". Mint(-) (9.2). There are five available in assorted colors. $15. (Auction #111, Lot 12.40).

AKRO AGATE COMPANY. Akroite. Lily Vase, No. 658. White with no color. Hard color to find. 4-1/4". Mint (9.7). There are five available in assorted colors. $13. (Auction #111, Lot 12.50).

AKRO AGATE COMPANY. Akroite. Oval Planter, No. 654. In great shape. Red and white. 6" x 3-1/4" x 2-3/8". Mint (9.9). $12. (Auction #119, Lot 19.10).

AKRO AGATE COMPANY. Akroite. Cornucopia, No. 765. Plain foot style. White, clear and green. In great shape. 3-1/4". Mint (9.9). $12. (Auction #111, Lot 6).

AKRO AGATE COMPANY. Akroite. Oval Planter, No. 654. In great shape. Green and white. 6" x 3-1/4" x 2-3/8". Mint (9.9). $12. (Auction #119, Lot 19).

AKRO AGATE COMPANY. Akroite. Shell Ashtray, No. 246. Green and white glass. Opalescent. 4" x 3-1/2". Mint (9.9). $10. (Auction #111, Lot 1).

AKRO AGATE COMPANY. Akroite. Leaf Ashtray, No. 245. Green and white. 4-1/8". Mint (9.9). $9. (Auction #111, Lot 26).

AKRO AGATE COMPANY. Akroite. Grecian Urn, No. 764. Orange and white. One small rim chip. 3-1/4". Near Mint(+) (8.9). $6. (Auction #111, Lot 31).

AKRO AGATE COMPANY. Akroware. Cereal Bowl. Interior Panel design. Large size. Lemonade and oxblood glass. Sixteen panels. $65. (Auction #144, Lot 33).

AKRO AGATE COMPANY. Akroware. An Akro No. 249 rectangular ashtray with short tabs. Akro logo on bottom. The glass is fluorescent. $65. (Auction #62, Lot 44).

AKRO AGATE COMPANY. **Akroware.** Saucer. Interior Panel design. Large size. Lemonade and oxblood glass. Sixteen panels. See Hardy 1st. $37. (Auction #144, Lot 31).

AKRO AGATE COMPANY. **Akroware.** Ashtray. Square. Oxblood swirl on translucent white. In great shape. Mint. There are two ashtrays. $28. (Auction #81, Lot 23).

AKRO AGATE COMPANY. **Akroware.** Ashtray. Square. Oxblood swirl on translucent white. In great shape. Mint. There are two ashtrays. $28. (Auction #81, Lot 23.20).

AKRO AGATE COMPANY. **Assorted.** Lot of three marbles. Two are corkscrew and one is a patch. The corkscrews are opaque orange base. $50. (Auction #149, Lot 35).

AKRO AGATE COMPANY. **Assorted.** Lot of three marbles. Two are corkscrew and one is a patch. The corkscrews are opaque orange base. $48. (Auction #149, Lot 35.20).

AKRO AGATE COMPANY. **Assorted.** Lot of five marbles. Shooter purple and yellow Popeye, shooter lemonade oxblood, shooter red and green. $47. (Auction #175, Lot 33).

AKRO AGATE COMPANY. **Assorted.** Lot of three marbles. Two are corkscrew and one is a patch. The corkscrews are opaque orange base. $40. (Auction #149, Lot 35.30).

AKRO AGATE COMPANY. **Assorted.** Lot of three marbles. Two are corkscrew and one is a patch. The corkscrews are opaque orange base. $35. (Auction #149, Lot 35.40).

AKRO AGATE COMPANY. **Assorted.** Lot of five marbles. Four corkscrews and an orange slag. The corkscrews include two two-color, color. $35. (Auction #115, Lot 14).

AKRO AGATE COMPANY. **Assorted.** Lot of three marbles. Three color corkscrew shooter. Red and light green on white. 27/32". Near Mint. $33. (Auction #136, Lot 12).

AKRO AGATE COMPANY. **Assorted.** Lot of two marbles. Two-color color-base corkscrew, 5/8", Mint (9.9). Helmet patch, "oxblood" stripe. $27. (Auction #133, Lot 9).

AKRO AGATE COMPANY. **Assorted.** Lot of three items. First is a piece of cullet glass. Second is three malformed reject corkscrews. . $26. (Auction #107, Lot 4).

AKRO AGATE COMPANY. **Assorted.** Lot of two marbles. A corkscrew and a patch. Both are the exact same early colors of orange and blue. $26. (Auction #129, Lot 3).

AKRO AGATE COMPANY. **Assorted.** Lot of six marbles. Includes a shooter patch oxblood (8.9), sparkler (8.5), and four ribbon corkscrew. $23. (Auction #106, Lot 3).

AKRO AGATE COMPANY. **Assorted.** Lot of three marbles. Blue and white corkscrew, fluorescent, 23/32", Mint (9.9). Yellow and translucent. $19. (Auction #103, Lot 19).

AKRO AGATE COMPANY. **Assorted.** Lot of five marbles. Four are Helmet Patch, one is a Ringer. One helmet has a subsurface moon. $15. (Auction #106, Lot 41).

AKRO AGATE COMPANY. **Assorted.** Lot of four marbles. Moss Agate, 5/8", Mint(-) (9.1). Ringer swirl, 5/8", Near Mint (8.5). Helmet. $6. (Auction #180, Lot 9).

AKRO AGATE COMPANY. **Assorted Ade.** Lot of three marbles. A lemonade, a limeade and a cherryade. Each has a minor defect. All are shooters. $65. (Auction #124, Lot 8).

AKRO AGATE COMPANY. **Assorted oxblood.** Lot of two marbles. Lemonade oxblood. 19/32". Near Mint(+) (8.8). Silver oxblood. 5/8". Near Mint(+). $55. (Auction #172, Lot 8).

AKRO AGATE COMPANY. **Assorted oxblood.** Lot of two marbles. First is a limeade oxblood shooter. Semi-opaque vaseline green glass with wispy . $55. (Auction #109, Lot 15).

AKRO AGATE COMPANY. **Assorted oxblood.** Lot of two marbles. Lemonade oxblood. One tiny flake. 19/32". Near Mint(+) (8.9). Other is patch oxblood. $50. (Auction #120, Lot 31).

AKRO AGATE COMPANY. **Assorted oxblood.** Lot of three marbles. A carnelian oxblood and two shooter patch oxbloods. All have some damage. 11/1. $42. (Auction #138, Lot 3).

AKRO AGATE COMPANY. **Assorted oxblood.** Lot of three marbles. A silver oxblood, a blue oxblood and a carnelian oxblood. All have damage. $42. (Auction #181, Lot 12).

AKRO AGATE COMPANY. **Assorted oxblood.** Lot of six marbles. Three swirl oxblood, a patch oxblood, a non-Akro swirl "oxblood" with blue swirl. $40. (Auction #177, Lot 31).

AKRO AGATE COMPANY. **Assorted oxblood.** Lot of two marbles. First is an orange oxblood. 23/32". Near Mint(-) (8.2). The other is a blue oxblood. $37. (Auction #113, Lot 2).

AKRO AGATE COMPANY. **Assorted oxblood.** Lot of three marbles. A silver oxblood and two lemonade (pale) oxbloods. 5/8" and 11/16". Near Mint(. $36. (Auction #178, Lot 36).

AKRO AGATE COMPANY. **Assorted oxblood.** Lot of two marbles. First is a silver oxblood. Nice oxblood on it. 5/8". Near Mint(+) (8.7). $35. (Auction #84, Lot 23).

AKRO AGATE COMPANY. **Assorted oxblood.** Lot of two marbles. Swirl oxblood. Nice marble. 19/32". Mint (9.8). Patch oxblood. Thin oxblood. 9/1. $25. (Auction #81, Lot 8).

AKRO AGATE COMPANY. **Blue oxblood.** Translucent milky white base. Nice spiral of translucent blue. Narrow oxblood spiral. In great shape. 23/32". Mint (9.9). $130. (Auction #185, Lot 46).

AKRO AGATE COMPANY. **Blue oxblood.** Shooter blue oxblood. Superior marble!!!! Translucent milky white base. Spiral of dark translucent blue. 3/4". Mint(-) (9.3). $120. (Auction #70, Lot 44).

AKRO AGATE COMPANY. **Blue oxblood.** Translucent milky white base. Nice spiral of translucent blue. Several tiny pit. 3/4. Near Mint(+) (8.9). $100. (Auction #153, Lot 45).

AKRO AGATE COMPANY. **Blue oxblood.** Beautiful example. Translucent milky white base. Spiral of translucent blue. Two spirals of oxblood. 5/8". Mint (9.9). $85. (Auction #126, Lot 39).

AKRO AGATE COMPANY. **Blue oxblood.** Superb example. Corkscrew. Thin oxblood. Pristine condition. 5/8". Mint (9.9). $80. (Auction #111, Lot 24).

AKRO AGATE COMPANY. **Blue oxblood.** Beautiful example. Translucent milky white base. Spiral of translucent blue. Two spirals of oxblood. 5/8". Mint (9.9). $75. (Auction #124, Lot 27).

AKRO AGATE COMPANY. **Blue oxblood.** Nice corkscrew blue oxblood. Translucent milky white base. Spiral of translucent blue. 23/32". Near Mint(+) (8.9). $70. (Auction #172, Lot 43).

AKRO AGATE COMPANY. **Blue oxblood.** Beautiful example. Translucent milky white base. Spiral of translucent blue. Spiral of oxblood. 5/8". Mint (9.9). $70. (Auction #136, Lot 47).

AKRO AGATE COMPANY. **Blue oxblood.** Very nice blue oxblood. Two tiny subsurface moons. No other damage. Clarksburg, WV, circa 1928-1938. . $65. (Auction #95, Lot 28).

AKRO AGATE COMPANY. **Blue oxblood.** Milky white base with translucent blue swirl and deep rich oxblood. Super example. Clarksburg, WV. 21/32". Mint (9.9). $65. (Auction #92, Lot 36).

AKRO AGATE COMPANY. **Blue oxblood.** Translucent milky white base. Wide spiral of translucent blue. Nice oxblood spiral. Thin burnt black. 11/16". Near Mint (8.6). $65. (Auction #181, Lot 39).

AKRO AGATE COMPANY. **Blue oxblood.** Translucent milky white base. Nice spiral of translucent blue. Nice oxblood spiral. 19/32". Near Mint(+) (8.9). $47. (Auction #98, Lot 20).

AKRO AGATE COMPANY. **Blue oxblood.** Translucent milky white base. Narrow swirl of translucent blue. Thinner swirl of oxblood. Clarksburg, WV. 19/32". Mint (9.9). $45. (Auction #140, Lot 38).

AKRO AGATE COMPANY. **Blue oxblood.** Translucent milky white base. Narrow spiral of translucent blue. Wider spiral of blue. 5/8". Mint (9.9). $45. (Auction #121, Lot 47).

AKRO AGATE COMPANY. **Blue oxblood.** Translucent milky white base. Very wide spiral of translucent blue. Nice oxblood spiral. 23/32". Near Mint(+) (8.9). $36. (Auction #56, Lot 20).

AKRO AGATE COMPANY. **Blue oxblood.** Nice example. Translucent milky white base. Opaque white swirl, translucent blue swirl and an oxblood. 19/32". Near Mint (8.6). $35. (Auction #76, Lot 43).

AKRO AGATE COMPANY. **Blue oxblood.** Translucent milky white base, translucent blue swirl and a rich oxblood swirl. Two subsurface moons. 21/32". Near Mint (8.5). $25. (Auction #61, Lot 20).

AKRO AGATE COMPANY. **Blueblood corkscrew.** Superior example of a blueblood, although slightly damaged. Base is opaque light blue. 5/8". Near Mint(+) (8.7). $40. (Auction #97, Lot 34).

AKRO AGATE COMPANY. **Carnelian.** Beautiful Carnelian shooter. In super shape. Very fluorescent. Clarksburg, WV, circa 1927-1935. 3/4". 3/4". Mint (9.9). $50. (Auction #118, Lot 14).

AKRO AGATE COMPANY. **Carnelian.** Super Akro Agate Carnelian. Very fluorescent and lots of brown. Clarksburg, WV, circa 1925-1935. 11/1. 11/16". Mint (9.9). $47. (Auction #91, Lot 1).

AKRO AGATE COMPANY. **Carnelian.** Super Akro Agate Carnelian. Very fluorescent and lots of brown. Clarksburg, WV, circa 1925-1935. 5/8". 5/8". Mint (9.9). $32. (Auction #164, Lot 28).

AKRO AGATE COMPANY. **Carnelian.** Beautiful Carnelian. Very fluorescent. In great shape. Clarksburg, WV, circa 1925-1935. 5/8". Mint (9. 5/8". Mint (9.9). $31. (Auction #94, Lot 10).

AKRO AGATE COMPANY. **Carnelian.** Nice example of an Akro Carnelian. Clarksburg, WV, circa 1925-1935. 11/16". Mint (9.9). 11/16". Mint (9.9). $30. (Auction #59, Lot 14).

AKRO AGATE COMPANY. **Carnelian.** Nice Akro Agate Carnelian. Very fluorescent and lots of brown. A sparkle and a tiny rough spot. Clarksburg, WV. 11/16". Mint(-) (9). $28. (Auction #173, Lot 7).

AKRO AGATE COMPANY. Carnelian. Super Akro Agate Carnelian. Very fluorescent and lots of brown. Clarksburg, WV, circa 1925-1935. 23/3. 23/32". Mint (9.9). $28. (Auction #128, Lot 3).

AKRO AGATE COMPANY. Carnelian. Very nice Akro Agate Carnelian. Very fluorescent and lots of brown. A few imperfections on the surface. 3/4". Mint(-) (9). $28. (Auction #126, Lot 3).

AKRO AGATE COMPANY. Carnelian. Beautiful Akro Carnelian. Fluorescent. Nice marble. Clarksburg, WV, circa 1925-1935. 21/32". Mint (9. 21/32". Mint (9.9). $27. (Auction #82, Lot 3).

AKRO AGATE COMPANY. Carnelian. Shooter Akro Agate Carnelian. Very fluorescent and lots of brown. Couple of sparkles. Clarksburg, WV,. 3/4". Mint (9). $27. (Auction #159, Lot 37).

AKRO AGATE COMPANY. Carnelian. Nice Akro Agate Carnelian. Very fluorescent and lots of brown. One small rough line. 11/16". Mint(-) (9.1). $26. (Auction #140, Lot 1).

AKRO AGATE COMPANY. Carnelian. Lot of two marbles. Akro Agate Carnelian. Very fluorescent and lots of brown. Clarksburg, WV. Mint . $26. (Auction #178, Lot 32).

AKRO AGATE COMPANY. Carnelian. Super Carnelian in a corkscrew pattern. Very fluorescent. One tiny pinprick. Clarksburg, WV. 11/16". Mint(-) (9.2). $25. (Auction #107, Lot 21).

AKRO AGATE COMPANY. Carnelian. Akro Agate Carnelian. Very fluorescent and lots of brown. Clarksburg, WV, circa 1925-1935. 11/16". 11/16". Mint (9.9). $24. (Auction #171, Lot 32).

AKRO AGATE COMPANY. Carnelian. Super Akro Agate Carnelian. Very fluorescent and lots of brown. Clarksburg, WV, circa 1925-1935. 5/8". 11/16". Mint (9.9). $24. (Auction #121, Lot 28).

AKRO AGATE COMPANY. Carnelian. Super Akro Agate Carnelian. Very fluorescent and lots of brown. One sparkle. Clarksburg, WV. 5/8". Mint(-) (9.2). $23. (Auction #145, Lot 44).

AKRO AGATE COMPANY. Carnelian. Excellent shooter Carnelian. Lots of brown. One sparkle. Clarksburg, WV, circa 1925-1935. 11/16". Min. 11/16". Mint(-) (9). $22. (Auction #80, Lot 2).

AKRO AGATE COMPANY. Carnelian. Very nice Carnelian. Very fluorescent. Clarksburg, WV, circa 1925-1935. 21/32". Mint (9.9). 21/32". Mint (9.9). $22. (Auction #116, Lot 18).

AKRO AGATE COMPANY. Carnelian. Beautiful example of a Carnelian. Very fluorescent. 5/8". Mint (9.9). $20. (Auction #111, Lot 18).

AKRO AGATE COMPANY. Carnelian. Lot of two marbles. Both are Carnelians. Very fluorescent. The larger has a flake and a sparkle. $17. (Auction #62, Lot 7).

AKRO AGATE COMPANY. Carnelian. Very nice example. Very fluorescent. One tiny sparkle. Clarksburg, WV, circa 1925-1935. 21/32". Mint(. 21/32". Mint(-) (9.2). $17. (Auction #101, Lot 8).

AKRO AGATE COMPANY. Carnelian. Super Akro Agate Carnelian. Very fluorescent and lots of brown. One tiny pit. Clarksburg, WV. 11/16". Mint(-) (9.1). $16. (Auction #152, Lot 22).

AKRO AGATE COMPANY. Carnelian. Excellent example of an Akro Carnelian. Very fluorescent. One sparkle. Clarksburg, WV, circa 1925. 21/32". Mint(-) (9.1). $16. (Auction #61, Lot 8).

AKRO AGATE COMPANY. Carnelian. Semi-opaque fluorescent light cream base. Opaque white swirls and translucent brown swirls. 3/4". Near Mint(+) (8.7). $15. (Auction #64, Lot 29).

AKRO AGATE COMPANY. Carnelian. Nice Akro Agate Carnelian. Very fluorescent and lots of brown. One sparkle. Clarksburg, WV. 11/16". Mint(-) (9.2). $12. (Auction #112, Lot 31).

AKRO AGATE COMPANY. Carnelian. Nice Carnelian. Very fluorescent. Lots of brown. One sparkle. Clarksburg, WV, circa 1927-1935. 11/16". 11/16". Mint(-) (9). $11. (Auction #110, Lot 28).

AKRO AGATE COMPANY. Carnelian. Akro Agate Carnelian. Very fluorescent and lots of brown. Buffed. Clarksburg, WV, circa 1925-1935. 11. Mint . $10. (Auction #171, Lot 36).

AKRO AGATE COMPANY. Carnelian oxblood. Semi-opaque white base. Lots of transparent brown swirling in the marble. Wide and rich oxblood swirl. 25/32". Mint (9.9). $280. (Auction #185, Lot 49).

AKRO AGATE COMPANY. Carnelian oxblood. A true Carnelian oxblood. Translucent milky ade base. Thin swirl of white. 3/4". Mint (9.8). $150. (Auction #155, Lot 47).

AKRO AGATE COMPANY. Carnelian oxblood. Translucent milky white base. Swirl of transparent brown, swirl of translucent brown. 21/32". Mint (9.9). $140. (Auction #178, Lot 47).

AKRO AGATE COMPANY. Carnelian oxblood. Translucent milky white base. Transparent light brown swirling in the marble. Rich oxblood swirl. 11/16". Mint (9.9). $140. (Auction #184, Lot 47).

AKRO AGATE COMPANY. Carnelian oxblood. Translucent milky white base with a translucent brown swirl and a nice oxblood swirl on the surface. 11/16". Mint (9.9). $120. (Auction #133, Lot 48).

AKRO AGATE COMPANY. Carnelian oxblood. Corkscrew design. Translucent milky white base. Wide translucent brown swirl on the surface. 5/8". Mint (9.9). $90. (Auction #140, Lot 43).

AKRO AGATE COMPANY. Carnelian oxblood. Excellent example. Translucent milky white base. Wide patch of translucent brown on one side. 11/16". Mint (9.9). $90. (Auction #167, Lot 40).

AKRO AGATE COMPANY. Carnelian oxblood. Nice carnelian oxblood. Translucent milky white base. Translucent red/brown swirl, translucent brown. 21/32". Mint (9.9). $80. (Auction #54, Lot 39).

AKRO AGATE COMPANY. Carnelian oxblood. Translucent milky white base. Wide translucent brown swirl on the surface. Thin lines of oxblood. 21/32". Mint (9.8). $70. (Auction #70, Lot 38).

AKRO AGATE COMPANY. Carnelian oxblood. Translucent milky white base. Swirl of transparent orange/brown, swirl of translucent brown. 3/4". Mint(-) (9.1). $55. (Auction #90, Lot 17).

AKRO AGATE COMPANY. Carnelian oxblood. Translucent milky white base. Lots of transparent brown swirling in the marble. Wide and rich oxblood. 3/4". Near Mint(-) (8). $32. (Auction #180, Lot 16).

AKRO AGATE COMPANY. Cherryade. Very hard to find Cherryade shooter. Fluorescent "ade" base with opaque wispy white swirls and trans. 31/32". Mint (9.9). $185. (Auction #125, Lot 49).

AKRO AGATE COMPANY. Cherryade. Very hard to find Cherryade shooter. Fluorescent "ade" base with a little bit of opaque wispy white . 1". Mint (9.9). $160. (Auction #144, Lot 50).

AKRO AGATE COMPANY. Cherryade. Super shooter size cherryade corkscrew. One of the nicest I have seen. Translucent fluorescent lemon. 1". Mint(-) (9). $150. (Auction #92, Lot 45).

AKRO AGATE COMPANY. Cherryade. Very hard to find Cherryade shooter. Fluorescent "ade" base with opaque wispy white swirls. 7/8". Near Mint(+) (8.9). $120. (Auction #93, Lot 43).

AKRO AGATE COMPANY. Cherryade. Very hard to find Cherryade shooter. Fluorescent "ade" base with opaque wispy white swirls. 1". Near Mint(+) (8.9). $110. (Auction #88, Lot 43).

AKRO AGATE COMPANY. Cherryade. Very hard to find Cherryade shooter. Fluorescent "ade" base with a little bit of opaque wispy white. 1". Mint(-) (9). $90. (Auction #136, Lot 49).

AKRO AGATE COMPANY. Cherryade. Hard to find Cherryade shooter. Fluorescent "ade" base with a little bit of opaque wispy white swirl. 31/32". Near Mint(+) (8.9). $85. (Auction #148, Lot 41).

AKRO AGATE COMPANY. Cherryade. Very hard to find Cherryade shooter. Fluorescent "ade" base with a little bit of opaque wispy white. 1". Near Mint(+) (8.9). $75. (Auction #131, Lot 42).

AKRO AGATE COMPANY. Cherryade. Hard to find Cherryade shooter. Fluorescent "ade" base with a little bit of opaque wispy white swirl. 15/16". Near Mint(+) (8.9). $60. (Auction #159, Lot 39).

AKRO AGATE COMPANY. Children's Dish Set. Small size set of eight boxed set. Play-Time Glass Dishes. Box side reads No. 1320 - B - Gypsy Tea. $160. (Auction #111, Lot 49).

AKRO AGATE COMPANY. Corkscrew. Experimental orange and blue corkscrew. These are very hard to find. Tiny partial moon at one end. 1". Near Mint(+) (8.9). $150. (Auction #75, Lot 44).

AKRO AGATE COMPANY. Corkscrew. Lot of six marbles. Four are three-color, two are four-color. Excellent assortment of colors. $110. (Auction #132, Lot 4).

AKRO AGATE COMPANY. Corkscrew. Lot of five marbles. All are three color corkscrew in the same color pattern. Excellent group of five. $100. (Auction #74, Lot 27).

AKRO AGATE COMPANY. Corkscrew. Lot of four marbles. All are three color Aces. Translucent white base. Spiral of egg yolk yellow. $100. (Auction #67, Lot 17).

AKRO AGATE COMPANY. Corkscrew. Lot of twelve marbles. All are corkscrews. Two limeades (Mint), a lemonade (Mint), two Ringers. $95. (Auction #69, Lot 22).

AKRO AGATE COMPANY. Corkscrew. Lot of nineteen marbles. Includes seventeen assorted corkscrews, a Peltier Peerless patch. $95. (Auction #115, Lot 24).

AKRO AGATE COMPANY. Corkscrew. Lot of twenty four marbles. Excellent assortment of corkscrews. Many types and colors. $90. (Auction #122, Lot 17).

AKRO AGATE COMPANY. Corkscrew. Three color corkscrew. Outstanding colors. Black, orange and yellow. In superb shape. Superior marble. 11/16". Mint (9.8). $90. (Auction #173, Lot 43).

AKRO AGATE COMPANY. Corkscrew. Outstanding four-color corkscrew. Semi-opaque white base. Spiral of translucent yellow. 25/32". Mint(-) (9.1). $90. (Auction #176, Lot 49).

AKRO AGATE COMPANY. Corkscrew. Three color corkscrew. Black with an opaque yellow spiral. Transparent red on the yellow. Double twist. 11/16". Mint (9.9). $90. (Auction #73, Lot 17).

AKRO AGATE COMPANY. **Corkscrew.** Super corkscrew. Opaque yellow base. One spiral of transparent black and one of transparent red. 21/32". Mint (9.9). $85. (Auction #110, Lot 46).

AKRO AGATE COMPANY. **Corkscrew.** Lot of five marbles. All are three-color. All the same color scheme and size, possibly same run. $85. (Auction #155, Lot 12).

AKRO AGATE COMPANY. **Corkscrew.** Lot of ten marbles. All are two-color color-base corkscrews. Five are Mint. 5/8" to 21/32". Mint. $85. (Auction #143, Lot 13).

AKRO AGATE COMPANY. **Corkscrew.** Five color corkscrew. Very hard to find. Semi-opaque white base. Wide spiral of green. 3/4". Near Mint(+) (8.9). $83. (Auction #134, Lot 26).

AKRO AGATE COMPANY. **Corkscrew.** Three color corkscrew in very rare coloring. Wide spiral of transparent navy blue, wide panel of red. 3/4". Mint(-) (9.1). $80. (Auction #113, Lot 47).

AKRO AGATE COMPANY. **Corkscrew.** Four color corkscrew. Hard to find. Semi-opaque white base. Snake of blue, snake of yellow and snake. 3/4". Mint (9.9). $80. (Auction #134, Lot 41).

AKRO AGATE COMPANY. **Corkscrew.** Lot of seventeen marbles. Assortment of corkscrews. Nice colors and designs. Almost all Mint. 19/32". $80. (Auction #106, Lot 20).

AKRO AGATE COMPANY. **Corkscrew.** Lot of sixteen corkscrews. Nice assortment of corkscrews. Includes a fluorescent ribbon, a tri-color. $80. (Auction #73, Lot 25).

AKRO AGATE COMPANY. **Corkscrew.** Lot of seven marbles. All are tri-color corkscrews. Includes two that do not have white. Clarksburg, WV. $80. (Auction #69, Lot 19).

AKRO AGATE COMPANY. **Corkscrew.** Lot of forty three marbles. Excellent assortment of colors and types of corkscrews. $80. (Auction #128, Lot 25).

AKRO AGATE COMPANY. **Corkscrew.** Lot of twenty five marbles. Assortment of designs and colors. Includes a Popeye and some shooters. $75. (Auction #108, Lot 14).

AKRO AGATE COMPANY. **Corkscrew.** Very unusual four color shooter. Translucent milky white base with opaque white swirl in it in a spiral. 1". Mint(-) (9.3). $75. (Auction #57, Lot 14).

AKRO AGATE COMPANY. **Corkscrew.** Lot of sixteen marbles. Assortment of two color. Some white, some not. Most are Mint. 5/8" to 15/16". $75. (Auction #95, Lot 19).

AKRO AGATE COMPANY. **Corkscrew.** Three color corkscrew. Opaque black, opaque yellow, transparent red. 3/4". Near Mint(+) (8.9). $70. (Auction #143, Lot 9).

AKRO AGATE COMPANY. **Corkscrew.** Rare corkscrew with oxblood. The corkscrew is a spiral of light blue and a spiral of dark blue. 5/8". Mint(-) (9). $70. (Auction #75, Lot 32).

AKRO AGATE COMPANY. **Corkscrew.** Lot of two marbles. Exceptional and rare pair of marbles from the same run. $70. (Auction #59, Lot 34).

AKRO AGATE COMPANY. **Corkscrew.** Superb two-color triple-twist shooter corkscrew. Opaque yellow and translucent red. Excellent pattern. 7/8". Mint(-) (9.2). $70. (Auction #183, Lot 42).

AKRO AGATE COMPANY. **Corkscrew.** Outstanding three color corkscrew. Yellow, light green and translucent light red. Shooter. 25/32". Mint (9.9). $70. (Auction #98, Lot 44).

AKRO AGATE COMPANY. **Corkscrew.** Lot of eight marbles. All are two-color color-base. Five are Mint. 5/8" to 21/32". Mint (9.9) to Near Mint. $70. (Auction #143, Lot 18).

AKRO AGATE COMPANY. **Corkscrew.** Lot of twenty marbles. Three white-base two-color, seventeen color-base two-color. Excellent assortment. $70. (Auction #177, Lot 7).

AKRO AGATE COMPANY. **Corkscrew.** Lot of ten marbles. Nice assortment of corkscrews including two-color, three-color, snakes and ribbons. $65. (Auction #120, Lot 16).

AKRO AGATE COMPANY. **Corkscrew.** Lot of thirty seven marbles. All are white base corkscrews. At least half have some damage. $65. (Auction #122, Lot 19).

AKRO AGATE COMPANY. **Corkscrew.** Lot of approximately forty five marbles. All are two-color, white-base corkscrews. $65. (Auction #157, Lot 23).

AKRO AGATE COMPANY. **Corkscrew.** A true five-color corkscrew. Semi-opaque white base. Narrow translucent yellow spiral. 3/4". Near Mint(+) (8.9). $62. (Auction #141, Lot 14).

AKRO AGATE COMPANY. **Corkscrew.** Lot of eleven marbles. Includes two-color corkscrews, Ribbons and snakes. Nice group. $60. (Auction #144, Lot 13).

AKRO AGATE COMPANY. **Corkscrew.** Four color corkscrew. Translucent milky white base. Corkscrew of transparent dark blue. 19/32". Mint (9.7). $60. (Auction #159, Lot 44).

AKRO AGATE COMPANY. **Corkscrew.** Lot of two marbles. Both are same run. A pair of the oddest corkscrews that I have ever seen. $60. (Auction #104, Lot 9).

AKRO AGATE COMPANY. **Corkscrew.** Superb four color corkscrew. Very unusual coloring. Opaque white, yellow and blue spirals. 5/8". Mint(-) (9). $60. (Auction #70, Lot 33).

AKRO AGATE COMPANY. **Corkscrew.** Beautiful three-color corkscrew. Opaque light green, opaque yellow and translucent red. Nice shooter. 13/16". Mint (9.7). $60. (Auction #129, Lot 17).

AKRO AGATE COMPANY. **Corkscrew.** Superior three color translucent shooter. Translucent milky white base. Opaque white wispy spiral. 31/32". Mint (9.9). $60. (Auction #109, Lot 48).

AKRO AGATE COMPANY. **Corkscrew.** Four color. Bleed causes a fifth. Opaque white base. Spirals on the surface of yellow and blue. 3/4". Mint(-) (9). $60. (Auction #136, Lot 41).

AKRO AGATE COMPANY. **Corkscrew.** Four color corkscrew. Orange, white, lavender and cream/tan. Nice shooter. Clarksburg, WV, circa 1870. 23/32". Mint (9.9). $60. (Auction #147, Lot 33).

AKRO AGATE COMPANY. **Corkscrew.** Three color corkscrew, sometimes referred to as an Indian blanket by collectors. Opaque black, opaque. 11/16". Mint (9.7). $60. (Auction #171, Lot 41).

AKRO AGATE COMPANY. **Corkscrew.** Lot of two marbles. Both are shooter size. One is transparent red on opaque yellow. $56. (Auction #117, Lot 17).

AKRO AGATE COMPANY. **Corkscrew.** Lot of six marbles. All are corkscrews. Blue on clear snake. Orange and yellow two color. $55. (Auction #80, Lot 6).

AKRO AGATE COMPANY. **Corkscrew.** Three color corkscrew. Thin opaque yellow, translucent black and transparent red. 25/32". Mint(-) (9.1). $55. (Auction #111, Lot 7).

AKRO AGATE COMPANY. **Corkscrew.** Four color corkscrew. Opaque white, translucent blue, translucent red. 23/32". Near Mint(+) (8.9). $55. (Auction #64, Lot 40).

AKRO AGATE COMPANY. **Corkscrew.** Lot of two marbles. Translucent opalescent white base with a translucent green spiral. Moonie corkscrew. $55. (Auction #75, Lot 40).

AKRO AGATE COMPANY. **Corkscrew.** Lot of forty seven. Excellent assortment of colors and types. All have some damage. $55. (Auction #175, Lot 21).

AKRO AGATE COMPANY. **Corkscrew.** Lot of twenty five marbles. Outstanding set of corkscrews. Five marbles each of five different color. $55. (Auction #164, Lot 24).

AKRO AGATE COMPANY. **Corkscrew.** Opaque white base. Wide spiral of translucent orange, narrower spiral of translucent pink. Odd color. 7/8". Mint (9.9). $55. (Auction #168, Lot 48).

AKRO AGATE COMPANY. **Corkscrew.** Lot of seven marbles. Assorted. Four tri-colors. Three of those are Mint. A red and green Popeye. $55. (Auction #69, Lot 17).

AKRO AGATE COMPANY. **Corkscrew.** Lot of nine marbles. Includes a red and yellow Popeye, blue and yellow Popeye, and assortment snakes. $52. (Auction #115, Lot 2).

AKRO AGATE COMPANY. **Corkscrew.** Lot of five marbles. All are shooters. Two are red on white. Two are black and blue spiral on white. $50. (Auction #155, Lot 35).

AKRO AGATE COMPANY. **Corkscrew.** Subtle four-color corkscrew. Opaque white base. Three colors brushed on the surface. 7/8". Mint (9.5). $50. (Auction #147, Lot 7).

AKRO AGATE COMPANY. **Corkscrew.** Lot of six marbles. Five are three color. One is a two color. All have some very minor damage. Nice. $50. (Auction #136, Lot 14).

AKRO AGATE COMPANY. **Corkscrew.** Super three color double twist shooter. Almost evenly sized spirals of opaque white, opaque light green. 27/32". Mint (9.5). $50. (Auction #70, Lot 18).

AKRO AGATE COMPANY. **Corkscrew.** Lot of five marbles. All are opaque white ribbons in root beer brown. Nice set for a line in a box. $50. (Auction #127, Lot 31).

AKRO AGATE COMPANY. **Corkscrew.** Three color corkscrew shooter. Apparently, this color combination is being referred to as an "Indian." 25/32". Mint (9.5). $50. (Auction #97, Lot 28).

AKRO AGATE COMPANY. **Corkscrew.** Lot of four marbles. All are translucent shooters. Three have a red spiral, one has a green spiral. $50. (Auction #132, Lot 9).

AKRO AGATE COMPANY. **Corkscrew.** Three color shooter. Opaque white, opaque black and transparent red. A beauty. 3/4". Mint(-) (9.2). $50. (Auction #148, Lot 32).

AKRO AGATE COMPANY. **Corkscrew.** Lot of eleven marbles. Ten are two-color color-base. One is a Ringer. 5/8" to 23/32". Almost all Mint condition. $50. (Auction #127, Lot 5).

AKRO AGATE COMPANY. Corkscrew. Unusual corkscrew. Translucent milky white base. Two triple twist double spirals of translucent orange. 11/16". Mint (9.9). $50. (Auction #59, Lot 18).

AKRO AGATE COMPANY. Corkscrew. Outstanding shooter corkscrew. Very rare design and coloring. Opaque white base. Three thin spirals. 15/16". Mint(-) (9). $50. (Auction #118, Lot 47).

AKRO AGATE COMPANY. Corkscrew. Lot of five marbles. Assortment of snakes and ribbons. Various shades of red and orange. 19/32" to 5". $50. (Auction #177, Lot 29).

AKRO AGATE COMPANY. Corkscrew. Lot of six marbles. Three are color base two-color, one is a three-color translucent. $50. (Auction #63, Lot 18).

AKRO AGATE COMPANY. Corkscrew. Lot of six marbles. All are shooters. Includes two Tomatoes, a Lemonade, a blue and white. $49. (Auction #161, Lot 22).

AKRO AGATE COMPANY. Corkscrew. Double-ingot three-color corkscrew. Opaque yellow, opaque black, transparent red. 25/32". Near Mint (8.6). $48. (Auction #176, Lot 39).

AKRO AGATE COMPANY. Corkscrew. Lot of three corkscrews. First is a red, blue and yellow tricolor. Some minor roughness. 23/32". Mint. $48. (Auction #85, Lot 19).

AKRO AGATE COMPANY. Corkscrew. Three-color corkscrew, referred to sometimes as an "Indian blanket". Opaque yellow, opaque black. 3/4". Near Mint(+) (8.9). $47. (Auction #178, Lot 46).

AKRO AGATE COMPANY. Corkscrew. Lot of three marbles. All are three-color corkscrew. White, translucent red, light blue. Mint(-) . $47. (Auction #149, Lot 27).

AKRO AGATE COMPANY. Corkscrew. Very nice three color corkscrew. Opaque white and translucent red corkscrew. Translucent blue on top. 11/16". Mint (9.9). $47. (Auction #73, Lot 1).

AKRO AGATE COMPANY. Corkscrew. Lot of fifteen marbles. All are corkscrews. Nice assortment. 19/32" to 21/32". Mint (9.9) to Near Mint. $47. (Auction #102, Lot 23).

AKRO AGATE COMPANY. Corkscrew. Lot of twelve marbles. All are snakes and ribbons. Assortment of colors. Ten are Mint. 19/32" to 21/32". $46. (Auction #177, Lot 9).

AKRO AGATE COMPANY. Corkscrew. Two-color color-base corkscrew. One of the hardest color combinations to find. Purple and light green. 5/8". Mint (9.9). $46. (Auction #146, Lot 46).

AKRO AGATE COMPANY. Corkscrew. Lot of four marbles. All are shooters. Green, white, red. Blue, white, red (2). Red on green. 25/32". $46. (Auction #136, Lot 3).

AKRO AGATE COMPANY. Corkscrew. Super three color double twist shooter. Almost evenly sized spirals of opaque white, opaque light green. 27/32". Mint (9.5). $46. (Auction #103, Lot 20).

AKRO AGATE COMPANY. Corkscrew. Looks like a purple and yellow Popeye, without the yellow. But, is really a Moonie Corkscrew. Equal. 9/16". Mint (9.9). $46. (Auction #87, Lot 42).

AKRO AGATE COMPANY. Corkscrew. Lot of twenty three marbles. All are white-base, two-color corkscrews. Nine are Mint. $45. (Auction #155, Lot 22).

AKRO AGATE COMPANY. Corkscrew. Lot of three marbles. Same three-color corkscrew in three different sizes (1/8" increments!). White. Mint. $45. (Auction #182, Lot 34).

AKRO AGATE COMPANY. Corkscrew. Lot of thirty one marbles. Nice assortment of colors. Almost all have some damage. 19/32" to 11/16". $45. (Auction #178, Lot 16).

AKRO AGATE COMPANY. Corkscrew. Very unusual four-color double ingot corkscrew. White, lavender, orange and red. Beauty. Clarksburg, WV. 11/16". Mint (9.9). $45. (Auction #131, Lot 1).

AKRO AGATE COMPANY. Corkscrew. Beautiful three color corkscrew. One half is a spiral of opaque light blue and one half is a spiral . 27/32". Mint(-) (9). $45. (Auction #129, Lot 11).

AKRO AGATE COMPANY. Corkscrew. Lot of fifteen corkscrews. All are white base with assorted color spirals. Excellent assortment. $45. (Auction #88, Lot 24).

AKRO AGATE COMPANY. Corkscrew. Very nice three-color double-ingot corkscrew. Light green, yellow and transparent red. 25/32". Near Mint(+) (8.7). $44. (Auction #185, Lot 42).

AKRO AGATE COMPANY. Corkscrew. Lot of twelve marbles. All are snakes and ribbons. Assortment of colors. Ten are Mint. 19/32" to 21/32". $44. (Auction #177, Lot 9.20).

AKRO AGATE COMPANY. Corkscrew. Lot of two marbles. Nice shooters. One is opaque yellow with a wide translucent red spiral. Feathering. $44. (Auction #106, Lot 46).

AKRO AGATE COMPANY. Corkscrew. Lot of nine marbles. Nice assortment of two-color and three-color opaque. $44. (Auction #151, Lot 4).

AKRO AGATE COMPANY. Corkscrew. Lot of twelve corkscrews. Five two color white base, four two-color color base, one three color. $44. (Auction #58, Lot 27).

AKRO AGATE COMPANY. Corkscrew. Lot of sixteen marbles. Assortment of two-color white base, two-color color base, snakes and ribbons. $44. (Auction #112, Lot 24).

AKRO AGATE COMPANY. Corkscrew. Super three color double twist shooter. Almost evenly sized spirals of opaque white, opaque light green. 27/32". Mint (9.5). $44. (Auction #103, Lot 20.10).

AKRO AGATE COMPANY. Corkscrew. Exceptional and rare marble. A spiral of translucent green in opalescent translucent white. Moonie. 23/32". Mint (9.9). $42. (Auction #118, Lot 43).

AKRO AGATE COMPANY. Corkscrew. Lot of six marbles. Three are red on yellow, 19/32", Mint (9.9 & 9.0). One is black on yellow. 19/32". $42. (Auction #83, Lot 18).

AKRO AGATE COMPANY. Corkscrew. Lot of twenty two marbles. About half are white base. Remainder are color base, translucent, ribbon. $42. (Auction #55, Lot 27).

AKRO AGATE COMPANY. Corkscrew. Very nice shooter three color corkscrew. Wide spiral of light blue, transparent red and yellow. 13/16". Mint(-) (9.3). $42. (Auction #85, Lot 16).

AKRO AGATE COMPANY. Corkscrew. Lot of twenty two marbles. Nice assortment of different types and colors of corkscrews. $42. (Auction #174, Lot 47).

AKRO AGATE COMPANY. Corkscrew. Lot of three marbles. Lot of three marbles. A red, black and yellow; a black and white; a red and yellow. $42. (Auction #151, Lot 7).

AKRO AGATE COMPANY. Corkscrew. Four-color corkscrew. White base. Wide transparent red spiral. Narrower very light yellow spiral. 23/32". Mint (9.9). $42. (Auction #140, Lot 41).

AKRO AGATE COMPANY. Corkscrew. Lot of five marbles. All are blue and yellow corkscrews. Nice set for a line in a box or tin. 21/32". $42. (Auction #127, Lot 26).

AKRO AGATE COMPANY. Corkscrew. Four color corkscrew. Opaque white with transparent red, opaque light green and translucent brown/green. 21/32". Mint (9.7). $42. (Auction #185, Lot 5).

AKRO AGATE COMPANY. Corkscrew. Lot of sixteen marbles. Nice assortment of two color corkscrews (two are three color). 5/8" to 23/32. $41. (Auction #102, Lot 5).

AKRO AGATE COMPANY. Corkscrew. Shooter three color. Opaque white base. Yellow spiral with a blue spiral next to it. Clarksburg, WV. 27/32". Mint (9.9). $41. (Auction #55, Lot 34).

AKRO AGATE COMPANY. Corkscrew. Four color corkscrew. Opaque white. Covered by yellow. Transparent blue spiral. 3/4". Near Mint (8.6). $40. (Auction #175, Lot 47).

AKRO AGATE COMPANY. Corkscrew. Lot of four marbles. All are three color shooters. Rare coloring and design. 3/4" (1) and 31/32" (3). $40. (Auction #178, Lot 35).

AKRO AGATE COMPANY. Corkscrew. Lot of ten marbles. Nice assortment of two-color color base, with two three-colors. Seven are Mint. $40. (Auction #117, Lot 1).

AKRO AGATE COMPANY. Corkscrew. Hard to find four-color corkscrew. Translucent milky white base. On surface is a spiral of translucent. 3/4". Near Mint (8.6). $40. (Auction #70, Lot 4).

AKRO AGATE COMPANY. Corkscrew. Lot of three marbles. Each is a two color corkscrew. Orange and blue. $40. (Auction #74, Lot 25).

AKRO AGATE COMPANY. Corkscrew. Three color corkscrew. Double twist. Creamy white base. Spiral of translucent orange. 11/16". Mint (9.9). $40. (Auction #168, Lot 35).

AKRO AGATE COMPANY. Corkscrew. Unusual four-color corkscrew. Translucent milky white base. Wispy opaque white, opaque light egg yolk. 31/32". Near Mint(+) (8.7). $40. (Auction #171, Lot 40).

AKRO AGATE COMPANY. Corkscrew. Lot of thirty five marbles. Assortment of two color corkscrews. Most are white-base. Most have damage. $40. (Auction #144, Lot 24).

AKRO AGATE COMPANY. Corkscrew. Super three color double twist shooter. Almost evenly sized spirals of opaque white. 27/32". Mint (9.5). $40. (Auction #92, Lot 28).

AKRO AGATE COMPANY. Corkscrew. Very interesting three color corkscrew. One half is a spiral of yellow, one half is a spiral of black. 23/32". Mint (9.7). $39. (Auction #124, Lot 35).

AKRO AGATE COMPANY. Corkscrew. Two color corkscrew. Red and purple. Shooter size. Nice one. Clarksburg, WV, circa 1928-1935. 3/4". M. 3/4". Mint (9.9). $39. (Auction #165, Lot 20).

AKRO AGATE COMPANY. Corkscrew. Lot of ten marbles. All are two-color white-base. Two are Mint. 19/32" to 5/8". Mint (9.9) to Near Mint. $39. (Auction #143, Lot 17).

AKRO AGATE COMPANY. Corkscrew. Beautiful three color corkscrew. One half is a spiral of opaque light blue. 27/32". Near Mint(+) (8.7). $39. (Auction #134, Lot 34).

AKRO AGATE COMPANY. Corkscrew. Super three color double twist shooter. Almost evenly sized spirals of opaque white. 27/32". Mint (9.5). $38. (Auction #87, Lot 34).

AKRO AGATE COMPANY. Corkscrew. Lot of ten marbles. Six are two-color color-base. Four are three-color. Two of those are red, black. $38. (Auction #182, Lot 22).

AKRO AGATE COMPANY. Corkscrew. Two color corkscrew shooter. Opaque light green and translucent red. Clarksburg, WV, circa 1928-1938. 29/32". Mint (9.6). $38. (Auction #179, Lot 19.20).

AKRO AGATE COMPANY. Corkscrew. Super three color double twist shooter. Almost evenly sized spirals of opaque white. 27/32". Mint (9.5). $38. (Auction #92, Lot 28.20).

AKRO AGATE COMPANY. Corkscrew. Two color corkscrew shooter. Opaque light green and translucent red. Clarksburg, WV, circa 1928-1938. 29/32". Mint (9.6). $38. (Auction #179, Lot 19).

AKRO AGATE COMPANY. Corkscrew. Lot of five marbles. All are two color corkscrews. No white in these. Nice group. Clarksburg, WV. $37. (Auction #69, Lot 20).

AKRO AGATE COMPANY. Corkscrew. Larger three color corkscrew. Opaque white base. Spiral of translucent red on the surface. 31/32". Mint(-) (9.1). $37. (Auction #148, Lot 39).

AKRO AGATE COMPANY. Corkscrew. Super three color corkscrew. White, transparent red and black spirals. Hard to find these in shooter. 13/16". Mint(-) (9.3). $37. (Auction #58, Lot 1).

AKRO AGATE COMPANY. Corkscrew. Lot of six marbles. All are three-color. Four are white-base. Three are Mint. 5/8". Mint (9.9) to Near Mint. $37. (Auction #143, Lot 15).

AKRO AGATE COMPANY. Corkscrew. Double ingot error. Was supposed to be a transparent red, opaque light green and opaque white corkscrew. 23/32". Mint (9.8). $37. (Auction #91, Lot 31).

AKRO AGATE COMPANY. Corkscrew. Four color corkscrew. Opaque white base. Spiral of orange, spiral of green. 5/8". Mint (9.9). $37. (Auction #142, Lot 24).

AKRO AGATE COMPANY. Corkscrew. Lot of five marbles. Two are blue and red on white, one is blue, orange and brown, one is red and black. $37. (Auction #141, Lot 38).

AKRO AGATE COMPANY. Corkscrew. Lot of twenty marbles. All are red spiral on white. A couple have minor hits. 5/8" to 23/32". Mint. $36. (Auction #146, Lot 24).

AKRO AGATE COMPANY. Corkscrew. Lot of four marbles. One red and yellow Popeye, two three-color, one two-color. 19/32" to 3/4". Near. $36. (Auction #175, Lot 31).

AKRO AGATE COMPANY. Corkscrew. Three color shooter. Odder colors. Opaque light green, transparent orange and opaque yellow. 25/32". Near Mint(+) (8.9). $36. (Auction #147, Lot 44).

AKRO AGATE COMPANY. Corkscrew. Exceptional marble. A spiral of translucent green in opalescent translucent white. Moonie corkscrews. $36. (Auction #134, Lot 43).

AKRO AGATE COMPANY. Corkscrew. Nice three color corkscrew. White, translucent red, light blue. A few little marks on the red. Nice. 13/16". Mint(-) (9). $36. (Auction #137, Lot 2).

AKRO AGATE COMPANY. Corkscrew. Nice three color corkscrew. White, translucent red, light blue. Nice shooter. Clarksburg, WV. 13/16". Mint (9.7). $36. (Auction #142, Lot 16).

AKRO AGATE COMPANY. Corkscrew. Very odd three color corkscrew. Opaque creamy white base. Blended wide spiral of transparent orange. 21/32". Mint (9.9). $36. (Auction #82, Lot 36).

AKRO AGATE COMPANY. Corkscrew. Double-ingot three-color corkscrew. Opaque white, transparent blue and transparent red. In great shape. 13/16". Mint (9.7). $35. (Auction #183, Lot 33).

AKRO AGATE COMPANY. Corkscrew. Opaque orange base. Blue spiral on it. There is another orange spiral on the blue. $35. (Auction #120, Lot 45).

AKRO AGATE COMPANY. Corkscrew. Lot of seven marbles. Three white-base two-color, three color-base two-color, one three-color. $35. (Auction #133, Lot 1).

AKRO AGATE COMPANY. Corkscrew. Double ingot error. Opaque yellow and translucent orange. Clarksburg, WV, circa 1928-1938. 25/32". Mint. 25/32". Mint (9.9). $35. (Auction #76, Lot 24).

AKRO AGATE COMPANY. Corkscrew. Outstanding three color corkscrew. Opaque white with a wide spiral of black. 3/4". Near Mint(+) (8.9). $35. (Auction #81, Lot 33).

AKRO AGATE COMPANY. Corkscrew. Lot of four marbles. Three opaque white ribbon in transparent red. One orange and white two-color. $35. (Auction #122, Lot 3).

AKRO AGATE COMPANY. Corkscrew. Odd coloring. Three color. Orange base. Transparent red spiral. Also, an odd green/gray spiral. 5/8". Mint (9.9). $35. (Auction #185, Lot 19).

AKRO AGATE COMPANY. Corkscrew. Three color corkscrew. Light green, yellow, transparent red and an additional transparent red spiral. 5/8". Mint (9.9). $35. (Auction #59, Lot 4).

AKRO AGATE COMPANY. Corkscrew. Lot of two marbles. Both are the same color scheme, but slightly different sizes. Translucent purple. $35. (Auction #109, Lot 34).

AKRO AGATE COMPANY. Corkscrew. Three color corkscrew. Opaque white base. Light blue spiral on the surface. Two transparent red spiral. 5/8". Mint (9.4). $35. (Auction #176, Lot 33).

AKRO AGATE COMPANY. Corkscrew. Three color corkscrew. Translucent milky white base with unmelted sand. Snake spiral of red. 21/32". Mint (9.9). $35. (Auction #185, Lot 17).

AKRO AGATE COMPANY. Corkscrew. Lot of two marbles. Both are shooter size. One is transparent red on opaque yellow. $35. (Auction #137, Lot 16).

AKRO AGATE COMPANY. Corkscrew. Lot of twelve marbles. All are orange spiral on white. A couple have some hits. 19/32" to 3/4". Mint. $35. (Auction #146, Lot 34).

AKRO AGATE COMPANY. Corkscrew. Three color corkscrew. White, light green and translucent red. Clarksburg, WV, circa 1928-1938. 13/16. 13/16". Mint (9.6). $35. (Auction #160, Lot 9).

AKRO AGATE COMPANY. Corkscrew. Lot of two marbles. Both are three-color corkscrews, sometimes referred to as "Indian Blanket". $35. (Auction #129, Lot 19).

AKRO AGATE COMPANY. Corkscrew. Lot of twenty nine marbles. Assortment of types and colors. Includes two limeades (one is a shooter). $35. (Auction #108, Lot 21).

AKRO AGATE COMPANY. Corkscrew. Three-color shooter. Very nice. Semi-opaque white base. Wide spiral of transparent orange. 23/32". Near Mint (8.6). $34. (Auction #141, Lot 49).

AKRO AGATE COMPANY. Corkscrew. Lot of two marbles. Both are two-color shooter. Red and green, 29/32", Near Mint(+) (8.7). $34. (Auction #143, Lot 3).

AKRO AGATE COMPANY. Corkscrew. Nice two color shooter. Opaque yellow base with a translucent red spiral. Nice marble. Clarksburg, WV. 15/16". Mint (9.7). $34. (Auction #70, Lot 31).

AKRO AGATE COMPANY. Corkscrew. Harder to find three-color corkscrew. Translucent milky white base. Spiral of opaque pale egg yolk yellow. 5/8". Mint (9.8). $34. (Auction #167, Lot 25).

AKRO AGATE COMPANY. Corkscrew. Lot of sixteen marbles. All are two color, white base. Almost all are Mint. 19/32" to 11/16". Mint. $34. (Auction #97, Lot 23).

AKRO AGATE COMPANY. Corkscrew. Lot of two marbles. Two color corkscrew shooter. Opaque light green and translucent red. 29/32". Mint (9.5). $34. (Auction #96, Lot 3).

AKRO AGATE COMPANY. Corkscrew. Red and yellow shooter. Two sparkles and small annealing fracture. Pre-Freese Improvement. 1". Near Mint(+) (8.9). $33. (Auction #159, Lot 22).

AKRO AGATE COMPANY. Corkscrew. Four-color corkscrew. Opaque white base. Transparent royal blue spiral, transparent red spiral, Opaque. 11/16". Mint(-) (9). $33. (Auction #183, Lot 11).

AKRO AGATE COMPANY. Corkscrew. Three color corkscrew. White, light green and translucent red. Extra twist on one end. One tiny sparkle. 27/32". Mint(-) (9.2). $33. (Auction #147, Lot 40).

AKRO AGATE COMPANY. Corkscrew. Lot of two marbles. Both are shooter-size, three-color translucent. First is milky translucent white. $33. (Auction #124, Lot 12).

AKRO AGATE COMPANY. Corkscrew. Triple twist shooter two-color. Opaque light green and translucent red/brown. Some scratching. 15/16". Near Mint(+) (8.9). $33. (Auction #154, Lot 34).

AKRO AGATE COMPANY. Corkscrew. Shooter translucent corkscrew. Translucent milky white base with opaque white spirals in it. Translucent. 31/32". Near Mint(+) (8.9). $33. (Auction #155, Lot 16).

AKRO AGATE COMPANY. Corkscrew. Lot of two marbles. Both are the same color pattern, just different sizes. $32. (Auction #147, Lot 14).

AKRO AGATE COMPANY. Corkscrew. Two color corkscrew in early colors. Orange base with transparent bright blue spiral. Creased. 23/32". Near Mint(+) (8.9). $32. (Auction #149, Lot 20.20).

AKRO AGATE COMPANY. Corkscrew. Two color corkscrew in early colors. Orange base with transparent bright blue spiral. Creased. 23/32". Near Mint(+) (8.9). $32. (Auction #149, Lot 20).

AKRO AGATE COMPANY. Corkscrew. Lot of sixteen marbles. All are green spiral on white. One fluorescent. Almost all Mint. $32. (Auction #151, Lot 26).

AKRO AGATE COMPANY. Corkscrew. Pretty three color corkscrew. Opaque white base. Snake of translucent green on it. 13/16". Mint (9.9). $32. (Auction #133, Lot 5).

AKRO AGATE COMPANY. Corkscrew. Lot of fourteen marbles. Twelve are two-color corkscrews, two are three-color corkscrews. $32. (Auction #161, Lot 25).

AKRO AGATE COMPANY. Corkscrew. Lot of fourteen marbles. All are Snakes and Ribbons. Nice group. Most have some damage. $32. (Auction #144, Lot 22).

AKRO AGATE COMPANY. Corkscrew. Three color corkscrew. White, light green and translucent red. Clarksburg, WV, circa 1928-1938. 13/16". Mint (9.6). $32. (Auction #160, Lot 9.20).

AKRO AGATE COMPANY. Corkscrew. Lot of six marbles. All are two-color color-base corkscrews. All have some damage. 5/8" to 21/32". $32. (Auction #178, Lot 8).

AKRO AGATE COMPANY. Corkscrew. Tri-color Ace. Translucent milky white base. Spiral of translucent blue and opaque light egg yolk yellow. 5/8". Mint (9.9). $32. (Auction #78, Lot 7).

AKRO AGATE COMPANY. Corkscrew. Lot of five marbles. Assortment of corkscrews. Includes a white-base two-color, two color-base. $32. (Auction #184, Lot 16).

AKRO AGATE COMPANY. Corkscrew. Lot of two marbles. Same coloring, different sizes. Interesting coloring. Spiral of green. $32. (Auction #62, Lot 36).

AKRO AGATE COMPANY. Corkscrew. Lot of four marbles. All are corkscrews. Green and yellow. Black and yellow. Green, brown and white. $32. (Auction #73, Lot 9).

AKRO AGATE COMPANY. Corkscrew. Lot of eleven marbles. Nice assortment of snakes and ribbons. 19/32" to 23/32". Three are Mint. Mint. $31. (Auction #161, Lot 19).

AKRO AGATE COMPANY. Corkscrew. Triple twist shooter two-color. Opaque light green and translucent red/brown. Some scratching. 15/16". Near Mint(+) (8.9). $31. (Auction #154, Lot 34.20).

AKRO AGATE COMPANY. Corkscrew. Very unusual corkscrew. Translucent milky white base. Spiral of translucent red, next to a spiral of. 3/4". Mint(-) (9). $31. (Auction #56, Lot 4).

AKRO AGATE COMPANY. Corkscrew. Lot of fifteen marbles. Eleven are corkscrews. Assorted types and colors. Four are actually Champion. $31. (Auction #155, Lot 23).

AKRO AGATE COMPANY. Corkscrew. Lot of twenty two marbles. Nice assortment of styles and colors. Four are Mint. Rest have damage. $31. (Auction #54, Lot 22).

AKRO AGATE COMPANY. Corkscrew. Very odd corkscrew. Shooter. Opaque white base with a transparent red patch and two translucent blue. 15/16". Near Mint (8.8). $31. (Auction #162, Lot 8).

AKRO AGATE COMPANY. Corkscrew. Lot of two marbles. Both are Ringer style. Both are translucent milky white base. $30. (Auction #154, Lot 19).

AKRO AGATE COMPANY. Corkscrew. Interesting three color corkscrew. Yellow base with a wide translucent red spiral. 31/32". Near Mint(+) (8.9). $30. (Auction #183, Lot 15).

AKRO AGATE COMPANY. Corkscrew. Opaque white base. Transparent gray corkscrew. Two small subsurface moons, but an odd color. Clarksburg, WV. 31/32". Near Mint(+) (8.8). $30. (Auction #177, Lot 41).

AKRO AGATE COMPANY. Corkscrew. Lot of thirty six marbles. Assortment of two color corkscrews. Many colors and styles represented. $30. (Auction #158, Lot 28).

AKRO AGATE COMPANY. Corkscrew. Lot of seven marbles. Assortment of corkscrews. Includes five three-color and two two-color corkscrew. $30. (Auction #92, Lot 11).

AKRO AGATE COMPANY. Corkscrew. Three color corkscrew. Translucent red spiral on opaque white. Very thin translucent yellow spiral. 5/8". Mint (9.9). $30. (Auction #78, Lot 18).

AKRO AGATE COMPANY. Corkscrew. Lot of two marbles. Both are shooters. Interesting pair. Both have the same yellow base. $30. (Auction #112, Lot 39).

AKRO AGATE COMPANY. Corkscrew. Lot of fifteen marbles. Assortment of two-color and three-color. Almost all have some damage. 19/32". $30. (Auction #141, Lot 28).

AKRO AGATE COMPANY. Corkscrew. Two color corkscrew. Opaque yellow and transparent red. Shooter. Has an extra translucent red spiral. 15/16". Mint(-) (9). $30. (Auction #85, Lot 23.20).

AKRO AGATE COMPANY. Corkscrew. Double ingot shooter corkscrew. Transparent red on white. Two marbles fell on the same roller. 27/32". Mint (9.9). $30. (Auction #83, Lot 12).

AKRO AGATE COMPANY. Corkscrew. Three color corkscrew. White, light green and translucent red. Double twist. Clarksburg, WV. 13/16".

Mint (9.9). $30. (Auction #111, Lot 19).

AKRO AGATE COMPANY. Corkscrew. Moonie corkscrew. Opalescent white base with a yellow snake on the surface. In great shape. Clarksburg, WV. 5/8". Mint (9.9). $30. (Auction #168, Lot 12).

AKRO AGATE COMPANY. Corkscrew. Triple twisted light green spiral on white. Super example!!! One very tiny rough spot. Clarksburg, WV. 11/16". Mint(-) (9.1). $30. (Auction #118, Lot 38).

AKRO AGATE COMPANY. Corkscrew. Lot of six marbles. Assortment of shooter corkscrews. Actually, one is a Moss Agate, not a corkscrew. $30. (Auction #112, Lot 16).

AKRO AGATE COMPANY. Corkscrew. Double ingot shooter corkscrew. Transparent red on white. Two marbles fell on the same roller. 27/32". Mint (9.9). $30. (Auction #83, Lot 12.20).

AKRO AGATE COMPANY. Corkscrew. Lot of two marbles. First is opaque yellow with translucent red. One tiny subsurface moon. 25/32". $30. (Auction #103, Lot 13).

AKRO AGATE COMPANY. Corkscrew. Two color corkscrew. Opaque yellow and transparent red. Shooter. Has an extra translucent red spiral. 15/16". Mint(-) (9). $30. (Auction #85, Lot 23).

AKRO AGATE COMPANY. Corkscrew. Light blue base. Semi-opaque thin yellow spiral. Very thin black spiral next to it. In great shape. 23/32". Mint (9.9). $30. (Auction #136, Lot 18).

AKRO AGATE COMPANY. Corkscrew. Lot of three marbles. Snake, white on green. Ribbon, white in red. Ribbon, white in amber. $30. (Auction #126, Lot 33).

AKRO AGATE COMPANY. Corkscrew. Very unusual corkscrew. I have never seen this one before. The base glass is semi-opaque very fluorescent. 19/32". Mint (9.9). $30. (Auction #98, Lot 4).

AKRO AGATE COMPANY. Corkscrew. Lot of four marbles. All are blue and yellow. A couple have some blending. 5/8" to 11/16". Mint (9.9). $30. (Auction #157, Lot 43).

AKRO AGATE COMPANY. Corkscrew. Lot of ten marbles. Assortment of corkscrews. Two color and translucents. All about 5/8" except one. $30. (Auction #84, Lot 20).

AKRO AGATE COMPANY. Corkscrew. Three-color corkscrew shooter. Opaque white, translucent light green, transparent red. Super looking . 7/8". Mint (9.9). $29. (Auction #173, Lot 12).

AKRO AGATE COMPANY. Corkscrew. Three color corkscrew. White, black and translucent red. One sparkle. Nice marble. Clarksburg, WV. 23/32". Mint(-) (9.1). $29. (Auction #76, Lot 18).

AKRO AGATE COMPANY. Corkscrew. Three color corkscrew. Opaque light blue and opaque yellow with a transparent red spiral on the yellow. 25/32". Near Mint(+) (8.8). $29. (Auction #149, Lot 14).

AKRO AGATE COMPANY. Corkscrew. Lot of eleven marbles. All are corkscrews. One three-color, the rest are two-color. $29. (Auction #178, Lot 4).

AKRO AGATE COMPANY. Corkscrew. Interesting three color corkscrew. Yellow base with a wide translucent red spiral. 31/32". Near Mint(+) (8.9). $29. (Auction #160, Lot 25.20).

AKRO AGATE COMPANY. Corkscrew. Interesting three color corkscrew. Yellow base with a wide translucent red spiral. 31/32". Near Mint(+) (8.9). $29. (Auction #165, Lot 33).

AKRO AGATE COMPANY. Corkscrew. Interesting three color corkscrew. Yellow base with a wide translucent red spiral. 31/32". Near Mint(+) (8.9). $29. (Auction #160, Lot 25).

AKRO AGATE COMPANY. Corkscrew. Interesting three color corkscrew. Yellow base with a wide translucent red spiral. 31/32". Near Mint(+) (8.9). $29. (Auction #165, Lot 33.20).

AKRO AGATE COMPANY. Corkscrew. Lot of six marbles. All are three color corkscrews. Five are white base. The color base is an Indian. $29. (Auction #127, Lot 8).

AKRO AGATE COMPANY. Corkscrew. Three color corkscrew. Opaque light blue and opaque yellow with a transparent red spiral on the yellow. 25/32". Near Mint(+) (8.8). $28. (Auction #149, Lot 14.20).

AKRO AGATE COMPANY. Corkscrew. Four color corkscrew. White, light green, light blue, light red. Nice pattern. Two tiny rough spots. 5/8". Near Mint(+) (8.9). $28. (Auction #156, Lot 40).

AKRO AGATE COMPANY. Corkscrew. Three color corkscrew. Opaque light blue and opaque yellow with a transparent red spiral on the yellow. 25/32". Near Mint(+) (8.8). $28. (Auction #149, Lot 14.40).

AKRO AGATE COMPANY. Corkscrew. Three color corkscrew. Opaque light blue and opaque yellow with a transparent red spiral on the yellow. 25/32". Near Mint(+) (8.8). $28. (Auction #149, Lot 14.30).

AKRO AGATE COMPANY. Corkscrew. Super four-color corkscrew. Semi-opaque white base. Spirals of translucent blue, yellow and olive green. 23/32". Near Mint(+) (8.9). $28. (Auction #152, Lot 48).

AKRO AGATE COMPANY. Corkscrew. Opaque light green and translucent dark red. Shooter size. Clarksburg, WV, circa 1928-1938. 15/16".

M. 15/16". Mint (9.9). $28. (Auction #76, Lot 23.20).

AKRO AGATE COMPANY. Corkscrew. Three color corkscrew. White, light blue, transparent red. Clarksburg, WV, circa 1928-1935. 11/16". M. 11/16". Mint (9.9). $28. (Auction #157, Lot 7).

AKRO AGATE COMPANY. Corkscrew. Lot of two marbles. One is translucent red on green, 15/16", Mint (9.3). The other is translucent red. $28. (Auction #130, Lot 20).

AKRO AGATE COMPANY. Corkscrew. Lot of two marbles. Two color corkscrew shooter. Opaque light green and translucent red. 29/32". Mint (9.5). $28. (Auction #98, Lot 10).

AKRO AGATE COMPANY. Corkscrew. Lot of three marbles. All are shooters. Translucent milky white, opaque white, red spiral, 1". Good . $28. (Auction #84, Lot 19).

AKRO AGATE COMPANY. Corkscrew. Lot of nine marbles. Nice assortment of two-color opaque, ribbons and snakes. $28. (Auction #151, Lot 2).

AKRO AGATE COMPANY. Corkscrew. Lot of five marbles. All are two color corkscrews with color base. 5/8" to 11/16". Mint (9.9) to Near Mint. $28. (Auction #75, Lot 20).

AKRO AGATE COMPANY. Corkscrew. Three-color corkscrew. Opaque white with a spiral of translucent light yellow. 5/8". Mint (9.7). $28. (Auction #176, Lot 15).

AKRO AGATE COMPANY. Corkscrew. Opaque light green and translucent dark red. Shooter size. Clarksburg, WV, circa 1928-1938. 15/16". Mint (9.9). $28. (Auction #76, Lot 23).

AKRO AGATE COMPANY. Corkscrew. Lot of seven marbles. Assortment of snake and ribbon corkscrews. Includes one triple twist. $27. (Auction #141, Lot 9).

AKRO AGATE COMPANY. Corkscrew. Lot of two marbles. Both are shooters. Both have a translucent white base with opaque white spirals. $27. (Auction #149, Lot 28).

AKRO AGATE COMPANY. Corkscrew. Ribbon corkscrew. Double twist. Transparent root beer brown base with opaque white ribbon. Shooter. 25/32". Mint (9.9). $27. (Auction #126, Lot 20).

AKRO AGATE COMPANY. Corkscrew. Three color corkscrew. White, light green and translucent red. Double twist. Clarksburg, WV. $27. (Auction #110, Lot 18).

AKRO AGATE COMPANY. Corkscrew. Three color corkscrew. White, light green and translucent red. Double twist. Clarksburg, WV. $27. (Auction #110, Lot 18.20).

AKRO AGATE COMPANY. Corkscrew. Three color shooter. Opaque white base. Wide spiral of transparent red. 27/32". Mint (8.6). $27. (Auction #168, Lot 41).

AKRO AGATE COMPANY. Corkscrew. Two color corkscrew. Very light lavender and translucent red. Nice marble. Clarksburg, WV, circa 1928. 3/4". Mint (9.7). $27. (Auction #78, Lot 40).

AKRO AGATE COMPANY. Corkscrew. Three color corkscrew. Opaque white, yellow and transparent red. Clarksburg, WV, circa 1928-1935. 21/. 21/32". Mint (9.9). $27. (Auction #129, Lot 25).

AKRO AGATE COMPANY. Corkscrew. Shooter two-color. Blue and white corkscrew. One area of annealing fractures. Clarksburg, WV. 31/32". Mint(-) (9.1). $26. (Auction #177, Lot 49).

AKRO AGATE COMPANY. Corkscrew. Three-color corkscrew. Opaque white with a spiral of translucent light yellow. 5/8". Mint (9.7). $26. (Auction #176, Lot 15.20).

AKRO AGATE COMPANY. Corkscrew. Lot of fourteen marbles. All are blue spiral on white. One fluorescent. Almost all Mint. $26. (Auction #151, Lot 12).

AKRO AGATE COMPANY. Corkscrew. Three-color corkscrew. Opaque white with a spiral of translucent light green. 5/8". Mint (9.7). $26. (Auction #176, Lot 9).

AKRO AGATE COMPANY. Corkscrew. Lot of seventeen corkscrews. All are white-base, two-color. A couple have some damage. 19/32". $26. (Auction #177, Lot 13).

AKRO AGATE COMPANY. Corkscrew. Three-color corkscrew. Opaque white base. Two spirals of opaque black, one spiral of transparent red. 11/16". Near Mint(+) (8.7). $26. (Auction #183, Lot 17).

AKRO AGATE COMPANY. Corkscrew. Red and yellow shooter. Some tiny subsurface moons and some roughness. Pre-Freese Improvement. 1". Near Mint(+) (8.7). $26. (Auction #121, Lot 9).

AKRO AGATE COMPANY. Corkscrew. Red and yellow Popeye. One tiny pit. Nice marble. Clarksburg, WV, circa 1927-1935. 11/16". Mint(-) (9). $26. (Auction #156, Lot 20).

AKRO AGATE COMPANY. Corkscrew. Three color corkscrew. White, light blue, transparent red. Clarksburg, WV, circa 1928-1935. 11/16". Mint (9.9). $26. (Auction #157, Lot 7.20).

AKRO AGATE COMPANY. Corkscrew. Three color corkscrew. Opaque light blue and opaque yellow with a transparent red spiral on the yel-

low. 25/32". Near Mint(+) (8.8). $26. (Auction #149, Lot 14.50).

AKRO AGATE COMPANY. Corkscrew. Lot of seven marbles. A nice assortment of snakes and ribbons. Two are Mint. 5/8" to 11/16". $26. (Auction #117, Lot 9).

AKRO AGATE COMPANY. Corkscrew. Opaque light green base with a translucent red/brown spiral. According to the consignor. 15/16". Mint (9.9). $26. (Auction #70, Lot 13).

AKRO AGATE COMPANY. Corkscrew. Opaque light green and translucent dark red. Shooter size. Clarksburg, WV, circa 1928-1938. 15/16". Mint (9.9). $26. (Auction #76, Lot 23.30).

AKRO AGATE COMPANY. Corkscrew. Green, light brown and light black corkscrew. Slightly flattened on one end. A couple of tiny sparkles. 25/32". Mint(-) (9.2). $26. (Auction #73, Lot 11).

AKRO AGATE COMPANY. Corkscrew. Lot of five marbles. Assortment of two-color color-base corkscrews. Nice group. All Mint. 5/8". $25. (Auction #111, Lot 14).

AKRO AGATE COMPANY. Corkscrew. Opaque white with a wide shallow transparent root beer brown spiral. Odd twist and fold to it. Clarksburg, WV. 25/32". Mint (9.9). $25. (Auction #73, Lot 32).

AKRO AGATE COMPANY. Corkscrew. Lot of five marbles. All are the same. All are opaque white base with an opaque blue spiral. Great shape. $25. (Auction #107, Lot 40).

AKRO AGATE COMPANY. Corkscrew. Lot of two marbles. The first is a three color. Red and white corkscrew. $25. (Auction #62, Lot 24).

AKRO AGATE COMPANY. Corkscrew. Nice shooter three color. There are four spirals, but three colors. Two gray/white spirals. 23/32". Mint(-) (9.1). $25. (Auction #63, Lot 4).

AKRO AGATE COMPANY. Corkscrew. Three color corkscrew. White, light green and translucent red. One small scratch. Clarksburg, WV. 13/16". Mint (9.5). $25. (Auction #145, Lot 27).

AKRO AGATE COMPANY. Corkscrew. Lot of two marbles. Both are Ringer. Translucent white base with opaque white wispy spiral. $25. (Auction #164, Lot 9).

AKRO AGATE COMPANY. Corkscrew. Very odd corkscrew. Looks opaque at first glance. Very dark, transparent cherry red base. 21/32". Near Mint(+) (8.9). $24. (Auction #66, Lot 18).

AKRO AGATE COMPANY. Corkscrew. Nice three color corkscrew. Opaque white and transparent red corkscrew. Nice opaque yellow spiral. 5/8". Mint(-) (9.1). $24. (Auction #73, Lot 3).

AKRO AGATE COMPANY. Corkscrew. Lot of four marbles. All are three color corkscrew in the same color pattern. Each is red, yellow. $24. (Auction #74, Lot 29).

AKRO AGATE COMPANY. Corkscrew. Opaque black and opaque white corkscrew. About half and half. Super looking marble. Shooter. Clarksburg, WV. 3/4". Mint (9.9). $24. (Auction #182, Lot 36).

AKRO AGATE COMPANY. Corkscrew. Lot of five marbles. Nice set of five. Perfect for a line in a tin or a box. $24. (Auction #179, Lot 15).

AKRO AGATE COMPANY. Corkscrew. Lot of seventeen corkscrews. All are white-base, two-color. A couple have some damage. 19/32". $24. (Auction #177, Lot 13.20).

AKRO AGATE COMPANY. Corkscrew. Lot of two marbles. First is a three color translucent. Milky white, translucent blue. $24. (Auction #119, Lot 25).

AKRO AGATE COMPANY. Corkscrew. Three-color corkscrew. Opaque white with a spiral of translucent light green. 5/8". Mint (9.7). $24. (Auction #176, Lot 9.20).

AKRO AGATE COMPANY. Corkscrew. Three color corkscrew. Opaque white base and opaque orange base. Spiral of green on the white. 5/8". Mint (9.9). $24. (Auction #151, Lot 31).

AKRO AGATE COMPANY. Corkscrew. Nice corkscrew. Orange and blue. Harder color combination to find. In great shape. Clarksburg, WV. 5/8". Mint (9.9). $24. (Auction #126, Lot 18).

AKRO AGATE COMPANY. Corkscrew. Red and yellow Popeye. One tiny pit. Nice marble. Clarksburg, WV, circa 1927-1935. 11/16". Mint(-) (9. 11/16". Mint(-) (9). $24. (Auction #156, Lot 20.20).

AKRO AGATE COMPANY. Corkscrew. Three color corkscrew. Opaque white, opaque yellow and translucent red. 21/32". Mint (9.9). $23. (Auction #80, Lot 14.20).

AKRO AGATE COMPANY. Corkscrew. Red and yellow shooter. Extra thin transparent red spiral on the yellow. Three tiny subsurface moons. 1". Near Mint(+) (8.9). $23. (Auction #64, Lot 10).

AKRO AGATE COMPANY. Corkscrew. Three color corkscrew. White base white translucent red/brown spiral and an orange/yellow spiral. 11/16". Mint (9.9). $23. (Auction #80, Lot 4).

AKRO AGATE COMPANY. Corkscrew. Shooter size red and green corkscrew. Several sparkles. Clarksburg, WV, circa 1928-1938. 15/16". Near Mint(+) (8.9). $23. (Auction #59, Lot 30).

AKRO AGATE COMPANY. Corkscrew. Shooter size red and yellow corkscrew. In great shape. Clarksburg, WV, circa 1928-1938. 29/32". Mint (9.9). $23. (Auction #58, Lot 23).

AKRO AGATE COMPANY. Corkscrew. Shooter three color corkscrew. Opaque white base. Wide spiral of transparent red. 25/32". Mint (9.7). $23. (Auction #90, Lot 4).

AKRO AGATE COMPANY. Corkscrew. Double ingot. This is a three color, sometimes called an "Indian blanket". A few tiny chips. Clarksburg, WV. 25/32". Near Mint (8.6). $23. (Auction #179, Lot 9).

AKRO AGATE COMPANY. Corkscrew. Lot of three marbles. Each is opaque white with transparent dark cranberry red. One is Mint. 5/8". $23. (Auction #179, Lot 6).

AKRO AGATE COMPANY. Corkscrew. Three color corkscrew. White, light green and translucent red. Clarksburg, WV, circa 1928-1938. 13/16. 13/16". Mint (9.6). $23. (Auction #165, Lot 13).

AKRO AGATE COMPANY. Corkscrew. Three color corkscrew. White, light green and translucent red. Annealing fractures at one pole. 27/32". Mint(-) (9). $23. (Auction #159, Lot 8).

AKRO AGATE COMPANY. Corkscrew. Three color corkscrew. Semi-opaque white base. Thin spiral of transparent yellow and thin spiral of . 25/32". Near Mint(+) (8.7). $23. (Auction #134, Lot 11).

AKRO AGATE COMPANY. Corkscrew. Shooter size red and yellow corkscrew. In great shape. Clarksburg, WV, circa 1928-1938. 29/32". Mint (9.9). $23. (Auction #58, Lot 23.20).

AKRO AGATE COMPANY. Corkscrew. Three color corkscrew. White, light green and translucent red. A little bit of dirt or metallic on t. 13/16". Mint (9.8). $22. (Auction #183, Lot 13).

AKRO AGATE COMPANY. Corkscrew. Hard to find four color corkscrew. White, light green, translucent red and orange. 23/32". Near Mint (8.6). $22. (Auction #116, Lot 7).

AKRO AGATE COMPANY. Corkscrew. Super snake corkscrew. Opaque yellow base with a snake of transparent red on the surface. 9/16". Mint (9.5). $22. (Auction #131, Lot 18).

AKRO AGATE COMPANY. Corkscrew. Nice three color corkscrew. White, translucent red, light green. A few marks on it. Nice shooter. 13/16". Mint(-) (9). $22. (Auction #149, Lot 31).

AKRO AGATE COMPANY. Corkscrew. Lot of ten marbles. All are white-base two-color corkscrews. Five are Mint. 5/8" to 23/32". Mint. $22. (Auction #143, Lot 11).

AKRO AGATE COMPANY. Corkscrew. Lot of five marbles. Four are two-color and one is three-color. Nice group. 19/32" to 23/32". Mint. $22. (Auction #123, Lot 5).

AKRO AGATE COMPANY. Corkscrew. Three color corkscrew. White base with light green spiral and orange/red spiral. Very odd coloring. 27/32". Mint(-) (9). $22. (Auction #182, Lot 25.20).

AKRO AGATE COMPANY. Corkscrew. Double ingot two-color corkscrew. Opaque yellow and transparent red. Beautiful example. 13/16". Mint(-) (9). $22. (Auction #185, Lot 7).

AKRO AGATE COMPANY. Corkscrew. Lot of two marbles. Both are baby blue base with yellow spiral. One is lighter blue than the other. $22. (Auction #151, Lot 49).

AKRO AGATE COMPANY. Corkscrew. Lot of three marbles. All are the same. Translucent milky white base. $22. (Auction #151, Lot 9).

AKRO AGATE COMPANY. Corkscrew. Very nice corkscrew, sometimes mistaken for an orange oxblood. Translucent milky white base. 5/8". Mint(-) (9.2). $22. (Auction #129, Lot 9).

AKRO AGATE COMPANY. Corkscrew. Lot of two marbles. Interesting color combination. Both are probably the same run. Opaque white. $22. (Auction #116, Lot 25).

AKRO AGATE COMPANY. Corkscrew. Three color. Black, orange and yellow. Very unusual coloring. Small chip, tiny chip and subsurface moon. 11/16". Near Mint (8.5). $22. (Auction #134, Lot 2).

AKRO AGATE COMPANY. Corkscrew. Translucent milky white base. Snake of orange/red on the surface. Shooter. In great shape. Nice marble. 23/32". Mint (9.9). $22. (Auction #143, Lot 7).

AKRO AGATE COMPANY. Corkscrew. Very interesting corkscrew. This is an opaque two-color in Popeye colors without the clear and white. 11/16". Near Mint(+) (8.8). $22. (Auction #153, Lot 28).

AKRO AGATE COMPANY. Corkscrew. Three color corkscrew. White, light green, transparent red. Clarksburg, WV, circa 1928-1935. 11/16". Mint (9.9). $22. (Auction #157, Lot 19).

AKRO AGATE COMPANY. Corkscrew. Opaque yellow base. Translucent red spiral. Narrow translucent orange spiral on the yellow. Subsurface. 15/16". Near Mint(+) (8.9). $22. (Auction #151, Lot 36).

AKRO AGATE COMPANY. Corkscrew. Lot of two marbles. One is blue and yellow. The other is green and dark orange. Both about 5/8". $22. (Auction #95, Lot 40).

AKRO AGATE COMPANY. Corkscrew. Double ingot two-color corkscrew. Opaque white and transparent red. One tiny pit. 27/32". Mint(-). 27/32". Mint(-) (9.2). $22. (Auction #111, Lot 29).

AKRO AGATE COMPANY. Corkscrew. Lot of five marbles. All are damaged. Two Aces, blue on translucent white, 15/16", Near Mint(+) (8.7). $22. (Auction #83, Lot 35).

AKRO AGATE COMPANY. Corkscrew. Three color corkscrew. White, light green and translucent red. Clarksburg, WV, circa 1928-1938. 13/16". Mint (9.6). $21. (Auction #165, Lot 13.20).

AKRO AGATE COMPANY. Corkscrew. Nice shooter three color. There are four spirals, but three colors. Two gray/white spirals. 23/32". Near Mint(+) (8.9). $21. (Auction #65, Lot 37).

AKRO AGATE COMPANY. Corkscrew. Nice two-color corkscrew. Light blue/slate gray with a yellow spiral. Very odd coloring. Clarksburg, WV. 5/8". Mint (9.9). $21. (Auction #146, Lot 9).

AKRO AGATE COMPANY. Corkscrew. Red and yellow Popeye. One tiny pit. Nice marble. Clarksburg, WV, circa 1927-1935. 11/16". Mint(-) (9). $21. (Auction #156, Lot 20.30).

AKRO AGATE COMPANY. Corkscrew. Shooter three color corkscrew. Opaque white base. Wide spiral of transparent red and a narrower one. 25/32". Mint (9.7). $21. (Auction #90, Lot 4.20).

AKRO AGATE COMPANY. Corkscrew. Red and yellow Popeye. One tiny pit. Nice marble. Clarksburg, WV, circa 1927-1935. 11/16". Mint(-) (9). $21. (Auction #156, Lot 20.50).

AKRO AGATE COMPANY. Corkscrew. Three color corkscrew. Opaque white, opaque yellow and translucent red. All spirals are about the same. 21/32". Mint (9.9). $21. (Auction #80, Lot 14).

AKRO AGATE COMPANY. Corkscrew. Red and yellow Popeye. One tiny pit. Nice marble. Clarksburg, WV, circa 1927-1935. 11/16". Mint(-) (9). $21. (Auction #156, Lot 20.40).

AKRO AGATE COMPANY. Corkscrew. Lot of seven marbles. Six are two-color white-base, one is a two-color color-base. One not Mint. 5/8". $21. (Auction #133, Lot 11).

AKRO AGATE COMPANY. Corkscrew. Three color corkscrew. White, light green and translucent red. Clarksburg, WV, circa 1928-1938. 5/8". $20. (Auction #82, Lot 9).

AKRO AGATE COMPANY. Corkscrew. Lot of three marbles. All are opaque white base with a spiral of blue on top of black. 19/32" to 21/32". $20. (Auction #146, Lot 39).

AKRO AGATE COMPANY. Corkscrew. Nice three color corkscrew. White, translucent red, light green. A few marks on it. Nice shooter. 13/16". Mint(-) (9). $20. (Auction #149, Lot 31.20).

AKRO AGATE COMPANY. Corkscrew. Nice three color corkscrew. White, translucent red, light green. A few marks on it. Nice shooter. 13/16". Mint(-) (9). $20. (Auction #149, Lot 31.30).

AKRO AGATE COMPANY. Corkscrew. Very unusual corkscrew. Semi-opaque milky white base. Spiral of translucent blue and translucent green. 3/4". Mint (9.9). $20. (Auction #85, Lot 37).

AKRO AGATE COMPANY. Corkscrew. Three color corkscrew. White, light green, transparent red. Clarksburg, WV, circa 1928-1935. 11/16". Mint (9.9). $20. (Auction #157, Lot 19.20).

AKRO AGATE COMPANY. Corkscrew. Lot of four marbles. All are Akro corkscrews. Opaque yellow and transparent red, opaque white. $20. (Auction #92, Lot 12).

AKRO AGATE COMPANY. Corkscrew. Lot of six marbles. Assortment of two-color and three-color corkscrews. All have some damage. $20. (Auction #138, Lot 7).

AKRO AGATE COMPANY. Corkscrew. Tomato Soup corkscrew. Translucent white base with opaque white spiral and translucent red spiral. 1". Near Mint(+) (8.9). $20. (Auction #118, Lot 33).

AKRO AGATE COMPANY. Corkscrew. Three color corkscrew. White, light green and translucent red. Clarksburg, WV, circa 1928-1938. 25/32". Mint (9.9). $20. (Auction #126, Lot 1).

AKRO AGATE COMPANY. Corkscrew. Three color corkscrew. White base with light green spiral and orange/red spiral. Very odd coloring. 27/32". Mint(-) (9). $20. (Auction #182, Lot 25).

AKRO AGATE COMPANY. Corkscrew. Lot of five marbles. Nice set of corkscrews. Includes a three-color translucent, a two-color translucent. $20. (Auction #118, Lot 5).

AKRO AGATE COMPANY. Corkscrew. Three color translucent. Translucent milky white base. One spiral of translucent blue. 19/32". Mint (9.9). $20. (Auction #124, Lot 25).

AKRO AGATE COMPANY. Corkscrew. Very nice corkscrew, sometimes mistaken for an orange oxblood. Translucent milky white base. Spiral. 5/8". Mint (9.9). $20. (Auction #132, Lot 2).

AKRO AGATE COMPANY. Corkscrew. Three color corkscrew. Very interesting example. Light blue, yellow and transparent orange. Excellent. 19/32". Mint (9.9). $20. (Auction #140, Lot 3).

AKRO AGATE COMPANY. Corkscrew. Lot of two marbles. These appear to be same run. Transparent milky white base. Double twist. 5/8". Near Mint (8.6). $20. (Auction #84, Lot 42).

AKRO AGATE COMPANY. Corkscrew. Lot of seventeen corkscrews. All are white-base, two-color. A couple have some damage. 19/32". $20. (Auction #177, Lot 13.30).

AKRO AGATE COMPANY. Corkscrew. Two-color corkscrew. Transparent red on green. Nice example. Clarksburg, WV, circa 1928-1935. 3/4". M. 3/4". Mint (9.9). $20. (Auction #130, Lot 14).

AKRO AGATE COMPANY. Corkscrew. Lot of two marbles. First is a three color. Opaque white, opaque yellow and transparent red. $20. (Auction #170, Lot 17).

AKRO AGATE COMPANY. Corkscrew. Lot of four marbles. All are ribbon corkscrews. Nice assortment of colors. One is Mint. 19/32". $20. (Auction #182, Lot 15).

AKRO AGATE COMPANY. Corkscrew. Three color corkscrew. Wide spirals of yellow and blue. Two narrow spirals of brown. In great shape. 11/16". Mint (9.9). $20. (Auction #130, Lot 5).

AKRO AGATE COMPANY. Corkscrew. Lot of two marbles. Both are opaque yellow and translucent red shooters. Both have tiny subsurface moons. $20. (Auction #88, Lot 10).

AKRO AGATE COMPANY. Corkscrew. Three color corkscrew. Opaque white, opaque yellow, transparent red. One tiny pit. 21/32". Near Mint. 21/32". Near Mint (8.9). $19. (Auction #96, Lot 13).

AKRO AGATE COMPANY. Corkscrew. Three color corkscrew. Opaque white, opaque yellow and translucent red. All spirals are about the same. 21/32". Mint (9.9). $19. (Auction #80, Lot 14.30).

AKRO AGATE COMPANY. Corkscrew. Interesting three color corkscrew. Yellow base with a wide translucent red spiral. 31/32". Near Mint(+) (8.9). $18. (Auction #168, Lot 16.30).

AKRO AGATE COMPANY. Corkscrew. Two color corkscrew shooter. Opaque light green and translucent red. One tiny annealing fracture. 29/32". Mint (9.5). $18. (Auction #65, Lot 10).

AKRO AGATE COMPANY. Corkscrew. Interesting three color corkscrew. Yellow base with a wide translucent red spiral. 31/32". Near Mint(+) (8.9). $18. (Auction #168, Lot 16.20).

AKRO AGATE COMPANY. Corkscrew. Interesting three color corkscrew. Yellow base with a wide translucent red spiral. 31/32". Near Mint(+) (8.9). $18. (Auction #168, Lot 16).

AKRO AGATE COMPANY. Corkscrew. Lot of eight marbles. Nice assortment of colors. All are two-color. 5/8" to 23/32". Mint (9.9) to Near Mint. $18. (Auction #123, Lot 3).

AKRO AGATE COMPANY. Corkscrew. Lot of two marbles. Same colors, different sizes. Both are translucent red in opaque yellow. $18. (Auction #127, Lot 32).

AKRO AGATE COMPANY. Corkscrew. Three color corkscrew. Red, yellow and thin white. Very nice marble. Some tiny pits. 13/16". Near Mint(+) (8.9). $18. (Auction #160, Lot 34.20).

AKRO AGATE COMPANY. Corkscrew. Lot of two marbles. Both are ribbons. One is transparent light blue with white ribbon. $18. (Auction #175, Lot 35).

AKRO AGATE COMPANY. Corkscrew. Three color corkscrew. White, light green and translucent red. Clarksburg, WV, circa 1928-1938. 5/8". $18. (Auction #82, Lot 9.20).

AKRO AGATE COMPANY. Corkscrew. Three color corkscrew. Red, yellow and thin white. Very nice marble. Some tiny pits. 13/16". Near Mint(+) (8.9). $18. (Auction #160, Lot 34).

AKRO AGATE COMPANY. Corkscrew. Opalescent translucent white base with a black snake on it. 5/8". Mint (9.9). $18. (Auction #76, Lot 11).

AKRO AGATE COMPANY. Corkscrew. Four color corkscrew shooter. Semi-opaque white base. Two narrow spirals of semi-opaque orange. 27/32". Near Mint (8.6). $18. (Auction #143, Lot 5).

AKRO AGATE COMPANY. Corkscrew. Two-color corkscrew. Opaque light green with transparent dark red spiral on it. One sparkle. 29/32". Near Mint(+) (8.9). $18. (Auction #145, Lot 17).

AKRO AGATE COMPANY. Corkscrew. Two-color corkscrew. Opaque light green with transparent dark red spiral on it. One sparkle. 29/32". Near Mint(+) (8.9). $18. (Auction #145, Lot 17.20).

AKRO AGATE COMPANY. Corkscrew. Two color corkscrew shooter. Opaque light green and translucent red. Some annealing fractures. 29/32". Mint (9). $17. (Auction #182, Lot 3).

AKRO AGATE COMPANY. Corkscrew. Four color corkscrew. White, light green, red and a narrow spiral of transparent brown. 11/16". Near Mint(+) (8.8). $17. (Auction #185, Lot 21).

AKRO AGATE COMPANY. Corkscrew. Shooter two-color corkscrew. Dull orange spiral on white. Interesting colors. 27/32". Near Mint(+) (8.9). $17. (Auction #183, Lot 1).

AKRO AGATE COMPANY. Corkscrew. Lot of twenty marbles. All corkscrews. Almost all white-base. Mostly two-color with a couple of three colors. $17. (Auction #172, Lot 26).

AKRO AGATE COMPANY. Corkscrew. Lot of seven marbles. All are white base two-color. Three red, two blue, one black, one green. 5/8". $17. (Auction #140, Lot 11).

AKRO AGATE COMPANY. Corkscrew. Three color corkscrew. Opaque white with a wide transparent red spiral on it. Narrow wispy blue spiral. 5/8". Mint (9.3). $17. (Auction #164, Lot 37).

AKRO AGATE COMPANY. Corkscrew. Unusual coloring. Thin orange spiral in black. One tiny manufacturing pit. Clarksburg, WV, circa 1928. 5/8". Mint(-) (9). $17. (Auction #122, Lot 48).

AKRO AGATE COMPANY. Corkscrew. Lot of nine marbles. Assortment of two-color corkscrews. 5/8" to 21/32". Five are Mint. Mint (9.9). $17. (Auction #109, Lot 20).

AKRO AGATE COMPANY. Corkscrew. Lot of three marbles. Each is a red, yellow and white three-color corkscrew. Each has annealing fractures. $17. (Auction #83, Lot 16).

AKRO AGATE COMPANY. Corkscrew. Very pretty three-color corkscrew. Opaque white with a translucent red spiral. 19/32". Mint (9.8). $17. (Auction #74, Lot 1).

AKRO AGATE COMPANY. Corkscrew. Four color corkscrew. Another hard one to find. Semi-opaque white base. Spiral of blue, spiral of green. 3/4". Near Mint (8.4). $17. (Auction #141, Lot 36).

AKRO AGATE COMPANY. Corkscrew. Four-color corkscrew. Marble is one-half translucent milky white, and one-half a spiral of opaque yellow. 21/32". Near Mint(+) (8.9). $17. (Auction #126, Lot 7).

AKRO AGATE COMPANY. Corkscrew. Opaque light green with a dark transparent red spiral. Similar to the 1" corkscrews. 5/8". Mint (9.9). $17. (Auction #77, Lot 35).

AKRO AGATE COMPANY. Corkscrew. Two color shooter corkscrew. Opaque light green base with a wide spiral on the surface of translucent. 15/16". Near Mint(+) (8.9). $16. (Auction #90, Lot 16.20).

AKRO AGATE COMPANY. Corkscrew. Very pretty ribbon corkscrew. Transparent clear base. Ribbon of light green. 5/8". Mint (9.5). $16. (Auction #138, Lot 8).

AKRO AGATE COMPANY. Corkscrew. Three color corkscrew shooter. Opaque white, opaque light blue, translucent red. A couple of sparkles. 13/16". Near Mint(+) (8.5). $16. (Auction #62, Lot 5).

AKRO AGATE COMPANY. Corkscrew. Red and yellow shooter. Subsurface moon. Pre-Freese Improvement, with tiny feathering at the poles. Near Mint(+) (8.9). $16. (Auction #110, Lot 24.20).

AKRO AGATE COMPANY. Corkscrew. Three color corkscrew. Opaque white base. Wide black spiral, slightly narrower transparent red spiral. 11/16". Mint (9.8). $16. (Auction #61, Lot 4).

AKRO AGATE COMPANY. Corkscrew. Lot of two marbles. Two snake corkscrews. Both are opaque yellow snakes on translucent white base. 5/8". Mint (9.9). $16. (Auction #65, Lot 8).

AKRO AGATE COMPANY. Corkscrew. Three color corkscrew. White, yellow and orange. Nice marble. Clarksburg, WV, circa 1928-1938. 5/8". Mint (9.9). $16. (Auction #75, Lot 2).

AKRO AGATE COMPANY. Corkscrew. Shooter in odd coloring. Creamy light cocoa opaque base with a wide surface spiral of transparent red. 27/32". Near Mint(+) (8.9). $16. (Auction #176, Lot 5.30).

AKRO AGATE COMPANY. Corkscrew. Shooter in odd coloring. Creamy light cocoa opaque base with a wide surface spiral of transparent red. 27/32". Near Mint(+) (8.9). $16. (Auction #176, Lot 5.20).

AKRO AGATE COMPANY. Corkscrew. Lot of twenty two marbles. Nice assortment. Almost all have some damage. 19/32" to 23/32". Mint (9.5). $16. (Auction #180, Lot 39).

AKRO AGATE COMPANY. Corkscrew. Shooter in odd coloring. Creamy light cocoa opaque base with a wide surface spiral of transparent red. 27/32". Near Mint(+) (8.9). $16. (Auction #176, Lot 5).

AKRO AGATE COMPANY. Corkscrew. Interesting corkscrew. Orange tinted opaque white with a transparent red spiral. Very nice. Clarksburg, WV. 23/32". Mint (9.7). $16. (Auction #96, Lot 1).

AKRO AGATE COMPANY. Corkscrew. Three color corkscrew. White with a light green and light blue spirals. Very nice marble. 5/8". Mint(-) (9). $16. (Auction #77, Lot 14).

AKRO AGATE COMPANY. Corkscrew. Lot of five marbles. All the same color and size, possibly same run. Nice line for a tin or box. $16. (Auction #155, Lot 8).

AKRO AGATE COMPANY. Corkscrew. Lot of two marbles. First is a Ringer, 5/8", Mint (9.9). The second is green and white. $16. (Auction #98, Lot 28).

AKRO AGATE COMPANY. Corkscrew. Three color corkscrew. Red, yellow and white. Very nice marble. Clarksburg, WV, circa 1928-1938. 23/32". Mint (9.8). $16. (Auction #78, Lot 1).

AKRO AGATE COMPANY. Corkscrew. Red and yellow shooter. Subsurface moon. Pre-Freese Improvement, with tiny feathering at the poles. Near Mint(+) (8.9). $16. (Auction #110, Lot 24).

AKRO AGATE COMPANY. Corkscrew. Three color corkscrew. White, light green and translucent red. Clarksburg, WV, circa 1928-1938. 5/8". $16. (Auction #82, Lot 9.30).

AKRO AGATE COMPANY. Corkscrew. Lot of two marbles. One is black on orange. 19/32". Mint (9.9). The other is black on white. 9/16". $15. (Auction #125, Lot 10).

AKRO AGATE COMPANY. Corkscrew. Lot of six marbles. Nice assortment of corkscrews. All two-color. Two are white base, rest are color. $15. (Auction #130, Lot 1).

AKRO AGATE COMPANY. Corkscrew. Two color corkscrew shooter. Opaque light green and translucent red. Dug at a Clarksburg dump site. 29/32". Mint (9.5). $15. (Auction #160, Lot 3.20).

AKRO AGATE COMPANY. Corkscrew. Odd corkscrew. White base. Black spiral on top of oxblood. Thin oxblood under the black. 5/8". Mint (8.7). $15. (Auction #66, Lot 16).

AKRO AGATE COMPANY. Corkscrew. Hard to find Moonie Corkscrew. Translucent opalescent white base with a translucent green spiral. 3/4". Near Mint(+) (8.9). $15. (Auction #77, Lot 37).

AKRO AGATE COMPANY. Corkscrew. Unusual coloring. Predominately opaque white. Transparent blue spiral on top of opaque black. 5/8". Near Mint (8.6). $15. (Auction #74, Lot 7).

AKRO AGATE COMPANY. Corkscrew. Lot of two marbles. Both are corkscrews. The first is an Imperial. Transparent brown. $15. (Auction #63, Lot 2).

AKRO AGATE COMPANY. Corkscrew. Nice three-color corkscrew. White, light blue and translucent red. Clarksburg, WV, circa 1928-1938. 21/32". Mint (9.9). $15. (Auction #110, Lot 12).

AKRO AGATE COMPANY. Corkscrew. Lot of two marbles. Both are double ingot shooter corkscrews. Red and white. 13/16" and 7/8". Mint(-). $15. (Auction #138, Lot 31).

AKRO AGATE COMPANY. Corkscrew. Lot of ten marbles. Assortment of snakes and ribbons. All have some damage. 19/32" to 5/8". Near Mint. $15. (Auction #138, Lot 28).

AKRO AGATE COMPANY. Corkscrew. Two color corkscrew shooter. Opaque light green and translucent red. Dug at a Clarksburg dump site. 29/32". Mint (9.5). $15. (Auction #160, Lot 3).

AKRO AGATE COMPANY. Corkscrew. Opaque yellow with transparent red spiral. Almost no twist to the marble. Has an annealing fracture. $15. (Auction #169, Lot 32).

AKRO AGATE COMPANY. Corkscrew. Three color corkscrew. White, light green and translucent red. Annealing fractures at one pole. 27/32". Mint(-) (9). $15. (Auction #161, Lot 38).

AKRO AGATE COMPANY. Corkscrew. Lot of two marbles. Both ribbon corkscrews. Opaque white ribbon in transparent aqua. Some tiny pits. $15. (Auction #185, Lot 38).

AKRO AGATE COMPANY. Corkscrew. Another odd colored corkscrew. Powder blue and yellow. Several sparkles. Clarksburg, WV, circa 1928. 21/32". Mint (9). $14. (Auction #76, Lot 31).

AKRO AGATE COMPANY. Corkscrew. Three color corkscrew. Opaque white, opaque black and translucent red. One tiny sparkle. Clarksburg, WV. 5/8". Mint(-) (9.1). $14. (Auction #139, Lot 35).

AKRO AGATE COMPANY. Corkscrew. Two color shooter corkscrew. Opaque light green base. 15/16". Near Mint(+) (8.9). $14. (Auction #90, Lot 16).

AKRO AGATE COMPANY. Corkscrew. Three color corkscrew. White, black and translucent red. Very little white. Nice marble. Clarksburg, WV. 11/16". Mint (9.9). $14. (Auction #103, Lot 10).

AKRO AGATE COMPANY. Corkscrew. Three color corkscrew. Opaque white base. Narrow yellow spiral on the surface. Very narrow green spiral. 5/8". Mint (9.9). $14. (Auction #146, Lot 7).

AKRO AGATE COMPANY. Corkscrew. Lot of two marbles. Both are corkscrews. First is a three color. Black, yellow and translucent red. $14. (Auction #60, Lot 11).

AKRO AGATE COMPANY. Corkscrew. Three color corkscrew. White base. Opaque green spiral and two opaque yellow spirals. In nice shape. 5/8". Mint(-) (9.2). $14. (Auction #70, Lot 36).

AKRO AGATE COMPANY. Corkscrew. Lot of two marbles. First is a snake. White on transparent cobalt blue. 5/8". Mint (9.9). $14. (Auction #63, Lot 11).

AKRO AGATE COMPANY. Corkscrew. Two color corkscrew shooter. Opaque light green and translucent red. Dug at a Clarksburg dump site. 29/32". Mint (9). $13. (Auction #168, Lot 2).

AKRO AGATE COMPANY. Corkscrew. Opaque white base. Black spiral on yellow. In great shape. A beauty. Clarksburg, WV, circa 1925-1935. $13. (Auction #95, Lot 3).

AKRO AGATE COMPANY. Corkscrew. Two color corkscrew shooter. Opaque light green and translucent red. Dug at a Clarksburg dump site. 29/32". Mint (9). $13. (Auction #168, Lot 2.30).

AKRO AGATE COMPANY. Corkscrew. Two color corkscrew shooter. Opaque light green and translucent red. Dug at a Clarksburg dump site. 29/32". Mint (9). $13. (Auction #168, Lot 2.20).

AKRO AGATE COMPANY. Corkscrew. Lot of five marbles. All are two-color white-base corkscrews. Nice assortment of colors. All are Mint. $12. (Auction #111, Lot 44).

AKRO AGATE COMPANY. Corkscrew. Lot of four marbles. All are yellow spiral on opaque white. Three Mint. 19/32" to 11/16". Mint (9.9). $12. (Auction #151, Lot 1).

AKRO AGATE COMPANY. Corkscrew. Lot of five marbles. All are black and white corkscrews, in assorted sizes. 5/8" to 15/16". Mint. $12. (Auction #119, Lot 1).

AKRO AGATE COMPANY. Corkscrew. Nice corkscrew in a hard to find color combination. Translucent milky white with opaque white spiral. 5/8". Mint(-) (9). $12. (Auction #116, Lot 21).

AKRO AGATE COMPANY. Corkscrew. Transparent red on opaque yellow, with an thin transparent orange spiral on the yellow. 15/16". Near Mint(+) (8.7). $12. (Auction #138, Lot 4).

AKRO AGATE COMPANY. Corkscrew. Lot of ten marbles. All are white-base two-color corkscrews. 5/8" to 13/16". Mint(-) (9.0) to Near Mint. $12. (Auction #127, Lot 37).

AKRO AGATE COMPANY. Corkscrew. Odd coloring. Three color corkscrew. Semi-opaque white base. Narrow spiral of transparent orange. 23/32". Near Mint(+) (8.8). $12. (Auction #134, Lot 16).

AKRO AGATE COMPANY. Corkscrew. Lot of three marbles. A snake, a ribbon and a two color. 19/32". to 5/8". Mint (9.9-9.4). $11. (Auction #95, Lot 9).

AKRO AGATE COMPANY. Corkscrew. Three color corkscrew. All three spirals are basically the same width. Light green, light yellow. 5/8". Near Mint(+) (8.7). $11. (Auction #167, Lot 16).

AKRO AGATE COMPANY. Corkscrew. Tri-color Ace corkscrew. Translucent milky white base with a spiral of translucent blue. 19/32". Mint(-) (9.1). $11. (Auction #83, Lot 4).

AKRO AGATE COMPANY. Corkscrew. Very nice corkscrew. White covered by translucent yellow, with a translucent brown spiral. 3/4". Near Mint(+) (8.7). $11. (Auction #98, Lot 18).

AKRO AGATE COMPANY. Corkscrew. Three color corkscrew. Not much of a twist. All three spirals are basically the same width. 5/8". Near Mint(+) (8.9). $10. (Auction #167, Lot 9).

AKRO AGATE COMPANY. Corkscrew. Lot of ten marbles. All are white-base two-color corkscrews. 5/8" to 3/4". Mint (9.9) to Near Mint. $10. (Auction #119, Lot 23).

AKRO AGATE COMPANY. Corkscrew. Odd two color corkscrew. Double twisted. Grayish/white spiral and a light green spiral. Both spirals. 11/16". Mint (9.4). $10. (Auction #105, Lot 12).

AKRO AGATE COMPANY. Corkscrew. Opaque white base. Black spiral on orange. In great shape. A beauty. Clarksburg, WV, circa 1925-1935. $10. (Auction #95, Lot 33).

AKRO AGATE COMPANY. Corkscrew. Yellow and black corkscrew. In great shape. Clarksburg, WV, circa 1928-1938. 19/32." Mint (9.9). $10. (Auction #66, Lot 5).

AKRO AGATE COMPANY. Corkscrew. Lot of three marbles. Orange on yellow, transparent red on white, transparent orange. $10. (Auction #90, Lot 20).

AKRO AGATE COMPANY. Corkscrew. Black and orange corkscrew. One pinprick. Clarksburg, WV, circa 1928-1935. 5/8". Mint(-) (9.0). 5/8". Mint(-) (9). $9. (Auction #154, Lot 30).

AKRO AGATE COMPANY. Corkscrew. Unusual two color corkscrew. Opaque brown/cream color base with a brown/orange translucent spiral. 5/8". Mint(-) (9.1). $9. (Auction #110, Lot 7).

AKRO AGATE COMPANY. Corkscrew. Lot of ten marbles. All are white-base. One is a two color. All have some damage. All about 5/8". $9. (Auction #138, Lot 12).

AKRO AGATE COMPANY. Corkscrew. Three color corkscrew. Orange and green. Thin spiral of transparent brown. One subsurface moon. 21/32". Near Mint(+) (8.8). $6. (Auction #185, Lot 13).

AKRO AGATE COMPANY. Corkscrew. Lot of two marbles. Ringer, 5/8", Mint(-) (9.1). Imperial, 19/32", Near Mint(+) (8.8). $5. (Auction #182, Lot 19).

AKRO AGATE COMPANY. Corkscrew. Translucent white base with a black spiral. Odd coloring. Has a small subsurface moon. Clarksburg, WV. 9/16". Near Mint(+) (8.8). $5. (Auction #60, Lot 13).

AKRO AGATE COMPANY. Corkscrew. Hard to find corkscrew. Early colors of orange and blue. Same colors as the large experimental corks. 5/8". Mint (9.6). $30. (Auction #137, Lot 33).

AKRO AGATE COMPANY. Cornelian. Very hard to find Akro Cornelian. Translucent red glass with white swirls. Similar to a Brick. 27/32". Near Mint(-) (8.2). $50. (Auction #180, Lot 19).

AKRO AGATE COMPANY. Cornelian. Very hard to find Akro Cornelian. Translucent red glass with white swirls. Similar to a Brick. 21/32". Mint(-) (9). $32. (Auction #95, Lot 44).

AKRO AGATE COMPANY. Cornelian. Opaque red and wispy white. Similar to a Brick, but not oxblood. Beauty. Clarksburg, WV, circa 1925. 11/16". Mint (9.9). $30. (Auction #102, Lot 45).

AKRO AGATE COMPANY. Cornelian. Opaque red and wispy white. Similar to a Brick, but not oxblood. Beauty. Clarksburg, WV, circa 1925. 11/16". Mint (9.9). $30. (Auction #102, Lot 45.10).

AKRO AGATE COMPANY. Cornelian. Opaque red and wispy white. Similar to a Brick, but not oxblood. Beauty. Clarksburg, WV, circa 1925. 11/16". Mint (9.9). $22. (Auction #106, Lot 47).

AKRO AGATE COMPANY. Cornelian. Opaque red and wispy white. Similar to a Brick, but not oxblood. Beauty. Clarksburg, WV, circa 1925. 11/16". Mint (9.9). $22. (Auction #106, Lot 47.10).

AKRO AGATE COMPANY. Cullet. Small plastic box, 3-3/4" x 2-5/8" x 1-1/8", filled with small pieces of cullet. $34. (Auction #161, Lot 29).

AKRO AGATE COMPANY. Cullet. Small plastic box, 3-3/4" x 2-5/8" x 1-1/8", filled with small pieces of cullet. $32. (Auction #161, Lot 29.20).

AKRO AGATE COMPANY. Cullet. Small plastic box, 3-3/4" x 2-5/8" x 1-1/8", filled with small pieces of cullet. $30. (Auction #111, Lot 34.20).

AKRO AGATE COMPANY. Cullet. Small plastic box, 3-3/4" x 2-5/8" x 1-1/8", filled with small pieces of cullet. $27. (Auction #111, Lot 34.10).

AKRO AGATE COMPANY. Cullet. Excellent large piece of cullet from the Akro factory. White, red, orange, black. About 7" x 4" x 2". $15. (Auction #132, Lot 29).

AKRO AGATE COMPANY. Cullet. Baggie of Akro cullet. Dug at the plant site. Mostly small pieces and malformed marbles. Some nice. $14. (Auction #143, Lot 19).

AKRO AGATE COMPANY. Egg yolk/blue oxblood hybrid. Very rare marble. Translucent milky white base, opaque egg yolk yellow swirls and translucent blue. 5/8". Mint (9.9). $300. (Auction #71, Lot 39).

AKRO AGATE COMPANY. Egg yolk oxblood. Semi-opaque white base with a wide egg yolk yellow swirl and a narrower oxblood swirl. A real beauty. 3/4". Mint(-) (9.1). $180. (Auction #169, Lot 47).

AKRO AGATE COMPANY. Egg yolk oxblood. Very nice swirl example. Translucent white base. Swirl of opaque egg yolk and swirl of rich oxblood. 3/4". Mint (9.9). $170. (Auction #124, Lot 45).

AKRO AGATE COMPANY. Egg yolk oxblood. Excellent example. Milky white base, opaque egg yolk yellow swirl, oxblood swirl. Surface is pristine. 19/32". Mint (9.9). $170. (Auction #142, Lot 46).

AKRO AGATE COMPANY. Egg yolk oxblood. Translucent milky white base. Large swirl of egg yolk yellow and nice swirl of oxblood. 11/16". Mint(-) (9.1). $150. (Auction #84, Lot 44).

AKRO AGATE COMPANY. Egg yolk oxblood. Very nice corkscrew example. Translucent white base. Spiral of opaque egg yolk and spiral of rich oxblood. 23/32". Mint(-) (9.2). $150. (Auction #156, Lot 38).

AKRO AGATE COMPANY. Egg yolk oxblood. Very nice corkscrew example. Translucent white base. Spiral of opaque egg yolk and spiral of rich oxblood. 23/32". Mint (9.9). $150. (Auction #140.10, Lot 48).

AKRO AGATE COMPANY. Egg yolk oxblood. Semi-opaque white base. Egg yolk swirl on the surface and dark oxblood next to it. Beautiful condition. 5/8". Mint (9.9). $120. (Auction #161, Lot 45).

AKRO AGATE COMPANY. Egg yolk oxblood. Semi-opaque white base with a wide egg yolk yellow swirl and a narrower oxblood swirl. A real beauty. 3/4". Mint(-) (9.1). $120. (Auction #107, Lot 47).

AKRO AGATE COMPANY. Egg yolk oxblood. Beautiful egg yolk oxblood. Translucent milky white base. Swirl of translucent egg yolk yellow. 5/8". Mint (9.9). $110. (Auction #59, Lot 40).

AKRO AGATE COMPANY. Egg yolk oxblood. Excellent example. Milky white base, opaque egg yolk yellow swirl, oxblood swirl. Surface is pristine. 19/32". Mint (9.9). $110. (Auction #129, Lot 38).

AKRO AGATE COMPANY. Egg yolk oxblood. Excellent example. Milky white base, opaque egg yolk yellow swirl, oxblood swirl. Surface is pristine. 19/32". Mint (9.9). $95. (Auction #111, Lot 38).

AKRO AGATE COMPANY. Egg yolk oxblood. Nice egg yolk oxblood. Translucent milky white base. Small swirl of opaque egg yolk yellow. 5/8". Mint (9.9). $85. (Auction #100, Lot 20).

AKRO AGATE COMPANY. Egg yolk oxblood. Superior example of an egg yolk. Translucent milky white base. Translucent yellow swirls. Nice oxblood. 19/32". Mint (9.9). $85. (Auction #68, Lot 44).

AKRO AGATE COMPANY. Egg yolk oxblood. Semi-opaque white base. Egg yolk swirl on the surface and a rich oxblood swirl on the surface. 23/32". Near Mint(+) (8.9). $80. (Auction #126, Lot 13).

AKRO AGATE COMPANY. Egg yolk oxblood. Translucent milky white base. Egg yolk swirl on the surface and a rich oxblood swirl on the surface. 3/4". Near Mint(+) (8.9). $80. (Auction #130, Lot 47).

AKRO AGATE COMPANY. Egg yolk oxblood. Translucent white base. Egg yolk swirl on the surface and a thin oxblood swirl on the surface. 5/8". Mint(-) (9). $65. (Auction #171, Lot 49).

AKRO AGATE COMPANY. Egg yolk oxblood. Semi-opaque white base. Egg yolk swirl on the surface and a rich oxblood swirl on the surface. 11/16". Near Mint(+) (8.8). $60. (Auction #134, Lot 39).

AKRO AGATE COMPANY. Egg yolk oxblood. Semi-opaque white base. Egg yolk and a light oxblood corkscrew on the surface Some minor chips. 11/16". Near Mint(+) . $28. (Auction #177, Lot 38).

AKRO AGATE COMPANY. Experimental Hero Patch. This is an experimental Hero patch. Opaque white base. Bright, actually electric, orange patch. 31/32". Mint (9.7). $90. (Auction #70, Lot 42).

AKRO AGATE COMPANY. Experimental patch. Opaque white base with a dark green patch covering almost half the marble. Very unusual patch. 1". Mint (9.9). $70. (Auction #71, Lot 31).

AKRO AGATE COMPANY. Experimental patch. Opaque white base with a dark green patch covering almost half the marble. Very unusual patch. 1". Mint (9.9). $65. (Auction #71, Lot 31.20).

AKRO AGATE COMPANY. Experimental patch. Shooter marble. Opaque white base with a small green and small yellow patch. Feathering at the seams. 31/32". Mint (9.9). $32. (Auction #77, Lot 29).

AKRO AGATE COMPANY. Experimental Patch. Gorgeous experimental patch. One side is orange and one side is light blue. These are very hard to find. 1-1/8". Mint(-) (9). $80. (Auction #71, Lot 28).

AKRO AGATE COMPANY. Fire Opal. Early Akro opaque marble. This one is bright orange. These were called Fire Opal by the company. 31/32". Near Mint(+) (8.9). $25. (Auction #129, Lot 15).

AKRO AGATE COMPANY. Flintie. Yellow Flintie. Opalescent yellow marble. Hard to find. Clarksburg, WV, circa 1925-1935. 5/8". Mint. 5/8". Mint (9.9). $43. (Auction #113, Lot 6).

AKRO AGATE COMPANY. Flintie. Yellow Flintie. Opalescent yellow marble. Hard to find. Clarksburg, WV, circa 1925-1935. 5/8". Mint. 5/8". Mint (9.9). $40. (Auction #113, Lot 6.20).

AKRO AGATE COMPANY. Flintie. Yellow Flintie. Opalescent yellow marble. Hard to find. Clarksburg, WV, circa 1925-1935. 5/8". Mint. 5/8". Mint (9.9). $35. (Auction #113, Lot 6.30).

AKRO AGATE COMPANY. Flintie. Yellow Flintie. Opalescent yellow marble. Hard to find. Clarksburg, WV, circa 1925-1935. 5/8". Mint. 5/8". Mint (9.9). $33. (Auction #145, Lot 2).

AKRO AGATE COMPANY. Flintie. Yellow Flintie. Opalescent yellow marble. Hard to find. Clarksburg, WV, circa 1925-1935. 5/8". Mint. 5/8". Mint (9.9). $33. (Auction #145, Lot 2.20).

AKRO AGATE COMPANY. Flintie. Yellow Flintie. Opalescent yellow marble. Hard to find. Clarksburg, WV, circa 1925-1935. 5/8". Mint. 5/8". Mint (9.9). $33. (Auction #145, Lot 2.30).

AKRO AGATE COMPANY. Flintie. Yellow Flintie. Very hard color to find. Opalescent yellow marble. Some tiny pits, two small subsurface. 11/16". Near Mint (8.6). $27. (Auction #83, Lot 36).

AKRO AGATE COMPANY. Game. "Akro Solitary Checkers". Red cardboard boxed game. Interior is cardboard solitaire-type game. $17. (Auction #143, Lot 35).

AKRO AGATE COMPANY. Helmet patch. Lot of thirty seven marbles. Nice assortment of colors. $55. (Auction #132, Lot 14).

AKRO AGATE COMPANY. Helmet patch. Lot of fourteen marbles. Nice assortment of colors. $36. (Auction #151, Lot 20).

AKRO AGATE COMPANY. Helmet patch. Lot of fourteen marbles. Nice assortment of colors. $36. (Auction #151, Lot 20.20).

AKRO AGATE COMPANY. Helmet patch. Lot of sixteen marbles. Nice assortment of helmet patches. About half have hit marks. 19/32" to 5/8". $32. (Auction #141, Lot 39).

AKRO AGATE COMPANY. Helmet patch. Lot of fourteen marbles. Nice assortment of colors. $27. (Auction #146, Lot 14).

AKRO AGATE COMPANY. Helmet patch. Lot of fourteen marbles. Nice assortment of colors. $27. (Auction #146, Lot 14.20).

AKRO AGATE COMPANY. Helmet patch. Lot of nine marbles. Assortment of helmet patch. All about 5/8". All Mint. $14. (Auction #80, Lot 26).

AKRO AGATE COMPANY. Helmet Patch. Lot of thirty seven marbles. Assortment of colors. Most have some damage. $48. (Auction #144, Lot 25).

AKRO AGATE COMPANY. Helmet Patch. Shooter helmet patch. Light blue transparent base. White helmet with a red stripe. Clarksburg, WV. 25/32". Mint (9.9). $19. (Auction #151, Lot 41).

AKRO AGATE COMPANY. Helmet Patch. Lot of five marbles. Assortment of colors. Nice group. 19/32" to 5/8". Mint (9.9-9.7). There are two. $16. (Auction #112, Lot 8.10).

AKRO AGATE COMPANY. Helmet Patch. Lot of five marbles. Assortment of colors. Nice group. 19/32" to 5/8". Mint (9.9-9.7). There are two. $16. (Auction #112, Lot 8).

AKRO AGATE COMPANY. Helmet Patch. Shooter helmet patch. Light brown transparent base. White helmet with a red stripe. 23/32". Mint(-) (9.2). $14. (Auction #85, Lot 3).

AKRO AGATE COMPANY. Helmet Patch. Lot of nine marbles. Assortment of colors. All around 19/32" and Mint (9.9-9.4). There are two sets. $14. (Auction #80, Lot 26.20).

AKRO AGATE COMPANY. Helmet Patch. Lot of eighteen marbles. Assortment of sizes and colors. About half have damage. 5/8" to 23/32". Mint. $12. (Auction #122, Lot 37).

AKRO AGATE COMPANY. Hybrid oxblood. Very rare oxblood. The base is pale limeade. Very fluorescent. Has one very small opaque white swirl. 25/32". Mint(-) (9). $195. (Auction #100, Lot 32).

AKRO AGATE COMPANY. Hybrid oxblood. Very unusual oxblood. This is a silver oxblood with an additional green swirl. Transparent silver. 3/4". Mint(-) (9). $140. (Auction #131, Lot 10).

AKRO AGATE COMPANY. Hybrid oxblood. Shooter size carnelian/egg yolk oxblood. Translucent milky brown/white base (fluorescent!!). Excellent. 3/4". Near Mint (8.5). $120. (Auction #84, Lot 33).

AKRO AGATE COMPANY. Imperial corkscrew. Nice shooter. Harder to find. Translucent milky white base. Opaque wispy white spiral. 23/32". Mint (9.9). $32. (Auction #69, Lot 41).

AKRO AGATE COMPANY. Kneepad. Very difficult to find. Kneepad. Brown rubberized exterior with purple piping and a felt interior. $110. (Auction #145, Lot 26).

AKRO AGATE COMPANY. Lemonade. Translucent "Ade" base. Semi-opaque wispy white, opaque bright yellow. One tiny manufacturing rough spot. 31/32". Mint(-) (9.2). $37. (Auction #171, Lot 42).

AKRO AGATE COMPANY. Lemonade. Lot of three marbles. All three are lemonades. Two have minor green next to the yellow. $36. (Auction #84, Lot 25).

AKRO AGATE COMPANY. Lemonade. Lot of three marbles. Two corkscrews and one swirl. One of the corkscrews has a subsurface moon. $29. (Auction #141, Lot 18).

AKRO AGATE COMPANY. Lemonade. Lot of three marbles. All are corkscrews. Each has a sparkle. 19/32". Mint(-) (9.2). $25. (Auction #56, Lot 5).

AKRO AGATE COMPANY. Lemonade. Lot of three marbles. All are lemonade corkscrews. Very fluorescent. All have minor damage. 5/8". $24. (Auction #130, Lot 34).

AKRO AGATE COMPANY. Lemonade. Lemonade corkscrew. Nice example. 19/32." Mint (9.9). $17. (Auction #111, Lot 9).

AKRO AGATE COMPANY. Lemonade corkscrew. Nice marble. Fluorescent lemonade base. Opaque white spiral. Nice oxblood swirl. One subsurface moon. 19/32". Near Mint(+) (8.9). $32. (Auction #56, Lot 10).

AKRO AGATE COMPANY. Lemonade oxblood. Superior example!!!. Base is very fluorescent lemonade translucent with a green tint. 25/32". Mint(-) (9.1). $130. (Auction #129, Lot 48).

AKRO AGATE COMPANY. Lemonade oxblood. Fluorescent lemonade base with translucent white swirls. Excellent oxblood swirls on the surface. 19/32". Mint (9.9). $110. (Auction #91, Lot 10).

AKRO AGATE COMPANY. Lemonade oxblood. Lemonade oxblood. However, this one has a greenish "ade" base, not a yellowish "ade" base. Corkscrew. 21/23". Mint(-) (9.1). $100. (Auction #170, Lot 48).

AKRO AGATE COMPANY. Lemonade oxblood. Lemonade oxblood shooter. Fluorescent lemonade base. Wispy opaque white swirls. Beautiful oxblood. 3/4". Near Mint(+) (8.9). $95. (Auction #88, Lot 41).

AKRO AGATE COMPANY. Lemonade oxblood. A beauty. Super example. Base is translucent fluorescent lemonade. Wispy white swirls in it. 5/8". Mint (9.9). $90. (Auction #93, Lot 30).

AKRO AGATE COMPANY. Lemonade oxblood. Superb example. Fluorescent vaseline lemonade base with wispy white swirls and gorgeous oxblood. 5/8". Mint (9.9). $85. (Auction #111, Lot 4).

AKRO AGATE COMPANY. Lemonade oxblood. Superb example. Fluorescent vaseline lemonade base with wispy white swirls and gorgeous oxblood. 5/8". Mint (9.9). $75. (Auction #129, Lot 27).

AKRO AGATE COMPANY. Lemonade oxblood. Translucent lemonade base. Translucent white swirls in it. Nice oxblood swirl on the surface. 5/8". Mint (9.9). $70. (Auction #124, Lot 37).

AKRO AGATE COMPANY. Lemonade oxblood. Superb example. Fluorescent vaseline lemonade base with wispy white swirls and gorgeous oxblood. 5/8". Mint (9.9). $70. (Auction #136, Lot 39).

AKRO AGATE COMPANY. Lemonade oxblood. Superb example. Fluorescent vaseline lemonade base with wispy white swirls and gorgeous

oxblood. 5/8". Mint (9.9). $70. (Auction #142, Lot 41).

AKRO AGATE COMPANY. Lemonade oxblood. Lot of two marbles. Fluorescent lemonade base with translucent white swirls. Excellent oxblood swirl. Mint. $70. (Auction #144, Lot 8).

AKRO AGATE COMPANY. Lemonade oxblood. Superb example. Fluorescent vaseline lemonade base with wispy white swirls and gorgeous oxblood. 5/8". Mint (9.9). $70. (Auction #137, Lot 31.20).

AKRO AGATE COMPANY. Lemonade oxblood. Translucent lemonade base. Translucent white swirls in it. Nice oxblood swirl on the surface. 5/8". Mint (9.9). $65. (Auction #126, Lot 16).

AKRO AGATE COMPANY. Lemonade oxblood. Fluorescent lemonade base with translucent white swirls. Excellent oxblood swirls on the surface. 19/32". Mint (9.9). $65. (Auction #96, Lot 27).

AKRO AGATE COMPANY. Lemonade oxblood. Superb example. Fluorescent vaseline lemonade base with wispy white swirls and gorgeous oxblood. 5/8". Mint (9.9). $65. (Auction #137, Lot 31).

AKRO AGATE COMPANY. Lemonade oxblood. Semi-opaque very fluorescent ade base with wispy white swirls and with oxblood swirls on the surface. 19/32". Mint (9.9). $65. (Auction #107, Lot 32).

AKRO AGATE COMPANY. Lemonade oxblood. Semi-opaque very fluorescent lemonade base with opaque white swirls and oxblood swirls. Very nice example. 5/8". Mint (9.7). $60. (Auction #65, Lot 28).

AKRO AGATE COMPANY. Lemonade oxblood. Nice example. Fluorescent vaseline lemonade base with wispy white swirls and gorgeous oxblood. 5/8". Mint (9.9). $60. (Auction #130, Lot 45).

AKRO AGATE COMPANY. Lemonade oxblood. Superb example. Fluorescent vaseline lemonade base with opaque white swirls and nice oxblood. 5/8". Mint (9.9). $60. (Auction #140, Lot 7).

AKRO AGATE COMPANY. Lemonade oxblood. Nice example. Fluorescent vaseline lemonade base with wispy white swirls and gorgeous oxblood. 5/8". Mint (9.1). $55. (Auction #131, Lot 30).

AKRO AGATE COMPANY. Lemonade oxblood. Nice example. Fluorescent vaseline lemonade base with wispy white swirls and gorgeous oxblood. 5/8". Mint (9.9). $55. (Auction #171, Lot 10).

AKRO AGATE COMPANY. Lemonade oxblood. Superior example. Fluorescent translucent "ade" base. Wispy white spiral in it. Rich oxblood spiral. 19/32". Mint (9.8). $55. (Auction #173, Lot 15).

AKRO AGATE COMPANY. Lemonade oxblood. Nice lemonade oxblood. Translucent fluorescent lemonade base. Wispy opaque white swirl in the marble. 5/8". Near Mint(+) (8.9). $55. (Auction #71, Lot 14).

AKRO AGATE COMPANY. Lemonade oxblood. Fluorescent translucent lemonade base with nice oxblood swirls on it. Has a sparkle. Clarksburg, WV. 19/32". Mint(-) (9). $50. (Auction #100, Lot 8).

AKRO AGATE COMPANY. Lemonade oxblood. Fluorescent translucent lemonade base with wispy white swirls. Nice oxblood swirling on the surface. 19/32". Mint (9.5). $48. (Auction #68, Lot 38).

AKRO AGATE COMPANY. Lemonade oxblood. Nice example. Fluorescent vaseline lemonade base with wispy white swirls and gorgeous oxblood. 5/8". Near Mint(+) (8.7). $25. (Auction #181, Lot 9).

AKRO AGATE COMPANY. Limeade. Lot of two marbles. Both are Limeades. One is a corkscrew, one is a swirl. Excellent pair. $60. (Auction #137, Lot 12).

AKRO AGATE COMPANY. Limeade. Nice limeade swirl. Very fluorescent. In great shape. Clarksburg, WV, circa 1927-1938. 5/8". Mint. 5/8". Mint (9.9). $29. (Auction #182, Lot 1).

AKRO AGATE COMPANY. Limeade. Beautiful example of a limeade. Very fluorescent. One sparkle. Clarksburg, WV, circa 1928-1938. 5/8". Mint(-) (9.2). $25. (Auction #129, Lot 32).

AKRO AGATE COMPANY. Limeade. Beautiful limeade swirl. Very fluorescent. Two tiny sparkles. 5/8". Mint(-) (9.2). 5/8". Mint(-) (9.2). $16. (Auction #111, Lot 25).

AKRO AGATE COMPANY. Limeade corkscrew. Lot of two marbles. Both are limeades. Corkscrew type. Both are very fluorescent. One has some sparkle. $35. (Auction #142, Lot 18).

AKRO AGATE COMPANY. Limeade corkscrew. Beautiful example of a limeade corkscrew. Clarksburg, WV, circa 1928-1938. 5/8". Mint (9.9). $26. (Auction #57, Lot 30).

AKRO AGATE COMPANY. Limeade oxblood. Rare marble. Translucent milky white base, lightly fluorescent. Opaque white swirls. 23/32". Near Mint(-) (8). $60. (Auction #133, Lot 8).

AKRO AGATE COMPANY. Limeade oxblood. A limeade swirl with wispy oxblood on the translucent green swirl. These are hard to find. 5/8". Near Mint (8.6). $50. (Auction #174, Lot 44).

AKRO AGATE COMPANY. Limeade oxblood. Excellent example. A limeade corkscrew with oxblood spirals on it. Overall light pitting. Clarksburg, WV. 5/8". Near Mint (8.3). $30. (Auction #128, Lot 34).

AKRO AGATE COMPANY. Milky oxblood. This is a very early example. I think it is one of the experimentals dug up by Roger Hardy. 23/32".

Mint (9.4). $57. (Auction #182, Lot 17).

AKRO AGATE COMPANY. Milky oxblood corkscrew. Early and rare example. Semi-opaque milky white base. One transparent spiral on it. Nice oxblood spiral. 21/32". Mint(-) (9). $50. (Auction #140, Lot 36).

AKRO AGATE COMPANY. Milky oxblood. Semi-opaque white base. Nice band of oxblood on it, in a "V" shape. One rough spot and two tiny flakes. 23/32". Near Mint(+) (8.9). $49. (Auction #117, Lot 43).

AKRO AGATE COMPANY. Milky oxblood. Semi-opaque white base. Opalescent. About half covered with excellent oxblood. One tiny sparkle. 5/8". Mint(-) (9.2). $46. (Auction #176, Lot 45).

AKRO AGATE COMPANY. Milky oxblood. Translucent white base. Nice swirls of oxblood on the surface and partially into the marble. 5/8". Mint (9.9). $45. (Auction #74, Lot 19).

AKRO AGATE COMPANY. Milky oxblood. Semi-opaque white base. Excellent swirling of oxblood. Clarksburg, WV, circa 1927-1935. 5/8". Mint (9.9). $45. (Auction #179, Lot 46).

AKRO AGATE COMPANY. Milky oxblood. Semi-opaque white base with exceptional oxblood on it. Superb example. Clarksburg, WV, circa 1925. 19/32". Mint (9.9). $38. (Auction #95, Lot 38).

AKRO AGATE COMPANY. Milky oxblood. Semi-opaque white base with exceptional oxblood on it. Superb example. Clarksburg, WV, circa 1925. 19/32". Mint (9.9). $36. (Auction #95, Lot 38.20).

AKRO AGATE COMPANY. Milky oxblood. Semi-opaque white base. About half covered with rich, textured oxblood. Outstanding example. Clarksburg, WV. 19/32". Mint (9.9). $35. (Auction #100, Lot 6).

AKRO AGATE COMPANY. Milky oxblood. Semi-opaque white base with exceptional oxblood on it. Superb example. Clarksburg, WV, circa 1925. 19/32". Mint (9.9). $34. (Auction #95, Lot 38.30).

AKRO AGATE COMPANY. Milky oxblood. Semi-opaque white base with lots of oxbloods swirling. Super example, one very tiny pit. Clarksburg, WV. 5/8". Mint (9.4). $29. (Auction #166, Lot 39).

AKRO AGATE COMPANY. Milky oxblood. Semi-opaque white base with nice oxblood swirling. In great shape. Nice marble. Clarksburg, WV. 19/32". Mint (9.9). $27. (Auction #56, Lot 8).

AKRO AGATE COMPANY. Milky oxblood. Super marble. Translucent white base with nice oxblood swirling on it. Excellent color to the base. 5/8". Mint (9.9). $26. (Auction #118, Lot 40).

AKRO AGATE COMPANY. Milky oxblood. Semi-opaque white base. Nice band of oxblood on it, in a "U" shape. Small flake and some calicification. 23/32". Near Mint(+) (8.9). $25. (Auction #174, Lot 42).

AKRO AGATE COMPANY. Milky oxblood. Translucent milky base with a rich oxblood swirl on it. Superb example. Clarksburg, WV, circa 1928. 5/8". Mint (9.9). $24. (Auction #109, Lot 46).

AKRO AGATE COMPANY. Milky oxblood. Semi-opaque white base. Thin swirls of oxblood. Small subsurface moon. Clarksburg, WV, circa 1927-1935. 19/32". Near Mint(+) (8.9). $22. (Auction #169, Lot 17).

AKRO AGATE COMPANY. Milky oxblood. Semi-opaque white base. Thin swirls of oxblood. A couple of sparkles. Clarksburg, WV, circa 1927-1935. 19/32". Near Mint(+) (8.9). $15. (Auction #144, Lot 5).

AKRO AGATE COMPANY. Milky oxblood. Reject milky oxblood. Misshapen marble. Semi-opaque white base with excellent oxblood. $12. (Auction #149, Lot 8).

AKRO AGATE COMPANY. Milky oxblood. Odder patch type. Translucent and opaque white base. Patch of oxblood on one side of the marble. 11/16". Near Mint (8.6). $7. (Auction #141, Lot 42).

AKRO AGATE COMPANY. Moonie. Very nice opalescent white Moonie. Tiny melt spot. Clarksburg, WV, circa 1927-1935. 5/8". Mint(-) (9.2). $15. (Auction #112, Lot 4).

AKRO AGATE COMPANY. Moonie. Very nice opalescent white Moonie. Tiny melt spot. Clarksburg, WV, circa 1927-1935. 5/8". Mint(-) (9.2). $15. (Auction #112, Lot 4.20).

AKRO AGATE COMPANY. Moonie. Very nice opalescent white Moonie. Tiny melt spot. Clarksburg, WV, circa 1927-1935. 5/8". Mint(-) (9.2). $15. (Auction #112, Lot 4.10).

AKRO AGATE COMPANY. Moonie corkscrew. Translucent white moonie core with opaque orange/yellow spiral. Super example. Hard to find. Clarksburg, WV. 23/32". Mint (9.9). $48. (Auction #96, Lot 31).

AKRO AGATE COMPANY. Moonie Corkscrew. Lot of four marbles. Each is a corkscrew. Translucent opalescent white base. 5/8". Mint (9.9). $42. (Auction #85, Lot 18).

AKRO AGATE COMPANY. Moss Agate. Lot of two marbles. Pair of shooter Moss Agates. Both are fluorescent moss base with translucent red. $46. (Auction #111, Lot 37).

AKRO AGATE COMPANY. Moss Agate. Lot of four marbles. All are Moss Agates. Transparent red patch on translucent moss agate brown/green. $15. (Auction #62, Lot 1).

AKRO AGATE COMPANY. Moss Agate. Hard to find shooter size Moss Agate. Translucent green/brown milky base. Very fluorescent. 1". Near

Mint(+) (8.9). $5. (Auction #61, Lot 16).

AKRO AGATE COMPANY. Orange oxblood. Translucent milky white base with translucent orange swirls and an oxblood swirl. In super shape. 3/4". Mint (9.9). $230. (Auction #111, Lot 43).

AKRO AGATE COMPANY. Orange oxblood. Harder to find orange oxblood. Translucent milky white base. Swirl of translucent orange. 23/32". Mint(-) (9). $170. (Auction #173, Lot 29).

AKRO AGATE COMPANY. Orangeade. Super shooter orangeade swirl. Semi-opaque fluorescent ade base. Wispy opaque white swirls. 1". Mint(-) (9). $135. (Auction #71, Lot 33).

AKRO AGATE COMPANY. Orangeade. Fluorescent Ade base. Opaque wispy white swirls. Orange/yellow opaque swirls. 19/32". Near Mint (8.6). $65. (Auction #166, Lot 47).

AKRO AGATE COMPANY. Orangeade. Hard to find shooter orangeade swirl. Very fluorescent. Several chips. Clarksburg, WV, circa 1928. 7/8". Good (7.60). $45. (Auction #75, Lot 34).

AKRO AGATE COMPANY. Orangeade/Lemonade hybrid. A superb example of an orangeade/lemonade hybrid swirl. Fluorescent translucent milky base. 21/32". Mint (9.9). $150. (Auction #61, Lot 41).

AKRO AGATE COMPANY. Original box. Original yellow Popeye box. Box is 6-3/4" x 3-5/8" x 3/4". It has Popeye on the covering. $1550. (Auction #79, Lot 39).

AKRO AGATE COMPANY. Original box. Original box of 50 No. 4 Heroes. Box is brown cardboard. Stenciled on the top is "50 - No. 4 Hero Mad. $1325. (Auction #79, Lot 40).

AKRO AGATE COMPANY. Original box. Original yellow Popeye box. Box is 6-3/4" x 3-5/8" x 3/4". It has Popeye on the cover, carrying marbles. $1100. (Auction #111, Lot 50).

AKRO AGATE COMPANY. Original box. Original " 25 No. 0 Cardinal Red" box, with all marbles. Box is red paper on cardboard. $775. (Auction #138, Lot 49).

AKRO AGATE COMPANY. Original box. Original No. 0 Cardinal Red box. Square cardboard box. Bottom is covered with white paper. $450. (Auction #179, Lot 49).

AKRO AGATE COMPANY. Original box. Original cardboard No. 230 box. Top has crisp colors. However, one small puncture. $350. (Auction #79, Lot 37).

AKRO AGATE COMPANY. Original box. Original cardboard box. Metal tabs at corners. End flap reads "100 Unique No. 0". Very well centered. $350. (Auction #111, Lot 40).

AKRO AGATE COMPANY. Original box. No. 250 cardboard box. Top is dirty and has some wear. Near Mint(+) (8.7). Bottom has some minor tear. $160. (Auction #127, Lot 49).

AKRO AGATE COMPANY. Original box. Original No. 32 cardboard sleeve. These are the larger light blue sleeves with two oval cutouts. Old. $150. (Auction #79, Lot 24).

AKRO AGATE COMPANY. Original box. An original No. 16 cardboard sleeve, with marbles. This is the thin blue cardboard sleeve. $150. (Auction #54, Lot 37).

AKRO AGATE COMPANY. Original box. Original "100 Tri Color No. 0" box. Red box. Metal corner tabs. One corner split. Excellent graphics. $140. (Auction #127, Lot 50).

AKRO AGATE COMPANY. Original box. Original No. 32 cardboard sleeve. These are the larger light blue sleeves with two oval cutouts. Old. $140. (Auction #79, Lot 24.20).

AKRO AGATE COMPANY. Original box. An original Akro Agate "100 YELLOW No" box. Boxes of Akro opaques are hard to find. And No. 00 (9. $140. (Auction #103, Lot 40).

AKRO AGATE COMPANY. Original box. Original Akro Agate No. 16 cardboard sleeve. Box is in Mint condition. No damage. Box is 3-3/4". $135. (Auction #79, Lot 23).

AKRO AGATE COMPANY. Original box. Original No. 32 cardboard sleeve. These are the larger light blue sleeves with two oval cutouts. Old. $130. (Auction #90, Lot 45).

AKRO AGATE COMPANY. Original box. Original No. 32 cardboard sleeve. These are the larger light blue sleeves with two oval cutouts. Old. $130. (Auction #105, Lot 24).

AKRO AGATE COMPANY. Original box. Original No. 32 cardboard sleeve. These are the larger light blue sleeves with two oval cutouts. Old. $130. (Auction #111, Lot 30).

AKRO AGATE COMPANY. Original box. Original Akro Agate No. 16 cardboard sleeve. Box is in Mint condition. No damage. Box is 3-3/4". $125. (Auction #79, Lot 23.20).

AKRO AGATE COMPANY. Original box. Original No. 32 cardboard sleeve. These are the larger light blue sleeves with two oval cutouts. Old. $120. (Auction #93, Lot 23).

AKRO AGATE COMPANY. Original box. Original No. 32 cardboard sleeve. These are the larger light blue sleeves with two oval cutouts.

Old. $120. (Auction #105, Lot 24.10).

AKRO AGATE COMPANY. Original box. Original Akro Agate No. 16 cardboard sleeve. Box is in Mint. Box is 3-3/4" x 3/4" x 3/4" and Mint. $120. (Auction #119, Lot 38).

AKRO AGATE COMPANY. Original box. Original Akro Agate No. 16 cardboard sleeve. Box is in Mint(-) condition with a small crush at one end. $100. (Auction #111, Lot 11).

AKRO AGATE COMPANY. Original box. An original No. 16 cardboard sleeve. Sleeve is in superb shape. Contains a red, brown, blue, green. $95. (Auction #62, Lot 42).

AKRO AGATE COMPANY. Original box. Very rare box. You almost never see this one. This is a very early , unnumbered red box. $80. (Auction #60, Lot 43).

AKRO AGATE COMPANY. Original box. Original Akro Agates Chinese Checkers box. This is the red box with the metal corner clasps. $46. (Auction #63, Lot 25).

AKRO AGATE COMPANY. Original box. Original tan Akro Agate Chinese Checkers box. No. 0. Printing on top is off center. $34. (Auction #79, Lot 26).

AKRO AGATE COMPANY. Original box. Original red Akro Agate Chinese Checkers box. No. 0. End flap is missing one metal tab. $27. (Auction #79, Lot 27).

AKRO AGATE COMPANY. Original box. Original tan box of "60 Game Marbles No. 00". Light blue printing on the cover and the end flap. $26. (Auction #169, Lot 36).

AKRO AGATE COMPANY. Original package. An original "25 No. 0 Akro Carnelians" box. Box top is paper covering cardboard. Paper is the emboss. $600. (Auction #143, Lot 49).

AKRO AGATE COMPANY. Original package. Tan cardboard box of "60 Game Marbles No. 00". Box is water stained with faded blue graphics. $26. (Auction #111, Lot 21).

AKRO AGATE COMPANY. Original package. Tan cardboard box of "60 Game Marbles No. 00". Box is in very nice shape with no water staining. $25. (Auction #121, Lot 23).

AKRO AGATE COMPANY. Original package. Tan cardboard box of "60 Game Marbles No. 00". Box is tape tear in corner, but good graphic. $18. (Auction #138, Lot 48).

AKRO AGATE COMPANY. Original tin. Original No. 200 tin. The tin is in very nice shape. Some minor rust spotting on the right hand side. $370. (Auction #171, Lot 50).

AKRO AGATE COMPANY. Original tin. An original No. 200 tin. The tin is empty. The top has some corrosion on the left hand side. $180. (Auction #79, Lot 30).

AKRO AGATE COMPANY. Oxblood corkscrew. Very rare marble. Three-color corkscrew. Opaque yellow, transparent red and oxblood. Nice spiral. 25/32". Mint (9.6). $400. (Auction #183, Lot 38).

AKRO AGATE COMPANY. Oxblood corkscrew. Transparent clear base. Ribbon of oxblood twisted 2-1/2 times. In great shape. Exceptional example! 5/8". Mint (9.9). $170. (Auction #167, Lot 45).

AKRO AGATE COMPANY. Oxblood corkscrew. One of the rarest oxblood corkscrews that I have ever seen. Opaque yellow base with a translucent red. 21/32". Near Mint (8.6). $50. (Auction #59, Lot 1).

AKRO AGATE COMPANY. Oxblood corkscrew. Two color corkscrew. Opaque orange base. Spiral of very dark oxblood on the orange. 5/8". Near Mint(+) (8.9). $40. (Auction #184, Lot 38).

AKRO AGATE COMPANY. Oxblood hybrid. Super orange/egg yolk oxblood hybrid. Translucent milky white base (one fluorescent spiral in it). 3/4". Mint(-) (9). $200. (Auction #156, Lot 47).

AKRO AGATE COMPANY. Patch. Experimental patch. One side is opaque white, one side is red. These are the same design as the blue. 3/4". Mint (9.9). $50. (Auction #111, Lot 33.10).

AKRO AGATE COMPANY. Patch. Experimental patch. One side is opaque white, one side is red. These are the same design as the blue. 3/4". Mint (9.9). $50. (Auction #111, Lot 33).

AKRO AGATE COMPANY. Patch. Experimental Hero patch. Opaque white base with bright orange patch. Rare! Feathering at seams. 31/32". Mint (9.9). $45. (Auction #111, Lot 15).

AKRO AGATE COMPANY. Patch. Orangeade patch. This is not a Moss Agate. It is an orangeade. 1". Near Mint(+) (8.7). $43. (Auction #130, Lot 43).

AKRO AGATE COMPANY. Patch. Very hard to find Hero. Opaque white base with transparent brown patch. Super marble, in great shape. 5/8". Mint (9.9). $42. (Auction #103, Lot 49).

AKRO AGATE COMPANY. Patch. Experimental Moss Agate patch. Translucent olive green base with a bright yellow patch. 11/16". Mint (9.9). $36. (Auction #111, Lot 20).

AKRO AGATE COMPANY. Patch. Lot of two marbles. Pair of experimental patches, dug at the plant site. Opalescent moonie base. 11/16".

Mint(-) (9). $32. (Auction #64, Lot 13).

AKRO AGATE COMPANY. Patch. Very unusual marble. This is actually a corkscrew that was made when the cup was not spinning. Opaque. 3/4". Mint (9.9). $32. (Auction #140, Lot 17).

AKRO AGATE COMPANY. Patch. Lot of twenty marbles. Nice set of patches. All are translucent milky white with a color patch on top. $20. (Auction #105, Lot 27).

AKRO AGATE COMPANY. Patch. Experimental patch. Hard to find. Fluorescent vaseline dark green translucent base. 11/16". Mint (9.4). $17. (Auction #93, Lot 6).

AKRO AGATE COMPANY. Patch. Lot of six marbles. All shooters. Two different color schemes. 15/16". Near Mint(+) (8.9) to Near Mint. $11. (Auction #138, Lot 22).

AKRO AGATE COMPANY. Patch. Excellent patch. This is the early orange and blue. Bright orange base with a mottled bright blue. 5/8". Near Mint(+) (8.9). $7. (Auction #170, Lot 3).

AKRO AGATE COMPANY. Patch oxblood. Shooter clear patch oxblood in hard to find colors. Wide oxblood patch on a marble that is one half. 31/32". Mint (9.9). $100. (Auction #83, Lot 44).

AKRO AGATE COMPANY. Patch oxblood. Superior shooter patch oxblood. Predominately clear base with a nice white patch and a smaller yellow. 1-1/16". Mint (9.9). $90. (Auction #131, Lot 12).

AKRO AGATE COMPANY. Patch oxblood. Opaque white base. Green patch on one side, oxblood patch next to it. A beauty, and huge! Clarksburg, WV. 1-1/16". Mint (9.9). $60. (Auction #148, Lot 18).

AKRO AGATE COMPANY. Patch oxblood. Large patch oxblood. Opaque white base. Wide blue band on one side. Narrower green band next to it. 1-1/16". Near Mint(+) (8.9). $60. (Auction #124, Lot 5).

AKRO AGATE COMPANY. Patch oxblood. I've categorized this as an Akro Agate, although some collectors believe that they are Vitro Agate. 31/32". Near Mint(+) (8.7). $55. (Auction #180, Lot 47).

AKRO AGATE COMPANY. Patch oxblood. Opaque white base. Several bands of translucent yellow and transparent aqua blue/green. Wide patch. 3/4". Mint(-) (9.1). $48. (Auction #74, Lot 17).

AKRO AGATE COMPANY. Patch oxblood. Lot of four marbles. Assortment of patch oxbloods. Two have blue patch, one has green patch. $46. (Auction #119, Lot 6).

AKRO AGATE COMPANY. Patch oxblood. Super shooter patch oxblood. Opaque white base. Green band on one side, oxblood band on the other. 7/8". Mint (9.9). $46. (Auction #58, Lot 12).

AKRO AGATE COMPANY. Patch oxblood. Shooter patch oxblood. Opaque white base. Blue band and a green band on it. 13/16". Mint (9.9). $45. (Auction #68, Lot 25).

AKRO AGATE COMPANY. Patch oxblood. Shooter patch oxblood. Opaque white base. Blue band and a green band on it. 13/16". Mint (9.9). $45. (Auction #68, Lot 25.20).

AKRO AGATE COMPANY. Patch oxblood. Shooter patch oxblood. Opaque white base. Band of oxblood on one side. Band of light green. 7/8". Mint (9.5). $40. (Auction #104, Lot 7).

AKRO AGATE COMPANY. Patch oxblood. Shooter size patch oxblood. Opaque white base. Oxblood band on one side, blue band on the other. 7/8". Mint (9.9). $34. (Auction #69, Lot 37).

AKRO AGATE COMPANY. Patch oxblood. Opaque white base. Wide band of translucent green covering half the surface. 27/32". Mint (9.9). $30. (Auction #90, Lot 11).

AKRO AGATE COMPANY. Patch oxblood. Lot of five marbles. All are patch oxblood. One not Mint. 9/16" to 5/8". Mint (9.9) & Near Mint(+) (. $24. (Auction #138, Lot 6).

AKRO AGATE COMPANY. Patch oxblood. Opaque white base. Green patch on one side, oxblood patch on the other. Very nice marble. Clarksburg, WV. 21/32". Mint (9.9). $18. (Auction #103, Lot 1).

AKRO AGATE COMPANY. Patch oxblood. Lot of two marbles. Both are patch oxblood. The larger has a faint oxblood patch. $17. (Auction #77, Lot 10).

AKRO AGATE COMPANY. Patch oxblood. Lot of three marbles. All are patch oxblood. Nice set with good oxblood. 19/32" (2) and 5/8". Mint (. $16. (Auction #54, Lot 3).

AKRO AGATE COMPANY. Patch oxblood. Lot of three marbles. All white base. Two have blue stripes, one has green stripe. All have nice oxblood. $15. (Auction #184, Lot 3).

AKRO AGATE COMPANY. Patch oxblood. Lot of two marbles. Semi-opaque white base. One has blue patch, one has green patch. $15. (Auction #178, Lot 33).

AKRO AGATE COMPANY. Patch oxblood. Lot of two marbles. Both are patch oxblood. One green stripe, one is a blue stripe. Small oxblood patch. $10. (Auction #68, Lot 32).

AKRO AGATE COMPANY. Patch oxblood. Opaque white base with colored bands covering about one-quarter of the marble. 5/8". Mint

(9.9). $10. (Auction #170, Lot 16).

AKRO AGATE COMPANY. Patch oxblood. Opaque white base with colored bands covering about one-quarter of the marble. 5/8". Mint (9.9). $8. (Auction #170, Lot 16.20).

AKRO AGATE COMPANY. Patch oxblood. Semi-opaque white base. Band of translucent blue on one side and wispy oxblood on the other. Clarksburg, WV. 9/16". Mint (9.9). $8. (Auction #97, Lot 7).

AKRO AGATE COMPANY. Patch oxblood. Opaque white base with colored bands covering about one-quarter of the marble. 5/8". Mint (9.9). $6. (Auction #170, Lot 16.30).

AKRO AGATE COMPANY. Popeye. Larger red and blue Popeye. Superior example. Clarksburg, WV, circa 1928-1938. 23/32". Mint (9.8). 23/32". Mint (9.8). $140. (Auction #74, Lot 44).

AKRO AGATE COMPANY. Popeye. Shooter purple and yellow Popeye. This one is a beauty. It is very difficult to find these purple. 23/32". Mint(-) (9.3). $130. (Auction #71, Lot 22).

AKRO AGATE COMPANY. Popeye. Hybrid Popeye. Red, purple and green brushed on the surface. The red is wide. 3/4". Near Mint(+) (8.9). $85. (Auction #131, Lot 44).

AKRO AGATE COMPANY. Popeye. Light blue and yellow Popeye. Not baby blue, but very light. Super looking marble. Clarksburg, WV. 5/8". Mint (9.9). $39. (Auction #156, Lot 2).

AKRO AGATE COMPANY. Popeye corkscrew. Very rare Popeye. Orange and green. The clear/white is mostly clear. There is a brown spiral between. 5/8". Mint (9.7). $260. (Auction #163, Lot 41).

AKRO AGATE COMPANY. Popeye corkscrew. Shooter size hybrid Popeye, in great shape. Wide spiral of translucent red. Narrow spirals of blue. 3/4". Mint(-) (9). $165. (Auction #185, Lot 34).

AKRO AGATE COMPANY. Popeye corkscrew. Purple and yellow shooter Popeye corkscrew. Hard to find. In super shape. Clarksburg, WV, circa 1928. 23/32". Mint (9.9). $150. (Auction #78, Lot 30).

AKRO AGATE COMPANY. Popeye corkscrew. Hybrid Popeye corkscrew. Shooter marble. The marble is predominately transparent clear and white. 3/4". Mint (9.9). $140. (Auction #64, Lot 43).

AKRO AGATE COMPANY. Popeye corkscrew. Hybrid Popeye corkscrew. Blue, yellow and orange. The blue and yellow have bled a little. 23/32". Near Mint(+) (8.9). $130. (Auction #138, Lot 27).

AKRO AGATE COMPANY. Popeye corkscrew. Lot of nine marbles. All are Popeyes. Two purple and yellow, two green and yellow, two green and red. $120. (Auction #102, Lot 10).

AKRO AGATE COMPANY. Popeye corkscrew. Red and blue Popeye. Super marble. One of the hardest colors to find. Clarksburg, WV, circa 1927-1935. 5/8". Mint (9.9). $120. (Auction #100, Lot 16).

AKRO AGATE COMPANY. Popeye corkscrew. Purple and yellow shooter. Very hard to find. Lots of swirling in this one. Great color. Super marble. 23/32". Mint (9.9). $120. (Auction #148, Lot 47).

AKRO AGATE COMPANY. Popeye corkscrew. Super hybrid Popeye. Green, red and yellow. Superior example. Surface in great shape. Clarksburg, WV. 5/8". Mint (9.9). $110. (Auction #137, Lot 48).

AKRO AGATE COMPANY. Popeye corkscrew. Rare type. Snake corkscrew. Transparent clear base. Spirals of wispy white, green and red on the surface. 5/8". Mint (9.7). $100. (Auction #184, Lot 42).

AKRO AGATE COMPANY. Popeye corkscrew. Gorgeous red, white and blue Popeye. The red is wide and the blue is thin. Both are brushed on the surface. 5/8". Mint (9.9). $100. (Auction #71, Lot 34.20).

AKRO AGATE COMPANY. Popeye corkscrew. Light blue and yellow shooter. Nice size. In great shape. Clarksburg, WV, circa 1928-1935. 23/32". Mint (9.9). $100. (Auction #118, Lot 10.10).

AKRO AGATE COMPANY. Popeye corkscrew. Lot of five marbles. Two red and yellow, one blue and yellow, one purple and yellow, one red and blue. $96. (Auction #166, Lot 14).

AKRO AGATE COMPANY. Popeye corkscrew. Gorgeous red, white and blue Popeye. The red is wide and the blue is thin. Both are brushed on the surface. 5/8". Mint (9.9). $95. (Auction #71, Lot 34).

AKRO AGATE COMPANY. Popeye corkscrew. Red and blue Popeye. Superb example. Blue and red just float on the surface. Clarksburg, WV. 5/8". Mint (9.9). $95. (Auction #93, Lot 40).

AKRO AGATE COMPANY. Popeye corkscrew. Red and blue Popeye. In great shape. Super marble. Clarksburg, WV, circa 1928-1938. 5/8". Mint (9.9). $95. (Auction #84, Lot 6).

AKRO AGATE COMPANY. Popeye corkscrew. Red and blue Popeye. The red and blue spirals are about the same width and are on the surface. 11/16". Mint (9.5). $90. (Auction #150, Lot 32).

AKRO AGATE COMPANY. Popeye corkscrew. Purple and yellow corkscrew. The purple is two bands side by side, one is light purple. 5/8". Mint (9.9). $90. (Auction #131, Lot 27).

AKRO AGATE COMPANY. Popeye corkscrew. Red and blue Popeye. Very nice coloring. Clarksburg, WV, circa 1927-1935. 11/16". Mint (9.8).

$85. (Auction #146, Lot 50).

AKRO AGATE COMPANY. Popeye corkscrew. Hard to find hybrid Popeye. Red, purple and yellow. The red is right on top of the purple. 5/8". Mint (9.9). $80. (Auction #73, Lot 44).

AKRO AGATE COMPANY. Popeye corkscrew. Red, yellow and green Popeye. Distinct spirals of each. In superb shape. Stunning example. Clarksburg, WV. 5/8". Mint (9.9). $80. (Auction #166, Lot 49).

AKRO AGATE COMPANY. Popeye corkscrew. Lot of three marbles. All are Popeyes. One is a green, yellow and blue hybrid (9.0). $80. (Auction #169, Lot 10).

AKRO AGATE COMPANY. Popeye corkscrew. Red and blue Popeye. Very nice coloring. Clarksburg, WV, circa 1927-1935. 11/16". Mint (9.8). $80. (Auction #146, Lot 50.30).

AKRO AGATE COMPANY. Popeye corkscrew. Lot of six marbles. Three red with yellow, one green and yellow, one red and green, one blue and yellow. $80. (Auction #125, Lot 34).

AKRO AGATE COMPANY. Popeye corkscrew. Blue and yellow Popeye corkscrew shooter. Hard to find. Superb marble. One very tiny pinprick. Clarksburg, WV. 23/32". Mint (9.6). $80. (Auction #106, Lot 36).

AKRO AGATE COMPANY. Popeye corkscrew. Red and blue Popeye. Very nice coloring. Clarksburg, WV, circa 1927-1935. 11/16". Mint (9.8). There a. 11/16". Mint (9.8). $80. (Auction #146, Lot 50.20).

AKRO AGATE COMPANY. Popeye corkscrew. Purple and yellow Popeye. Dark purple. Nice marble. Clarksburg, WV, circa 1927-1935. 5/8". Mint (9.9). $80. (Auction #123, Lot 45).

AKRO AGATE COMPANY. Popeye corkscrew. Red and blue Popeye. Nice marble. One small pit. Clarksburg, WV, circa 1927-1935. 21/32". Near Mint(+) (8.9). $76. (Auction #151, Lot 38.20).

AKRO AGATE COMPANY. Popeye corkscrew. Red and blue Popeye. Nice marble. One small pit. Clarksburg, WV, circa 1927-1935. 21/32". Near Mint(+) (8.9). $76. (Auction #151, Lot 38).

AKRO AGATE COMPANY. Popeye corkscrew. Red and blue Popeye. Nice marble. One small pit. Clarksburg, WV, circa 1927-1935. 21/32". Near Mint(+) (8.9). $76. (Auction #151, Lot 38.30).

AKRO AGATE COMPANY. Popeye corkscrew. Lot of seven marbles. Nice group. Two red and yellow, one green and yellow, one fluorescent green. $75. (Auction #174, Lot 33).

AKRO AGATE COMPANY. Popeye corkscrew. Purple and yellow Popeye. Beautiful example. Clarksburg, WV, circa 1927-1935. 5/8". Mint (9.9). $75. (Auction #137, Lot 46).

AKRO AGATE COMPANY. Popeye corkscrew. Very hard to find powder blue and yellow Popeye. Beautiful color. Tiny annealing fracture. Clarksburg, WV. 58". Mint(-) (9.2). $75. (Auction #66, Lot 43).

AKRO AGATE COMPANY. Popeye corkscrew. Purple and yellow Popeye. Superior example. Clarksburg, WV, circa 1928-1938. 21/32". Mint (9.9). $75. (Auction #73, Lot 40).

AKRO AGATE COMPANY. Popeye corkscrew. Purple and yellow Popeye. This one is a beautiful example. Clarksburg, WV, circa 1927-1935. 5/8". Mint (9.9). $71. (Auction #134, Lot 10).

AKRO AGATE COMPANY. Popeye corkscrew. Shooter red and blue Popeye. Several tiny pits, flakes and chips. Large size. Clarksburg, WV. 3/4". Near Mint (8.6). $70. (Auction #173, Lot 20).

AKRO AGATE COMPANY. Popeye corkscrew. Hybrid Popeye corkscrew. Green, red and yellow Popeye. Lots of clear/white. Wide spiral of yellow. 23/32". Mint(-) (9). $70. (Auction #91, Lot 12).

AKRO AGATE COMPANY. Popeye corkscrew. Red, white and blue Popeye corkscrew. A real beauty. These are hard to find. A couple of tiny pits. 5/8". Mint(-) (9). $70. (Auction #78, Lot 37).

AKRO AGATE COMPANY. Popeye corkscrew. Blue and yellow Popeye shooter. Surface in great shape. Clarksburg, WV, circa 1928-1938. 23/32". Mint (9.9). $70. (Auction #82, Lot 43).

AKRO AGATE COMPANY. Popeye corkscrew. Purple and yellow Popeye. Beautiful example. Clarksburg, WV, circa 1927-1935. 5/8". Mint (9.9). $70. (Auction #137, Lot 46.20).

AKRO AGATE COMPANY. Popeye corkscrew. Purple and yellow Popeye. This one is a beauty, in super shape. Clarksburg, WV, circa 1928-1935. 19/32". Mint (9.9). $70. (Auction #121, Lot 12).

AKRO AGATE COMPANY. Popeye corkscrew. Lot of six marbles. Two red and yellow, two green and yellow, one blue and yellow, one orange and yellow. $70. (Auction #122, Lot 31).

AKRO AGATE COMPANY. Popeye corkscrew. Lot of six marbles. Three red and yellow, one green and red, two blue and yellow. All have some damage. $70. (Auction #125, Lot 12).

AKRO AGATE COMPANY. Popeye corkscrew. Purple and yellow Popeye. Super example. Clarksburg, WV, circa 1927-1935. 5/8". Mint (9.9). $70. (Auction #170, Lot 39).

AKRO AGATE COMPANY. Popeye corkscrew. Red and yellow shooter corkscrew. Large size, in great shape. One tiny manufacturing pit.

Clarksburg, WV. 3/4". Mint(-) (9.2). $70. (Auction #56, Lot 14).

AKRO AGATE COMPANY. Popeye corkscrew. Red and green shooter Popeye. In excellent shape. Clarksburg, WV, circa 1928-1938. 23/32". Mint (9.9). $70. (Auction #59, Lot 28).

AKRO AGATE COMPANY. Popeye corkscrew. Hybrid Popeye corkscrew. Red, yellow and green. A sparkle and a pinprick. Super marble. Clarksburg WV. 21/32". Mint(-) (9). $65. (Auction #81, Lot 6).

AKRO AGATE COMPANY. Popeye corkscrew. Lot of two marbles. Red and yellow Popeye. Green and yellow Popeye. Clarksburg, WV, circa 1928-1938. 11/16". Mint (9.9). $65. (Auction #64, Lot 26).

AKRO AGATE COMPANY. Popeye corkscrew. Shooter red and yellow Popeye. Excellent colors. Very hard to find shooter Popeyes. 23/32". Mint(-) (9). $65. (Auction #57, Lot 18).

AKRO AGATE COMPANY. Popeye corkscrew. Lot of four marbles. All are Popeye corkscrews. Red and blue, 21/32", Near Mint (8.6). Red and green. $65. (Auction #161, Lot 35).

AKRO AGATE COMPANY. Popeye corkscrew. Purple and yellow. Super marble. 5/8". Mint (9.9). There are two marbles available. 5/8". Mint (9.9). $65. (Auction #111, Lot 47).

AKRO AGATE COMPANY. Popeye corkscrew. Red and blue Popeye. One tiny pit (may actually be from manufacturing). 11/16". Mint(-) (9). $65. (Auction #111, Lot 8).

AKRO AGATE COMPANY. Popeye corkscrew. Purple and yellow Popeye. Purple on the yellow. Ribbon style. Outstanding example. Clarksburg, WV. 5/8". Mint (9.9). $65. (Auction #164, Lot 43).

AKRO AGATE COMPANY. Popeye corkscrew. Lot of three marbles. Blue and yellow Popeye. Very nice. They appear to be same run. $65. (Auction #151, Lot 6).

AKRO AGATE COMPANY. Popeye corkscrew. Lot of five marbles. All are blue and yellow Popeyes. Each has annealing fractures. 19/32" to 21/32". $65. (Auction #73, Lot 19).

AKRO AGATE COMPANY. Popeye corkscrew. Lot of six marbles. Four red and yellow, one green and red, one translucent white with blue and egg yolk. $65. (Auction #125, Lot 4).

AKRO AGATE COMPANY. Popeye corkscrew. Purple and yellow Popeye. Beautiful example. Clarksburg, WV, circa 1927-1935. 5/8". Mint (9.9). $65. (Auction #137, Lot 46.30).

AKRO AGATE COMPANY. Popeye corkscrew. Purple and yellow Popeye. Very light purple. A number of tiny pinpricks and pits on the surface. Clarksburg, WV. 21/32". Near Mint(+) (8.9). $61. (Auction #145, Lot 39).

AKRO AGATE COMPANY. Popeye corkscrew. Purple and yellow. Super marble. 5/8". Mint (9.9). There are two marbles available. 5/8". Mint (9.9). $60. (Auction #111, Lot 47.10).

AKRO AGATE COMPANY. Popeye corkscrew. Red and green. Excellent example, as the red, green and white all lay on the surface. 21/32". Mint (9.8). $60. (Auction #97, Lot 36).

AKRO AGATE COMPANY. Popeye corkscrew. Red and blue Popeye. One tiny subsurface moon and some tiny sparkles. Clarksburg, WV, circa 1927-1935. 5/8". Near Mint(+) (8.7). $60. (Auction #153, Lot 32).

AKRO AGATE COMPANY. Popeye corkscrew. Lot of two marbles. Both are purple and yellow corkscrews. 21/32" & Near Mint (8.4). 11/16" & Near Mint. $60. (Auction #76, Lot 12).

AKRO AGATE COMPANY. Popeye corkscrew. Red and green shooter. Hard to find this large. Two sparkles. Nice marble. Clarksburg, WV, circa 1928. 3/4". Mint(-) (9). $60. (Auction #56, Lot 35).

AKRO AGATE COMPANY. Popeye corkscrew. Purple and yellow Popeye. Thin yellow. Very nice marble. Clarksburg, WV, circa 1928-1938. 5/8". Mint (9.9). $56. (Auction #67, Lot 29).

AKRO AGATE COMPANY. Popeye corkscrew. Red and green shooter. Couple of tiny pinpricks. Clarksburg, WV, circa 1928-1935. 3/4". Mint(-) (9.0). $55. (Auction #121, Lot 4).

AKRO AGATE COMPANY. Popeye corkscrew. Lot of two marbles. These are blended color Popeye corkscrews. One is blue and yellow. $55. (Auction #57, Lot 37).

AKRO AGATE COMPANY. Popeye corkscrew. Red and blue Popeye. Excellent coloring and pattern. Two sparkles. Clarksburg, WV, circa 1927-1935. 5/8". Mint(-) (9). $55. (Auction #156, Lot 34).

AKRO AGATE COMPANY. Popeye corkscrew. Purple and yellow Popeye. One tiny sparkle. Very nice. Clarksburg, WV, circa 1927-1935. 21/32". Mint(-) (9.1). $55. (Auction #154, Lot 29).

AKRO AGATE COMPANY. Popeye corkscrew. Hard to find hybrid Popeye corkscrew. Red, green and a thin spiral of yellow. One tiny flake. 11/16". Near Mint(+) (8.9). $55. (Auction #57, Lot 35).

AKRO AGATE COMPANY. Popeye corkscrew. Green and yellow on a fluorescent white/clear base. Rare marble. Clarksburg, WV, circa 1928-1938. 5/8". Mint (9.9). $55. (Auction #65, Lot 35).

AKRO AGATE COMPANY. Popeye corkscrew. Purple and yellow Popeye. In great shape. Clarksburg, WV, circa 1928-1938. 5/8". Mint (9.8). $50. (Auction #68, Lot 43).

AKRO AGATE COMPANY. Popeye corkscrew. Purple and yellow Popeye. Nice shape. Clarksburg, WV, circa 1928-1938. 5/8". Mint (9.5). $50. (Auction #59, Lot 26).

AKRO AGATE COMPANY. Popeye corkscrew. Purple and yellow Popeye. One minuscule scratch and a tiny sparkle. Clarksburg, WV, circa 1928-1938. 5/8". Mint (9.2). $50. (Auction #85, Lot 42).

AKRO AGATE COMPANY. Popeye corkscrew. Red and green shooter Popeye. Sparkle. Clarksburg, WV, circa 1928-1938. 23/32". Mint(-) (9.1). $50. (Auction #94, Lot 42).

AKRO AGATE COMPANY. Popeye corkscrew. Purple and yellow Popeye. Very nice marble. Clarksburg, WV, circa 1927-1935. 5/8". Mint (9.9). $50. (Auction #155, Lot 19).

AKRO AGATE COMPANY. Popeye corkscrew. Red and blue Popeye. One very tiny, very shallow flake. Excellent marble nonetheless. Clarksburg, WV. $50. (Auction #181, Lot 37).

AKRO AGATE COMPANY. Popeye corkscrew. Purple and yellow. Beautiful pattern. One tiny sparkle and one tiny pit. Clarksburg, WV, circa 1928. 5/8". Near Mint(+) (8.9). $50. (Auction #97, Lot 31).

AKRO AGATE COMPANY. Popeye corkscrew. Blue and yellow shooter. Stunning example. Lots of white. The blue is translucent and just laying on. 23/32". Mint(-) (9). $50. (Auction #129, Lot 40).

AKRO AGATE COMPANY. Popeye corkscrew. Lot of four marbles. Two are green and yellow, one red and yellow, one blue and yellow. $50. (Auction #101, Lot 44).

AKRO AGATE COMPANY. Popeye corkscrew. Hybrid Popeye corkscrew. Red and blue spirals on the outside. Yellow spiral in the interior. 19/32". Near Mint (8.4). $50. (Auction #148, Lot 11).

AKRO AGATE COMPANY. Popeye corkscrew. Purple and yellow Popeye. Has one strand of purple in the yellow, as well as the wider purple band. 5/8". Mint (9.4). $50. (Auction #152, Lot 26).

AKRO AGATE COMPANY. Popeye corkscrew. Red and yellow Popeye. Shooter. Excellent example. Clarksburg, WV, circa 1927-1935. 23/32". Mint (9.9). $49. (Auction #179, Lot 35).

AKRO AGATE COMPANY. Popeye corkscrew. Red and yellow Popeye corkscrew. Very nice shooter marble. Wide clear panel. One tiny pit. 3/4". Mint(-) (9.2). $49. (Auction #71, Lot 10).

AKRO AGATE COMPANY. Popeye corkscrew. Lot of two marbles. Both are red and green Popeye. 11/16" & Mint (9.9). 3/4" & Near Mint(+) (8.9). $48. (Auction #179, Lot 43).

AKRO AGATE COMPANY. Popeye corkscrew. Red and yellow Popeye. Shooter. Nice marble. Clarksburg, WV, circa 1927-1935. 3/4". Mint (9.7). $47. (Auction #134, Lot 21).

AKRO AGATE COMPANY. Popeye corkscrew. Light blue and yellow shooter. Nice size. Annealing fracture running down the blue. Clarksburg, WV. 23/32". Mint(-) (9). $47. (Auction #156, Lot 17).

AKRO AGATE COMPANY. Popeye corkscrew. Green and yellow fluorescent Popeye. Fluorescent ones are very hard to find. This one is in great shape. 5/8". Mint (9.9). $47. (Auction #126, Lot 43).

AKRO AGATE COMPANY. Popeye corkscrew. Blue and yellow Popeye corkscrew. Super marble. Clarksburg, WV, circa 1928-1938. 11/16". Mint (9.9). $47. (Auction #81, Lot 19.20).

AKRO AGATE COMPANY. Popeye corkscrew. Blue and yellow Popeye corkscrew. Super marble. Clarksburg, WV, circa 1928-1938. 11/16". Mint (9.9). $47. (Auction #81, Lot 19.30).

AKRO AGATE COMPANY. Popeye corkscrew. Red and yellow shooter Popeye. Super pattern. A couple of sparkles. Clarksburg, WV, circa 1928-1938. 23/32". Mint(-) (9.1). $46. (Auction #106, Lot 43).

AKRO AGATE COMPANY. Popeye corkscrew. Yellow and blue shooter. Clear panel. Very nice example. A couple of sparkles. Clarksburg, WV. 23/32". Mint (9.2). $42. (Auction #134, Lot 24).

AKRO AGATE COMPANY. Popeye corkscrew. Red and yellow Popeye shooter. Manufacturing dimple at one end. Clarksburg, WV, circa 1928-1935. 23/32". Mint (9.7). $42. (Auction #96, Lot 42).

AKRO AGATE COMPANY. Popeye corkscrew. Shooter yellow and green. One tiny subsurface moon, but still an outstanding example. Clarksburg, WV. 3/4". Near Mint(+) (8.9). $41. (Auction #181, Lot 33).

AKRO AGATE COMPANY. Popeye corkscrew. Blue and yellow shooter. Small fold at top and a tiny subsurface moon. 3/4". Near Mint(+) (8.9). $41. (Auction #111, Lot 3).

AKRO AGATE COMPANY. Popeye corkscrew. Red and yellow shooter. Pristine. 23/32". Mint (9.9). $41. (Auction #111, Lot 46).

AKRO AGATE COMPANY. Popeye corkscrew. Lot of three marbles. Two are red and yellow, one is blue and yellow. All have some damage. 21/32". $40. (Auction #132, Lot 7).

AKRO AGATE COMPANY. **Popeye corkscrew.** Yellow and baby blue. The baby blue is thin. A couple of sparkles. Clarksburg, WV, circa 1928-1938. 5/8". Mint (9). $40. (Auction #77, Lot 42).

AKRO AGATE COMPANY. **Popeye corkscrew.** Purple and yellow Popeye. A beauty. One very tiny rough spot. Clarksburg, WV, circa 1927-1935. 5/8". Mint(-) (9.2). $40. (Auction #171, Lot 38).

AKRO AGATE COMPANY. **Popeye corkscrew.** Lot of four marbles. All are nice Popeyes, but they each have some damage. Green & yellow shooter. $40. (Auction #94, Lot 22).

AKRO AGATE COMPANY. **Popeye corkscrew.** Shooter red and green Popeye. One tiny pinprick on it. Superb marble. Clarksburg, WV, circa 1928-1938. 23/32". Mint(-) (9.2). $40. (Auction #81, Lot 12).

AKRO AGATE COMPANY. **Popeye corkscrew.** Blue and yellow Popeye. Very nice pattern. Shooter. A pinprick and a tiny subsurface moon. Clarksburg, WV. 3/4". Near Mint(+) (8.9). $40. (Auction #150, Lot 10).

AKRO AGATE COMPANY. **Popeye corkscrew.** Blue and yellow Popeye. In great shape. Clarksburg, WV, circa 1927-1935. 5/8". Mint (9.9). $39. (Auction #153, Lot 5.20).

AKRO AGATE COMPANY. **Popeye corkscrew.** Blue and yellow Popeye. In great shape. Clarksburg, WV, circa 1927-1935. 5/8". Mint (9.9). $39. (Auction #153, Lot 5).

AKRO AGATE COMPANY. **Popeye corkscrew.** Shooter red and green Popeye. A couple of tiny pits, a tiny subsurface moon and a couple of tiny sparkles. 3/4". Near Mint(+) (8.9). $39. (Auction #182, Lot 27).

AKRO AGATE COMPANY. **Popeye corkscrew.** Lot of three marbles. Two red and yellow Popeyes, one green and red Popeye. 19/32" to 5/8". Near Mint. $38. (Auction #155, Lot 5).

AKRO AGATE COMPANY. **Popeye corkscrew.** Blue and yellow shooter corkscrew. One small flake at the top. Clarksburg, WV, circa 1928-1938. 3/4". Near Mint(+) (8.8). $38. (Auction #59, Lot 13).

AKRO AGATE COMPANY. **Popeye corkscrew.** Lot of four marbles. Three are red and yellow. There is also a shooter blue and yellow. $37. (Auction #181, Lot 25).

AKRO AGATE COMPANY. **Popeye corkscrew.** Lot of five marbles. Three red and yellow, one green and yellow, one blue and yellow. 19/32" to 21/32". $37. (Auction #178, Lot 7).

AKRO AGATE COMPANY. **Popeye corkscrew.** Beautiful red and yellow Popeye. Great marble. Clarksburg, WV, circa 1928-1938. 11/16". Mint (9.9). $37. (Auction #63, Lot 29).

AKRO AGATE COMPANY. **Popeye corkscrew.** Purple and yellow Popeye. Light purple. One small subsurface moon. Clarksburg, WV, circa 1927-1935. 11/16". Near Mint(+) (8.9). $37. (Auction #150, Lot 44).

AKRO AGATE COMPANY. **Popeye corkscrew.** Green and yellow Popeye. Thin green. Just barely a shooter. Clarksburg, WV, circa 1928-1935. 23/32". Mint (9.9). $37. (Auction #118, Lot 45).

AKRO AGATE COMPANY. **Popeye corkscrew.** Red and yellow shooter Popeye. Super pattern. Has one tiny chip. Still, a superb looking marble. 3/4". Near Mint(+) (8.9). $37. (Auction #160, Lot 38).

AKRO AGATE COMPANY. **Popeye corkscrew.** Green and yellow shooter. Stunning example. Lots of white. The green is translucent. 23/32". Mint(-) (9). $37. (Auction #129, Lot 30).

AKRO AGATE COMPANY. **Popeye corkscrew.** Lot of three marbles. All are Popeyes. Red and yellow, green and yellow, blue and yellow. $36. (Auction #106, Lot 32).

AKRO AGATE COMPANY. **Popeye corkscrew.** Blue and yellow Popeye. In nice shape. Clarksburg, WV, circa 1928-1935. 19/32". Mint (9.9). $36. (Auction #118, Lot 18).

AKRO AGATE COMPANY. **Popeye corkscrew.** Blue and yellow Popeye. In great shape. Clarksburg, WV, circa 1927-1935. 5/8". Mint (9.9). $36. (Auction #153, Lot 5.30).

AKRO AGATE COMPANY. **Popeye corkscrew.** Lot of two marbles. Red and green, 5/8", Near Mint(+) (8.9). Blue and yellow, 5/8", Near Mint(+) $36. (Auction #177, Lot 36).

AKRO AGATE COMPANY. **Popeye corkscrew.** Shooter blue and yellow. A couple of subsurface moons. Clarksburg, WV, circa 1927-1935. 3/4". Near Mint (8.6). $35. (Auction #162, Lot 32).

AKRO AGATE COMPANY. **Popeye corkscrew.** Lot of three marbles. Two are red and yellow. One is blue and yellow. $35. (Auction #140, Lot 5).

AKRO AGATE COMPANY. **Popeye corkscrew.** Red and green Popeye. Very nice. Clarksburg, circa 1927-1935. 21/32". Mint (9.9). $35. (Auction #140, Lot 34).

AKRO AGATE COMPANY. **Popeye corkscrew.** Red and yellow Popeye. Shooter. One sparkle. Clarksburg, WV, circa 1928-1938. 23/32". Mint(-) (9.2). $35. (Auction #104, Lot 3).

AKRO AGATE COMPANY. **Popeye corkscrew.** Lot of three marbles. All three are red and yellow Popeyes. One is Mint, one has a pit. $35. (Auction #63, Lot 16).

AKRO AGATE COMPANY. **Popeye corkscrew.** Green and yellow Popeye. Lots of white. A beauty. Clarksburg, WV, circa 1928-1938. 11/16". Mint (9.9). $35. (Auction #71, Lot 16).

AKRO AGATE COMPANY. **Popeye corkscrew.** Red and yellow Popeye. One spiral is clear. There is some mixing of the white and red. 19/32". Mint (9.9). $35. (Auction #137, Lot 37.20).

AKRO AGATE COMPANY. **Popeye corkscrew.** Purple and yellow Popeye. Light purple. Clarksburg, WV, circa 1927-1935. 21/32". Buffed. $35. (Auction #181, Lot 18).

AKRO AGATE COMPANY. **Popeye corkscrew.** Red and yellow shooter Popeye. One tiny pit, and some melted air holes. Clarksburg, WV, circa 1928. 3/4". Mint(-) (9). $35. (Auction #62, Lot 18).

AKRO AGATE COMPANY. **Popeye corkscrew.** Red and yellow Popeye. One spiral is clear. There is some mixing of the white and red. 19/32". Mint (9.9). $35. (Auction #137, Lot 37).

AKRO AGATE COMPANY. **Popeye corkscrew.** This marble is marginally a hybrid. It is a green and yellow Popeye. Very thin band of red. 21/32". Mint (9.9). $34. (Auction #62, Lot 23).

AKRO AGATE COMPANY. **Popeye corkscrew.** Odd Popeye. Perhaps from the end of a run. A red and yellow. Just one wispy strand of white. 5/8". Mint (9.9). $34. (Auction #73, Lot 36).

AKRO AGATE COMPANY. **Popeye corkscrew.** Blue and yellow Popeye. Very nice. Clarksburg, WV, circa 1927-1935. 5/8". Mint (9.9). $34. (Auction #159, Lot 27).

AKRO AGATE COMPANY. **Popeye corkscrew.** Green and yellow Popeye. The yellow is a ribbon, the green and white are snakes. One tiny melt spot. 19/32". Mint(-) (9.2). $34. (Auction #183, Lot 3).

AKRO AGATE COMPANY. **Popeye corkscrew.** Red and green Popeye. Gorgeous marble. Clarksburg, WV, circa 1927-1935. 5/8". Mint (9.9). $34. (Auction #159, Lot 17).

AKRO AGATE COMPANY. **Popeye corkscrew.** Purple and yellow Popeye. One tiny pit. Clarksburg, WV, circa 1928-1938. 21/32". Near Mint(+) (8.9). $34. (Auction #104, Lot 1).

AKRO AGATE COMPANY. **Popeye corkscrew.** Interesting hybrid shooter. Almost all brushed red. There is a small spiral of yellow, white, green. 23/32". Near Mint(+) (8.7). $33. (Auction #62, Lot 40).

AKRO AGATE COMPANY. **Popeye corkscrew.** Red and yellow Popeye. In great shape. Clarksburg, WV, circa 1928-1935. 11/16". Mint (9.9). $33. (Auction #133, Lot 39).

AKRO AGATE COMPANY. **Popeye corkscrew.** Red and green Popeye. Gorgeous pattern. Clarksburg, WV, circa 1928-1938. 11/16". Mint (9.9). $33. (Auction #68, Lot 27).

AKRO AGATE COMPANY. **Popeye corkscrew.** Green and yellow Popeye. Clarksburg, WV, circa 1928-1938. 5/8". Mint (9.9). $32. (Auction #76, Lot 39).

AKRO AGATE COMPANY. **Popeye corkscrew.** Red and yellow Popeye. One spiral is clear. There is some mixing of the white and red. 19/32". Mint (9.9). $32. (Auction #137, Lot 37.30).

AKRO AGATE COMPANY. **Popeye corkscrew.** Red and green Popeye. In great shape. Clarksburg, WV, circa 1928-1935. 5/8". Mint (9.9). $32. (Auction #118, Lot 20).

AKRO AGATE COMPANY. **Popeye corkscrew.** Red and green shooter Popeye. Annealing fracture in the red. Clarksburg, WV, circa 1927-1935. 3/4". Mint(-) (9). $32. (Auction #143, Lot 44).

AKRO AGATE COMPANY. **Popeye corkscrew.** Red and green Popeye. Gorgeous marble. Clarksburg, WV, circa 1927-1935. 5/8". Mint (9.9). $32. (Auction #159, Lot 17.30).

AKRO AGATE COMPANY. **Popeye corkscrew.** Red and green Popeye. Gorgeous marble. Clarksburg, WV, circa 1927-1935. 5/8". Mint (9.9). $32. (Auction #159, Lot 17.40).

AKRO AGATE COMPANY. **Popeye corkscrew.** Red and green Popeye. Gorgeous marble. Clarksburg, WV, circa 1927-1935. 5/8". Mint (9.9). $32. (Auction #159, Lot 17.20).

AKRO AGATE COMPANY. **Popeye corkscrew.** Red and green Popeye. Clarksburg, WV, circa 1927-1935. 5/8". Mint (9.9). $32. (Auction #149, Lot 34).

AKRO AGATE COMPANY. **Popeye corkscrew.** Red and yellow Popeye. In great shape. Clarksburg, WV, circa 1928-1938. 5/8". Mint (9.9). $32. (Auction #71, Lot 18).

AKRO AGATE COMPANY. **Popeye corkscrew.** Blue and yellow Popeye. Nice marble. Clarksburg, WV, circa 1927-1935. 11/16". Mint (9.7). $31. (Auction #184, Lot 20).

AKRO AGATE COMPANY. **Popeye corkscrew.** Lot of two marbles. Both are green and yellow. Each has a tiny pit. 5/8". Mint(-) (9.1). $31. (Auction #111, Lot 5).

AKRO AGATE COMPANY. **Popeye corkscrew.** Odd Popeye. Transparent clear base. Snake spirals on the surface of translucent red, translucent gre. 21/32". Mint(-) (9). $31. (Auction #142, Lot 32).

AKRO AGATE COMPANY. **Popeye corkscrew.** Green and red. Superior coloring and design. 5/8". Mint (9.9). There are three available. 5/8". Mint (9.9). $31. (Auction #111, Lot 16).

AKRO AGATE COMPANY. **Popeye corkscrew.** Red and yellow Popeye. Has a thin orange band laying on the yellow. In great shape. Clarksburg, WV. 21/32". Mint (9.9). $31. (Auction #100, Lot 4).

AKRO AGATE COMPANY. **Popeye corkscrew.** Red and yellow Popeye. A beauty. Clarksburg, WV, circa 1927-1935. 23/32". Mint (9.9). $31. (Auction #163, Lot 33).

AKRO AGATE COMPANY. **Popeye corkscrew.** Odd Popeye. Transparent clear base. Snake spirals on the surface of translucent red, translucent green. 21/32". Mint(-) (9). $31. (Auction #142, Lot 32.10).

AKRO AGATE COMPANY. **Popeye corkscrew.** Red and yellow Popeye. Great example. Clarksburg, WV, circa 1927-1935. 5/8". Mint (9.9). $30. (Auction #170, Lot 11).

AKRO AGATE COMPANY. **Popeye corkscrew.** Blue and yellow Popeye corkscrew. One tiny pit and a tiny scratch. Clarksburg, WV, circa 1928-1938. 11/16". Mint(-) (9.2). $30. (Auction #169, Lot 35).

AKRO AGATE COMPANY. **Popeye corkscrew.** Blue and yellow Popeye. One tiny pit. Clarksburg, WV, circa 1927-1935. 5/8". Mint(-) (9). $30. (Auction #159, Lot 33).

AKRO AGATE COMPANY. **Popeye corkscrew.** Red and yellow Popeye. One spiral is clear. There is some mixing of the white and red. 19/32". Mint (9.9). $30. (Auction #137, Lot 37.80).

AKRO AGATE COMPANY. **Popeye corkscrew.** Red and yellow Popeye. One spiral is clear. There is some mixing of the white and red. 19/32". Mint (9.9). $30. (Auction #137, Lot 37.40).

AKRO AGATE COMPANY. **Popeye corkscrew.** Red and yellow Popeye. One spiral is clear. There is some mixing of the white and red. 19/32". Mint (9.9). $30. (Auction #137, Lot 37.50).

AKRO AGATE COMPANY. **Popeye corkscrew.** Red and yellow Popeye. One spiral is clear. There is some mixing of the white and red. 19/32". Mint (9.9). $30. (Auction #137, Lot 37.70).

AKRO AGATE COMPANY. **Popeye corkscrew.** Green and yellow Popeye. 5/8". Mint (9.9). There are two marbles available. 5/8". Mint (9.9). $30. (Auction #149, Lot 16).

AKRO AGATE COMPANY. **Popeye corkscrew.** Red and yellow Popeye. One spiral is clear. There is some mixing of the white and red. 19/32". Mint (9.9). $30. (Auction #137, Lot 37.90).

AKRO AGATE COMPANY. **Popeye corkscrew.** Red and green Popeye. The red and green are brushed on the surface. Clarksburg, WV, circa 1927-1935. 5/8". Mint (9.9). $30. (Auction #145, Lot 33).

AKRO AGATE COMPANY. **Popeye corkscrew.** Red and green Popeye. Nice marble. Translucent red spiral and translucent green spiral on the surface. 5/8". Mint (9.3). $30. (Auction #104, Lot 33).

AKRO AGATE COMPANY. **Popeye corkscrew.** Blue and yellow Popeye. Super marble. Clarksburg, WV, circa 1927-1935. 5/8". Mint (9.9). $30. (Auction #158, Lot 35).

AKRO AGATE COMPANY. **Popeye corkscrew.** Red and yellow Popeye. Nice clear spiral. Gorgeous example. Clarksburg, WV, circa 1928-1938. 5/8". Mint (9.9). $30. (Auction #92, Lot 34).

AKRO AGATE COMPANY. **Popeye corkscrew.** Red and yellow Popeye. One spiral is clear. There is some mixing of the white and red. 19/32". Mint (9.9). $30. (Auction #137, Lot 37.60).

AKRO AGATE COMPANY. **Popeye corkscrew.** Lot of two marbles. Both are the same. Both yellow and green. Both are fluorescent!! $30. (Auction #148, Lot 16).

AKRO AGATE COMPANY. **Popeye corkscrew.** Transparent clear with a snake of wispy white, a snake of red and a snake of green. 5/8". Mint(-) (9.2). $30. (Auction #165, Lot 7).

AKRO AGATE COMPANY. **Popeye corkscrew.** Red, white and blue Popeye. One flake and a couple of tiny pits. Clarksburg, WV, circa 1928-1938. 19/32". Near Mint(+) (8.7). $30. (Auction #54, Lot 10).

AKRO AGATE COMPANY. **Popeye corkscrew.** Navy blue and yellow Popeye corkscrew. Nice clear panel. Clarksburg, WV, circa 1928-1938. 21/32". Mint (9.9). $30. (Auction #78, Lot 15).

AKRO AGATE COMPANY. **Popeye corkscrew.** Red and yellow Popeye. In great shape. Clarksburg, WV, circa 1928-1938. 5/8". Mint (9.9). $30. (Auction #71, Lot 18.20).

AKRO AGATE COMPANY. **Popeye corkscrew.** Red and yellow Popeye. In great shape. Clarksburg, WV, circa 1928-1938. 5/8". Mint (9.9). $30. (Auction #71, Lot 18.30).

AKRO AGATE COMPANY. **Popeye corkscrew.** Red and green Popeye. Nice clear panel. Super marble. Clarksburg, WV, circa 1928-1938. 21/32". Mint (9.9). $30. (Auction #66, Lot 11).

AKRO AGATE COMPANY. **Popeye corkscrew.** Green and red. Superior coloring and design. 5/8". Mint (9.9). There are three available. 5/8". Mint (9.9). $29. (Auction #111, Lot 16.30).

AKRO AGATE COMPANY. **Popeye corkscrew.** Green and yellow Popeye. Extra very thin spiral of green. Nice pattern. One sparkle. Clarksburg, WV. 11/16". Mint(-) (9.1). $29. (Auction #137, Lot 5).

AKRO AGATE COMPANY. **Popeye corkscrew.** Green and yellow Popeye. Great example. Clarksburg, WV, circa 1927-1935. 5/8". Mint (9.9). $29. (Auction #170, Lot 14.20).

AKRO AGATE COMPANY. **Popeye corkscrew.** Lot of three marbles. Red and green, mis-shaped, 5/8", Near Mint(8.6). Purple and yellow, 5/8". $29. (Auction #181, Lot 1).

AKRO AGATE COMPANY. **Popeye corkscrew.** Purple and yellow Popeye. A few tiny pits and very tiny chips. Clarksburg, WV, circa 1927-1935. 5/8". Near Mint (8.5). $29. (Auction #173, Lot 1).

AKRO AGATE COMPANY. **Popeye corkscrew.** Blue and yellow Popeye. In great shape. Clarksburg, WV, circa 1927-1935. 5/8". Mint (9.9). $29. (Auction #167, Lot 3).

AKRO AGATE COMPANY. **Popeye corkscrew.** Transparent red, transparent green and translucent white spiral snakes on transparent clear. Clarksburg, WV. 5/8". Mint (9.9). $29. (Auction #63, Lot 13).

AKRO AGATE COMPANY. **Popeye corkscrew.** Red and green Popeye. Lots of clear. Very nice marble. Clarksburg, WV, circa 1927-1935. 11/16". Mint (9.7). $29. (Auction #109, Lot 8).

AKRO AGATE COMPANY. **Popeye corkscrew.** Green and red. Superior coloring and design. 5/8". Mint (9.9). There are three available. 5/8". Mint (9.9). $29. (Auction #111, Lot 16.20).

AKRO AGATE COMPANY. **Popeye corkscrew.** Green and yellow Popeye. Nice marble. Clarksburg, WV, circa 1927-1935. 5/8". Mint (9.8). $29. (Auction #184, Lot 17).

AKRO AGATE COMPANY. **Popeye corkscrew.** Green and yellow Popeye. Great example. Clarksburg, WV, circa 1927-1935. 5/8". Mint (9.9). $29. (Auction #170, Lot 14).

AKRO AGATE COMPANY. **Popeye corkscrew.** Red and green Popeye. Great example. Clarksburg, WV, circa 1927-1935. 5/8". Mint (9.9). $28. (Auction #170, Lot 31.40).

AKRO AGATE COMPANY. **Popeye corkscrew.** Blue and white Popeye. In great shape. Clarksburg, WV, circa 1928-1938. 5/8". Mint (9.9). $28. (Auction #55, Lot 7).

AKRO AGATE COMPANY. **Popeye corkscrew.** Red and yellow Popeye. In great shape. Thin red. Wispy white. Clarksburg, WV, circa 1928-1935. 5/8". Mint (9.9). $28. (Auction #126, Lot 10).

AKRO AGATE COMPANY. **Popeye corkscrew.** Lot of two marbles. Red and yellow Popeye. Each has a tiny defect. 5/8". Mint(-) (9.0). $28. (Auction #124, Lot 1).

AKRO AGATE COMPANY. **Popeye corkscrew.** Red and green Popeye. Great example. Clarksburg, WV, circa 1927-1935. 5/8". Mint (9.9). $28. (Auction #170, Lot 31.30).

AKRO AGATE COMPANY. **Popeye corkscrew.** Red and yellow Popeye. Clarksburg OH, circa 1927-1935. 5/8". Mint (9.9). $28. (Auction #153, Lot 40).

AKRO AGATE COMPANY. **Popeye corkscrew.** Red and yellow Popeye. Clarksburg OH, circa 1927-1935. 5/8". Mint (9.9). $28. (Auction #153, Lot 40.20).

AKRO AGATE COMPANY. **Popeye corkscrew.** Green and yellow Popeye. 5/8". Mint (9.9). There are two marbles available. 5/8". Mint (9.9). $28. (Auction #149, Lot 16.20).

AKRO AGATE COMPANY. **Popeye corkscrew.** Red and yellow Popeye. Clarksburg OH, circa 1927-1935. 5/8". Mint (9.9). $28. (Auction #153, Lot 40.30).

AKRO AGATE COMPANY. **Popeye corkscrew.** Green and yellow Popeye. Nice design, beautiful marble. Clarksburg, WV, circa 1927-1935. 5/8". Mint (9.9). $28. (Auction #153, Lot 8).

AKRO AGATE COMPANY. **Popeye corkscrew.** Green and yellow Popeye. Great example. Clarksburg, WV, circa 1927-1935. 5/8". Mint (9.9). $27. (Auction #170, Lot 14.30).

AKRO AGATE COMPANY. **Popeye corkscrew.** Red and green Popeye. Shooter size. Two tiny subsurface moon. Surface fracture in the red spiral. Cl. 3/4". Near Mint (8.6). $27. (Auction #140, Lot 21).

AKRO AGATE COMPANY. **Popeye corkscrew.** Red and green Popeye. Super marble. Clarksburg, WV, circa 1928-1938. 5/8". Mint (9.9). $27. (Auction #85, Lot 13).

AKRO AGATE COMPANY. **Popeye corkscrew.** Red and green Popeye. Excellent example. Clarksburg, WV, circa 1927-1935. 5/8". Mint (9.9). $27. (Auction #130, Lot 10).

AKRO AGATE COMPANY. **Popeye corkscrew.** Green and yellow Popeye. Very nice marble. Clarksburg, WV, circa 1928-1938. 5/8". Mint (9.9). $27. (Auction #80, Lot 30).

AKRO AGATE COMPANY. **Popeye corkscrew.** Green and yellow Popeye. Superb marble. Clarksburg, WV, circa 1928-1938. 21/32". Mint (9.9). $27. (Auction #66, Lot 39).

AKRO AGATE COMPANY. **Popeye corkscrew.** Red and green Popeye. Nice marble. Translucent red spiral and translucent green spiral on the surface. 5/8". Mint (9.9). $27. (Auction #82, Lot 33.30).

AKRO AGATE COMPANY. **Popeye corkscrew.** Green and yellow Popeye. Very nice marble. Clarksburg, WV, circa 1928-1938. 5/8". Mint (9.9). $27. (Auction #80, Lot 30.20).

AKRO AGATE COMPANY. **Popeye corkscrew.** Red and green Popeye. Some minor blending of the red and green. A couple of tiny sparkles on the surface. 11/16". Mint(-) (9). $27. (Auction #71, Lot 4).

AKRO AGATE COMPANY. **Popeye corkscrew.** Blue and white. A beauty. 5/8". Mint (9.9). Two examples available. 5/8". Mint (9.9). $27. (Auction #111, Lot 28).

AKRO AGATE COMPANY. **Popeye corkscrew.** Green and yellow Popeye. Great example. Clarksburg, WV, circa 1927-1935. 5/8". Mint (9.9). $27. (Auction #170, Lot 14.50).

AKRO AGATE COMPANY. **Popeye corkscrew.** Red and green Popeye. One tiny sparkle. 21/32". Clarksburg, WV, circa 1870-1915. Mint(-) (9.0). 21/32". $27. (Auction #69, Lot 39).

AKRO AGATE COMPANY. **Popeye corkscrew.** Red and yellow Popeye. Great example. Clarksburg, WV, circa 1927-1935. 5/8". Mint (9.9). $27. (Auction #170, Lot 11.30).

AKRO AGATE COMPANY. **Popeye corkscrew.** Blue and white. A beauty. 5/8". Mint (9.9). Two examples available. 5/8". Mint (9.9). $27. (Auction #111, Lot 28.20).

AKRO AGATE COMPANY. **Popeye corkscrew.** Red and green Popeye. Nice marble. Translucent red spiral and translucent green spiral on the surface. 5/8". Mint (9.9). $27. (Auction #82, Lot 33.20).

AKRO AGATE COMPANY. **Popeye corkscrew.** Green and yellow Popeye. Great example. Clarksburg, WV, circa 1927-1935. 5/8". Mint (9.9). $27. (Auction #170, Lot 14.40).

AKRO AGATE COMPANY. **Popeye corkscrew.** Red and yellow Popeye. Great example. Clarksburg, WV, circa 1927-1935. 5/8". Mint (9.9). $27. (Auction #170, Lot 11.20).

AKRO AGATE COMPANY. **Popeye corkscrew.** Green and yellow Popeye. Very nice marble. Clarksburg, WV, circa 1928-1938. 5/8". Mint (9.9). $27. (Auction #80, Lot 30.30).

AKRO AGATE COMPANY. **Popeye corkscrew.** Green and yellow shooter. Wide yellow, wide clear, narrow green. Four tiny pinprick, a sparkle. 3/4". Near Mint(+) (8.9). $26. (Auction #110, Lot 4).

AKRO AGATE COMPANY. **Popeye corkscrew.** Red and green Popeye. Great example. Clarksburg, WV, circa 1927-1935. 5/8". Mint (9.9). $26. (Auction #170, Lot 31.50).

AKRO AGATE COMPANY. **Popeye corkscrew.** Red and yellow Popeye. Clarksburg, WV, circa 1827-1935. 5/8". Mint (9.9). $26. (Auction #179, Lot 11).

AKRO AGATE COMPANY. **Popeye corkscrew.** Red and yellow Popeye corkscrew. Wide clear panel. A beauty. Clarksburg, WV, circa 1928-1938. 21/32". Mint (9.9). $26. (Auction #78, Lot 4).

AKRO AGATE COMPANY. **Popeye corkscrew.** Red and yellow Popeye. In great shape. Clarksburg, WV, circa 1927-1935. 5/8". Mint (9.9). $26. (Auction #107, Lot 1).

AKRO AGATE COMPANY. **Popeye corkscrew.** Blue and yellow Popeye. In great shape. Clarksburg, WV, circa 1928-1938. 21/32". Mint (9.9). $26. (Auction #67, Lot 27).

AKRO AGATE COMPANY. **Popeye corkscrew.** Red and yellow Popeye. Wide clear panel. A beauty. Clarksburg, WV, circa 1928-1938. 5/8". Mint (9.9). $26. (Auction #91, Lot 29).

AKRO AGATE COMPANY. **Popeye corkscrew.** Red and yellow Popeye. 5/8". Mint (9.9). Three marbles available. 5/8". Mint (9.9). $25. (Auction #111, Lot 2.20).

AKRO AGATE COMPANY. **Popeye corkscrew.** Red and yellow Popeye. 5/8". Mint (9.9). Three marbles available. 5/8". Mint (9.9). $25. (Auction #111, Lot 2.10).

AKRO AGATE COMPANY. **Popeye corkscrew.** Red and yellow Popeye. Great example. Clarksburg, WV, circa 1927-1935. 5/8". Mint (9.9). $25. (Auction #170, Lot 11.50).

AKRO AGATE COMPANY. **Popeye corkscrew.** Red and yellow Popeye. 5/8". Mint (9.9). Three marbles available. 5/8". Mint (9.9). $25. (Auction #111, Lot 2).

AKRO AGATE COMPANY. **Popeye corkscrew.** Red and green Popeye. Beautiful example. One very tiny sparkle. Clarksburg, WV, circa 1927-1935. 5/8". 5/8". Mint (9.9). $25. (Auction #110, Lot 16).

AKRO AGATE COMPANY. **Popeye corkscrew.** Red and green Popeye. One sparkle. Clarksburg, WV, circa 1927-1935. 11/16". Mint(-) (9.2). $25. (Auction #101, Lot 4).

AKRO AGATE COMPANY. **Popeye corkscrew.** Yellow and green Popeye. Some minor blending to create a thin tan spiral too. In great shape. 5/8". Mint (9.9). $25. (Auction #98, Lot 6).

AKRO AGATE COMPANY. **Popeye corkscrew.** Red and yellow Popeye. Great example. Clarksburg, WV, circa 1927-1935. 5/8". Mint (9.9). $25. (Auction #170, Lot 11.40).

AKRO AGATE COMPANY. **Popeye corkscrew.** Navy blue and yellow Popeye. Narrow blue and yellow. Tons of white. Nice example. 21/32". Near Mint(+) (8.9). $25. (Auction #156, Lot 9).

AKRO AGATE COMPANY. **Popeye corkscrew.** Red and yellow. Very nice. Clarksburg, WV, circa 1927-1935. 19/32." Mint (9.9). $25. (Auction #158, Lot 4).

AKRO AGATE COMPANY. **Popeye corkscrew.** Green and yellow Popeye. Nice marble. Surface in great shape. Clarksburg, WV, circa 1928-1938. 19/32." Mint (9.9). $25. (Auction #67, Lot 40).

AKRO AGATE COMPANY. **Popeye corkscrew.** Blue and yellow Popeye. One tiny pit. Clarksburg, WV, circa 1927-1935. 11/16". Mint(-) (9). $24. (Auction #146, Lot 5.20).

AKRO AGATE COMPANY. **Popeye corkscrew.** Fluorescent yellow and green Popeye. Subsurface moon, some sparkles and a tiny flake. Clarksburg, WV. 58". Near Mint (8.4). $24. (Auction #92, Lot 26).

AKRO AGATE COMPANY. **Popeye corkscrew.** Red and yellow Popeye. Clarksburg, WV, circa 1827-1935. 5/8". Mint (9.9). $24. (Auction #179, Lot 11.20).

AKRO AGATE COMPANY. **Popeye corkscrew.** Blue and yellow Popeye. One tiny pit. Clarksburg, WV, circa 1927-1935. 11/16". Mint(-) (9). $24. (Auction #146, Lot 5).

AKRO AGATE COMPANY. **Popeye corkscrew.** Blue and yellow Popeye. One tiny pit. Clarksburg, WV, circa 1927-1935. 11/16". Mint(-) (9). $24. (Auction #146, Lot 5.30).

AKRO AGATE COMPANY. **Popeye corkscrew.** Red and green Popeye. Wide clear panel. In great shape. Clarksburg, WV, circa 1928-1938. 21/32". Mint (9.9). $24. (Auction #90, Lot 14).

AKRO AGATE COMPANY. **Popeye corkscrew.** Green and yellow Popeye. Lots of white in the clear. Clarksburg, WV, circa 1928-1938. 5/8". Mint (9.9). $24. (Auction #58, Lot 18).

AKRO AGATE COMPANY. **Popeye corkscrew.** Red and yellow Popeye. Shooter. Subsurface moon, some sparkles and a pit. Clarksburg, WV, circa 1927. 23/32". Near Mint(+) (8.7). $24. (Auction #167, Lot 12).

AKRO AGATE COMPANY. **Popeye corkscrew.** Blue and yellow Popeye corkscrew. One tiny pit and a tiny scratch. Clarksburg, WV, circa 1928-1938. 11/16". Mint(-) (9.2). $24. (Auction #104, Lot 14).

AKRO AGATE COMPANY. **Popeye corkscrew.** Red and yellow Popeye. Very nice marble. Clarksburg, WV, circa 1927-1935. 5/8". Mint (9.9). $23. (Auction #159, Lot 10).

AKRO AGATE COMPANY. **Popeye corkscrew.** Red and yellow Popeye. Nice marble. Clarksburg, WV, circa 1870-1915. 5/8". Mint (9.9). $23. (Auction #139, Lot 39).

AKRO AGATE COMPANY. **Popeye corkscrew.** Red and yellow Popeye. Nice marble. Clarksburg, WV, circa 1927-1935. 5/8". Mint (9.7). $23. (Auction #184, Lot 12).

AKRO AGATE COMPANY. **Popeye corkscrew.** Red and yellow Popeye. Very nice marble. Clarksburg, WV, circa 1927-1935. 5/8". Mint (9.9). $23. (Auction #159, Lot 10.20).

AKRO AGATE COMPANY. **Popeye corkscrew.** Navy blue and yellow Popeye. Narrow blue and yellow. Tons of white. Nice example. 21/32". Near Mint(+) (8.9). $22. (Auction #156, Lot 9.20).

AKRO AGATE COMPANY. **Popeye corkscrew.** Red and yellow Popeye. Clarksburg, WV, circa 1827-1935. 5/8". Mint (9.9). $22. (Auction #179, Lot 11.30).

AKRO AGATE COMPANY. **Popeye corkscrew.** Red and yellow Popeye. 5/8". Mint (9.9). There are two marbles available. 5/8". Mint (9.9). $22. (Auction #149, Lot 1.20).

AKRO AGATE COMPANY. **Popeye corkscrew.** Red and yellow Popeye. 5/8". Mint (9.9). There are two marbles available. 5/8". Mint (9.9). $22. (Auction #149, Lot 1).

AKRO AGATE COMPANY. **Popeye corkscrew.** Blue and yellow Popeye. One tiny sparkle. Clarksburg, WV, circa 1927-1935. 5/8". Mint(-) (9.2). 5/8". Mint(-) (9.2). $22. (Auction #98, Lot 14).

AKRO AGATE COMPANY. **Popeye corkscrew.** Red and yellow Popeye. One tiny subsurface moon. Clarksburg, WV, circa 1927-1935. 23/32". Near Mint(+) (8.9). $22. (Auction #162, Lot 10).

AKRO AGATE COMPANY. **Popeye corkscrew.** Red and yellow Popeye corkscrew. A couple of very tiny sparkles. Clarksburg, WV, circa 1928-1938. 11/16". Mint(-) (9.2). $22. (Auction #104, Lot 31).

AKRO AGATE COMPANY. **Popeye corkscrew.** Red and yellow Popeye. Thin red. Almost no white in the clear. A beauty. Clarksburg, WV, circa 1927. 5/8". Mint (9.9). $22. (Auction #131, Lot 3).

AKRO AGATE COMPANY. **Popeye corkscrew.** Green and yellow Popeye. One sparkle. Very nice marble. Clarksburg, WV, circa 1928-1938. 5/8". Mint(-) (9.2). $22. (Auction #104, Lot 17).

AKRO AGATE COMPANY. Popeye corkscrew. Green and yellow Popeye corkscrew. One sparkle. Clarksburg, WV, circa 1928-1938. 21/32". Mint(-) (9.1). $22. (Auction #78, Lot 16).

AKRO AGATE COMPANY. Popeye corkscrew. Blue and yellow Popeye. One tiny pit. Clarksburg, WV, circa 1928-1938. 5/8". Mint(-) (9). $21. (Auction #69, Lot 35).

AKRO AGATE COMPANY. Popeye corkscrew. Shooter Popeye corkscrew. Light red and light green. Thin coloring. Ribbon type. Very unusual. 23/32". Near Mint(+) (8.9). $21. (Auction #127, Lot 7).

AKRO AGATE COMPANY. Popeye corkscrew. Dark blue and yellow. Lots of white. Thin band of green, created by the blending of the blue and yellow. 5/8". Near Mint(+) (8.9). $20. (Auction #109, Lot 31).

AKRO AGATE COMPANY. Popeye corkscrew. Red and yellow Popeye. Some very minor pits and a couple of sparkles. Clarksburg, WV, circa 1928-1938. 19/32". Mint(-) (9). $20. (Auction #85, Lot 34).

AKRO AGATE COMPANY. Popeye corkscrew. Red and yellow Popeye. In nice shape with just one small manufacturing spot on it. Clarksburg, WV. 5/8". Mint(-) (9). $20. (Auction #118, Lot 1).

AKRO AGATE COMPANY. Popeye corkscrew. Red and yellow Popeye. Very thin red. Very little white. Clarksburg, WV, circa 1927-1935. 5/8". Mint (9.9). $20. (Auction #160, Lot 20).

AKRO AGATE COMPANY. Popeye corkscrew. Green and red Popeye. A couple of tiny sparkles. Clarksburg, WV, circa 1870-1915. 11/16". Mint(-) (9). $20. (Auction #154, Lot 7).

AKRO AGATE COMPANY. Popeye corkscrew. Red and green Popeye. Great example. Clarksburg, WV, circa 1927-1935. 5/8". Mint (9.9). $20. (Auction #170, Lot 31).

AKRO AGATE COMPANY. Popeye corkscrew. Red and blue Popeye. Several flakes on it. Clarksburg, WV, circa 1927-1935. 11/16". Near Mint (8.4). $20. (Auction #110, Lot 9).

AKRO AGATE COMPANY. Popeye corkscrew. Blue and yellow Popeye. Nice one. One tiny melt spot. Clarksburg, WV, circa 1870-1915. 5/8". Mint(-) (9). $20. (Auction #139, Lot 12).

AKRO AGATE COMPANY. Popeye corkscrew. Red and green Popeye. Great example. Clarksburg, WV, circa 1927-1935. 5/8". Mint (9.9). $20. (Auction #170, Lot 31.20).

AKRO AGATE COMPANY. Popeye corkscrew. Blue and yellow Popeye. Nice marble. One tiny sparkle. 5/8". Mint(-) (9.1). $20. (Auction #123, Lot 19).

AKRO AGATE COMPANY. Popeye corkscrew. Red and yellow Popeye. Beautiful example. Clarksburg, WV, circa 1928-1938. 5/8". Mint (9.8). $20. (Auction #92, Lot 1).

AKRO AGATE COMPANY. Popeye corkscrew. Blue and yellow Popeye. Clarksburg, WV, circa 1928-1938. 5/8". Mint (9.9). $19. (Auction #68, Lot 3).

AKRO AGATE COMPANY. Popeye corkscrew. Red and green Popeye. Has two sparkles. Clarksburg, WV, circa 1928-1938. 21/32". Mint(-) (9). $19. (Auction #65, Lot 24).

AKRO AGATE COMPANY. Popeye corkscrew. Red and yellow Popeye. Very nice. One piece of unmelted sand. Clarksburg, WV, circa 1927-1935. 5/8". Mint (9.8). $19. (Auction #161, Lot 3).

AKRO AGATE COMPANY. Popeye corkscrew. Blue and yellow Popeye. One barely visible subsurface moon. Clarksburg, WV, circa 1928-1938. 21/32". Near Mint(+) (8.9). $18. (Auction #62, Lot 29).

AKRO AGATE COMPANY. Popeye corkscrew. Lot of two marbles. One red and green, one red and yellow. Each has a chip, subsurface moons. $18. (Auction #148, Lot 3).

AKRO AGATE COMPANY. Popeye corkscrew. Green and yellow Popeye. Nice pattern. Couple of tiny pinpricks. Clarksburg, WV, circa 1928-1938. 21/32". Near Mint(+) (8.9). $17. (Auction #87, Lot 36).

AKRO AGATE COMPANY. Popeye corkscrew. Red and yellow Popeye. One pinprick. Clarksburg, WV, circa 1927-1935. 5/8". Mint(-) (9.1). $17. (Auction #140, Lot 13).

AKRO AGATE COMPANY. Popeye corkscrew. Red and yellow Popeye. One sparkle. Clarksburg, WV, circa 1928-1938. 5/8". Mint(-) (9.1). $16. (Auction #83, Lot 8).

AKRO AGATE COMPANY. Popeye corkscrew. Red and yellow Popeye. Two sparkles. Clarksburg, WV, circa 1927-1935. 11/16". Near Mint(+) (8.9). $16. (Auction #98, Lot 35).

AKRO AGATE COMPANY. Popeye corkscrew. Green and yellow Popeye. Nice augur style. Small annealing fracture. 11/16". Mint(-) (9). $16. (Auction #124, Lot 14).

AKRO AGATE COMPANY. Popeye corkscrew. Red and green Popeye. A tiny subsurface moon, a sparkle on it and some scratching. Clarksburg, WV. 11/16". Near Mint(+) (8.9). $16. (Auction #82, Lot 10).

AKRO AGATE COMPANY. Popeye corkscrew. Red and yellow Popeye. In great shape. Clarksburg, WV, circa 1927-1935. 5/8". Mint (9.9). $15. (Auction #110, Lot 26).

AKRO AGATE COMPANY. Popeye corkscrew. Red and yellow Popeye. A tiny pit and tiny flake. Clarksburg, WV, circa 1927-1935. 5/8". Near Mint(+) (8.7). $12. (Auction #166, Lot 20).

AKRO AGATE COMPANY. Popeye corkscrew. Blue and yellow Popeye. Clarksburg, WV, circa 1927-1935. 19/32". Lightly buffed. $9. (Auction #139, Lot 30).

AKRO AGATE COMPANY. Popeye patch. Fluorescent green and yellow Popeye. Almost no twist to the marble, it is a patch. Very fluorescent . 3/4". Near Mint(+) (8.9). $110. (Auction #131, Lot 46).

AKRO AGATE COMPANY. Popeye patch. Hard to find Popeye patch. This is not the more common Vitro look-alike. Red and green with white. 21/32". Mint (9.9). $65. (Auction #146, Lot 43).

AKRO AGATE COMPANY. Popeye Patch. A very rare and genuine Popeye Patch. Very unusual. Almost impossible to find. 5/8". Mint (9.9). $80. (Auction #61, Lot 43).

AKRO AGATE COMPANY. Ribbon core. Transparent very light green, very fluorescent glass with an opaque white ribbon double twisted. 11/16". Mint (9.9). $22. (Auction #103, Lot 32).

AKRO AGATE COMPANY. Ribbon corkscrew. Lot of four marbles. All are triple twist ribbon corkscrew, possibly same run. Opaque white ribbon. 5/8". Mint (9.9). $90. (Auction #95, Lot 36).

AKRO AGATE COMPANY. Ribbon corkscrew. Wow!!! Stunning double twist ribbon corkscrew. Transparent clear base. Ribbon is opaque yellow. 5/8". Mint (9.9). $72. (Auction #67, Lot 34).

AKRO AGATE COMPANY. Ribbon corkscrew. Lot of five marbles. All are the same color and pattern. Transparent clear base. Opaque yellow ribbon. $37. (Auction #142, Lot 36).

AKRO AGATE COMPANY. Ribbon corkscrew. Double twist ribbon corkscrew. Transparent clear base. Opaque yellow ribbon. 5/8". Mint (9.9). $36. (Auction #131, Lot 38).

AKRO AGATE COMPANY. Ribbon corkscrew. Two and a half twist ribbon corkscrew. Transparent red base with an opaque white ribbon. 21/32". Mint (9.9). $35. (Auction #121, Lot 31).

AKRO AGATE COMPANY. Ribbon corkscrew. Superb triple twist ribbon corkscrew. Transparent red base glass. White ribbon, twisted three times. 21/32". Mint (9.9). $34. (Auction #67, Lot 37).

AKRO AGATE COMPANY. Ribbon corkscrew. Transparent fluorescent vaseline yellow base. Opaque white ribbon. Triple twist. In super shape. 23/32". Mint (9.9). $34. (Auction #75, Lot 11).

AKRO AGATE COMPANY. Ribbon corkscrew. A real beauty!! Transparent clear base. Ribbon of opaque yellow, with a snake of opaque red. 5/8". Mint (9.9). $34. (Auction #143, Lot 45).

AKRO AGATE COMPANY. Ribbon corkscrew. Lot of three marbles. Yellow double twist in clear, one tiny pit, 5/8", Mint(-) (9.0). $30. (Auction #67, Lot 15).

AKRO AGATE COMPANY. Ribbon corkscrew. Super small corkscrew. Fluorescent transparent vaseline yellow base with a translucent white ribbon. 9/16". Mint (9.9). $30. (Auction #107, Lot 39).

AKRO AGATE COMPANY. Ribbon corkscrew. Triple twist ribbon corkscrew. Blue ribbon in clear. Clarksburg, WV, circa 1928-1935. 5/8". Mint (9.9). $29. (Auction #120, Lot 7).

AKRO AGATE COMPANY. Ribbon corkscrew. Transparent clear base Ribbon of semi-opaque yellow in the center. Snake of translucent white. 5/8". Mint(-) (9.1). $29. (Auction #133, Lot 43).

AKRO AGATE COMPANY. Ribbon corkscrew. Lot of four marbles. All are ribbon corkscrews. Nice assortment of colors. 5/8" to 21/32". Mint (9.9). $28. (Auction #118, Lot 31).

AKRO AGATE COMPANY. Ribbon corkscrew. Transparent clear bubble filled base with an oxblood ribbon. Some tiny chips and tiny moons. 5/8". Near Mint (8.4). $27. (Auction #152, Lot 4).

AKRO AGATE COMPANY. Ribbon corkscrew. Double twist ribbon corkscrew. Transparent orange base with opaque white ribbon. In great shape. 5/8". Mint (9.9). $26. (Auction #145, Lot 31).

AKRO AGATE COMPANY. Ribbon corkscrew. Transparent fluorescent vaseline base with a double twist opaque white ribbon. Clarksburg, WV. 11/16". Mint (9.9). $25. (Auction #63, Lot 33).

AKRO AGATE COMPANY. Ribbon corkscrew. Transparent vaseline base (very fluorescent) with a wide opaque white ribbon. 11/16". Mint (9.9). $25. (Auction #61, Lot 29).

AKRO AGATE COMPANY. Ribbon corkscrew. Lot of four marbles. All are transparent clear base. Two are white ribbons, one green ribbon. $24. (Auction #157, Lot 46).

AKRO AGATE COMPANY. Ribbon corkscrew. Lot of two marbles. Both are yellow ribbons in transparent clear. One is a double twist. $24. (Auction #62, Lot 20).

AKRO AGATE COMPANY. Ribbon corkscrew. Lot of two marbles. First is dark transparent red with a translucent white ribbon. $23. (Auction #69, Lot 4).

AKRO AGATE COMPANY. Ribbon corkscrew. Lot of two marbles. Both are transparent vaseline yellow fluorescent base with an opaque white ribbon. $22. (Auction #77, Lot 27).

AKRO AGATE COMPANY. Ribbon corkscrew. Fluorescent transparent vaseline yellow base. Opaque white ribbon. In great shape. A beauty! Clarksburg, WV. 11/16". Mint (9.9). $22. (Auction #70, Lot 8).

AKRO AGATE COMPANY. Ribbon corkscrew. Lot of two marbles. Pair of double twist ribbon corkscrews. Both in transparent clear base. $21. (Auction #61, Lot 34).

AKRO AGATE COMPANY. Ribbon corkscrew. Transparent lavender base with an opaque yellow ribbon. Not completely through the base lavender. 19/32". Mint (9.9). $20. (Auction #113, Lot 22).

AKRO AGATE COMPANY. Ribbon corkscrew. Lot of two marbles. Same run. Odd colors. Translucent milky white with an opaque orange ribbon. Each. $20. (Auction #83, Lot 42).

AKRO AGATE COMPANY. Ribbon corkscrew. Fluorescent transparent vaseline yellow base with an opaque white ribbon. Clarksburg, WV, circa 1928. 19/32". Mint (9.9). $20. (Auction #69, Lot 31).

AKRO AGATE COMPANY. Ribbon corkscrew. Transparent clear base with a baby blue ribbon. Double twist. Beautiful marble. Clarksburg, WV. 5/8". Mint (9.9). $20. (Auction #75, Lot 6).

AKRO AGATE COMPANY. Ribbon corkscrew. Fluorescent transparent tan and opaque white. Nice marble. Augur type spiral. Clarksburg, WV. 19/32". Mint (9.9). $19. (Auction #73, Lot 5).

AKRO AGATE COMPANY. Ribbon corkscrew. Triple twist ribbon corkscrew. Transparent clear base. Thin ribbon of opaque yellow with a brown edge. 5/8". Near Mint(+) (8.8). $19. (Auction #67, Lot 3).

AKRO AGATE COMPANY. Ribbon corkscrew. Very nice marble. Transparent clear base. Ribbon of opaque yellow. Thin snake on the remaining clear. 5/8". Mint (9.9). $19. (Auction #149, Lot 30.20).

AKRO AGATE COMPANY. Ribbon corkscrew. Transparent clear base. Opaque white ribbon with yellow on one side. So from the top it looks yellow. 21/32". Mint (9.9). $19. (Auction #111, Lot 42).

AKRO AGATE COMPANY. Ribbon corkscrew. Very nice marble. Transparent clear base. Ribbon of opaque yellow. Thin snake on the remaining clear. 5/8". Mint (9.9). $19. (Auction #149, Lot 30).

AKRO AGATE COMPANY. Ribbon corkscrew. Lot of two marbles. Both are opaque yellow ribbon in transparent clear. One has an extra spiral. $18. (Auction #92, Lot 38).

AKRO AGATE COMPANY. Ribbon corkscrew. Transparent clear base with a translucent green ribbon. Augur style. A beauty. Clarksburg, WV. 5/8". Mint (9.9). $18. (Auction #76, Lot 4).

AKRO AGATE COMPANY. Ribbon corkscrew. Very nice marble. Transparent clear base. Ribbon of opaque yellow. Thin snake on the remaining clear. 5/8". Mint (9.9). $17. (Auction #149, Lot 30.30).

AKRO AGATE COMPANY. Ribbon corkscrew. Transparent cherry red base with thin opaque white ribbon. Two and one half twists. One tiny sparkle. 111/6". Mint(-) (9). $16. (Auction #155, Lot 39).

AKRO AGATE COMPANY. Ribbon corkscrew. Hard to find four-twist ribbon corkscrew. Transparent orange base with thin opaque white corkscrew. 21/32". Near Mint(+) (8.9). $16. (Auction #112, Lot 33).

AKRO AGATE COMPANY. Ribbon corkscrew. Lot of four marbles. All transparent clear base. One yellow, one light blue, two green. $16. (Auction #98, Lot 8).

AKRO AGATE COMPANY. Ribbon corkscrew. Odd coloring. Translucent green base with an opaque white ribbon, double twisted. Clarksburg, WV. 5/8". Mint (9.9). $15. (Auction #83, Lot 32).

AKRO AGATE COMPANY. Ribbon corkscrew. Very nice marble. Transparent clear base. Ribbon of opaque yellow. Thin snake on the remaining clear. 5/8". Mint (9.9). $15. (Auction #137, Lot 4).

AKRO AGATE COMPANY. Ribbon corkscrew. Transparent yellow base. Very fluorescent. Opaque white augur ribbon. Surface in great shape. 9/16". Mint (9.9). $15. (Auction #66, Lot 36).

AKRO AGATE COMPANY. Ribbon corkscrew. Translucent milky white base with a translucent milky green ribbon. Super marble. Clarksburg, WV. 5/8". Mint (9.9). $12. (Auction #145, Lot 48).

AKRO AGATE COMPANY. Ribbon corkscrew. Transparent blue glass with three twists. A couple of very tiny pinpricks. A beauty. Clarksburg, WV. 19/32". Near Mint(+) (8.9). $12. (Auction #164, Lot 3).

AKRO AGATE COMPANY. Ribbon corkscrew. Transparent clear base. Opaque white ribbon with a narrow yellow spiral on it. Narrow white snake on. 5/8". Mint (9.9). $12. (Auction #164, Lot 14).

AKRO AGATE COMPANY. Ribbon corkscrew. Transparent brown base with an opaqe white ribbon. The ribbon is completely in the marble. 29/32". Near Mint (8.6). $11. (Auction #62, Lot 8).

AKRO AGATE COMPANY. Ribbon corkscrew. Transparent clear base with a double twist baby blue ribbon. 5/8". Mint (9.9). $11. (Auction #111, Lot 27).

AKRO AGATE COMPANY. Ribbon corkscrew. Very nice "augur style" ribbon corkscrew. Transparent orange base (harder to find). 11/16". Near Mint(+) (8.8). $10. (Auction #61, Lot 10).

AKRO AGATE COMPANY. Ringer. Lot of two marbles. Both are Ringers. They are the harder to find non-red color. Translucent milky white. $35. (Auction #66, Lot 31).

AKRO AGATE COMPANY. Ringer corkscrew. Lot of nineteen marbles. All are Ringer corkscrews. Translucent milky base with wispy opaque white. $75. (Auction #84, Lot 17).

AKRO AGATE COMPANY. Silver oxblood. Outstanding and superior example. Shooter! Translucent silver base. Wispy opaque white swirls. Beaut. 3/4". Mint (9.9). $120. (Auction #181, Lot 41).

AKRO AGATE COMPANY. Silver oxblood. Shooter silver oxblood. Translucent silver base with wispy opaque white and a nice oxblood swirl. 3/4". Mint(-) (9). $90. (Auction #73, Lot 42).

AKRO AGATE COMPANY. Silver oxblood. Translucent silver base with translucent white swirls and with nice oxblood swirls on the surface. 19/32". Mint (9.9). $80. (Auction #93, Lot 37).

AKRO AGATE COMPANY. Silver oxblood. Translucent silver base with translucent white swirls and with nice oxblood swirls on the surface. 19/32". Mint (9.9). $75. (Auction #93, Lot 37.20).

AKRO AGATE COMPANY. Silver oxblood. Superior silver oxblood shooter. Translucent silver milky base with wispy white swirls. Excellent oxblood. 23/32". Mint (9.9). $75. (Auction #131, Lot 15).

AKRO AGATE COMPANY. Silver oxblood. Translucent milky white base. Semi-opaque white swirls. Excellent oxblood swirl on the top. 3/4". Near Mint (8.5). $60. (Auction #133, Lot 19).

AKRO AGATE COMPANY. Silver oxblood. Translucent milky silver base. Swirls of opaque white in it. Swirls of oxblood on the surface. 21/32". Mint (9.9). $60. (Auction #137, Lot 44).

AKRO AGATE COMPANY. Silver oxblood. Translucent milky silver base. Swirls of opaque white in it. Swirls of oxblood on the surface. 21/32". Mint (9.9). $55. (Auction #137, Lot 44.30).

AKRO AGATE COMPANY. Silver oxblood. Translucent milky silver base. Swirls of opaque white in it. Swirls of oxblood on the surface. 21/32". Mint (9.9). $55. (Auction #137, Lot 44.20).

AKRO AGATE COMPANY. Silver oxblood. Translucent silver base. Semi-opaque white swirls. Excellent oxblood swirl on the top. 19/32". Mint (9.9). $50. (Auction #182, Lot 44).

AKRO AGATE COMPANY. Silver oxblood. Lot of two marbles. Translucent milky white base. Semi-opaque white swirls. Nice oxblood swirl. Mint . $50. (Auction #144, Lot 16).

AKRO AGATE COMPANY. Silver oxblood. Translucent silver base with translucent white swirls and with nice oxblood swirls on the surface. 5/8". Mint (9.9). $46. (Auction #91, Lot 32).

AKRO AGATE COMPANY. Silver oxblood. Translucent silver base with translucent white swirls and with nice oxblood swirls on the surface. 5/8". Mint (9.9). $46. (Auction #91, Lot 32.20).

AKRO AGATE COMPANY. Silver oxblood. Translucent milky silver base. Swirls of opaque white in it. Swirls of oxblood on the surface. 21/32". Mint (9.9). $45. (Auction #126, Lot 34).

AKRO AGATE COMPANY. Silver oxblood. Translucent milky silver base. Swirls of opaque white in it. Swirls of oxblood on the surface. 21/32". Mint (9.9). $44. (Auction #129, Lot 29).

AKRO AGATE COMPANY. Silver oxblood. Translucent milky white base. Semi-opaque white swirls. Nice oxblood swirl on the top. Excellent. 19/32". Mint (9.9). $41. (Auction #96, Lot 29).

AKRO AGATE COMPANY. Silver oxblood. Silver oxblood. Translucent milky silver base with opaque white swirls. Small, rich oxblood swirl. 11/16". Mint(-) (9). $40. (Auction #84, Lot 39).

AKRO AGATE COMPANY. Silver oxblood. Translucent silver base. Wispy white swirls in it. Nice oxblood swirls on the surface. Two sparkles. 21/32". Mint(-) (9). $40. (Auction #68, Lot 31).

AKRO AGATE COMPANY. Silver oxblood. Translucent milky silver base. Swirls of opaque white in it. Swirls of oxblood on the surface. 21/32". Mint (9.9). $39. (Auction #124, Lot 29).

AKRO AGATE COMPANY. Silver oxblood. Translucent milky white base. Semi-opaque white swirls. Nice oxblood swirl on the top. Excellent. 19/32". Mint (9.9). $38. (Auction #136, Lot 35).

AKRO AGATE COMPANY. Silver oxblood. Translucent milky white base. Semi-opaque white swirls. Nice oxblood swirl on the top. Superior. 19/32". Mint (9.9). $37. (Auction #155, Lot 41).

AKRO AGATE COMPANY. Silver oxblood. Translucent milky white base. Opaque white swirls in the marble and oxblood red swirls on the surface. 19/32". Mint(-) (9.2). $37. (Auction #67, Lot 13).

AKRO AGATE COMPANY. Silver oxblood. Translucent milky white base. Semi-opaque white swirls. Nice oxblood swirl on the top. Excellent. 19/32". Mint (9.9). $35. (Auction #166, Lot 41).

AKRO AGATE COMPANY. Silver oxblood. Translucent milky white base. Semi-opaque white swirls. Superior oxblood swirl on the top. Excellent. 19/32". Mint (9.9). $35. (Auction #127, Lot 43).

AKRO AGATE COMPANY. Silver oxblood. Translucent milky white base. Semi-opaque white swirls. Nice oxblood swirl on the top. Excellent. 19/32". Mint (9.9). $34. (Auction #95, Lot 6).

AKRO AGATE COMPANY. Silver oxblood. Translucent milky white base. Semi-opaque white swirls. Nice oxblood swirl on the top. One sparkle. 19/32". Mint(-) (9.1). $33. (Auction #171, Lot 44).

AKRO AGATE COMPANY. Silver oxblood. Translucent milky white base. Semi-opaque white swirls. Nice oxblood swirl on the top. Excellent. 19/32". Mint (9.9). $32. (Auction #144, Lot 1).

AKRO AGATE COMPANY. Silver oxblood. Translucent milky white base. Semi-opaque white swirls. Nice oxblood swirl on the top. Excellent. 19/32". Mint (9.9). $32. (Auction #97, Lot 39).

AKRO AGATE COMPANY. Silver oxblood. Translucent milky white base. Semi-opaque white swirls. Nice oxblood swirl on the top. 5/8". Mint(-) (9.2). $32. (Auction #142, Lot 30).

AKRO AGATE COMPANY. Silver oxblood. Translucent milky white base. Semi-opaque white swirls. Nice oxblood swirl on the top. Excellent. 19/32". Mint (9.9). $32. (Auction #144, Lot 47).

AKRO AGATE COMPANY. Silver oxblood. Translucent milky white base. Opaque white swirls in the marble and oxblood red swirls on the surface. 19/32". Mint(-) (9). $30. (Auction #67, Lot 7).

AKRO AGATE COMPANY. Silver oxblood. Translucent milky white base. Semi-opaque white swirls. Nice oxblood swirl on the top. Superior example. 19/32". Mint (9.9). $30. (Auction #150, Lot 7).

AKRO AGATE COMPANY. Silver oxblood. Translucent milky white base. Semi-opaque white swirls. Nice oxblood swirl on the top. Excellent. 19/32". Mint (9.9). $30. (Auction #98, Lot 2).

AKRO AGATE COMPANY. Silver oxblood. Translucent milky white base. Semi-opaque white swirls. Nice oxblood swirl on the top. Nice example. 21/32". Mint (9.6). $29. (Auction #183, Lot 31).

AKRO AGATE COMPANY. Silver oxblood. Translucent milky white base. Semi-opaque white swirls. Nice oxblood swirl on the top. Excellent. 19/32". Mint (9.9). $27. (Auction #141, Lot 16).

AKRO AGATE COMPANY. Silver oxblood. Translucent silver white base. Semi-opaque white swirls. Nice oxblood swirl on the top. Excellent. 19/32". Mint (9.9). $26. (Auction #149, Lot 43).

AKRO AGATE COMPANY. Silver oxblood. Translucent milky white base. Semi-opaque white swirls. Nice oxblood swirl on the top. 21/32". Near Mint(+) (8.9). $24. (Auction #153, Lot 14).

AKRO AGATE COMPANY. Silver oxblood. Translucent milky silver base. Swirls of opaque white in it. Swirls of oxblood on the surface. 5/8". Mint(-) (9.2). $23. (Auction #142, Lot 38).

AKRO AGATE COMPANY. Slag. One of the largest Akro green slags that I have ever seen. And in super condition. Transparent green. 1-1/4". Mint(-) (9.1). $100. (Auction #100, Lot 34).

AKRO AGATE COMPANY. Slag. Lot of thirty one marbles. Assortment of colors including brown, green, blue, purple, yellow, red. $100. (Auction #68, Lot 21).

AKRO AGATE COMPANY. Slag. Lot of seven marbles. All are Akro slags, and all are shooters. Blue, 27/32", Mint (9.9). Very light. $100. (Auction #64, Lot 20).

AKRO AGATE COMPANY. Slag. Large blue slag. One of the biggest I have ever seen. In super shape. Ill-formed "9". 1-1/4". Near Mint(+) (8.9). $80. (Auction #81, Lot 26).

AKRO AGATE COMPANY. Slag. Lot of ten marbles. Three brown, three green, two blue, purple, red. Nice set. 19/32" to 1-1/16". Mint. $70. (Auction #175, Lot 2).

AKRO AGATE COMPANY. Slag. Lot of nineteen marbles. Includes two brown, three green, three purple, two blue, four red, three aqua. $65. (Auction #73, Lot 27).

AKRO AGATE COMPANY. Slag. Green slag. Large. Excellent swirling pattern. Several tiny rough spots, but no chips or flakes. 1-1/4". Near Mint(+) (8.9). $60. (Auction #167, Lot 30).

AKRO AGATE COMPANY. Slag. Early Akro. Orange slag. "True" orange, not a light red. Very hard to find. Super example. 19/32". Mint (9.9). $60. (Auction #182, Lot 12).

AKRO AGATE COMPANY. Slag. Green slag shooter. Nice example. One small sparkle and one tiny pit. Akron, OH, circa 1925-1935. 31/32". Mint(-) (9). $55. (Auction #107, Lot 37).

AKRO AGATE COMPANY. Slag. Lot of three marbles. All are green slags. They are early Akro. All are shooters! $55. (Auction #116, Lot 4).

AKRO AGATE COMPANY. Slag. Large, early slag. I believe this is Akro and not M.F. Christensen, because of the shade of brown. 1-1/4". Mint(-) (9.2). $50. (Auction #107, Lot 24).

AKRO AGATE COMPANY. Slag. Lot of thirteen marbles. All are red slags. Almost all have some minor damage. $50. (Auction #164, Lot 22).

AKRO AGATE COMPANY. Slag. Very early Akro slag. Brown slag. Loads of white in the brown. In great shape. Super pattern. Clarksburg, WV. 1". Mint (9.9). $50. (Auction #124, Lot 43).

AKRO AGATE COMPANY. Slag. I believe that this is a very early Akro Agate slag, and not M.F. Christensen. It exhibits a poor "9". 1-3/16". Mint(-) (9.1). $50. (Auction #110, Lot 43).

AKRO AGATE COMPANY. Slag. Lot of twenty eight marbles. All are Akro slags. Fifteen green, four blue, six purple, a red, a brow. $49. (Auction #181, Lot 28).

AKRO AGATE COMPANY. Slag. Lot of twenty-eight marbles. All are Akro. Nine brown, eight green (one shooter), seven purple. $48. (Auction #159, Lot 21).

AKRO AGATE COMPANY. Slag. Lot of seven marbles. Nice assortment of large slags. Two blue, two brown, two green and a clear. $45. (Auction #120, Lot 23).

AKRO AGATE COMPANY. Slag. Very early Akro slag. Blue slag. Loads of white in the blue. In great shape. Super pattern. Clarksburg, WV. 7/8". Mint (9.9). $42. (Auction #124, Lot 39).

AKRO AGATE COMPANY. Slag. Early red slag shooter. Lazy "9" on the top, cut-off line on side, nice tail. Super coloring. 13/16". Mint (9.9). $41. (Auction #140, Lot 45).

AKRO AGATE COMPANY. Slag. Lot of four marbles. All are red slags. Nice assortment. Real beauties. One has sparkles. 5/8" to 23. $40. (Auction #130, Lot 36).

AKRO AGATE COMPANY. Slag. Lot of twenty marbles. All are Akro slags. Two brown, three purple, five blue, one aqua, four clear. $38. (Auction #106, Lot 22).

AKRO AGATE COMPANY. Slag. Lot of five marbles. Assortment of shooters. Two brown, a purple, a blue, and an Alley Agate. $38. (Auction #95, Lot 10).

AKRO AGATE COMPANY. Slag. Lot of four marbles. All are shooters. Brown, blue, purple, green. Several are early. 25/32", 29/32". $37. (Auction #128, Lot 38).

AKRO AGATE COMPANY. Slag. Lot of four marbles. All are shooter slags. Blue, 7/8", Mint(-) (9.0). Brown, 13/16", Near Mint(+). $37. (Auction #160, Lot 13).

AKRO AGATE COMPANY. Slag. Shooter blue slag. Nice lazy "9" on the top. A small subsurface moon at the bottom. 1-1/8". Near Mint (8.6). $36. (Auction #183, Lot 19).

AKRO AGATE COMPANY. Slag. Nice orange slag. Early Akro marble. Clarksburg, WV, circa 1920-1930. 21/32". Mint (9.9). 21/32". Mint (9.9). $36. (Auction #54, Lot 9).

AKRO AGATE COMPANY. Slag. Large green slag. Some small rough spots, one small flake, a couple of small subsurface moons. 1-1/4". Near Mint (8.6). $36. (Auction #116, Lot 31).

AKRO AGATE COMPANY. Slag. Lot of nineteen marbles. One corkscrew, eighteen slags. Purple, brown, green, blue, clear. $35. (Auction #128, Lot 28).

AKRO AGATE COMPANY. Slag. Shooter slag. Green. Nice "9" on the top. Cutoff line off to the side of the bottom. Some sparkles. 1-3/16". Near Mint (8.5). $33. (Auction #183, Lot 27).

AKRO AGATE COMPANY. Slag. Lot of twenty one marbles. Assortment of slags including brown, blue, green, red, purple. $32. (Auction #157, Lot 40).

AKRO AGATE COMPANY. Slag. Lot of seven marbles. All are Akro slags. Includes two green, two red, two brown, one purple. 19/32". $31. (Auction #172, Lot 19).

AKRO AGATE COMPANY. Slag. Super slag. Blue and white slag. Mostly blue. Very large size of a blue. Has one small flake. 1". Near Mint(+) (8.9). $30. (Auction #58, Lot 19).

AKRO AGATE COMPANY. Slag. Lot of twenty four marbles. Four yellow, two aqua, one red, twelve green, five brown. 5/8" to 11/16". $30. (Auction #108, Lot 16).

AKRO AGATE COMPANY. Slag. Lot of fifteen marbles. All are slags. Seven brown, five blue, one aqua, one green, one red. $30. (Auction #106, Lot 21).

AKRO AGATE COMPANY. Slag. Shooter size Cardinal Red slag. This one is in great shape. Again, hard to find these in this condition. 25/32". Mint (9.5). $30. (Auction #58, Lot 2).

AKRO AGATE COMPANY. Slag. Nice shooter red slag. Clarksburg, WV, circa 1925-1935. 13/16". Mint (9.9). 13/16". Mint (9.9). $30. (Auction #120, Lot 41).

AKRO AGATE COMPANY. Slag. Lot of seven marbles. All are brown slags. Mostly Akro, with a couple of M.F. Christensen. $30. (Auction #133, Lot 3).

AKRO AGATE COMPANY. Slag. Gorgeous red shooter slag. In great shape. Clarksburg, WV, circa 1927-1935. 7/8". Mint (9.9). $30. (Auction #146, Lot 10).

AKRO AGATE COMPANY. Slag. Lot of twenty marbles. Brown, green, purple, blue, yellow, clear. All have some damage. 5/8" to 23/32". $28. (Auction #178, Lot 12).

AKRO AGATE COMPANY. Slag. Shooter brown slag. Nice example. A couple of tiny chips. Lightly buffed. 1-3/16". $28. (Auction #171, Lot 33).

AKRO AGATE COMPANY. Slag. Clear slag. Early Akro. Possibly hand-gathered. "9" on the top with a trailing tail. Two tiny pinpricks. 27/32". Mint(-) (9). $26. (Auction #147, Lot 3).

AKRO AGATE COMPANY. Slag. Brown slag. I believe this is an early Akro, not an M.F. Christensen. Very nice. 1-3/16". Near Mint(+) (8.7). $25. (Auction #123, Lot 41).

AKRO AGATE COMPANY. Slag. Lot of twelve marbles. Two brown, two blue, two purple, two green, two red (both Mint), an aqua. $25. (Auction #169, Lot 5).

AKRO AGATE COMPANY. Slag. Lot of six marbles. Five are Akro, one is Christensen Agate. Akros are yellow, green and three brown. $25. (Auction #144, Lot 20).

AKRO AGATE COMPANY. Slag. Orange slag. Very early example. Almost completely white. One tiny airhole and one tiny subsurface moons. 11/16". Near Mint(+) (8.9). $24. (Auction #65, Lot 13).

AKRO AGATE COMPANY. Slag. Lot of six marbles. Assortment of purple slags. Assorted sizes. 19/32" to 7/8". Mint (9.9) to Near Mint. $24. (Auction #111, Lot 13).

AKRO AGATE COMPANY. Slag. Lot of five marbles. All are early Akro slags. Three brown, one green, one blue. 19/32" to 23/32". $23. (Auction #147, Lot 16).

AKRO AGATE COMPANY. Slag. Lot of eight marbles. Nice assortment of Akro slags (one M.F. Christensen). Two blue, two purple. $22. (Auction #141, Lot 5).

AKRO AGATE COMPANY. Slag. Orange slag. Very early example. Almost completely white. Shooter size. Has some sparkles. 27/32". Near Mint(+) (8.7). $21. (Auction #65, Lot 5).

AKRO AGATE COMPANY. Slag. Very early brown slag. I believe this is Akro and not M.F. Christensen because of the lack of a seam. 7/8". Mint(-) (9.1). $21. (Auction #90, Lot 8).

AKRO AGATE COMPANY. Slag. Lot of five marbles. All are brown slags. 19/32" to 13/16". Mint (9.9) to Near Mint(+) (8.9). $20. (Auction #129, Lot 1).

AKRO AGATE COMPANY. Slag. Purple slag. Excellent, large shooter. Clarksburg, WV, circa 1925-1935. 29/32". Mint (9.7). 29/32". Mint (9.7). $20. (Auction #167, Lot 18).

AKRO AGATE COMPANY. Slag. Lot of four marbles. All are shooter slags. Two green, one purple, one blue. All about 7/8". All Near Mint. $18. (Auction #139, Lot 8).

AKRO AGATE COMPANY. Slag. Lot of two marbles. Both are shooter slags. Early slags. First is brown. "Seedy" glass. $17. (Auction #181, Lot 16).

AKRO AGATE COMPANY. Slag. Lot of thiry one marbles. Ten brown, six green, five purple, four aqua, two red, two yellow. $17. (Auction #171, Lot 30).

AKRO AGATE COMPANY. Slag. Lot of fourteen marbles. All are Akro slags. Five purple, five red, two blue, one green, one yellow. $17. (Auction #161, Lot 24).

AKRO AGATE COMPANY. Slag. Green slag. Nice "9" on the top. Not a lot of white in this one. Has one tiny chip. Clarksburg, WV. 13/16". Near Mint(+) (8.9). $17. (Auction #148, Lot 10).

AKRO AGATE COMPANY. Slag. Lot of four slags. All beautiful Akros. Brown, purple, green, red. 5/8" to 11/16". Mint (9.9). $17. (Auction #122, Lot 34).

AKRO AGATE COMPANY. Slag. Yellow slag. Very fluorescent. Two barely visible subsurface moon. Clarksburg, WV, circa 1925-1935. 2. 23/32". Near Mint(+) (8.9). $17. (Auction #64, Lot 8).

AKRO AGATE COMPANY. Slag. Red slag. Very nice, early one. Lots of white blankets on the surface. One tiny sparkle. Clarksburg, WV. 5/8". Mint(-) (9.1). $16. (Auction #100, Lot 29).

AKRO AGATE COMPANY. Slag. Lot of six marbles. Three green (one small one has sparkles), two red (smaller has haziness). $16. (Auction #97, Lot 18).

AKRO AGATE COMPANY. Slag. Large clear slag. It is almost impossible to find clear ones this large. Numerous subsurface moons. 1-3/16". Good(+) (7.70). $14. (Auction #75, Lot 14).

AKRO AGATE COMPANY. Slag. Early Akro slag. Very light lavender and white. A couple of sparkles. Clarksburg, WV, circa 1922-1927. 21/32". Near Mint(+) (8.9). $14. (Auction #134, Lot 4).

AKRO AGATE COMPANY. Slag. Lot of two marbles. The harder to find Akro clear slags. One has a couple of tiny sparkles. 21/32". $14. (Auction #97, Lot 12).

AKRO AGATE COMPANY. Slag. Early Akro aqua slag. In great shape. Clarksburg, WV, circa 1925-1930. 21/32". Mint (9.9). $13. (Auction #110, Lot 2).

AKRO AGATE COMPANY. Slag. Lot of five marbles. One red slag, three orange slags, one Vitro Agate patch. Two slags are Mint. $11. (Auction #125, Lot 9).

AKRO AGATE COMPANY. Slag. Lot of nine marbles. All are earlier slags. Four red, One orange, one blue, one green, one purple. $11. (Auction #146, Lot 31).

AKRO AGATE COMPANY. Slag. Clear slag. Super example. Clarksburg, WV, circa 1922-1927. 11/16". Mint (9.9). $11. (Auction #156, Lot 22).

AKRO AGATE COMPANY. Slag. Lot of three marbles. All are green slags. Three different sizes. 15/16" & Mint(-) (9.0), 13/16" & Mint. $9. (Auction #165, Lot 1).

AKRO AGATE COMPANY. Slag. Lot of two marbles. Both are clear slags. One has a tiny subsurface moon. Clarksburg, WV, circa 1925. $9. (Auction #69, Lot 6).

AKRO AGATE COMPANY. Slag. Lot of two marbles. Both are early Akro slags. Green. Poor "9"s. Minor cutoff type lines on the side. $8. (Auction #75, Lot 1).

AKRO AGATE COMPANY. Slag. Lot of two marbles. Both are shooter slags. One blue, one brown. 1-1/16". Good(+) (7.9). $7. (Auction #180, Lot 2).

AKRO AGATE COMPANY. Slag. Lot of three marbles. All are Akro. Two are aqua and one is red. One of the aqua has some hits. $7. (Auction #149, Lot 5).

AKRO AGATE COMPANY. Slag. Very early Akro clear slag. The glass was too cool when the marble was made, so there is folding. 3/4". Mint (9.5). $5. (Auction #81, Lot 14).

AKRO AGATE COMPANY. Snake corkscrew. Lot of five marbles. Transparent dark brown base with an opaque yellow snake on the surface. Nice se. $70. (Auction #78, Lot 25).

AKRO AGATE COMPANY. Snake corkscrew. Lot of five marbles. All the same color. Great for a line in a tin or box. Transparent bubble-filled. $44. (Auction #138, Lot 14).

AKRO AGATE COMPANY. Snake corkscrew. Transparent cobalt blue base with a triple twist opaque white snake going just below the surface. 25/32". Mint(-) (8.9). $42. (Auction #129, Lot 7).

AKRO AGATE COMPANY. Snake corkscrew. Unusual example. Transparent cherry red base. Wide snake of opaque white. Narrow snake of orange rig. 5/8". Mint (9.9). $39. (Auction #137, Lot 42).

AKRO AGATE COMPANY. Snake corkscrew. Very oddly colored marble. Translucent milky white base. There is a translucent powder blue spiral. 21/32". Mint (9.7). $30. (Auction #76, Lot 26).

AKRO AGATE COMPANY. Snake corkscrew. Transparent dark brown core with a thin opaque yellow spiral on the surface. Clarksburg, WV. 19/32". Mint (9.9). $22. (Auction #76, Lot 37).

AKRO AGATE COMPANY. Snake corkscrew. Lot of two marbles. Both are transparent light brown base. One has an opaque white snake. $19. (Auction #80, Lot 18).

AKRO AGATE COMPANY. Snake corkscrew. Transparent brown with a thin double twisted opaque yellow snake. In great shape. Clarksburg, WV. 5/8". Mint (9.9). $15. (Auction #61, Lot 12).

AKRO AGATE COMPANY. Snake corkscrew. Lot of four marbles. All are snake corkscrew. Two white on clear, one light blue on clear. $14. (Auction #100, Lot 1).

AKRO AGATE COMPANY. Snake corkscrew. Transparent clear base with blue snake. Clarksburg, WV, circa 1928-1935. 5/8". Mint (9.9). $13. (Auction #157, Lot 14.20).

AKRO AGATE COMPANY. Snake corkscrew. Transparent clear base with blue snake. Clarksburg, WV, circa 1928-1935. 5/8". Mint (9.9). $13. (Auction #157, Lot 14.30).

AKRO AGATE COMPANY. Snake corkscrew. Transparent clear base with blue snake. Clarksburg, WV, circa 1928-1935. 5/8". Mint (9.9). $13. (Auction #157, Lot 14).

AKRO AGATE COMPANY. Snake corkscrew. Transparent clear base. Snake of green on the surface, with a thin snake of wispy white. 5/8". Mint(-) (9). $11. (Auction #130, Lot 12).

AKRO AGATE COMPANY. Snake corkscrew. Gorgeous snake. Transparent very fluorescent vaseline yellow base. Double twist opaque white snake. 21/32". Mint (9.9). $10. (Auction #68, Lot 1).

AKRO AGATE COMPANY. Sparkler. A beauty!!! Blue, yellow, white, brown and green in the core. In great shape. Clarksburg, WV. 11/16". Mint (9.9). $50. (Auction #96, Lot 5).

AKRO AGATE COMPANY. Sparkler. Nice coloring. Lots of white. In great shape. Clarksburg, WV, circa 1925-1935. 5/8". Mint (9.9). $50. (Auction #141, Lot 12).

AKRO AGATE COMPANY. Sparkler. Beautiful example. Lots of color. One tiny pit. 5/8". Mint (9.0). $44. (Auction #111, Lot 10).

AKRO AGATE COMPANY. Sparkler. Nice example of a Sparkler. Transparent clear with wispy white, yellow, green, blue, orange and red. 5/8". Near Mint(+) (8.9). $43. (Auction #63, Lot 31).

AKRO AGATE COMPANY. Sparkler. Nice sparkler. Blue, green, red, yellow and white in the core. The surface has some wispy white. 9/16". Mint (9.9). $42. (Auction #81, Lot 29).

AKRO AGATE COMPANY. Sparkler. An Akro Sparkler shooter. Very hard to find shooter Sparklers. Transparent clear base. Wisps of white. 3/4". Near Mint(+) (8.9). $42. (Auction #59, Lot 20).

AKRO AGATE COMPANY. Sparkler. Excellent Sparkler. Nice coloring. Has some wispy white on the exterior, but not opalescent. 21/32". Mint (9.8). $40. (Auction #138, Lot 13).

AKRO AGATE COMPANY. Sparkler. Unusual opalescent Sparkler. Translucent opalescent base glass with colored interior bands. 21/32". Mint (9.9). $40. (Auction #56, Lot 7).

AKRO AGATE COMPANY. Sparkler. Excellent Sparkler. Great coloring. Outstanding pattern and coloring. Small subsurface moon. Clarksburg, WV. 19/32". Near Mint(+) (8.9). $40. (Auction #181, Lot 20).

AKRO AGATE COMPANY. Sparkler. Excellent example. Blue, green, red, brown and white. Beautiful. Clarksburg, WV, circa 1925-1935. 5/8". Mint (9.9). $38. (Auction #103, Lot 7).

AKRO AGATE COMPANY. Sparkler. Nice sparkler. Great color in the interior. Surface has very light wispy white on it. In great shape. 21/32". Mint (9.9). $37. (Auction #58, Lot 15).

AKRO AGATE COMPANY. Sparkler. Gorgeous little Sparkler. Almost completely filled by red, orange, blue, brown and white. 9/16". Mint(-) (9). $35. (Auction #65, Lot 33).

AKRO AGATE COMPANY. Sparkler. Excellent Sparkler. Great coloring. Has some wispy white on the exterior, but not opalescent. 21/32". Mint (9.8). $35. (Auction #57, Lot 2).

AKRO AGATE COMPANY. Sparkler. Nice sparkler. Blue, green, red, yellow and white in the core. The surface has wispy white on it. 9/16". Mint (9.9). $35. (Auction #80, Lot 37).

AKRO AGATE COMPANY. Sparkler. Nice coloring. Little white. Slightly flat near the bottom on one side. Clarksburg, WV, circa 1925-19. 5/8". Mint (9.8). $32. (Auction #156, Lot 6).

AKRO AGATE COMPANY. Sparkler. Core of white, yellow, black, brown, light blue. One tiny subsurface moon. Clarksburg, WV, circa 1925. 5/8". Near Mint(+) (8.9). $32. (Auction #84, Lot 3).

AKRO AGATE COMPANY. Sparkler. Super colors on this one. Almost completely filled with color. Very little clear showing. Has a tiny. 5/8". Near Mint(+) (8.9). $26. (Auction #57, Lot 9).

AKRO AGATE COMPANY. Sparkler. Very nice example. Nice coloring. Small flat spot, small annealing fracture and two sparkles. Clarksburg, WV. 5/8". Near Mint (8.6). $23. (Auction #76, Lot 8).

AKRO AGATE COMPANY. Sparkler. Transparent clear base. Lots of white, some color. Has a few tiny chips and pits on it. Clarksburg, WV. 11/16". Near Mint (8.6). $21. (Auction #171, Lot 2).

AKRO AGATE COMPANY. Sparkler. Very nice with a variety of colors in the core. A tiny pit and a small rough spot on the surface. 5/8". Near Mint(+) (8.9). $17. (Auction #167, Lot 34).

AKRO AGATE COMPANY. Sparkler. Nice example. White, yellow, green and brown in transparent clear. One tiny annealing fracture. Clarksburg, WV. 21/32". Near Mint(+) (8.9). $17. (Auction #61, Lot 19).

AKRO AGATE COMPANY. Sparkler. Coloring on one side of the marble. White, green, yellow, brown, black. A couple of tiny chips. 11/16". Near Mint (8.5). $14. (Auction #162, Lot 4).

AKRO AGATE COMPANY. Sparkler. Nice coloring. Lots of white. Slightly flat near the bottom on one side. Clarksburg, WV, circa 1925. 5/8". Mint (9.8). $12. (Auction #90, Lot 1).

AKRO AGATE COMPANY. Swirl. Very unusual marble. This is a four color. Rare, you almost always see this type in three colors. 7/8". Near Mint (8.6). $50. (Auction #84, Lot 21.30).

AKRO AGATE COMPANY. Swirl. Very unusual marble. This is a four color. Rare, you almost always see this type in three colors. 7/8". Near Mint (8.6). $50. (Auction #84, Lot 21).

AKRO AGATE COMPANY. Swirl. Very unusual marble. This is a four color. Rare, you almost always see this type in three colors. 7/8". Near Mint (8.6). $50. (Auction #84, Lot 21.20).

AKRO AGATE COMPANY. Swirl. Lot of two marbles. Excellent pair of three-color swirls. Each is translucent milky white. $50. (Auction #103, Lot 18).

AKRO AGATE COMPANY. Swirl. Very unusual shooter swirl. I have never seen this one before. Probably experimental. 15/16". Near Mint(+) (8.7). $49. (Auction #137, Lot 38).

AKRO AGATE COMPANY. Swirl. Tri-color swirl shooter. Translucent milky white base. Swirls of trnaslucent dark blue. 1". Mint(-) (9). $49. (Auction #139, Lot 47).

AKRO AGATE COMPANY. Swirl. Lot of two marbles. Both are translucent milky white base. Swirls of translucent blue and opaque egg yolk. $45. (Auction #179, Lot 33).

AKRO AGATE COMPANY. Swirl. "Tomato Soup" swirl. Milky white, opaque white, translucent red. Not fluorescent. 5/8". Mint (9.9). $27. (Auction #121, Lot 13).

AKRO AGATE COMPANY. Swirl. Lot of two marbles. Both are tri-color swirl. Translucent milky base. Translucent dark blue swirl. $20. (Auction #62, Lot 33).

AKRO AGATE COMPANY. Swirl. Tri-color swirl. Translucent milky white, translucent dark blue and opaque egg yolk yellow. 19/32". Mint(-) (9). $14. (Auction #82, Lot 14).

AKRO AGATE COMPANY. Swirl oxblood. Opaque white base about half covered by oxblood. A beauty. 19/32." Mint (9.9). $50. (Auction #111, Lot 23).

AKRO AGATE COMPANY. Swirl oxblood. Opaque white base with a very nice oxblood swirl. Super marble. Clarksburg, WV, circa 1930-1940. 19/3. 19/32". Mint (9.9). $41. (Auction #173, Lot 17).

AKRO AGATE COMPANY. Swirl oxblood. Opaque white base. Nice oxblood swirl on one side of it. 5/8". Mint (9.9). $41. (Auction #117, Lot 13).

AKRO AGATE COMPANY. Swirl oxblood. Very unusual swirl oxblood. Base is opaque white with transparent green and clear swirl. 5/8". Mint (9.9). $40. (Auction #74, Lot 11.20).

AKRO AGATE COMPANY. Swirl oxblood. Very unusual swirl oxblood. Base is opaque white with transparent green and clear swirl. 5/8". Mint (9.9). $40. (Auction #74, Lot 11).

AKRO AGATE COMPANY. Swirl oxblood. Opaque white base. About one quarter covered with rich oxblood. Clarksburg, WV, circa 1930-1940. 19/32". Mint (9.9). $40. (Auction #116, Lot 33).

AKRO AGATE COMPANY. Swirl oxblood. Opaque white base with a nice oxblood swirl on it. Clarksburg, WV, circa 1930-1940. 21/32". Mint (9.7. 21/32". Mint (9.7). $40. (Auction #55, Lot 14).

AKRO AGATE COMPANY. Swirl oxblood. Opaque white base with a very nice oxblood swirl. Super marble. Clarksburg, WV, circa 1930-1940. 19/32". Mint (9.9). $39. (Auction #173, Lot 17.20).

AKRO AGATE COMPANY. Swirl oxblood. Superior example. Opaque white base with exceptional swirling on half of the marble. In great shape. 5/8". Mint (9.9). $35. (Auction #156, Lot 14).

AKRO AGATE COMPANY. Swirl oxblood. Opaque white base. Very dark, rich oxblood. Really nice marble. Clarksburg, WV, circa 1930-1940. 19/32". Mint (9.9). $34. (Auction #58, Lot 36).

AKRO AGATE COMPANY. Swirl oxblood. Opaque white base with a nice swirl of oxblood on about half the surface. Clarksburg, WV, circa 1930. 5/8". Mint (9.9). $34. (Auction #119, Lot 10).

AKRO AGATE COMPANY. Swirl oxblood. Superior example. Opaque white base with exceptional swirling on most of the marble. In great shape. 5/8". Mint (9.9). $32. (Auction #121, Lot 2).

AKRO AGATE COMPANY. Swirl oxblood. Opaque white base. Excellent oxblood swirl. Clarksburg, WV, circa 1930-1940. 5/8". Mint (9.9). $32. (Auction #59, Lot 10).

AKRO AGATE COMPANY. Swirl oxblood. Opaque white. Thin oxblood swirls. Clarksburg, WV, circa 1930-1940. 19/32." Mint (9.9). $32. (Auction #137, Lot 20).

AKRO AGATE COMPANY. Swirl oxblood. Opaque white base with nice rich oxblood swirled on one side of it. Clarksburg, WV, circa 1930-1940. 19/32". Mint (9.9). $30. (Auction #103, Lot 44).

AKRO AGATE COMPANY. Swirl oxblood. Opaque white base. Three oxblood ribbons on it. In great shape. Clarksburg, WV, circa 1930-1935. 5/8". Mint (9.9). $29. (Auction #161, Lot 2).

AKRO AGATE COMPANY. Swirl oxblood. Opaque white base with swirls of oxblood. Very nice. Clarksburg, WV, circa 1930-1935. 5/8". Mint (9.9). $28. (Auction #177, Lot 47.20).

AKRO AGATE COMPANY. Swirl oxblood. Opaque white base with swirls of oxblood. Very nice. Clarksburg, WV, circa 1930-1935. 5/8". Mint (9.9). $28. (Auction #177, Lot 47).

AKRO AGATE COMPANY. Swirl oxblood. Very nice example. Opaque white base with nice oxblood swirling on most of the marble. 5/8". Mint (9.9). $28. (Auction #145, Lot 15).

AKRO AGATE COMPANY. Swirl oxblood. Opaque white base with swirls of oxblood. Very nice. Clarksburg, WV, circa 1930-1935. 5/8". Mint (9.9). $28. (Auction #172, Lot 4.20).

AKRO AGATE COMPANY. Swirl oxblood. Opaque white base with swirls of oxblood. Very nice. Clarksburg, WV, circa 1930-1935. 19/32". Mint (9.9). $27. (Auction #184, Lot 5).

AKRO AGATE COMPANY. Swirl oxblood. Opaque white base. Nice, rich oxblood swirl on one side. A beauty. Clarksburg, WV, circa 1930-1935. 5/8". Mint (9.9). $27. (Auction #170, Lot 9).

AKRO AGATE COMPANY. Swirl oxblood. Opaque white base with swirls of oxblood. Very nice. Clarksburg, WV, circa 1930-1935. 19/32". Mint (9.9). $27. (Auction #184, Lot 5.20).

AKRO AGATE COMPANY. Swirl oxblood. Opaque white base with swirls of oxblood. Very nice. Clarksburg, WV, circa 1930-1935. 5/8". Mint (9.9). $27. (Auction #176, Lot 11).

AKRO AGATE COMPANY. Swirl oxblood. Opaque white base with rich swirl of oxblood. Very nice. Clarksburg, WV, circa 1930-1935. 5/8". Mint (9.9). $27. (Auction #167, Lot 20).

AKRO AGATE COMPANY. Swirl oxblood. Opaque white. Thin oxblood swirls. Clarksburg, WV, circa 1930-1940. 5/8". Mint (9.9). $26. (Auction #88, Lot 3).

AKRO AGATE COMPANY. Swirl oxblood. Beautiful example. Opaque white base with exceptional swirling on one side of the marble. 5/8". Mint (9.9). $26. (Auction #150, Lot 14).

AKRO AGATE COMPANY. Swirl oxblood. Opaque white base with swirls of oxblood. Very nice. Clarksburg, WV, circa 1930-1935. 5/8". Mint (9.9). $26. (Auction #177, Lot 47.30).

AKRO AGATE COMPANY. Swirl oxblood. Opaque white base with swirls of oxblood. Very nice. Clarksburg, WV, circa 1930-1935. 5/8". Mint (9.9). $25. (Auction #164, Lot 1).

AKRO AGATE COMPANY. Swirl oxblood. Opaque white base with swirls of oxblood. Very nice. Clarksburg, WV, circa 1930-1935. 5/8". Mint (9.9). $25. (Auction #164, Lot 1.20).

AKRO AGATE COMPANY. Swirl oxblood. Opaque white base. Nice, rich oxblood swirl on one side. A beauty. Clarksburg, WV, circa 1930-1935. 5/8". Mint (9.9). $25. (Auction #170, Lot 9.20).

AKRO AGATE COMPANY. Swirl oxblood. Opaque white base with swirls of oxblood. Very nice. Clarksburg, WV, circa 1930-1935. 5/8". Mint (9.9). $25. (Auction #164, Lot 1.30).

AKRO AGATE COMPANY. Swirl oxblood. Opaque white base with swirls of oxblood. Very nice. Clarksburg, WV, circa 1930-1935. 5/8". Mint (9.9). $25. (Auction #172, Lot 4).

AKRO AGATE COMPANY. Swirl oxblood. Opaque white base with swirls of oxblood. Very nice. Clarksburg, WV, circa 1930-1935. 5/8". Mint (9.9). $24. (Auction #172, Lot 4.30).

AKRO AGATE COMPANY. Swirl oxblood. Opaque white. Thin oxblood swirls. Clarksburg, WV, circa 1930-1940. 5/8". Mint (9.9). 5/8". Mint (9.9). $24. (Auction #88, Lot 3.20).

AKRO AGATE COMPANY. Swirl oxblood. Opaque white base with a very nice oxblood swirl. Super marble. Clarksburg, WV, circa 1930-1940. 19/32". Mint (9.9). $23. (Auction #77, Lot 4).

AKRO AGATE COMPANY. Swirl oxblood. Nice example. Opaque white base with swirls of oxblood on one side of the marble. In great shape. 5/8". Mint (9.9). $23. (Auction #152, Lot 11).

AKRO AGATE COMPANY. Swirl oxblood. Opaque white base. About one-third covered by rich, dark, oxblood. In great shape. Clarksburg, WV. 5/8". Mint (9.9). $23. (Auction #100, Lot 14).

AKRO AGATE COMPANY. Swirl oxblood. Opaque white base with oxblood swirling. Nice marble. Clarksburg, WV, circa 1930-1940. 19/32". Mint (. 19/32". Mint (9.9). $22. (Auction #123, Lot 47.20).

AKRO AGATE COMPANY. Swirl oxblood. Opaque white base. Nice, rich oxblood swirl on one side. A beauty. Clarksburg, WV, circa 1930-1935. 5/8". Mint (9.9). $22. (Auction #170, Lot 9.30).

AKRO AGATE COMPANY. Swirl oxblood. Opaque white base with oxblood swirling. Nice marble. Clarksburg, WV, circa 1930-1940. 19/32". Mint (9.9). $22. (Auction #123, Lot 47).

AKRO AGATE COMPANY. Swirl oxblood. Opaque white base with thin oxblood swirls. Clarksburg, WV, circa 1930-1935. 5/8". Mint (9.9). $19. (Auction #125, Lot 7).

AKRO AGATE COMPANY. Swirl oxblood. Lot of two marbles. Both opaque white with thin swirls of oxblood. Each has a few tiny pits. $19. (Auction #149, Lot 2).

AKRO AGATE COMPANY. Swirl oxblood. Opaque white base with narrow oxblood swirls on it. Clarksburg, WV, circa 1930-1935. 5/8". Mint (9.9). $19. (Auction #163, Lot 35).

AKRO AGATE COMPANY. Swirl oxblood. Lot of two marbls. Opaque white base with oxblood swirls. Both have some damage. 5/8". Near Mint. $18. (Auction #123, Lot 7).

AKRO AGATE COMPANY. Swirl oxblood. Opaque white base with a very nice oxblood swirl. Super marble. Clarksburg, WV, circa 1930-1940. 19/32". Mint (9.9). $18. (Auction #182, Lot 23).

AKRO AGATE COMPANY. Swirl oxblood. Very nice example. Opaque white base with exceptional swirling on one side of the marble. 5/8". Mint (9.9). $17. (Auction #154, Lot 40).

AKRO AGATE COMPANY. Swirl oxblood. Opaque white base with narrow oxblood swirls on it. Clarksburg, WV, circa 1930-1935. 5/8". Mint (9.9). $17. (Auction #163, Lot 35.30).

AKRO AGATE COMPANY. Swirl oxblood. Opaque white base with narrow oxblood swirls on it. Clarksburg, WV, circa 1930-1935. 5/8". Mint (9.9). $17. (Auction #163, Lot 35.20).

AKRO AGATE COMPANY. Swirl oxblood. Opaque white base. Wide swirl of oxblood in a patch pattern on just half the marble. 3/4". Near Mint (8.3). $17. (Auction #141, Lot 33).

AKRO AGATE COMPANY. Swirl oxblood. Opaque white base with oxblood swirls on one side of the marble. In great shape. Clarksburg, WV. 5/8". Mint (9.9). $16. (Auction #118, Lot 7).

AKRO AGATE COMPANY. Swirl oxblood. Opaque white base with a very nice oxblood swirl. Super marble. Clarksburg, WV, circa 1930-1940. 19/32". Mint (9.9). $16. (Auction #182, Lot 23.20).

AKRO AGATE COMPANY. Swirl oxblood. Opaque white base with thin oxblood swirls. Some tiny roughness on it. Clarksburg, WV, circa 1930. 9/16". Near Mint(+) (8.7). $12. (Auction #87, Lot 14).

AKRO AGATE COMPANY. Swirl oxblood. Opaque white base. Thin swirls of oxblood. One pinprick and one sparkle. Clarksburg, WV, circa 1930. 5/8". Mint(-) (9). $12. (Auction #148, Lot 7).

AKRO AGATE COMPANY. Swirl oxblood. Semi-opaque white base with loads of oxblood swirls on it. Super oxblood. Great looking marble. 5/8". Near Mint(+) (8.9). $11. (Auction #109, Lot 39).

CHRISTENSEN AGATE COMPANY. American Agate. Large size. Electric red swirled in semi-opaque white. Mostly red. Beautiful. 13/16". Near Mint (8.6). $50. (Auction #182, Lot 8).

CHRISTENSEN AGATE COMPANY. American Agate. Beautiful example of a small American Agate. Semi-opaque white and electric red swirled. 19/32". Mint (9.7). $50. (Auction #169, Lot 43).

CHRISTENSEN AGATE COMPANY. American Agate. Beautiful American Agate. Opaque white with electric red swirls. Probably hand-gathered. 23/32". Mint (9.9). $42. (Auction #119, Lot 44).

CHRISTENSEN AGATE COMPANY. American Agate. Electric red swirled in semi-opaque white. Cambridge, OH, circa 1927-1929. 23/32". Mint (9.9). $38. (Auction #138, Lot 9).

CHRISTENSEN AGATE COMPANY. American Agate. Small American Agate. Almost all electric red, with just a bit of translucent white. 17/32". Mint(-) (9.2). $35. (Auction #80, Lot 8).

CHRISTENSEN AGATE COMPANY. American Agate. Exceptional example. Electric red swirled in semi-opaque white. Cambridge, OH, circa 1927-1929. 5/8". Mint (9.9). $30. (Auction #55, Lot 4).

CHRISTENSEN AGATE COMPANY. American Agate. Super example. Predominately electric red with some translucent white mixed in. In great shape. Cambridge, OH. 11/16". Mint (9.9). $30. (Auction #121, Lot 18).

CHRISTENSEN AGATE COMPANY. American Agate. Very nice example. Electric red swirled in semi-opaque white. Probably hand-gathered. 23/32. Mint (9.5). $27. (Auction #152, Lot 42).

CHRISTENSEN AGATE COMPANY. American Agate. Nice example. Electric red swirled in semi-opaque white. Light pitting. Cambridge, OH, circa 1927. 11/16". Near Mint (8.6). $18. (Auction #128, Lot 44).

CHRISTENSEN AGATE COMPANY. Assorted. Lot of two marbles. First is an electric yellow slag, 19/32", Near Mint (8.4). $32. (Auction #84, Lot 26).

CHRISTENSEN AGATE COMPANY. Assorted. Lot of four marbles. A three-color swirl, two two-color swirls, one electrice striped opaque. $25. (Auction #175, Lot 8).

CHRISTENSEN AGATE COMPANY. Assorted. Lot of three marbles. All are Christensen Agate swirls. Three different colors and patterns. $24. (Auction #158, Lot 13).

CHRISTENSEN AGATE COMPANY. Bloodie. Super Bloodie. Opaque white base with swirls of transparent blood red and some translucent brown. 21/32". Mint (9.9). $90. (Auction #93, Lot 33).

CHRISTENSEN AGATE COMPANY. Bloodie. Nice Bloodie. Opaque white base with swirls of transparent blood red and some translucent brown. 21/32". Mint (9.9). $71. (Auction #148, Lot 34).

CHRISTENSEN AGATE COMPANY. Bloodie. Nice Bloodie. Opaque white base with swirls of transparent blood red and some translucent brown. 21/32". Near Mint(+) (8.9). $41. (Auction #184, Lot 22).

CHRISTENSEN AGATE COMPANY. Cobra. Transparent clear base with electric yellow and lavender stretched flakes. $105. (Auction #71, Lot 38).

CHRISTENSEN AGATE COMPANY. Diaper fold swirl. Transparent clear base. Some swirls of bright white in the marble. One seam. Diaper fold

example. 5/8". Mint (9.9). $70. (Auction #169, Lot 21).
CHRISTENSEN AGATE COMPANY. **Diaper fold swirl.** Transparent clear base. Some swirls of bright white in the marble. One seam. Diaper fold example. 5/8". Mint (9.9). $29. (Auction #107, Lot 43).
CHRISTENSEN AGATE COMPANY. **Electric slag.** Hard to find electric yellow slag. Transparent electric yellow base with opaque white swirls. 19/32". Mint(-) (9). $50. (Auction #173, Lot 45).
CHRISTENSEN AGATE COMPANY. **Flame Bloodie.** Very hard to find Bloodie exhibiting a Flame Swirl pattern. Opaque white base. Swirls of transparent. 5/8". Mint (9.9). $200. (Auction #74, Lot 16).
CHRISTENSEN AGATE COMPANY. **Flame swirl.** Three color flame swirl. Outstanding example. Opaque light blue base. Dull red and gray/black swirls. 19/32". Mint (9.8). $320. (Auction #159, Lot 48).
CHRISTENSEN AGATE COMPANY. **Flame swirl.** Three color flame swirl. Opaque white base. Swirls of orange edged by light salmon. 21/32". Mint (9.9). $130. (Auction #129, Lot 46).
CHRISTENSEN AGATE COMPANY. **Flame swirl.** Nice example!! Orange and salmon swirls and flames on white. Excellent design. 5/8". Mint (9.9). $120. (Auction #152, Lot 46).
CHRISTENSEN AGATE COMPANY. **Flame swirl.** Gorgeous Flame swirl, in great shape. Orange swirls and flames on opaque yellow. 5/8". Mint (9.5). $120. (Auction #57, Lot 43).
CHRISTENSEN AGATE COMPANY. **Flame swirl.** Christensen Agate Flame. Dark orange swirls and flames on opaque white. 21/32". Mint (9.8). $110. (Auction #124, Lot 33).
CHRISTENSEN AGATE COMPANY. **Flame swirl.** Beautiful flame swirl. Opaque pink/white base. Completely covered by lavender and yellow swirls. 19/32". Near Mint(-) (8.7). $90. (Auction #143, Lot 43).
CHRISTENSEN AGATE COMPANY. **Flame swirl.** Very nice flame. Orange swirls and flames on yellow. About a dozen flame tips. 5/8". Near Mint(+) (8.7). $80. (Auction #104, Lot 36).
CHRISTENSEN AGATE COMPANY. **Flame swirl.** Nice example!! Orange swirls and flames on white. Excellent design. One very tiny flake. 5/8". Near Mint (8.6). $80. (Auction #55, Lot 8).
CHRISTENSEN AGATE COMPANY. **Flame swirl.** Outstanding flame swirl. Opaque white base with orange swirls. About ten flame tips. Some sparkles. 21/32". Mint(-) (9). $75. (Auction #98, Lot 48).
CHRISTENSEN AGATE COMPANY. **Flame swirl.** Very nice flame. Orange swirls and flames on yellow. About a dozen flame tips. 5/8". Mint(-) (9). $60. (Auction #54, Lot 43).
CHRISTENSEN AGATE COMPANY. **Flame swirl.** Very nice flame swirl. These are hard to find. Orange swirls on white. About eighteen flame tips. 5/8". Near Mint(+) (8.8). $56. (Auction #113, Lot 15).
CHRISTENSEN AGATE COMPANY. **Flame swirl.** Orange flames and swirls on light green. About a dozen flame tips. Nice swirling. Two moons. 21/32". Near Mint (8.4). $45. (Auction #119, Lot 4).
CHRISTENSEN AGATE COMPANY. **Flame Swirl.** Outstanding example of a Flame Swirl. Brown/gray swirls on light blue. About a dozen flame tips. 19/32". Mint (9.9). $320. (Auction #164, Lot 49).
CHRISTENSEN AGATE COMPANY. **Flame Swirl.** Opaque white base with transparent dark red and opaque mustard yellow swirls. 19/32". Near Mint (8.4). $100. (Auction #163, Lot 11).
CHRISTENSEN AGATE COMPANY. **Guinea.** Authentic Guinea. Blue base. Transparent cobalt blue covered completely by colored flecks. 11/16". Mint (9.9). $450. (Auction #91, Lot 45).
CHRISTENSEN AGATE COMPANY. **Guinea.** Super example. Transparent clear base. Single seam. Open panel opposite that seam. 5/8". Mint (9.9). $440. (Auction #167, Lot 49).
CHRISTENSEN AGATE COMPANY. **Guinea.** Excellent Guinea. Transparent cobalt blue base with stretched light blue, green, white, orange. 9/16". Mint (9.7). $435. (Auction #56, Lot 45).
CHRISTENSEN AGATE COMPANY. **Guinea.** Transparent blue base. Completely covered by flecks of color. Includes light blue, orange, light green. 17/32". Mint (9.9). $400. (Auction #112, Lot 50).
CHRISTENSEN AGATE COMPANY. **Guinea.** Blue base Guinea. Two seam. Has an open panel on about one-third of the marble. Lavender, orange, yellow. 33/64". Mint (9.9). $390. (Auction #78, Lot 42).
CHRISTENSEN AGATE COMPANY. **Guinea.** Super Guinea. Transparent blue base. Single seam. Splotches of yellow, light green, orange, lavender. 5/8". Mint (9.9). $390. (Auction #128, Lot 50).
CHRISTENSEN AGATE COMPANY. **Guinea.** Transparent clear base Guinea. Two seam. Covered with tiny specks of lavender, orange, yellow. 11/16". Mint (9.1). $385. (Auction #185, Lot 44).
CHRISTENSEN AGATE COMPANY. **Guinea.** Gorgeous Guinea. Slightly larger size than typical. Transparent clear base. Stretched flecks of white. 21/32". Mint(-) (9). $380. (Auction #81, Lot 45).
CHRISTENSEN AGATE COMPANY. **Guinea.** Beautiful Guinea. Two seam design. Transparent clear base. Overall coloring of yellow, lavender. 21/32". Mint (9.8). $375. (Auction #183, Lot 49).
CHRISTENSEN AGATE COMPANY. **Guinea.** Transparent clear base. Two seam example. Colored splotches covering about ninety percent of the surface. 21/32". Mint (9.9). $370. (Auction #110, Lot 44).
CHRISTENSEN AGATE COMPANY. **Guinea.** Beautiful Guinea. Two seam design. Transparent clear base. Overall coloring. 21/32". Near Mint(+) (8.9). $350. (Auction #65, Lot 43).
CHRISTENSEN AGATE COMPANY. **Guinea.** Beautiful Guinea. Two seam design. Transparent clear base. Covered with color. Predominately orange. 9/16". Mint (9.9). $345. (Auction #104, Lot 50).
CHRISTENSEN AGATE COMPANY. **Guinea.** A beautiful Guinea. Guaranteed authentic. Transparent clear base. Yellow, light blue, orange, black. 17/32". Mint (9.9). $330. (Auction #71, Lot 45).
CHRISTENSEN AGATE COMPANY. **Guinea.** Transparent clear base. Single seam example. Open panel about ten percent of the surface. 21/32". Mint(-) (9). $330. (Auction #169, Lot 49).
CHRISTENSEN AGATE COMPANY. **Guinea.** Beautiful Guinea. Single seam design. Transparent clear base. Overall coloring. 5/8". Mint(-) (9.1). $325. (Auction #143, Lot 48).
CHRISTENSEN AGATE COMPANY. **Guinea.** Blue base Guinea. Two seams. Completely covered by light green, light blue, electric orange, lavende. 19/32". Mint(-) (9). $315. (Auction #100, Lot 46).
CHRISTENSEN AGATE COMPANY. **Guinea.** Transparent clear base. Flecks of yellow, green, orange, black, lavender and white. One seam. 21/32". Near Mint(+) (8.9). $250. (Auction #115, Lot 50).
CHRISTENSEN AGATE COMPANY. **Guinea/Cobra hybrid.** Rare marble. I've gotta call this a Guinea/Cobra hybrid. Single seam example. 9/16". Mint (9.7). $700. (Auction #85, Lot 44).
CHRISTENSEN AGATE COMPANY. **Handgathered swirl.** A very rare handgathered four color swirl. Pastel colors. White, light blue, darker blue and pink. 23/32". Mint (9.7). $310. (Auction #71, Lot 36).
CHRISTENSEN AGATE COMPANY. **Handgathered swirl.** A very rare handgathered two color swirl. Light lavender with dark lavender swirls. 19/32. Mint (9.7). $155. (Auction #134, Lot 37).
CHRISTENSEN AGATE COMPANY. **Moonie.** Very rare Christensen Agate Company marble. This marble is hand-gathered. Technically, it is a slag. 21/32". Mint (9.3). $180. (Auction #173, Lot 39).
CHRISTENSEN AGATE COMPANY. **Slag.** Rare peach slag. Superior coloring. Gorgeous transparent peach color. Translucent and opaque white. 7/8". Mint(-) (9.2). $320. (Auction #149, Lot 49).
CHRISTENSEN AGATE COMPANY. **Slag.** Very hard to find electric orange slag. Transparent clear base with electric orange swirls in it. 5/8". Mint (9.9). $190. (Auction #128, Lot 48).
CHRISTENSEN AGATE COMPANY. **Slag.** One of the largest Christensen Agate slags I have ever seen. Aqua. Two seam. White brushed on one side. 31/32". Mint (9.9). $160. (Auction #100, Lot 22).
CHRISTENSEN AGATE COMPANY. **Slag.** Electric yellow slag. Hard to find. This is an even harder no seam swirl example. Possibly hand-gathered. 11/16". Mint (9.9). $130. (Auction #140, Lot 49).
CHRISTENSEN AGATE COMPANY. **Slag.** Electric yellow slag. Two seams. Base is transparent electric yellow. Swirls of translucent white. 5/8". Mint (9.9). $90. (Auction #88, Lot 18).
CHRISTENSEN AGATE COMPANY. **Slag.** Shooter yellow slag. In excellent shape. Very hard to find. Transparent dark yellow with opaque white. 27/32". Mint (9.9). $85. (Auction #108, Lot 39).
CHRISTENSEN AGATE COMPANY. **Slag.** Lot of three marbles. All are peewee slags. Very hard to find. Purple, amber (almost yellow) and red. $85. (Auction #150, Lot 17).
CHRISTENSEN AGATE COMPANY. **Slag.** Electric yellow slag. Very hard to find. Transparent electric yellow base. Opaque white swirls. 21/32". Mint (9.6). $80. (Auction #66, Lot 37).
CHRISTENSEN AGATE COMPANY. **Slag.** Lot of three marbles. All are peewee slags. Very hard to find. Purple, amber and orange. 13/32" to 7/16". $80. (Auction #142, Lot 14).
CHRISTENSEN AGATE COMPANY. **Slag.** Lot of three marbles. All are peewee slags. Very hard to find. Purple, amber and red. 13/32" to 7/16". $80. (Auction #166, Lot 45).
CHRISTENSEN AGATE COMPANY. **Slag.** Very hard to find peach slag. This one is a nice shooter size. A beauty, but it has two flakes. 15/16". Near Mint (8.5). $75. (Auction #121, Lot 14).
CHRISTENSEN AGATE COMPANY. **Slag.** Dark yellow slag. Transparent dark yellow base with opaque white swirls. Hard color to find. 7/8". Near Mint (8.8). $72. (Auction #133, Lot 13).
CHRISTENSEN AGATE COMPANY. **Slag.** Electric yellow slag. Hard to find. Single seam example. Possibly hand-gathered. Surface is super. 5/8". Mint (9.9). $70. (Auction #162, Lot 43).
CHRISTENSEN AGATE COMPANY. **Slag.** Electric yellow. Transparent clear base. Two seam. Filled with electric yellow swirls. 19/32". Mint

(9.9). $65. (Auction #170, Lot 34).

CHRISTENSEN AGATE COMPANY. Slag. Lot of three marbles. All are peewee slags. Very hard to find. Purple, amber and red. 13/32" to 7/16". $61. (Auction #139, Lot 6).

CHRISTENSEN AGATE COMPANY. Slag. Peach slag. Shooter size. This is the peach color that is very close to a very light brown. 1-1/16". Near Mint(+) (8.8). $60. (Auction #142, Lot 34).

CHRISTENSEN AGATE COMPANY. Slag. Lot of four marbles. Aqua, 3/4", Near Mint (8.3). Brown, 23/32", Near Mint (8.5). Green, 3/4", Near Mint. $45. (Auction #184, Lot 28).

CHRISTENSEN AGATE COMPANY. Slag. Purple slag. One seam. Peewee. Cambridge, OH, circa 1927-1929. 7/16". Mint (9.9). $42. (Auction #76, Lot 17).

CHRISTENSEN AGATE COMPANY. Slag. Lot of two marbles. Both are peewee slags. One is red and one is purple. Cambridge, OH, circa 1927. $40. (Auction #69, Lot 2).

CHRISTENSEN AGATE COMPANY. Slag. Peewee brown slag. One seam. Hard to find. Cambridge, OH, circa 1927-1929. 7/16". Mint (9.9). $39. (Auction #76, Lot 20).

CHRISTENSEN AGATE COMPANY. Slag. Electric yellow slag. Hard to find. Single seam, exhibiting a small diaper fold on one side. 5/8". Near Mint(+) (8.7). $37. (Auction #161, Lot 46).

CHRISTENSEN AGATE COMPANY. Slag. Red slag. Large one, hard to find. Single seam. Has three large manufacturing melt spots. 31/32". Near Mint (8.5). $37. (Auction #184, Lot 36).

CHRISTENSEN AGATE COMPANY. Slag. Hard to find electric yellow slag. Transparent electric yellow glass with semi-opaque white swirls. 19/32". Near Mint(+) (8.9). $37. (Auction #100, Lot 31).

CHRISTENSEN AGATE COMPANY. Slag. Tiny peewee slag. Yellow. Nice marble. Hard to find. Cambridge, OH, circa 1927-1929. 7/16". Mint (9.9). $35. (Auction #69, Lot 43).

CHRISTENSEN AGATE COMPANY. Slag. Two seam amber slag. Lots of white. Great example. Two seam ones are hard to find. Cambridge, OH. 5/8". Mint (9.9). $34. (Auction #159, Lot 19).

CHRISTENSEN AGATE COMPANY. Slag. Peewee brown slag. One seam. Hard to find. Cambridge, OH, circa 1927-1929. 7/16". Mint (9.9). $30. (Auction #77, Lot 7).

CHRISTENSEN AGATE COMPANY. Slag. Super slag. Light transparent lavender with opaque white swirling. Single seam design. Excellent. 9/16". Mint (9.9). $27. (Auction #140, Lot 9).

CHRISTENSEN AGATE COMPANY. Slag. Lot of two marbles. Both are two seam slags. One is electric yellow. One is light green. $26. (Auction #120, Lot 43).

CHRISTENSEN AGATE COMPANY. Slag. Green slag. Two seam example. Two tiny flakes. Cambridge, OH, circa 1927-1929. 17/32". Near Mint(+) (8.7). $20. (Auction #169, Lot 3).

CHRISTENSEN AGATE COMPANY. Slag. Purple slag. One seam. Peewee. Cambridge, OH, circa 1927-1929. 7/16". Mint (9.9). $20. (Auction #77, Lot 33).

CHRISTENSEN AGATE COMPANY. Slag. Lot of two marbles. Orange slag, two seam, peewee, 15/32", Mint(-) (9.2). Green slag, two seam, 19/32". $20. (Auction #122, Lot 5).

CHRISTENSEN AGATE COMPANY. Slag. Yellow slag. Not electric, but still a very distinctive color. Two seam design. 9/16". Near Mint(+) (8.9). $20. (Auction #184, Lot 7).

CHRISTENSEN AGATE COMPANY. Slag. Lot of two marbles. Electric yellow, single seam, some chips, 5/8", Near Mint (8.6). Red slag. $18. (Auction #104, Lot 5).

CHRISTENSEN AGATE COMPANY. Slag. Peewee purple slag. Two seam. Lots of white on one hemisphere. Hard size to find. Cambridge, OH. 15/32". Mint (9.9). $17. (Auction #66, Lot 30).

CHRISTENSEN AGATE COMPANY. Slag. Lot of three marbles. Green, blue and brown. All have subsurface moons and hits. $15. (Auction #68, Lot 7).

CHRISTENSEN AGATE COMPANY. Slag. Electric yellow slag. Hard to find. This is an even harder two-seam example. One small moon. Cambridge, OH. 5/8". Near Mint (8.6). $12. (Auction #76, Lot 7).

CHRISTENSEN AGATE COMPANY. Slag. Transparent green base. Opaque white on the surface and in the marble. Two seam example. Very nice. 11/16". Mint (9.6). $12. (Auction #150, Lot 37).

CHRISTENSEN AGATE COMPANY. Slag. Lot of two marbles. First is a clear slag. Two seam. Subsurface moon. Very bright. 21/32". Near Mint. $10. (Auction #90, Lot 5).

CHRISTENSEN AGATE COMPANY. Slag. Hard to find peewee fluorescent yellow slag. Transparent yellow/green base. Very fluorescent. Opaque. 1/2". Near Mint(+) (8.9). $10. (Auction #105, Lot 10).

CHRISTENSEN AGATE COMPANY. Slag. Lot of two marbles. Electric yellow, single seam, some chips, 5/8", Near Mint (8.6). $10. (Auction #56, Lot 31).

CHRISTENSEN AGATE COMPANY. Slag. Green slag. Two seam example. Two tiny flakes. Cambridge, OH, circa 1927-1929. 17/32". Near Mint(+) (8.7). $6. (Auction #106, Lot 7).

CHRISTENSEN AGATE COMPANY. Striped opaque. Opaque light blue base. Thin swirls of electric orange with some black. Two seam marble. Cambridge, OH. 5/8". Mint (9.9). $75. (Auction #88, Lot 7).

CHRISTENSEN AGATE COMPANY. Striped opaque. Opaque black base with yellow brushed on one side. Diaper fold pattern. Cambridge, OH, circa 1927-1929. 19/32". Mint (9.9). $60. (Auction #82, Lot 34).

CHRISTENSEN AGATE COMPANY. Striped opaque. Very nice example. Opaque black base with bands and blankets of electric yellow. Single seam. 9/16". Mint (9.9). $50. (Auction #107, Lot 35).

CHRISTENSEN AGATE COMPANY. Striped opaque. Two seam marble. Light blue base with brown/orange bands and swirls covering almost the entire surface. 9/16". Mint (9.9). $47. (Auction #66, Lot 15).

CHRISTENSEN AGATE COMPANY. Striped opaque. Superior electric striped opaque. Bright opaque white base. Electric orange bands and striping. 21/32". Mint (9.9). $45. (Auction #143, Lot 40).

CHRISTENSEN AGATE COMPANY. Striped opaque. Electric yellow striping on opaque black. Super marble. Cambridge, OH, circa 1927-1929. 19/32". Mint . 19/32". Mint (9.9). $40. (Auction #127, Lot 40).

CHRISTENSEN AGATE COMPANY. Striped opaque. Opaque white base with striping of electric orange. Single seam. Very nice example. One very tiny pinprick. 5/8". Mint(-) (9.1). $39. (Auction #148, Lot 45).

CHRISTENSEN AGATE COMPANY. Striped opaque. Two seam example. Opaque light green base. Lots of opaque electric orange bands and blankets. 5/8". Mint (9.9). $38. (Auction #91, Lot 6).

CHRISTENSEN AGATE COMPANY. Striped opaque. Opaque light blue base with electric yellow and green stripes. Two seam example. Odd coloring. Cambridge, OH. 9/16". Mint (9.9). $37. (Auction #98, Lot 16).

CHRISTENSEN AGATE COMPANY. Striped opaque. Poor diaper fold. Bright light blue base with electric orange striping. Two seams. Very nice marble. 19/32". Mint (9.9). $35. (Auction #105, Lot 37).

CHRISTENSEN AGATE COMPANY. Striped opaque. Two seam example. Opaque light green base with some electric orange striping on it. 21/32". Mint (9.9). $32. (Auction #92, Lot 6).

CHRISTENSEN AGATE COMPANY. Striped opaque. Opaque black base with electric yellow bands on one side. Two seam. Very lightly buffed. $30. (Auction #185, Lot 36).

CHRISTENSEN AGATE COMPANY. Striped opaque. Opaque white base. Electric orange stripes. Three tiny pinpricks. Two seam example. Nice one. Cambridge, OH. 21/32". Mint(-) (9). $26. (Auction #98, Lot 30).

CHRISTENSEN AGATE COMPANY. Striped opaque. Lot of two marbles. Both are opaque light blue base with thin gray striping. 19/32" & 5/8". Near Mint. $22. (Auction #115, Lot 37).

CHRISTENSEN AGATE COMPANY. Striped opaque. Electric orange and dark green stripes on opaque light green. Two seam design. Two very tiny flakes. 5/8. Near Mint(+) (8.9). $22. (Auction #60, Lot 20).

CHRISTENSEN AGATE COMPANY. Striped opaque. Electric orange on opaque light green. Two seam design. Several very tiny flakes. Cambridge, OH. 5/8. Near Mint(+) (8.8). $18. (Auction #60, Lot 30).

CHRISTENSEN AGATE COMPANY. Striped opaque. Electric orange striping on one side of a blue base marble. Two seam. Some tiny pitting. 21/32". Near Mint(+) (8.7). $15. (Auction #163, Lot 4).

CHRISTENSEN AGATE COMPANY. Striped opaque. Lot of two marbles. Both are the same coloring. Opaque black base with electric yellow bands on both. $10. (Auction #57, Lot 11).

CHRISTENSEN AGATE COMPANY. Striped opaque. Opaque white base. Two seam. One side has electric orange striping. Large blown out airhole. 19/32". Near Mint(+) (8.8). $5. (Auction #178, Lot 43).

CHRISTENSEN AGATE COMPANY. Striped transparent. Transparent clear base with white brushed on both sides. Two seam design. In great shape. 3/4". Mint (9.9). $47. (Auction #75, Lot 38).

CHRISTENSEN AGATE COMPANY. Striped transparent. An excellent shooter example. In great shape!!! Transparent clear base with white banding. 13/16". Mint (9.9). $41. (Auction #58, Lot 38).

CHRISTENSEN AGATE COMPANY. Striped transparent. Transparent green base. One side has wide bands of opaque white. Three tiny pinpricks. Cambridge, OH. 21/32". Mint(-) (9). $40. (Auction #131, Lot 32).

CHRISTENSEN AGATE COMPANY. Striped transparent. Transparent brown base with opaque white striping on one side. One seam. Super example. 3/4". Mint(-) (9). $40. (Auction #88, Lot 28).

CHRISTENSEN AGATE COMPANY. Striped transparent. Transparent cherry red base. Stripes and blankets of white on most of the surface. Two seam design. 19/32". Mint (9.9). $37. (Auction #149, Lot 45).

CHRISTENSEN AGATE COMPANY. Striped Transparent. Transparent orange base with opaque white bands on both hemispheres. Two seam marble. In nice shape. 5/8". Mint (9.5). $49. (Auction #64, Lot 2).

CHRISTENSEN AGATE COMPANY. Swirl. Very rare hand gathered swirl. This marble is from the same consignor as the pastel blue and pink. 21/32". Mint (9.7). $320. (Auction #78, Lot 45).

CHRISTENSEN AGATE COMPANY. Swirl. A superb three color swirl. Outstanding design to the marble. Opaque black, brown/red and yellow. 5/8". Mint(-) (9.2). $190. (Auction #81, Lot 41).

CHRISTENSEN AGATE COMPANY. Swirl. Very hard to find four-color swirl. Opaque white, yellow, red and brown. Super swirling. 3/4". Near Mint(+) (8.7). $140. (Auction #164, Lot 16).

CHRISTENSEN AGATE COMPANY. Swirl. Two color swirl. Excellent pattern. Yellow and black. Some minor flame tips. Excellent marble. Cambridge, OH. 19/32". Mint (9.9). $130. (Auction #126, Lot 41).

CHRISTENSEN AGATE COMPANY. Swirl. Excellent pattern on this one. Three color. Light blue base completely covered by swirls of yellow. 5/8". Near Mint(+) (8.9). $120. (Auction #92, Lot 32).

CHRISTENSEN AGATE COMPANY. Swirl. Red swirls on two-tone blue. Shooter size. Very rare! Some sparkles. Still, a real beauty. 25/32". Near Mint(+) (8.9). $110. (Auction #184, Lot 44).

CHRISTENSEN AGATE COMPANY. Swirl. Superb swirl, almost a flame. Opaque red, edged in brown, on light blue. Exceptional design. 21/32". Mint (9.5). $110. (Auction #56, Lot 43).

CHRISTENSEN AGATE COMPANY. Swirl. Three color swirl. Nice pattern. Two "turkey heads" on it. Yellow base with red swirl. 5/8". Near Mint(-) (8.2). $85. (Auction #169, Lot 13).

CHRISTENSEN AGATE COMPANY. Swirl. Excellent three color swirl. Super coloring. Opaque white with swirls of yellow and lavender. 5/8". Mint (9.9). $80. (Auction #91, Lot 37).

CHRISTENSEN AGATE COMPANY. Swirl. A very rare pastel swirl. Pastel colors. White, light blue, darker blue and pink. 21/32". Mint (9.7). $80. (Auction #142, Lot 48).

CHRISTENSEN AGATE COMPANY. Swirl. Lot of two marbles. First is a Flame Swirl. Orange flames and swirls on light green. 19/32", Near Mint. $80. (Auction #163, Lot 14).

CHRISTENSEN AGATE COMPANY. Swirl. Three color swirl. Green base with brown/red swirls edged by brown/gray. Cambridge, OH, circa 1927-1929. 21/32". Mint (9.9). $75. (Auction #145, Lot 12).

CHRISTENSEN AGATE COMPANY. Swirl. Three color swirl. Green base with orange/red swirls edged by brown/gray. Cambridge, OH, circa 1927. 21/32". Mint (9.9). $75. (Auction #137, Lot 35).

CHRISTENSEN AGATE COMPANY. Swirl. Nice turkey. Brown swirl on light blue. A couple of tiny pits. Very nice. Cambridge, OH, circa 1927. 5/8". Mint(-) (9). $70. (Auction #181, Lot 14).

CHRISTENSEN AGATE COMPANY. Swirl. Hard to find three-color swirl. Several flame tips. Opaque white base. Light green and orange swirls. 5/8". Near Mint(+) (8.9). $70. (Auction #104, Lot 41).

CHRISTENSEN AGATE COMPANY. Swirl. Lot of three marbles. All are red swirl on green. Cambridge, OH, circa 1927-1929. 5/8" to 21/32". Mint. $65. (Auction #74, Lot 23).

CHRISTENSEN AGATE COMPANY. Swirl. Three color swirl. Green base with brown/red swirls edged by brown/gray. Cambridge, OH, circa 1927. 21/32". Mint (9.9). $65. (Auction #145, Lot 12.20).

CHRISTENSEN AGATE COMPANY. Swirl. Three-color Swirl. Very unusual coloring. Green base with opaque brown and translucent brown swirling. 21/32". Mint (9.9). $57. (Auction #129, Lot 36).

CHRISTENSEN AGATE COMPANY. Swirl. Three color swirl. Opaque blue base with wide red swirling (vivid). Red has brown edging. 11/16". Mint (9.9). $55. (Auction #136, Lot 8).

CHRISTENSEN AGATE COMPANY. Swirl. Three color swirl. Opaque light green base. Swirls of light red and light gray on the marble. 5/8". Mint (9.9). $55. (Auction #142, Lot 28).

CHRISTENSEN AGATE COMPANY. Swirl. Three color swirl. Light blue base. Swirls of mustard and gray. One tiny manufacturing pit. Cambridge, OH. 5/8". Mint (9.5). $55. (Auction #64, Lot 33).

CHRISTENSEN AGATE COMPANY. Swirl. Super three color swirl. Lavender base with yellow and gray swirls. One small sparkle. Super coloring. 5/8". Mint(-) (9). $55. (Auction #133, Lot 45).

CHRISTENSEN AGATE COMPANY. Swirl. Very nice three color swirl. Opaque white base. Loads of swirling of pink and yellow. Excellent coloring. 5/8". Near Mint(+) (8.9). $55. (Auction #109, Lot 40).

CHRISTENSEN AGATE COMPANY. Swirl. Lot of three marbles. Nice set. Bloodie, 21/32", Mint(-) (9.0). Red on blue. 21/32", Mint (9.9). Red. $50. (Auction #56, Lot 29).

CHRISTENSEN AGATE COMPANY. Swirl. Very nice two color swirl. Red on light blue. Excellent pattern with just the barest hint of turkey. 9/16". Mint (9.9). $50. (Auction #133, Lot 21).

CHRISTENSEN AGATE COMPANY. Swirl. Subtle four color swirl with a minor flame design. The base is two different shades of light blue. 25/32". Near Mint(+) (8.7). $50. (Auction #173, Lot 41).

CHRISTENSEN AGATE COMPANY. Swirl. Lot of four marbles. Includes a Bloodie, and three other two-color swirls. All have some damage. 19/32". $47. (Auction #161, Lot 11).

CHRISTENSEN AGATE COMPANY. Swirl. Shooter size three-color swirl. Light green base with red and brown swirls. Surface has been buffed. $46. (Auction #162, Lot 21).

CHRISTENSEN AGATE COMPANY. Swirl. Three color swirl. Opaque white with salmon and light gray swirls. One subsurface moon. Nice marble. 11/16". Near Mint(+) (8.9). $46. (Auction #133, Lot 40).

CHRISTENSEN AGATE COMPANY. Swirl. Lot of three marbles. Red on yellow, red on green, brown on green. All three are in great shape. $42. (Auction #55, Lot 1).

CHRISTENSEN AGATE COMPANY. Swirl. Red swirls on yellow. Shooter. Exhibits some flame tipping. Nice marble and hard to find. Cambridge, OH. 23/32". Mint (9.9). $40. (Auction #113, Lot 39).

CHRISTENSEN AGATE COMPANY. Swirl. Three color swirl. Green base with orange/red swirls edged by brown/gray. Cambridge, OH, circa 1927. 21/32". Mint (9.9). $40. (Auction #136, Lot 30).

CHRISTENSEN AGATE COMPANY. Swirl. A super two-color swirl. Excellent pattern on it. Black base with yellow swirls. Superb example. Cambridge, OH. 5/8". Mint (9.9). $37. (Auction #58, Lot 40).

CHRISTENSEN AGATE COMPANY. Swirl. Lot of three marbles. All are two color swirls. Red on blue, red on green, brown/red and purple. $35. (Auction #81, Lot 4).

CHRISTENSEN AGATE COMPANY. Swirl. Beautiful Christensen Agate swirl. Light blue base with red swirls. Excellent coloring and pattern. 19/32". Mint (9.4). $32. (Auction #109, Lot 16).

CHRISTENSEN AGATE COMPANY. Swirl. Two color swirl. Green swirls on yellow. A couple of sparkles. Very nice marble. Cambridge, OH. 5/8". Mint(-) (9.1). $32. (Auction #145, Lot 37).

CHRISTENSEN AGATE COMPANY. Swirl. Lot of three marbles. Red on green, orange on green, green on white. Cambridge, OH, circa 1927-1929. $32. (Auction #104, Lot 21).

CHRISTENSEN AGATE COMPANY. Swirl. Two color swirl. Yellow swirls on black. Some cold roll lines. Nice marble. Cambridge, OH, circa 1927. 19/32". Mint (9.7). $32. (Auction #93, Lot 27).

CHRISTENSEN AGATE COMPANY. Swirl. Two color swirl. Red swirls on blue. Very nice. Cambridge, OH, circa 1927-1929. 5/8". Mint (9.9). $31. (Auction #149, Lot 19).

CHRISTENSEN AGATE COMPANY. Swirl. Two color swirl. Yellow on light blue. One turkey head. Cambridge, OH, circa 1927-1929. 21/32". Mint . 21/32". Mint (9.9). $30. (Auction #167, Lot 27).

CHRISTENSEN AGATE COMPANY. Swirl. Three color swirl. Opaque light blue base. Ruddy red swirl edged by brown. One tiny flat spot. Cambridge, OH. 5/8". Mint(-) (9.2). $30. (Auction #60, Lot 32).

CHRISTENSEN AGATE COMPANY. Swirl. Lot of two marbles. Three color swirl. Yellow, green, some red. 19/32". Near Mint (8.3). Three colors. $30. (Auction #120, Lot 6).

CHRISTENSEN AGATE COMPANY. Swirl. Lot of three marbles. A two color swirl, and two three-color swirls. 19/32" to 21/32". Near Mint(+) . $29. (Auction #177, Lot 34).

CHRISTENSEN AGATE COMPANY. Swirl. Super two-color swirl. Yellow swirls on light blue base. Swirls exhibit flame tips. One tiny sparkle. 21/32". Mint(-) (9.1). $29. (Auction #153, Lot 10).

CHRISTENSEN AGATE COMPANY. Swirl. Two-color swirl. Red on green. Nice swirl. Cambridge, OH, circa 1927-1929. 21/32". Mint (9.7). $28. (Auction #159, Lot 31).

CHRISTENSEN AGATE COMPANY. Swirl. Two color swirl. Red swirls on light green. In superb shape. Very nice marble. Cambridge, OH. 5/8". Mint (9.9). $27. (Auction #118, Lot 12).

CHRISTENSEN AGATE COMPANY. Swirl. Lot of ten marbles. Five are Christensen Agate two-color swirls. Nice assortment. Most have some damage. $26. (Auction #152, Lot 7).

CHRISTENSEN AGATE COMPANY. Swirl. Two color swirl. Yellow on light blue. A couple of tiny flakes. Cambridge, OH, circa 1927-1929. 5/8". Near Mint(+) (8.7). $26. (Auction #162, Lot 14).

CHRISTENSEN AGATE COMPANY. Swirl. Lot of three marbles. Red on green, orange on green, green on white. Cambridge, OH, circa 1927-1929. $25. (Auction #54, Lot 20).

CHRISTENSEN AGATE COMPANY. Swirl. Three color swirl. Red and brown swirls on light blue. One sparkle. Nice pattern. Cambridge, OH. 21/32". Mint(-) (9). $25. (Auction #130, Lot 41).

CHRISTENSEN AGATE COMPANY. Swirl. Very nice two color swirl. Opaque black with orange swirls. Very nice. Some cold roll lining. Cambridge, OH. 19/32". Mint (9.7). $25. (Auction #98, Lot 33).

CHRISTENSEN AGATE COMPANY. Swirl. Two color swirl. Red on green. Cambridge, OH, circa 1927-1929. 11/16". Mint (9.9). $24. (Auction #82, Lot 27).

CHRISTENSEN AGATE COMPANY. Swirl. Yellow swirls on a gray base. Harder color combination to find. Buffed marble. Cambridge, OH. $24. (Auction #117, Lot 48).

CHRISTENSEN AGATE COMPANY. Swirl. Two color swirl. Yellow swirl on black. One sparkle. Cambridge, OH, circa 1928-1929. 21/32". Mint(-) (9.1). $22. (Auction #67, Lot 9).

CHRISTENSEN AGATE COMPANY. Swirl. Two color swirl. Green with light red swirl. One tiny sparkle. Cambridge, OH, circa 1927-1929. 5/8". Mint (9.3). $22. (Auction #164, Lot 12).

CHRISTENSEN AGATE COMPANY. Swirl. Red swirls on green base. Three flame tips. A couple of sparkles. Cambridge, OH, circa 1927-1929. 5/8". Mint(-) (9). $22. (Auction #152, Lot 29).

CHRISTENSEN AGATE COMPANY. Swirl. Two color swirl. Pale yellow on black. Surface in great shape. Cambridge, OH, circa 1927-1929. 5/8". Mint (9.9). $21. (Auction #113, Lot 9).

CHRISTENSEN AGATE COMPANY. Swirl. Lot of two marbles. Both are two color. One is red on yellow, other is green on yellow. Nice pair. $21. (Auction #169, Lot 19).

CHRISTENSEN AGATE COMPANY. Swirl. Very nice two color swirl. Red on blue. Excellent coloring. Some light pitting. 19/32". Near Mint (8.6). $20. (Auction #126, Lot 27).

CHRISTENSEN AGATE COMPANY. Swirl. Lot of six marbles. Nice assortment of swirls, including an electric. 19/32" to 11/16". Near Mint (8.6). $20. (Auction #178, Lot 2).

CHRISTENSEN AGATE COMPANY. Swirl. Two color swirl. Brown/red on blue. One tiny sparkle. Cambridge, OH, circa 1927-1929. 5/8". Mint(-) (9). $20. (Auction #149, Lot 41).

CHRISTENSEN AGATE COMPANY. Swirl. Three color swirl. Super turkey head swirl. Opaque white base with swirls of electric orange. 5/8". Near Mint(+) (8.9). $19. (Auction #96, Lot 17).

CHRISTENSEN AGATE COMPANY. Swirl. Lot of four marbles. Assortment of two color swirls. 5/8". Mint (9.9) to Near Mint(+) (8.8). $19. (Auction #115, Lot 18).

CHRISTENSEN AGATE COMPANY. Swirl. Three color swirl. Light green, light yellow and thin light brown. Has a small scratch. 5/8". Mint(-) (9.2). $19. (Auction #117, Lot 38).

CHRISTENSEN AGATE COMPANY. Swirl. Two color swirl. Red swirls on yellow. Super marble. Cambridge, OH, circa 1928-1929. 5/8". Mint (9.9). $18. (Auction #100, Lot 10).

CHRISTENSEN AGATE COMPANY. Swirl. Green swirl on yellow. One tiny annealing fracture, but the surface is wet. Cambridge, OH, circa 1927. 19/32". Mint (9.5). $18. (Auction #182, Lot 7).

CHRISTENSEN AGATE COMPANY. Swirl. Two color swirl. Yellow swirls on light blue. A couple of tiny pinpricks. Nice example. Cambridge, OH. 21/32". Mint(-) (9). $17. (Auction #93, Lot 13).

CHRISTENSEN AGATE COMPANY. Swirl. Nice two color swirl. Light green swirls on yellow. In great shape. Cambridge, OH, circa 1927-1928. 5/8". Mint (9.7). $17. (Auction #59, Lot 38).

CHRISTENSEN AGATE COMPANY. Swirl. Lot of three marbles. All are two color swirls. All have minor damage. 19/32" to 11/16". Near Mint. $14. (Auction #125, Lot 2).

CHRISTENSEN AGATE COMPANY. Swirl. Orange/red swirl on opaque white. Nice swirl. Cambridge, OH, circa 1927-1929. 5/8". Mint (9.9). $14. (Auction #95, Lot 31).

CHRISTENSEN AGATE COMPANY. Swirl. Pretty two-color swirl. Orange swirls on yellow. Has a sparkle. Cambridge, OH, circa 1927-1929. 5/8". Mint(-) (9.1). $14. (Auction #124, Lot 10).

CHRISTENSEN AGATE COMPANY. Swirl. Orange swirls on opaque yellow. Nice example. Slightly out of round. Cambridge, OH, circa 1927-1929. 19/32". Mint (9.8). $13. (Auction #112, Lot 6).

CHRISTENSEN AGATE COMPANY. Swirl. Lot of four marbles. All are two color swirls. All have damage. 19/32" to 5/8". Near Mint (8.6) to Good. $12. (Auction #141, Lot 20).

CHRISTENSEN AGATE COMPANY. Swirl. Nice two color swirl. About half white and half bright orange. I wouldn't call it electric orange. 19/32". Mint(-) (9). $1. (Auction #59, Lot 15).

CHRISTENSEN AGATE COMPANY. Swirl Flame. Three-color swirl flame. Opaque light blue base. Red/brown swirls edged by very light brown. 5/8". Near Mint(+) (8.9). $100. (Auction #154, Lot 45).

CONTEMPORARY HANDMADE. Lot of five marbles. Assortment of contemporary marbles mimicking Christensen Agates and a Peltier. $70. (Auction #179, Lot 37).

CONTEMPORARY HANDMADE. Lot of five marbles. All are torchmade. Unknown maker or makers. None is signed. Indian, Joseph Coat. $65. (Auction #174, Lot 46).

CONTEMPORARY HANDMADE. Lot of two marbles. Both are lampworked. Superman, 19/32". Multicolor swirl, 7/8". Both Mint (9.9). $62. (Auction #83, Lot 14).

CONTEMPORARY HANDMADE. Lot of four marbles. All lampworked. Three are similar to Christensen Agates Guineas. $55. (Auction #125, Lot 17).

CONTEMPORARY HANDMADE. End of day cloud. Transparent clear base. Subsurface layer of opaque white and opaque turquoise. 1-5/8". Mint (9.9). $50. (Auction #86, Lot 7).

CONTEMPORARY HANDMADE. Lot of two marbles. First is a Davis balloon. Signed "Jim Davis". 1-5/8". Mint (9.9). Second is a Joseph Coat. $48. (Auction #175, Lot 19).

CONTEMPORARY HANDMADE. Lot of four marbles. All are various designs with oxblood cullet in them. All lampworked. $42. (Auction #143, Lot 10).

CONTEMPORARY HANDMADE. Lot of six marbles. All lampworked. All are swirls that are similar to Christensen Agates. Nice work. $36. (Auction #125, Lot 6).

CONTEMPORARY HANDMADE. Lot of five marbles. All lampworked. Three are swirls that are similar to Christensen Agates. $35. (Auction #125, Lot 29).

CONTEMPORARY HANDMADE. Lot of five marbles. All lampworked. Three are swirls that are similar to Christensen Agates. $32. (Auction #125, Lot 29.10).

CONTEMPORARY HANDMADE. Four layer latticinio core swirl. Beautiful. Unsigned. American, age unknown, but recent. 1-3/16". Mint (9.9). $32. (Auction #166, Lot 31).

CONTEMPORARY HANDMADE. Opaque white base with a subsurface layer of bands in various rainbow colors. Overglaze of clear. 15/16". Mint (9.9). $30. (Auction #101, Lot 16).

CONTEMPORARY HANDMADE. Lampworked. Similar to Christensen Agates Guinea. Nice work. Unsigned. $28. (Auction #141, Lot 19).

CONTEMPORARY HANDMADE. Lot of two marbles. Both are torchmade, maker is unknown. One is a corkscrew with lutz. 21/32", Mint. $28. (Auction #169, Lot 34).

CONTEMPORARY HANDMADE. Lot of four marbles. All are swirls. All lampworked. One has lutz. Excellent assortment. Unsigned. $27. (Auction #172, Lot 18).

CONTEMPORARY HANDMADE. Unidentified maker. Probably Scott Patrick. Lampworked Guinea. Unsigned. American, circa 1997-1998. 21/32". Mint (9.9). $27. (Auction #135, Lot 33).

CONTEMPORARY HANDMADE. Unknown maker. White ribbon core with lutz. Outer layer is alternating transparent pink bands. 1-3/16". Mint (9.7). $24. (Auction #183, Lot 8).

CONTEMPORARY HANDMADE. Guinea. Transparent green base. Unknown maker. Not signed. American, circa 1997-1998. 21/32". Mint (9.9). $22. (Auction #167, Lot 29).

CONTEMPORARY HANDMADE. Contemporary Guinea. Unknown maker. Blue base. 21/32". Mint (9.9). $22. (Auction #179, Lot 8).

CONTEMPORARY HANDMADE. Lampworked marble. Unknown maker, unsigned. Black ribbons on red. Looks like a Peltier Wasp. 3/4". Mint (9.9). $20. (Auction #158, Lot 32).

CONTEMPORARY HANDMADE. Lampworked marble. Unsigned. Unknown maker. Inner core is two blue bands with lutz on them. 31/32". Mint (9.7). $20. (Auction #152, Lot 10).

CONTEMPORARY HANDMADE. Lot of three marbles. All are lampworked. Unsigned, maker unknown. Nice set. 19/32" to 7/8". Mint. $19. (Auction #127, Lot 9).

CONTEMPORARY HANDMADE. Unknown maker. Not signed. Possibly Jody Fine. Transparent clear base. 15/16". Mint (9.9). $18. (Auction #83, Lot 40).

CONTEMPORARY HANDMADE. Unknown maker. Probably Gibson Glass, but it is right-hand twist. Onionskin of assorted colors. 1-9/16". Mint (9.9). $18. (Auction #143, Lot 23).

CONTEMPORARY HANDMADE. Lot of two marbles. Both are swirls. Unknown maker, possibly Jody Fine. 15/16" and 1-1/16". Mint. $18. (Auction #172, Lot 7).

CONTEMPORARY HANDMADE. White sulphide disk with the numeral "4" on it. Slightly off center. Handmade. Unsigned. 1-9/16". Mint (9.9). $15. (Auction #72, Lot 6).

CONTEMPORARY HANDMADE. Unsigned, unknown maker. Opaque white marble with four lutz bands. 23/32". Mint (9.7). $15. (Auction #97, Lot 2).

CONTEMPORARY HANDMADE. Lampworked. Great replica of a ribbon corkscrew. Opaque white and transparent green ribbons. 5/8". Mint

(9.9). $14. (Auction #141, Lot 35).

CONTEMPORARY HANDMADE. Handpainted glazed pottery. Blue star on either pole with red rings on the circumference. Handmade. 1-1/4". Mint (9.9). $14. (Auction #72, Lot 10).

CONTEMPORARY HANDMADE. Contemporary painted pottery. Opaque white base with six black and red bullseyes. Nice one. Unsigned. 1-31/6". Mint (9.9). $7. (Auction #179, Lot 23).

CONTEMPORARY HANDMADE. Slag. Black and white. Has some rough spots on it. Handmade. Maker unknown. Circa 1985-1995. 1-1/2". Near Mint (8.6). $5. (Auction #72, Lot 7).

CONTEMPORARY HANDMADE. Unknown maker. Opaque white base. Two pink bands and two aventurine black. Possibly Gibson Glass. 1-5/16". Mint (9.9). $2. (Auction #135, Lot 19).

CONTEMPORARY HANDMADE. Andrew Davis. Sulphide. Figure of a locomotive. Large figure filling the marble. One small air bubble. 1-13/16". Mint (9.7). $75. (Auction #167, Lot 5).

CONTEMPORARY HANDMADE. Andrew Davis. Cloud type. Transparent clear with a surface layer of opaque white with opaque green spots. Signed. 1-9/16". Mint (9.9). $30. (Auction #158, Lot 29).

CONTEMPORARY HANDMADE. Andrew Davis. Random pattern of red and green on black with lutz. Signed "A.D". 1-5/8". Mint (9.9). $28. (Auction #175, Lot 13).

CONTEMPORARY HANDMADE. Andrew Davis. Onionskin with mica. Aqua base with brown/red splotches. Some mica on core. Signed "AD". American. 1-3/4". Mint (9.9). $22. (Auction #170, Lot 27).

CONTEMPORARY HANDMADE. Andy Davis. Clambroth. Opaque black base with yellow bands. Signed "A D". 1-1/2". Mint (9.9). $70. (Auction #153, Lot 29).

CONTEMPORARY HANDMADE. Art Seymour. Interesting marble and cane set. Includes a latticino core swirl, a portion of cane. $75. (Auction #167, Lot 41).

CONTEMPORARY HANDMADE. Beetem Glass. A Beetem Globe marble. Very large. This is a replica of the planet Earth. Dichroic continents. 3-1/4". Mint (9.9). $270. (Auction #135, Lot 40).

CONTEMPORARY HANDMADE. Beetem Glass. Prototype Filigrana. Subsurface layer of alternating bands of aventurine green and aventurine green. 2-1/2". Mint (9.9). $250. (Auction #135, Lot 39).

CONTEMPORARY HANDMADE. Bill Murray. Joseph Coat. Prototype marble. Transparent clear base. Subsurface layer of blue, orange and green. 2-1/4". Mint (9.9). $110. (Auction #176, Lot 23).

CONTEMPORARY HANDMADE. Bob Dane. Two panel cloud. Very nice. Old Dane marbles are hard to find. 2-1/8". Mint (9.9). $40. (Auction #135, Lot 4).

CONTEMPORARY HANDMADE. Bob Dane. Transparent clear base with a wide subsurface band of blue, pink, black and white. Unsigned. 1-5/8". Mint (9.9). $37. (Auction #114, Lot 24).

CONTEMPORARY HANDMADE. Bob Dane. Subsurface layer of blue with some white and yellow strands on it. Unsigned. 1-3/8". Mint (9.9). $22. (Auction #135, Lot 31).

CONTEMPORARY HANDMADE. Bob Dane. Single ribbon core swirl. Very pretty. Unsigned. Handmade by Bob Dane. American, circa 1998. 1-3/16". Mint (9.9). $20. (Auction #139, Lot 13).

CONTEMPORARY HANDMADE. Boyd Miller. Ribbon core with two floating bands of lutz. Signed "BAM 98". 1-11/16". Mint (9.9). $26. (Auction #164, Lot 23).

CONTEMPORARY HANDMADE. Boyd Miller. Ribbon core with two floating bands of lutz. Signed "BAM 98". 1-11/16". Mint (9.9). $23. (Auction #135, Lot 3).

CONTEMPORARY HANDMADE. Boyer Glassworks. End of day cloud lutz. Very colorful. Light sprinkling of lutz. This one is a beauty!!! Handmade. 2-1/8". Mint (9.9). $65. (Auction #165, Lot 43).

CONTEMPORARY HANDMADE. Boyer Glassworks. Millefiori marble. Transparent clear base. Subsurface layer of aventurine green embedded. 2". Mint (9.9). $50. (Auction #99, Lot 9).

CONTEMPORARY HANDMADE. Boyer Glassworks. Single red flower with green leaves. A beauty. Signed on bottom "Boyer 1989" (possibly 1984). 1-3/16". Mint (9.9). $30. (Auction #86, Lot 17).

CONTEMPORARY HANDMADE. Boyer Glassworks. Onionskin lutz. Transparent clear base. Subsurface layer of transparent dark purple, lobed. 1-1/2". Mint (9.9). $30. (Auction #86, Lot 5).

CONTEMPORARY HANDMADE. Boyer Glassworks. Ribbon swirl. Three layer. Ribbon is single and thin. Middle layer of strands. 1-1/4". Mint (9.9). $21. (Auction #86, Lot 14).

CONTEMPORARY HANDMADE. Brookside Glass. Large marble. Transparent clear base. Subsurface layer of alternating black and yellow narrow bands. 2-3/16". Mint (9.9). $51. (Auction #182, Lot 28).

CONTEMPORARY HANDMADE. Brookside Glass. Clambroth. Black base with white strands. Signed "BG JMT 98" (John M Talmadge). 2-1/

4". Mint (9.9). $45. (Auction #135, Lot 35).

CONTEMPORARY HANDMADE. Brookside Glass. Onionskin core with a subsurface layer of assorted color splotches. Very nice. Signed "BG JMT 98". 2-1/4". Mint (9.9). $45. (Auction #135, Lot 27).

CONTEMPORARY HANDMADE. California Glass Studios. Swirl. Transparent clear base with a ribbon core of alternating horizontal bands of opaque black. 1-15/16". Mint (9.9). $30. (Auction #121, Lot 27).

CONTEMPORARY HANDMADE. California Glass Studio. Fat ribbon of dichroic silver, impregnated with transparent cranberry red splotches. Nice marble. 1-13/16". Mint (9.9). $29. (Auction #114, Lot 9).

CONTEMPORARY HANDMADE. California Glass Studios. Silver Spiral. Transparent clear base with a ribbon core of alternating horizontal bands. 1-15/16". Mint (9.9). $25. (Auction #99, Lot 8).

CONTEMPORARY HANDMADE. Cape Cod Glass. Superb marble. White latticinio core. Outer layer is alternating bands of red or blue, on lutz. 1-1/2". Mint (9.9). $160. (Auction #72, Lot 35).

CONTEMPORARY HANDMADE. Cape Cod Glass. Very nice crown filligree design. Transparent clear base. White latticinio core. 1-1/16". Mint (9.9). $72. (Auction #173, Lot 33).

CONTEMPORARY HANDMADE. Cape Cod Glass. Crown Filligree design. Core of yellow latticinio. Outer layer is six twisted bands. 1". Mint (9.9). $27. (Auction #114, Lot 12).

CONTEMPORARY HANDMADE. China. Modern glazed handpainted china. Three sets of two bands. Two each of black, gray and red. 1-1/16". Mint (9.5). $12. (Auction #109, Lot 1).

CONTEMPORARY HANDMADE. China. Lot of two marbles. Both are handpainted lined glazed chinas. Two different color schemes. $8. (Auction #149, Lot 15).

CONTEMPORARY HANDMADE. Crystal Myths. Paperweight style marble. Orange, yellow and green frog on a lutz ground, rimmed by green leaves. 1-7/8". Mint (9.9). $70. (Auction #129, Lot 24).

CONTEMPORARY HANDMADE. Crystal Myths. Paperweight type. Transparent clear glass. Lutz and black snake floating above three black and yellow. 2". Mint (9.9). $32. (Auction #86, Lot 29).

CONTEMPORARY HANDMADE. Crystal Myths. Lampworked marble. Paperweight style. Transparent clear base. Outer layer of opaque blue. 1-1/16". Mint (9.9). $28. (Auction #86, Lot 13).

CONTEMPORARY HANDMADE. Crystal Myths. Transparent clear base. Subsurface layer of colored blankets, dichroic and black fleur de lis. 1-1/8". Mint (9.9). $18. (Auction #114, Lot 16).

CONTEMPORARY HANDMADE. Crystal Myths. Lampworked marble. Transparent clear marble. Outer layer on the base of a six sided star in white. 15/16". Mint (9.9). $17. (Auction #86, Lot 19).

CONTEMPORARY HANDMADE. Crystal Myths. Lampworked marble. Paperweight style. Transparent clear base. Outer layer of black and yellow. 15/16". Mint (9.9). $12. (Auction #99, Lot 19).

CONTEMPORARY HANDMADE. Cuneo Furance/Steve Maslach. Alternating white and orange latticinio core. Four outer bands of black and white strands. Unsigned. 1-5/16". Mint (9.9). $24. (Auction #167, Lot 13).

CONTEMPORARY HANDMADE. Cuneo Furnace/Maslach Glass. Lot of seven marbles. Excellent assortment of swirls. Super group. None are signed. American. $85. (Auction #102, Lot 47).

CONTEMPORARY HANDMADE. Cuneo Furnace/Steve Maslach. Lot of two marbles. White latticinio core swirl, 1-5/16", Mint (9.9). Solid core swirl, 1-1/8". Mint. $40. (Auction #151, Lot 8).

CONTEMPORARY HANDMADE. Cuneo Furnace/Steve Maslach. Lot of two marbles. Ribbon swirl, 1-5/16", Mint (9.9). Ribbon swirl, 1-1/8". Mint (9.9). Both unsign. $32. (Auction #146, Lot 28).

CONTEMPORARY HANDMADE. Cuneo Furnace/Steve Maslach. Superb ribbon core. Ribbon consists of yellow, white. blue, aqua, purple and lavender bands. 1-7/16". Mint (9.9). $27. (Auction #176, Lot 21).

CONTEMPORARY HANDMADE. Cuneo Furnace/Maslach Glass. Three layer swirl. Core is lavender covered white solid core. Middle layer is transparent lavender. 1-5/8". Mint (9.9). $27. (Auction #99, Lot 13).

CONTEMPORARY HANDMADE. Cuneo Furnace/Steve Maslach. Very nice ribbon core swirl. Beautiful marble. Not signed. American, circa 1987-1997. 1-1/16". Mint (9.9). $27. (Auction #143, Lot 1).

CONTEMPORARY HANDMADE. Cuneo Furnace/Steve Maslach. Nice ribbon core swirl. Older marble, based on the collection it came from. American, circa 1980. 1-1/16". Mint (9.9). $25. (Auction #158, Lot 10).

CONTEMPORARY HANDMADE. Cuneo Furnace/Steve Maslach. Lot of two marbles. Ribbon swirl, 1-5/16", Mint (9.9). Ribbon swirl, 1-1/8". Mint (9.9). Both unsign. $25. (Auction #146, Lot 23).

CONTEMPORARY HANDMADE. Cuneo Furnace/Steve Maslach. Lot of two marbles. Ribbon swirl, 1-5/16", Mint (9.9). Ribbon swirl, 1-1/8". Mint (9.9). Both unsign. $23. (Auction #146, Lot 17).

CONTEMPORARY HANDMADE. Cuneo Furnace/Steve Maslach. Single ribbon core swirl. Two outer bands consisting of strands. Yellows. oranges, olive green. 1-1/16". Mint (9.9). $23. (Auction #148, Lot 6).

CONTEMPORARY HANDMADE. Cuneo Furnace/Maslach Glass. Lot of two marbles. Both are lobed solid core swirls, caged by latticinio outer layer. Nice pair. $23. (Auction #99, Lot 20).

CONTEMPORARY HANDMADE. Cuneo Furnace/Steve Maslach. Lot of two marbles. Ribbon swirl, 1-5/16", Mint (9.9). Yellow latticinio core swirl, 1-1/8". Mint (9). $21. (Auction #146, Lot 1).

CONTEMPORARY HANDMADE. Cuneo Furnace/Steve Maslach. Ribbon core swirl. Two sets of outer strands. Nice marble. In great shape. Unsigned. American. 29/32". Mint (9.9). $14. (Auction #152, Lot 3).

CONTEMPORARY HANDMADE. Cuneo Furnace/Maslach Glass. Ribbon core swirl with a cage of white strands. Tiny subsurface moon. Unsigned. 1-3/8". Near Mint(+) (8.9). $14. (Auction #135, Lot 23).

CONTEMPORARY HANDMADE. David Salazar. Experimental design, not put into production. Large, transparent cranberry red marble. 1-7/8". Mint (9.9). $385. (Auction #86, Lot 33).

CONTEMPORARY HANDMADE. David Salazar. Prototype Moon and Stars. This marble has a blue moon and stars in white. Early Salazar prototype. 1-7/16". Mint (9.9). $175. (Auction #86, Lot 28).

CONTEMPORARY HANDMADE. David Salazar. Experimental aquarium scene. Paperweight type marble. Transparent clear base. Bottom layer is opaque. 1-5/8". Mint (9.9). $150. (Auction #99, Lot 35).

CONTEMPORARY HANDMADE. David Salazar. Prototype Moon and Stars. This marble has a yellow moon and white stars on blue. Only five stars. 1-5/16". Mint (9.9). $100. (Auction #99, Lot 31).

CONTEMPORARY HANDMADE. David Salazar. Aquarium scene. Paperweight type marble. Transparent clear base. Bottom layer is transparent light blue. 1-7/8". Mint (9.9). $100. (Auction #99, Lot 6).

CONTEMPORARY HANDMADE. David Salazar. Hummingbird paperweight marble. Transparent clear base. Multi-layer design. Back layer is dichroic. 1-11/16". Mint (9.9). $100. (Auction #148, Lot 29).

CONTEMPORARY HANDMADE. David Salazar. Aquarium scene. Paperweight type marble. Transparent clear base. Bottom layer is transparent light blue. 1-3/4". Mint (9.9). $95. (Auction #104, Lot 48).

CONTEMPORARY HANDMADE. David Salazar. Beautiful multilevel design of a plant with two red flowers. White background. Very pretty. Handmade. 1-5/8". Mint (9.9). $90. (Auction #72, Lot 4).

CONTEMPORARY HANDMADE. David Salazar. Very dark translucent blue base. Yellow crescent moon and white stars all around the surface. 1-13/16". Mint (9.9). $90. (Auction #72, Lot 34).

CONTEMPORARY HANDMADE. David Salazar. Hummingbird paperweight marble. Transparent clear base. Multi-layer design. Back layer is dichroic. 1-11/16". Mint (9.9). $85. (Auction #72, Lot 31).

CONTEMPORARY HANDMADE. David Salazar. Aquarium scene. Paperweight type marble. Transparent clear base. Bottom layer is transparent light blue. 1-3/4". Mint (9.9). $70. (Auction #86, Lot 24).

CONTEMPORARY HANDMADE. David Salazar. Miniature aquarium scene. Paperweight type. Transparent clear front. Dichroic blue back. 7/8". Mint (9.9). $45. (Auction #86, Lot 30).

CONTEMPORARY HANDMADE. Davis Handmade Marbles. Superb very large Davis marble. Six lobed onionskin with lutz. A beauty. Signed "Jim Davis". America. 2-3/4". Mint (9.9). $70. (Auction #168, Lot 28).

CONTEMPORARY HANDMADE. Davis Handmade Marbles. Sulphide of a seal pup in transparent tinted vaseline yellow glass. Signed on bottom "Jim Davis". America. 2-1/4". Mint (9.9). $50. (Auction #162, Lot 29).

CONTEMPORARY HANDMADE. Davis Handmade Marbles. Sulphide. Teddy bear, head cocked to one side. Signed on bottom "Jim Davis". American, circa 1985. 1-7/16". Mint (9.9). $48. (Auction #182, Lot 21).

CONTEMPORARY HANDMADE. Davis Handmade Marbles. Sulphide. Figure of a standing angel boy/girl (?) singing, holding a book. Figure fills the entire marble. 2-1/4". Mint (9.9). $46. (Auction #150, Lot 21).

CONTEMPORARY HANDMADE. Davis Handmade Marbles. Onionskin. White core with blue and pink. Nice left hand twist. Signed "Jim Davis". American. $42. (Auction #153, Lot 15).

CONTEMPORARY HANDMADE. Davis Handmade Marbles. Nice "Balloon" type. Predominately blue and yellow, with some green. Signed on bottom "Jim Davis". 1-11/16". Mint (9.9). $42. (Auction #118, Lot 24).

CONTEMPORARY HANDMADE. Davis Handmade Marbles. Experimental marble, not intended for production, according to Jim Davis. Onionskin cloud. 1-7/16". Mint (9.9). $40. (Auction #114, Lot 17).

CONTEMPORARY HANDMADE. Davis Handmade Marbles. Lot of two marbles. Both are swirls. Both signed on bottom "Jim Davis". Divided core swirl. $38. (Auction #174, Lot 3).

CONTEMPORARY HANDMADE. Davis Handmade Marbles. Beach ball. Subsurface opaque white layer with panel of transparent red, transparent green. 1-7/8". Mint (9.9). $36. (Auction #150, Lot 26).

CONTEMPORARY HANDMADE. Davis Handmade Marbles. Crazy Indian. Green and red bands swirled in black. Handmade by Andrew Davis. Signed "AD". American,. 1-7/16". Mint (9.9). $34. (Auction #120, Lot 14).

CONTEMPORARY HANDMADE. Davis Handmade Marbles. Very unusual first-off-cane marble. Transparent clear base. Subsurface layer of alternating red band. 1-1/2". Mint (9.9). $32. (Auction #173, Lot 26).

CONTEMPORARY HANDMADE. Davis Handmade Marbles. Lot of two marbles. Both are signed on the bottom "Jim Davis". Both are onionskin type, one has lutz. $32. (Auction #174, Lot 8).

CONTEMPORARY HANDMADE. Davis Handmade Marbles. Rare design for Davis. Naked single ribbon core. Pink ribbon with some blue. Signed "Jim Davis". American. 1-1/2". Mint (9.9). $30. (Auction #121, Lot 20).

CONTEMPORARY HANDMADE. Davis Handmade Marbles. Banded latticino. Take-off on a Matthews' Population marble. Experimental design for Davis. Signed. 1-5/8". Mint (9.9). $30. (Auction #124, Lot 21).

CONTEMPORARY HANDMADE. Davis Handmade Marbles. Snakeskin type. Pink, green, white, purple. Signed "Jim Davis". American, circa 1998-1997. 1-5/8". Mint (9.9). $26. (Auction #166, Lot 25).

CONTEMPORARY HANDMADE. Davis Handmade Marbles. Narrow onionskin core. Subsurface spiral of air bubble. Nice design. Experimental. Signed "Jim Davis". 1-1/2". Mint (9.9). $25. (Auction #135, Lot 32).

CONTEMPORARY HANDMADE. Davis Handmade Marbles. Unusual marble. Subsurface layer of white and green. Two wide bands of black, one wide band of blue. 1-1/2". Mint (9.9). $24. (Auction #135, Lot 22).

CONTEMPORARY HANDMADE. Davis Handmade Marbles. Lot of two marbles. Both are confetti-type. The first is signed on bottom "Jim Davis". 1-7/8". Mint . $23. (Auction #174, Lot 22).

CONTEMPORARY HANDMADE. Davis Handmade Marbles. Peacock design. Transparent clear base with lavender, light blue and white peacock feather design. 1-9/16". Mint (9.9). $23. (Auction #139, Lot 29).

CONTEMPORARY HANDMADE. Davis Handmade Marbles. White and dichroic green double ribbon swirl. Experimental design, not a standard production item. 1-1/2". Mint (9.9). $23. (Auction #135, Lot 5).

CONTEMPORARY HANDMADE. Davis Handmade Marbles. Experimental marble, not intended for production according to Andrew Davis. Guinea style. 1-1/2". Mint (9.9). $22. (Auction #114, Lot 10).

CONTEMPORARY HANDMADE. Davis Handmade Marbles. Lot of two marbles. Both are onionskin type. Nice pair. Both signed "Jim Davis". 1-1/2" & 1-5/8". Mint. $22. (Auction #175, Lot 17).

CONTEMPORARY HANDMADE. Davis Handmade Marbles. Experimental marble, not intended for production, according to Jim Davis. Transparent blue subsurface. 1-7/16". Mint (9.9). $22. (Auction #164, Lot 19).

CONTEMPORARY HANDMADE. Davis Handmade Marbles. Clambroth. Brown core with red and yellow bands. One tiny subsurface moon. Signed "AD" (Andy Davis). 1-7/16". Near Mint(+) (8.9). $22. (Auction #135, Lot 7).

CONTEMPORARY HANDMADE. Davis Handmade Marbles. Experimental marble, not intended for production, according to Jim Davis. Transparent blue subsurface. 1-7/16". Mint (9.9). $22. (Auction #114, Lot 7).

CONTEMPORARY HANDMADE. Davis Handmade Marbles. Davis Peacock marble. Predominately earth tones. American, circa 1992-1997. 1-1/4". Mint (9.9). $21. (Auction #162, Lot 7).

CONTEMPORARY HANDMADE. Davis Handmade Marbles. Onionskin lutz. Two layers. Very nice marble. Signed. American, circa 1992-1997. 1-1/4". Mint (9.9). $20. (Auction #140, Lot 2).

CONTEMPORARY HANDMADE. Davis Handmade Marbles. Peacock design. Greens, browns, whites. Signed "Jim Davis". American, circa 1990-1998. 1-9/16". Mint (9.9). $20. (Auction #165, Lot 24).

CONTEMPORARY HANDMADE. Davis Handmade Marbles. Transparent clear base. Pink and white snakeskin filling the lower half of the marble. Signed "Jim Davis". 1-29/32". Mint (9.9). $17. (Auction #179, Lot 27).

CONTEMPORARY HANDMADE. Davis Handmade Marbles. Red and gray subsurface snakeskin. Nice marble. American, circa 1992-1997. Signed "Jim Davis". 1-1/2". Mint (9.9). $17. (Auction #136, Lot 24).

CONTEMPORARY HANDMADE. Davis Handmade Marbles. Nice Snakeskin. Red, green and yellow. Nice marble. Signed "Jim Davis". American, circa 1987-1997. 1-1/8". Mint (9.9). $17. (Auction #142, Lot 1).

CONTEMPORARY HANDMADE. **Davis Handmade Marbles.** End of day onionskin. Transparent green on white. Handmade and signed "Jim Davis". American. 1-1/2". Mint (9.7). $16. (Auction #107, Lot 13).

CONTEMPORARY HANDMADE. **Davis Handmade Marbles.** Interesting design. Looks like blue and white flower or tree bud in transparent clear. 1-1/4". Mint (9.9). $13. (Auction #141, Lot 4).

CONTEMPORARY HANDMADE. **Davis Handmade Marbles.** Ribbon core swirl. Ribbon is blue, white and red. Unusual design for Davis. Signed "Jim Davis". Date. 1-1/2". Mint (9.9). $12. (Auction #114, Lot 1).

CONTEMPORARY HANDMADE. **Davis Handmade Marbles.** Purple and white cone in a transparent base. Nice design. Signed "Jim Davis". American, circa 1990. 1-1/2". Mint (9.9). $10. (Auction #135, Lot 20).

CONTEMPORARY HANDMADE. **Douglas Sweet.** Planet marble. Handmade. Signed "Sweet". A beauty. Circa 1990-1995. 1-9/16". Mint (9.9). $90. (Auction #72, Lot 2).

CONTEMPORARY HANDMADE. **Dudley Giberson.** Gorgeous ribbon core swirl. Several lutz bands in the swirl. The remainder are pastel blue. 1-3/16". Mint (9.9). $70. (Auction #72, Lot 14).

CONTEMPORARY HANDMADE. **Dudley Giberson.** Very pretty single ribbon swirl. One half is purple and blue, the other half is gold lutz. Some white. 1-1/16". Mint (9.9). $65. (Auction #99, Lot 18).

CONTEMPORARY HANDMADE. **Dudley Giberson.** Very pretty single ribbon swirl. Opaque white with purple edges and a green lutz center. Handmade. 1-1/16". Mint (9.9). $50. (Auction #72, Lot 26).

CONTEMPORARY HANDMADE. **Dudley Giberson.** Ribbon core swirl, with lutz. Superb marble. Gorgeous!! Very thin ribbon core, filling the marble. 1-1/16". Mint (9.9). $48. (Auction #140, Lot 37).

CONTEMPORARY HANDMADE. **Dudley Giberson.** Super ribbon lutz. Transparent clear base. Ribbon is opaque white with a yellow latticinio center. 1-1/8". Mint (9.9). $46. (Auction #145, Lot 34).

CONTEMPORARY HANDMADE. **Dudley Giberson.** Naked single ribbon core swirl. Ribbon is as wide as the marble and razor thin. Center is opaque purple. 1-1/16". Mint (9.9). $40. (Auction #116, Lot 29).

CONTEMPORARY HANDMADE. **Dudley Giberson.** Ribbon core swirl. Single ribbon. Center is five dark transparent red strands. 1-1/16". Mint (9.9). $40. (Auction #86, Lot 12).

CONTEMPORARY HANDMADE. **Dudley Giberson.** Ribbon lutz. Transparent clear base. Wide ribbon. Lavender on one side, lutz on the other. Signed. 1-3/16". Mint (9.9). $35. (Auction #170, Lot 46).

CONTEMPORARY HANDMADE. **Earthenware.** Lot of two marbles. One is a glazed china painted with primitive flowers. 1-9/16". Mint (9.9). $15. (Auction #115, Lot 25).

CONTEMPORARY HANDMADE. **Fritz Glass.** Limited Edition! These are called "Crazy Indians". Opaque black base with subsurface orange strands. 1-9/16". Mint (9.9). $170. (Auction #99, Lot 28).

CONTEMPORARY HANDMADE. **Fritz Glass.** Limited Edition prototype! This called a "Confetti". Transparent amber base. 1-9/16". Mint (9.9). $160. (Auction #99, Lot 32).

CONTEMPORARY HANDMADE. **Fritz Glass.** Limited Edition! These are called "Crazy Indians". Opaque black base with subsurface orange strands. 1-9/16". Mint (9.9). $110. (Auction #99, Lot 27).

CONTEMPORARY HANDMADE. **Fritz Glass.** Limited Edition! These are called "Crazy Indians". Opaque black base with subsurface white strands. 1-9/16". Mint (9.9). $105. (Auction #114, Lot 28).

CONTEMPORARY HANDMADE. **Fritz Glass.** Limited Edition prototype! This called a "Half and Half". Top half is a Joseph Coat. 1-9/16". Mint (9.9). $90. (Auction #99, Lot 34).

CONTEMPORARY HANDMADE. **Fritz Glass.** Limited Edition! Indian. Opaque black base with subsurface orange strands. 1-9/16". Mint (9.9). $85. (Auction #114, Lot 23).

CONTEMPORARY HANDMADE. **Fritz Glass.** Prototype of the "Half and Half". Not in production yet. Top half is a Joseph Coat of various colors. 1-9/16". Mint (9.9). $65. (Auction #135, Lot 38).

CONTEMPORARY HANDMADE. **Fritz Glass.** Prototype of the "Half and Half". Not in production yet. Top half is a Joseph Coat of blue and orange. 1-9/16". Mint (9.9). $55. (Auction #114, Lot 34).

CONTEMPORARY HANDMADE. **Fritz Glass.** Joseph Coat swirl. Superb coloring. Left hand twist with reverse twist on top. Signed "Fritz 98". 1-9/16". Mint (9.9). $50. (Auction #139, Lot 27).

CONTEMPORARY HANDMADE. **Fritz Glass.** Solid core swirl. Two panels of orange and two of blue, separated by yellow bands. Signed "F 98" 1-9/16". Mint (9.9). $33. (Auction #135, Lot 13).

CONTEMPORARY HANDMADE. **Fritz Lauenstein.** Solid core swirl. Four panel solid core. Pink, orange, blue and green. Outer layer is a cage of orange. 1-5/8". Mint (9.9). $55. (Auction #86, Lot 9).

CONTEMPORARY HANDMADE. **Fritz Lauenstein.** Beach ball. A panel of yellow, one of blue and one of orange, separated by three black panels. 1-5/8". Mint (9.9). $45. (Auction #86, Lot 26).

CONTEMPORARY HANDMADE. **Fulton-Parker Glass.** Desert Devil. Transparent clear base. Subsurface layer of three wide aventurine red panels. 1-1/2". Mint (9.9). $65. (Auction #159, Lot 29).

CONTEMPORARY HANDMADE. **Fulton-Parker Glass.** Transparent clear base. Subsurface layer of four panels of green aventurine, separated by opaque yellow. 1-5/16". Mint (9.9). $55. (Auction #86, Lot 15).

CONTEMPORARY HANDMADE. **Fulton Parker Glass.** Desert Devil. Transparent clear glass base with subsurface layer of three bands of translucent red. 1-1/8". Mint (9.9). $50. (Auction #114, Lot 14).

CONTEMPORARY HANDMADE. **Fulton-Parker Glass.** Ribbon core swirl. Transparent blue ribbon core with a lutz band on it. Outer layer of three lutz bands. 1-7/16". Mint (9.9). $32. (Auction #86, Lot 3).

CONTEMPORARY HANDMADE. **Fulton Parker Glass.** "SuperMarble". Two subsurface bands of red and two of blue, separated by yellow. "Superman" colors. 1-9/16". Mint (9.9). $30. (Auction #135, Lot 26).

CONTEMPORARY HANDMADE. **Fulton Parker Glass.** Transparent clear base. Layer of transparent dichroic running through one side of the equatorial plane. 1-5/16". Mint (9.9). $30. (Auction #99, Lot 15).

CONTEMPORARY HANDMADE. **Geoffrey Beetem.** Globe marble. Stunning example of modern glasswork. Transparent clear base. 2-1/16". Mint (9.9). $310. (Auction #86, Lot 35).

CONTEMPORARY HANDMADE. **Geoffrey Beetem.** Super ribbon lutz. Transparent clear base. Fat ribbon consisting of translucent green. 1-5/8". Mint (9.9). $100. (Auction #86, Lot 31).

CONTEMPORARY HANDMADE. **Geoffrey Beetem Designs.** Stardust V-Lobe. Two lobed panels of opaque blue, separated by red and yellow bands. 1-7/8". Mint (9.9). $80. (Auction #99, Lot 11).

CONTEMPORARY HANDMADE. **Geoffrey Beetem Designs.** Stardust Clambroth. Subsurface layer of bands in various dichroic colors, separated by strands. 1-3/8". Mint (9.9). $41. (Auction #114, Lot 26).

CONTEMPORARY HANDMADE. **Geoffrey Beetem.** Ribbon core swirl. Core is bands of white and aqua, with two lutz bands, and a pink band in the center. 1-5/8". Mint (9.9). $35. (Auction #72, Lot 28).

CONTEMPORARY HANDMADE. **Gibson Glass.** Lobed onionskin. Green, blue and pink on white. Eight very deep lobes. Surface in great shape. Unsigned. 1-3/4". Mint (9.9). $37. (Auction #93, Lot 24).

CONTEMPORARY HANDMADE. **Gibson Glass.** Three layer latticinio core swirl. Transparent clear glass. Opaque white latticinio core. 1-3/4". Mint (9.9). $34. (Auction #103, Lot 22).

CONTEMPORARY HANDMADE. **Gibson Glass.** Lobed onionskin. Numerous colors. Unsigned. American, circa 1980-1998. 2". Mint (9.9). $34. (Auction #165, Lot 22).

CONTEMPORARY HANDMADE. **Gibson Glass.** Green and yellow onionskin. Unsigned. American, circa 1985-1995. 1-5/16". Mint (9.9). $33. (Auction #157, Lot 25).

CONTEMPORARY HANDMADE. **Gibson Glass.** Huge blue and white slag. Very nice marble. West Virginia, circa 1985-1995. 1-7/8". Mint (9.9). $33. (Auction #104, Lot 27).

CONTEMPORARY HANDMADE. **Gibson Glass.** Blue slag. Transparent blue and opaque white. Nice pattern. Large marble. Unsigned. 1-15/16". Mint (9.9). $32. (Auction #86, Lot 1).

CONTEMPORARY HANDMADE. **Gibson Glass.** Sulphide. Clear glass. Painted kitten (Siamese) playing with a blue ball of yarn. Large figure. 2-1/8". Mint (9.9). $32. (Auction #86, Lot 20.10).

CONTEMPORARY HANDMADE. **Gibson Glass.** Onionskin. White core with bands of translucent colors. Nice marble. Unsigned. Circa 1988-1993. 1-3/4". Mint (9.9). $30. (Auction #114, Lot 4).

CONTEMPORARY HANDMADE. **Gibson Glass.** Sulphide. Clear glass. Painted kitten (Siamese) playing with a blue ball of yarn. Large figure. 2-1/8". Mint (9.9). $30. (Auction #86, Lot 20).

CONTEMPORARY HANDMADE. **Gibson Glass.** Two panel onionskin. White core. Red panel and blue panel. Lobed. Minor scratches. Unsigned. America. 2". Mint (9.5). $27. (Auction #138, Lot 24).

CONTEMPORARY HANDMADE. **Gibson Glass.** Divided core swirl. Nice pastel colors. American, circa 1988-1993. 1-1/2". Mint (9.9). $27. (Auction #122, Lot 18).

CONTEMPORARY HANDMADE. **Gibson Glass.** Brown and white onionskin. Unsigned. American, circa 1985-1995. 1-5/8". Mint (9.9). $25. (Auction #157, Lot 44).

CONTEMPORARY HANDMADE. **Gibson Glass.** Beach ball. Subsurface opaque white layer with panel of transparent red, transparent green. 1-7/8". Mint (9.9). $24. (Auction #99, Lot 3).

CONTEMPORARY HANDMADE. **Gibson Glass.** Banded swirl. Pinks, blues and greens. Unsigned. American, circa 1985-1995. 1-3/4". Mint (9.9). $22. (Auction #157, Lot 5).

CONTEMPORARY HANDMADE. **Gibson Glass.** Solid core. Transparent red core. Outer layer is white bands and a couple of colored ones. No twist. 1-1/2". Mint (9.9). $22. (Auction #86, Lot 4).

CONTEMPORARY HANDMADE. **Gibson Glass.** Snakeskin. White base with green and brown skin. In great shape. Unsigned. Odd. 1-3/4". Mint (9.9). $22. (Auction #131, Lot 25).

CONTEMPORARY HANDMADE. **Gibson Glass.** Green and white onionskin. Unsigned. American, circa 1985-1995. 1-7/16". Mint (9.9). $21. (Auction #157, Lot 12).

CONTEMPORARY HANDMADE. **Gibson Glass.** Snakeskin. White base with green, orange, blue and brown skin. In great shape. Unsigned. American. 1-5/16". Mint (9.9). $21. (Auction #133, Lot 12).

CONTEMPORARY HANDMADE. **Gibson Glass.** "Feather" design. Opaque white base. Surface is coverd by bands of transparent green. 1-5/8". Mint (9.9). $20. (Auction #86, Lot 6).

CONTEMPORARY HANDMADE. **Gibson Glass.** Four panel onionskin. Two panels each of translucent white or translucent green. American. 1-1/2". Mint (9.9). $20. (Auction #122, Lot 13).

CONTEMPORARY HANDMADE. **Gibson Glass.** Two level onionskin. In earthy tones. Unsigned. American, circa 1980-1998. 1-5/16". Mint (9.9). $19. (Auction #165, Lot 5).

CONTEMPORARY HANDMADE. **Gibson Glass.** Snakeskin. Blues and greys on white. Very nice marble. Unsigned. West Virginia, circa 1985-1995. 1-3/4". Mint (9.9). $19. (Auction #130, Lot 26).

CONTEMPORARY HANDMADE. **Gibson Glass.** Transparent clear base with translucent orange and white onionskin. Unsigned. American, circa 1992. 1-1/2". Mint (9.9). $18. (Auction #124, Lot 26).

CONTEMPORARY HANDMADE. **Gibson Glass.** Solid core swirl with colored outer bands. Unsigned. American, circa 1987-1997. 1-13/16". Mint (9.9). $17. (Auction #128, Lot 26).

CONTEMPORARY HANDMADE. **Gibson Glass.** Eight lobe onionskin. Red skin on white core. Unsigned. American, circa 1975-1995. 1-13/16". Mint (9.9). $13. (Auction #135, Lot 1).

CONTEMPORARY HANDMADE. **Gibson Glass.** Onionskin. Orange and white. Fracture running from pole to pole on one side. Unsigned. American. 1-3/4". Near Mint(+) (8.9). $8. (Auction #157, Lot 36).

CONTEMPORARY HANDMADE. **Gibson Glass.** Onionskin. White core with bands of translucent red. Nice marble. Unsigned. Two large fractures. 1-3/4". Near Mint (8.6). $7. (Auction #133, Lot 25).

CONTEMPORARY HANDMADE. **Gossamer Studios.** Complex marble. White and lavender ribbon core swirl. Fills the marble. 1-7/16". Mint (9.9). $125. (Auction #114, Lot 8).

CONTEMPORARY HANDMADE. **Grablow Glass.** Paperweight style of a rose flower in transparent clear glass. Aventurine green petals at the base. 2-1/4". Mint (9.8). $160. (Auction #142, Lot 22).

CONTEMPORARY HANDMADE. **Grablow Glass.** Transparent clear base. Opaque white free form swirl in center. Subsurface layer of controlled air bubbles. 2-1/8". Mint (9.9). $80. (Auction #156, Lot 29).

CONTEMPORARY HANDMADE. **Greg Hoglin.** Lampworked. Interesting paperweight style marble. Transparent clear base. Equatorial band of blue. 1-1/16". Mint (9.9). $70. (Auction #167, Lot 23).

CONTEMPORARY HANDMADE. **Greg Hoglin.** Yellow base. Three clown faces on it. Very colorful. Fun marble. Lampworked. Unsigned. American. 25/32". Mint (9.9). $42. (Auction #135, Lot 30).

CONTEMPORARY HANDMADE. **Harry Bessett.** White latticino core swirl with a cage of transparent outer strands. Signed "HB". Nice one. American. 1-1/4". Mint (9.9). $20. (Auction #151, Lot 43).

CONTEMPORARY HANDMADE. **Harry Boyer.** End of day lutz. Very colorful. Lots of lutz. This one is a beauty!!! Handmade. Signed "Boyer". 1-1/2". Mint (9.9). $75. (Auction #72, Lot 3).

CONTEMPORARY HANDMADE. **Harry Boyer.** Paperweight flower marble. Has a green four-leaf clover with three multi-color flowers floating above. 1-11/16". Mint (9.9). $60. (Auction #72, Lot 33).

CONTEMPORARY HANDMADE. **Harry Boyer.** Paperweight flower marble. Has a green four-leaf clover with three multi-color flowers floating above. 1-1/2". Mint (9.9). $40. (Auction #99, Lot 14).

CONTEMPORARY HANDMADE. **Harry Boyer.** White latticinio core swirl with transparent color outer bands. Handmade. Signed "Boyer". Circa 1992. 1-7/16". Mint (9.9). $20. (Auction #72, Lot 25).

CONTEMPORARY HANDMADE. **Hart's of Glass.** Joseph Coat swirl with lutz. A beauty. Signature cane of a red heart in the bottom (Jim Hart). American. 1-5/8". Mint (9.9). $45. (Auction #135, Lot 14).

CONTEMPORARY HANDMADE. **House of Marbles.** Red subsurface fleur de lis pattern. There is a beautiful layer of mica below the red. Handmade. 1-9/16". Mint (9.9). $41. (Auction #72, Lot 5).

CONTEMPORARY HANDMADE. **Hulet Glass.** Super paperweight type marble. Blue silhouette on white of a child shooting a marble!!! 1-7/16". Mint (9.9). $120. (Auction #114, Lot 35).

CONTEMPORARY HANDMADE. **J. Fine Glass.** Large ribbon core swirl. Opaque razor thin single ribbon. One face has bands of primary colors on it. 2-1/4". Mint (9.9). $85. (Auction #162, Lot 23).

CONTEMPORARY HANDMADE. **J. Fine Glass.** Lot of two marbles. Same design and color in two different sizes. Nice pair. Three vane ribbon. $30. (Auction #99, Lot 5).

CONTEMPORARY HANDMADE. **J. Fine Glass.** Lot of two marbles. Both are ribbon core swirls with caged outer layers. Unsigned. American. $30. (Auction #121, Lot 5).

CONTEMPORARY HANDMADE. **J. Fine Glass.** Single ribbon core swirl. Multi-colored core. Unsigned. American, circa 1985-1995. 1-1/4". Mint (9.8). $26. (Auction #171, Lot 19).

CONTEMPORARY HANDMADE. **J. Fine Glass.** Lot of two marbles. Unsigned, but I think they are Jody Fine. One is a solid core. $25. (Auction #169, Lot 9).

CONTEMPORARY HANDMADE. **J. Fine Glass.** Lot of two marbles. Both are vaned solid core. Two different color schemes. Nice pair. Unsigned. 7/8". Mint (9.9). $20. (Auction #114, Lot 18).

CONTEMPORARY HANDMADE. **J. Fine Glass.** Lot of two marbles. Both are vaned solid core. Two different color schemes. Nice pair. Unsigned. 7/8". Mint (9.9). $19. (Auction #153, Lot 39).

CONTEMPORARY HANDMADE. **J. Fine Glass.** Superb ribbon core swirl. Fills the marble. Triple twist. Has strands of orange yellow too. 7/8". Mint (9.9). $18. (Auction #150, Lot 5).

CONTEMPORARY HANDMADE. **J. Fine Glass.** Lot of two marbles. Both are ribbon core swirls. Two different styles. Both unsigned. $17. (Auction #135, Lot 9).

CONTEMPORARY HANDMADE. **J. Fine Glass.** Ribbon core swirl. Very pretty. Unsigned. Produced by Jody Fine. American, circa 1975-1995. 1-1/16". Mint (9.9). $15. (Auction #135, Lot 18).

CONTEMPORARY HANDMADE. **Jerry Park.** Subsurface pink layer with black spots. Lampworked. Signed "JP 98". 1-1/16". Mint (9.9). $16. (Auction #135, Lot 11).

CONTEMPORARY HANDMADE. **Jim Cooprider.** Very interesting double ribbon double twisted corkscrew. Transparent gray and translucent orange. 31/32". Mint (9.9). $39. (Auction #86, Lot 16).

CONTEMPORARY HANDMADE. **Jim Davis.** Snakeskin with lutz. Handmade and signed "Jim Davis" on the bottom. Nice marble. American. 1-1/2". Mint (9.9). $60. (Auction #59, Lot 22).

CONTEMPORARY HANDMADE. **Jim Davis.** Lot of two marbles. Both left hand twist. One is a snakeskin. The other is an end of day. $47. (Auction #61, Lot 22).

CONTEMPORARY HANDMADE. **Jim Davis.** "Peacock" marble. Huge Peacock, one of the largest I have ever seen. Subsurface layer of transparent. 2-1/4". Mint (9.9). $45. (Auction #86, Lot 23).

CONTEMPORARY HANDMADE. **Jim Davis.** Nice lobed onionskin. Bright colors. Three lobes. Some lutz. Each has an air bubble in it. Signed. 1-9/16". Mint (9.9). $43. (Auction #55, Lot 24).

CONTEMPORARY HANDMADE. **Jim Davis.** Snakeskin. Left hand twist. Nice marble. Signed on bottom "Jim Davis". American, circa 1990-1996. 1-1/2". Mint (9.9). $40. (Auction #58, Lot 28).

CONTEMPORARY HANDMADE. **Jim Davis.** Snakeskin. Orange, red and blue. Handmade. Signed "Jim Davis". 1-5/16". Mint (9.9). $39. (Auction #74, Lot 39).

CONTEMPORARY HANDMADE. **Jim Davis.** Snakeskin. Very colorful, rainbow colors. Handmade. Signed "Jim Davis". West Virginia, circa 1992. 1-9/16". Mint (9.9). $36. (Auction #69, Lot 26).

CONTEMPORARY HANDMADE. **Jim Davis.** Left hand twist cased snakeskin with lutz. Assorted colors. Super marble. Handmade. Signed "Jim Davis". 1-9/16". Mint (9.9). $35. (Auction #63, Lot 23).

CONTEMPORARY HANDMADE. **Jim Davis.** Six lobed onionskin. The lobe peaks are a brown and green earth tones. The lobe troughs are blues. 1-1/2". Mint (9.9). $35. (Auction #99, Lot 23).

CONTEMPORARY HANDMADE. **Jim Davis.** Snakeskin marble. Cased in clear. Assorted colors. Handmade. Signed "Jim Davis". American. 1-9/16". Mint (9.9). $33. (Auction #67, Lot 22).

CONTEMPORARY HANDMADE. **Jim Davis.** Peacock pattern. White core with loads of colors and lutz on it. Handmade. Signed "Jim Davis". 1-9/16". Mint (9.9). $32. (Auction #72, Lot 29).

CONTEMPORARY HANDMADE. **Jim Davis.** "Peacock" marble. Transparent clear base. Transparent purple on opaque brown on opaque white. 1-7/16". Mint (9.9). $30. (Auction #86, Lot 10).

CONTEMPORARY HANDMADE. **Jim Davis.** Snakeskin. Multicolor with lutz. Very unusual for Davis. Handmade. Signed "Jim Davis". American. 1-1/2". Mint (9.9). $30. (Auction #85, Lot 22).

CONTEMPORARY HANDMADE. **Jim Davis.** Snakeskin. Pink on white. Handmade and signed on bottom "Jim Davis". West Virginia, circa 1992-1997. 1-5/8". Mint (9.9). $30. (Auction #83, Lot 26).

CONTEMPORARY HANDMADE. **Jim Davis.** Snakeskin. Cased. Thin bands. Nice marble. Handmade and signed on the bottom "Jim Davis". American. 1-9/16". Mint (9.9). $28. (Auction #64, Lot 21).

CONTEMPORARY HANDMADE. **Jim Davis.** Peppermint swirl. Handmade and signed on the bottom "Jim Davis". 1-3/16". Mint (9.9). $28. (Auction #87, Lot 29).

CONTEMPORARY HANDMADE. **Jim Davis.** Snakeskin. Pink on white. Handmade and signed on bottom "Jim Davis". West Virginia, circa 1992-1997. 1-5/8". Mint (9.9). $27. (Auction #83, Lot 26.10).

CONTEMPORARY HANDMADE. **Jim Davis.** Jim Davis snakeskin. White with shades of green. Handmade and signed "Jim Davis". American. 1-1/2". Mint (9.9). $27. (Auction #81, Lot 35.10).

CONTEMPORARY HANDMADE. **Jim Davis.** Jim Davis snakeskin. White with shades of green. Handmade and signed "Jim Davis". American. 1-1/2". Mint (9.9). $25. (Auction #81, Lot 35).

CONTEMPORARY HANDMADE. **Jim Davis.** Peacock marble. Predominately grays and blues, with some pink. Handmade. Signed "Jim Davis". 1-9/16". Mint (9.9). $25. (Auction #72, Lot 9).

CONTEMPORARY HANDMADE. **Jim Davis.** Snakeskin. Predominately blue. Handmade. Signed "Jim Davis". American, circa 1992-1997. 1-3/8". Mint (9.9). $24. (Auction #68, Lot 34).

CONTEMPORARY HANDMADE. **Jim Davis.** Davis "Peacock" pattern. White and lavender. Handmade. Signed "Jim Davis". American, circa 1992-1997. 1-5/8". Mint (9.9). $24. (Auction #66, Lot 26).

CONTEMPORARY HANDMADE. **Jim Davis.** Peacock marble. Blue on white. Handmade. Signed "Jim Davis". West Virginia, circa 1992-1997. 1-1/2". Mint (9.9). $22. (Auction #78, Lot 23).

CONTEMPORARY HANDMADE. **Jim Davis.** Snakeskin marble. Predominately greens and yellow, with some pink. Handmade. Signed "Jim Davis". 1-5/8". Mint (9.9). $20. (Auction #72, Lot 1).

CONTEMPORARY HANDMADE. **Jim Davis.** Transparent clear base marble with subsurface layer of white glass. Lobed, with loops of red and blue. 1-1/2". Mint (9.9). $20. (Auction #99, Lot 10).

CONTEMPORARY HANDMADE. **Jim Davis.** Snakeskin. White with blue and red. Handmade and signed "Jim Davis". American, circa 1992-1997. 1-1/2". Mint (9.9). $20. (Auction #84, Lot 12).

CONTEMPORARY HANDMADE. **Jim Davis.** Snakeskin. Predominately green, with white and some blue. Handmade and signed "Jim Davis". American. $19. (Auction #99, Lot 2).

CONTEMPORARY HANDMADE. **Jim Davis.** Snakeskin. Predominately pink, with white and green. Handmade and signed "Jim Davis". American. $17. (Auction #82, Lot 16).

CONTEMPORARY HANDMADE. **Jim Davis.** Lot of two marbles. Both are transparent clear base with a free-form design of stretched bright color. $17. (Auction #149, Lot 32).

CONTEMPORARY HANDMADE. **Jim Davis.** Onionskin. Opaque white and transparent green onionskin. Left hand twist. Handmade, signed "Jim Davis". 1-5/8". Mint (9.9). $15. (Auction #92, Lot 19).

CONTEMPORARY HANDMADE. **Jim Davis.** Snakeskin. Purple on white with spirals of tiny air bubbles. Handmade and signed on bottom "Jim Davis". 1-5/8". Mint (9.9). $12. (Auction #99, Lot 7).

CONTEMPORARY HANDMADE. **Jim Hart.** Entire core is bubble filled translucent light blue. Subsurface layer of alternating lutz. 1-9/16". Mint (9.9). $50. (Auction #114, Lot 22).

CONTEMPORARY HANDMADE. **Jim Hart.** Transparent clear base. Core of opaque black with dichroic flakes on it. Lutz jellyfish hovering. 1-5/8". Mint (9.9). $32. (Auction #114, Lot 5).

CONTEMPORARY HANDMADE. **Jim Murray.** Joseph Coat swirl. Subsurface layer of alternating opaque white and dark transparent red bands. 1-7/16". Mint (9.9). $30. (Auction #133, Lot 46).

CONTEMPORARY HANDMADE. **Jody Fine.** Banded swirl. Gorgeous design. One half white strands and one half copper color strands. Nice twist. 7/8". Mint (9.9). $46. (Auction #72, Lot 12).

CONTEMPORARY HANDMADE. **Jody Fine.** Lot of three marbles. All are the same design and size, in three different color patterns. Four lobe. $42. (Auction #92, Lot 15).

CONTEMPORARY HANDMADE. **Jody Fine.** Nice single ribbon swirl. Wide, thin ribbon, double twisted. Fills the marble. The ribbon is multicolored. 1-5/8". Mint (9.9). $27. (Auction #86, Lot 2).

CONTEMPORARY HANDMADE. **Jody Fine.** Solid core swirl. Multicolor. Handmade. Unsigned, but made at Fine Art Glass. Circa 1988-1993. 1-1/4". Mint (9.9). $24. (Auction #72, Lot 24).

CONTEMPORARY HANDMADE. **Jody Fine.** A real beauty. Lobed solid core. Translucent white core with color strands on the lobe peaks. 29/32". Mint (9.9). $23. (Auction #72, Lot 21).

CONTEMPORARY HANDMADE. **Jody Fine.** Four lobed solid core. Very deep lobes. Vane type. Two lobes are dark blue and two are light blue. 29/32". Mint (9.9). $18. (Auction #107, Lot 42.40).

CONTEMPORARY HANDMADE. **Jody Fine.** Four lobed solid core. Very deep lobes. Vane type. Two lobes are dark blue and two are light blue. 29/32". Mint (9.9). $18. (Auction #107, Lot 42).

CONTEMPORARY HANDMADE. **Jody Fine.** White latticinio core swirl, around a multicolor latticinio core swirl. 15/16". Mint (9.9). $17. (Auction #86, Lot 18).

CONTEMPORARY HANDMADE. **Jody Fine.** Lobed solid cores swirl with and outer layer of one half bands and one half strands. Very colorful. 1-1/8". Mint (9.9). $17. (Auction #72, Lot 15).

CONTEMPORARY HANDMADE. **Jody Fine.** Four lobed solid core. Very deep lobes. Vane type. Two lobes are dark blue and two are light blue. 29/32". Mint (9.9). $16. (Auction #107, Lot 42.20).

CONTEMPORARY HANDMADE. **Jody Fine.** Four lobed solid core. Very deep lobes. Vane type. Two lobes are dark blue and two are light blue. 29/32". Mint (9.9). $14. (Auction #107, Lot 42.30).

CONTEMPORARY HANDMADE. **Joe St. Clair.** Very hard to find St. Clair marble. Green slag. A beauty. Distinctive coloring and design. Signed. 2-1/16". Mint (9.9). $130. (Auction #155, Lot 42).

CONTEMPORARY HANDMADE. **Joe St. Clair.** Sulphide. Transparent clear base. White disk with a relief bull on it, "Taurus" and signed "Nonie". 2". Mint (9.9). $80. (Auction #99, Lot 33).

CONTEMPORARY HANDMADE. **John Gilvey.** Very unusual scenic paperweight type. Transparent clear with a desert scene. 1-9/16". Mint (9.9). $100. (Auction #114, Lot 33).

CONTEMPORARY HANDMADE. **John Hamon Miller.** Solid core. Three lobes. Fat purple core. Each lobe peak has a band of yellow and black on it. 1-13/16". Mint (9.9). $46. (Auction #185, Lot 14).

CONTEMPORARY HANDMADE. **John Hamon Miller.** Solid core swirl with aventurine green bands. Naked solid core. Very pretty. Signed "JHM 98". 2-1/4". Mint (9.5). $42. (Auction #135, Lot 25).

CONTEMPORARY HANDMADE. **John Hamon Miller.** Lobed four-panel onionskin. Some subsurface lutz. Very pretty. Signed "JHM 98". 1-9/16". Mint (9.9). $30. (Auction #159, Lot 24).

CONTEMPORARY HANDMADE. **Josh Simpson.** Outstanding example of an "Inhabited World" marble. Transparent clear base. "Planet" in the lower half. 1-7/8". Mint (9.9). $80. (Auction #174, Lot 45).

CONTEMPORARY HANDMADE. **Josh Simpson.** Planet type. "Uninhabited World". Nice design. Unsigned. American, circa 1980-1990. 1-7/16". Mint (9.9). $30. (Auction #174, Lot 26).

CONTEMPORARY HANDMADE. **Josiah Simpson.** Superb example of a Simpson "Planet". Swirling blue oceans with large brown and green continents. 1-13/16". Mint (9.9). $65. (Auction #114, Lot 29).

CONTEMPORARY HANDMADE. **Kaimana Glass.** Transparent clear with a subsurface layer of opaque blue. On the blue are dichroic shapes. 2". Mint (9.9). $60. (Auction #99, Lot 4).

CONTEMPORARY HANDMADE. **Karen Federici.** Torchmade glass marble, simulating a scenic rose china. Great idea!!!!. Opaque white base. 1-1/16". Mint (9.9). $42. (Auction #173, Lot 11).

CONTEMPORARY HANDMADE. **Karen Federici.** Nice paperweight style marble. Yellow flower with green leaves. Very nicely done. Signed on bottom. 15/16". Mint (9.9). $42. (Auction #178, Lot 44).

CONTEMPORARY HANDMADE. **Karen Federici.** Lampworked marble. Black base. Green surface layer. Spaced white, blue and black flowers. 31/32". Mint (9.9). $38. (Auction #159, Lot 7).

CONTEMPORARY HANDMADE. **Karen Federici.** Opaque white with blue roses around the equator and circular designs at either pole. Signed on bottom. 31/32". Mint (9.9). $27. (Auction #182, Lot 11).

CONTEMPORARY HANDMADE. **Karuna Glass.** Confetti. Subsurface layer of dark purple covered by small confetti pieces of dichroic. A beauty. 1-13/16". Mint (9.9). $34. (Auction #135, Lot 15).

CONTEMPORARY HANDMADE. **Karuna Glass.** Opaque black marble with subsurface strips of dichroic in assorted bright colors. Signed "Sweet". 1-1/2". Mint (9.9). $25. (Auction #114, Lot 2).

CONTEMPORARY HANDMADE. **Kelly O'Grady.** Paperweight type. Beautiful flower in earth tones. Nice work! Lampworked. Signed on the bottom "K 98". 1-1/4". Mint (9.9). $45. (Auction #114, Lot 19).

CONTEMPORARY HANDMADE. **Lewis & Jennifer Wilson.** Gorgeous orange dragon standing on lutz boulders on a blue ground. In great shape. Handmade. Signed . 1-15/16". Mint (9.9). $110. (Auction #72, Lot 30).

CONTEMPORARY HANDMADE. **Lunberg Studios.** A Lunberg Studios "World Marble Classic". Excellent glass rendition of the Earth in a thick casing. 2-1/2". Mint (9.9). $160. (Auction #170, Lot 49).

CONTEMPORARY HANDMADE. **Lundberg Studios.** Transparent clear glass. Green kelp, blue anemone and a blue and yellow angelfish. Signed "SL CAG 97". 2". Mint (9.9). $75. (Auction #114, Lot 6).

CONTEMPORARY HANDMADE. **Mark Matthews.** Opaque banded lutz. Subsurface layer of opaque orange with six narrow pink bands.

1-1/8". Mint (9.9). $150. (Auction #86, Lot 34).

CONTEMPORARY HANDMADE. Mark Matthews. Gorgeous onionskin. Transparent clear core. Subsurface layer of opaque white. Very satiny finish. 1-13/16". Mint (9.9). $135. (Auction #72, Lot 32).

CONTEMPORARY HANDMADE. Mark Matthews. Opaque banded lutz. Purple base. Light purple bands. Two wide white edged lutz bands. 1-3/16". Mint (9.9). $110. (Auction #72, Lot 27).

CONTEMPORARY HANDMADE. Mark Matthews. Ribbon core swirl. Thin single ribbon of transparent dark green on opaque white. 1-3/4". Mint (9.9). $65. (Auction #86, Lot 25).

CONTEMPORARY HANDMADE. Mark Matthews. Left hand twist peppermint swirl with mica. Beautiful marble. Handmade by Mark Matthews. Signed. 5/8". Mint (9.9). $57. (Auction #63, Lot 5).

CONTEMPORARY HANDMADE. Mark Matthews. Left hand twist peppermint swirl with mica. Beautiful marble. Handmade by Mark Matthews. Signed. 5/8". Mint (9.9). $55. (Auction #63, Lot 5.20).

CONTEMPORARY HANDMADE. Mark Matthews. Spearmint swirl with mica. Beautiful. Handmade. Signed with the Matthews logo. Circa 1992-1997. 1/2". Mint (9.9). $50. (Auction #72, Lot 17).

CONTEMPORARY HANDMADE. Mark Matthews. Peewee peppermint swirl with mica. Opaque white core. Two translucent blue bands with mica. 15/32". Mint (9.9). $50. (Auction #59, Lot 12).

CONTEMPORARY HANDMADE. Mark Matthews. Left hand twist peppermint swirl with mica. Beautiful marble. Handmade by Mark Matthews. Signed. 5/8". Mint (9.9). $50. (Auction #63, Lot 5.30).

CONTEMPORARY HANDMADE. Mark Matthews. Peppermint swirl. With mica. Another beauty. Handmade. Signed with the Matthews logo. Circa 1992. 15/32". Mint (9.9). $45. (Auction #72, Lot 19).

CONTEMPORARY HANDMADE. Mark Matthews. Left hand twist peppermint swirl with mica. Beautiful marble. Handmade by Mark Matthews. Signed. 5/8". Mint (9.9). $45. (Auction #105, Lot 49).

CONTEMPORARY HANDMADE. Mark Matthews. Spearmint swirl with mica. Beautiful. Handmade. Signed with the Matthews logo. Circa 1992-1997. 5/8". Mint (9.9). $36. (Auction #90, Lot 38).

CONTEMPORARY HANDMADE. Matthews Art Glass. Superior lobed onionskin. Transparent clear base. Opaque white subsurface layer. Seven loads. Loops. 1-15/16". Mint (9.9). $180. (Auction #99, Lot 30).

CONTEMPORARY HANDMADE. Matthews Art Glass. A Mark Matthews experimental Beach Ball. He never put this into production. Panels of blue, yellow. 2-1/8". Mint (9.9). $175. (Auction #114, Lot 31).

CONTEMPORARY HANDMADE. Matthews Art Glass. Very unusual. Opaque black base with a surface layer of Tiffany-favrille type iridescent swirling. 1-7/8". Mint (9.9). $155. (Auction #135, Lot 37).

CONTEMPORARY HANDMADE. Matthews Art Glass. "Cube Squared". Transparent clear marble with air inclusions of three squares and a cube. Signed "Ma. 2". Mint (9.9). $110. (Auction #135, Lot 24).

CONTEMPORARY HANDMADE. Matthews Art Glass. Super swirl. Solid core swirl. The core is three panels. Each panel is opaque yellow. 1-3/4". Mint (9.9). $100. (Auction #137, Lot 25).

CONTEMPORARY HANDMADE. Matthews Art Glass. Ribbon core swirl. Single ribbon green and aqua. Outer layer is two bands of blue. Well designed. 1-1/2". Mint (9.9). $100. (Auction #131, Lot 22).

CONTEMPORARY HANDMADE. Matthews Art Glass. Beautiful marble. Transparent clear base. Subsurface layer of baby blue glass with seven lobes in it. 1-3/4". Mint (9.9). $90. (Auction #133, Lot 34).

CONTEMPORARY HANDMADE. Matthews Art Glass. Gorgeous cased clambroth type. Transparent clear base. Subsurface layer of transparent dark lavender. 1-7/16". Mint (9.9). $90. (Auction #145, Lot 47).

CONTEMPORARY HANDMADE. Matthews Art Glass. Super marble. Transparent clear core. Layer of opaque light green on that. 1-7/16". Mint (9.9). $80. (Auction #140, Lot 30).

CONTEMPORARY HANDMADE. Matthews Art Glass. Ribbon core swirl. Beautiful marble. Matthews does outstanding work. Signed on the bottom. 1-7/16". Mint (9.9). $75. (Auction #135, Lot 34).

CONTEMPORARY HANDMADE. Matthews Art Glass. Spearmint swirl with mica. Subsurface layer of opaque white. Two bands of transparent green. 1/2". Mint (9.9). $37. (Auction #114, Lot 20).

CONTEMPORARY HANDMADE. Michael Edmondson. Contemporary Beach Ball design. Thirteen panels, include a lutz panel. Left hand twist. Lampworked. 1-1/16". Mint (9.9). $31. (Auction #120, Lot 34).

CONTEMPORARY HANDMADE. Mike Edmondson. Lot of two marbles. One is a swirl of yellow, orange and black. Signature/date cane "ME 97". 27/32". $65. (Auction #167, Lot 10).

CONTEMPORARY HANDMADE. Murano Glass. Transparent clear base. Sulphide of a pig on a yellow ground. One small scratch on the top. 2-1/8". Mint(-) (9). $120. (Auction #99, Lot 25).

CONTEMPORARY HANDMADE. Nadine MacDonald. Lot of three marbles. All are handpainted chinas. All are jack-o-lanterns! Assorted faces. $50. (Auction #156, Lot 21.20).

CONTEMPORARY HANDMADE. Nadine MacDonald. Lot of three marbles. All are handpainted chinas. All are jack-o-lanterns! Assorted faces. $50. (Auction #156, Lot 21).

CONTEMPORARY HANDMADE. Nadine MacDonald. Lot of four marbles. All are handpainted chinas. All are jack-o-lanterns! One is incised. $32. (Auction #156, Lot 10.20).

CONTEMPORARY HANDMADE. Nadine MacDonald. Lot of four marbles. All are handpainted chinas. All are jack-o-lanterns! One is incised. $30. (Auction #156, Lot 10).

CONTEMPORARY HANDMADE. Nadine MacDonald. Lot of two marbles. Both are handpainted chinas. Similar Christmas motif of poinsettias. $22. (Auction #172, Lot 11).

CONTEMPORARY HANDMADE. Nadine MacDonald. Handpainted glazed pottery. Christmas design. Candy cane, snowman, stocking, gift and holly leaves. 1-1/8". Mint (9.9). $20. (Auction #170, Lot 29.30).

CONTEMPORARY HANDMADE. Nadine MacDonald. Handpainted glazed pottery. Christmas design. Candy cane, snowman, stocking, gift and holly leaves. 1-1/8". Mint (9.9). $20. (Auction #170, Lot 29).

CONTEMPORARY HANDMADE. Nadine MacDonald. Handpainted glazed pottery. Christmas design. Candy cane, snowman, stocking, gift and holly leaves. 1-1/8". Mint (9.9). $20. (Auction #170, Lot 29.20).

CONTEMPORARY HANDMADE. Nadine MacDonald. Handpainted glazed pottery. Christmas design. Candy cane and holly leaves on red. Signed "N.M.". 25/32". Mint (9.9). $17. (Auction #170, Lot 13.30).

CONTEMPORARY HANDMADE. Nadine MacDonald. Handpainted glazed pottery. Christmas design. Candy cane and holly leaves on red. Signed "N.M.". 25/32". Mint (9.9). $17. (Auction #170, Lot 13.20).

CONTEMPORARY HANDMADE. Nadine MacDonald. Handpainted glazed pottery. Christmas design. Candy cane and holly leaves on red. Signed "N.M.". 25/32". Mint (9.9). $16. (Auction #170, Lot 13).

CONTEMPORARY HANDMADE. Nadine MacDonald. Handpainted glazed pottery. Christmas design. Candy cane, red bow and holly leaves on white. Signed. 27/32". Mint (9.9). $14. (Auction #172, Lot 16).

CONTEMPORARY HANDMADE. Nadine MacDonald. Handpainted glazed pottery. Christmas design. Candy cane, red bow and holly leaves on white. Signed. 27/32". Mint (9.9). $12. (Auction #172, Lot 16.20).

CONTEMPORARY HANDMADE. Nick Dougher. Lampworked cloud. Semi-opaque white base. Overall clouds of green, blue, red and yellow. Handmade. 1-5/8". Mint (9.9). $32. (Auction #99, Lot 29).

CONTEMPORARY HANDMADE. Pottery. Lot of four marbles. Four handpainted glazed pottery marbles. Modern, maker unknown. Line and bullseye. $30. (Auction #158, Lot 20).

CONTEMPORARY HANDMADE. Pottery. Lot of six marbles. All are handpainted glazed pottery marbles. Modern, maker unknown. $24. (Auction #166, Lot 27).

CONTEMPORARY HANDMADE. Richard Dinardo. Ribbon core swirl. White core. Outer layer is a cage of white strands. Very nice. Signed "Dinardo 84". 1-9/16". Mint (9.9). $65. (Auction #135, Lot 36).

CONTEMPORARY HANDMADE. Richard Dinardo. Beautiful solid core swirl. Opaque white core. Outer layer is a cage of two triple twisted bands. 1-11/16". Mint (9.3). $30. (Auction #114, Lot 21).

CONTEMPORARY HANDMADE. Richard Dinardo. Banded swirl. Transparent clear base with subsurface bands of black, blue, red, yellow and green. 1-3/8". Mint (9.9). $27. (Auction #99, Lot 24).

CONTEMPORARY HANDMADE. Robert Dane. Banded swirl. Transparent clear base. Four subsurface bands of yellow, black and green. 1-5/16". Mint (9.9). $45. (Auction #99, Lot 21).

CONTEMPORARY HANDMADE. Robert Lichtman. Left hand twist onionskin. Various shades of blue, pink and green on white. Superior marble. Signed. 1-5/16". Mint (9.9). $40. (Auction #86, Lot 27).

CONTEMPORARY HANDMADE. Roger Hoglin. Paperweight type. Nine canes, sitting on a base of lutz, which is on a base of blue and white. 31/32". Mint (9.9). $30. (Auction #114, Lot 15).

CONTEMPORARY HANDMADE. Rolf & Genie Wald. Beach ball. This one is a beauty, with one lutz panel amongst the color ones. Handmade. Signed. 1-7/16". Mint (9.9). $75. (Auction #72, Lot 11).

CONTEMPORARY HANDMADE. Rolf & Genie Wald. Lutz lobed solid core. Three panels. One is green lutz, one is purple lutz and one is brown lutz. 1-3/8". Mint (9.9). $75. (Auction #72, Lot 22).

CONTEMPORARY HANDMADE. Rolf & Genie Wald. Odd marble. This is an end of cane Joseph's Coat with lutz and mica. 1-1/8". Mint (9.9). $55. (Auction #72, Lot 13).

CONTEMPORARY HANDMADE. Rolf & Genie Wald. Beach ball. Six panels, all the same size. No twist. White, green, red, yellow, blue, orange. Signed. 1-7/16". Mint (9.9). $55. (Auction #86, Lot 21.10).

CONTEMPORARY HANDMADE. Rolf & Genie Wald. Beach ball. Six panels, all the same size. No twist. White, green, red, yellow, blue, orange. Signed. 1-7/16". Mint (9.9). $50. (Auction #86, Lot 21).

CONTEMPORARY HANDMADE. Rolf & Genie Wald. End of day onionskin with mica. Very nice marble. Handmade. Signed "Wald 95". American, circa 1995. 1-1/2". Mint (9.9). $50. (Auction #99, Lot 1).

CONTEMPORARY HANDMADE. Rolf & Genie Wald. Peewee Beach Ball! Beautiful. Handmade. Signed "Wald 93". 7/16". Mint (9.9). $44. (Auction #72, Lot 18).

CONTEMPORARY HANDMADE. Rolf & Genie Wald. Wald experimental! Folded Beach Ball. This is a six panel beach ball that is folded over. Panels. 1-7/16". Mint (9.9). $42. (Auction #114, Lot 3).

CONTEMPORARY HANDMADE. Rolf & Genie Wald. Ribbon core swirl. Gold lutz on one side, transparent light blue on the other. Rainbow edge strands. 1-3/8". Mint (9.9). $40. (Auction #99, Lot 12).

CONTEMPORARY HANDMADE. Rolf & Genie Wald. Ribbon core swirl. Gold lutz ribbon. Rainbow edge strands. Orange strands offsetting one face. Handmade. 1-7/16". Mint (9.9). $35. (Auction #72, Lot 8).

CONTEMPORARY HANDMADE. Rolf & Genie Wald. End of day onionskin with mica. Very nice marble. Handmade. Signed "Wald 95". Circa 1995. 1-1/2". Mint (9.9). $35. (Auction #72, Lot 23).

CONTEMPORARY HANDMADE. Rolf & Genie Wald. A Beach Ball. Six panels: Blue, yellow, white, green, red, lutz. Each panel is about the same size. 1-1/16". Mint (9.9). $34. (Auction #99, Lot 17).

CONTEMPORARY HANDMADE. Rolf & Genie Wald. Beach Ball. Six panels: red, yellow, blue, orange, lutz and green. Signed "Wald 97". 1-1/8". Mint (9.9). $32. (Auction #114, Lot 13).

CONTEMPORARY HANDMADE. Rolf & Genie Wald. Wald experimental! Folded Beach Ball. This is a six panel beach ball that is folded over. Panels. 27/32". Mint (9.9). $32. (Auction #184, Lot 14).

CONTEMPORARY HANDMADE. Rolf & Genie Wald. Spinner. Purple lutz core. A beauty. Handmade. Signed "Wald 97". 1-1/8". Mint (9.9). $29. (Auction #72, Lot 20).

CONTEMPORARY HANDMADE. Rolf & Genie Wald. Solid core with mica. Core is two bands of white, one of purple and one of orange. Subsurface layer. 1-1/8". Mint (9.9). $27. (Auction #86, Lot 11).

CONTEMPORARY HANDMADE. Rolf & Genie Wald. Smaller Beach Ball. Handmade. Signed "Wald 94". 7/8". Mint (9.9). $22. (Auction #83, Lot 31).

CONTEMPORARY HANDMADE. Rolf & Genie Wald. Peewee Spinner. With lutz. A beauty. Handmade. Signed "Wald 93". Circa 1993. 15/32". Mint (9.9). $21. (Auction #72, Lot 16).

CONTEMPORARY HANDMADE. Rolf & Genie Wald. This is a "square shooter". A Wald ribbon lutz, made into a cube. $16. (Auction #114, Lot 11).

CONTEMPORARY HANDMADE. Rolf and Genie Wald. Ribbon core swirl. With a blue aventurine face. Very pretty. Signed "Wald 92". 1-7/16". Mint (9.9). $42. (Auction #135, Lot 6).

CONTEMPORARY HANDMADE. Rolf and Genie Wald. Folded Spinner. Subsurface layer of lutz with colored strands on it. Folded over. Experimental. Signed. 1-1/16". Mint (9.9). $30. (Auction #135, Lot 29).

CONTEMPORARY HANDMADE. Rolf and Genie Wald. Single ribbon core swirl. One face is purple lutz. Nice marble. Signed "Wald 92". 1-1/16". Mint (9.9). $26. (Auction #171, Lot 9).

CONTEMPORARY HANDMADE. Rolf and Genie Wald. Experimental. Ribbon core swirl that is folded over. Gold lutz on one face. Signed "Wald 98". 1-1/16". Mint (9.9). $25. (Auction #135, Lot 10).

CONTEMPORARY HANDMADE. Salazar Art Glass. Very hard to find mid-1980s David Salazar marble. Transparent clear glass. Blue dichroic background. 2-1/4". Mint (9.9). $160. (Auction #173, Lot 28).

CONTEMPORARY HANDMADE. Salazar Art Glass. Very hard to find mid-1980s David Salazar marble. Transparent clear glass. Blue dichroic background. 1-1/2. Mint (9.9). $150. (Auction #181, Lot 49).

CONTEMPORARY HANDMADE. Salazar Art Glass. Super Iris marble. Paperweight style. Dichroic blue base. Two layer Iris with blue flowers and green. 1-3/4". Mint (9.9). $130. (Auction #156, Lot 39).

CONTEMPORARY HANDMADE. Salazar Art Glass. Aquarium scene. Paperweight type marble. Transparent clear base. 1-7/8". Mint (9.9). $110. (Auction #124, Lot 30).

CONTEMPORARY HANDMADE. Salazar Art Glass. Blue Parrot in a tree with green leaves, all in front of an orange moon. With blue dichroic background. 1-5/8". Mint (9.9). $100. (Auction #135, Lot 16).

CONTEMPORARY HANDMADE. Salazar Art Glass. Seascape. Blue whale swimming amongst green kelp and white anemones, against a blue dichroic background. 1-11/16". Mint (9.9). $100. (Auction #114, Lot 25).

CONTEMPORARY HANDMADE. Salazar Art Glass. An aquarium scene. Multi-level paperweight marble. Dichroic irridescent blue back. 1-3/4".

Mint (9.9). $75. (Auction #174, Lot 48).

CONTEMPORARY HANDMADE. Salazar Art Glass. Pansy. Three blue and lavender pansies with green leaves. With blue dichroic background. A beauty. 1-13/16". Mint (9.9). $75. (Auction #178, Lot 48).

CONTEMPORARY HANDMADE. Salazar Art Glass. Transparent cobalt blue base. Two bands of colored strands alternating with two bands of dichroic. 1-11/16". Mint (9.9). $50. (Auction #114, Lot 32).

CONTEMPORARY HANDMADE. Salazar Art Glass. Salazar Heart design. Interior wispy white and blue bands. Red heart in the top center. A beauty. 1-5/8". Mint (9.9). $44. (Auction #114, Lot 30).

CONTEMPORARY HANDMADE. Salazar Art Glass. "Moon and Stars". Blue opaque with yellow crescent moon and white stars. Signed "DPS 3/93". 1-1/4". Mint (9.9). $37. (Auction #135, Lot 28).

CONTEMPORARY HANDMADE. Salazar Art Glass. Very interesting swirl. Not a typical design for Salazar. Ribbon swirl. Core is brown. 1-11/16". Mint (9.9). $32. (Auction #185, Lot 39).

CONTEMPORARY HANDMADE. Salazar Art Glass. Salazar Jack-o-lantern. Orange pumpkin with an aventurine green stem and black eyes, nose and mouth. 29/32". Mint (9.9). $26. (Auction #159, Lot 41).

CONTEMPORARY HANDMADE. Salazar Art Glass. Clambroth style. Semi-opaque red, blue and white base. Bands of yellow. Signed on the bottom. 1-1/2". Mint (9.9). $24. (Auction #134, Lot 28).

CONTEMPORARY HANDMADE. Salazar Art Glass. Salazar Pumpkin. Orange pumpkin with an aventurine green stem and black eyes, nose and mouth. 31/32". Mint (9.9). $24. (Auction #184, Lot 35).

CONTEMPORARY HANDMADE. Salazar Art Glass. Clambroth. Transparent dark brown base with orange bands. Handmade by Jesse Siegel. 1-5/8". Mint (9.9). $22. (Auction #166, Lot 42).

CONTEMPORARY HANDMADE. Salazar Art Glass. Ribbon core swirl, with a snakeskin outer band. Very unusual design. Signed "DPSG 9/97 JS". 1-5/8". Mint (9.9). $20. (Auction #135, Lot 17).

CONTEMPORARY HANDMADE. Sara Creekmore. Dichroic cat face floating above a green dichroic base. Signed "Sara 98". 1-9/16". Mint (9.9). $30. (Auction #135, Lot 2).

CONTEMPORARY HANDMADE. Shipwrecked Glass. Transparent lavender with subsurface dichroic patches. Signed "NOR". American, circa 1995-1998. 1-5/16". Mint (9.9). $25. (Auction #135, Lot 8).

CONTEMPORARY HANDMADE. Steve Maslach. Ribbon core swirl. Orange ribbon, edged by yellow bands. Very pretty. Nice marble. Unsigned. 1-1/16". Mint (9.9). $26. (Auction #86, Lot 22).

CONTEMPORARY HANDMADE. Steve Maslach. Latticinio core swirl. Two panels of gray, one of white, one of blue. Two outer sets of black strand. 1-1/16". Mint (9.9). $18. (Auction #86, Lot 8).

CONTEMPORARY HANDMADE. T.C. Robertson. Very unusual marble. Called a Plated Marble. Transparent clear base. Latticinio core. 2-1/8". Mint (9.9). $170. (Auction #99, Lot 22).

CONTEMPORARY HANDMADE. T.C. Robertson. Large, interesting marble. Three layer. Inner core is white latticinio ribbon. Middle layer is yellow. 3". Mint (9.7). $75. (Auction #153, Lot 21).

CONTEMPORARY HANDMADE. T.C. Robertson. Large, interesting marble. Fat ribbon core. Lutz in assorted colors on the core. 3". Mint (9.8). $47. (Auction #162, Lot 28).

CONTEMPORARY HANDMADE. T.C. Robertson. Transparent clear base with a subsurface layer of blue, red, pink and dichroic bands. Unsigned. 1-5/8". Mint (9.9). $40. (Auction #114, Lot 27).

CONTEMPORARY HANDMADE. T.C. Robertson. Transparent clear base filled with transparent red curtains and some opaque white. Unsigned. America. 2-1/4". Mint (9.7). $39. (Auction #166, Lot 29).

CONTEMPORARY HANDMADE. T.C. Robertson. Transparent clear base. Solid core of transparent red. Middle layer of ghost air bubbles. 1-11/16". Mint (9.9). $30. (Auction #176, Lot 27).

CONTEMPORARY HANDMADE. T.C. Robertson. Ribbon core swirl. Thin translucent ribbon. Ouer layer is two very wide bands of transparent red. 1-3/4". Mint (9). $9. (Auction #148, Lot 27).

CONTEMPORARY HANDMADE. Teign Valley Glass. Transparent clear base. Two layers of pink and white in a fleur de lis pattern. Handmade, but unsigned. 1-1/2". Mint (9.9). $25. (Auction #99, Lot 16).

CONTEMPORARY HANDMADE. Terry Crider. End of day onionskin with mica. Transparent clear base. Subsurface layer of opaque white. 1-3/4". Mint (9.9). $37. (Auction #99, Lot 26).

CONTEMPORARY HANDMADE. William Burchfeld. Cape Cod Glass. Crown and filligreen design. White latticinio core. 1". Mint (9.9). $80. (Auction #86, Lot 32).

CONTEMPORARY HANDMADE. Woodchuck Glass. Lot of three marbles. All paperweight style. Two flowers and a free-form. Signature cane in bottom. Mint . $45. (Auction #166, Lot 6).

CONTEMPORARY HANDMADE. Woodchuck Glass. Excellent lampworked marble. Black and white swirl in transparent clear. 1-1/16". Mint (9.9). $22. (Auction #172, Lot 14).

CONTEMPORARY HANDMADE. Woodchuck Glass. Lot of two marbles. Both are ribbon core swirl. Signatures cane reading "ME 98" (Mike Edmondson). 29/32". Mint (9.9). $22. (Auction #169, Lot 30).

CONTEMPORARY HANDMADE. Woodchuck Glass. Lot of four marbles. All are multicolor swirls. All lampworked. Two have signature canes reading "ME". $22. (Auction #172, Lot 9).

CONTEMPORARY HANDMADE. Woodchuck Glass. Red subsurface layer with several wide millefiori canes. Signature cane in bottom reading "ME 97". 29/32". Mint (9.9). $13. (Auction #135, Lot 12).

CONTEMPORARY HANDMADE. Woodchuck Glass. Swirled slag of yellow, blue, red, black and clear. Signature cane reading "ME 97" (Mike Edmondson). 29/32". Mint (9.9). $11. (Auction #135, Lot 21).

END OF DAY. Very unusual end of day marble. 3/4". Near Mint(+) (8.7). $110. (Auction #181, Lot 17).

END OF DAY. Blizzard. One of the finest looking examples of a blizzard onionskin that I have ever seen. Transparent clear . $330. (Auction #154, Lot 47).

END OF DAY. Cloud. Superior cloud end of day, in absolutely stunning condition!!! Transparent clear base. Core is opaque. 1-7/16". Mint (9.9). $575. (Auction #159, Lot 50).

END OF DAY. Cloud. Superior three-panel end-of-cane (first off) Cloud. Rare marble, excellent opportunity. Opaque white. 13/16". Near Mint(+) (8.9). $300. (Auction #156, Lot 46).

END OF DAY. Cloud. Rare single-pontil Cloud. Probably hand-gathered. Opaque white core coming almost all the way to the. 5/8". Near Mint(+) (8.9). $250. (Auction #162, Lot 48).

END OF DAY. Cloud. Lot of two marbles. Again, you could classify these as clouds, or possibly onionskins. Matched pair. $190. (Auction #163, Lot 47).

END OF DAY. Cloud. Superior cloud! Translucent white and yellow core. Completely covered by unstretched transparent pin. 7/8". Near Mint(+) (8.7). $180. (Auction #158, Lot 48).

END OF DAY. Cloud. Stunning single pontil end of day cloud in ribbon form. Fantastic looking marble. $175. (Auction #154, Lot 15).

END OF DAY. Cloud. Very rare. Single pontil, first-of-cane, cloud in ribbon form, with mica. Transparent clear base. 15/16". Good(+) (7.80). $110. (Auction #176, Lot 4).

END OF DAY. Cloud. Super single-pontil first-off-cane cloud. Transparent clear base. Opaque white core with clouds. 11/16". Near Mint (8.6). $100. (Auction #181, Lot 42).

END OF DAY. Cloud. Very rare end of cane cloud. Transparent clear base. Subsurface core of opaque yellow. 25/32". Near Mint(-) (8.1). $90. (Auction #69, Lot 36).

END OF DAY. Cloud. Outstanding cloud, but heavily polished. Likely was a single pontil, hand-gather, but you can't tell. $90. (Auction #165, Lot 23).

END OF DAY. Cloud. Very nice left-twist, shrunken core, cloud. Transparent clear base. Opaque white core. 25/32". Near Mint(+) (8.9). $70. (Auction #153, Lot 9).

END OF DAY. Cloud. Single pontil cloud. Rare marble. Transparent clear base. Mushroom cloud of opaque white rising. 23/32". Good (7.50). $37. (Auction #140, Lot 8).

END OF DAY. Mist. Interesting marble. Transparent clear base. Core is two thin ribbons of multicolor bands. 1-5/8". Near Mint(+) (8). $80. (Auction #89, Lot 20).

END OF DAY. Onionskin. This is one of the finest marbles that I have ever had at auction. Four-panel, four-lobe onionskin. 1-17/32". Mint(-) (9.1). $1350. (Auction #167, Lot 50).

END OF DAY. Onionskin. Superior end of day onionskin with mica. Opaque white core with stretched splotches of blue and green. 1-5/16". Mint (9.8). $600. (Auction #145, Lot 50).

END OF DAY. Onionskin. A fantastic onionskin. Very rare. Subsurface layer of stretched bands and splotches of white, pink. 25/32". Mint (9.8). $525. (Auction #142, Lot 49).

END OF DAY. Onionskin. Absolutely outstanding end of day onionskin with mica. Core is predominately yellow bands. 3/4". Near Mint(+) (8.9). $450. (Auction #105, Lot 50).

END OF DAY. Onionskin. Absolutely outstanding example!!! Stunning! Opaque white core. Skin of translucent dark green. 1-9/16". Mint(-) (9.2). $400. (Auction #182, Lot 50).

END OF DAY. Onionskin. A very rare end of cane (first off cane) four panel onionskin. 25/32". Near Mint(+) (8.8). $350. (Auction #80, Lot 45).

END OF DAY. Onionskin. Very rare onionskin. Larger size. Opaque white core. Stretched splotches of blue and red on it. 1-1/2". Good (7.90). $330. (Auction #147, Lot 26).

END OF DAY. Onionskin. This may be the most fantastic small onionskin I have ever seen. Very rare. Left hand twist! 23/32". Mint(-) (9.1). $285. (Auction #100, Lot 50).

END OF DAY. Onionskin. Superb marble and unusual. The entire core of the marble is transparent green. 1-7/16". Near Mint(+) (8.9). $280. (Auction #89, Lot 45).

END OF DAY. Onionskin. Not sure what to call this one. Transparent clear base. It has no core. There is a subsurface layer. $250. (Auction #116, Lot 17).

END OF DAY. Onionskin. Super looking large onionskin. Opaque white base. 1-7/8". Near Mint(+) (8.8). $240. (Auction #88, Lot 45).

END OF DAY. Onionskin. Superior and exceptional example. Opaque yellow core. Bands of transparent pink and transparent green. 29/32". Mint (9.9). $185. (Auction #121, Lot 16).

END OF DAY. Onionskin. Stunning, and very rare, end of day onionskin with mica. Core is predominately ruddy red with white. $185. (Auction #98, Lot 47).

END OF DAY. Onionskin. Some collectors refer to these as coreless onionskins. Transparent clear base with a subsurface layer. 27/32". Mint(-) (9.1). $180. (Auction #164, Lot 48).

END OF DAY. Onionskin. Very hard to find first-off-cane onionskin. Transparent clear base. This is actually a six panel onionskin. 23/32". Near Mint(+) (8.2). $160. (Auction #88, Lot 8).

END OF DAY. Onionskin. Super eight panel onionskin, but it has some condition problems. Subtle panelling. Opaque white core. 1-15/16". Good(+) (7.90). $160. (Auction #148, Lot 30).

END OF DAY. Onionskin. Extremely rare peewee onionskin. Actually, this is the only one of this kind that I have ever seen. 1/2". Mint (9.9). $160. (Auction #85, Lot 17).

END OF DAY. Onionskin. You might classify this one as a cloud. Opaque white core. Spots of dark blue and some pink covering. 1-1/8". Near Mint(+) (8.7). $150. (Auction #163, Lot 40).

END OF DAY. Onionskin. End of day onionskin. Transparent clear base. Subsurface layer of stretched bands of yellow, red. 1-3/16". Near Mint (8.6). $150. (Auction #89, Lot 47).

END OF DAY. Onionskin. Large end of day onionskin with mica. Opaque yellow core with pink onionskin. Nice sprinkling of mica. 1-11/16". Good(+) (7.90). $150. (Auction #94, Lot 50).

END OF DAY. Onionskin. Superior end of day onionskin. Outstanding addition to any collection. Transparent clear base. 21/32". Mint (9.9). $140. (Auction #90, Lot 35).

END OF DAY. Onionskin. Lot of six marbles. All are large onionskins. All have significant damage. 1-1/2" to 2-1/16". Good. $140. (Auction #101, Lot 32).

END OF DAY. Onionskin. I never know what to call these, but I guess onionskin is as good as anything else. 7/8". Near Mint (8.3). $125. (Auction #154, Lot 33).

END OF DAY. Onionskin. Outstanding example. Opaque yellow core with green skin. Super spiral twist at the top. 11/16". Mint (9.9). $120. (Auction #118, Lot 39).

END OF DAY. Onionskin. Lot of six marbles. All are end of day onionskins. All have damage. Nice assortment of colors. 13/16. $115. (Auction #144, Lot 23).

END OF DAY. Onionskin. Super onionskin. Transparent green and opaque yellow. Some clear spaces on one side. 21/32". Mint (9.7). $110. (Auction #80, Lot 5).

END OF DAY. Onionskin. Superior end of cane onionskin. Transparent clear base. Loops and bands of white, yellow, brown. 11/16". Near Mint(+) (8.9). $110. (Auction #100, Lot 13).

END OF DAY. Onionskin. Superior peewee end of day onionskin. Opaque yellow core with transparent red on it. 15/32". Mint (9.9). $110. (Auction #88, Lot 36).

END OF DAY. Onionskin. Lot of six marbles. Assortment of onionskins. Includes two four-panels. All have some damage to them. $110. (Auction #89, Lot 18).

END OF DAY. Onionskin. Lot of six marbles. Assortment of onionskins. Includes a cloud and a four panel. All have some damage. $110. (Auction #89, Lot 16).

END OF DAY. Onionskin. Four panel onionskin with a generous coating of mica. Odd colors. Two panels are pink on white. $110. (Auction #165, Lot 11).

END OF DAY. Onionskin. Very unusual onionskin. Opaque yellow two band core. Subsurface layer of semi-opaque white, pink. 11/16". Mint (9.4). $110. (Auction #145, Lot 40).

END OF DAY. Onionskin. Very nice onionskin. Opaque white core. Transparent blue on the almost the whole core. 1-5/16". Mint (9.9). $100. (Auction #74, Lot 40).

END OF DAY. Onionskin. Fat yellow core. Skin of transparent pink. Surface in superb condition. Exceptional example! 7/8". Mint (9.9). $100. (Auction #183, Lot 37).

END OF DAY. Onionskin. Superior end of day onionskin with mica. Probably from near the end of the cane. 11/16". Near Mint(+) (8.7). $100. (Auction #70, Lot 43).

END OF DAY. Onionskin. Gorgeous four panel onionskin. Two panels of transparent pink and blue on white. 21/32". Mint (9.9). $100. (Auction #57, Lot 34).

END OF DAY. Onionskin. This one is a beauty. Opaque white core. Covered by stretched splotches of blue, pink. 1-9/16". Near Mint(+) (8.8). $100. (Auction #138, Lot 21).

END OF DAY. Onionskin. Stunning, left hand twist onionskin. Opaque white base, with stretched blue and pink on it. 11/16". Mint (9.9). $95. (Auction #56, Lot 42).

END OF DAY. Onionskin. Superb onionskin. Opaque white core with some clear spaces. Transparent dark blue on the white. 29/32". Mint(-) (9). $95. (Auction #87, Lot 35).

END OF DAY. Onionskin. Transparent green, and a little blue, on opaque white. One tiny sparkle. A beauty! Germany. 11/16". Mint(-) (9.2). $86. (Auction #74, Lot 37).

END OF DAY. Onionskin. Onionskin with mica. Opaque white core. Overall transparent light pink. A band of green. 17/32". Mint (9.5). $85. (Auction #164, Lot 42).

END OF DAY. Onionskin. Super onionskin with mica. Core is completely pink on white. A couple of pieces of mica on the core. 25/32". Mint(-) (9.1). $85. (Auction #126, Lot 46).

END OF DAY. Onionskin. Transparent clear base. Opaque dark green inner core. Outer core of opaque yellow. 21/32". Mint (9.1). $85. (Auction #89, Lot 3).

END OF DAY. Onionskin. Very unusual core. Mixture of translucent white, transparent yellow, transparent pink. 9/16". Mint (9.8). $85. (Auction #130, Lot 48).

END OF DAY. Onionskin. Transparent blue on opaque white, with some pink and green. Surface in great shape. Gorgeous marble! 19/32". Mint (9.9). $85. (Auction #65, Lot 39).

END OF DAY. Onionskin. First off cane four panel onionskin. Opaque white core. Two panels of pink, one of green, one of blue. 9/16". Mint (9.9). $85. (Auction #125, Lot 46).

END OF DAY. Onionskin. Transparent blue on white, with two pink bands. Surface in great shape. A beauty. Germany, circa 1870s. 17/32". Mint (9.9). $85. (Auction #76, Lot 9).

END OF DAY. Onionskin. White core with transparent green all over it. A band of blue too. Surface in great shape. Germany. 21/32". Mint (9.9). $85. (Auction #77, Lot 28).

END OF DAY. Onionskin. Lot of three marbles. Assortment of onionskins. All are pink on white. One is a shrunken core. $80. (Auction #161, Lot 15).

END OF DAY. Onionskin. Outstanding onionskin with mica. Opaque white core. Transparent pink/red skin. 13/16". Near Mint(+) (8.9). $80. (Auction #179, Lot 42).

END OF DAY. Onionskin. Lot of four marbles. Nice assortment of onionskins. Two are four-panel. Three are left-hand twists! $80. (Auction #144, Lot 18).

END OF DAY. Onionskin. Translucent blue on white. In superb shape. Germany, circa 1870-1915. 19/32." Mint (9.9). $80. (Auction #75, Lot 33).

END OF DAY. Onionskin. Odd onionskin. The core is a combination of opaque mustard yellow and transparent dark blue. 11/16". Mint (9.8). $80. (Auction #159, Lot 43).

END OF DAY. Onionskin. Super onionskin. Very odd coloring. Opaque white and yellow, with a little transparent pink. 19/32". Mint (9.9). $75. (Auction #96, Lot 38).

END OF DAY. Onionskin. Opaque yellow core. Skin of transparent pink. One blue band. An absolute beauty!!! Germany. 3/4". Mint (9.9). $75. (Auction #176, Lot 40).

END OF DAY. Onionskin. Very hard to find two panel onionskin with shrunken core. Very lightly tinted blue base glass. Opaque. 17/32". Mint (9.7). $75. (Auction #77, Lot 1).

END OF DAY. Onionskin. Translucent green on white. Also, a little pink and green. Peewee. A beauty. Germany, circa 1870-1915. 15/32". Mint (9.9). $75. (Auction #75, Lot 37).

END OF DAY. Onionskin. Core of transparent pink on opaque white. Surface in great shape. Germany, circa 1870-1915. 19/32." Mint (9.9). $75. (Auction #83, Lot 37).

END OF DAY. Onionskin. Nice onionskin with odd coloring. Translucent white core. Stretched bands of blue. 11/16". Mint (9.9). $75. (Auction #154, Lot 12).

END OF DAY. Onionskin. Superb onionskin. Opaque white core with transparent light green on it. Surface is pristine. 11/16". Mint (9.9). $75. (Auction #103, Lot 5).

END OF DAY. Onionskin. Unusual type of onionskin. Opaque white core. Bands and strands of semi-opaque red and orange covering. 11/16". Mint(-) (9.2). $75. (Auction #181, Lot 34).

END OF DAY. Onionskin. Very pretty peewee onionskin. Translucent white and cherry red core. One thin yellow band. 15/32". Mint (9.9). $70. (Auction #107, Lot 17).

END OF DAY. Onionskin. Transparent blue bands on opaque white. Surface in superb shape. Germany, circa 1870-1915. 19/32". Mint (9.9). $70. (Auction #61, Lot 18).

END OF DAY. Onionskin. Lot of three marbles. All are onionskins, middle size is a four-panel. 7/8" & Near Mint(-) (8.1). $70. (Auction #106, Lot 15).

END OF DAY. Onionskin. A beauty. Opaque white core covered by transparent pink. Surface in great shape. Germany, circa 1870. 9/16". Mint (9.9). $70. (Auction #91, Lot 9).

END OF DAY. Onionskin. Super peewee marble. Translucent white core with one band of blue. Interesting coloring. Germany. 1/2". Mint (9.9). $65. (Auction #126, Lot 42).

END OF DAY. Onionskin. Lot of three marbles. All are four panel onionskins. All are white core with two pink panels. $65. (Auction #128, Lot 13).

END OF DAY. Onionskin. Interesting onionskin from near the end of the cane. Subsurface layer of white and orange. 21/32". Mint (9.7). $65. (Auction #139, Lot 41).

END OF DAY. Onionskin. Rare coloring. Core is opaque mustard yellow, almost completely covered by red. 9/16". Mint (9.6). $65. (Auction #64, Lot 39).

END OF DAY. Onionskin. Blue skin on white core. Very pretty marble. Germany, circa 1870-1915. 21/32". Mint (9.9). $65. (Auction #136, Lot 34).

END OF DAY. Onionskin. Superb peewee onionskin, in an odd color. Translucent white core. 1/2". Mint (9.9). $65. (Auction #121, Lot 7).

END OF DAY. Onionskin. Lot of four onionskins. Assorted colors. All have some damage. 9/16" to 23/32". Near Mint (8.5) to Near Mint. $65. (Auction #157, Lot 22).

END OF DAY. Onionskin. Opaque yellow core covered by transparent green. One red band. Surface is in superb shape! Excellent. 11/16". Mint (9.9). $65. (Auction #63, Lot 40).

END OF DAY. Onionskin. Gorgeous marble! Semi-opaque white core with transparent light lime green skin. 5/8". Mint (9.9). $65. (Auction #153, Lot 11).

END OF DAY. Onionskin. Opaque white core with bands of blue, pink and some green. Some clear spaces in the white. Very nice. 25/32". Mint (9.5). $65. (Auction #184, Lot 46).

END OF DAY. Onionskin . Yellow core with transparent pink. A couple of tiny pits. Germany, circa 1870-1915. 21/32". Mint(-) (9). $61. (Auction #76, Lot 28).

END OF DAY. Onionskin. Lot of three marbles. All are onionskins. Smaller marbles. Assorted coloring. All have slight damage. $60. (Auction #122, Lot 29).

END OF DAY. Onionskin. Very pretty marble. Opaque yellow core. Completely covered by a skin of translucent green. 21/32". Mint (9.6). $60. (Auction #176, Lot 12).

END OF DAY. Onionskin. Gorgeous onionskin. Opaque white core with transparent blue and green bands on it. Surface in great. 19/32". Mint (9.9). $60. (Auction #82, Lot 19).

END OF DAY. Onionskin. Opaque white core. Pink skin with one band of blue. A beauty. Germany, circa 1870-1915. 19/32". Mint (9.9). $60. (Auction #137, Lot 15).

END OF DAY. Onionskin. Interesting onionskin in ribbon form. Transparent clear base. Opaque white core. 25/32". Near Mint(+) (8.2). $60. (Auction #157, Lot 29).

END OF DAY. Onionskin. Opaque white core with transparent pink on it. In super shape. Germany, circa 1870-1915. 23/32". Mint (9.9). $60. (Auction #164, Lot 36).

END OF DAY. Onionskin. Opaque white core. Three-quarters is covered by transparent blue. 9/16". Mint (9.9). $60. (Auction #167, Lot 6).

END OF DAY. Onionskin. Super marble. Core is opaque white and yellow. Skin is transparent pink with two narrow blue bands. 21/32". Mint (9.9). $60. (Auction #123, Lot 46).

END OF DAY. Onionskin. Transparent dark blue on opaque white. One pink band. Has a small melt spot on it. Germany. 9/16". Mint (9.5). $60. (Auction #80, Lot 33).

END OF DAY. Onionskin. Opaque yellow core with some pink on it. Lots of clear spaces in the core. Possibly from near an end. 11/16". Mint

(9.9). $60. (Auction #140, Lot 39).

END OF DAY. Onionskin. Mustard yellow core with some pink bands and a few green ones. A couple of tiny manufacturing pits. 23/32". Mint(-) (9.3). $60. (Auction #96, Lot 33).

END OF DAY. Onionskin. Another rare marble. Peewee two panel onionskin from near the end of the cane. Core is opaque white. 15/32". Near Mint(+) (8.7). $60. (Auction #61, Lot 33).

END OF DAY. Onionskin. Opaque white core with blue skin. Some green. A beauty. Germany, circa 1870-1915. 9/16". Mint (9.9). $56. (Auction #139, Lot 17).

END OF DAY. Onionskin. Opaque white core covered by transparent blue skin. One melt spot. 23/32". Mint (9.3). $55. (Auction #98, Lot 32).

END OF DAY. Onionskin. Beautiful onionskin. Opaque white core with a skin of transparent green. One tiny melt spot. 5/8". Mint (9.5). $55. (Auction #153, Lot 20).

END OF DAY. Onionskin. Opaque subsurface layer with some narrow bands of transparent pink, transparent blue. 9/16". Mint (9.9). $55. (Auction #133, Lot 38).

END OF DAY. Onionskin. Lot of two marbles. First is blue and white, 25/32", Near Mint(+) (8.8). The second is pink and white. $55. (Auction #149, Lot 12).

END OF DAY. Onionskin. Opaque white core with blue bands and a couple of light green ones. Tiny air bubbles in the glass. 21/32". Mint(-) (9.2). $55. (Auction #57, Lot 4).

END OF DAY. Onionskin. Transparent clear base. Translucent yellow core with some transparent pink on it. Surface in great shape. 19/32". Mint (9.9). $55. (Auction #90, Lot 33).

END OF DAY. Onionskin. Opaque white core with light blue skin. Two pink bands. Surface has a tiny flake. Germany. 9/16". Near Mint(+) (8.9). $55. (Auction #117, Lot 44).

END OF DAY. Onionskin. Opaque white core with transparent green skin. Germany, circa 1870-1915. 19/32." Mint (9.9). $55. (Auction #103, Lot 35).

END OF DAY. Onionskin. Lot of three marbles. All are onionskins. Assorted colors. 19/32". Near Mint(+) (8.8). $55. (Auction #177, Lot 28).

END OF DAY. Onionskin. Another beauty. Opaque white core with overall bands of transparent pink. 5/8". Mint (9.9). $55. (Auction #153, Lot 37).

END OF DAY. Onionskin. End of day onionskin. Transparent clear base. Subsurface layer of stretched bands of gray, yellow. 1-3/16". Near Mint(-) (8). $55. (Auction #89, Lot 14).

END OF DAY. Onionskin. Very nice onionskin. Opaque yellow core. Completely covered by transparent pink banding. 13/16". Near Mint(+) (8.7). $55. (Auction #143, Lot 42).

END OF DAY. Onionskin. Opaque white core. Blue skin with one pink band. Two tiny melt spots. Germany, circa 1870-1915. 11/16". Mint (9.7). $55. (Auction #147, Lot 13).

END OF DAY. Onionskin. Superb example of a shrunken core onionskin. Opaque white and transparent green core. Very shrunken. 15/32". Mint (9.9). $55. (Auction #95, Lot 41).

END OF DAY. Onionskin. Opaque white core. Transparent lime green skin. A beauty. Two melt spots. Germany, circa 1870-1915. 21/32". Mint(-) (9.2). $55. (Auction #148, Lot 15).

END OF DAY. Onionskin. Superior left hand twist onionskin. One of the finest I have ever seen. Opaque white core. 17/32". Mint(-) (9.1). $55. (Auction #106, Lot 45).

END OF DAY. Onionskin. Opaque white core. Transparent dark blue skin. One band of pink. Very nice marble. Germany. 21/32". Mint (9.7). $55. (Auction #148, Lot 17).

END OF DAY. Onionskin. Lot of three marbles. All are four-panel. One is in blue glass (rare). All have damage. 31/32". $55. (Auction #174, Lot 31).

END OF DAY. Onionskin. Gorgeous marble. Opaque white core. Transparent pink bands overall, with some blue and green too. Germany. 9/16". Mint (9.9). $51. (Auction #152, Lot 45).

END OF DAY. Onionskin. Opaque white core with pink skin. Very nice example. Germany, circa 1870-1915. 9/16". Mint (9.9). $51. (Auction #184, Lot 39).

END OF DAY. Onionskin. Gorgeous marble. Opaque yellow core with some clear spaces. Bands and spots of pink on the core. 11/16". Mint (9.9). $51. (Auction #155, Lot 45).

END OF DAY. Onionskin. I never know what to call these, but I guess onionskin is as good as anything else. 25/32". Near Mint (8.3). $50. (Auction #157, Lot 2).

END OF DAY. Onionskin. Interesting onionskin in ribbon form. Transparent clear base. Opaque white core. 25/32". Near Mint(+) (8.2). $50. (Auction #122, Lot 32).

END OF DAY. Onionskin. Super onionskin. Opaque white core. Almost completely covered by yellow, green, blue and pink. Great. 5/8". Near Mint(+) (8.9). $50. (Auction #73, Lot 43).

END OF DAY. Onionskin. Peewee. Almost a Joseph's Coat. Outstanding onionskin. Opaque yellow core, almost completely covered. 1/2". Mint (9.9). $50. (Auction #82, Lot 26).

END OF DAY. Onionskin. A super shrunken core onionskin. Opaque white core with transparent light green bands and some pink. 3/4". Near Mint(+) (8.9). $50. (Auction #55, Lot 18).

END OF DAY. Onionskin. Peewee. Green, blue and pink on white. Very nice marble. Germany, circa 1870-1915. 1/2". Mint (9.9). $50. (Auction #67, Lot 36).

END OF DAY. Onionskin. Very interesting peewee onionskin. Opaque white core. Covered with transparent blue and green bands. 15/32". Mint (9.9). $50. (Auction #123, Lot 6).

END OF DAY. Onionskin. Lot of five marbles. All are damaged. 17/32" to 13/16". Near Mint (8.6) to Good(+) (7.8). $50. (Auction #101, Lot 39).

END OF DAY. Onionskin. Small shrunken core onionskin. Probably from near an end of the cane. Transparent clear base. 17/32". Mint (9.9). $50. (Auction #88, Lot 15).

END OF DAY. Onionskin. A beauty!!!! Subsurface layer of translucent pink and white. Tiny manufacturing spot near the bottom. 19/32". Mint (9.7). $50. (Auction #122, Lot 36).

END OF DAY. Onionskin. Opaque white and transparent pink core. Lots of clear space. In great shape. Germany, circa 1870-1915. 17/32". Mint (9.9). $50. (Auction #166, Lot 36).

END OF DAY. Onionskin. Very rare first-off-cane end of day onionskin in ribbon form. Transparent clear base. Core is opaque. 3/4". Good (7.60). $50. (Auction #136, Lot 28).

END OF DAY. Onionskin. Super peewee onionskin with a shrunken core, from near an end of the cane. Core is opaque white. 1/2". Mint (9.9). $50. (Auction #131, Lot 39).

END OF DAY. Onionskin. Lot of five marbles. Nice assortment of paneled and non-panelled. All have damage. 21/32" to 29/32". $50. (Auction #92, Lot 13).

END OF DAY. Onionskin. Another interesting onionskin. Transparent clear base. Core is translucent white. 19/32". Mint (9.9). $48. (Auction #93, Lot 31).

END OF DAY. Onionskin. Excellent onionskin. Opaque white core with light green skin. One tiny manufacturing pit. 11/16". Mint (9.7). $48. (Auction #124, Lot 38).

END OF DAY. Onionskin. Opaque white base with transparent pink skin. Germany, circa 1870-1915. 17/32". Mint (9.9). $48. (Auction #146, Lot 42.30).

END OF DAY. Onionskin. Opaque white base with transparent pink skin. Germany, circa 1870-1915. 17/32". Mint (9.9). $48. (Auction #146, Lot 42.20).

END OF DAY. Onionskin. Opaque white base with transparent pink skin. Germany, circa 1870-1915. 17/32". Mint (9.9). $48. (Auction #146, Lot 42).

END OF DAY. Onionskin. Opaque white and pink onionskin peewee. A beauty. Small spot of melted glass on one side. Germany. 1/2". Mint (9.7). $47. (Auction #126, Lot 30).

END OF DAY. Onionskin. Opaque white core with transparent blue skin. Surface in great shape. 9/16". Mint (9.7). $47. (Auction #117, Lot 35).

END OF DAY. Onionskin. Nice onionskin. Core is transparent white, translucent yellow and transparent pink. 17/32". Mint (9.9). $47. (Auction #162, Lot 33).

END OF DAY. Onionskin. Peewee. Opaque white core with transparent green skin. In great shape. Germany, circa 1870-1915. 1/2". Mint (9.9). $47. (Auction #89, Lot 43).

END OF DAY. Onionskin. Transparent blue on opaque white core. Super example. Germany, circa 1870-1915. 9/16". Mint (9.8). $47. (Auction #164, Lot 27).

END OF DAY. Onionskin. Hard to find example. Base glass is light blue. Opaque white core. Skin of pink and blue. 9/16". Mint(-) (9). $47. (Auction #145, Lot 10).

END OF DAY. Onionskin. Opaque white core with dark blue skin. In great shape. Germany, circa 1870-1915. 19/32." Mint (9.9). $47. (Auction #118, Lot 4).

END OF DAY. Onionskin. Superb shrunken core onionskin. Opaque white core. Three green splotches on it. 9/16". Mint (9.9). $47. (Auction #160, Lot 26).

END OF DAY. Onionskin. Super pastel color onionskin. Opaque white core. Transparent bands of green, blue and pink. 11/16". Mint (9.9).

$46. (Auction #131, Lot 31).

END OF DAY. Onionskin. Opaque white base. Blue skin. Surface in great shape. Germany, circa 1870-1915. 21/32". Mint (9.9). $46. (Auction #169, Lot 42).

END OF DAY. Onionskin. Opaque white base with transparent green skin. Peewee. Germany, circa 1870-1915. 15/32". Mint (9.9). $45. (Auction #151, Lot 42.30).

END OF DAY. Onionskin. Very unusual coloring. Opaque white base covered by transparent green bands. Bands of opaque yellow. $45. (Auction #171, Lot 37).

END OF DAY. Onionskin. Opaque white base. Blue skin. Surface in great shape. Germany, circa 1870-1915. 21/32". Mint (9.9). $45. (Auction #129, Lot 26).

END OF DAY. Onionskin. Opaque white base with transparent green skin. Peewee. Germany, circa 1870-1915. 15/32". Mint (9.9). $45. (Auction #151, Lot 42.20).

END OF DAY. Onionskin. Opaque white base with transparent green skin. Peewee. Germany, circa 1870-1915. 15/32". Mint (9.9). $45. (Auction #151, Lot 42).

END OF DAY. Onionskin. Opaque white core. Skin of transparent green and transparent turquoise splotches with a little pink. 1-5/16". Good (7.50). $45. (Auction #125, Lot 20).

END OF DAY. Onionskin. Opaque white core with blue skin. One pink band. Beautiful example. Germany, circa 1870-1915. 19/32." Mint (9.9). $45. (Auction #124, Lot 23).

END OF DAY. Onionskin. Transparent pink on opaque yellow core. One tiny melt spot. Beauty. Germany, circa 1870-1915. 9/16". Mint (9.6). $45. (Auction #164, Lot 17).

END OF DAY. Onionskin. Opaque white base with transparent blue skin. Germany, circa 1870-1915. 17/32". Mint (9.9). $44. (Auction #146, Lot 38.40).

END OF DAY. Onionskin. Opaque white base with transparent blue skin. Germany, circa 1870-1915. 17/32". Mint (9.9). $44. (Auction #146, Lot 38).

END OF DAY. Onionskin. Opaque white base with transparent blue skin. Germany, circa 1870-1915. 17/32". Mint (9.9). $44. (Auction #146, Lot 38.20).

END OF DAY. Onionskin. Opaque white base with transparent blue skin. Germany, circa 1870-1915. 17/32". Mint (9.9). $44. (Auction #146, Lot 38.30).

END OF DAY. Onionskin. Opaque white core. Covered by transparent pink. Two blue bands. One air hole. A beauty. Germany. 21/32". Mint (9.4). $43. (Auction #155, Lot 40).

END OF DAY. Onionskin. Lot of two marbles. First is a four panel. Pink on yellow, blue on white. Some pitting. 21/32". Near Mint. $42. (Auction #97, Lot 1).

END OF DAY. Onionskin. Peewee. Green and blue on white. A beauty. Almost no twist. Germany, circa 1870-1915. 1/2". Mint (9.9). $42. (Auction #88, Lot 11).

END OF DAY. Onionskin. Pink on yellow onionskin. Core slightly shrunken on one side. Super marble. Germany, circa 1870-1915. 5/8". Mint (9.7). $42. (Auction #67, Lot 39).

END OF DAY. Onionskin. Very nice end of day onionskin. Opaque white core with transparent pink on it. Lots of clear space. 9/16". Mint (9.9). $42. (Auction #129, Lot 35).

END OF DAY. Onionskin. Opaque white core with pink skin. A few bands of blue and green. Very pretty marble. Germany. 9/16". Mint (9.7). $42. (Auction #124, Lot 19).

END OF DAY. Onionskin. Opaque white core with pink skin. Has some yellow too. Surface in nice shape with one tiny flat spot. 19/32". Mint (9.8). $42. (Auction #140, Lot 32).

END OF DAY. Onionskin. Yellow core with transparent pink skin. Surface is pristine. Stunning. Slightly shrunken on one side. 19/32". Mint (9.9). $41. (Auction #113, Lot 36).

END OF DAY. Onionskin. Peewee onionskin. Opaque yellow core. Transparent green skin on it. Nice one. Germany, circa 1870-19. 1/2". Mint (9.7). $41. (Auction #129, Lot 16).

END OF DAY. Onionskin. Opaque white core with transparent green and some pink. Shrunken core on one side. Tight twist. 1/2". Near Mint(+) (8.9). $41. (Auction #120, Lot 46).

END OF DAY. Onionskin. Very nice onionskin. Opaque white core with transparent green skin and some transparent blue. Superb. 9/16". Mint (9.9). $41. (Auction #96, Lot 12).

END OF DAY. Onionskin. Opaque white core with transparent pink skin and some very light blue. Some clear spaces in the white. 11/16". Mint(-) (9.2). $41. (Auction #142, Lot 17).

END OF DAY. Onionskin. Opaque white core. Blue skin. Very nice example. Germany, circa 1870-1915. 9/16". Mint (9.9). $40. (Auction

#100, Lot 33).

END OF DAY. Onionskin. Opaque white core with transparent bands of pink, green, orange and blue. Almost no twist. Melt spot. 5/8". Mint(-) (9). $40. (Auction #166, Lot 46).

END OF DAY. Onionskin. Lot of two marbles. First is a two panel. Opaque white core. Two panels of pink and two of blue. $40. (Auction #105, Lot 14).

END OF DAY. Onionskin. Beautiful onionskin. Peewee. Opaque white core. Transparent green skin. Germany, circa 1870-1915. 15/32". Mint (9.7). $40. (Auction #131, Lot 7).

END OF DAY. Onionskin. Translucent yellow and translucent pink core. Very earthy toned. Slightly shrunken on one side. 11/16". Mint(-) (9). $39. (Auction #103, Lot 31).

END OF DAY. Onionskin. Nice onionskin. Blue and white core. In great shape. Peewee. Compare to Lot #38. Germany, circa 1870. 15/32". Mint (9.9). $38. (Auction #97, Lot 41).

END OF DAY. Onionskin. Translucent white core with transparent light green on it. Surface has two small melt spots. 5/8". Mint (9). $38. (Auction #167, Lot 33).

END OF DAY. Onionskin. Odd type. Transparent clear core. Opaque white layer covering that. 11/16". Near Mint (8.6). $38. (Auction #68, Lot 28).

END OF DAY. Onionskin. Opaque white core with dark blue skin. A little green in it too. Germany, circa 1870-1915. 5/8". Mint (9.9). $38. (Auction #125, Lot 43).

END OF DAY. Onionskin. Opaque yellow core with pink skin. A beauty!! One manufacturing pit. Germany, circa 1870-1915. 5/8". Mint (9.7). $37. (Auction #128, Lot 40).

END OF DAY. Onionskin. Opaque white base with transparent pink skin. Germany, circa 1870-1915. 17/32". Mint (9.9). $37. (Auction #151, Lot 50.20).

END OF DAY. Onionskin. Opaque white base with transparent pink skin. Germany, circa 1870-1915. 17/32". Mint (9.9). $37. (Auction #151, Lot 50).

END OF DAY. Onionskin. Opaque white base with transparent pink skin. Germany, circa 1870-1915. 17/32". Mint (9.9). $37. (Auction #151, Lot 50.30).

END OF DAY. Onionskin. Peewee end of day onionskin. White core. Covered by translucent blue with one pink band and one yellow. 15/32". Mint(-) (9). $37. (Auction #104, Lot 34).

END OF DAY. Onionskin. Lot of two marbles. First is a pink on yellow onionskin with mica. 25/32". Near Mint(-) (8.1). $36. (Auction #112, Lot 7).

END OF DAY. Onionskin. Transparent clear base. Core is transparent blue and translucent white bands. Some clear spaces. 9/16". Mint (9.9). $36. (Auction #93, Lot 28).

END OF DAY. Onionskin. Opaque white base completely covered with transparent pink. There are tiny black spots on the core. 19/32". Mint (9.4). $36. (Auction #83, Lot 9).

END OF DAY. Onionskin. Translucent white core covered by transparent blue with some pink and a little green. 11/16". Mint(-) (9). $36. (Auction #88, Lot 42).

END OF DAY. Onionskin. Gorgeous end of day onionskin. Opaque white core with transparent dark blue skin. No twist. 21/32". Mint (9.9). $35. (Auction #109, Lot 35).

END OF DAY. Onionskin. Nice peewee onionskin. Transparent blue on white. Tiny marble. Germany, circa 1870-1915. 7/16". Mint (9.7). $35. (Auction #54, Lot 32).

END OF DAY. Onionskin. Opaque white core with transparent pink stretched bands. Core is slightly shrunken on one side. 21/32". Mint(-) (9.1). $35. (Auction #60, Lot 36).

END OF DAY. Onionskin. In nice shape with a shrunken core. Opaque white core. Transparent light green on one side. 3/4". Near Mint(+) (8.9). $35. (Auction #131, Lot 45).

END OF DAY. Onionskin. Opaque white core with blue thin skin. Slightly shrunken on one side. Germany, circa 1870-1915. 9/16". Mint (9.9). $35. (Auction #100, Lot 15).

END OF DAY. Onionskin. Opaque white core, covered by transparent green. A couple of pink bands. One small moon. 19/32". Near Mint (8.6). $35. (Auction #87, Lot 10).

END OF DAY. Onionskin. Lot of two marbles. Nice pair of onionskin. Excellent coloring. Both have been polished, the pontils. $34. (Auction #164, Lot 4).

END OF DAY. Onionskin. Opaque white core with transparent blue onion. Pristine surface. 9/16". Mint (9.9). $34. (Auction #98, Lot 19).

END OF DAY. Onionskin. Opaque white core with blue skin. One tiny pit. Germany, circa 1870-1915. 9/16". Mint(-) (9.1). $34. (Auction #183, Lot 9).

END OF DAY. Onionskin. Lot of two marbles. First is transparent green on white. Large annealing fractures on one side. 1". $34. (Auction #108, Lot 37).

END OF DAY. Onionskin. Lot of two marbles. One is blue on white, one is green on white. Both have some damage. 25/32". Near Mint. $33. (Auction #180, Lot 42).

END OF DAY. Onionskin. Opaque white core with transparent pink skin. Has one tiny pit. Nice marble. Germany, circa 1870-1915. 21/32". Mint(-) (9). $32. (Auction #145, Lot 5).

END OF DAY. Onionskin. Nice onionskin. Blue and white core. In great shape. Compare to Lot #41. Germany, circa 1870-1915. 9/16". Mint (9.9). $32. (Auction #97, Lot 38).

END OF DAY. Onionskin. Opaque white core. Transparent green skin with a pink band. Large flake on one side (5/8"). 1-5/16". Good (7.50). $32. (Auction #134, Lot 22).

END OF DAY. Onionskin. Peewee onionskin. Opaque white core. Transparent pink skin. Very nice. Germany, circa 1870-1915. 15/32". Mint (9.8). $32. (Auction #146, Lot 47).

END OF DAY. Onionskin. Opaque white core with a thin layer of very light transparent green. Very pretty. One tiny pit. Germany. 17/32". Mint(-) (9.2). $31. (Auction #173, Lot 30).

END OF DAY. Onionskin. Opaque white core with blue skin. Both pontils are ground. Germany, circa 1870-1915. 19/32". Mint (9.5). $31. (Auction #182, Lot 16).

END OF DAY. Onionskin. Interesting shrunken core end of day onionskin. Transparent clear base. Core of translucent white. 21/32". Near Mint(+) (8.9). $30. (Auction #93, Lot 11).

END OF DAY. Onionskin. Opaque white and transparent blue core. Deep crease on one side of the core. One small pit on the surface. 17/32". Near Mint(+) (8.9). $30. (Auction #184, Lot 11).

END OF DAY. Onionskin. Opaque white core, transparent pink skin. A few tiny pits and very tiny chips. Germany, circa 1870. 19/32". Near Mint (8.6). $30. (Auction #181, Lot 2).

END OF DAY. Onionskin. Opaque white core with transparent blue and pink. Top pontil is cold rolled. In great shape. Germany. 9/16". Mint (9.6). $29. (Auction #95, Lot 11).

END OF DAY. Onionskin. Opaque white core with several blue bands and some pink on it. Very nice marble. Germany, circa 1870. 17/32". Mint (9.8). $28. (Auction #142, Lot 35).

END OF DAY. Onionskin. Opaque white core. Blue skin. Slightly shrunken on one side. One tiny pinprick. Very pretty marble. 19/32". Mint(-) (9). $27. (Auction #142, Lot 6).

END OF DAY. Onionskin. Opaque white base. Transparent pink skin. A couple of tiny pits. Germany, circa 1870-1915. 19/32". Mint(-) (9). $27. (Auction #181, Lot 10).

END OF DAY. Onionskin. Opaque white core with overall transparent blue and one band of red. 5/8". Mint(-) (9.1). $27. (Auction #83, Lot 3).

END OF DAY. Onionskin. Transparent blue skin on opaque white. Some minor surface wear. Germany, circa 1870-1915. 9/16". Mint(-) (9). $27. (Auction #95, Lot 8).

END OF DAY. Onionskin. Peewee onionskin. Transparent blue on opaque white. One narrow green band. Tiny subsurface moon. 15/32". Near Mint (8.6). $26. (Auction #80, Lot 15).

END OF DAY. Onionskin. Core is translucent white and yellow. Covered by translucent pink skin. 17/32". Mint(-) (9.1). $24. (Auction #156, Lot 15).

END OF DAY. Onionskin. Opaque white core covered by transparent pink. A couple of tiny pits on the surface. Germany. 21/32". Near Mint(+) (8.9). $24. (Auction #87, Lot 6).

END OF DAY. Onionskin. Lot of four marbles. Assortment of onionskins. All have been used. 25/32" to 7/8". Near Mint(-) (8.0). $22. (Auction #171, Lot 16).

END OF DAY. Onionskin. Transparent pink stretched splotches on opaque yellow. This would be a stunning example. 11/16". Near Mint(+) (8.9). $22. (Auction #61, Lot 9).

END OF DAY. Onionskin. Opaque white core. Pink skin. Two slight lobes. Mica on the core. There is overall haziness. 11/16". Good (7.40). $20. (Auction #102, Lot 36).

END OF DAY. Onionskin. Interesting onionskin. Opaque white core. A few thin bands of pink and a few green. Small fracture. 21/32". Near Mint(+) (8.9). $20. (Auction #118, Lot 34).

END OF DAY. Onionskin. Lot of two marbles. First is transparent pink on white. Overall haziness and tiny moons. 21/32". Good. $14. (Auction #54, Lot 7).

END OF DAY. Onionskin cloud. And yet one more stunning marble. Transparent clear base. 21/32". Mint (9.7). $450. (Auction #124, Lot 50).

END OF DAY. Onionskin with mica. Stunning marble. Very rare. Two-panel "blizzard mica" onionskin. Transparent clear base. $600. (Auction #89, Lot 48).

END OF DAY. Onionskin with mica. Nice small onionskin with mica. Transparent pink and dark green stretched bands on opaque yellow. 17/32". Near Mint(+) (8.9). $35. (Auction #61, Lot 28).

END OF DAY. paneled Cloud. Unbelievable and very rare four panel cloud. In super shape. A very rare find!!! Two panels of yellow. 21/32". Mint(-) (9.2). $380. (Auction #113, Lot 42).

END OF DAY. paneled onionskin. Absolutely stunning four-panel onionskin with mica and slight lobing. Transparent clear glass. 2-3/16". Mint(-) (9.1). $1600. (Auction #183, Lot 50).

END OF DAY. paneled onionskin. Absolutely stunning four-panel onionskin, in superior condition. 2". Mint(-) (9.2). $725. (Auction #176, Lot 50).

END OF DAY. paneled onionskin. Outstanding example. Four-panel onionskin. Opaque white core. Two panels of transparent green splotches. 1-11/16". Mint(-) (9). $410. (Auction #169, Lot 50).

END OF DAY. paneled onionskin. Wow!! This is one of the rarest onionskins I have ever seen. Three panel onionskin with mica!! 7/8". Near Mint(+) (8.9). $390. (Auction #91, Lot 44).

END OF DAY. paneled onionskin. Superior and outstanding example of a four panel onionskin. Surface is pristine. Stunning example. 1-9/16". Mint (9.8). $365. (Auction #126, Lot 50).

END OF DAY. paneled onionskin. One of the finest looking end of days that I have ever seen. Four panels. Two panels are translucent. 1-5/8". Near Mint(+) (8.9). $290. (Auction #85, Lot 45).

END OF DAY. paneled onionskin. Larger onionskin. Very clear marble. Great coloring. Four panels. Opaque white core. 1-11/16". Near Mint(+) (8.7). $230. (Auction #113, Lot 32).

END OF DAY. paneled onionskin. I've classified this as an onionskin, although obviously it is a very odd one. 21/32". Mint(-) (9.2). $220. (Auction #80, Lot 41).

END OF DAY. paneled onionskin. Rare larger four-panel left-twist onionskin. Opaque white core. Two panels of pink, one of blue. 1-9/16". Near Mint(+) (8.7). $220. (Auction #153, Lot 48).

END OF DAY. paneled onionskin. Very unusual, superb onionskin. Transparent clear base. Opaque white core. Has one panel of orange. 21/32". Mint (9.9). $220. (Auction #90, Lot 44).

END OF DAY. paneled onionskin. Four panel onionskin. Opaque white core. Two panels are transparent pink, two are transparent green. 1-1/4". Near Mint(+) (8.9). $220. (Auction #149, Lot 48).

END OF DAY. paneled onionskin. Four panel onionskin with mica. Large. Opaque white core. Two wide panels of transparent pink dots. $220. (Auction #107, Lot 44).

END OF DAY. paneled onionskin. Opaque yellow core with two white panels of pink and two narrow panels of green. Lots of mica. 21/32". Mint (9.9). $190. (Auction #137, Lot 47).

END OF DAY. paneled onionskin. I have classified this as a paneled onionskin, although it exhibits some characteristics of a Joseph Coat. 7/8". Mint(-) (9.2). $180. (Auction #173, Lot 44).

END OF DAY. paneled onionskin. Four panel onionskin. Opaque white core. Two panels of blue and two of pink. This one is a beauty. 1-9/16". Near Mint(+) (8.9). $160. (Auction #71, Lot 37).

END OF DAY. paneled onionskin. Huge four panel onionskin. Polished. Opaque white core. Two panels of pink splotches, two of turquoise. $150. (Auction #122, Lot 24).

END OF DAY. paneled onionskin. Hard to find left-hand twist, four panel onionskin. Two panels are light blue on white. 23/32". Mint (9.8). $150. (Auction #78, Lot 38).

END OF DAY. paneled onionskin. Super four-panel onionskin. Two wide panels of transparent red on opaque yellow. 15/16". Mint (9.9). $140. (Auction #85, Lot 10).

END OF DAY. paneled onionskin. Four panel onionskin. Mustard yellow core. Two pink panels and two green panels. In nice shape. Germany. 7/8". Mint (9.9). $140. (Auction #112, Lot 14).

END OF DAY. paneled onionskin. Four-panel onionskin. Left-hand twist. Opaque white core. Two wide panels of pink, two narrow panels. 1-1/16". Near Mint(+) (8.7). $140. (Auction #161, Lot 48).

END OF DAY. paneled onionskin. Very rare four-panel onionskin. Each panel is a different color. Each is about the same width. 19/32". Near Mint(+) (8.9). $140. (Auction #87, Lot 41).

END OF DAY. paneled onionskin. Superb four-panel onionskin. Fat opaque white core. Two panels of transparent green with some blue. 31/32". Mint (9.9). $140. (Auction #129, Lot 43).

END OF DAY. paneled onionskin. Opaque yellow core with two white panels of pink and two narrow panels of green. A few pieces of mica. 11/16". Mint (9.9). $135. (Auction #137, Lot 6).

END OF DAY. paneled onionskin. Two panel onionskin. Opaque white core. Transparent green on one side, transparent pink on the other. 19/32". Mint (9.9). $130. (Auction #73, Lot 37).

END OF DAY. paneled onionskin. Opaque yellow core with two wide panels of pink and two narrow panels of green. A fair amount of mica. 11/16". Mint (9.9). $130. (Auction #162, Lot 45).

END OF DAY. paneled onionskin. Large four-panel onionskin. Base glass has a light blue tint. Two panels of blue on white. 1-5/8". Near Mint (8.5). $130. (Auction #97, Lot 45).

END OF DAY. paneled onionskin. Left-hand twist four-panel onionskin with some lobing. Opaque white core. Two panels of pink. 15/16". Near Mint (8.4). $125. (Auction #168, Lot 39).

END OF DAY. paneled onionskin. Very nice four-panel onionskin with mica. Fat white core. Two wide panels of pink. 13/16". Mint (9.7). $120. (Auction #183, Lot 45).

END OF DAY. paneled onionskin. Four panel onionskin. Outstanding example. Opaque white core. Two panels of blue with some pink. 1-1/16". Mint(-) (9). $120. (Auction #179, Lot 40).

END OF DAY. paneled onionskin. Opaque yellow core with two white panels of pink and two narrow panels of green. Some nice mica. 21/32". Mint (9.9). $110. (Auction #145, Lot 45).

END OF DAY. paneled onionskin. Lot of two marbles. First is four panel, 1-5/8", Near Mint(-) (8.1). Other is also four panel, 1-7/8". $110. (Auction #94, Lot 13).

END OF DAY. paneled onionskin. Hard to find five panel onionskin. Two panels of blue on white. Two of pink on yellow. 1-9/16". Near Mint (8.3). $110. (Auction #130, Lot 27).

END OF DAY. paneled onionskin. Beautiful four panel onionskin. Two panels are blue on white, the other two are pink on yellow. 3/4". Near Mint(+) (8.9). $105. (Auction #81, Lot 34).

END OF DAY. paneled onionskin. Nice left hand twist, four panel onionskin. White core. Two panels of blue and two of pink. 1-9/16". Near Mint (8.5). $100. (Auction #58, Lot 29).

END OF DAY. paneled onionskin. Opaque whtie core. Two wide panels of transparent pink, two narrow panels of transparent blue. 7/8". Mint (9.9). $100. (Auction #82, Lot 42).

END OF DAY. paneled onionskin. Four panel onionskin. Probably from the start of the cane. Opaque white core. Two panels of blue. 23/32". Mint (9.8). $100. (Auction #121, Lot 32).

END OF DAY. paneled onionskin. Four-panel onionskin with mica. Opaque white core. Two wide panels of pink, two narrower panels of blue. 23/32". Mint(-) (9). $100. (Auction #154, Lot 43).

END OF DAY. paneled onionskin. Hard to find six-panel onionskin. Each panel is about the same width. Two each of pink on yellow. 11/16". Mint(-) (9). $100. (Auction #107, Lot 22).

END OF DAY. paneled onionskin. Larger four-panel onionskin. Opaque white core. Two panels of blue, two panels of pink on yellow. 1-1/2". Near Mint (8.3). $100. (Auction #112, Lot 17).

END OF DAY. paneled onionskin. Larger four-panel onionskin with mica. Opaque white core. Two pink bands and two blue bands. $100. (Auction #106, Lot 48).

END OF DAY. paneled onionskin. This one is a absolute beauty. Opaque white core. Two wide panels of transparent blue. Two narrow panels. $100. (Auction #145, Lot 36).

END OF DAY. paneled onionskin. Six-panel onionskin. Opaque white core. Two panels of yellow with some pink and green on it. 21/32". Mint (9.9). $90. (Auction #159, Lot 18).

END OF DAY. paneled onionskin. Four panel onionskin. Opaque yellow core. Two wide panels of transparent pink. 1-1/2". Near Mint (8.5). $90. (Auction #89, Lot 22).

END OF DAY. paneled onionskin. Very unusual four panel onionskin with mica. One wide panel of pink on yellow, one wide panel of pink. 7/8". Near Mint (8.5). $85. (Auction #120, Lot 35).

END OF DAY. paneled onionskin. Unsual onionskin. Two panels of white and two panels of yellow. The yellow has transparent pink. 21/32". Mint (9.9). $85. (Auction #147, Lot 1).

END OF DAY. paneled onionskin. Four panel onionskin. Opaque white core. Two wide panels of pink, two narrow panels of blue. 25/32". Mint (9.9). $85. (Auction #136, Lot 36).

END OF DAY. paneled onionskin. Superb four panel onionskin. Two panels are pink on white. Two are green on yellow. 21/32". Near Mint(+) (8.9). $80. (Auction #116, Lot 46).

END OF DAY. paneled onionskin. Four panel onionskin. Two are pink and yellow, two are blue and white. Surface in great shape. 9/16". Mint (9.9). $80. (Auction #78, Lot 36).

END OF DAY. paneled onionskin. Four-panel onionskin. Opaque yellow core. Two wide panels of green, two narrow panels of red. 13/16". Near Mint(+) (8.9). $80. (Auction #173, Lot 2).

END OF DAY. paneled onionskin. Lot of three marbles. All are four-panel onionskins. Nice group. 19/32" to 29/32". Mint(-) (9.0) to Near Mint. $80. (Auction #161, Lot 20).

END OF DAY. paneled onionskin. Hard to find lobed onionskin. White core. Two pink panels, two blue panels. Each panel has a lobe. 9/16". Mint (9.7). $80. (Auction #136, Lot 4).

END OF DAY. paneled onionskin. Lot of five marbles. All are four-panel onionskin. Assortment of colors. All have some damage. 23/32". $80. (Auction #157, Lot 30).

END OF DAY. paneled onionskin. Four panel onionskin. Core is mustard yellow. There are two transparent pink panels. 23/32". Mint (9.7). $80. (Auction #70, Lot 41).

END OF DAY. paneled onionskin. Two panel onionskin with a little mica. Opaque yellow core. Two wide panels of pink, two narrow panels. 1-1/8". Near Mint (8.3). $75. (Auction #163, Lot 15).

END OF DAY. paneled onionskin. Opaque yellow core with two white panels of pink and two narrow panels of green. 21/32". Mint (9.9). $75. (Auction #155, Lot 48).

END OF DAY. paneled onionskin. Opaque yellow core with two wide panels of pink and two narrow panels of green. Some mica. 11/16". Mint (9.9). $75. (Auction #162, Lot 20).

END OF DAY. paneled onionskin. Very hard to find end of cane (first-off-cane) four panel onionskin. Opaque white core. 21/32". Mint (9.9). $75. (Auction #113, Lot 38).

END OF DAY. paneled onionskin. Four panel onionskin. Two wide panels of pink on white. One narrow panel of blue on white. 7/8". Near Mint (8.6). $70. (Auction #128, Lot 47).

END OF DAY. paneled onionskin. Four panel onionskin. Opaque white core. Two panels are transparent red and two are transparent blue. 7/8". Near Mint (8.6). $65. (Auction #103, Lot 24).

END OF DAY. paneled onionskin. Four panel onionskin. Two panels are pink on white (one has a green band). 9/16". Mint (9.8). $65. (Auction #67, Lot 14).

END OF DAY. paneled onionskin. Super four-panel onionskin. Very interesting marble. Core is opaque white. 5/8". Mint (9.5). $65. (Auction #88, Lot 27).

END OF DAY. paneled onionskin. Lot of two marbles. Both are four-panel. First is two blue and white panels. $65. (Auction #94, Lot 37).

END OF DAY. paneled onionskin. Four panel onionskin. Shooter size. Super example. Opaque white core. Two wide panels of pink. 29/32". Mint(-) (9). $65. (Auction #105, Lot 47).

END OF DAY. paneled onionskin with mica. Four-panel onionskin. Opaque white core. Two wide panels of transparent pink and two narrow panels. 5/8". Mint (9.9). $65. (Auction #89, Lot 42).

END OF DAY. paneled onionskin. Subtle four-panel onionskin. Two wide panels of translucent green and translucent white. 21/32". Mint (9.9). $65. (Auction #81, Lot 9).

END OF DAY. paneled onionskin. Beautiful peewee onionskin. Two wide panels of transparent pink on opaque white and two narrow panels. 15/32". Mint (9.9). $65. (Auction #89, Lot 41).

END OF DAY. paneled onionskin. Four-panel onionskin. Opaque white core with two panels of blue and two of pink. 7/8". Mint (9.6). $60. (Auction #159, Lot 9).

END OF DAY. paneled onionskin. Four panel, left hand twist onionskin. Opaque white core. Two panels are pink. 11/16". Mint (9.5). $60. (Auction #115, Lot 47).

END OF DAY. paneled onionskin. Very pretty four panel onionskin with mica. Two wide panels of pink on white. 7/8". Near Mint (8.4). $60. (Auction #120, Lot 32).

END OF DAY. paneled onionskin. Four panel onionskin. Two panels are blue on white, two are pink on white. Surface in superb shape. 21/32". Mint (9.9). $60. (Auction #85, Lot 14).

END OF DAY. paneled onionskin. Opaque yellow core with two white panels of pink and two narrow panels of green. Some mica. 11/16". Near Mint(+) (8.9). $60. (Auction #140, Lot 46).

END OF DAY. paneled onionskin. Odd onionskin. Two panels are transparent pink on yellow. One panel is transparent pink on white. 21/32". Mint(-) (9.3). $60. (Auction #62, Lot 28).

END OF DAY. paneled onionskin. Four panel onionskin. Yellow core. Two wide panels of pink. Two narrower panels of green and blue. 1-1/8". Near Mint (8.6). $60. (Auction #157, Lot 49).

END OF DAY. paneled onionskin. Four-panel left-hand twist onionskin with mica. Very unusual marble. Opaque white core. 29/32". Near Mint(-) (8). $60. (Auction #120, Lot 44).

END OF DAY. paneled onionskin. Super four-panel lobed onionskin. Two panels are opaque white with transparent blue, two are opaque. 21/32". Near Mint(+) (8.9). $60. (Auction #156, Lot 8).

END OF DAY. paneled onionskin. Four panel onionskin. Opaque white core. Two panels of yellow and pink. Two panels of blue. 3/4". Near Mint(+) (8.7). $58. (Auction #90, Lot 18).

END OF DAY. paneled onionskin. Core of transparent pink on opaque yellow. Two panels of green. One very tiny melt spot. Tight twist. 11/16". Mint (9.5). $56. (Auction #150, Lot 13).

END OF DAY. paneled onionskin. Four panel onionskin. Opaque white core. Two wide panels of pink. Two narrow panels of blue. 11/16". Mint (9.9). $55. (Auction #134, Lot 44).

END OF DAY. paneled onionskin. Four panel onionskin. Opaque white core. Two wide panels of transparent red. 21/32". Near Mint(+) (8.9). $55. (Auction #176, Lot 48).

END OF DAY. paneled onionskin. Very unusual marble. Core is opaque white. Two wide bands of transparent blue form two narrow panels. 13/16". Near Mint (8.3). $55. (Auction #121, Lot 41).

END OF DAY. paneled onionskin. Four panel onionskin. Peewee. Opaque white core. Two wide panels of pink, two narrow panels of blue. 15/32". Mint (9.9). $55. (Auction #131, Lot 2).

END OF DAY. paneled onionskin. Pastel colors. Opaque white core. Two panels are transparent aqua green and two are transparent pink. 3/4". Near Mint(+) (8.9). $55. (Auction #69, Lot 30).

END OF DAY. paneled onionskin. Lot of three marbles. All are shooter four-panel onionskins. Nice assortment of colors and styles. $55. (Auction #144, Lot 14).

END OF DAY. paneled onionskin. Four-panel left-hand twist onionskin with a reverse twist on top. Opaque white core. 13/16". Mint(-) (9). $55. (Auction #172, Lot 49).

END OF DAY. paneled onionskin. Very rare three-panel left-hand twist onionskin. Opaque white core. One panel of pink, one green. 7/8". Near Mint(-) (8.1). $55. (Auction #120, Lot 42).

END OF DAY. paneled onionskin. Lot of four marbles. All are four-panel. Assorted color schemes. All have damage. 23/32" to 25/32". $51. (Auction #157, Lot 42).

END OF DAY. paneled onionskin. Gorgeous marble. Opaque white base with two panels of turquoise green and two panels of pink. 21/32". Mint (9.8). $50. (Auction #170, Lot 42).

END OF DAY. paneled onionskin. Four panel onionskin. White core. Two panels of pink and two of blue. Overall chips. Germany. 2". Good(-) (7). $50. (Auction #102, Lot 24).

END OF DAY. paneled onionskin. Four panel onionskin. Opaque white core. Two panels of light green, two panels of pink. Nice twist. 3/4". Mint (9.3). $50. (Auction #115, Lot 11).

END OF DAY. paneled onionskin. Hard to find six-panel onionskin. Opaque white core. Three panels of transparent blue. 19/32". Mint(-) (9.1). $50. (Auction #169, Lot 16).

END OF DAY. paneled onionskin. Superb four-panel onionskin. Transparent clear base. Core is two white panels of transparent pink. 17/32". Mint (9.9). $50. (Auction #89, Lot 5).

END OF DAY. paneled onionskin. Four panel onionskin. Interesting design. Two panels of pink bands on yellow. 23/32". Near Mint(+) (8.9). $50. (Auction #140, Lot 4).

END OF DAY. paneled onionskin. Tiny marble. Opaque white core. Two panels with pink stripes, two with blue stripes. 15/32". Mint (9.9). $50. (Auction #134, Lot 17).

END OF DAY. paneled onionskin. Opaque white core. Two panels of transparent pink and two of transparent green. Surface is pristine. 23/32". Mint (9.9). $48. (Auction #98, Lot 43).

END OF DAY. paneled onionskin. Four panel onionskin. Opaque white core. Two pink panels and two blue panels. Two minor lobes. 11/16". Mint (9.9). $47. (Auction #129, Lot 31).

END OF DAY. paneled onionskin. Very subtle marble. Opaque white core. Two panels are transparent pink, two are light transparent green. 21/32". Near Mint(+) (8.9). $46. (Auction #82, Lot 35).

END OF DAY. paneled onionskin. Interesting four-panel onionskin from near an end of the cane. Translucent white core. 3/4". Near Mint(+) (8.9). $46. (Auction #179, Lot 32).

END OF DAY. paneled onionskin. Rare four panel onionskin in ribbon form. Opaque white core. Two wide panels with pink. 31/32". Good(+) (7.80). $45. (Auction #144, Lot 37).

END OF DAY. paneled onionskin. Four panel onionskin. Opaque white core with lots of clear spaces. Two panels of pink and two of blue. 9/16". Mint (9.9). $45. (Auction #145, Lot 30).

END OF DAY. paneled onionskin. Very pretty four-panel onionskin. Opaque white base. Two thin panels of blue, two wider of pink. 9/16". Mint (9.9). $44. (Auction #131, Lot 33).

END OF DAY. paneled onionskin. Rare two-panel left-hand twist onionskin. Opaque white core. One wide panel of pink. 5/8". Near Mint(+) (8.9). $44. (Auction #150, Lot 31).

END OF DAY. paneled onionskin. Nice four panel onionskin. Two wide panels of translucent white. 9/16". Mint (9.9). $44. (Auction #92, Lot 2).

END OF DAY. paneled onionskin. Four panel. Two panels of blue on white and two or pink on yellow. Two small melt spots. Germany. 21/32". Mint(-) (9.2). $44. (Auction #95, Lot 5).

END OF DAY. paneled onionskin. Four-panel onionskin. Two panels of pink on yellow, two of blue on white. Small chip. Germany. 1/2". Near Mint(+) (8.7). $43. (Auction #117, Lot 42).

END OF DAY. paneled onionskin. Very pretty example. Four panel onionskin. Opaque white core. Two panels of pastel blue. 17/32". Mint(-) (9). $43. (Auction #130, Lot 46).

END OF DAY. paneled onionskin. Four panel onionskin. Opaque white core with lots clear spaces. Two wide panels of transparent pink. 3/4". Near Mint(+) (8.9). $43. (Auction #84, Lot 41).

END OF DAY. paneled onionskin. Four-panel peewee onionskin. Odd coloring. Opaque white base. Two panels are transparent green. 1/2". Mint(-) (9.2). $42. (Auction #104, Lot 40).

END OF DAY. paneled onionskin. Four-panel onionskin. Tight twist. Very pretty. Opaque white core. Two panels of transparent turquoise. 21/32". Mint (9.7). $42. (Auction #154, Lot 38).

END OF DAY. paneled onionskin. Four-panel onionskin. Yellow core. Two panels of green, two of red. Overall surface haziness. 1-5/16". Good(+) (7.90). $41. (Auction #171, Lot 5).

END OF DAY. paneled onionskin. Four-panel onionskin. Opaque white core. Two wide pink on yellow panels and two narrow blue on white. 1-1/16". Good(+) (7.90). $41. (Auction #181, Lot 26).

END OF DAY. paneled onionskin. Opaque yellow core with two wide panels of pink and two narrow panels of green. Nice twist. 11/16". Mint (9.5). $40. (Auction #145, Lot 18).

END OF DAY. paneled onionskin. Four panel peewee onionskin. Opaque white core. Two panels of pink, one of blue, one of green. 15/32". Mint (9.7). $40. (Auction #134, Lot 5).

END OF DAY. paneled onionskin. Four-panel peewee onionskin. Odd coloring. Opaque white base. Two panels are transparent green. 1/2". Mint(-) (9.2). $40. (Auction #66, Lot 40).

END OF DAY. paneled onionskin. Four panel onionskin. Overall mustard yellow core. A narrow panel of blue and a narrow panel of blue. 11/16". Mint (9.9). $39. (Auction #116, Lot 15).

END OF DAY. paneled onionskin. Beautiful four panel onionskin. Opaque white core. Two panels of pink and two of blue. 21/32". Mint(-) (9). $37. (Auction #129, Lot 8).

END OF DAY. paneled onionskin. Subtle paneled onionskin. Core of overall white. Two wide panels of blue. 19/32". Mint (9.9). $37. (Auction #92, Lot 41).

END OF DAY. paneled onionskin. Four panel onionskin. Opaque white base. Two panels of pink, two of turquoise. Very pretty marble. 11/16". Mint (9.4). $37. (Auction #156, Lot 35).

END OF DAY. paneled onionskin. Four panel onionskin. Two white panels with pink and some blue. Those are narrow. 25/32". Near Mint(+) (8.9). $36. (Auction #142, Lot 45).

END OF DAY. paneled onionskin. Four-panel onionskin. Opaque white core. Two panels of blue, two of pink. One melt spot. Nice marble. 19/32". Mint (9.9). $36. (Auction #173, Lot 18).

END OF DAY. paneled onionskin. Opaque white core. Two white panels of pink, two narrow panels of light blue. No twist. Crease. 9/16". Mint (9.9). $35. (Auction #120, Lot 8).

END OF DAY. paneled onionskin. Four-panel peewee onionskin. Yellow core. Two panels of pink, two of green. One tiny subsurface moon. 1/2". Near Mint(+) (8.9). $35. (Auction #151, Lot 39).

END OF DAY. paneled onionskin. Four panel onionskin. Two panels are light green on white. Two are light pink and yellow on white. 19/32". Near Mint (8.6). $35. (Auction #118, Lot 21).

END OF DAY. paneled onionskin. Four panel onionskin. Opaque white base with some clear spaces. Two wide panels of pink. 11/16". Mint (9.4). $35. (Auction #144, Lot 43).

END OF DAY. paneled onionskin. Four panel onionskin. Opaque white core. Two panels of transparent pink and two of transparent blue. 21/32". Mint(-) (9.2). $35. (Auction #148, Lot 44).

END OF DAY. paneled onionskin. Four-panel onionskin. Opaque white core. Two narrow panels of turquoise, two wide panels of pink. 21/32". Mint(-) (9). $34. (Auction #181, Lot 40).

END OF DAY. paneled onionskin. Opaque white core. Two narrow bands of transparent turquoise, two wide bands of transparent pink. 21/32". Mint (9.7). $34. (Auction #98, Lot 11).

END OF DAY. paneled onionskin. Four panel onionskin. Opaque white core. Two panels of pink, two of blue. Some subsurface moons. 25/32". Near Mint (8.6). $34. (Auction #172, Lot 5).

END OF DAY. paneled onionskin. Nice small four-panel onionskin. Opaque white core. Two panels of transparent pink. 9/16". Mint (9.9). $33. (Auction #100, Lot 7).

END OF DAY. paneled onionskin. Four panel onionskin. Opaque white core with two narrow panels of pink and two wide panels of pink. 11/16". Near Mint(+) (8.9). $32. (Auction #109, Lot 13).

END OF DAY. paneled onionskin. Very nice onionskin. Opaque white core. Two wide panels of blue, two narrow panels of green. 21/32". Mint(-) (9.2). $32. (Auction #105, Lot 5).

END OF DAY. paneled onionskin. Four panel onionskin. Opaque white core. Two narrow panels of light blue. 9/16". Mint (9.9). $32. (Auction #142, Lot 2).

END OF DAY. paneled onionskin. Opaque yellow core. Two panels of pink and two of green. Some pits and sparkles on the surface. Germany. 5/8". Near Mint(+) (8.8). $31. (Auction #137, Lot 34).

END OF DAY. paneled onionskin. Interesting marble. Four panels. Two are opaque white with transparent yellow. 15/16". Near Mint (8.6). $30. (Auction #144, Lot 4).

END OF DAY. paneled onionskin. Four panel onionskin. Opaque mustard/yellow base. Two wide panels of pink, two narrow panels of green. 21/32". Near Mint (8.6). $28. (Auction #171, Lot 35).

END OF DAY. paneled onionskin. Four panel onionskin. Opaque white core. Two panels are transparent pink, two are transparent green. 21/32". Near Mint (8.6). $27. (Auction #126, Lot 4).

END OF DAY. paneled onionskin. Four panel onionskin. Two wide panels of green on white, two narrow panels of green on yellow. 3/4". Near Mint (8.6). $26. (Auction #134, Lot 15).

END OF DAY. paneled onionskin. Four-panel onionskin. Two white panels and two yellow panels. Overall skin of transparent pink. 19/32". Near Mint(+) (8.8). $25. (Auction #182, Lot 6).

END OF DAY. paneled onionskin. Very pretty four panel onionskin. Opaque white core. Two panels of pink, two of green. 5/8". Near Mint (8.6). $22. (Auction #107, Lot 5).

END OF DAY. paneled Onionskin. Superior example of an end of cane paneled onionskin. This is from the start of the cane. Four-panel. 13/16". Mint(-) (9). $150. (Auction #170, Lot 50).

END OF DAY. paneled Onionskin. Base glass is tinted lightly blue. Core is opaque white. Two panels of transparent pink. 19/32". Near Mint(+) (8.9). $45. (Auction #84, Lot 27).

END OF DAY. Ribbon onionskin. Extremely rare ribbon onionskin. Transparent clear base. Two opposing subsurface panels. 27/32". Near Mint(+) (8.7). $460. (Auction #93, Lot 42).

END OF DAY. Uncased. For lack of a better description, I've gotta call this an uncased end of day. 21/32". Mint(-) (9). $125. (Auction #153, Lot 44).

END OF DAY. Uncased. For lack of a better description, I've gotta call this an uncased end of day. 21/32". Mint(-) (9). $90. (Auction #61, Lot 44).

LUTZ. Assorted. Lot of two marbles. Both have some damage. Banded lutz, aqua base, white bands. 25/32", Good(+) (7.9). $95. (Auction #102, Lot 46).

LUTZ. Banded. Transparent clear base. Four light green bands. Two white-edged lutz bands. 1-1/8". Near Mint(+) (8.9). $400. (Auction #182, Lot 48).

LUTZ. Banded. Transparent ice-blue base. Two white-edged lutz bands. Four white bands. Tiny air hole. 21/32". Mint (9.7). $345. (Auction #112, Lot 49).

LUTZ. Banded. Super banded lutz. Transparent clear base. Four bands of light blue. Two white-edged lutz bands. 7/8". Mint (9.8). $300. (Auction #150, Lot 47).

LUTZ. Banded. Rare coloring. Semi-opaque custard tan base. Four blue bands. Two white edged lutz bands. 21/32". Near Mint(+) (8.7). $290. (Auction #101, Lot 54).

LUTZ. Banded. This is one of the only banded lutzes I have ever seen. 15/32". Mint (9.9). $275. (Auction #59, Lot 44).

LUTZ. Banded. Shooter colored glass banded lutz. Transparent blue base. Four white bands and two white edged lutz . 27/32". Near Mint (8.6). $190. (Auction #156, Lot 30).

LUTZ. Banded. Superior example. Transparent blue base, filled with lots of tiny air bubbles. Four white bands. 9/16". Mint (9.9). $190. (Auction #154, Lot 35).

LUTZ. Banded. Shooter colored glass banded lutz. Transparent blue base. Four white bands and two white edged lutz . 27/32". Near Mint(+) (8.9). $180. (Auction #109, Lot 37.10).

LUTZ. Banded. Transparent clear. Four blue bands. Two white edged lutz bands. Surface in great shape. 29/32". Mint (9.8). $180. (Auction #155, Lot 50).

LUTZ. Banded. Transparent clear base. Two white-edged lutz band. Four light blue bands. Surface in great shape. 21/32". Mint (9.9). $165. (Auction #131, Lot 47).

LUTZ. Banded. Large banded lutz. Transparent clear base. Two white-edged lutz bands. Four blue bands. 1-3/8". Good(+) (7.90). $160. (Auction #130, Lot 50).

LUTZ. Banded. Excellent example. Transparent clear base. Two lutz bands, edged by opaque white. 23/32". Mint (9.8). $150. (Auction #118, Lot 50).

LUTZ. Banded. Shooter colored glass banded lutz. Transparent blue base. Four orange bands and two white edged lutz. 25/32". Good(+) (7.90). $150. (Auction #123, Lot 40).

LUTZ. Banded. Lot of two marbles. Both are large lutzes, but damaged. First is transparent clear with four red bands. $140. (Auction #89, Lot 34).

LUTZ. Banded. Transparent clear base. Four lavender bands. Two white-edged lutz bands. 13/16". Near Mint(+) (8.9). $140. (Auction #163, Lot 39).

LUTZ. Banded. Transparent clear base. Four red bands. Two white edged lutz bands. Surface in great shape. Germany. 11/16". Mint (9.9). $140. (Auction #101, Lot 48).

LUTZ. Banded. Transparent clear base. Four light blue bands. Two white-edged lutz bands. 13/16". Near Mint(+) (8.8). $130. (Auction #163, Lot 12).

LUTZ. Banded. Transparent clear base. Four light green bands. Two white-edged lutz bands. One melt spot. 11/16". Mint(-) (9.2). $120. (Auction #183, Lot 43).

LUTZ. Banded. Transparent clear base. Two wide white-edged lutz bands, four thin light blue bands. One tiny moon. 19/32". Near Mint(+) (8.9). $120. (Auction #100, Lot 37).

LUTZ. Banded. Transparent clear base. Two white-edged lutz bands. Four light blue bands. One small melt spot. 21/32". Mint(-) (9.1). $110. (Auction #112, Lot 40).

LUTZ. Banded. Rare coloring and size. Translucent blue base. Four white bands and two white-edged lutz bands. 29/32". Good(+) (7.70). $81. (Auction #180, Lot 18).

LUTZ. Banded. Shooter colored glass banded lutz. Transparent blue base. Four orange bands and two white edged lutz. 25/32". Good(+) (7.90). $80. (Auction #169, Lot 33).

LUTZ. Banded. Transparent clear base. Four red bands and two white-edged lutz bands. Two tiny shallow chips. 27/32". Near Mint(+) (8.7). $80. (Auction #175, Lot 40).

LUTZ. Banded. Transparent clear base. Four yellow bands, two white edged lutz bands. Surface has some tiny flakes. 27/32". Near Mint (8.6). $80. (Auction #76, Lot 38).

LUTZ. Banded. Transparent clear base. Four light blue bands. Two white-edged lutz bands. Marble is oval. 23/32". Near Mint(+) (8.9). $70. (Auction #160, Lot 19).

LUTZ. Banded. Transparent banded lutz. Four orange bands, two white-edged lutz bands. Overall chips. Germany. 7/8". Good (7.40). $46. (Auction #177, Lot 30).

LUTZ. Banded. Transparent clear base. Four light blue bands. Two white edged lutz bands. Several chips. 3/4". Good(-) (7). $38. (Auction #55, Lot 6).

LUTZ. Banded. Transparent clear. Four blue bands. Overall chips with a subsurface moon. Germany, circa 1870-1915. 11/16". Good(-) (7.20). $30. (Auction #108, Lot 2).

LUTZ. End of day onionskin. Superior onionskin lutz. Core is a subsurface layer of translucent white covered by transparent pink. 5/8". Mint (9.9). $450. (Auction #83, Lot 43).

LUTZ. End of day onionskin. Superior end of day onionskin lutz. Core is white with transparent light blue, light pink. 21/32". Mint (9.7). $435. (Auction #103, Lot 50).

LUTZ. End of day onionskin. Stunning example of an onionskin lutz, in super shape. Opaque white core. Two wide panels of pink. 3/4". Mint (9.5). $420. (Auction #149, Lot 50).

LUTZ. End of day onionskin. Absolutely outstanding example. One of the most colorful I have ever seen. 11/16". Mint (9.9). $375. (Auction #124, Lot 48).

LUTZ. End of day onionskin. Opaque white core with lutz bands on it. Great sparkling and shimmering. 23/32". Mint (9.9). $375. (Auction #81, Lot 42).

LUTZ. End of day onionskin. Superior example. Opaque yellow core. Overall cover of lutz with some heavy bands. Gorgeous. 11/16". Mint (9.9). $340. (Auction #167, Lot 46).

LUTZ. End of day onionskin. Super example. Fat opaque white core. Covered with transparent pink and some green. 13/16". Near Mint(+) (8.9). $340. (Auction #185, Lot 50).

LUTZ. End of day onionskin. Superb onionskin lutz. Core is translucent yellow. Has several good bands of lutz on it. 21/32". Mint (9.5). $310. (Auction #78, Lot 43).

LUTZ. End of day onionskin. A stunning marble. Opaque core with bands of transparent green and a couple of transparent blue. 9/16". Mint (9.9). $300. (Auction #121, Lot 42).

LUTZ. End of day onionskin. Multicolor onionskin base with very heavy lutz on it. Base is yellow, orange, white, blue and red. 17/32". Mint(-) (9). $290. (Auction #63, Lot 44).

LUTZ. End of day onionskin. Superior example. Inner core of green and white. Subsurface layer of opaque white and transparent green. 21/32". Mint (9.8). $285. (Auction #95, Lot 45).

LUTZ. End of day onionskin. Stunning example!!! Opaque white base. Bands of green, yellow and blue on the core. 21/32". Mint (9.9). $250. (Auction #115, Lot 49).

LUTZ. End of day onionskin. A beautiful shooter onionskin lutz. Opaque white core with transparent green on it. 7/8". Near Mint(+) (8.9). $235. (Auction #102, Lot 48).

LUTZ. End of day onionskin. Super example. Shrunken core onionskin lutz! Core is opaque white with some pink, blue and green bands. 9/16". Mint (9.6). $220. (Auction #129, Lot 49).

LUTZ. End of day onionskin. A beautiful marble. Opaque core with bands of transparent green and a couple of transparent blue. 9/16". Mint (9.7). $175. (Auction #122, Lot 50).

LUTZ. End of day onionskin. White, blue and green core. Lots of lutz sprinkled on the core, including one chunk of unground lutz. 21/32". Near Mint (8.6). $170. (Auction #104, Lot 49).

LUTZ. End of day onionskin. Super example. Shrunken core onionskin lutz! Core is opaque white with some pink, blue and green bands. 9/16". Mint (9.6). $160. (Auction #142, Lot 42).

LUTZ. End of day onionskin. Large and what was once a beautiful onionskin lutz. Transparent white core with green, pink and blue. 1-5/16". $150. (Auction #122, Lot 38).

LUTZ. End of day onionskin. Four panel onionskin. Opaque white base. Two panels of light green, two of blue. Covered by lutz. 21/32". Near Mint(-) (8). $130. (Auction #115, Lot 40).

LUTZ. End of day onionskin. Beautful marble. Translucent yellow core. Transparent green skin. About a half dozen bands of lutz. 21/32". Near Mint(+) (8.9). $130. (Auction #107, Lot 46).

LUTZ. End of day onionskin. This is a really a superb large onionskin with a band of lutz. Core is opaque white. 1-3/16". Near Mint(-) (8). $120. (Auction #130, Lot 11).

LUTZ. End of day onionskin. Opaque yellow and white core with lutz on it. Very nice shimmering. One blown-out air hole. 11/16". Near Mint (8.6). $110. (Auction #162, Lot 15).

LUTZ. End of day onionskin. Lot of two marbles. Both are onionskin lutzes. Yellow core with pink and green. Lots of lutz. $110. (Auction #101, Lot 41).

LUTZ. End of day onionskin. Translucent yellow core with lutz on it. Very nice shimmering. One large blown-out air hole. 9/16". Near Mint (8.5). $100. (Auction #130, Lot 42).

LUTZ. End of day onionskin. Opaque white core covered by transparent green and by lutz. One side has a large manufacturing crease. 17/32". Mint(-) (9). $80. (Auction #117, Lot 37).

LUTZ. End of day onionskin. Large end of day onionskin lutz. Opaque yellow core with bands of pink and green. 1-1/16". Good(-) (7.30). $75. (Auction #106, Lot 49).

LUTZ. End of day onionskin. White, blue and green core. Lots of lutz sprinkled on the core, including one chunk of unground lutz. 21/32". Near Mint (8.6). $65. (Auction #60, Lot 27).

LUTZ. End of day onionskin. Translucent white, pink and green core. Shrunken on one side. Some nice bands of lutz on the core. 9/16". Near Mint (8.3). $60. (Auction #177, Lot 50).

LUTZ. Indian. One of the rarest types of lutz, if not the rarest. Stunning example of a swirl-type Indian Lutz. 19/32". Mint (9.8). $700. (Auction #173, Lot 50).

LUTZ. Indian. One of the rarest types of lutz, if not the rarest. Stunning example of a swirl-type Indian Lutz. 19/32". Mint (9.8). $580. (Auction #148, Lot 50).

LUTZ. Indian. Another superior example. Opaque black core. Two narrow bands of yellow and white. 19/32". Mint(-) (9). $435. (Auction #147, Lot 48).

LUTZ. Indian. Large Indian lutz! Opaque black core. Two wide bands of lutz on the core. Two narrower bands of color. 1-1/16". Good(+) (7.80). $200. (Auction #181, Lot 48).

LUTZ. Indian. This was a superb Indian lutz, once upon a time. Opaque black core. One band of transparent red. 19/32". Collectible . $42. (Auction #165, Lot 14).

LUTZ. Mist. Shooter green mist lutz. Hard size to find. Transparent green core. 25/32". Mint(-) (9). $405. (Auction #74, Lot 45).

LUTZ. Mist. Hard to find peewee mist lutz. Transparent green base. Subsurface bands of lutz. 15/32". Near Mint (8.6). $100. (Auction #174, Lot 49).

LUTZ. Onionskin. Opaque white core with a fine sprinkling of lutz on the core and several heavier bands. 9/16". Mint (9.9). $170. (Auction #84, Lot 45).

LUTZ. Onionskin. Large onionskin lutz! Opaque white core with blue skin. Some pink. $170. (Auction #115, Lot 10).

LUTZ. Opaque banded. Extremely rare, first off cane, opaque banded lutz. The first I have ever seen. Opaque black base. 21/32". Mint (9.9). $490. (Auction #125, Lot 50).

LUTZ. Opaque banded. Opaque black base. Four orange bands. Two lutz filled, white edged bands. Has one manufacturing melt. 9/16". Mint(-) (9). $300. (Auction #65, Lot 45).

LUTZ. Opaque banded. Opaque black base. Four orange bands, two white edged lutz bands. Transparent clear casing. 11/16". Mint(-) (9). $280. (Auction #184, Lot 45).

LUTZ. Opaque banded. Very unusual and oddly colored opaque banded lutz. These are hard to find anyway. Opaque black base. 21/32". Near Mint(+) (8.9). $280. (Auction #96, Lot 45).

LUTZ. Opaque banded. Opaque black core. Subsurface are four light blue bands and two white-edged lutz bands. 21/32". Near Mint(+) (8.9). $220. (Auction #154, Lot 41).

LUTZ. Opaque banded. Opaque black base. Subsurface layer has two white-edged lutz bands with four blue bands. $190. (Auction #97, Lot 35).

LUTZ. Opaque banded. Opaque black base. Four blue and green bands and two white-edged lutz bands. 27/32". Near Mint(-) (8). $160. (Auction #172, Lot 40).

LUTZ. Opaque banded. Semi-opaque blue base. Four white bands and two lutz bands edged in white. Several flakes. 25/32". Good(+) (7.90). $100. (Auction #174, Lot 29).

LUTZ. Opaque banded. Opaque black base. Four red bands, two white edged lutz bands. Transparent clear casing. 21/32". Good (7.60). $90. (Auction #175, Lot 34).

LUTZ. Opaque Banded. Opaque black base. Two white edged lutz bands on the base. Four light blue bands. 25/32". Near Mint(+) (8.8). $270. (Auction #168, Lot 36).

LUTZ. Ribbon. Shooter, in great shape. Transparent clear base. Opaque white core. 7/8". Mint(-) (9.1). $700. (Auction #168, Lot 49).

LUTZ. Ribbon. Beautiful ribbon lutz, in outstanding condition. Superior example. Transparent clear base. 9/16". Mint (9.9). $500. (Auction #93, Lot 45).

LUTZ. Ribbon. Stunning lutz!!!! You won't find a ribbon much better. The ribbon fills almost the entire core. 21/32". Mint (9.8). $480. (Auction #113, Lot 50).

LUTZ. Ribbon. Stunning lutz!!!! You won't find a ribbon much better. The ribbon fills almost the entire core. 21/32". Mint (9.6). $470. (Auction #55, Lot 45).

LUTZ. Ribbon. Ribbon core lutz in colored glass. The base glass is blue. Ribbon is fat and opaque white. 21/32". Near Mint(+) (8.9). $410. (Auction #140, Lot 50).

LUTZ. Ribbon. Superior shooter ribbon lutz, which unfortunately has one moon. Transparent lavender base glass. 7/8". Near Mint(+) (8.9). $400. (Auction #100, Lot 44).

LUTZ. Ribbon. Ribbon core lutz in colored glass. The base glass is amber. Ribbon is fat and opaque white. 21/32". Mint (9.7). $385. (Auction #134, Lot 50).

LUTZ. Ribbon. Ribbon core lutz in colored glass. The base glass is blue. Ribbon is fat and opaque white. 21/32". Mint (9.7). $370. (Auction #161, Lot 50).

LUTZ. Ribbon. Ribbon core lutz in colored glass. The base glass is green. Ribbon is fat and opaque white. 5/8". Mint (9.9). $370. (Auction #153, Lot 50).

LUTZ. Ribbon. Ribbon core lutz in colored glass. The base glass is amber. Ribbon is fat and opaque white. 5/8". Mint (9.9). $350. (Auction #156, Lot 50).

LUTZ. Ribbon. Ribbon core lutz in colored glass. The base glass is green. Ribbon is fat and opaque white. 5/8". Mint (9.9). $340. (Auction #164, Lot 50).

LUTZ. Ribbon. Super ribbon lutz. Double ribbon. Each is translucent yellow. Edged by bands of lutz edged by white. 19/32". Mint (9.5). $335. (Auction #120, Lot 50).

LUTZ. Ribbon. Shooter ribbon lutz. Single ribbon of transparent cranberry. Edges are wide lutz bands, edged in white. $300. (Auction #158, Lot 50).

LUTZ. Ribbon. Ribbon core lutz in colored glass. The base glass is green. Ribbon is fat and opaque white. 5/8". Mint (9.9). $290. (Auction #175, Lot 50).

LUTZ. Ribbon. Large ribbon lutz. One of the largest I have seen. Base is transparent honey brown. 1-9/16". Good (7.50). $270. (Auction #77, Lot 41).

LUTZ. Ribbon. Ribbon core lutz in colored glass. The base glass is light blue. Ribbon is fat and opaque white. 21/32". Mint(-) (9.2). $270. (Auction #181, Lot 50).

LUTZ. Ribbon . Transparent amber yellow glass. Opaque white ribbon. Flat ribbon, not a wide fat one. 21/32". Near Mint(+) (8.9). $220. (Auction #160, Lot 29).

LUTZ. Ribbon. Transparent clear glass. Two ribbons of semi-opaque yellow. 11/16". Near Mint(+) (8.7). $220. (Auction #180, Lot 50).

LUTZ. Ribbon. Very pretty ribbon core lutz. Double ribbon. One ribbon is translucent vaseline yellow. 9/16". Near Mint(+) (8.7). $220. (Auction #68, Lot 45).

LUTZ. Ribbon. Transparent green glass. Opaque white ribbon, edged with nice lutz. One tiny moon and one pinprick. 19/32". Near Mint(+) (8.7). $190. (Auction #71, Lot 44).

LUTZ. Ribbon. Transparent green base. Fat single ribbon opaque white ribbon core. Each edge is a wide band of lutz. 19/32". Near Mint(+) (8.9). $180. (Auction #117, Lot 50).

LUTZ. Ribbon. Ribbon core lutz in colored glass. The base glass is purple. This is a very hard color to find. 21/32". Near Mint(-) (8.1). $170. (Auction #59, Lot 31).

LUTZ. Ribbon. Transparent clear base. Opaque white ribbon. Covered on both face by transparent pink. Wide lutz band. 21/32". Near Mint(+) (8.9). $160. (Auction #172, Lot 44).

LUTZ. Ribbon. Double ribbon. One face is yellow, one is light blue. Edged by lutz bands with white edging. 11/16". Near Mint (8.3). $155. (Auction #128, Lot 43).

LUTZ. Ribbon. Ribbon lutz in a very hard to find color. Opaque orange ribbon. Edged but lutz bands with white edging. 11/16". Good(+) (7.90). $140. (Auction #94, Lot 41).

LUTZ. Ribbon. Transparent amber base glass. Opaque white ribbon with lutz bands edged in white. Subsurface moon. 9/16". Near Mint(-) (8). $125. (Auction #125, Lot 45).

LUTZ. Ribbon. Pretty ribbon, but surface is not Mint. Transparent cranberry ribbon The ribbon is edged on both sides. 19/32". Near Mint (8.5). $125. (Auction #139, Lot 46).

LUTZ. Ribbon. Nice ribbon lutz. Transparent clear base. One ribbon is translucent yellow, the other is translucent. 5/8". Mint. $110. (Auction #141, Lot 48).

LUTZ. Ribbon. Very pretty ribbon, but surface is not Mint. Opaque white ribbon core. 21/32". Near Mint(-) (8.2). $100. (Auction #110, Lot 33).

LUTZ. Ribbon. Opaque white ribbon. Transparent pink band on one face, transparent green band on the other. 11/16". Good(-) (7.20). $60. (Auction #163, Lot 31).

LUTZ. Ribbon. From near an end of the cane. Transparent emerald green base. Opaque white core. Narrow core. 21/32". Good(+) (7.90). $47. (Auction #166, Lot 38).

LUTZ. Ribbon core. Beautiful lutz. Double ribbon core. One ribbon is translucent yellow. The other is opaque light blue. 19/32". Near Mint(+) (8.9). $260. (Auction #67, Lot 44).

LUTZ. Ribbon core. Transparent aqua blue glass. Opaque white ribbon. Lutz edging. Lots of tiny air bubbles in the glass. 25/32". Near Mint (8.6). $140. (Auction #141, Lot 41).

LUTZ. Ribbon core. Nice lutz. Double ribbon core. One ribbon is translucent yellow. The other is opaque light blue. 9/16". Near Mint(-) (8). $95. (Auction #69, Lot 42).

LUTZ. Solid core mist. Opaque black core. Core is completely covered by lutz. Cased by transparent clear. 21/32". Near Mint(+) (8.9). $475. (Auction #142, Lot 47).

M.F. CHRISTENSEN & SON COMPANY. This is a very odd item. Not a marble. This is a brick with a small hole in the bottom. 25/32". Mint (9.3). $30. (Auction #61, Lot 25).

M.F. CHRISTENSEN & SON COMPANY. Assorted. Lot of three marbles. Brick, nice black swirl, 5/8", Near Mint(-) (8.1). Brick, white swirl. 21/32". $44. (Auction #90, Lot 25).

M.F. CHRISTENSEN & SON COMPANY. Assorted. Lot of two marbles. Brick, 21/32", Near Mint(+) (8.7). Brown slag, 11/16", Mint (9.9). $26. (Auction #115, Lot 6).

M.F. CHRISTENSEN & SON COMPANY. Brick. Green brick. Exceptional example. Translucent dark green and oxblood swirled together. Ill-formed "9". 21/32". Mint (9.5). $250. (Auction #90, Lot 39).

M.F. CHRISTENSEN & SON COMPANY. Brick. Superior example. Oxblood red, white and black. Stunning marble. Excellent swirling and pattern. 3/4". Mint (9.8). $250. (Auction #164, Lot 47).

M.F. CHRISTENSEN & SON COMPANY. Brick. Large brick. Oxblood red with some white and a little black mixed in. A few small cold roll spots. 7/8". Near Mint(+) (8.8). $180. (Auction #137, Lot 50).

M.F. CHRISTENSEN & SON COMPANY. Brick. Superior shooter green brick. One of the nicest I have ever seen. Almost all oxblood red. 25/32". Mint (9.1). $170. (Auction #71, Lot 20).

M.F. CHRISTENSEN & SON COMPANY. Brick. Superb Brick. Predominately very rich oxblood with some white swirled in and a little black. "9". 13/16". Mint(-) (9.2). $160. (Auction #140, Lot 47).

M.F. CHRISTENSEN & SON COMPANY. Brick. Shooter size marble. Lots of white. An absolute beauty. Two tiny melt pits. Nice cut-off line. Akron. 25/32". Mint(-) (9.1). $160. (Auction #94, Lot 47).

M.F. CHRISTENSEN & SON COMPANY. Brick. Dark opaque oxblood-red, almost purple hued, with white blankets on it. Superb pattern. 19/32". Mint (9.9). $160. (Auction #67, Lot 43).

M.F. CHRISTENSEN & SON COMPANY. Brick. Beautiful brick. Oxblood red with thin spirals of black and dark green. Nice "9" at the top. 27/32". Mint(-) (9.1). $160. (Auction #185, Lot 47).

M.F. CHRISTENSEN & SON COMPANY. Brick. Exceptional brick!! Oxblood red swirled with white and some black. Has a nice cut-off line. 19/32". Mint (9.9). $140. (Auction #55, Lot 19).

M.F. CHRISTENSEN & SON COMPANY. Brick. Super brick. Almost completely dark oxblood red, with some black and white mixed in. Small fold. 11/16". Mint (9.7). $130. (Auction #87, Lot 44).

M.F. CHRISTENSEN & SON COMPANY. Brick. Very hard to find large brick. Superior example. Excellent hand-gather. Could almost be a horizontal. 27/32". Near Mint(+) (8.7). $130. (Auction #173, Lot 22).

M.F. CHRISTENSEN & SON COMPANY. Brick. Super, shooter brick. Mostly oxblood red with a few wisps of black. Excellent, thin white "9". 27/32". Near Mint(+) (8.9). $120. (Auction #158, Lot 39).

M.F. CHRISTENSEN & SON COMPANY. Brick. Superb black brick. The marble is swirled oxblood-red and black with a very little white. Dark. 21/32". Mint (9.7). $110. (Auction #91, Lot 8).

M.F. CHRISTENSEN & SON COMPANY. Brick. Combination of oxblood red, white and black. Excellent swirl. "9" on one end and cutoff line. 25/32". Mint (9.9). $110. (Auction #105, Lot 48).

M.F. CHRISTENSEN & SON COMPANY. Brick. Super brick. Oxblood red. White and some black swirled in. Great "9". Surface in great shape. 21/32". Mint (9.9). $110. (Auction #101, Lot 53).

M.F. CHRISTENSEN & SON COMPANY. Brick. Oxblood red, with some white. Lots of black/green mixed in. Gorgeous marble. Akron, OH, circa 1914. 21/32". Mint (9.7). $100. (Auction #59, Lot 42).

M.F. CHRISTENSEN & SON COMPANY. Brick. Swirled pattern of oxblood red and translucent green. Nice pattern on it. Overall very light hazines. 23/32". Near Mint(+) (8.8). $100. (Auction #126, Lot 45).

M.F. CHRISTENSEN & SON COMPANY. Brick. Very nice brick. Predominately oxblood red with some black swirl. White patch on the bottom. 23/32". Mint (9.7). $100. (Auction #96, Lot 39).

M.F. CHRISTENSEN & SON COMPANY. Brick. Superior example. Exceptional coloring and pattern. Super "9" and tail. 5/8". Mint (9.8). $100. (Auction #158, Lot 49).

M.F. CHRISTENSEN & SON COMPANY. Brick. Beautiful brick. Oxblood red with black swirls. Surface is pristine. Akron, OH, circa 1914-1917. 5/8". 5/8". Mint (9.9). $95. (Auction #116, Lot 47).

M.F. CHRISTENSEN & SON COMPANY. Brick. Excellent brick. Oxblood red, lots of white and some green swirls. The ones with green are hard to find. 21/32". Mint(-) (9.3). $85. (Auction #112, Lot 46).

M.F. CHRISTENSEN & SON COMPANY. Brick. Beautiful brick. Combination of oxblood red, white and black. Shooter. Has some very tiny pits. 13/16". Near Mint (8.6). $85. (Auction #183, Lot 44).

M.F. CHRISTENSEN & SON COMPANY. Brick. One of the larger bricks I have seen in a while. Super pattern and style. Oxblood red with black swirl. 7/8". Near Mint (8.6). $85. (Auction #153, Lot 41).

M.F. CHRISTENSEN & SON COMPANY. Brick. Predominately oxblood-red with some black and some white. Nice pattern. One tiny pinprick. Akron, OH. 5/8". Mint(-) (9.1). $80. (Auction #66, Lot 33).

M.F. CHRISTENSEN & SON COMPANY. Brick. Mostly a mixture of oxblood-red and black. A wispy white spiral on the upper half of the marble. 34/36". Mint(-) (9). $80. (Auction #64, Lot 4).

M.F. CHRISTENSEN & SON COMPANY. Brick. Large brick. A beauty. Oxblood red with thin swirls of black. A very thin spiral of transparent green. 27/32". Mint(-) (9). $80. (Auction #121, Lot 43).

M.F. CHRISTENSEN & SON COMPANY. Brick. Superior example. Swirls of oxblood red, white and black. A couple of bits of burnt dirt on the surface. 21/32". Mint (9.9). $80. (Auction #107, Lot 34).

M.F. CHRISTENSEN & SON COMPANY. Brick. Superb Brick. Oxblood red with some white and black. "9" on the top and cutoff line on the bottom. 5/8". Mint (9.9). $80. (Auction #93, Lot 15).

M.F. CHRISTENSEN & SON COMPANY. Brick. Super brick. Oxblood red with loads of white and a little black. Excellent swirling and pattern. 19/32". Mint (9.9). $80. (Auction #109, Lot 36).

M.F. CHRISTENSEN & SON COMPANY. Brick. Nice brick, in great shape. Oxblood red with some white and a little black. Nice pattern. Akron, OH. 21/32". Mint (9.9). $75. (Auction #170, Lot 38).

M.F. CHRISTENSEN & SON COMPANY. Brick. Nice brick. Oxblood red and black. Two pinpricks and some light scratches. Akron, OH, circa 1914-1917. 21/32". Near Mint(+) (8.9). $75. (Auction #147, Lot 42).

M.F. CHRISTENSEN & SON COMPANY. Brick. Oxblood-red with white and some transparent green swirling throughout. Very nice tail and nice texture. 23/32". Mint(-) (9.1). $70. (Auction #156, Lot 45).

M.F. CHRISTENSEN & SON COMPANY. Brick. Oxblood red, some white, some black. Excellent coloring and texture. Super marble!!!! Akron, OH. 5/8". Mint (9.9). $70. (Auction #155, Lot 46).

M.F. CHRISTENSEN & SON COMPANY. Brick. Very nice brick. Predominately oxblood-red with some black and white. A couple of tiny pinpricks. 21/32". Mint(-) (9). $65. (Auction #166, Lot 43).

M.F. CHRISTENSEN & SON COMPANY. Brick. Interesting glass on this one. Swirled oxblood red, black, white and clear. 11/16". Near Mint(+) (8.9). $65. (Auction #113, Lot 45).

M.F. CHRISTENSEN & SON COMPANY. Brick. Oxblood red with lots of black. Some white. Nice "9" and trailing tail. Akron, OH, circa 1914-1917. 5. 5/8". Mint (9.9). $65. (Auction #150, Lot 39).

M.F. CHRISTENSEN & SON COMPANY. Brick. Beautiful Brick. Oxblood red with wispy white. Nice pattern with a "9" and a cut-off line. 19/32". Mint (9.9). $65. (Auction #112, Lot 35).

M.F. CHRISTENSEN & SON COMPANY. Brick. Lot of two marbles. Nice pair of bricks. Both are oxblood red, black and white. Both have some damage. $60. (Auction #133, Lot 16).

M.F. CHRISTENSEN & SON COMPANY. Brick. Beautiful swirling of oxblood red, white and black. Super looking marble. A couple of tiny pinpricks. 21/32". Mint(-) (9). $60. (Auction #134, Lot 13).

M.F. CHRISTENSEN & SON COMPANY. Brick. Oxblood red with white. A little black in it. Super design. Surface in excellent shape. Akron, OH. 21/32". Mint (9.9). $60. (Auction #136, Lot 43).

M.F. CHRISTENSEN & SON COMPANY. Brick. Nice shooter. Oxblood red with thin black spirals. One very tiny rub spot. Akron, OH, circa 1914-1917. 25/32". Mint(-) (9.1). $60. (Auction #152, Lot 44).

M.F. CHRISTENSEN & SON COMPANY. Brick. Interesting brick. Dark oxblood red base. Almost completely covered by blankets of white. 11/16". Near Mint(+) (8.7). $56. (Auction #184, Lot 1).

M.F. CHRISTENSEN & SON COMPANY. Brick. Shooter brick. Oxblood red with a thin black spiral. One tiny rough spot. Very nice. Akron, OH. 25/32". Near Mint(+) (8.9). $55. (Auction #119, Lot 48).

M.F. CHRISTENSEN & SON COMPANY. Brick. Nice brick. Mostly oxblood red, with some white and black. Nice pattern. A couple of very tiny pits. 19/32". Mint(-) (9.1). $55. (Auction #103, Lot 46).

M.F. CHRISTENSEN & SON COMPANY. Brick. Nice Brick. Oxblood red with some very thin transparent green. One tiny pinprick. Akron, OH. 21/32". Mint (9.3). $55. (Auction #131, Lot 34).

M.F. CHRISTENSEN & SON COMPANY. Brick. Nice brick. Oxblood red with swirls of white. Surface in great shape. Excellent example. Akron, OH. 5/8". Mint (9.9). $50. (Auction #141, Lot 46).

M.F. CHRISTENSEN & SON COMPANY. Brick. Oxblood-red with a nice white swirl in the top and black filaments throughout. Very nice tail. 5/8". Mint(-) (9.1). $45. (Auction #68, Lot 36).

M.F. CHRISTENSEN & SON COMPANY. Brick. Shooter size. Predominately oxblood red, with some black in it. A little bit of white at the top. 25/32". Near Mint (8.4). $44. (Auction #122, Lot 7).

M.F. CHRISTENSEN & SON COMPANY. Brick. Shooter Brick. Predominately oxblood red with just a little black spiraling. Some light pitting. 13/16". Near Mint(+) (8.7). $41. (Auction #130, Lot 8).

M.F. CHRISTENSEN & SON COMPANY. Brick. Lot of two marbles. Both are Bricks. Both have some damage. 3/4". Near Mint (8.3 & 8.2). $40. (Auction #102, Lot 7).

M.F. CHRISTENSEN & SON COMPANY. Brick. Nice brick. Great texture. Light oxblood red and thin black. Surface has been very lightly buffed. $40. (Auction #75, Lot 13).

M.F. CHRISTENSEN & SON COMPANY. Brick. Marble is oxblood red, mottled with some black, with some black and white swirls. "9" pattern. 11/16". Mint(-) (9). $36. (Auction #148, Lot 37).

M.F. CHRISTENSEN & SON COMPANY. Brick. Mostly oxblood red with a little white and a little black. A couple of tiny pinpricks on the surface.

5/8". Mint (9.2). $35. (Auction #131, Lot 28).

M.F. CHRISTENSEN & SON COMPANY. Brick. Small Brick. Lots of black in the oxblood red. Some white. Buffed. Akron, OH, circa 1914-1917. 19/32". $28. (Auction #137, Lot 9).

M.F. CHRISTENSEN & SON COMPANY. Brick. One-half of a brick marble. This is a factory reject. It is one-half of the marble. $27. (Auction #149, Lot 4).

M.F. CHRISTENSEN & SON COMPANY. Brick. Dark oxblood red with some black and white swirls. Some tiny chips and pits, some haziness. Akron, OH. 5/8". Near Mint (8.3). $26. (Auction #151, Lot 32).

M.F. CHRISTENSEN & SON COMPANY. Brick. Odd brick. Almost completely the same shade of oxblood red, with just a few thin black swirls. 5/8". Near Mint(+) (8.9). $24. (Auction #141, Lot 7).

M.F. CHRISTENSEN & SON COMPANY. Brick. Lot of two marbles. Both are nice bricks. One has a large fracture (it may have been glued back together). $22. (Auction #94, Lot 8).

M.F. CHRISTENSEN & SON COMPANY. Brick. Oxblood red and white. Nice pattern. Very lightly buffed. Has some tiny pits left on it. Some annealing. $19. (Auction #169, Lot 45).

M.F. CHRISTENSEN & SON COMPANY. Brick. Combination of oxblood red, white and black. Nice swirling. Has two small rough spots. Akron, OH. 5/8". Near Mint(+) (8.7). $30. (Auction #177, Lot 44).

M.F. CHRISTENSEN & SON COMPANY. Imperial Jade. Extremely rare M.F. Christensen Opaque. Light green. Marketed as Imperial Jade by company. 21/32". Mint(-) (9.1). $140. (Auction #58, Lot 43).

M.F. CHRISTENSEN & SON COMPANY. Imperial Jade. Extremely rare M.F. Christensen Opaque. Light green. Marketed as Imperial Jade by the company. 21/32". Mint(-) (9). $110. (Auction #134, Lot 49).

M.F. CHRISTENSEN & SON COMPANY. Opaque. Dark blue opaque. Has a "9" and tail pattern. This is the first dark blue M.F. Christensen opaque. 21/32". Mint (9.9). $220. (Auction #87, Lot 40).

M.F. CHRISTENSEN & SON COMPANY. Opaque. Very hard to find Imperial Jade. Opaque white. "9" on the top, spiraling to the bottom. M.F. Christensen. 11/16". Mint (9.8). $150. (Auction #167, Lot 47).

M.F. CHRISTENSEN & SON COMPANY. Opaque. Very hard to find Imperial Jade. Opaque white. Very faint "9" on the top, spiraling to the bottom. 5/8". Near Mint(+) (8.9). $105. (Auction #152, Lot 50).

M.F. CHRISTENSEN & SON COMPANY. Opaque. Light blue M.F. Christensen opaque. I can barely make out a spiral on the top. 5/8". Mint (9.5). $50. (Auction #152, Lot 20).

M.F. CHRISTENSEN & SON COMPANY. Opaque slag. Extremely unusual marble. Exhibits the exact same pattern as Lot #6, but the colors are purple and yellow. 19/32". Mint (9.9). $70. (Auction #85, Lot 9).

M.F. CHRISTENSEN & SON COMPANY. Opaque slag. Lot of two marbles. I have classified these as M.F. Christensen, although I have never seen the yellow. $50. (Auction #90, Lot 43).

M.F. CHRISTENSEN & SON COMPANY. Opaque slag. Again, it is not known if these are M.F. Christensen, Christensen Agate or Akro. Pattern is MFC. 9/16". Mint (9.9). $39. (Auction #66, Lot 9).

M.F. CHRISTENSEN & SON COMPANY. Opaque slag. These usually appear as pinch pontil transitionals. Swirl of opaque bright red and opaque white. 21/32". Near Mint(+) (8.9). $14. (Auction #147, Lot 9).

M.F. CHRISTENSEN & SON COMPANY. Oxblood slag. Very dark transparent green slag, with some swirls of oxblood in it. Surface in great shape. 23/32". Mint (9.9). $165. (Auction #117, Lot 46).

M.F. CHRISTENSEN & SON COMPANY. Slag. Calling this marble a slag does not do it justice, although technically that is what it is. 5/8". Mint (9.9). $180. (Auction #100, Lot 43).

M.F. CHRISTENSEN & SON COMPANY. Slag. This is one of the largest slags that I have ever seen in Mint condition. 1-1/4". Mint (9.7). $135. (Auction #60, Lot 37).

M.F. CHRISTENSEN & SON COMPANY. Slag. Rare orange slag. Superior example. One of the finest M.F.Christensen slags that I have ever seen. 13/16". Mint(-) (9). $90. (Auction #88, Lot 31).

M.F. CHRISTENSEN & SON COMPANY. Slag. Very nice, and large, slag. Brown slag. Excellent white patterning. Outstanding marble. Poor "9". 1-5/16". Near Mint(+) (8.9). $80. (Auction #105, Lot 45).

M.F. CHRISTENSEN & SON COMPANY. Slag. Wow! Another large slag. This one is green. Nice "9" and very nice patterning. 1-9/16". Near Mint (8.4). $66. (Auction #63, Lot 24).

M.F. CHRISTENSEN & SON COMPANY. Slag. Superior shooter size brown slag. Excellent marble. Has two tiny spots. 1-1/16". Mint (9.5). $65. (Auction #95, Lot 42).

M.F. CHRISTENSEN & SON COMPANY. Slag. Lot of two marbles. Both are larger slags. Poor 9's, but nice cutoff lines. Each has some very minor damage. $65. (Auction #117, Lot 23).

M.F. CHRISTENSEN & SON COMPANY. Slag. Large green slag. Nice "9" on the top with a very good cutoff line on the bottom. One small flake. 1-3/16". Near Mint (8.6). $65. (Auction #147, Lot 12).

M.F. CHRISTENSEN & SON COMPANY. Slag. Nice larger green slag. Nice "9" on one end and a "cut-off" line on the other end. 1-1/8". Near Mint(+) (8.9). $65. (Auction #55, Lot 31).

M.F. CHRISTENSEN & SON COMPANY. Slag. Large green slag. Excellent "9" and cutoff line. One subsurface moon, right on the top. Akron, OH. 1-1/16". Near Mint(+) (8.9). $55. (Auction #145, Lot 46).

M.F. CHRISTENSEN & SON COMPANY. Slag. Gorgeous large blue slag. "Lazy" "9" with very little white showing. Nice cutoff line. 1". Mint (9.5). $55. (Auction #105, Lot 40).

M.F. CHRISTENSEN & SON COMPANY. Slag. Large brown slag. Nice example. The white is predominately on the bottom half of the marble. 1-3/16". Mint(-) (9). $46. (Auction #153, Lot 30).

M.F. CHRISTENSEN & SON COMPANY. Slag. Gorgeous shooter size red slag. Nice "9" and tail. In great shape. Superb marble. Akron, OH. 25/32". Mint (9.9). $45. (Auction #54, Lot 33).

M.F. CHRISTENSEN & SON COMPANY. Slag. Nice large green slag. Excellent "9" on the top, and an M.F. Christensen cutoff line on the bottom. 1-1/16". Near Mint (8.6). $44. (Auction #61, Lot 27).

M.F. CHRISTENSEN & SON COMPANY. Slag. Lot of eight marbles. Seven are M.F. Christensen slags, the other is an Akro slag. Three purple. $42. (Auction #63, Lot 17).

M.F. CHRISTENSEN & SON COMPANY. Slag. Hard to find clear slag. Transparent clear base with opaque white swirled in. 11/16". Mint (9.9). $40. (Auction #62, Lot 14).

M.F. CHRISTENSEN & SON COMPANY. Slag. Large brown slag. Nice "9" and cutoff line. Several subsurface moons. Akron, OH, circa 1914-1917. 1-3/16". Near Mint (8.6). $40. (Auction #122, Lot 1).

M.F. CHRISTENSEN & SON COMPANY. Slag. Purple slag. Poor "9" on the top, but super cut-off line on the bottom. In great shape. Akron, OH. 7/8". Mint (9.8). $40. (Auction #182, Lot 40).

M.F. CHRISTENSEN & SON COMPANY. Slag. Large brown slag. Poor "9" on one end, but a nice cut-off line on the other. Akron, OH, circa 1914. 31/32". Mint (9.7). $39. (Auction #70, Lot 12).

M.F. CHRISTENSEN & SON COMPANY. Slag. Lot of two marbles. First is a clear slag. Some pitting. Shooter. 29/32". Near Mint (8.6). $38. (Auction #88, Lot 1).

M.F. CHRISTENSEN & SON COMPANY. Slag. Green slag. Large. Interesting "9" on the top. Faint cutoff line on the bottom. 1-1/4". Near Mint(-) (8.2). $37. (Auction #185, Lot 9).

M.F. CHRISTENSEN & SON COMPANY. Slag. Transparent dark cobalt blue slag. Shooter. White swirling deep in side the marble. One small flake. 1-1/16". Near Mint(+) (8.9). $35. (Auction #159, Lot 4).

M.F. CHRISTENSEN & SON COMPANY. Slag. Lot of nine marbles. All are slags with nice "9s on them. One is light purple, the rest are brown. $35. (Auction #102, Lot 13).

M.F. CHRISTENSEN & SON COMPANY. Slag. Blue slag. Very nice "9" and a cutoff line. Has two sparkles on it. 27/32". Mint(-) (9). $32. (Auction #57, Lot 20).

M.F. CHRISTENSEN & SON COMPANY. Slag. Brown slag. An ill-formed horizontal slag. Nice white spiraling four. 1-3/16". Near Mint (8.5). $32. (Auction #62, Lot 27).

M.F. CHRISTENSEN & SON COMPANY. Slag. Lot of three shooter slags. One brown, one green, one blue. All have nice "9"s and cut-off lines. $32. (Auction #150, Lot 19).

M.F. CHRISTENSEN & SON COMPANY. Slag. Early, odd slag. Brown, completely filled with air bubbles. Thin, wispy white "9" on the surface. 21/32". Mint (9.9). $31. (Auction #83, Lot 28).

M.F. CHRISTENSEN & SON COMPANY. Slag. Opaque white and transparent red opaque slag. Excellent design. Super M.F. Christensen cutoff line. 21/32". Mint (9.7). $31. (Auction #85, Lot 6).

M.F. CHRISTENSEN & SON COMPANY. Slag. Green slag. Excellent "9" and cutoff line. One tiny pit on the bottom. A beauty. Akron, OH. 29/32". Mint(-) (9.2). $30. (Auction #101, Lot 11).

M.F. CHRISTENSEN & SON COMPANY. Slag. Brown slag. Very nice design. In great shape. Shooter. Akron, OH, circa 1915-1917. 7/8". Mint (9.9). $29. (Auction #154, Lot 4).

M.F. CHRISTENSEN & SON COMPANY. Slag. Lot of three marbles. All are brown slag. 1-1/4" & Good(-) (7.2). 1-3/16" & Near Mint (8.5). 7/8". $27. (Auction #180, Lot 32).

M.F. CHRISTENSEN & SON COMPANY. Slag. Brown slag. Superior "9" and cutoff line. Superb example. Akron, OH, circa 1914-1917. 25/32". Mint (9.9). $27. (Auction #100, Lot 12).

M.F. CHRISTENSEN & SON COMPANY. Slag. Brown slag. Shooter. Nice "9" and a long cut-off line. Just a couple of very tiny sparkles. Akron, OH. 27/32". Mint (9.5). $25. (Auction #155, Lot 7).

M.F. CHRISTENSEN & SON COMPANY. Slag. Rare colored slag. Transparent smokey gray base with swirls of translucent white. Nice "9" and

cutoff line. 19/32". Near Mint (8.4). $25. (Auction #95, Lot 37).

M.F. CHRISTENSEN & SON COMPANY. Slag. Blue slag. Beautiful shade of blue. Nice wispy white swirl on it. Forms a wide "9" at the top. 31/32". Near Mint(+) (8.8). $24. (Auction #149, Lot 10).

M.F. CHRISTENSEN & SON COMPANY. Slag. Exceptional example of a M.F. Christensen green slag. Superb "9" on the top, M.F. Christensen cutoff line. 21/32". Mint (9.9). $23. (Auction #60, Lot 7).

M.F. CHRISTENSEN & SON COMPANY. Slag. Super brown slag. Transparent brown base with loads of white in it. Superb "9" on the top. Very nice. 7/8". Near Mint(+) (8.9). $23. (Auction #91, Lot 26).

M.F. CHRISTENSEN & SON COMPANY. Slag. Lot of seven marbles. Includes five M.F. Christensen brown slags. Also, includes a blue bennington. $23. (Auction #115, Lot 9).

M.F. CHRISTENSEN & SON COMPANY. Slag. Blue slag. Super "9" on it. End a cutoff line. Akron, OH, circa 1914-1917. 21/32". Mint (9.9). $22. (Auction #67, Lot 31).

M.F. CHRISTENSEN & SON COMPANY. Slag. Large green slag. Nice marble. Exceptional "9" and very nice cutoff line. 15/16". Near Mint(+) (8.7). $20. (Auction #68, Lot 42).

M.F. CHRISTENSEN & SON COMPANY. Slag. Brown slag shooter. Super "9". Nice tail. Dark brown. One tiny sparkle. Akron, OH, circa 1913-1916. 25/32". Mint(-) (9). $20. (Auction #57, Lot 6).

M.F. CHRISTENSEN & SON COMPANY. Slag. Brown shooter size slag. Possibly early Akro Agate. One tiny chip, one small rough spot. 1-1/16". Near Mint (8.6). $20. (Auction #65, Lot 7).

M.F. CHRISTENSEN & SON COMPANY. Slag. Green slag. Good lazy "9", excellent cut-off line. Two blown out air holes. Akron, OH, circa 1912. 31/32". Mint(-) (9). $15. (Auction #139, Lot 37).

M.F. CHRISTENSEN & SON COMPANY. Slag. Brown slag. Excellent design. Nice "9" and a good cutoff line. Small flake and a few tiny pits. Akron, OH. 29/32". Near Mint (8.5). $15. (Auction #67, Lot 11).

M.F. CHRISTENSEN & SON COMPANY. Slag. Lot of two marbles. Beautiful shooter brown slag. A couple of tiny pits and chips on it. 31/32". Near Mint. $12. (Auction #172, Lot 1).

M.F. CHRISTENSEN & SON COMPANY. Slag. Nice example of a brown slag. Nicely hand gathered. Good "9" and cut-off line. Akron, OH, circa 1914. 5/8". Mint (9.9). $12. (Auction #126, Lot 36).

M.F. CHRISTENSEN & SON COMPANY. Slag. Lot of three marbles. All the same size. One brown, two green. Each has some damage. 11/16". Near Mint. $9. (Auction #140, Lot 28).

MARBLE KING, INC. Lot of approximately one hundred twenty five marbles. About half are Marble King Rainbows. $45. (Auction #177, Lot 27).

MARBLE KING, INC. Cloth "Marble King Tournament Assortment" bag. Berry Pink Industries. Small stain at bottom. $33. (Auction #83, Lot 22).

MARBLE KING, INC. Pamphlet that accompanied the Tournament Assortment. Copyright 1965 by Marble King. $16. (Auction #83, Lot 21).

MARBLE KING, INC. Lot of eight marbles. Six are modern Marble King two-patch yellow on white. Other two are Vitro. $1. (Auction #151, Lot 21).

MARBLE KING, INC. Advertising bags. Lot of two items. Both are Morton Salt headers. Black print and checkerboard on orange on white card. $60. (Auction #174, Lot 11).

MARBLE KING, INC. Advertising package. Poly bag. Header label advertising Borden Co. Light yellow cardboard, printed in red. $49. (Auction #176, Lot 28).

MARBLE KING, INC. Assorted. Lot of six marbles. Assortment. Two hybrid Rainbows (5/8)", hybrid Rainbow shooter, modern hybrid Rainbow. $13. (Auction #65, Lot 18).

MARBLE KING, INC. Assorted Rainbow. Lot of five marbles. Bumblebee (yellow and black), Wasp (red and black), Cub Scout (blue and yellow). $55. (Auction #54, Lot 26).

MARBLE KING, INC. Assorted Rainbow. Lot of five marbles. Bumblebee (yellow and black), Wasp (red and black), Cub Scout (blue and yellow). $50. (Auction #54, Lot 26.20).

MARBLE KING, INC. Assorted Rainbow. Lot of five marbles. Bumblebee (yellow and black), Wasp (red and black), Cub Scout (blue and yellow). $50. (Auction #54, Lot 26.30).

MARBLE KING, INC. Assorted Rainbow. Lot of five marbles. Bumblebee (yellow and black), Wasp (red and black), Cub Scout (blue and yellow). $44. (Auction #55, Lot 23).

MARBLE KING, INC. Assorted Rainbow. Lot of five marbles. Bumblebee (yellow and black), Wasp (red and black), Cub Scout (blue and yellow). $40. (Auction #55, Lot 23.30).

MARBLE KING, INC. Assorted Rainbow. Lot of five marbles. Bumblebee (yellow and black), Wasp (red and black), Cub Scout (blue and yellow). $40. (Auction #55, Lot 23.20).

MARBLE KING, INC. Assorted Rainbow. Lot of two marbles. The first is a two color Rainbow Girl Scout. Alternating green and yellow patch . $18. (Auction #61, Lot 17).

MARBLE KING, INC. Bengal Tiger. I have seen this color combination referred to as a Bengal Tiger or a Captain Marvel. This is a Bumblebee. 31/32". Mint (9.9). $120. (Auction #98, Lot 50).

MARBLE KING, INC. Berry Pink. This type is popularly referred to as a Berry Pink. Two seam patch. Base is transparent clear. 1". Near Mint(+) (8.8). $40. (Auction #170, Lot 12).

MARBLE KING, INC. Blended. Blue and red blended spiderman. Bands of red and blue on opaque white. Paden City, WV, date unknown. 5/8. Mint (9.7). $55. (Auction #160, Lot 6).

MARBLE KING, INC. Blended. Lot of two marbles. Both are blended. First is a blended Spiderman. 19/32". Second is a blended Ruby. $40. (Auction #172, Lot 6).

MARBLE KING, INC. Blended. Blended dragonfly. Blended blue and green bands. Paden City, WV, circa 1990-1997. 19/32." Mint (9.9). $21. (Auction #74, Lot 21).

MARBLE KING, INC. Bumblebee. Lot of fifty three marbles. All are yellow and black patch and ribbon Rainbow Bumblebees. $60. (Auction #54, Lot 25).

MARBLE KING, INC. Bumblebee. Lot of forty one marbles. All are Rainbow Bumblebee. Black and yellow. All about 5/8". $60. (Auction #93, Lot 25).

MARBLE KING, INC. Bumblebee. Lot of thirty three marbles. Two color Marble King Rainbow Bumblebee. Black and yellow patch and ribbon. $50. (Auction #123, Lot 29).

MARBLE KING, INC. Bumblebee. Peewee two color Rainbow Bumblebee. Yes, they exist. I was not aware of any when my previous book was published. 7/16". Near Mint (8.6). $50. (Auction #172, Lot 48).

MARBLE KING, INC. Bumblebee. Lot of forty seven marbles. All are two-color yellow and black Rainbow Bumblebees. 19/32" to 5/8". Mint. $46. (Auction #128, Lot 30.10).

MARBLE KING, INC. Bumblebee. Lot of thirty eight marbles. All are black and yellow patch and ribbon Bumblebees. All about 5/8". $46. (Auction #77, Lot 23).

MARBLE KING, INC. Bumblebee. Lot of forty seven marbles. All are two-color yellow and black Rainbow Bumblebees. 19/32" to 5/8". Mint. $46. (Auction #128, Lot 30).

MARBLE KING, INC. Bumblebee. Lot of three marbles. Two color Marble King Rainbow Bumblebee. 31/32", 21/32", 19/32". Mint (9.9-9.5). $35. (Auction #123, Lot 39).

MARBLE KING, INC. Bumblebee. Lot of fifteen marbles. All are two color Rainbow Bumblebees. Black and yellow. Paden City, WV. $32. (Auction #98, Lot 24.10).

MARBLE KING, INC. Bumblebee. Lot of fifteen marbles. All are two color Rainbow Bumblebees. Black and yellow. Paden City, WV. $30. (Auction #98, Lot 24).

MARBLE KING, INC. Bumblebee. Lot of fifteen marbles. All are two-color Rainbow Bumblebee patch and ribbon. Black and yellow patch. $27. (Auction #175, Lot 16).

MARBLE KING, INC. Bumblebee. Lot of fifteen marbles. All are two color Rainbow Bumblebees. Black and yellow. Paden City, WV. $27. (Auction #100, Lot 28).

MARBLE KING, INC. Bumblebee. Shooter two color Rainbow Bumblebee. Yellow and black patch and ribbon. Paden City, WV, circa 1955. 31/32". Mint (9.8). $26. (Auction #180, Lot 46).

MARBLE KING, INC. Bumblebee. Lot of fifteen marbles. All are two-color patch and ribbon Rainbow Bumblebees, black and yellow. 5/8. $24. (Auction #163, Lot 18).

MARBLE KING, INC. Bumblebee. Lot of fifteen marbles. All are two color Rainbow Bumblebees. Black and yellow. Paden City, WV. $23. (Auction #109, Lot 23).

MARBLE KING, INC. Bumblebee. Lot of fifteen marbles. All are two color Rainbow Bumblebees. Black and yellow. Paden City, WV. $23. (Auction #109, Lot 23.10).

MARBLE KING, INC. Bumblebee. Lot of fifteen marbles. All are two color Rainbow Bumblebees. Black and yellow. Paden City, WV. $22. (Auction #113, Lot 31.20).

MARBLE KING, INC. Bumblebee. Lot of twenty two marbles. All are two-color yellow and black Rainbow Bumblebees. 5/8" to 3/4". $22. (Auction #119, Lot 11).

MARBLE KING, INC. Bumblebee. Lot of fifteen marbles. All are two color Rainbow Bumblebees. Black and yellow. Paden City, WV. $22. (Auction #113, Lot 31).

MARBLE KING, INC. Bumblebee. Lot of twenty four marbles. All are two color Rainbow Bumblebees. Yellow and black patch and ribbon. $22. (Auction #112, Lot 25).

MARBLE KING, INC. Bumblebee. Lot of seven marbles. All are two color patch and ribbon Rainbow Bumblebees. 5/8". Mint (9.9) to Near Mint. $19. (Auction #166, Lot 1).

MARBLE KING, INC. Bumblebee. Lot of two marbles. Both are two color Marble King Rainbow Bumblebees in two different sizes. Yellow. $15. (Auction #127, Lot 41).

MARBLE KING, INC. Bumblebee. Lot of fourteen marbles. All are two color Rainbow Bumblebees. Yellow and black patch and ribbon. $14. (Auction #101, Lot 24).

MARBLE KING, INC. Bumblebee. Lot of fifteen marbles. All are two color Rainbow Bumblebees. Black and yellow. Paden City, WV. $12. (Auction #105, Lot 29).

MARBLE KING, INC. Bumblebee. Lot of seven marbles. All are yellow and black patch & ribbon Rainbow Bumblebees. Paden City, WV. $12. (Auction #69, Lot 18).

MARBLE KING, INC. Bumblebee. Odd three color patch and ribbon Rainbow Bumblebee. Opaque white base. Patch and ribbon each of black. 5/8". Near Mint(+) (8.9). $11. (Auction #159, Lot 6).

MARBLE KING, INC. Bumblebee. Lot of five marbles. All are black and yellow Bumblebees. Largest has a large airhole. $10. (Auction #181, Lot 21).

MARBLE KING, INC. Catseye. Shooter St. Mary's catseye. Transparent clear base. Four vane design. Orange and yellow. 31/32". Near Mint(+) (8.9). $39. (Auction #153, Lot 49).

MARBLE KING, INC. Catseye. A St. Mary's shooter catseye. Transparent white. Dull red vanes edged by blue. Shooters are hard to find. 29/32". Mint (9.5). $30. (Auction #75, Lot 9).

MARBLE KING, INC. Catseye. A hard to find shooter St. Mary's catseye. Transparent clear base. Four vanes. 31/32". Mint (9.5). $25. (Auction #55, Lot 44).

MARBLE KING, INC. Catseye. Super St. Mary's Cat's Eye. Transparent clear base with four vane catseye. One plane is opaque blue. 5/8". Mint (9.7). $17. (Auction #63, Lot 41).

MARBLE KING, INC. Catseye. Super St. Mary's Cat's Eye. Transparent clear base with four vane catseye. One plane is opaque blue. 5/8". Mint (9.7). $15. (Auction #63, Lot 41.20).

MARBLE KING, INC. Catseye. Super St. Mary's Cat's Eye. Transparent clear base with four vane catseye. One plane is opaque blue. 5/8". Mint (9.7). $13. (Auction #63, Lot 41.30).

MARBLE KING, INC. Catseye. St. Mary's catseye. One plane is yellow, the other is blue. Surface in great shape. St. Mary's WV. 5/8". Mint (9.9). $12. (Auction #78, Lot 10).

MARBLE KING, INC. Cub Scout. Lot of eleven marbles. All are two color patch and ribbon Rainbow Cub Scouts. Blue and yellow. $49. (Auction #158, Lot 25).

MARBLE KING, INC. Cub Scout. Lot of six marbles. All are two color Marble King Rainbow Cub Scouts. Blue and yellow patch and ribbon. $36. (Auction #123, Lot 27).

MARBLE KING, INC. Cub Scout. Lot of six marbles. All are two color Marble King Rainbow Cub Scouts. Blue and yellow patch and ribbon. $34. (Auction #123, Lot 27.10).

MARBLE KING, INC. Cub Scout. Lot of fourteen marbles. Two color Cub Scout Rainbows. Blue and yellow patch and ribbon. $30. (Auction #112, Lot 37).

MARBLE KING, INC. Cub Scout. Lot of seven marbles. All are Cub Scouts. Blue and yellow patch and ribbon. All about 5/8". All Mint. $25. (Auction #141, Lot 29.20).

MARBLE KING, INC. Cub Scout. Lot of seven marbles. All are Cub Scouts. Blue and yellow patch and ribbon. All about 5/8". All Mint. $25. (Auction #141, Lot 29).

MARBLE KING, INC. Cub Scout. Lot of three marbles. All are Rainbow Cub Scouts, blue and yellow. One is a shooter, 3/4", Near Mint. $24. (Auction #94, Lot 20).

MARBLE KING, INC. Cub Scout. Lot of three marbles. All are blue and yellow patch and ribbon Cub Scouts. $18. (Auction #148, Lot 12).

MARBLE KING, INC. Cub Scout. Lot of three marbles. All are blue and yellow patch and ribbon Cub Scouts. 19/32" to 5/8". Mint(9.9-9.5). $17. (Auction #169, Lot 1).

MARBLE KING, INC. Cub Scout. Two color patch and ribbon Rainbow Cub Scout. Yellow patch and ribbon with blue patch and ribbon. 5/8". Mint (9.9). $10. (Auction #182, Lot 20.20).

MARBLE KING, INC. Cub Scout. Two color patch and ribbon Rainbow Cub Scout. Yellow patch and ribbon with blue patch and ribbon. 5/8". Mint (9.9). $10. (Auction #182, Lot 20).

MARBLE KING, INC. Cub Scout. Two color patch and ribbon Rainbow Cub Scout. Yellow patch and ribbon with blue patch and ribbon. 5/8". Mint (9.9). $8. (Auction #182, Lot 20.40).

MARBLE KING, INC. Cub Scout. Two color patch and ribbon Rainbow Cub Scout. Yellow patch and ribbon with blue patch and ribbon. 5/8". Mint (9.9). $8. (Auction #182, Lot 20.30).

MARBLE KING, INC. Cub Scout. Two color patch and ribbon Rainbow Cub Scout. Yellow patch and ribbon with blue patch and ribbon. 5/8". Mint (9.9). $7. (Auction #153, Lot 19.20).

MARBLE KING, INC. Cub Scout. Two color patch and ribbon Rainbow Cub Scout. Yellow patch and ribbon with blue patch and ribbon. 5/8". Mint (9.9). $7. (Auction #153, Lot 19).

MARBLE KING, INC. Cub Scout. Two color patch and ribbon Rainbow Cub Scout. Yellow patch and ribbon with blue patch and ribbon. 5/8". Mint (9.9). $5. (Auction #153, Lot 19.40).

MARBLE KING, INC. Cub Scout. Two color patch and ribbon Rainbow Cub Scout. Yellow patch and ribbon with blue patch and ribbon. 5/8". Mint (9.9). $5. (Auction #153, Lot 19.30).

MARBLE KING, INC. Dragonfly. Patch and ribbon Rainbow Dragonfly. Light green and light black veneered on white. 5/8". Mint(-) (9.2). $70. (Auction #75, Lot 3).

MARBLE KING, INC. Girl Scout. Two color patch and ribbon Rainbow Girl Scout. Yellow and green patch and ribbon. 5/8". Mint (9.9). $22. (Auction #137, Lot 1).

MARBLE KING, INC. Girl Scout. Two color patch and ribbon Rainbow Girl Scout. Yellow and green patch and ribbon. 5/8". Mint (9.9). $20. (Auction #137, Lot 1.20).

MARBLE KING, INC. Girl Scout. Two color patch and ribbon Rainbow Girl Scout. Yellow and green patch and ribbon. Paden City, WV. 5/8". Mint (9.9). $20. (Auction #164, Lot 31).

MARBLE KING, INC. Girl Scout. Two color patch and ribbon Rainbow Girl Scout. Yellow and green patch and ribbon. 5/8". Mint (9.9). $18. (Auction #137, Lot 1.30).

MARBLE KING, INC. Girl Scout. Two color patch and ribbon Rainbow Girl Scout. Yellow and green patch and ribbon. Paden City, WV. 5/8". Mint (9.9). $18. (Auction #176, Lot 17).

MARBLE KING, INC. Girl Scout. Two color Rainbow Girl Scout. Opaque white base. Veneered patches and ribbons of green and yellow. 5/8". Mint (9.9). $17. (Auction #88, Lot 38).

MARBLE KING, INC. Girl Scout. Two color patch and ribbon Rainbow Girl Scout. Yellow and green patch and ribbon. 5/8". Mint (9.9). $16. (Auction #137, Lot 1.40).

MARBLE KING, INC. Girl Scout. Two color patch and ribbon Rainbow Girl Scout. Yellow and green patch and ribbon. 5/8". Mint (9.9). $16. (Auction #137, Lot 1.50).

MARBLE KING, INC. Girl Scout. Two color Rainbow Girl Scout. Opaque white base. Veneered patches and ribbons of green and yellow. 5/8". Mint (9.9). $15. (Auction #88, Lot 38.30).

MARBLE KING, INC. Girl Scout. Two color Rainbow Girl Scout. Opaque white base. Veneered patches and ribbons of green and yellow. 5/8". Mint (9.9). $15. (Auction #88, Lot 38.20).

MARBLE KING, INC. Girl Scout. Two color Rainbow Girl Scout. Green and yellow patch and ribbon. Paden City, WV, circa 1955-1965. 5/8". Mint (9.9). $12. (Auction #112, Lot 11).

MARBLE KING, INC. Girl Scout. Two color patch and ribbon Rainbow Girl Scout. Yellow and green patch and ribbon. Paden City, WV. 5/8". Mint (9.9). $12. (Auction #120, Lot 1).

MARBLE KING, INC. Girl Scout. Two color patch and ribbon Rainbow Girl Scout. Yellow and green patch and ribbon. Paden City, WV. 5/8". Mint (9.9). $10. (Auction #120, Lot 1.20).

MARBLE KING, INC. Girl Scout. Two color patch and ribbon Rainbow Girl Scout. Yellow and green patch and ribbon. Subsurface moon. 5/8". Near Mint(+) (8.9). $7. (Auction #171, Lot 6.30).

MARBLE KING, INC. Girl Scout. Two color patch and ribbon Rainbow Girl Scout. Yellow and green patch and ribbon. Subsurface moon. 5/8". Near Mint(+) (8.9). $5. (Auction #171, Lot 6.20).

MARBLE KING, INC. Girl Scout. Two color patch and ribbon Rainbow Girl Scout. Yellow and green patch and ribbon. Subsurface moon. 5/8". Near Mint(+) (8.9). $3. (Auction #171, Lot 6).

MARBLE KING, INC. Green Hornet. Rare two-color patch and ribbon Rainbow Green Hornet. It is very hard to find vintage examples. 5/8". Mint (9.9). $380. (Auction #150, Lot 49).

MARBLE KING, INC. Green Hornet. Rare two-color patch and ribbon Rainbow Green Hornet. It is very hard to find vintage examples. 5/8". Mint (9.9). $325. (Auction #150, Lot 49.20).

MARBLE KING, INC. Green Hornet/Bumblebee. Very rare Green Hornet/Bumblebee shooter!!This is a shooter Bumblebee with green on top of the yellow. 7/8". Mint (9.9). $220. (Auction #65, Lot 38).

MARBLE KING, INC. Hybrid Rainbow. Cub Scout/Girl Scout hybrid. Two bands each of green, blue and yellow. Some white in one blue band. 9/16". Mint (9.6). $50. (Auction #101, Lot 47).

MARBLE KING, INC. Original bag. Poly bag. Red on white label. "RAINBOW 40 Marble King Marbles 40". Includes some bumblebees. $56. (Auction #178, Lot 17).

MARBLE KING, INC. Original bag. Original cloth Tournament Assortment bag. Includes twenty seven of the original marbles. $30. (Auction #101, Lot 27).

MARBLE KING, INC. Original bag. Poly bag. Label reads "RAINBOWS / 14 Marble King Marbles 14". White on red. The numbers are in black. $28. (Auction #152, Lot 33).

MARBLE KING, INC. Original bag. Poly bag. Red on white label. "RAINBOW 14 Marble King Marbles 14". Includes a couple of bumblebees. $19. (Auction #178, Lot 14).

MARBLE KING, INC. Original bag. Tournament Assortment poly bag. Empty. No marbles. Still has drawstring. Some rubbing on front. Near Mint. $12. (Auction #95, Lot 20).

MARBLE KING, INC. Original bag. Lot of five items. All are empty plastic bags. Printed on the front are The Incredible Hulk and Spiderman. $10. (Auction #120, Lot 28).

MARBLE KING, INC. Original bag. Poly bag. Twenty five count of catseyes. In nice shape. Paden City, WV, circa 1965-1980. Mint (9.5). $9. (Auction #67, Lot 24).

MARBLE KING, INC. Original bag. Poly bag. Twenty five count of catseyes. Small tape tear on label. Paden City, WV, circa 1965-1980. Mint. $7. (Auction #115, Lot 27.70).

MARBLE KING, INC. Original bag. Poly bag. Twenty five count of catseyes. In nice shape. Paden City, WV, circa 1965-1980. Mint (9.5). $7. (Auction #67, Lot 24.30).

MARBLE KING, INC. Original bag. Poly bag. Twenty five count of catseyes. Small tape tear on label. Paden City, WV, circa 1965-1980. Mint. $7. (Auction #115, Lot 27.80).

MARBLE KING, INC. Original bag. Poly bag. Twenty five count of catseyes. Small tape tear on label. Paden City, WV, circa 1965-1980. Mint. $7. (Auction #115, Lot 27.20).

MARBLE KING, INC. Original bag. Poly bag. Twenty five count of catseyes. Small tape tear on label. Paden City, WV, circa 1965-1980. Mint. $7. (Auction #115, Lot 27.60).

MARBLE KING, INC. Original bag. Poly bag. Twenty five count of catseyes. Small tape tear on label. Paden City, WV, circa 1965-1980. Mint. $7. (Auction #115, Lot 27.30).

MARBLE KING, INC. Original bag. Poly bag. Twenty five count of catseyes. Small tape tear on label. Paden City, WV, circa 1965-1980. Mint. $7. (Auction #115, Lot 27.40).

MARBLE KING, INC. Original bag. Poly bag. Twenty five count of catseyes. In nice shape. Paden City, WV, circa 1965-1980. Mint (9.5). $7. (Auction #67, Lot 24.20).

MARBLE KING, INC. Original bag. Poly bag. Twenty five count of catseyes. Small tape tear on label. Paden City, WV, circa 1965-1980. Mint. $7. (Auction #115, Lot 27).

MARBLE KING, INC. Original bag. Poly bag. Twenty five count of catseyes. In nice shape. Paden City, WV, circa 1965-1980. Mint (9.5). $7. (Auction #67, Lot 24.50).

MARBLE KING, INC. Original bag. Poly bag. Twenty five count of catseyes. In nice shape. Paden City, WV, circa 1965-1980. Mint (9.5). $7. (Auction #67, Lot 24.40).

MARBLE KING, INC. Original bag. Marble King Tournament Assortment. This is the empty poly bag, with drawstring. Paden City, WV. $4. (Auction #79, Lot 20).

MARBLE KING, INC. Original bag. An original Marble King Tournament Assortment poly bag. No marbles. Smaller size. With red drawstring. $3. (Auction #127, Lot 47).

MARBLE KING, INC. Original Bag. Original poly bag of "100 Rainbow Marble King Marbles". Nice bag, in great shape, as is the label. $110. (Auction #65, Lot 21).

MARBLE KING, INC. Original Bag. Original poly bag of "100 Rainbow Marble King Marbles". Nice bag, in great shape, as is the label. $80. (Auction #100, Lot 26).

MARBLE KING, INC. Original Bag. Original poly bag of "40 Rainbow Marble King Marbles". Nice bag, in great shape, as is the label. $46. (Auction #100, Lot 25).

MARBLE KING, INC. Original bags . Lot of three items. First is an original Mr. Peanut poly bag. This one is genuine. $75. (Auction #79, Lot 14).

MARBLE KING, INC. Original bags. Lot of seven items. All are a original bags. A great assortment of poly bags spanning the past thirty years. $50. (Auction #79, Lot 18).

MARBLE KING, INC. Original bags. Lot of three items. Three poly bags. Each contains twenty clearies. Paper label. Nice bags. Paden City, WV. $22. (Auction #56, Lot 21).

MARBLE KING, INC. Original bags. Lot of three items. Three poly bags. Each contains twenty clearies. Paper label. Nice bags. Paden City, WV. $20. (Auction #56, Lot 21.20).

MARBLE KING, INC. Original bags. Lot of three items. Three poly bags. Each contains twenty clearies. Paper label. Nice bags. Paden City, WV. $15. (Auction #56, Lot 21.40).

MARBLE KING, INC. Original bags. Lot of three items. Three poly bags. Each contains twenty clearies. Paper label. Nice bags. Paden City, WV. $15. (Auction #56, Lot 21.30).

MARBLE KING, INC. Original bags. Lot of three items. Three poly bags. Each contains twenty clearies. Paper label. Nice bags. Paden City, WV. $15. (Auction #56, Lot 21.60).

MARBLE KING, INC. Original bags. Lot of three items. Three poly bags. Each contains twenty clearies. Paper label. Nice bags. Paden City, WV. $15. (Auction #56, Lot 21.50).

MARBLE KING, INC. Original bags. Lot of three items. Three poly bags. Each contains twenty clearies. Paper label. Nice bags. Paden City, WV. $14. (Auction #64, Lot 24).

MARBLE KING, INC. Original bags. Lot of three items. Three poly bags. Each contains twenty clearies. Paper label. Nice bags. Paden City, WV. $10. (Auction #56, Lot 21.80).

MARBLE KING, INC. Original bags. Lot of three items. Three poly bags. Each contains twenty clearies. Paper label. Nice bags. Paden City, WV. $10. (Auction #56, Lot 21.70).

MARBLE KING, INC. Original box. Hard to find Berry Pink Industries chinese checkers box. No. 65 box. Yellow cardboard. $26. (Auction #171, Lot 21).

MARBLE KING, INC. Original box. Original cardboard Chinko-Checko-Marblo box. Berry Pink, Inc. Box is missing the corner clips on one. $22. (Auction #79, Lot 25).

MARBLE KING, INC. Original package. Original advertising mesh bag for Morton's Salt. Contains sixteen Peltier Rainbos. $70. (Auction #119, Lot 36).

MARBLE KING, INC. Original package. Original poly bag of forty marbles. White cardboard label printed in black over orange. $45. (Auction #173, Lot 25).

MARBLE KING, INC. Original package. Poly bag of "85 Cat's Eye Marbles 85". Red printing on white label. Attached is a pamphlet. $44. (Auction #133, Lot 22.20).

MARBLE KING, INC. Original package. Poly bag of "85 Cat's Eye Marbles 85". Red printing on white label. Attached is a pamphlet. $44. (Auction #133, Lot 22.30).

MARBLE KING, INC. Original package. Poly bag of "85 Cat's Eye Marbles 85". Red printing on white label. Attached is a pamphlet. $44. (Auction #133, Lot 22.40).

MARBLE KING, INC. Original package. Poly bag of "85 Cat's Eye Marbles 85". Red printing on white label. Attached is a pamphlet. $44. (Auction #133, Lot 22).

MARBLE KING, INC. Original package. Poly bag of "85 Cat's Eye Marbles 85". Red printing on white label. Attached is a pamphlet. $44. (Auction #133, Lot 22.50).

MARBLE KING, INC. Original package. Lot of four items. Super group. All are catseye packages. Four different types. $42. (Auction #178, Lot 22).

MARBLE KING, INC. Original package. An original Mr. Peanuts poly advertising bag. This bag is genuine. Contains fourteen 5/8" common swirl. $32. (Auction #170, Lot 24).

MARBLE KING, INC. Original package. An original Mr. Peanuts poly advertising bag. This bag is genuine. Contains fourteen 5/8" common swirl. $30. (Auction #88, Lot 21.20).

MARBLE KING, INC. Original package. An original Mr. Peanuts poly advertising bag. This bag is genuine. Contains fourteen 5/8" common swirl. $30. (Auction #88, Lot 21).

MARBLE KING, INC. Original package. Poly bag. Header label is white, printed in black with orange trim. One side reads "Marble King". $30. (Auction #172, Lot 29).

MARBLE KING, INC. Original package. Cloth Marble King Tournament Assortment bag. No marbles. Bag is about 9" x 8" (sight). Near Mint(+). $28. (Auction #132, Lot 36).

MARBLE KING, INC. Original package. Poly bag. Header label is white, printed in black with orange trim. One side reads "Marble King". $28. (Auction #172, Lot 29.20).

MARBLE KING, INC. Original package. Poly bag. Header label is white, printed in black with orange trim. One side reads "Marble King". $26. (Auction #172, Lot 29.30).

MARBLE KING, INC. Original package. Poly bag of "19 Glass Marbles 19". Orange label. Reverse reads "Marble King". Package contains 5/8". $22. (Auction #84, Lot 15).

MARBLE KING, INC. Original package. Lot of two items. Both are "J" blister packs. Red cardboard sheet printed with the company name and . $22. (Auction #170, Lot 23).

MARBLE KING, INC. Original package. Poly bag. 50 count. Modern Rainbos. Bag is Mint, as are marbles. $21. (Auction #132, Lot 33).

MARBLE KING, INC. Original package. Poly bag. Header label is white, printed in black with orange trim. One side reads "Marble King". $21. (Auction #184, Lot 24.50).

MARBLE KING, INC. Original package. Poly bag. Header label is white, printed in black with orange trim. One side reads "Marble King". $21. (Auction #184, Lot 24).

MARBLE KING, INC. Original package. Poly bag. Header label is white, printed in black with orange trim. One side reads "Marble King". $21. (Auction #184, Lot 24.40).

MARBLE KING, INC. Original package. Poly bag. Header label is white, printed in black with orange trim. One side reads "Marble King". $21. (Auction #184, Lot 24.30).

MARBLE KING, INC. Original package. Poly bag. Header label is white, printed in black with orange trim. One side reads "Marble King". $21. (Auction #184, Lot 24.20).

MARBLE KING, INC. Original package. Lot of two items. Both are "J" blister packs. Red cardboard sheet printed with the company name. $20. (Auction #170, Lot 23.20).

MARBLE KING, INC. Original package. An original Mr. Peanuts poly advertising bag. This bag is genuine. Contains fourteen 5/8" common swirl. $15. (Auction #120, Lot 22).

MARBLE KING, INC. Original package. An original poly bag of "60 Marble King Glass Marbles". Fifty nine 5/8" Rainbows and patches. $14. (Auction #60, Lot 26).

MARBLE KING, INC. Original package. A poly bag of twenty five catseyes. Includes a shooter. Red and black on white cardboard header. $11. (Auction #106, Lot 25).

MARBLE KING, INC. Original package. Poly bag of "8 count Bowlers". Paden City, WV, circa 1970-1990. Mint (9.7). $11. (Auction #66, Lot 27).

MARBLE KING, INC. Original package. Lot of ten items. Poly bag of twenty five catseyes. Includes a shooter. Red and black on white cardboard. $10. (Auction #125, Lot 25).

MARBLE KING, INC. Original package. A poly bag of twenty five catseyes. Includes a shooter. Red and black on white cardboard header. $9. (Auction #106, Lot 25.20).

MARBLE KING, INC. Original package. Poly bag of eight Bowlers. Two patch, white base. Paden City, 1975-1995. Mint (9.9). $6. (Auction #175, Lot 27).

MARBLE KING, INC. Original package. Poly bag. Cardboard header label. 6 count Big Boy. All shooter clearies. Recent bag. Mint (9.7). $6. (Auction #172, Lot 23).

MARBLE KING, INC. Original package. Poly bag of eight Bowlers. Two patch, white base. Paden City, 1975-1995. Mint (9.9). $6. (Auction #175, Lot 27.30).

MARBLE KING, INC. Original package. Poly bag of eight Bowlers. Two patch, white base. Paden City, 1975-1995. Mint (9.9). $6. (Auction #175, Lot 27.40).

MARBLE KING, INC. Original package. Poly bag of eight Bowlers. Two patch, white base. Paden City, 1975-1995. Mint (9.9). $6. (Auction #175, Lot 27.50).

MARBLE KING, INC. Original package. Poly bag of eight Bowlers. Two patch, white base. Paden City, 1975-1995. Mint (9.9). $6. (Auction #175, Lot 27.20).

MARBLE KING, INC. Original package. Poly bag. Cardboard header label. 6 count Big Boy. All shooter clearies. Recent bag. Mint (9.7). $5. (Auction #172, Lot 23.30).

MARBLE KING, INC. Original package. Modern 25-count. Two-patch marbles. Modern label. Mint (9.9). $5. (Auction #178, Lot 21).

MARBLE KING, INC. Original package. Poly bag. Cardboard header label. 6 count Big Boy. All shooter clearies. Recent bag. Mint (9.7). $5. (Auction #172, Lot 23.20).

MARBLE KING, INC. Original package. A poly bag of twenty five catseyes. Includes a shooter. Red and black on white cardboard header. $5. (Auction #106, Lot 25.30).

MARBLE KING, INC. Original package. A poly bag of twenty five catseyes. Includes a shooter. Red and black on white cardboard header. $3. (Auction #102, Lot 33).

MARBLE KING, INC. Original package. A poly bag of twenty five catseyes. Includes a shooter. Red and black on white cardboard header.

$1. (Auction #102, Lot 33.50).

MARBLE KING, INC. Original package. A poly bag of twenty five catseyes. Includes a shooter. Red and black on white cardboard header. $1. (Auction #102, Lot 33.40).

MARBLE KING, INC. Original package. A poly bag of twenty five catseyes. Includes a shooter. Red and black on white cardboard header. $1. (Auction #102, Lot 33.30).

MARBLE KING, INC. Original package. A poly bag of twenty five catseyes. Includes a shooter. Red and black on white cardboard header. $1. (Auction #102, Lot 33.20).

MARBLE KING, INC. Original packages. Lot of ten items. Poly bag of twenty five catseyes. Labels have some water damage. White label. $24. (Auction #87, Lot 24).

MARBLE KING, INC. Pamphlet. Pamphlet titled "The Game of Marbles" by Shirley "Windy" Allen. 20 pages. Gives rules of Ringer. $22. (Auction #132, Lot 31).

MARBLE KING, INC. Patch. Veneered patch. Opaque white base. Wide patch of orange, smaller patch of green. 19/32". Mint (9.7). $30. (Auction #156, Lot 18).

MARBLE KING, INC. Patch. Odd two color patch. Opaque black base. Thin red band at either pole. Vitro Agate type pattern. 19/32". Near Mint(+) (8.9). $8. (Auction #159, Lot 15).

MARBLE KING, INC. Patch. Transparent dark green base. Wispy translucent white inside the marble. Comes to just below the surface. 19/32". Mint(-) (9). $7. (Auction #159, Lot 26).

MARBLE KING, INC. Premium. Poly tube containing five Marble King catseyes. Marbles are all about 5/8". Tube is about 3". Mint. $6. (Auction #170, Lot 26.30).

MARBLE KING, INC. Premium. Poly tube containing five Marble King catseyes. Marbles are all about 5/8". Tube is about 3". Mint. $6. (Auction #170, Lot 26.40).

MARBLE KING, INC. Premium. Poly tube containing five Marble King catseyes. Marbles are all about 5/8". Tube is about 3". Mint. $6. (Auction #170, Lot 26).

MARBLE KING, INC. Premium. Poly tube containing five Marble King catseyes. Marbles are all about 5/8". Tube is about 3". Mint. $6. (Auction #170, Lot 26.20).

MARBLE KING, INC. Rainbow. Two color Rainbow. Sometimes referred to as a "Poor Man's Watermelon". Opaque white base. 9/16". Mint(-) (9.1). $95. (Auction #172, Lot 39).

MARBLE KING, INC. Rainbow. Modern green hornet/bumblebee hybrid. Opaque white base. Black equatorial band. Yellow patches. 7/8". Mint (9.9). $85. (Auction #131, Lot 48).

MARBLE KING, INC. Rainbow. Hybrid Rainbow. Sometimes referred to as a "Captain Marvel". Opaque white base, coverd by yellow. 5/8". Mint(-) (9). $60. (Auction #58, Lot 16).

MARBLE KING, INC. Rainbow. Lot of about one hundred fifty marbles. All are white base Rainbows. Two, three and four-color. $55. (Auction #144, Lot 28).

MARBLE KING, INC. Rainbow. Lot of eighteen marbles. Eight Bumblebees, seven Cub Scouts, three Wasps. All about 5/8". $55. (Auction #174, Lot 25).

MARBLE KING, INC. Rainbow. Lot of approximately ninety marbles. Assortment of three and four color white base Rainbows. $50. (Auction #87, Lot 22).

MARBLE KING, INC. Rainbow. Lot of ten marbles. Five are blue on white Rainbows. 5/8". Mint to Near Mint. $44. (Auction #120, Lot 18).

MARBLE KING, INC. Rainbow. Lot of twenty two marbles. Assortment four color Rainbows, with two Wasps. Most are 5/8". $44. (Auction #132, Lot 19).

MARBLE KING, INC. Rainbow. Lot of eighty marbles. All are Rainbow patch and ribbons. Fifty four are blue, yellow and green on white. $44. (Auction #70, Lot 24).

MARBLE KING, INC. Rainbow. Lot of sixteen marbles. Five Bumblebees and eleven Wasps. All are vintage patch and ribbon. 19/32". $42. (Auction #144, Lot 40.20).

MARBLE KING, INC. Rainbow. Lot of eighteen marbles. Ten Bumblebees (one not Mint), seven Wasps (one not Mint), one Cub Scout. $42. (Auction #141, Lot 24).

MARBLE KING, INC. Rainbow. Lot of five marbles. Assortment of Rainbow hybrid types. These were all dug at a West Virginia site. $40. (Auction #172, Lot 17).

MARBLE KING, INC. Rainbow. Lot of six marbles. All are two color Rainbow patch and ribbons. A Bumblebee, Cub Scout, Girl Scout. $40. (Auction #62, Lot 15).

MARBLE KING, INC. Rainbow. Lot of one hundred sixty one marbles. All are Rainbow patch and ribbon. Forty are red on white. $36. (Auction #70, Lot 25).

MARBLE KING, INC. Rainbow. Unusual Rainbow. Patch and ribbon of baby blue and brown/red. A couple of sparkles and a small annealing. 19/32". Mint(-) (9.2). $36. (Auction #156, Lot 7).

MARBLE KING, INC. Rainbow. Lot of thirty four marbles. Includes five Bumblebees, a Cub Scout shooter, a Wasp, a few Rainbow Red. $35. (Auction #180, Lot 26).

MARBLE KING, INC. Rainbow. Lot of sixteen marbles. Five Bumblebees and eleven Wasps. All are vintage patch and ribbon. 19/32". $35. (Auction #144, Lot 40).

MARBLE KING, INC. Rainbow. Unusual Rainbow. Transparent blue base with an opaque red patch and ribbon. A few very tiny pinpoint. 19/32". Mint(-) (9). $35. (Auction #156, Lot 1).

MARBLE KING, INC. Rainbow. Lot of eleven marbles. Five Cub Scouts and six Bumblebees. All are Mint (9.9-9.5). 5/8" to 23/32". $34. (Auction #80, Lot 10).

MARBLE KING, INC. Rainbow. Lot of five marbles. All are white base Rainbows. Each has a patch and ribbon. $34. (Auction #161, Lot 16).

MARBLE KING, INC. Rainbow. Five color patch and ribbon Rainbow. Opaque white base. Patch and ribbon of several colors. 5/8". Near Mint(+) (8.8). $32. (Auction #159, Lot 13).

MARBLE KING, INC. Rainbow. Lot of thirty five marbles. All are white base Rainbow. Many are three color, some are four color. $32. (Auction #141, Lot 27).

MARBLE KING, INC. Rainbow. Lot of five marbles. Three Cub Scouts, one Wasp, one hybrid (green on red, yellow, white). 19/32". $32. (Auction #184, Lot 26).

MARBLE KING, INC. Rainbow. Lot of fifty marbles. All are four color Rainbows. White base. Three colored bands. $30. (Auction #68, Lot 15).

MARBLE KING, INC. Rainbow. Lot of seven marbles. Wonderful assortment of hybrid Rainbows. Assorted multiple colors on white. $30. (Auction #58, Lot 25).

MARBLE KING, INC. Rainbow. Lot of two marbles. Both are shooters. One is a Wasp (red and black). Thin white line next to one blue. $28. (Auction #120, Lot 37).

MARBLE KING, INC. Rainbow. Lot of fifteen marbles. Nine 5/8" Bumblebees, one 1" Bumblebee, three modern 5/8" Cub Scouts, one 5/8". $26. (Auction #95, Lot 18).

MARBLE KING, INC. Rainbow. Lot of five marbles. Two Cub Scouts, a Bumblebee, two modern Tigers. 19/32" to 5/8". Mint (9.9-9.7). $25. (Auction #184, Lot 34).

MARBLE KING, INC. Rainbow. Lot of three marbles. Anemic Cub Scout shooter. Lots of white. 23/32". Mint(-) (9.0). Second is white. $25. (Auction #88, Lot 16).

MARBLE KING, INC. Rainbow. Lot of two marbles. Nice pair of hybrids. One is yellow with one ribbon of blue and one of black. $24. (Auction #175, Lot 45).

MARBLE KING, INC. Rainbow. Spiderman patch. One side is red, other is slate blue/gray. Overall annealing fractures on the red. 19/32". Near Mint(+) (8.9). $24. (Auction #156, Lot 16).

MARBLE KING, INC. Rainbow. Lot of nine marbles. Two Girl Scouts, seven Cub Scouts. 5/8" to 23/32" (1). About half Mint. $22. (Auction #132, Lot 11).

MARBLE KING, INC. Rainbow. Lot of five marbles. Wasp, 3/4", Mint (9.9). Two Bumblebees, 5/8", Mint (9.9). Two Girl Scouts, 5/8". $20. (Auction #82, Lot 1).

MARBLE KING, INC. Rainbow. Lot of twelve marbles. Seven Bumblebees, three Wasps, two modern two-patch wasps. 5/8" to 21/32". Mint. $19. (Auction #83, Lot 27).

MARBLE KING, INC. Rainbow. Opaque white base. Overall blue in bands of various shades of blue. Red/brown patch, red ribbon. 5/8". Mint (9.2). $19. (Auction #156, Lot 44).

MARBLE KING, INC. Rainbow. Lot of eleven marbles. Nice Bumblebees, one Wasp, one two-color white base. Most are Mint. 5/8". $18. (Auction #122, Lot 44).

MARBLE KING, INC. Rainbow. Lot of two marbles. Both are shooter size hybrid Rainbows. One is a yellow patch and ribbon. $18. (Auction #152, Lot 1).

MARBLE KING, INC. Rainbow. Lot of twenty two marbles. One Cub Scout, six Bumblebees, fifteen three-color on white. All about 5/8". $18. (Auction #112, Lot 23).

MARBLE KING, INC. Rainbow. Lot of three marbles. Three shooter multicolor Rainbows. 7/8". Mint (9.9). $18. (Auction #83, Lot 19).

MARBLE KING, INC. Rainbow. Lot of forty nine marbles. Includes six vintage Bumblebees and forty three modern Wasps. $17. (Auction #144, Lot 34).

MARBLE KING, INC. Rainbow. Lot of two marbles. Both are shooter white-base Rainbows. One has red patch and ribbon with some blue.

$14. (Auction #161, Lot 8).

MARBLE KING, INC. Rainbow. Lot of ten marbles. Five are modern two-patch Cub Scouts. Five are vintage patch and ribbon Bumblebee. $14. (Auction #158, Lot 7).

MARBLE KING, INC. Rainbow. Lot of five marbles. All are white base, multicolor Rainbows. All have green aventurine bands. $13. (Auction #170, Lot 18).

MARBLE KING, INC. Rainbow. Lot of three marbles. All are shooter size Rainbows. Red on white, blue on white, and green on white. $13. (Auction #58, Lot 24).

MARBLE KING, INC. Rainbow. Lot of two marbles. Both are shooters. One is a Cub Scout. One side of the blue ribbon. $12. (Auction #152, Lot 14).

MARBLE KING, INC. Rainbow. Lot of four marbles. Three are Rainbows in assorted colors. The last is a Vitro All-Red. 11/16". $11. (Auction #109, Lot 2).

MARBLE KING, INC. Rainbow. Lot of seven marbles. All are two color Rainbow Bumblebees. Black and yellow. One has a chip. $9. (Auction #92, Lot 16).

MARBLE KING, INC. Rainbow. Lot of twenty four marbles. One is a newer Wasp, the rest are three and four color white base. $7. (Auction #112, Lot 27).

MARBLE KING, INC. Rainbow. White base. Aventurine green patch and ribbon with a hint of blue. Paden City, WV, circa 1960-1975. 5/8". Mint (9.9). $3. (Auction #66, Lot 3).

MARBLE KING, INC. Rainbow Red. Lot of eight marbles. All are shooters. Excellent assortment of Rainbow Reds. 7/8". All Mint. $45. (Auction #123, Lot 31).

MARBLE KING, INC. Rainbow Red. Lot of twelve marbles. All are Rainbow Reds. All about 5/8". Almost all Mint. $13. (Auction #138, Lot 10).

MARBLE KING, INC. Spiderman. A very hard to find Spiderman Rainbow. Blue and red patch and ribbon on opaque white. Has an oxblood. 19/32". Mint (9.9). $200. (Auction #57, Lot 45).

MARBLE KING, INC. Spiderman. Superb example of a Spiderman. Vintage marble, not a reproduction. Alternating blue and red patch. 5/8". Mint(-) (9.1). $140. (Auction #67, Lot 45).

MARBLE KING, INC. Spiderman. Two color patch and ribbon Rainbow Spiderman. A patch and ribbon of blue and a patch and ribbon of blue. 19/32". Mint(-) (9). $70. (Auction #153, Lot 47).

MARBLE KING, INC. Tiger. Two-color Rainbow Tiger shooter. Opaque white base. Black and orange patch and ribbon. White bands. 7/8". Mint (9.9). $130. (Auction #178, Lot 39).

MARBLE KING, INC. Tiger. Extremely rare two color Rainbo Tiger. Two seam marble. Orange almost completely covered by black. 5/8". Mint (9.9). $49. (Auction #65, Lot 4).

MARBLE KING, INC. Tiger. Two color Rainbow Tiger. Orange and black patch and ribbon. Paden City, WV, circa 1955-1965. 19/32." Mint (9.9). $32. (Auction #121, Lot 19).

MARBLE KING, INC. Tiger. Two color Rainbow Tiger. Orange and black patch and ribbon. Paden City, WV, circa 1955-1965. 19/32." Mint (9.9). $30. (Auction #121, Lot 19.10).

MARBLE KING, INC. Tiger. Two color Rainbow Tiger. Orange and black. Nice example. Paden City, WV, circa 1950-1965. 5/8". Mint (9.9). $30. (Auction #94, Lot 1).

MARBLE KING, INC. Tiger. Two color Rainbow Tiger. Orange and black. Nice example. Paden City, WV, circa 1950-1965. 5/8". Mint (9.9). $27. (Auction #166, Lot 3).

MARBLE KING, INC. Tiger. Two color Rainbow Tiger. Orange and black. Nice example. Paden City, WV, circa 1950-1965. 5/8". Mint (9.9). $24. (Auction #141, Lot 1).

MARBLE KING, INC. Tiger. Two color Rainbow Tiger. Orange and black. Nice example. Paden City, WV, circa 1950-1965. 5/8". Mint (9.9). $23. (Auction #161, Lot 10).

MARBLE KING, INC. Tiger. Two color Rainbow Tiger. Orange and black patch and ribbon. Paden City, WV, circa 1955-1965. 19/32." Mint (9.9). $23. (Auction #113, Lot 19.20).

MARBLE KING, INC. Tiger. Two color Rainbow Tiger. Orange and black patch and ribbon. Paden City, WV, circa 1955-1965. 19/32." Mint (9.9). $23. (Auction #113, Lot 19).

MARBLE KING, INC. Tiger. Two color Rainbow Tiger. Orange and black. Nice example. Paden City, WV, circa 1950-1965. 5/8". Mint (9.9). $22. (Auction #167, Lot 14.20).

MARBLE KING, INC. Tiger. Two color Rainbow Tiger. Orange and black. Nice example. Paden City, WV, circa 1950-1965. 5/8". Mint (9.9). $22. (Auction #144, Lot 3.20).

MARBLE KING, INC. Tiger. Two color Rainbow Tiger. Orange and black. Nice example. Paden City, WV, circa 1950-1965. 5/8". Mint (9.9). $22. (Auction #167, Lot 14).

MARBLE KING, INC. Tiger. Two color Rainbow Tiger. Orange and black alternating patch and ribbon. Some annealing spidering. 5/8". Mint (9.7). $22. (Auction #61, Lot 6).

MARBLE KING, INC. Tiger. Two color Rainbow Tiger. Orange and black patch and ribbon. Paden City, WV, circa 1955-1965. 19/32." Mint (9.9). $21. (Auction #113, Lot 19.30).

MARBLE KING, INC. Tiger. Two color Rainbow Tiger. Orange and black. Nice example. Paden City, WV, circa 1950-1965. 5/8". Mint (9.9). $20. (Auction #144, Lot 3).

MARBLE KING, INC. Tiger. Two color patch and ribbon Rainbow Tiger. A black patch and ribbon, and an orange patch and ribbon. 19/32". Mint (9.9). $20. (Auction #153, Lot 36).

MARBLE KING, INC. Tiger. Two color patch and ribbon Rainbow Tiger. A black patch and ribbon, and an orange patch and ribbon. 19/32". Mint (9.9). $20. (Auction #153, Lot 36.20).

MARBLE KING, INC. Tiger. Two color Rainbow Tiger. Orange and black. Orange is a little light. Some tiny pinpricking. 5/8". Mint (9.9). $19. (Auction #148, Lot 5.20).

MARBLE KING, INC. Tiger. Two color Rainbow Tiger. Orange and black. Orange is a little light. Some tiny pinpricking. 5/8". Mint (9.9). $19. (Auction #148, Lot 5).

MARBLE KING, INC. Tiger. Two color Rainbow Tiger. Orange and black. Blown out airhole and annealing fractures. Paden City, WV. 5/8". Near Mint(+) (8.9). $14. (Auction #169, Lot 11).

MARBLE KING, INC. Tournament Assortment. Large drawstring heavy gauge poly bag. Contains about eighty Marble King marbles. $39. (Auction #55, Lot 28).

MARBLE KING, INC. Wasp. Two color Rainbow Wasp shooter. Black and red patch and ribbon. Nice shooter, hard to find. Paden City, WV. 29/32". Mint (9.9). $60. (Auction #102, Lot 41).

MARBLE KING, INC. Wasp. Lot of nine marbles. All are two color Rainbow Wasps. Red and black patch and ribbon. All about 5/8". $50. (Auction #123, Lot 13).

MARBLE KING, INC. Wasp. Two color patch and ribbon Rainbow Wasp with white showing. Shooter. Opaque white base with patch. 1". Mint(-) (9). $20. (Auction #159, Lot 1).

MARBLE KING, INC. Wasp. Two color Marble King Rainbow Wasp. Red and black patch and ribbon, over opaque white. Paden City, WV. 5/8". Mint (9.9). $12. (Auction #179, Lot 21.20).

MARBLE KING, INC. Wasp. Two color Marble King Rainbow Wasp. Red and black patch and ribbon, over opaque white. Paden City, WV. 5/8". Mint (9.9). $12. (Auction #179, Lot 21).

MARBLE KING, INC. Wasp. Two color Marble King Rainbow Wasp. Red and black patch and ribbon, over opaque white. Paden City, WV. 5/8". Mint (9.9). $10. (Auction #179, Lot 21.40).

MARBLE KING, INC. Wasp. Two color Marble King Rainbow Wasp. Red and black patch and ribbon, over opaque white. Paden City, WV. 5/8". Mint (9.9). $10. (Auction #179, Lot 21.30).

MARBLE KING, INC. Wasp. Two color Marble King Rainbow Wasp. Red and black patch and ribbon, over opaque white. Paden City, WV. 5/8". Mint (9.9). $10. (Auction #179, Lot 21.50).

MARBLE KING, INC. Wasp. Two color Rainbow Wasp. Shooter size. Opaque white base with patch and ribbon of black and red. 31/32". Near Mint(+) (8.9). $9. (Auction #171, Lot 18).

MARBLE KING, INC. Wasp. Two color Rainbow Wasp. Shooter size. Opaque white base with patch and ribbon of black and red. 31/32". Near Mint(+) (8.9). $9. (Auction #171, Lot 18.20).

MARBLE KING, INC. Watermelon. Rare marble!!! Very, very difficult to find! This is an excellent example with super symmetry. 19/32". Mint (9.9). $700. (Auction #129, Lot 50).

MASTER MARBLE/GLASS COMPANY. Bag. Leather marble pouch. Front has a multicolor Indian head with "Master Made Marbles" printed. $50. (Auction #121, Lot 24).

MASTER MARBLE/GLASS COMPANY. Catseye. Very interesting Master Glass Company catseye error. These are two catseyes that are fused together. $7. (Auction #63, Lot 7).

MASTER MARBLE/GLASS COMPANY. Clear Sunburst. Very nice marble, about one-half filled with color. Transparent clear base. Colors include white, green. 23/32". Mint (9.9). $22. (Auction #144, Lot 44).

MASTER MARBLE/GLASS COMPANY. Clear Sunburst. Very nice marble, about three-quarters filled with color. Transparent clear base. 23/32". Near Mint(+) (8.8). $17. (Auction #142, Lot 3).

MASTER MARBLE/GLASS COMPANY. Clear Sunburst. Very nice marble, about one half filled with color. Transparent clear base. Colors include white, green. 11/16". Mint(-) (9). $7. (Auction #151, Lot 29).

MASTER MARBLE/GLASS COMPANY. Cloudie. Shooter size Cloudie. Translucent white base with semi-opaque orange/red patch. 15/16". Mint(-) (9). $23. (Auction #96, Lot 10).

MASTER MARBLE/GLASS COMPANY. Comet. Harder to find three color patch. This one is a shooter. Semi-opaque yellow base with an orange patch. 27/32". Mint (9.9). $30. (Auction #87, Lot 7).

MASTER MARBLE/GLASS COMPANY. Comet. Transparent brown on opaque yellow. One rough spot. Clarksburg, WV, circa 1931-1941. 3/4". Near Mint(+) (8.9). $7. (Auction #180, Lot 17).

MASTER MARBLE/GLASS COMPANY. Game rules. Very hard to find folded card with "OFFICIAL RULES The National Marble Tournament Game of RINGER". $38. (Auction #129, Lot 22).

MASTER MARBLE/GLASS COMPANY. Meteor. Excellent Meteor. Opaque yellow base with opaque red covering about seventy five percent of the surface. 3/4". Near Mint(+) (8.9). $5. (Auction #102, Lot 2).

MASTER MARBLE/GLASS COMPANY. Opaque. Lot of two marbles. Both are Master Marble or Master Glass chinese checker marbles. Opaque lavender. $6. (Auction #87, Lot 9).

MASTER MARBLE/GLASS COMPANY. Original bag. Original poly bag of nineteen catseyes. Master Glass Company. Orange paper label. Clarksburg, WV. $18. (Auction #140, Lot 23).

MASTER MARBLE/GLASS COMPANY. Original bag. Original poly bag of nineteen catseyes. Master Glass Company. Orange paper label. Clarksburg, WV. $18. (Auction #140, Lot 23.40).

MASTER MARBLE/GLASS COMPANY. Original bag. Original poly bag of nineteen catseyes. Master Glass Company. Orange paper label. Clarksburg, WV. $18. (Auction #140, Lot 23.30).

MASTER MARBLE/GLASS COMPANY. Original bag. Original poly bag of nineteen catseyes. Master Glass Company. Orange paper label. Clarksburg, WV. $18. (Auction #140, Lot 23.20).

MASTER MARBLE/GLASS COMPANY. Original bag. Original poly bag of nineteen catseyes. Master Glass Company. Orange paper label. Clarksburg, WV. $17. (Auction #155, Lot 29).

MASTER MARBLE/GLASS COMPANY. Original bag. Original poly bag of nineteen catseyes. Master Glass Company. Orange paper label. Clarksburg, WV. $17. (Auction #155, Lot 29.20).

MASTER MARBLE/GLASS COMPANY. Original bag. Original poly bag of nineteen catseyes. Master Glass Company. Orange paper label. Clarksburg, WV. $15. (Auction #155, Lot 29.40).

MASTER MARBLE/GLASS COMPANY. Original bag. Original poly bag of nineteen catseyes. Master Glass Company. Orange paper label. Clarksburg, WV. $15. (Auction #140, Lot 23.50).

MASTER MARBLE/GLASS COMPANY. Original bag. Original poly bag of nineteen catseyes. Master Glass Company. Orange paper label. Clarksburg, WV. $15. (Auction #155, Lot 29.30).

MASTER MARBLE/GLASS COMPANY. Original bag. Original poly bag of nineteen catseyes. Master Glass Company. Orange paper label. Clarksburg, WV. $14. (Auction #107, Lot 26).

MASTER MARBLE/GLASS COMPANY. Original bag. Original poly bag of nineteen catseyes. Master Glass Company. Orange paper label. Clarksburg, WV. $14. (Auction #107, Lot 26.20).

MASTER MARBLE/GLASS COMPANY. Original bag. Original poly bag of nineteen catseyes. Master Glass Company. Orange paper label. Clarksburg, WV. $14. (Auction #107, Lot 26.10).

MASTER MARBLE/GLASS COMPANY. Original bag. Original poly bag of nineteen catseyes. Master Glass Company. Orange paper label. Clarksburg, WV. $12. (Auction #97, Lot 25).

MASTER MARBLE/GLASS COMPANY. Original bag. Original poly bag of nineteen catseyes. Master Glass Company. Orange paper label. Clarksburg, WV. $12. (Auction #97, Lot 25.20).

MASTER MARBLE/GLASS COMPANY. Original bag. Original poly bag of nineteen catseyes. Master Glass Company. Orange paper label. Clarksburg, WV. $12. (Auction #107, Lot 26.50).

MASTER MARBLE/GLASS COMPANY. Original bag. Original poly bag of nineteen catseyes. Master Glass Company. Orange paper label. Clarksburg, WV. $12. (Auction #107, Lot 26.40).

MASTER MARBLE/GLASS COMPANY. Original bag. Original poly bag of nineteen catseyes. Master Glass Company. Orange paper label. Clarksburg, WV. $9. (Auction #97, Lot 25.30).

MASTER MARBLE/GLASS COMPANY. Original bag. Original poly bag of catseyes. Contains twenty catseyes, all about 9/16". $7. (Auction #79, Lot 29.60).

MASTER MARBLE/GLASS COMPANY. Original bag. Original poly bag of catseyes. Contains twenty catseyes, all about 9/16". $7. (Auction #79, Lot 29.40).

MASTER MARBLE/GLASS COMPANY. Original bag. Original poly bag of nineteen catseyes. Master Glass Company. Orange paper label. Clarksburg, WV. $7. (Auction #97, Lot 25.40).

MASTER MARBLE/GLASS COMPANY. Original bag. Original poly bag of nineteen catseyes. Master Glass Company. Orange paper label. Clarksburg, WV. $7. (Auction #97, Lot 25.50).

MASTER MARBLE/GLASS COMPANY. Original bag. Original poly bag of catseyes. Contains twenty catseyes, all about 9/16". $7. (Auction #79, Lot 29).

MASTER MARBLE/GLASS COMPANY. Original bag. Original poly bag of catseyes. Contains twenty catseyes, all about 9/16". $7. (Auction #79, Lot 29.30).

MASTER MARBLE/GLASS COMPANY. Original bag. Original poly bag of catseyes. Contains twenty catseyes, all about 9/16". $7. (Auction #79, Lot 29.50).

MASTER MARBLE/GLASS COMPANY. Original bag. Original poly bag of catseyes. Contains twenty catseyes, all about 9/16". $7. (Auction #79, Lot 29.20).

MASTER MARBLE/GLASS COMPANY. Original bag. Original poly bag. Five shooter clearies. Bag has a paper label reading "Master Marbles / Master Glass". $4. (Auction #79, Lot 1).

MASTER MARBLE/GLASS COMPANY. Original box. An original No. 10 box. Double size of the more common No. 5 box. Red, white and blue with oval cutouts. $205. (Auction #160, Lot 21).

MASTER MARBLE/GLASS COMPANY. Original box. An original No. 10 box. Double size of the more common No. 5 box. Red, white and blue with oval cutouts. $185. (Auction #85, Lot 25).

MASTER MARBLE/GLASS COMPANY. Original box. An original No. 10 box. Double size of the more common No. 5 box. Red, white and blue with oval cutouts. $150. (Auction #79, Lot 31).

MASTER MARBLE/GLASS COMPANY. Original box. An original No. 10 box. Double size of the more common No. 5 box. Red, white and blue with oval cutouts. $120. (Auction #96, Lot 24).

MASTER MARBLE/GLASS COMPANY. Original box. An original No. 6 box. I can't ever recall having seen this one before. This is a small "Sunbeam" box. $110. (Auction #91, Lot 41).

MASTER MARBLE/GLASS COMPANY. Original box. Original No. 13 box. Rectangular "sunbeam" box with oval cutouts. Master Glass Co. Contains thirteen. $70. (Auction #130, Lot 32).

MASTER MARBLE/GLASS COMPANY. Original box. Original No. 13 box. Rectangular "sunbeam" box with oval cutouts. Master Glass Co. Contains thirteen. $65. (Auction #117, Lot 28).

MASTER MARBLE/GLASS COMPANY. Original box. An original No. 6 box. You hardly ever see this size. This is a small "Sunbeam" box. Master logo. $65. (Auction #163, Lot 43).

MASTER MARBLE/GLASS COMPANY. Original box. Original Master Glass No. 5 box. Red white and blue with oval cutouts. Box has a couple of tears. $30. (Auction #81, Lot 24).

MASTER MARBLE/GLASS COMPANY. Original box. Original No. 60 cardboard sleeve. Cellophane panel top. Red and green graphics. Box has edge wear. $16. (Auction #106, Lot 16).

MASTER MARBLE/GLASS COMPANY. Original box. Original No. 60 cardboard sleeve. Cellophane panel top. Red and green graphics. Box has edge wear. $16. (Auction #106, Lot 16.10).

MASTER MARBLE/GLASS COMPANY. Original package. Original stock box. Cardboard box. Top has Master logo with marbles on top. Yellow and black printing. $300. (Auction #132, Lot 40).

MASTER MARBLE/GLASS COMPANY. Original package. Original No. 13 Master Marble advertising box. This is a rectangular box. Five oval cutouts. $125. (Auction #83, Lot 23).

MASTER MARBLE/GLASS COMPANY. Original package. Original No. 13 Master Marble box. This is a rectangular box. Five oval cutouts in the top. $75. (Auction #179, Lot 30).

MASTER MARBLE/GLASS COMPANY. Original package. Lot of two items. Both are Master Glass No. 5 cardboard boxes. Both about 6" x 5" x 5/8" (sight). $20. (Auction #132, Lot 32).

MASTER MARBLE/GLASS COMPANY. Patch. Lot of thirty one marbles. Almost all are Master Comets. All red on yellow. Nice group. All about 5/8". $44. (Auction #151, Lot 16).

MASTER MARBLE/GLASS COMPANY. Patch. Lot of five marbles. All are Master Marble Comets. Each is a different color. Red on green, red on white. $42. (Auction #162, Lot 24).

MASTER MARBLE/GLASS COMPANY. Patch. Lot of five marbles. All are Master Marble Comets. Each is a different color. Red on green, red on white. $39. (Auction #162, Lot 24.20).

MASTER MARBLE/GLASS COMPANY. Patch. Lot of three marbles. Three Comets. Each a different color combination. Clarksburg, WV, circa 1932. $27. (Auction #76, Lot 14).

MASTER MARBLE/GLASS COMPANY. Patch. Lot of three marbles. Two are Comet patches. One is orange on blue, the other is red on green. $25. (Auction #58, Lot 22).

MASTER MARBLE/GLASS COMPANY. Patch. Lot of five marbles. Three Comets and a Cloudie. 19/32" to 21/32". Mint (9.9-9.7). $20. (Auction #75, Lot 18).

MASTER MARBLE/GLASS COMPANY. **Patch.** Lot of three marbles. Two Comets and a Cloudie. Nice set. Clarksburg, WV, circa 1932-1942. 5/8". Mint. $14. (Auction #69, Lot 14).

MASTER MARBLE/GLASS COMPANY. **Sunburst.** Lot of eleven marbles. Nice assortment of Sunbursts. All opaque. Assorted colors. 5/8" to 11/16". $80. (Auction #106, Lot 14).

MASTER MARBLE/GLASS COMPANY. **Sunburst.** Lot of twenty eight marbles. Assortment of Master Glass Sunbursts. with some Master Marble Sunbursts. $75. (Auction #132, Lot 15).

MASTER MARBLE/GLASS COMPANY. **Sunburst.** Lot of seven marbles. Great assortment of opaque Sunbursts. Clarksburg, WV, circa 1932-1942. 5/8". $75. (Auction #69, Lot 10).

MASTER MARBLE/GLASS COMPANY. **Sunburst.** Lot of six marbles. All are Sunbursts. Later type. Green or blue with wispy white. Clarksburg, WV. $55. (Auction #64, Lot 17).

MASTER MARBLE/GLASS COMPANY. **Sunburst.** Lot of nineteen marbles. Assortment of colors and styles. Some have clear panels. 5/8" to 11/16". Mint. $50. (Auction #144, Lot 32).

MASTER MARBLE/GLASS COMPANY. **Sunburst.** Lot of twenty nine marbles. Assortment of Master Glass Sunbursts. 5/8" to 23/32". Almost all Mint. $45. (Auction #132, Lot 13).

MASTER MARBLE/GLASS COMPANY. **Sunburst.** Lot of five marbles. All are Sunbursts. Nice group. Clarksburg, WV, circa 1931-1941. 11/16" to 23/32". $43. (Auction #75, Lot 16).

MASTER MARBLE/GLASS COMPANY. **Sunburst.** Lot of nine marbles. All are Sunbursts. Nice assortment. 21/32" to 23/32". Mint (9.9-9.5). $37. (Auction #180, Lot 7).

MASTER MARBLE/GLASS COMPANY. **Sunburst.** Lot of fourteen marbles. All are Sunbursts. Mostly later Master Glass Sunbursts, predominately shade. $37. (Auction #112, Lot 26).

MASTER MARBLE/GLASS COMPANY. **Sunburst.** Lot of fifteen marbles. Assortment of Master Marble Sunbursts and patches. All about 11/16". $35. (Auction #151, Lot 27).

MASTER MARBLE/GLASS COMPANY. **Sunburst.** Lot of six marbles. Nice assortment of opaque Sunbursts. 11/16" to 3/4". Mint (9.9). $32. (Auction #102, Lot 35).

MASTER MARBLE/GLASS COMPANY. **Sunburst.** Lot of fifteen marbles. Assortment of Master Marble Sunbursts and patches. All about 11/16". $32. (Auction #151, Lot 27.20).

MASTER MARBLE/GLASS COMPANY. **Sunburst.** Lot of thirteen marbles. All are Master Glass Sunbursts. Assorted shades of green. All about 11/16". $30. (Auction #151, Lot 11).

MASTER MARBLE/GLASS COMPANY. **Sunburst.** Lot of three marbles. All are clear Sunbursts. Nice variety of coloring. Clarksburg, WV, circa 1932. $29. (Auction #59, Lot 7).

MASTER MARBLE/GLASS COMPANY. **Sunburst.** Lot of ten marbles. Later Sunbursts. Assorted shades of green, clear, white and brown. 19/32" to 5/8". $28. (Auction #83, Lot 20).

MASTER MARBLE/GLASS COMPANY. **Sunburst.** Lot of thirteen marbles. All are Master Glass Sunbursts. Assorted shades of green. All about 11/16". $28. (Auction #151, Lot 11.20).

MASTER MARBLE/GLASS COMPANY. **Sunburst.** Lot of ten marbles. All are Master Marble Sunbursts. Assorted shades of green. All about 11/16". $26. (Auction #146, Lot 22.20).

MASTER MARBLE/GLASS COMPANY. **Sunburst.** Lot of ten marbles. All are Master Marble Sunbursts. Assorted shades of green. All about 11/16". $26. (Auction #146, Lot 22).

MASTER MARBLE/GLASS COMPANY. **Sunburst.** Lot of four marbles. All are clear Sunbursts! One is Mint. 5/8" to 11/16". Mint (9.9) to Near Mint(+). $26. (Auction #180, Lot 4).

MASTER MARBLE/GLASS COMPANY. **Sunburst.** Lot of ten marbles. All are Master Marble Sunbursts. Assorted shades of green. All about 11/16". $24. (Auction #146, Lot 22.30).

MASTER MARBLE/GLASS COMPANY. **Sunburst.** Lot of two marbles. Nice pair of Sunbursts. Same basic color scheme. 5/8". Mint (9.9). $22. (Auction #123, Lot 17).

MASTER MARBLE/GLASS COMPANY. **Sunburst.** Master Glass Company patch. Dark green base with opaque white brushed on one half of the marble. 5/8". Mint (9.9). $20. (Auction #88, Lot 20).

MASTER MARBLE/GLASS COMPANY. **Sunburst.** Exceptional example of a clear Sunburst. Transparent clear base, almost completely filled by filament. 34". Mint(-) (9.1). $19. (Auction #58, Lot 9).

MASTER MARBLE/GLASS COMPANY. **Sunburst.** Lot of eight marbles. All are Master Glass Sunbursts. Assorted shades of green. All about 11/16". $19. (Auction #146, Lot 16.20).

MASTER MARBLE/GLASS COMPANY. **Sunburst.** Clear Sunburst. Looks just like a sparkler, but the colors are too dull. Super example! Clarksburg, WV. 5/8". Mint (9.7). $19. (Auction #138, Lot 17).

MASTER MARBLE/GLASS COMPANY. **Sunburst.** Lot of eight marbles. All are Master Glass Sunbursts. Assorted shades of green. All about 11/16". $19. (Auction #146, Lot 16).

MASTER MARBLE/GLASS COMPANY. **Sunburst.** Lot of eight marbles. All are Master Glass Sunbursts. Assorted shades of green. All about 11/16". $17. (Auction #146, Lot 16.40).

MASTER MARBLE/GLASS COMPANY. **Sunburst.** Lot of eight marbles. All are Master Glass Sunbursts. Assorted shades of green. All about 11/16". $17. (Auction #146, Lot 16.30).

MASTER MARBLE/GLASS COMPANY. **Sunburst.** A Tigereye Sunburst. Transparent base. Translucent orange, white and black bands. Harder to find. 19/32". Mint (9.9). $15. (Auction #55, Lot 11).

MASTER MARBLE/GLASS COMPANY. **Sunburst.** Excellent example of a clear Sunburst. Transparent clear with a baby blue patch, white patch. 5/8". Near Mint(+) (8.9). $13. (Auction #107, Lot 19).

MASTER MARBLE/GLASS COMPANY. **Sunburst.** Clear Sunburst. Transparent clear, translucent orange, opaque light blue and opaque white. 23/32". Mint (9.9). $12. (Auction #110, Lot 41).

MASTER MARBLE/GLASS COMPANY. **Sunburst.** Clear Sunburst. Orange, blue and white in clear. Clarksburg, WV, circa 1932-1941. 5/8". Mint (9.5). $11. (Auction #76, Lot 2).

MASTER MARBLE/GLASS COMPANY. **Sunburst.** Shooter clear sunburst. One tiny subsurface moon and a tiny annealing fracture. Clarksburg, WV. 3/4". Near Mint(+) (8.9). $11. (Auction #82, Lot 31).

MASTER MARBLE/GLASS COMPANY. **Sunburst.** Clear Sunburst. Transparent clear with light blue and light yellow. In great shape. Super example. 11/16". Mint (9.9). $10. (Auction #97, Lot 26).

MASTER MARBLE/GLASS COMPANY. **Tigereye.** I haven't had one of these in a cyberauction for a while. Clear Sunburst. 5/8". Mint (9.9). $32. (Auction #180, Lot 15).

MISCELLANEOUS. Assortment for reproduction ephemera from Akro Agate. Includes a "Jobbers' Wholesale Price List" 192. $40. (Auction #95, Lot 23).

MISCELLANEOUS. Lot of three items. Golden Rule Marble, white. Fortune telling marble. Razor sharpener. Nice group. $35. (Auction #57, Lot 26).

MISCELLANEOUS. Lot of six items. "Chinko-Checkers" board, fiberboard, framed, circa late 1930s, Good (7.9). $20. (Auction #101, Lot 37).

MISCELLANEOUS. Ground goldstone sphere. Brown goldstone. Manmade marble, glass with finely ground copper flecks. 1". Mint (9.9). $20. (Auction #61, Lot 5).

MISCELLANEOUS. Packaged marble-related item. Includes the printed poem "The Legend of the Kindness Marble" by Cathy. $11. (Auction #168, Lot 23).

MISCELLANEOUS. Lot of three items. Small framed Rockwell Marble Players (6" x 6"). Leather pouch stamped "Grub Stake". $9. (Auction #155, Lot 27).

MISCELLANEOUS. Reproduction envelope. A return business size envelope from the M.F. Christensen & Son Company. $8. (Auction #95, Lot 22).

MISCELLANEOUS. The lid form a Sundae Cup of Heilemann's ice cream. Send 1 lid in plus 25 cents and get a bag of Marbles. $4. (Auction #78, Lot 21.40).

MISCELLANEOUS. The lid form a Sundae Cup of Heilemann's ice cream. Send 1 lid in plus 25 cents and get a bag of Marbles. $4. (Auction #78, Lot 21.20).

MISCELLANEOUS. The lid form a Sundae Cup of Heilemann's ice cream. Send 1 lid in plus 25 cents and get a bag of Marbles. $4. (Auction #78, Lot 21.30).

MISCELLANEOUS. The lid form a Sundae Cup of Heilemann's ice cream. Send 1 lid in plus 25 cents and get a bag of Marbles. $4. (Auction #78, Lot 21.60).

MISCELLANEOUS. The lid form a Sundae Cup of Heilemann's ice cream. Send 1 lid in plus 25 cents and get a bag of Marbles. $4. (Auction #78, Lot 21.50).

MISCELLANEOUS. The lid form a Sundae Cup of Heilemann's ice cream. Send 1 lid in plus 25 cents and get a bag of Marbles. $4. (Auction #78, Lot 21).

MISCELLANEOUS. Metal sphere. It is either hollow or a very light metal. Not sure which. No "X". Odd item. Unknown. 1". Mint (9.5). $3. (Auction #69, Lot 11).

MISCELLANEOUS. The lid form a Sundae Cup of Heilemann's ice cream. Send 1 lid in plus 25 cents and get a bag of Marbles. $2. (Auction #123, Lot 25).

MISCELLANEOUS. The lid form a Sundae Cup of Heilemann's ice cream. Send 1 lid in plus 25 cents and get a bag of Marbles. $2. (Auction #123, Lot 25.20).

MISCELLANEOUS. Advertisement. A full page ad from the Confectioners' Journal for "SMITH'S PHEN-HUNCH MARBLE GUM". $95. (Auction #147, Lot 20).

MISCELLANEOUS. Advertisement. Page 843 from the December 1926 issue of Child Life. Advertisement from Wolverine Supply. $5. (Auction #127, Lot 22).

MISCELLANEOUS. Advertising bag. Very rare cloth bag. I have only seen one of other of these. This is a bag that contained the marble. $130. (Auction #91, Lot 23).

MISCELLANEOUS. Advertising bag. Very rare cloth bag. I have only seen one of other of these. This is a bag that contained the marble. $120. (Auction #168, Lot 21).

MISCELLANEOUS. Advertising marble. Opaque white marble with the Pepsi logo on it. Modern. About 1". Mint(-) (9). $1. (Auction #94, Lot 4).

MISCELLANEOUS. Advertising Marbles. Lot of six marbles. All made by Lucky Dog. All on yellow or black. $17. (Auction #54, Lot 23).

MISCELLANEOUS. Agate. Hard to find marble. Dyed handcut agate. Dyed blue agate. White bullseye on top. Nice faceting. 13/16". Mint (9.9). $150. (Auction #170, Lot 45).

MISCELLANEOUS. Agate. Outstanding handcut banded agate!!! Green, white and brown bands. And one thin red band!!! Very hard. 23/32". Near Mint(+) (8.9). $130. (Auction #96, Lot 14).

MISCELLANEOUS. Agate. Lot of fourteen marbles. All are handcut agates. Nice assortment of banded and carnelian. $115. (Auction #132, Lot 3).

MISCELLANEOUS. Agate. Rare handcut black agate. Almost all black, with two white bands. Superior faceting. Well-polished. 5/8". Mint (9.9). $110. (Auction #176, Lot 44).

MISCELLANEOUS. Agate. Lot of five marbles. All are handcut agates. These are pristine. $110. (Auction #67, Lot 18).

MISCELLANEOUS. Agate. Lot of five marbles. An assortment of hand cut agates. All banded. Superior design to these marbles. $85. (Auction #73, Lot 29).

MISCELLANEOUS. Agate. Hand cut agate. Banded consisting of various bands in assorted shades of brown/red, with a white band. 15/16". Mint (9.5). $80. (Auction #179, Lot 34).

MISCELLANEOUS. Agate. Superb large hand cut banded agate. Carnelian red/brown and white. Nice faceting. Large marble. 1-1/16". Mint (9.9). $75. (Auction #105, Lot 43).

MISCELLANEOUS. Agate. Lot of seven marbles. All are handcut agate. Assortment of carnelian and banded. $70. (Auction #64, Lot 19).

MISCELLANEOUS. Agate. Hand cut agate. Very interesting. Banded in various shades of red/brown. One side has brown and black. 13/16". Mint (9.9). $60. (Auction #183, Lot 20).

MISCELLANEOUS. Agate. Banded agate. Very odd color. Green on top, then a band of white, then blue on the bottom. $60. (Auction #121, Lot 39).

MISCELLANEOUS. Agate. Superb hand cut banded black agate. Natural black, not dyed. 23/32". Mint (9.7). $55. (Auction #91, Lot 19).

MISCELLANEOUS. Agate. Lot of five marbles. All are hand cut agates. All are Mint! Banded and carnelian. 1/2" to 3/4". Mint. $55. (Auction #94, Lot 6).

MISCELLANEOUS. Agate. Beautiful banded agate. Hand cut. Nice faceting. In great shape. One tiny flat spot. 3/4". Mint (9.5). $55. (Auction #176, Lot 20).

MISCELLANEOUS. Agate. Hand cut black agate. Some white bands. Excellent faceting. Very hard to find. Germany, circa 1850. 21/32". Mint (9.9). $50. (Auction #105, Lot 13).

MISCELLANEOUS. Agate. Lot of three marbles. All banded agate. All hand cut. 7/16" to 17/32". Mint (9.9). $50. (Auction #134, Lot 3).

MISCELLANEOUS. Agate. Lot of eleven marbles. Includes an assortment of banded agate, carnelian agate, gray agate. $46. (Auction #94, Lot 14).

MISCELLANEOUS. Agate. Hand cut black banded agate. Very little white. Super faceting. A beauty. Germany, circa 1850-1920. 23/32". Mint (9.9). $45. (Auction #98, Lot 5).

MISCELLANEOUS. Agate. Lot of two marbles. Both are handcut agates. Orange/brown and translucent white. Nice pair. Germany,. $44. (Auction #172, Lot 13).

MISCELLANEOUS. Agate. Black banded agate. Rare color. Not dyed. Hand cut. This one is old. Very nice. Germany, circa 1850. 5/8". Mint (9.5). $42. (Auction #74, Lot 36).

MISCELLANEOUS. Agate. Lot of three marbles. All are handcut banded agates. One is a hard to find black and translucent white. $41. (Auction #152, Lot 17).

MISCELLANEOUS. Agate. Hand cut banded agate. Large one. Great faceting. Some crystal spots. In super shape. Germany. 1-3/16". Mint

(9.7). $41. (Auction #127, Lot 42).

MISCELLANEOUS. Agate. Hand cut banded agate. White, translucent white, red and brown bands. Nice faceting. 13/16". Mint (9.8). $40. (Auction #160, Lot 37).

MISCELLANEOUS. Agate. Nice large agate. Red, gray and brown banded pattern. Machine ground. A beauty. 1-5/16". Mint (9.9). 1-5/16". Mint (9.9). $39. (Auction #185, Lot 8).

MISCELLANEOUS. Agate. Hand cut banded agate. Red/brown, brown and white. Excellent faceting. In great shape. Germany. 29/32". Mint (9.9). $37. (Auction #154, Lot 37).

MISCELLANEOUS. Agate. Handcut banded agate. Superior pattern. White, brown and gray bands. Excellent polish. Germany. 5/8". Mint (9.9). $37. (Auction #170, Lot 19).

MISCELLANEOUS. Agate. Black agate. Hand cut. Bullseye. Beauty. One tiny chip that was a flaw in the stone. Germany. 9/16". Mint (9.5). $37. (Auction #158, Lot 44).

MISCELLANEOUS. Agate. Lot of three. All are hand cut agates. All three are banded. The largest has hit marks. 17/32", 9/16". $36. (Auction #88, Lot 6).

MISCELLANEOUS. Agate. Hand cut banded agate. Red/brown and translucent white. Excellent faceting. Great marble. Germany. 21/32". Mint (9.7). $36. (Auction #154, Lot 46).

MISCELLANEOUS. Agate. Lot of thirteen marbles. All are hand cut agates. All have been played with. 1/2" to 5/8". Mint(-). $35. (Auction #125, Lot 14).

MISCELLANEOUS. Agate. Exceptional shooter size handcut carnelian agate. Nice brown/red carnelian color. Some inclusions. 15/16". Mint (9.9). $35. (Auction #168, Lot 20).

MISCELLANEOUS. Agate. Handcut banded agate. Great faceting. A beauty. Germany, circa 1850-1920. 23/32". Mint (9.9). $32. (Auction #156, Lot 32).

MISCELLANEOUS. Agate. Handcut banded agate. Translucent milky and opaque white bands. Excellent marble. 1/2". Mint (9.6). $32. (Auction #167, Lot 28).

MISCELLANEOUS. Agate. Lot of four marbles. All are hand cut carnelian agates. Germany, circa 1820-1920. 11/16" to 7/8". Mint. $32. (Auction #87, Lot 15).

MISCELLANEOUS. Agate. Handcut agate. Brown, orange and white banded agate. Shooter. Nice faceting. One as made defect. Germany. 15/16". Mint (9.5). $32. (Auction #149, Lot 44).

MISCELLANEOUS. Agate. Beautiful hand cut banded agate. Brown and white. Nice white bullseye on the top. Super shooter. Germany. 7/8". Mint (9.7). $30. (Auction #93, Lot 12).

MISCELLANEOUS. Agate. Banded agate. Hand cut. Excellent fine faceting. Brown, white and black. Shooter. Nice marble. Germany. 7/8". Mint (9.9). $30. (Auction #106, Lot 37).

MISCELLANEOUS. Agate. Handcut agate. Outstanding example. Top third is a crystal panel, then several bands of white. 13/16". Mint (9.9). $26. (Auction #184, Lot 15).

MISCELLANEOUS. Agate. Hand cut agate. Translucent creamy white, with some light brown splotches and an opaque white bullseye. 25/32". Mint (9.9). $26. (Auction #168, Lot 38).

MISCELLANEOUS. Agate. Brown banded agate sphere. In great shape. Modern, machine cut. Origin and age unknown. 1-3/8". Mint (9.9). $26. (Auction #131, Lot 24).

MISCELLANEOUS. Agate. Banded agate. Hand cut. Nice example. Germany, circa 1850-1915. 5/8". Mint (9.9). $25. (Auction #73, Lot 34).

MISCELLANEOUS. Agate. Hand cut agate. One-half translucent milky white, one-half translucent light brown. Nice faceting. 13/16". Mint (9.7). $22. (Auction #171, Lot 1).

MISCELLANEOUS. Agate. Hand cut carnelian agate. Excellent faceting. Two small gouges. 13/16". Mint (9.9). $22. (Auction #153, Lot 34).

MISCELLANEOUS. Agate. Dyed blue agate. Machine ground. Origin and age unknown. 7/8". Mint (9.9). $22. (Auction #103, Lot 42).

MISCELLANEOUS. Agate. Dyed blue banded agate. White bullseye on the top. Probably machine ground. Origin and age unknown. 13/16". Mint (9.9). $22. (Auction #106, Lot 44).

MISCELLANEOUS. Agate. Lot of three marbles. All three are handcut agates. Two are banded, ones is carnelian. $20. (Auction #117, Lot 16).

MISCELLANEOUS. Agate. Hand cut banded agate. Excellent faceting. Small gouges on one side. 11/16". Mint (9.3). $20. (Auction #162, Lot 2).

MISCELLANEOUS. Agate. Lot of three marbles. First is a gray agate, machine cut, 15/16", Mint (9.9). Second is a black band. $20. (Auction #163, Lot 1).

MISCELLANEOUS. Agate. Handcut banded agate. Traslucent brown and semi-transparent white. Very nice faceting. Germany. 15/32". Mint (9.9). $18. (Auction #185, Lot 18).

MISCELLANEOUS. Agate. Lot of two marbles. Both are modern machine cut. One is an orange and white banded agate. $18. (Auction #107, Lot 29).

MISCELLANEOUS. Agate. Lot of three. All are hand cut agates. All three are banded. The largest has hit marks. 17/32", 9/16". $17. (Auction #104, Lot 23).

MISCELLANEOUS. Agate. Beautiful white banded agate. Looks to be machine cut, not hand cut. Opaque white banding. 23/32". Mint (9.9). $17. (Auction #105, Lot 22).

MISCELLANEOUS. Agate. Nice large hand-cut banded agate. Brown and white. Excellent faceting. This one has been used. 1-1/16". Near Mint(+) (8.9). $17. (Auction #100, Lot 3).

MISCELLANEOUS. Agate. Lot of two marbles. First is hand cut carnelian. 15/16". Near Mint (8.6). Second is white banded. $17. (Auction #106, Lot 9).

MISCELLANEOUS. Agate. Shooter hand cut banded agate. Clear, white and brown. Nice faceting. Overall tiny subsurface hit mark. 1-1/16". Near Mint (8.5). $15. (Auction #106, Lot 5).

MISCELLANEOUS. Agate. Hand cut banded agate. Beautiful. Germany, circa 1850-1920. 9/16". Mint (9.9). $14. (Auction #159, Lot 2).

MISCELLANEOUS. Agate. Hand cut banded agate. Orange/brown and white. Nice faceting. One manufacturing gouge on it. Germany. 21/32". Mint (9.5). $14. (Auction #164, Lot 15).

MISCELLANEOUS. Agate. Lot of three items. Handcut agate. All are carnelian agates. All have been used. 25/32" to 7/8". Near Mint. $14. (Auction #171, Lot 11).

MISCELLANEOUS. Agate. Hand cut banded agate. Beautiful. Germany, circa 1850-1920. 9/16". Mint (9.9). $12. (Auction #159, Lot 2.20).

MISCELLANEOUS. Agate. Hand cut banded agate. Beautiful. Germany, circa 1850-1920. 9/16". Mint (9.9). $12. (Auction #159, Lot 2.40).

MISCELLANEOUS. Agate. Hand cut banded agate. Beautiful. Germany, circa 1850-1920. 9/16". Mint (9.9). $12. (Auction #159, Lot 2.30).

MISCELLANEOUS. Agate. Machine ground agate. Creamy banded agate with a green inclusion. 11/16". Mint (9.9). $12. (Auction #185, Lot 2).

MISCELLANEOUS. Agate. Lot of two marbles. Both are banded agates. One brown, one black. Both are modern machine ground. $10. (Auction #110, Lot 8).

MISCELLANEOUS. Agate. Hand cut banded agate. Beautiful. Germany, circa 1850-1920. 9/16". Mint (9.9). $10. (Auction #159, Lot 2.50).

MISCELLANEOUS. Agate. Hand cut agate shooter. Banded brown patch on a gray agate. Nice faceting. Has some subsurface hit marks. 27/32". Near Mint (8.6). $10. (Auction #116, Lot 14).

MISCELLANEOUS. Agate. Hand cut banded agate. Beautiful. Germany, circa 1850-1920. 9/16". Mint (9.9). $10. (Auction #159, Lot 2.60).

MISCELLANEOUS. Agate. Lot of three marbles. All are hand cut carnelian agates. All have seen use. 11/16" to 23/32". Near Mint. $10. (Auction #161, Lot 4).

MISCELLANEOUS. Agate. Handcut carnelian agate. Some original gouges from making. One small subsurface moon. Germany. 5/8". Near Mint(+) (8.9). $10. (Auction #184, Lot 37).

MISCELLANEOUS. Agateware. This is a Victorian shoe hook puller with a hand cut agate. About 4-1/2" long. Has a hook at one end. $80. (Auction #121, Lot 25).

MISCELLANEOUS. Article. Framed magazine article. "Not All Grown-Ups Let You Win". No date. $7. (Auction #138, Lot 37).

MISCELLANEOUS. Artwork. Print of a painting by Don Grzybowski. Still life depicting apple, books, marble pouch with marbles . $250. (Auction #138, Lot 50).

MISCELLANEOUS. Artwork. Print of a painting by Don Grzybowski. Still life depicting pouches and marbles. $190. (Auction #143, Lot 50).

MISCELLANEOUS. Atomic Marble. Small sealed envelope presumably containing one machine made clearie. Labeled as "ATOMIC MARBLE". $5. (Auction #147, Lot 28).

MISCELLANEOUS. Bagatelle. Lot of three items. Lindstrom's Poker Ball Pin Game. Wooden. Probably 1930s. Mint(-).$85. (Auction #122, Lot 41.10).

MISCELLANEOUS. Ballot Box. Walnut ballot box. Sliding top. In great shape. Box is 9" x 5-1/2" x 4". Handle is 5". $50. (Auction #108, Lot 26).

MISCELLANEOUS. Ballot Box. Walnut ballot box. Lifting top. In great shape. Box is 9" x 6" x 4". Handle is 5". $50. (Auction #108, Lot 25).

MISCELLANEOUS. Book. Mark Randall and Dennis Webb. "Greenberg's Guide to Marbles". First Edition. 1988. Hard cover. 118 p. $85. (Auction #158, Lot 21).

MISCELLANEOUS. Book. "Marble Collectors Society of America Price Guide". Paperback, 28 pages. Copyright 1985, first edition. $70. (Auction #156, Lot 23).

MISCELLANEOUS. Book. Lot of two items. First is "Chinas: Hand-Painted Marbles of the Late 19th Century" by Jeff Carkskadden. $50. (Auction #184, Lot 25).

MISCELLANEOUS. Book. Lot of two items. First is "Chinas: Hand-Painted Marbles of the Late 19th Century" by Jeff Carkskadden. $50. (Auction #184, Lot 25.20).

MISCELLANEOUS. Book. Mark Randall and Dennis Webb. "Greenberg's Guide to Marbles". First Edition. 1988. Hard cover. 118 p. $50. (Auction #178, Lot 31).

MISCELLANEOUS. Book. "Kate Greenaway's Book of Games". Published in Great Britain by Frederick Warne & Co., Ltd. Hardcover. $45. (Auction #147, Lot 21).

MISCELLANEOUS. Book. Akro Agate by Dr. Budd Appleton. Copyright 1972. Small price guide on Akro Agate items. $37. (Auction #71, Lot 24).

MISCELLANEOUS. Book. "Little Men" By Louisa May Alcott. 1940 edition. Inside cover has an illustration of boys playing marbles. $37. (Auction #92, Lot 25).

MISCELLANEOUS. Book. "Collecting Antique Marbles" by Paul Baumann. Paperback, first edition, 1970, sixth printing 1984. $36. (Auction #138, Lot 41).

MISCELLANEOUS. Book. The Great American Marble Book by Fred Ferretti. First printing September 1973. $35. (Auction #71, Lot 23).

MISCELLANEOUS. Book. "Collecting Antique Marbles". Second edition. Paul Baumann. Published 1991. In very nice shape. $31. (Auction #119, Lot 30).

MISCELLANEOUS. Book. "Marble Collectors Society of America Price Guide". Paperback, 28 pages. Copyright 1985, third edition. $30. (Auction #127, Lot 17).

MISCELLANEOUS. Book. "Quiet Boy" by Lela and Rufus Waltrip. 1962. Cover shows two boys shooting marbles. $24. (Auction #92, Lot 24).

MISCELLANEOUS. Book. "Collectable Machine-Made Marbles" by Larry Castle and Marlow Peterson. Copyright 1989. $22. (Auction #138, Lot 43).

MISCELLANEOUS. Book. "Knuckles Down!" By Cathy C. Runyan. Small 36 page paperback book on various marble games. Copyright. $20. (Auction #127, Lot 19).

MISCELLANEOUS. Book. Marbles: Identification and Price Guide by Mel Morrison and Carl Terison. $20. (Auction #65, Lot 22).

MISCELLANEOUS. Book. "Chinas: Hand-painted Marbles of the Late 19th Century" by Jeff Carskadden and Richard Gartley. Copy. $20. (Auction #164, Lot 25).

MISCELLANEOUS. Book. "Chinas: Hand-painted Marbles of the Late 19th Century" by Jeff Carskadden and Richard Gartley. Copy. $20. (Auction #164, Lot 25.20).

MISCELLANEOUS. Book. "The Great American Marble Book", by Fred Ferretti. Copyright 1973, Workman Publishing Company. $20. (Auction #156, Lot 24).

MISCELLANEOUS. Book. "I Spy - Super Challenger!". Published by Scholastic Books, copyright 1997, first printing. $14. (Auction #64, Lot 25.20).

MISCELLANEOUS. Book. "I Spy - Super Challenger!". Published by Scholastic Books, copyright 1997, first printing. $14. (Auction #64, Lot 25).

MISCELLANEOUS. Book. "I Spy - Super Challenger!". Published by Scholastic Books, copyright 1997, first printing. $12. (Auction #64, Lot 25.30).

MISCELLANEOUS. Book. "Everett Grist's Machine Made & Contemporary Marbles". Copyright 1992. Paperback, 92 pages. $12. (Auction #127, Lot 18).

MISCELLANEOUS. Book. "Marbles: The Guide to Machine Made Marbles" 2nd edition. Larry Castle and Marlow Peterson. Autographed. $10. (Auction #119, Lot 29).

MISCELLANEOUS. Book. "I Spy - Super Challenger!". Published by Scholastic Books, copyright 1997, first printing. $10. (Auction #64, Lot 25.40).

MISCELLANEOUS. Book. Everett Grist "Marbles: Identification and Values", Third Edition, 1992, price update 1994. Paperback. $7. (Auction #158, Lot 22).

MISCELLANEOUS. Book. "Antique and Collectible Marbles" by Everett Grist. Second edition. Copyright 1988. $5. (Auction #138, Lot 42).

MISCELLANEOUS. Book. "Everett Grist's Big Book of Marbles". Hard cover. 1993. Spine is cracked. Includes a framed picture. $2. (Auction #143, Lot 29).

MISCELLANEOUS. Booklet. "All About Marbles and 20 Games to Play". Small paperback pamphlet. Produced by House of Marbles. $10. (Auction #95, Lot 21).

MISCELLANEOUS. Booklet. "All About Marbles and 20 Games to Play". Small paperback pamphlet. Produced by House of Marbles. $7. (Auction #95, Lot 21.30).

MISCELLANEOUS. Booklet. "All About Marbles and 20 Games to Play". Small paperback pamphlet. Produced by House of Marbles. $7. (Auction #95, Lot 21.20).

MISCELLANEOUS. Booklet. "All About Marbles and 20 Games to Play". Small paperback pamphlet. Produced by House of Marbles. $5. (Auction #95, Lot 21.40).

MISCELLANEOUS. Calendar. The 1994 Calendar from the Marine Corps Reserve Toys for Tots Foundation. $2. (Auction #119, Lot 31).

MISCELLANEOUS. Candy tin. Small candy tin with Norman Rockwell's "The Champion" on the top. Fairly recent. Made in England. $9. (Auction #127, Lot 20).

MISCELLANEOUS. Candy tin. Small candy tin with Norman Rockwell's "The Champion" on the top. Fairly recent. Made in England. $9. (Auction #151, Lot 24).

MISCELLANEOUS. Carpet Ball. Nice carpet ball. White base. Pink flower design. In great shape. 3-1/4". Mint (9.3). $200. (Auction #167, Lot 21).

MISCELLANEOUS. Carpet Ball. Nice carpet ball. White base. Twelve red lines on each axis. In great shape. England, circa 1880. 3-1/4". Mint (9.7). $120. (Auction #179, Lot 26).

MISCELLANEOUS. Carpet Ball. Nice carpet ball. White base. Black flower design. In great shape with just one small chip. England. 3-1/4". Near Mint(+) (8.9). $100. (Auction #172, Lot 21).

MISCELLANEOUS. Carpet Ball. Nice carpet ball. White base. Twelve yellow lines on each axis. In very nice shape. 3-1/4". Near Mint(+) (8.9). $95. (Auction #162, Lot 22).

MISCELLANEOUS. Carpet Ball. Nice carpet ball. White base. Brown crown and thistle design. 3-1/4". Near Mint(+) (8.9). $70. (Auction #181, Lot 30).

MISCELLANEOUS. Christmas Ornament. 1997 Hallmark Keepsake Ornament. Plaque depicting Norman Rockwell's "The Champion". $12. (Auction #112, Lot 20).

MISCELLANEOUS. Christmas Ornament. 1997 Hallmark Keepsake Ornament. Plaque depicting Norman Rockwell's "The Champion". $11. (Auction #146, Lot 19).

MISCELLANEOUS. Christmas Ornament. 1997 Hallmark Keepsake Ornament. Plaque depicting Norman Rockwell's "The Champion". $10. (Auction #136, Lot 21).

MISCELLANEOUS. Christmas Ornament. 1997 Hallmark Keepsake Ornament. Plaque depicting Norman Rockwell's "The Champion". $10. (Auction #88, Lot 14).

MISCELLANEOUS. Christmas Ornament. 1997 Hallmark Keepsake Ornament. Plaque depicting Norman Rockwell's "The Champion". $9. (Auction #151, Lot 23).

MISCELLANEOUS. Cigarette card. Cigarette card. Front depicts a boy knuckling down (not wearing any shoes) at a sidewalk with two boys. $95. (Auction #133, Lot 50).

MISCELLANEOUS. Codd bottle. Codd bottle. Glass marble in neck. "W.H. Grafton Wellington" on one side. "Dan Ryland Sole Makers". $27. (Auction #87, Lot 25).

MISCELLANEOUS. Codd bottle. Small Codd bottle. Transparent green glass. Glass marble in the neck. Rubber washer. $23. (Auction #102, Lot 27).

MISCELLANEOUS. Codd bottle. Codd bottle. Glass marble in neck. Completely unmarked except for "TZ" on the base. Age unknown. $22. (Auction #123, Lot 21).

MISCELLANEOUS. Codd Bottle. Collection of eleven Codd Bottles. These are the glass bottles with pinched necks and marbles in the neck. $140. (Auction #136, Lot 23).

MISCELLANEOUS. Display. Lot of about thirty items. Thin strips of oak with counter sunk holes for displaying marbles. Assortment. $3. (Auction #143, Lot 25).

MISCELLANEOUS. Display box. Nice display box/carrying case. Rectangular. Cherry. Top is laser engraved with "The Official Popeye". $65. (Auction #153, Lot 24).

MISCELLANEOUS. Display item. Small metal "globe holder". You put marble in the middle and screw the braces to hold it. 4" high. $11. (Auction #127, Lot 13).

MISCELLANEOUS. Display items. Lot of two display items. First is a partitioned display box for hanging on a wall or laying on a table. $7. (Auction #108, Lot 29).

MISCELLANEOUS. Eggs. Lot of seven. Ok, they are not marbles, but they are marble eggs. The stone marble, cut into egg shape. $22. (Auction #172, Lot 22).

MISCELLANEOUS. Ephemera. New member packet from the Marble Collectors Society of America. Includes Dr. Shaeffer's membership. $7. (Auction #138, Lot 40).

MISCELLANEOUS. Fantasy bags. Lot of three bags. These are a set of the "Alox Agate" "Army" "Navy" and "Air Force" fantasy bags. $2. (Auction #79, Lot 17).

MISCELLANEOUS. First Day Cover. First Day Cover from Jugoslavia. Stamp depicts a boy shooting marbles. Postmarked April 29, 1989. $20. (Auction #154, Lot 22).

MISCELLANEOUS. First Day Cover. First Day Cover from Jugoslavia. Stamp depicts a boy shooting marbles. Postmarked April 29, 1989. $18. (Auction #154, Lot 22.20).

MISCELLANEOUS. Fisher Jewel Tray. Has patent number on the bottom. Marbles are early Vitro opalescent orange. 3-1/4". Mint (9.7). $42. (Auction #138, Lot 25).

MISCELLANEOUS. Fisher Jewel Tray. Has patent number on the bottom. Marbles are opaque light blue. 3-1/4". Mint (9.7). $27. (Auction #163, Lot 19).

MISCELLANEOUS. Fisher Jewel Tray. Early example. Only has the design patent number on the bottom. Marbles are early Vitro. 3-1/4". Mint (9.7). $22. (Auction #112, Lot 18).

MISCELLANEOUS. Flower frog. Glass flower frog. 5" diameter. Clear glass. One center hole, five holes around that, and 10 holes. $12. (Auction #80, Lot 24.20).

MISCELLANEOUS. Flower frog. Glass flower frog. 5" diameter. Clear glass. One center hole, five holes around that, and 10 holes. $12. (Auction #80, Lot 24).

MISCELLANEOUS. Flower frog. Glass flower frog. About 6-1/2" diameter. Sixteen 5/8" holes. Mint (9.9). $4. (Auction #174, Lot 15).

MISCELLANEOUS. Flower frog. Glass flower frog. About 6-1/2" diameter. Sixteen 5/8" holes. Mint (9.9). $4. (Auction #174, Lot 15.20).

MISCELLANEOUS. Flower frogs. Lot of two items. Two clear glass flower frogs. These are circular glass domes with numerous holes. $69. (Auction #59, Lot 32).

MISCELLANEOUS. Flower frogs. Lot of three items. Three flower frogs. Folks use these to display marbles on. $21. (Auction #175, Lot 24).

MISCELLANEOUS. Frog. Glass flower frog. 5" diameter. Has nineteen 19/32" holes. Excellent marble display piece. Mint (9.9). $6. (Auction #90, Lot 31).

MISCELLANEOUS. Frog. Glass flower frog. 5" diameter. Has nineteen 19/32" holes. Excellent marble display piece. Mint (9.9). $4. (Auction #104, Lot 28).

MISCELLANEOUS. Frog. Glass flower frog. 5" diameter. Has nineteen 19/32" holes. Excellent marble display piece. Mint (9.9). $4. (Auction #90, Lot 31.20).

MISCELLANEOUS. Frogs. Lot of three items. Three glass frogs. All are circular, 4" to 6" diameter. All are Mint. $9. (Auction #119, Lot 21).

MISCELLANEOUS. Game. "BA TA CLAN Nŏuveau Jeu Chinois". French game. Cardboard box. Interior has a temple (paper on wood). $165. (Auction #160, Lot 23).

MISCELLANEOUS. Game. Very old game, in the original box. Cardboard box is 2-1/2" x 1-3/4" x 1". Cardboard box slides out. $130. (Auction #100, Lot 48).

MISCELLANEOUS. Game. This has to be one of the finest Whirl-It games I have seen. Wood board (light wood), about 10" diameter. $125. (Auction #168, Lot 27).

MISCELLANEOUS. Game. Older game. Wooden shooter type score game. Shooting portion is 12" x 7-1/2" x 1". Probably walnut. $120. (Auction #154, Lot 26).

MISCELLANEOUS. Game. Original boxed Solitaire game. Red leatherized paper on cardboard for the box top and bottom. $120. (Auction #105, Lot 26).

MISCELLANEOUS. Game. Very hard to find "Red, White and Blue" game. German game. Red cardboard box. Printing in silver. $110. (Auction #79, Lot 38).

MISCELLANEOUS. Game. Lot of nine items. Eight are chinese checker boards. Assortment including Hop Ching, Pressman, Balla. $80. (Auction #155, Lot 26).

MISCELLANEOUS. Game. Nice boxed solitaire-type game. Cardboard box and game board. Yellow cover with red printing. "SOLO-". $60. (Auction #147, Lot 22).

MISCELLANEOUS. Game. Original Czechoslovakian glass fortune telling marble, in the original box, with the original instrument. $55. (Auction #155, Lot 31).

MISCELLANEOUS. Game. "Skill-Bowl-Game". German. Small wood ramp 5-1/2" x 5-1/2" with six score holes. Wood ball 15/16". $55. (Auction #154, Lot 24).

MISCELLANEOUS. Game. English "Solitaire" game. Red cardboard box. Silver printing on cover. The cover has a waterstain. $50. (Auction #79, Lot 36).

MISCELLANEOUS. Game. "Mosaic Outfit" by Standard Toykraft Products, Inc. Copyright 1937. Cover is four color. $50. (Auction #163, Lot 22).

MISCELLANEOUS. Game. Lot of four games. All are various ramp shooter games. Assorted sizes. All are metal. $50. (Auction #138, Lot 36).

MISCELLANEOUS. Game. Spot Shot by Wolverine Supply. Red and white shooting game. Metal. No marble. In great shape. $44. (Auction #143, Lot 30).

MISCELLANEOUS. Game. "Skill Ball Marble Game" in original box. Marx Company. Blue metal skill ball target. No marbles. $44. (Auction #119, Lot 20).

MISCELLANEOUS. Game. "Mosaic". No. 1190 Made by Transogram Co. Inc. New York. This is the small version. Cardboard box. $40. (Auction #79, Lot 33).

MISCELLANEOUS. Game. "Mosaic". No. 1196 Made by Transogram Co. Inc. New York. This is the large version. Cardboard box. $38. (Auction #79, Lot 34).

MISCELLANEOUS. Game. "Hop Ching Chinese Checkers". I have never seen this particular one before. Boxed cardboard set. $37. (Auction #121, Lot 22.20).

MISCELLANEOUS. Game. "Hop Ching Chinese Checkers". I have never seen this particular one before. Boxed cardboard set. $35. (Auction #121, Lot 22).

MISCELLANEOUS. Game. "Hop Ching Chinese Checkers". I have never seen this particular one before. Boxed cardboard set. $32. (Auction #121, Lot 22.30).

MISCELLANEOUS. Game. Exceptional game set. "Modern Game Assortment" "Hop-Ching Chinese Checkers / Backgammon / Checkers /. $31. (Auction #149, Lot 40).

MISCELLANEOUS. Game. "Snap 'N Score". Wolverine Supply. In very nice shape. Part of the base has been re-painted. Metal. $30. (Auction #138, Lot 34).

MISCELLANEOUS. Game. Unidentified manufacturer. Lever tower type score game. Metal. Nice coloring 10" high, 8" long. $30. (Auction #138, Lot 32).

MISCELLANEOUS. Game. Chinese Checker board with marbles. Fiberboard chinese checker board in an original metal edging. $29. (Auction #123, Lot 23).

MISCELLANEOUS. Game. "Mosaic". No. 1190 Made by Transogram Co. Inc. New York. This is the small version. Cardboard box. $28. (Auction #168, Lot 25).

MISCELLANEOUS. Game. Metal "Snap Skee Ball Game". Skee-ball type game. No manufacturer printed one the game. $25. (Auction #119, Lot 22).

MISCELLANEOUS. Game. Tic-Tac-Toe No. 228 by Baldwin Manfacturing. Metal game. Tic-tac-toe game in middle. Tray for marbles. $23. (Auction #146, Lot 20).

MISCELLANEOUS. Game. "Hi-Score Marble Game". Metal. Unidentified manufacturer. Missing score cups. 12" long, 6" high. $23. (Auction #138, Lot 33).

MISCELLANEOUS. Game. "Nymph Mosaic". Made in Germany. Cardboard box. Bottom has a wooden square in it for separating the marbles. $22. (Auction #154, Lot 25).

MISCELLANEOUS. Game. "Marble-head Game". "The exciting game of a marble landslide". Complete and in original box. 1969. $21. (Auction #79, Lot 28).

MISCELLANEOUS. Game. Bagatelle. "Lucky 7 Four 4 Game Poosh-M-Up". Unidentified maker. Composition board and metal. $20. (Auction #138, Lot 35).

MISCELLANEOUS. Game. Cardboard box game. "3 Marble Games" by Whitman Publishing. No. 3910. Cardboard tray inside. $18. (Auction #132, Lot 39).

MISCELLANEOUS. Game. "WAHOO" game board. We had the box with the marbles and dice for this game a few auctions ago. $17. (Auction #149, Lot 25).

MISCELLANEOUS. Game. Lot of four games. All are plastic bagatelles. Circa 1960s. "Circus Days", "Little Hunter". $17. (Auction #119, Lot 18).

MISCELLANEOUS. Game. "Lucky Shot" by Whitman. Cardboard box and game. Metal shooter. Marble is missing. Catapult type game. $17. (Auction #138, Lot 39).

MISCELLANEOUS. Game. Lot of two items. Both are plastic bagatelles. One is "Football Game". No manufacturer listed. $15. (Auction #149, Lot 23).

MISCELLANEOUS. Game. Tri-Tac-Toe in original box. By Hoi Polloi Inc. Circa 1970s. Three level tic-tac-toe game. Plexiglas. $11. (Auction #155, Lot 28).

MISCELLANEOUS. Game. "CatchEm" by Rosebud Art Co., N.Y., U.S.A. Game is a cardboard board with graphic of a pond scene. $10. (Auction #143, Lot 28).

MISCELLANEOUS. Game. "Chinese Checkers" Whitman Publishing. Cardboard box containing cardboard game board. $9. (Auction #127, Lot 23).

MISCELLANEOUS. Game. "Target Ball" " A Game of Skill" "Ball Shooting Catapult game". Whitman Company. 1963. Includes four. $3. (Auction #119, Lot 33).

MISCELLANEOUS. Game. "Basket-Bounce" Cardboard card with a plastic covered playing area. Two "snappers" at the bottom. $2. (Auction #127, Lot 21).

MISCELLANEOUS. Game board. Exceptional Solitaire board. Wood, probably maple or beech. Probably English. Very nicely made! $162. (Auction #156, Lot 27).

MISCELLANEOUS. Game board. Old wood General Grant solitaire board. Mahogany. Very nicely made with good piping and grooves. $91. (Auction #147, Lot 23).

MISCELLANEOUS. Game board. Old wood General Grant solitaire board. Mahogany. Very nicely made. Little wear. $80. (Auction #153, Lot 23).

MISCELLANEOUS. Game board. Old wood General Grant solitaire board. Mahogany. Very nicely made with good piping and grooves. $75. (Auction #168, Lot 26).

MISCELLANEOUS. Game board. Wooden solitaire board. Not too old. Unknown wood. Holes accommodate approximately 7/8" to 1" marble. $9. (Auction #177, Lot 15).

MISCELLANEOUS. Games. Lot of three items. First is a fiberboard and steel bagatelle by Gotham called the "Gotham All-Star". $21. (Auction #108, Lot 30).

MISCELLANEOUS. Gear shift knob. Nice gear shift knob. Electric red and opaque white. Looks just like a giant flattened American Agate. 2". Mint (9.9). $65. (Auction #176, Lot 22).

MISCELLANEOUS. Gear Shift Knob. Green and white slag glass gear shift knob. Unknown manufacturer. Nice "9" on one side. Metal thread. 1-3/8". Near Mint(+) (8.9). $35. (Auction #165, Lot 18).

MISCELLANEOUS. Golden Rule marble. Golden Rule marble. Blue plastic marble. Metal band around the equator with the golden rule on it. 25/32". Mint (9.9). $17. (Auction #179, Lot 41).

MISCELLANEOUS. Jewelry. Solid core swirl in a sterling silver cage, with a sterling silver chain. Nice item. Swirl is 1-1/8". $175. (Auction #108, Lot 36).

MISCELLANEOUS. Jewelry. Brooch handmade by Larry Castle. Sterling silver brooch in a classic Art Deco design. $85. (Auction #147, Lot 25).

MISCELLANEOUS. Jewelry. Marble pin. Small safety pin type pin with two bangles hanging from it the bangle cages. $55. (Auction #87, Lot 21).

MISCELLANEOUS. Jewelry. Very unusual necklace. This is circa late 1930s or early 1940s. $50. (Auction #148, Lot 26).

MISCELLANEOUS. Jewelry. Very unusual bracelet. This is circa late 1930s or early 1940s. $45. (Auction #155, Lot 10).

MISCELLANEOUS. Jewelry. Small kaleidoscope on a chain. Kaleidoscope is about six inches long. Holds about a 5/8" marble. $30. (Auction #143, Lot 41).

MISCELLANEOUS. Jewelry. Marble pin. Small safety pin type pin with two bangles hanging from it. Each bangle contains a 5/8". $21. (Auction #116, Lot 6).

MISCELLANEOUS. Jewelry. Lot of six items. Three sets of cuff links or tuxedo shirt buttons. Two sets have glass clearies. $21. (Auction #138, Lot 29).

MISCELLANEOUS. Magazine. Life magazine, May 10 1937. Cover features the classic photo a boy knuckling down, cap askance. $47. (Auction #163, Lot 21).

MISCELLANEOUS. Magazine. Life magazine, May 10 1937. Cover features the classic photo a boy knuckling down, cap askance. $45. (Auction #137, Lot 27).

MISCELLANEOUS. Magazine. Life magazine, May 10 1937. Cover features the classic photo a boy knuckling down, cap askance. $41. (Auction #143, Lot 27).

MISCELLANEOUS. Magazine. Child Life, March 1941. Picture depicts a girl winning at Ringer, while the losing boy scratches his head. $40. (Auction #148, Lot 22).

MISCELLANEOUS. Magazine. April 1988 issue of Smithsonian. Cover story on marbles. "As playthings and pricey objets d'art". $39. (Auction #71, Lot 25).

MISCELLANEOUS. Magazine. Life magazine, May 10 1937. Cover features the classic photo a boy knuckling down, cap askance. $37. (Auction #148, Lot 21).

MISCELLANEOUS. Magazine. April 1988 issue of Smithsonian. Cover story on marbles. "As playthings and pricey objets d'art." $37. (Auction #71, Lot 25.20).

MISCELLANEOUS. Magazine. Life magazine, May 10 1937. Cover features the classic photo a boy knuckling down, cap askance. $36. (Auction #98, Lot 21).

MISCELLANEOUS. Magazine. April 1988 issue of Smithsonian. Cover story on marbles. "As playthings and pricey objets d'art." $32. (Auction #100, Lot 21.10).

MISCELLANEOUS. Magazine. April 1988 issue of Smithsonian. Cover story on marbles. "As playthings and pricey objets d'art." $32. (Auction #100, Lot 21).

MISCELLANEOUS. Magazine. September 1977 issue of Yankee magazine. Includes an eleven-page article on marbles with pictures. $30. (Auction #159, Lot 23).

MISCELLANEOUS. Magazine. April 1977 issue of "Hobbies: The Magazine of Collectors". Cover story is "Marbles - Another Fun Hobby". $26. (Auction #118, Lot 30).

MISCELLANEOUS. Magazine. April 1988 issue of Smithsonian. Cover story on marbles. "As playthings and pricey objets d'art." $25. (Auction #138, Lot 38).

MISCELLANEOUS. Magazine. May 1972 issue of The Antiques Journal. Cover story is "Don't Lose Your Marbles'. $22. (Auction #119, Lot 32).

MISCELLANEOUS. Magazine. April 1988 issue of Smithsonian. Cover story on marbles. "As playthings and pricey objets d'art." $22. (Auction #167, Lot 22).

MISCELLANEOUS. Magazine. April 1988 issue of Smithsonian. Cover story on marbles. "As playthings and pricey objets d'art." $22. (Auction #126, Lot 22).

MISCELLANEOUS. Magazine. November/December 1932 issue of Popular Home Craft: The Home Workshop Magazine. Includes an article. $20. (Auction #87, Lot 26).

MISCELLANEOUS. Magazine. Life magazine, April 30 1965. Includes an ad for Kellogg's Corn Flakes that has a girl shooting marbles. $20. (Auction #91, Lot 21).

MISCELLANEOUS. Magazine. April 1988 issue of Smithsonian. Cover story on marbles. "As playthings and pricey objets d'art." $20. (Auction #126, Lot 22.20).

MISCELLANEOUS. Magazine. April 1988 issue of Smithsonian. Cover story on marbles. "As playthings and pricey objets d'art." $19. (Auction #178, Lot 30.20).

MISCELLANEOUS. Magazine. April 1988 issue of Smithsonian. Cover story on marbles. "As playthings and pricey objets d'art." $19. (Auction #178, Lot 30).

MISCELLANEOUS. Magazine. Life magazine, April 30 1965. Includes an ad for Kellogg's Corn Flakes that has a girl shooting marbles. $18. (Auction #91, Lot 21.20).

MISCELLANEOUS. Magazine. June 26, 1950 issue of Life. Includes a two page article on the National Marbles Tournament. $12. (Auction #66, Lot 23).

MISCELLANEOUS. Magazine. Life magazine, April 30 1965. Includes an ad for Kellogg's Corn Flakes that has a girl shooting marbles. $10. (Auction #91, Lot 21.30).

MISCELLANEOUS. Magazine. Life Magazine, June 22 1942. Contains an article on "Marbles-Mad Beloit Crowns a New Mibs King". $10. (Auction #102, Lot 29).

MISCELLANEOUS. Magazine. Life Magazine, June 22 1942. Contains an article on "Marbles-Mad Beloit Crowns a New Mibs King". $7. (Auction #102, Lot 29.10).

MISCELLANEOUS. Magazine. Colliers, July 14 1951. Includes an article on wartime displaced persons coming to the U.S. $5. (Auction #102, Lot 30).

MISCELLANEOUS. Magazine ad. April 30, 1965 issue of Life magazine. Full page ad for Kellogg's Corn Flakes depicting a girl knuckling down. $16. (Auction #136, Lot 29).

MISCELLANEOUS. Magazine ad. April 30, 1965 issue of Life magazine. Full page ad for Kellogg's Corn Flakes depicting a girl knuckling down. $14. (Auction #136, Lot 29.20).

MISCELLANEOUS. Magazine cover. Cover from the March 28, 1925 issue of The Saturday Evening Post. $42. (Auction #80, Lot 21).

MISCELLANEOUS. Magazine cover. Cover from the March 10, 1923 issue of The Country Gentleman. Shows an older gentleman shooting a marble. $36. (Auction #92, Lot 23).

MISCELLANEOUS. Magazine cover. Cover from the Woman's Home Companion June 1949. Boy shooting marbles with a girl cheering him on. $28. (Auction #92, Lot 22).

MISCELLANEOUS. Magazine cover. Cut cover from the June 1949 issue of Woman's Home Companion. Shows a boy knuckling down. $21. (Auction #78, Lot 20).

MISCELLANEOUS. Marble holder. Marble Minder by Dyer Products Company. Plastic belt looped marble holder. Contains twenty Vitro Agate. $18. (Auction #119, Lot 34).

MISCELLANEOUS. Marble holder. "Marble-Matic Marble Bank". Blue plastic beltloop holder. ABout 5" x 5". Mint (9.7). Includes thirty. $12. (Auction #127, Lot 46).

MISCELLANEOUS. Marble pouch. Lot of eleven items. Assorment of pouches. Includes leather, and two vinyl. $120. (Auction #132, Lot 37).

MISCELLANEOUS. Marble pouch. Black rubberized cloth. Orange piping. The front is printed in orange. "Lucky Boy Glass Marbles". $90. (Auction #163, Lot 50).

MISCELLANEOUS. Marble pouch. Older pouch in superior shape. This pouch is pristine! Two tone deerskin. Embossed with an Indian. $55. (Auction #147, Lot 24).

MISCELLANEOUS. Marble pouch. Green rubberized cloth. Red piping. The front is printed in black. "Champion Glass Marbles". $50. (Auction #148, Lot 24).

MISCELLANEOUS. Marble pouch. Hard to find marble purse. Rubberized felt with metal clasp on top. Printed in white with a graphic. $50. (Auction #132, Lot 38).

MISCELLANEOUS. Marble pouch. Nice pouch. This is a Lucky Boy pouch. Black rubberized material on cloth. Printed white head. $39. (Auction #62, Lot 39).

MISCELLANEOUS. Marble pouch. Black rubberized cloth. White piping. The front is printed in white. "Champion Glass Marbles". $38. (Auction #148, Lot 23).

MISCELLANEOUS. Marble pouch. Tan leather marble pouch. Six panels. With burgundy drawstring. In great shape. Probably 1940s. $26. (Auction #93, Lot 20).

MISCELLANEOUS. Marble pouch. Lot of four items. All are marble pouches. One is vinyl, in its original packaging. $20. (Auction #143, Lot 31).

MISCELLANEOUS. Marble pouch. Leather marble pouch. Front is printed "Marbles" with several marbles on it. $19. (Auction #117, Lot 27).

MISCELLANEOUS. Marble pouch. Nice vinyl on textile pouch. Burgundy fake leather on one side, silver fake leather on the other. $12. (Auction #137, Lot 29).

MISCELLANEOUS. Marble pouch. Leather bag. Printed on front "Marbles" with some marbles. Embossed under that is "Jackson Lake Lodge". $10. (Auction #123, Lot 24).

MISCELLANEOUS. Marble shooter. Metal marble shooter. Spring loaded. This is a blue one. About 3-1/2" long. Circa 1930s. $28. (Auction #119, Lot 17).

MISCELLANEOUS. Marble shooter. Large size red metal marble shooter. 4-1/2" long. Mint (9.5). American, circa 1930-1940. $24. (Auction #87, Lot 23).

MISCELLANEOUS. Marble shooter. "Mar-Bo-Gun". Red plastic spring loaded marble shooter. Holds about a dozen marbles. American. $21. (Auction #130, Lot 25).

MISCELLANEOUS. Marble shooter. Mar-Bo-Gun marble shooter. Red plastic shooter. Includes twelve common swirls. In nice shape. $18. (Auction #170, Lot 22.20).

MISCELLANEOUS. Marble shooter. Mar-Bo-Gun marble shooter. Red plastic shooter. Includes twelve common swirls. In nice shape. $18. (Auction #170, Lot 22.30).

MISCELLANEOUS. Marble shooter. Mar-Bo-Gun marble shooter. Red plastic shooter. Includes twelve common swirls. In nice shape. $18. (Auction #170, Lot 22).

MISCELLANEOUS. Marble shooter. Mar-Bo-Gun marble shooter. Red plastic shooter. Includes twelve common swirls. In nice shape. $18. (Auction #170, Lot 22.40).

MISCELLANEOUS. Marble shooter. Metal marble shooter. Spring loaded. This is the red one. Larger size. 4-1/2". Mint (9.7). $15. (Auction #127, Lot 39).

MISCELLANEOUS. Marble shooter. Lot of two items. Both are metal marble shooters. One is red, one is blue. The blue has rust. $14. (Auction #132, Lot 22).

MISCELLANEOUS. Marble shooter. Metal marble shooter. Spring loaded. This is a blue one. About 3-1/2" long. Circa 1930s. $12. (Auction #152, Lot 36).

MISCELLANEOUS. Mineral. Lot of two mineral spheres. Both are onyx. 2" & 2-7/8". Mint (9.9). $110. (Auction #178, Lot 18).

MISCELLANEOUS. Mineral. Lot of four spheres. All are dyed agate. Machine cut. Blue, green, brown and turquoise. Hard to find. $80. (Auction #56, Lot 25).

MISCELLANEOUS. Mineral. Lot of four spheres. Two blue dyed agates and two green dyed agates. Beauties and hard to find. $65. (Auction #59, Lot 23).

MISCELLANEOUS. Mineral. Mahogany obsidian sphere. Beauty. 2-3/4". Mint (9.9). $60. (Auction #178, Lot 13).

MISCELLANEOUS. Mineral. Malachite sphere. Nice design and pattern. Machine cut. Age and origin unknown. 1-3/8". Mint (9.9). $55. (Auction #133, Lot 29).

MISCELLANEOUS. Mineral. Lot of four spheres. Four black dyed agates. Beauties and hard to find. 1-3/16", 1-1/16", 27/32", 13/16". $50. (Auction #69, Lot 23).

MISCELLANEOUS. Mineral. Lot of four spheres. Two blue dyed agates and two green dyed agates. Beauties and hard to find. 1-3/16". $43. (Auction #63, Lot 20).

MISCELLANEOUS. Mineral. Beautiful tigereye sphere. Probably machine ground. Great shimmering. Origin and age unknown. 1-5/16. 1-1/16". Mint (9.9). $40. (Auction #150, Lot 22).

MISCELLANEOUS. Mineral. Lot of three spheres. All are banded agate. One brown, two red. Three beauties. Machine ground. $40. (Auction #140, Lot 25).

MISCELLANEOUS. Mineral. Black dyed agate. Banded agate. Machine cut. Exceptional patterns. Age and origin unknown. 1-5/16". 1-1/16". Mint (9.9). $38. (Auction #150, Lot 27).

MISCELLANEOUS. Mineral. Tigereye sphere. Excellent shimmering. Two tiny subsurface moons. 1-3/16". Near Mint(+) (8.9). $37. (Auction #176, Lot 30).

MISCELLANEOUS. Mineral. Lot of two spheres. Both are banded agate. One green/brown, the other blue. Super design. Modern. 1". $36. (Auction #166, Lot 11).

MISCELLANEOUS. Mineral. Green dyed agate. Banded agate. Nice crystal panel. Machine cut. Age and origin unknown. 1-3/16". Mint (9.9). $35. (Auction #142, Lot 11).

MISCELLANEOUS. Mineral. Beautiful tigereye sphere. Probably machine ground. Great shimmering. Origin and age unknown. 1-1/16". Mint (9.9). $35. (Auction #116, Lot 9).

MISCELLANEOUS. Mineral. Sphere of agatized petrified wood. Green, brown and red. A beauty. Age and origin unknown. Machine. 1-1/2". Mint (9.9). $32. (Auction #133, Lot 30).

MISCELLANEOUS. Mineral. Tigereye sphere. Excellent shimmering. Machine cut. 27/32". Mint (9.9). $32. (Auction #128, Lot 33).

MISCELLANEOUS. Mineral. Hard to find blue tigereye. A beauty. Origin and age unknown. 3/4". Mint (9.9). $32. (Auction #155, Lot 11).

MISCELLANEOUS. Mineral. Tigereye sphere. Large sphere. Very nice shimmering. Age and origin unknown. 1-11/16". Mint (9.9). $32. (Auction #68, Lot 12).

MISCELLANEOUS. Mineral. Obsidian sphere. Nice shimmering at either end. 1-3/4". Mint (9.5). $30. (Auction #178, Lot 15).

MISCELLANEOUS. Mineral. Lot of twenty four spheres. Assortment of agate, onyx and marble. One agate is handcut, rest are machine made. $30. (Auction #174, Lot 5).

MISCELLANEOUS. Mineral. Blue dyed agate. Banded agate. Nice crystal panel. Machine cut. Age and origin unknown. 1-3/16". Mint (9.9). $30. (Auction #139, Lot 11).

MISCELLANEOUS. Mineral. Lot of two marbles. Both are dyed banded agate. Both machine cut. One brown, one blue. Nice pair. 1". $30. (Auction #136, Lot 27).

MISCELLANEOUS. Mineral. Lot of two spheres. Goldstone, 25/32", Mint (9.9). Malachite, some large facets, 23/32", Mint(-) (9). $28. (Auction #141, Lot 37).

MISCELLANEOUS. Mineral. Mahogany obsidian sphere. Opaque brown with mottled black. Very nice. Looks to be about 3" or so. $27. (Auction #68, Lot 17).

MISCELLANEOUS. Mineral. Lot of two spheres. Both are black obsidian. Shimmering at either pole. 1-1/2" & 1-7/8". Mint (9.9). $27. (Auction #122, Lot 23).

MISCELLANEOUS. Mineral. Tigereye sphere. Nice shimmering. Origin and age unknown. 23/32". Mint (9.5). $26. (Auction #92, Lot 35).

MISCELLANEOUS. Mineral. Hand cut brown tigereye. Older marble, my guess would be turn of the century. Probably made in Germany. 21/32". Mint(-) (9). $25. (Auction #54, Lot 1).

MISCELLANEOUS. Mineral. Large tigereye. Nice shimmering. Machine ground. One tiny hit mark. 1-5/16". Mint(-) (9). $24. (Auction #174, Lot 40).

MISCELLANEOUS. Mineral. Tigereye sphere. Beautiful shimmering. Age unknown. 27/32". Mint (9.5). $24. (Auction #87, Lot 32).

MISCELLANEOUS. Mineral. Lot of twenty spheres. Assortment of various minerals. All tiny. 1/4" to 3/8". Mint (9.9). $23. (Auction #60, Lot 12).

MISCELLANEOUS. Mineral. Mineral sphere. Sandstone, commonly called picture stone. Very odd to find this as a sphere. 2-1/4". Mint (9.9). $22. (Auction #73, Lot 30).

MISCELLANEOUS. Mineral. Lot of two marbles. Both are onyx. 11/16" & 3/4". Mint (9.9). $21. (Auction #166, Lot 18).

MISCELLANEOUS. Mineral. Lot of two spheres. Both are jasper. 15/16". Mint (9.9). $20. (Auction #178, Lot 38).

MISCELLANEOUS. Mineral. Lot of two spheres. Both are banded agate. One gray/brown, the other red/brown. Super design. Modern. $16. (Auction #78, Lot 6).

MISCELLANEOUS. Mineral. Lot of three spheres. All are rose quartz. 15/16", 27/32", 25/32". Mint (9.9). $16. (Auction #178, Lot 41).

MISCELLANEOUS. Mineral. Lot of two spheres. Both are banded agate. One light brown and one dark brown. Nice pattern on each. $15. (Auction #80, Lot 16).

MISCELLANEOUS. Mineral. Beautiful tigereye sphere. Probably machine ground. Great shimmering. Origin and age unknown. 25/32". Mint (9.9). $14. (Auction #142, Lot 23).

MISCELLANEOUS. Mineral. Machine cut mineral sphere. Unknown stone. Appears to be some sort of fossilized marble. 1-3/16". Mint (9.9). $13. (Auction #92, Lot 8).

MISCELLANEOUS. Mineral. Blue dyed agate. Banded agate. Machine cut. Age and origin unknown. 1-1/16". Mint (9.9). $12. (Auction #145, Lot 4).

MISCELLANEOUS. Mineral. Onyx sphere. Nice coloring. Probably Mexican. 1-3/8". Mint (9.9). $12. (Auction #124, Lot 15).

MISCELLANEOUS. Mineral. Beautiful tigereye sphere. Probably machine ground. Great shimmering. Origin and age unknown. 5/8". Mint (9.9). $10. (Auction #145, Lot 19).

MISCELLANEOUS. Mineral. Tiny sphere of snowflake obsidian. Age and origin unknown. 7/16". Mint (9.9). $9. (Auction #146, Lot 8).

MISCELLANEOUS. Mineral. Nice rose quartz sphere. Machine cut. Origin and age unknown. 25/32". Mint (9.9). $7. (Auction #60, Lot 2).

MISCELLANEOUS. Original box. Original cardboard box. Orange. Top reads "Marbles and Dice / for playing / WAHOO / Made in USA / Pa. $31. (Auction #131, Lot 23).

MISCELLANEOUS. Original package. An original box of peewee foil clays. The box is cardboard with red graphics. $140. (Auction #147, Lot 27).

MISCELLANEOUS. Perfume package. One of the oddest marble-related items that I have ever had. Small cardboard tube. $47. (Auction #176, Lot 29.20).

MISCELLANEOUS. Perfume package. One of the oddest marble-related items that I have ever had. Small cardboard tube. $47. (Auction #176, Lot 29).

MISCELLANEOUS. Picture. Framed print of Norman Rockwell's The Champion. Circa 1980s. 10-1/2" x 12-1/2". Mint (9.9). $19. (Auction #108, Lot 28).

MISCELLANEOUS. Picture. Framed print of Norman Rockwell's The Champion. Circa 1980s. 9" x 7". Mint (9.9) (Still shrink wrapped). $17. (Auction #108, Lot 27).

MISCELLANEOUS. Picture. Color xerocopy. Illustration from a book. Reads "Rip Van Winkle and his Playmates." Depicts Rip Van Winkle. $1. (Auction #154, Lot 23).

MISCELLANEOUS. Postcard. This is a postcard that I have never seen before. The postcard is Germany, printed in 1905. $80. (Auction #81, Lot 25).

MISCELLANEOUS. Postcard. I have never seen this postcard before. It is cream paper, embossed, with blue highlights. $45. (Auction #101, Lot 31).

MISCELLANEOUS. Postcard. Well known postcard depicting two boys playing marbles. Unused. In great shape. $32. (Auction #170, Lot 30).

MISCELLANEOUS. Postcard. Well known postcard depicting two boys playing marbles. Back is postmarked 1909. $30. (Auction #87, Lot 27).

MISCELLANEOUS. Postcard. Well known postcard depicting two boys playing marbles. Back is postmarked 1908. $19. (Auction #142, Lot 21).

MISCELLANEOUS. Pouch. Soft leather marble pouch. Printed "EAGLE HOTEL / W.W. HEATH, Prop. / Haverhill, Mass." $20. (Auction #156, Lot 25).

MISCELLANEOUS. Pouch. Lot of four vinyl pouches. All read "101 Marbles" "Made in Taiwan". Fairly recent. $3. (Auction #102, Lot 28).

MISCELLANEOUS. Premium. Cellophane tube containing Assortment of Vitro Agate, Marble King and Champion. $21. (Auction #139, Lot 21).

MISCELLANEOUS. Premium. Cellophane tube containing Assortment of Vitro Agate, Marble King and Champion. $19. (Auction #139, Lot 21.20).

MISCELLANEOUS. Premium. Cellophane tube containing Assortment of Vitro Agate, Marble King and Champion. $15. (Auction #139, Lot 21.30).

MISCELLANEOUS. Premium. Cellophane tube containing Assortment of Vitro Agate, Marble King and Champion. $11. (Auction #139, Lot 21.40).

MISCELLANEOUS. Premium. Cellophane tube containing Assortment of Vitro Agate, Marble King and Champion. $10. (Auction #125, Lot 28.20).

MISCELLANEOUS. Premium. Cellophane tube containing Assortment of Vitro Agate, Marble King and Champion. $10. (Auction #125, Lot 28).

MISCELLANEOUS. Premium. Cellophane tube containing Assortment of Vitro Agate, Marble King and Champion. $9. (Auction #139, Lot 21.50).

MISCELLANEOUS. Premium. Cellophane tube containing Assortment of Vitro Agate, Marble King and Champion. $7. (Auction #125, Lot 28.50).

MISCELLANEOUS. Premium. Cellophane tube containing Assortment of Vitro Agate, Marble King and Champion. $7. (Auction #125, Lot 28.40).

MISCELLANEOUS. Premium. Cellophane tube containing Assortment of Vitro Agate, Marble King and Champion. $7. (Auction #125, Lot 28.30).

MISCELLANEOUS. Print. Framed print of two young children playing marbles. This is actually the bottom half of a magazine. $15. (Auction #155, Lot 25).

MISCELLANEOUS. Razor sharpener. Metal razor sharpener. Two red clearies. Includes the original insert fro "Crystal Razor Sharpener". $22. (Auction #119, Lot 39).

MISCELLANEOUS. Razor sharpener. Metal razor sharpener. Some rust. Has two lavender clearies. Mint (9.5). $21. (Auction #93, Lot 19).

MISCELLANEOUS. Razor sharpener. Primitive metal razor sharpener. Remnants of white paint on it. Has two Heaton swirls. $10. (Auction #75, Lot 28).

MISCELLANEOUS. Reflector. Truck reflector that uses clearie marbles. Hexagonal heavy metal base. Has nine 3/4" red clearies. $17. (Auction #169, Lot 23).

MISCELLANEOUS. Reproduction box. Reproduction of the yellow Peltier Picture Marbles 12-count box. Includes a red insert for holding. $70. (Auction #168, Lot 22).

MISCELLANEOUS. Ring. Sterling silver ring with a cabochon that is made from a Peltier tri-color. Very pretty. Size 6-1/2". $30. (Auction #107, Lot 45).

MISCELLANEOUS. Solitaire board. Plastic resin board. Set up as a solitaire board. There are four "Greek" faces incised in the playing surface. $140. (Auction #131, Lot 21).

MISCELLANEOUS. Solitaire game. Modern solitaire board with malachite spheres. 7" diameter walnut solitaire board. Modern. $85. (Auction #128, Lot 31).

MISCELLANEOUS. Stationery. A letter from The Gropper Onyx Marble Company on its letterhead. To is printed with "The GROPPER ONYX". $40. (Auction #154, Lot 21).

MISCELLANEOUS. Steelie. Shooter hollow steelie. Excellent "X". In great shape. Probably American, probably 1910-1930. 1". Mint (9.9). $55. (Auction #91, Lot 15).

MISCELLANEOUS. Steelie. Shooter size hollow steelie. Nice "X". In great shape. American, circa 1910-1940. 31/32". Mint (9.7). $47. (Auction #66, Lot 6).

MISCELLANEOUS. Steelie. Nice shooter steelie. Hollow marble. Nice "X" on surface. American, 1900-1930. 1". Mint (9.8). $40. (Auction #97, Lot 9).

MISCELLANEOUS. Steelie. Nice shooter steelie. This one is actually made of brass, not steel, which is very odd. Hollow marble. 27/32". Mint (9.9). $35. (Auction #140, Lot 16).

MISCELLANEOUS. Steelie. Nice shooter steelie. Hollow marble. Nice "X" on surface. American, 1900-1930. 1". Mint (9.8). $35. (Auction #78, Lot 8).

MISCELLANEOUS. Steelie. Nice shooter steelie. Hollow marble. Nice "X" on surface. American, 1900-1930. 1". Mint (9.8). $35. (Auction #68, Lot 4).

MISCELLANEOUS. Steelie. Nice shooter steelie. Hollow marble. Nice "X" on surface. American, 1900-1930. 1". Mint (9.8). $34. (Auction #83, Lot 41).

MISCELLANEOUS. Steelie. Nice shooter steelie. Hollow marble. Nice "X" on surface. American, 1900-1930. 1". Mint (9.8). $32. (Auction #110, Lot 25).

MISCELLANEOUS. Steelie. Hollow steelie. Nice "X". Some minor corrosion. Origin and date unknown. 5/8". Mint(-) (9). $25. (Auction #119, Lot 8).

MISCELLANEOUS. Steelie. Nice shooter steelie. Hollow marble. Nice "X" on surface. American, 1900-1930. 1". Mint (9.8). $22. (Auction #145, Lot 41).

MISCELLANEOUS. Steelie. Nice shooter steelie. Hollow marble. Nice "X" on surface. Some oxidation on the surface. American. 5/8". Mint (9.4). $19. (Auction #168, Lot 32).

MISCELLANEOUS. Steelie. Lot of two marbles. Both are steelies. Both are hollow and have barely visible "X"s on them. America. $19. (Auction #59, Lot 5).

MISCELLANEOUS. Steelie. Hollow steelie. Nice "X". Some minor corrosion. Origin and date unknown. 5/8". Mint(-) (9). $17. (Auction #130, Lot 16).

MISCELLANEOUS. Steelie. Hollow steelie. Nice "X". Minimal rust. Origin and age unknown. 5/8". Mint (9.9). $14. (Auction #161, Lot 34).

MISCELLANEOUS. Steelie. Lot of four marbles. All are hollow steelies. All have "X"s. They are all rusty. 19/32". Mint(-) (9). $13. (Auction #141, Lot 10).

MISCELLANEOUS. Stone. Lot of two items. Both are ground stone spheroids. Some sort of rock. $32. (Auction #127, Lot 12).

MISCELLANEOUS. Tigereye. Very nice tigereye sphere. Nice shimmering to it. 1". Mint (9.9). $15. (Auction #82, Lot 8).

MISCELLANEOUS. Tile. Very rare Dutch (Delft?) tile. I have only seen one other of these. $150. (Auction #98, Lot 22).

MISCELLANEOUS. Tournament medal. Gold medal. "National Marble Tournament" "1937". Reverse reads "Champion ARK-LA-TEX Marbles Tournament". $675. (Auction #150, Lot 50).

MISCELLANEOUS. Tournament medal. Silver medal. Image of two boys shooting marbles in front of a bleacher of spectators. $400. (Auction #160, Lot 48).

MISCELLANEOUS. Tournament medal. Bronze medal. "National Marble Tournament" "1934". Plaque-style with eagle over top. $350. (Auction #142, Lot 50).

MISCELLANEOUS. Tournament medal. Bronze medal. "National Marble Tournament" "1935". Plaque-style with eagle over top. $270. (Auction #126, Lot 47).

MISCELLANEOUS. Tournament medal. Hard to find tournament medal. Bronze. Octagonal rectangle. Front reads "United States Marble Shooting Tournament". $240. (Auction #155, Lot 49).

MISCELLANEOUS. Tournament medal. Bronze medal. "National Marble Tournament" "1937". Plaque-style with eagle over top. $230. (Auction #110, Lot 49).

MISCELLANEOUS. Tournament medal. Pinback tournament medal. Reads "School Award" "VFW" "National Marble Tournament". Brass medal. VFW. $170. (Auction #147, Lot 49).

MISCELLANEOUS. Tournament pinback. Tournament pin from 1940. Celluloid pin. Reads "Star Times Player 1940 Marble Tournament". Pin is 29/32". Mint (9.7). $49. (Auction #176, Lot 37).

MISCELLANEOUS. Tournament pinback. Tournament pin from 1940. Celluloid pin. Reads "Star Times Player 1940 Marble Tournament". Pin is 29/32". Mint (9.7). $47. (Auction #98, Lot 38).

MISCELLANEOUS. Tournament pinback. Tournament pin from 1940. Celluloid pin. Reads "Star Times Player 1940 Marble Tournament". Pin is 29/32". Mint (9.7). $45. (Auction #98, Lot 38.10).

MISCELLANEOUS. Tournament pinback. Tournament pin from 1940. Celluloid pin. Reads "Star Times Player 1940 Marble Tournament". Pin is 29/32". Mint (9.7). $44. (Auction #183, Lot 26).

MISCELLANEOUS. Tournament pinback. Tournament pin from 1940. Celluloid pin. Reads "Star Times Player 1940 Marble Tournament". Pin is 29/32". Mint (9.7). $38. (Auction #116, Lot 35).

MISCELLANEOUS. Tournament pinback. Tournament pin from 1940. Celluloid pin. Reads "Star Times Player 1940 Marble Tournament". Pin is 29/32". Mint (9.7). $37. (Auction #124, Lot 3).

MISCELLANEOUS. Tournament pinback. Tournament pin from 1940. Celluloid pin. Reads "Star Times Player 1940 Marble Tournament". Pin is 29/32". Mint (9.7). $37. (Auction #81, Lot 31).

MISCELLANEOUS. Tournament pinback. Tournament pin from 1940. Celluloid pin. Reads "Star Times Player 1940 Marble Tournament". Pin is 29/32". Mint (9.7). $37. (Auction #81, Lot 31.10).

MISCELLANEOUS. Tournament pinback. Tournament pin from 1940. Celluloid pin. Reads "Star Times Player 1940 Marble Tournament". Pin is 29/32". Mint (9.7). $35. (Auction #90, Lot 40).

MISCELLANEOUS. Tournament ribbon. Very rare tournament ribbon. Red ribbon, about 5" long by 1-1/2" wide. Printed in gold. $300. (Auction #168, Lot 24).

MISCELLANEOUS. Tournament Trophy. Silverplated marble tournament trophy from 1928. Loving cup style. Front is engraved "WINNER...". $410. (Auction #154, Lot 49).

MISCELLANEOUS. Toy. A Limited Edition toy 1957 "International R-190 Full Rack Stake Truck" Printed on both sides. $180. (Auction #71, Lot 26).

MISCELLANEOUS. Toy. A Limited Edition toy 1957 "International R-190 Full Rack Stake Truck" Printed on both sides. $170. (Auction #71, Lot 26.10).

MISCELLANEOUS. Toy. A Limited Edition toy 1957 "International R-190 Full Rack Stake Truck" Printed on both sides. $120. (Auction #137, Lot 26).

MISCELLANEOUS. Toy. A Limited Edition toy 1957 "International R-190 Full Rack Stake Truck" Printed on both sides. $110. (Auction #182, Lot 49).

MISCELLANEOUS. Toy. A Limited Edition toy 1957 "International R-190 Full Rack Stake Truck" Printed on both sides. $100. (Auction #153, Lot 22).

MISCELLANEOUS. Toy. A Limited Edition toy 1957 "International R-190 Full Rack Stake Truck" Printed on both sides. $95. (Auction #96, Lot 21).

MISCELLANEOUS. Toy. A Limited Edition toy 1957 "International R-190 Full Rack Stake Truck" Printed on both sides. $85. (Auction #121, Lot 21).

MISCELLANEOUS. Toy. A Limited Edition toy 1957 "International R-190 Full Rack Stake Truck" Printed on both sides. $75. (Auction #115, Lot 26).

MISCELLANEOUS. Toy. Wyandotte Toys egg laying chicken. It works. Some scratching on the chicken. $32. (Auction #127, Lot 24).

MISCELLANEOUS. Toy. Japanese "Parachute" toy. Made in Japan. Thin plastic red and white parachute with an American flag. $16. (Auction #79, Lot 7).

NON-GLASS HANDMADE. Lot of nine marbles. Three benningtons and six pottery. One pottery has a purple band. $50. (Auction #108, Lot 18).

NON-GLASS HANDMADE. Lot of sixteen marbles and a cloth pouch. Fifteen of the marbles are unglazed china. $42. (Auction #106, Lot 17).

NON-GLASS HANDMADE. Lot of thirteen marbles. Assortment of non-glass. Three natural clay, two dyed clay, four bennington. $32. (Auction #149, Lot 38).

NON-GLASS HANDMADE. Lot of twenty eight marbles. Assortment of clays and chinas. Only a couple are glazed. $24. (Auction #81, Lot 22).

NON-GLASS HANDMADE. Lot of twenty eight marbles. Assortment of clays and chinas. Only a couple are glazed. $24. (Auction #82, Lot 23).

NON-GLASS HANDMADE. Lot of six marbles. Blue bennington, fancy bennington, handpainted china, two clays, and a machine made. $17. (Auction #106, Lot 11).

NON-GLASS HANDMADE. Lot of six spheres. Two limestone, one agate, one dense plastic or rubber, one malachite, one rose quartz. $14. (Auction #143, Lot 20).

NON-GLASS HANDMADE. Agate. Handcut banded agate. Excellent faceting. Very nice example. Germany, circa 1850-1920. 25/32". Mint (9.7). $30. (Auction #141, Lot 8).

NON-GLASS HANDMADE. Agate. Handcut banded agate. Red/brown and white, with some clear spots. Nice faceting. Germany, circa 1870. 23/32". Mint (9.9). $26. (Auction #148, Lot 14).

NON-GLASS HANDMADE. Agate. Handcut banded agate. Brown and white. Bullseye at either end. A few tiny hit marks on it. Germany. 5/8". Near Mint(+) (8.8). $22. (Auction #147, Lot 15).

NON-GLASS HANDMADE. Agate. Hand-cut banded agate. Excellent faceting. A couple of hit spots. Germany, circa 1820-1920. 21/32". Near Mint(+) (8.9). $17. (Auction #140, Lot 14).

NON-GLASS HANDMADE. Assorted. Lot of approximately one hundred twenty five marbles. Includes textile marble bag. This is an assortment. $85. (Auction #90, Lot 23).

NON-GLASS HANDMADE. Assorted. Lot of three marbles. Excellent assortment. Includes a handpainted china, a lined crockery. $70. (Auction #170, Lot 37).

NON-GLASS HANDMADE. Assorted. Lot of thirty seven marbles. Quite an assortment of clay, pottery, crockery and china. $56. (Auction #80, Lot 25).

NON-GLASS HANDMADE. Assorted. Lot of forty three marbles. Assortment of Benningtons, Chinas and Crockery. Mostly Benningtons. $55. (Auction #125, Lot 26).

NON-GLASS HANDMADE. Assorted. Lot of twenty six marbles. Excellent assortment of non-chinas. Includes benningtons, clays and pottery. $47. (Auction #123, Lot 28).

NON-GLASS HANDMADE. Assorted. Lot of eleven marbles. Five benningtons, six splatter crockery. All are Mint. 5/8" to 7/8". Mint. $42. (Auction #128, Lot 24).

NON-GLASS HANDMADE. Assorted. Lot of four marbles. Two unglazed painted china, a glazed painted china and a dyed clay. 9/16". $38. (Auction #109, Lot 9).

NON-GLASS HANDMADE. Assorted. Lot of twenty five marbles. Assortment of benningtons, chinas and crockery. 1/2" to 11/16". Mint. $36. (Auction #127, Lot 10).

NON-GLASS HANDMADE. Assorted. Lot of approximately one hundred thirty marbles. Mostly clays and dyed clays with some foil clays. $33. (Auction #174, Lot 12).

NON-GLASS HANDMADE. Assorted. Lot of thirty marbles. Eleven clay and nineteen limestone. All are 1/2" to 5/8". $22. (Auction #89, Lot 26).

NON-GLASS HANDMADE. Assorted. Lot of four marbles. Brown bennington, 1-7/16", Near Mint(+) (8.9). Brown bennington, 1-1/16", Mint. $21. (Auction #163, Lot 17).

NON-GLASS HANDMADE. Assorted. Lot of eighteen marbles. Seventeen are unglazed china, one is a bennington. Most of the unglazed. $16. (Auction #139, Lot 25).

NON-GLASS HANDMADE. Assorted. Lot of approximately sixty five marbles. Large modern bennington, about 3", Near Mint (8.5). $14. (Auction #132, Lot 30).

NON-GLASS HANDMADE. Assorted. Lot of seven marbles. Two brown benningtons, three blue benningtons, one multicolor and one dyed clay. $9. (Auction #172, Lot 34).

NON-GLASS HANDMADE. Bennington. Rare bennington. One side is brown, one side is blue. Half and half benningtons are hard to find. 25/32". Mint (9.9). $100. (Auction #160, Lot 44).

NON-GLASS HANDMADE. Bennington. Shooter size pink bennington. It is hard to find pink benningtons, but shooter sizes are even harder. 25/32". Near Mint(+) (8.9). $75. (Auction #137, Lot 10).

NON-GLASS HANDMADE. Bennington. One of the largest benningtons that I have ever seen. Blue bennington. In perfect shape. 1-7/16". Mint (9.9). $65. (Auction #104, Lot 38).

NON-GLASS HANDMADE. Bennington. Lot of ten marbles. All are brown benningtons. They range in size from 3/4" to 1-1/16". Germany. $61. (Auction #84, Lot 16).

NON-GLASS HANDMADE. Bennington. Lot of ten marbles. All are pink fancy benningtons. Pink base with brown and blue splotches. $55. (Auction #54, Lot 21).

NON-GLASS HANDMADE. Bennington. Lot of thirty two marbles. All are peewee benningtons. Nineteen blue, eight fancy and five brown. $50. (Auction #87, Lot 18).

NON-GLASS HANDMADE. Bennington. Lot of thirty four marbles. Assortment of brown and blue benningtons. 1/2" to 3/4". Mint (9.9-9.5). $46. (Auction #133, Lot 27).

NON-GLASS HANDMADE. Bennington. Shooter green bennington. Bennington base with green glaze (and one brown patch. Nice eyes. Germany. 1". Mint (9.9). $45. (Auction #158, Lot 19).

NON-GLASS HANDMADE. Bennington. Shooter fancy bennington. Super example. Large. Great coloring. Germany, circa 1850-1920. 1-5/16". Mint (9.9). $41. (Auction #137, Lot 43).

NON-GLASS HANDMADE. Bennington. Green bennington. Harder to find color. Opaque white base, covered by brown. 25/32". Mint (9.9). $41. (Auction #60, Lot 8).

NON-GLASS HANDMADE. Bennington. Lot of five marbles. All are pink benningtons. One has a small chip. 17/32". Mint (9.9) to Near Mint. $40. (Auction #96, Lot 7).

NON-GLASS HANDMADE. Bennington. One of the largest fancy benningtons that I have ever seen. Brown and blue splotches and a little green. 1-1/2". Near Mint(+) (9.9). $39. (Auction #67, Lot 23).

NON-GLASS HANDMADE. Bennington. Shooter fancy bennington. White base with blue, brown and some green. Lots of blue. In great shape. 1-1/16". Mint (9.9). $37. (Auction #173, Lot 16.20).

NON-GLASS HANDMADE. Bennington. Lot of seven marbles. All are fancy benningtons. 1/2" to 1". Mint (9.9). $37. (Auction #94, Lot 38).

NON-GLASS HANDMADE. Bennington. Shooter fancy bennington. White base with blue, brown and some green. Lots of blue. In great shape. 1-1/16". Mint (9.9). $37. (Auction #173, Lot 16).

NON-GLASS HANDMADE. Bennington. Lot of three marbles. All are brown benningtons. All are large. 1-3/8" to 1-7/16". Mint (9.9-9.4). $37. (Auction #119, Lot 16).

NON-GLASS HANDMADE. Bennington. Shooter white bennington. Bennington base with white glaze. Nice eyes. Germany, circa 1850-1920. 1". Mint (9.9). $35. (Auction #158, Lot 18).

NON-GLASS HANDMADE. Bennington. Lot of eleven marbles. Assortment of brown and blue benningtons. Nice set. Germany, circa 1850-1920. $32. (Auction #98, Lot 26).

NON-GLASS HANDMADE. Bennington. Lot of ten marbles. Assortment of brown and blue benningtons. 1/2" to 13/16". Mint (9.9-9.5). $32. (Auction #100, Lot 27).

NON-GLASS HANDMADE. Bennington. Lot of twenty marbles. All are blue or brown benningtons. 1/2" to 3/4". Mint (9.9-9.7). $31. (Auction #161, Lot 26).

NON-GLASS HANDMADE. Bennington. Lot of thirty five marbles. Assortment of blue and brown benningtons. 17/32" to 3/4". Mint (9.9-9.7). $31. (Auction #130, Lot 30).

NON-GLASS HANDMADE. Bennington. Lot of approximately sixty marbles. Assortment of Bennington, pottery and some clays. 1/2" to 13/16". $30. (Auction #101, Lot 33).

NON-GLASS HANDMADE. Bennington. Lot of twenty one marbles. All are blue bennington. 1/2" to 15/16". Mint (9.9-9.5). $29. (Auction #119, Lot 13).

NON-GLASS HANDMADE. Bennington. Shooter fancy bennington. White base with blue, brown. Lots of blue. In great shape. Germany. 1-1/16". Mint (9.9). $28. (Auction #179, Lot 24.20).

NON-GLASS HANDMADE. Bennington. Shooter fancy bennington. White base with blue and brown. Germany, circa 1860-1920. 29/32". Mint (9.6). $28. (Auction #182, Lot 13).

NON-GLASS HANDMADE. Bennington. Shooter fancy bennington. White base with blue, brown. Lots of blue. In great shape. Germany. 1-1/16". Mint (9.9). $28. (Auction #179, Lot 24).

NON-GLASS HANDMADE. Bennington. Lot of two marbles. One is brown with green spots. 15/16". Mint. The other is just a brown bennington. $27. (Auction #73, Lot 18).

NON-GLASS HANDMADE. Bennington. Pink base fancy bennington. Peewee. Germany, circa 1850-1920. 13/32". Mint (9.9). $25. (Auction #151, Lot 46).

NON-GLASS HANDMADE. Bennington. Large brown bennington. Germany, circa 1850-1920. 1-7/16". Mint (9.9). $24. (Auction #87, Lot 30).

NON-GLASS HANDMADE. Bennington. Lot of nine marbles. Four blue and five brown. Four are 19/32" to 11/16". The other five are 7/8". $22. (Auction #174, Lot 10).

NON-GLASS HANDMADE. Bennington. Large brown bennington. Some green splotches on it. Germany, circa 1850-1920. 1-3/8". Mint (9.9). $22. (Auction #92, Lot 39).

NON-GLASS HANDMADE. Bennington. Lot of two marbles. Both are shooter benningtons. One blue, one brown. Nice pair. Germany. $21. (Auction #183, Lot 6).

NON-GLASS HANDMADE. Bennington. Pink fancy bennington. Light pink base. Splotches of brown and blue. Peewee marble. Super. Germany. 15/32". Mint (9.9). $21. (Auction #78, Lot 19.30).

NON-GLASS HANDMADE. Bennington. Lot of thirteen marbles. Assortment of brown and blue benningtons. 5/8" to 3/4". Mint (9.9-9.5). $21. (Auction #95, Lot 16).

NON-GLASS HANDMADE. Bennington. Pink fancy bennington. Light pink base. Splotches of brown and blue. Peewee marble. Super. Germany. 15/32". Mint (9.9). $21. (Auction #78, Lot 19.20).

NON-GLASS HANDMADE. Bennington. Pink fancy bennington. Light pink base. Splotches of brown and blue. Peewee marble. Super. Germany. 15/32". Mint (9.9). $21. (Auction #78, Lot 19).

NON-GLASS HANDMADE. Bennington. Lot of two marbles. Both are shooters. One blue, one brown. Blue has some hit marks on it. Both 1-3/8". $20. (Auction #148, Lot 25).

NON-GLASS HANDMADE. Bennington. Lot of three marbles. All are brown benningtons, about the same size. One is Mint. 1-3/8". Mint (9.9). $20. (Auction #133, Lot 32).

NON-GLASS HANDMADE. Bennington. Green bennington. Some small flakes on the surface. Nice "eyes". Germany, circa 1850-1920. 11/16". Near Mint(+) (8.9). $20. (Auction #137, Lot 22).

NON-GLASS HANDMADE. Bennington. Lot of twenty eight marbles. All are blue benningtons. 1/2" to 11/16". Mint (9.9-9.7). $20. (Auction #145, Lot 22).

NON-GLASS HANDMADE. Bennington. Lot of two marbles. Both shooters. One brown and one blue. Both the exact same size. $20. (Auction #113, Lot 1).

NON-GLASS HANDMADE. Bennington. Larger, shooter brown bennington. Germany, circa 1850-1920. 1-1/4". Mint (9.9). $19. (Auction #113, Lot 11).

NON-GLASS HANDMADE. Bennington. Large blue bennington. Germany, cira 1850-1920. 1-5/16". Mint (9.5). $19. (Auction #94, Lot 2).

NON-GLASS HANDMADE. Bennington. Shooter fancy bennington. White base with blue, brown and some green. Lots of blue. In great shape. 27/32". Mint (9.9). $19. (Auction #142, Lot 4).

NON-GLASS HANDMADE. Bennington. Lot of nine marbles. One blue bennington, two brown, six fancy benningtons. Nice assortment. 9/16". $19. (Auction #54, Lot 30).

NON-GLASS HANDMADE. Bennington. Lot of six marbles. Brown and blue benningtons. Germany, circa 1850-1920. 17/32" to 13/16". Mint. $18. (Auction #166, Lot 30).

NON-GLASS HANDMADE. Bennington. Lot of ten marbles. Six brown, three blue, one fancy. 1/2" to 5/8". Mint (9.9-9.3). $18. (Auction #140, Lot 12).

NON-GLASS HANDMADE. Bennington. Shooter fancy bennington. White base with blue, brown and some green. Lots of blue. In great shape. 27/32". Mint (9.9). $17. (Auction #142, Lot 4.20).

NON-GLASS HANDMADE. Bennington. Nice fancy bennington. Blue and brown splotches on white. Germany, circa 1850-1920. 23/32". Mint (9.7). $17. (Auction #60, Lot 4).

NON-GLASS HANDMADE. Bennington. Brown shooter bennington. Germany, circa 1850-1915. 1-5/16". Mint (9.9). $17. (Auction #74, Lot 28).

NON-GLASS HANDMADE. Bennington. Lot of six marbles. Three brown, two blue and one crockery (not a bennington). 3/4" to 7/8". Mint (9.9). $17. (Auction #113, Lot 20).

NON-GLASS HANDMADE. Bennington. Large blue bennington shooter. Germany, circa 1850-1920. 1-5/16". Mint (9.9). $17. (Auction #89, Lot 12).

NON-GLASS HANDMADE. Bennington. Gorgeous shooter fancy bennington. White base with brown, blue and green splotches. Super shape. $16. (Auction #54, Lot 27).

NON-GLASS HANDMADE. Bennington . Lot of seven marbles. All are peewee fancy bennington. Germany, circa 1850-1920. 15/32" to 1/2". Mint. $16. (Auction #148, Lot 28.20).

NON-GLASS HANDMADE. Bennington . Lot of seven marbles. All are peewee fancy bennington. Germany, circa 1850-1920. 15/32" to 1/2". Mint. $16. (Auction #148, Lot 28).

NON-GLASS HANDMADE. Bennington. Very unusual fancy bennington. Almost completely covered by blue and green. No brown on this marble. 17/32". Mint (9.5). $16. (Auction #150, Lot 18).

NON-GLASS HANDMADE. Bennington. Gorgeous shooter fancy bennington. White base with brown, blue and green splotches. Super shape. $16. (Auction #54, Lot 27.30).

NON-GLASS HANDMADE. Bennington. Gorgeous shooter fancy bennington. White base with brown, blue and green splotches. Super shape. $16. (Auction #54, Lot 27.20).

NON-GLASS HANDMADE. Bennington. Lot of three marbles. These are the splattered type. Each is a white to cream base. One is splattered. $16. (Auction #113, Lot 23).

NON-GLASS HANDMADE. Bennington. Gorgeous shooter fancy bennington. White base with brown, blue and green splotches. Super shape. $16. (Auction #54, Lot 27.50).

NON-GLASS HANDMADE. Bennington. Gorgeous shooter fancy bennington. White base with brown, blue and green splotches. Super shape. $16. (Auction #54, Lot 27.40).

NON-GLASS HANDMADE. Bennington. Superb shooter fancy bennington. Outstanding example. Germany, circa 1870-1915. 27/32". Mint (9.9). $14. (Auction #116, Lot 12).

NON-GLASS HANDMADE. Bennington. Lot of twenty six marbles. All are brown bennington. 19/32" to 7/8". Mint (9.9-9.5). $14. (Auction #143, Lot 21).

NON-GLASS HANDMADE. Bennington. Lot of nine marbles. Eight are white bennington (no color on them), one is a black bennington. $14. (Auction #108, Lot 32).

NON-GLASS HANDMADE. Bennington. Lot of ten marbles. Assortment of brown and blue Benningtons. 1/2" to 19/32". Mint (9.9-9.7). $14. (Auction #109, Lot 19).

NON-GLASS HANDMADE. Bennington. Lot of twenty six marbles. All are brown bennington. 19/32" to 7/8". Mint (9.9-9.5). $14. (Auction #143, Lot 21.20).

NON-GLASS HANDMADE. Bennington. Light pink base. Splotches of blue and brown on it. Hard to find. Germany, circa 1870-1915. 5/8". Mint (9.9). $13. (Auction #139, Lot 9).

NON-GLASS HANDMADE. Bennington. Blue bennington. Nice example. Germany, circa 1870-1915. 1". Mint (9.9). $13. (Auction #76, Lot 3).

NON-GLASS HANDMADE. Bennington. Lot of nine marbles. Eight are white bennington (no color on them), one is a black bennington. $12. (Auction #108, Lot 32.30).

NON-GLASS HANDMADE. Bennington. Lot of nine marbles. Eight are white bennington (no color on them), one is a black bennington. $12. (Auction #108, Lot 32.20).

NON-GLASS HANDMADE. Bennington. Large brown bennington. 1-9/16". Near Mint(+) (8.8). 1-9/16". Near Mint(+) (8.8). $12. (Auction #125, Lot 30).

NON-GLASS HANDMADE. Bennington. Brown bennington. Nice shooter. Germany, circa 1870-1915. 1-1/16". Mint (9.9). $11. (Auction #101, Lot 2).

NON-GLASS HANDMADE. Bennington. Lot of two marbles. Both are fancy benningtons. Nice pair. Germany, circa 1870-1915. 23/32". Mint (9.9). $11. (Auction #101, Lot 12).

NON-GLASS HANDMADE. Bennington. Lot of nine marbles. Eight are white bennington (no color on them), one is a black bennington. $10. (Auction #108, Lot 32.40).

NON-GLASS HANDMADE. Bennington. Fancy bennington. Germany, circa 1850-1920. 9/16". Mint (9.9). $9. (Auction #163, Lot 7.20).

NON-GLASS HANDMADE. Bennington. Fancy bennington. Germany, circa 1850-1920. 9/16". Mint (9.9). $9. (Auction #163, Lot 7).

NON-GLASS HANDMADE. Bennington. Brown bennington. Very nice example. Germany, circa 1870-1915. 23/32". Mint (9.9). $5. (Auction #128, Lot 10).

NON-GLASS HANDMADE. Bennington. Lot of five marbles. All are blue benningtons. 5/8" to 13/16". Mint (9.9-9.7). $5. (Auction #102, Lot 16).

NON-GLASS HANDMADE. Bennington. Brown bennington. Super example. Germany, circa 1850-1920. 23/32". Mint (9.9). $5. (Auction #107, Lot 18).

NON-GLASS HANDMADE. Bennington. Brown bennington. Superb example in great shape. Germany, circa 1850-1920. 21/32". Mint (9.9). $1. (Auction #110, Lot 6).

NON-GLASS HANDMADE. Carpet ball. Opaque white base with intersecting brown lines. This is genuine and old. Some minor hit marks. 3-1/2". Near Mint(+) (8.8). $95. (Auction #128, Lot 21).

NON-GLASS HANDMADE. China. Very hard to find King's Rose china. Opaque white china. Painted on one side. 11/16". Mint (9.9). $400. (Auction #160, Lot 46).

NON-GLASS HANDMADE. China. Rare handpainted china. Unglazed. Six-vane red pinwheel on each pole. Five green bands around the equator. 3/4". Mint (9.7). $195. (Auction #173, Lot 49).

NON-GLASS HANDMADE. China. Lot of thirty three marbles. Ten are helix on either pole and crow's feet on equator, four are bulls. $160. (Auction #62, Lot 45).

NON-GLASS HANDMADE. China. Large unglazed handpainted china. Has six bullseyes, perfectly spaced at the axis poles. Two green. 1-5/16". Mint (9.7). $130. (Auction #94, Lot 17).

NON-GLASS HANDMADE. China. Exceptional china!!!! Three equidistantly spaced lines, encircling poles. One is light blue. 13/16". Mint (9.5). $130. (Auction #64, Lot 45).

NON-GLASS HANDMADE. China. Lot of seventy marbles. Almost all are glazed chinas. A few pottery and crockery in here too. $95. (Auction #94, Lot 27).

NON-GLASS HANDMADE. China. Unglazed, handpainted china. Each pole has a black helix. The equator has red crows feet. 1-1/4". Mint (9.5). $85. (Auction #101, Lot 51).

NON-GLASS HANDMADE. China. Excellent unglazed handpainted china. Four lines on each axis. Olive green, currant red and orange. 25/32". Mint (9.8). $85. (Auction #141, Lot 45).

NON-GLASS HANDMADE. China. A handpainted china. Super marble. Opaque white. Has four black lines on the equator. 23/32". Mint (9.7). $80. (Auction #58, Lot 37).

NON-GLASS HANDMADE. China. Lot of seven marbles. All are handpainted glazed chinas. Bullseyes and equatorial spiral. Excellent. $80. (Auction #123, Lot 12).

NON-GLASS HANDMADE. China. Lot of ten marbles. All are glazed, handpainted china. Each has three bullseyes on it. Nice set. Germany. $70. (Auction #92, Lot 20).

NON-GLASS HANDMADE. China. Lot of ten marbles. All are glazed, handpainted china. Each has three bullseyes on it. Nice set. Germany. $65. (Auction #92, Lot 20.20).

NON-GLASS HANDMADE. China. Beautiful unglazed handpainted china. Four intersecting lines on each axis. One is green. 1-3/16". Mint (9.9). $65. (Auction #116, Lot 41).

NON-GLASS HANDMADE. China. Lot of ten marbles. All are glazed, handpainted china. Each has three bullseyes on it. Nice set. Germany. $65. (Auction #92, Lot 20.30).

NON-GLASS HANDMADE. China. Lot of seven marbles. All are handpainted, glazed china. Includes intersecting lines. $65. (Auction #93, Lot 18).

NON-GLASS HANDMADE. China. Very interesting handpainted unglazed china. Large marble. There are four sets of six stranded bands. 1-3/8". Mint (9.9). $55. (Auction #101, Lot 6).

NON-GLASS HANDMADE. China. Lot of two marbles. Super pair of handpainted unglazed chinas. Both are intersecting lines. $55. (Auction #103, Lot 17).

NON-GLASS HANDMADE. China. Handpainted china. Excellent marble. Two wedgewood blue lines around the equator. Red pinwheel. 19/32". Mint (9.7). $55. (Auction #129, Lot 47).

NON-GLASS HANDMADE. China. Handpainted, unglazed china. Three lines on each axis. One set of black, one of dark green. 25/32". Mint (9.9). $55. (Auction #162, Lot 11).

NON-GLASS HANDMADE. China. Very nice handpainted china. Unusual coloring. A green pinwheel at either pole. Five black lines. 5/8". Mint (9.9). $50. (Auction #147, Lot 11).

NON-GLASS HANDMADE. China. Glazed handpainted china. Red pinwheel on either side. Pinwheels are hard to find. 13/16". Mint (9.6). $47. (Auction #59, Lot 27).

NON-GLASS HANDMADE. China. Glazed handpainted china. Black spiral covering one side of the marble. Red crow foot on the other side. 3/4". Mint (9.9). $46. (Auction #150, Lot 2).

NON-GLASS HANDMADE. China. Unglazed handpainted china. Super marble. Crisp painting. Three lines on each axis. Red, blue or green. 1-1/16". Mint (9.7). $44. (Auction #126, Lot 11).

NON-GLASS HANDMADE. China. Beautiful handpainted glazed china. Six bullseyes. Two each of red, green and blue. 29/32". Mint (9.3). $43. (Auction #148, Lot 2).

NON-GLASS HANDMADE. China. Lot of two marbles. Both are handpainted glazed chinas. One is green and orange spirals on two axes. $41. (Auction #123, Lot 38).

NON-GLASS HANDMADE. China. Lot of two marbles. Super pair of glazed, handpainted chinas. Both have six bullseyes. $40. (Auction #91, Lot 34).

NON-GLASS HANDMADE. China. Handpainted unglazed china. Six bullseyes. Two green, two red, two black. One on each of the six axes. 25/32". Mint(-) (9.2). $40. (Auction #183, Lot 34).

NON-GLASS HANDMADE. China. Unglazed handpainted china. Super marble. Good painting. Three spaced lines on each axis. Red, orange. 23/32". Mint (9.6). $37. (Auction #185, Lot 48).

NON-GLASS HANDMADE. China. Beautiful handpainted glazed china. Interesting design. Green bullseye on either pole. Red crows feet. 19/32". Mint (9.9). $37. (Auction #152, Lot 43).

NON-GLASS HANDMADE. China. Glazed, handpainted china. Each pole has a blue helix. The equator has red crows feet. 11/16". Mint (9.8). $37. (Auction #162, Lot 44).

NON-GLASS HANDMADE. China. Lot of seventeen marbles. All are unglazed china. Several are painted. 15/16" to 5/8". Mint (9.9). $36. (Auction #125, Lot 36).

NON-GLASS HANDMADE. China. Unglazed handpainted china. Super marble. Crisp painting. Two lines on each axis. Red, blue or green. 11/16". Mint (9.7). $36. (Auction #107, Lot 6).

NON-GLASS HANDMADE. China. Beautiful glazed handpainted china in a harder to find pattern. Light blue spiral at either pole. 1/2". Mint (9.9). $35. (Auction #59, Lot 36).

NON-GLASS HANDMADE. China. Handpainted unglazed china. Black bullseye on either pole. Red bands and lines around the equator. 1". Mint (9.9). $34. (Auction #98, Lot 31).

NON-GLASS HANDMADE. China. Unglazed, handpainted china. The poles each have a helix of green, the equator has red crows feet. 23/32". Mint (9.9). $33. (Auction #91, Lot 14).

NON-GLASS HANDMADE. China. Lot of five marbles. All are glazed chinas. Spirals or intersecting lines. 17/32" to 23/32". Mint. $32. (Auction #125, Lot 5).

NON-GLASS HANDMADE. China. Shooter size unglazed china. Porcelain marble, very dense. Has four lines on each of the three axes. 1-1/16". Mint(-) (9.1). $31. (Auction #154, Lot 20).

NON-GLASS HANDMADE. China. Glazed handpainted china. One band on each axis. One is red, one blue, one dark green. 23/32". Mint (9.7). $31. (Auction #165, Lot 42).

NON-GLASS HANDMADE. China. Large handpainted unglazed china marble. Intersecting lines. Each axis has three lines on it. 1-7/16". Near

Mint (8.5). $30. (Auction #115, Lot 23).

NON-GLASS HANDMADE. China. Handpainted unglazed china. Colors have faded. Outstanding and rare design. 13/16". Mint (9.5). $30. (Auction #165, Lot 47).

NON-GLASS HANDMADE. China. Very nice handpainted china. Unglazed. Red crows feet around the equator. Green leaves on either pole. 23/32". Mint (9.8). $30. (Auction #84, Lot 11).

NON-GLASS HANDMADE. China. Lot of two marbles. Both are handpainted and glazed. One is a red helix on one pole with green leave. $30. (Auction #121, Lot 8).

NON-GLASS HANDMADE. China. Outstanding example of a handpainted unglazed china. Spiral of blue on one axis, red on another. 23/32". Mint (9.9). $27. (Auction #98, Lot 42).

NON-GLASS HANDMADE. China. Glazed handpainted china. Green pinwheel on each side. Fairly light on each side. 17/32". Mint (9.9). $27. (Auction #59, Lot 6).

NON-GLASS HANDMADE. China. Lot of two marbles. Excellent pair. Same pattern, in complementary colors. One has a black spiral. $26. (Auction #153, Lot 42).

NON-GLASS HANDMADE. China. Beautiful handpainted glazed china. Six bullseyes. Two each of red, green and black. 5/8". Mint (9.9). $24. (Auction #152, Lot 16).

NON-GLASS HANDMADE. China. Nice shooter unglazed handpainted china. Three lines on each axis. Blue, green and red. Some dirt. 31/32". Mint (9.4). $24. (Auction #105, Lot 16).

NON-GLASS HANDMADE. China. Unglazed handpainted china. Red spiral on one axis. Black spirals on the other two axes. 3/4". Mint (9.9). $23. (Auction #96, Lot 4).

NON-GLASS HANDMADE. China. Handpainted unglazed china. Purple helix on either pole, green crowfeet around the equator. 31/32". Mint (9.9). $23. (Auction #165, Lot 37).

NON-GLASS HANDMADE. China. Handpainted, unglazed china. Two lines on each axis. One set of black, one of dark green. 23/32". Mint (9.9). $22. (Auction #93, Lot 7).

NON-GLASS HANDMADE. China. Glazed handpainted china. Black spiral on the equator, red spiral perpendicular around the poles. 3/4". Mint (9.9). $22. (Auction #156, Lot 28.20).

NON-GLASS HANDMADE. China. Glazed handpainted china. Black spiral on the equator, red spiral perpendicular around the poles. 3/4". Mint (9.9). $22. (Auction #156, Lot 28).

NON-GLASS HANDMADE. China. Lot of two marbles. One has two intersecting lines, one has three sets. Both are glazed. 1" and 3/4". $22. (Auction #128, Lot 18).

NON-GLASS HANDMADE. China. Glazed handpainted china. Spiral of light blue on one axis, spiral of red on another and spiral of blue. 5/8". Mint (9.6). $21. (Auction #164, Lot 11).

NON-GLASS HANDMADE. China. Unglazed, handpainted china. Three lines on each axes, one has red, one has blue, one has green. 31/32". Mint (9.5). $20. (Auction #124, Lot 6).

NON-GLASS HANDMADE. China. Nice glazed handpainted china. Two lines of green and two of orange. One set of green crows-feet. 25/32". Mint(-) (9). $20. (Auction #120, Lot 30).

NON-GLASS HANDMADE. China. Interesting glazed handpainted china. There are four bullseyes around the equator. Two blue. 9/16". Mint (9.5). $20. (Auction #154, Lot 13).

NON-GLASS HANDMADE. China. Unglazed handpainted china. Red bullseye on either pole with green leaves around the equator. 23/32". Mint(-) (9). $19. (Auction #142, Lot 13).

NON-GLASS HANDMADE. China. Lot of approximately sixty marbles. All are unglazed. Almost all are unpainted. 1/2" to 3/4". Mint. $18. (Auction #101, Lot 26).

NON-GLASS HANDMADE. China. Lot of three marbles. All three are glazed, handpainted. Each is a white base with faded bullseyes. 5/8". Mint (9.9). $17. (Auction #117, Lot 5).

NON-GLASS HANDMADE. China. Lot of eleven marbles. All are unglazed chinas. Most are painted with simple lines. 15/32" to 9/16". $15. (Auction #161, Lot 23).

NON-GLASS HANDMADE. China. Glazed handpainted china. Red line on equator. Light blue line pole to pole. Peewee. Beauty. Germany. 7/1". Mint (9.9). $15. (Auction #155, Lot 38).

NON-GLASS HANDMADE. China. Lot of eleven marbles. All are unglazed chinas. Most are painted with simple lines. 15/32" to 9/16". $15. (Auction #161, Lot 23.20).

NON-GLASS HANDMADE. China. Unglazed handpainted china. Three lines on each axis. One axis has green, one has blue, one has red. 13/16". Mint (9.5). $14. (Auction #165, Lot 34).

NON-GLASS HANDMADE. China. Handpainted glazed china. Spiral of red and perpendicular spiral of green. Germany, circa 1850-1920.

1". Mint (9.7). $12. (Auction #171, Lot 39).

NON-GLASS HANDMADE. China. Lot of eight marbles. All are unglazed chinas. Most are painted with simple lines. 15/32" to 9/16". $11. (Auction #152, Lot 24.30).

NON-GLASS HANDMADE. China. Handpainted glazed china. Three bullseyes. One blue, one red, one black. Black is faded. 21/32". Mint (9.7). $10. (Auction #158, Lot 11).

NON-GLASS HANDMADE. China. Lot of three marbles. All are unglazed. All have assorted intersecting lines. They are all dirty. $10. (Auction #139, Lot 1).

NON-GLASS HANDMADE. China. Handpainted unglazed china. Light red helix on one pole. Crow's feet on the other. In nice shape. Germany. 5/8". Mint (9.9). $10. (Auction #66, Lot 2).

NON-GLASS HANDMADE. China. Glazed, handpainted china. Red helix on one side. Green crowsfoot on the other. Germany, circa 1870. 9/16". Mint (9.8). $9. (Auction #166, Lot 19).

NON-GLASS HANDMADE. China. Lot of eight marbles. All are unglazed chinas. Most are painted with simple lines. 15/32" to 9/16". $9. (Auction #152, Lot 24).

NON-GLASS HANDMADE. China. Lot of eight marbles. All are unglazed chinas. Most are painted with simple lines. 15/32" to 9/16". $9. (Auction #152, Lot 24.20).

NON-GLASS HANDMADE. Clay. Lot of approximately one hundred fifty marbles. Assorted dyed and natural clay. All about 9/16". $45. (Auction #138, Lot 45).

NON-GLASS HANDMADE. Clay. Lot of approximately three hundred marbles. All are dyed clays. All are peewees. $37. (Auction #119, Lot 27).

NON-GLASS HANDMADE. Clay. Lot of approximately two hundred marbles. All are clays. Most are natural. Some dyed. Germany or U.S. $30. (Auction #56, Lot 24).

NON-GLASS HANDMADE. Clay. Lot of fifty marbles. Assortment of dyed clays. A few undyed. Nice set. Germany, circa 1850-1920. $27. (Auction #162, Lot 25.20).

NON-GLASS HANDMADE. Clay. Lot of one hundred marbles. Assortment of dyed clays. A few undyed. Nice set. Germany, circa 1850. $26. (Auction #130, Lot 21).

NON-GLASS HANDMADE. Clay. Lot of one hundred marbles. Assortment of dyed clays. A few undyed. Nice set. Germany, circa 1850. $26. (Auction #130, Lot 21.20).

NON-GLASS HANDMADE. Clay. Lot of fifty marbles. Assortment of dyed clays. A few undyed. Nice set. Germany, circa 1850-1920. $25. (Auction #162, Lot 25).

NON-GLASS HANDMADE. Clay. Lot of one hundred marbles. Assortment of dyed clays. A few undyed. Nice set. Germany, circa 1850. $24. (Auction #130, Lot 21.30).

NON-GLASS HANDMADE. Clay. Very unusual marble. Painted clay. Painted to resemble an eight panel beach ball. Two are wide purple. 13/16". Near Mint (8.6). $24. (Auction #123, Lot 33).

NON-GLASS HANDMADE. Clay. Lot of approximately ninety clays. Almost all dyed, some natural. Almost all Mint. German and American. $22. (Auction #158, Lot 24).

NON-GLASS HANDMADE. Clay. Lot of fifty marbles. Assortment of dyed clays. A few undyed. Nice set. Germany, circa 1850-1920. $20. (Auction #162, Lot 25.40).

NON-GLASS HANDMADE. Clay. Lot of fifty marbles. Assortment of dyed clays. A few undyed. Nice set. Germany, circa 1850-1920. $20. (Auction #162, Lot 25.30).

NON-GLASS HANDMADE. Clay. Green dyed clay. Large size. In great shape. Nice marble. German or American, circa 1880-1920. 1-3/16". Mint (9.9). $11. (Auction #67, Lot 4).

NON-GLASS HANDMADE. Crockery. Lined crockery. Blue and green lines swirled on opaque white. This is one of the largest that I have. 1-1/16". Mint (9.9). $120. (Auction #124, Lot 42).

NON-GLASS HANDMADE. Crockery. Lined crockery. Blue and green lines swirled on opaque white. Glazed, one salt spot. 1-1/9". Mint (9.9). $80. (Auction #136, Lot 48).

NON-GLASS HANDMADE. Crockery. Gorgeous lined crockery. Pale green lines on white. Glazed. Super pattern. In great shape. 21/32". Mint (9.9). $61. (Auction #54, Lot 34).

NON-GLASS HANDMADE. Crockery. Lot of four marbles. All are glazed lined crockery. Opaque white base with green and blue swirling. $48. (Auction #58, Lot 30).

NON-GLASS HANDMADE. Crockery. Lot of four marbles. All are glazed lined crockery. Opaque white base with green and blue swirling. $46. (Auction #58, Lot 30.20).

NON-GLASS HANDMADE. Crockery. Lot of four marbles. All are lined crockery. Excellent patterns and markings. Blue and green swirls. $29.

(Auction #90, Lot 26).

NON-GLASS HANDMADE. Crockery. Lot of three marbles. All three are lined crockery. One is glazed, two are not. Probably American. $25. (Auction #122, Lot 25).

NON-GLASS HANDMADE. Crockery. Lot of three marbles. All three are lined crockery. One is glazed, two are not. Probably American. $25. (Auction #122, Lot 25.10).

NON-GLASS HANDMADE. Crockery. Splatterware marble. White base splattered with blue and green. Glazed. Super example. Shooter. 1-1/8". Mint (9.9). $24. (Auction #170, Lot 4).

NON-GLASS HANDMADE. Crockery. Splatterware marble. White base splattered with blue and green. Glazed. Super example. Shooter. 1-1/8". Mint (9.9). $24. (Auction #170, Lot 4.20).

NON-GLASS HANDMADE. Crockery. Lot of five marbles. Assortment of lined and splattered crockery. Glazed and unglazed. $22. (Auction #128, Lot 8).

NON-GLASS HANDMADE. Crockery. Painted crockery. Olive brown marble with red splatter. Odd coloring. Germany, circa 1850-1920. 1-1/16". Mint (9.9). $22. (Auction #89, Lot 6).

NON-GLASS HANDMADE. Crockery. Very nice lined crockery marble. Glazed. Opaque white with smeared blue and green lines. 27/32". Mint (9.9). $21. (Auction #179, Lot 2).

NON-GLASS HANDMADE. Crockery. Lot of two marbles. Both are lined crockery. White base with green and blue lines. Glazed. $21. (Auction #85, Lot 28).

NON-GLASS HANDMADE. Crockery. Very nice glazed lined crockery. Green and blue lines smeared on a white base. Nicely glazed. 29/32". Mint (9.9). $20. (Auction #149, Lot 6).

NON-GLASS HANDMADE. Crockery. Nice lined crockery. Opaque white base. Thin lines of light green and light blue. Glazed. 23/32". Mint (9.9). $20. (Auction #109, Lot 41).

NON-GLASS HANDMADE. Crockery. Lot of three marbles. All are lined crockery. Opaque white base with blue and green lines. 21/32". $17. (Auction #113, Lot 7).

NON-GLASS HANDMADE. Crockery. Lined crockery. Opaque white base with blue and green lines. Superb example. Has a few dirt spots. 13/16". Mint (9.7). $15. (Auction #65, Lot 27).

NON-GLASS HANDMADE. Crockery. Very nice smaller lined crockery marble. Glazed. Opaque white with blue and green lines. 19/32". Mint (9.9). $13. (Auction #147, Lot 2).

NON-GLASS HANDMADE. Crockery. Lot of two marbles. Both are crockery with blue and green splotches. Germany, possibly American. $12. (Auction #82, Lot 15).

NON-GLASS HANDMADE. Crockery. White base with blue and green lines and smears. Glazed. Nice example. Probably American, possible German. 3/4". Mint (9.9). $10. (Auction #169, Lot 38).

NON-GLASS HANDMADE. Crockery. White base with blue and green lines and smears. Glazed. Nice example. Probably American, possible German. 3/4". Mint (9.9). $10. (Auction #102, Lot 34).

NON-GLASS HANDMADE. Crockery. Opaque white base with a couple of thin lines of blue and green. Still has dirt on it. Probably American. 3/4". Mint (9.7). $10. (Auction #68, Lot 22).

NON-GLASS HANDMADE. Crockery. Unglazed line crockery. Opaque white with light green lines. Remnants of glaze remain. Surface glaze. 21/32". Mint (8.7). $10. (Auction #68, Lot 2).

NON-GLASS HANDMADE. Crockery. Glazed. Opaque white base with green and blue lines. Rough spot on one side where it touched another. 21/32". Mint(-) (9.2). $9. (Auction #55, Lot 20).

NON-GLASS HANDMADE. Crockery. This marble originally was glazed, but the glaze has worn off. Opaque white base with swirls of blue. 25/32". Mint (9.3). $7. (Auction #60, Lot 33).

NON-GLASS HANDMADE. Crockery. Lined crockery. Blue and green lines on white. Very dirty. German or American, circa 1850-1920. 27/32". Mint(-) (9). $5. (Auction #136, Lot 15).

NON-GLASS HANDMADE. Crockery. Handpainted, glazed crockery. White base with splotches of green and blue. Very nice. Possibly German. 11/16". Mint (9.9). $5. (Auction #184, Lot 31).

NON-GLASS HANDMADE. Indian. Nice, larger Indian. Opaque black base. Two bands covering about twenty percent of the surface. Odd. 13/16". Near Mint(+) (8.9). $120. (Auction #64, Lot 44).

NON-GLASS HANDMADE. Original box. Original box of twelve clay marbles. Box is strawboard. Faintly printed on the cover is "Germany. $240. (Auction #79, Lot 35).

NON-GLASS HANDMADE. Original box. Original box of twelve clay marbles. Box is strawboard. No printing on the cover. Box is 3-3/4" x 3". $200. (Auction #143, Lot 47).

NON-GLASS HANDMADE. Original box. Original box of about one hundred benningtons. Box is strawpaper with metal staples at the cor-ner. $150. (Auction #129, Lot 23).

NON-GLASS HANDMADE. Pottery. Glazed crockery with purple and red painted around the marble. Some roughness at the "eyes". America. 25/32". Mint (9.7). $22. (Auction #183, Lot 24).

NON-GLASS HANDMADE. Pottery. Fired pottery. Dyed pink/purple with purple brushed around the equator. Probably American. 11/16". Mint (9.7). $19. (Auction #61, Lot 11).

NON-GLASS HANDMADE. Pottery. Glazed crockery with purple painted around the equator. Some roughness at the "eyes". American. 31/32". Mint (9.5). $15. (Auction #74, Lot 5).

NON-GLASS HANDMADE. Pottery. Glazed lined pottery. Opaque white base with smeared green and blue lines. Nice marble. Possibly Germany. 3/4". Mint (9.9). $14. (Auction #71, Lot 7.20).

NON-GLASS HANDMADE. Pottery. Glazed lined pottery. Opaque white base with smeared green and blue lines. Nice marble. Possibly Germany. 3/4". Mint (9.9). $14. (Auction #71, Lot 7).

NON-GLASS HANDMADE. Pottery. Glazed lined pottery. Opaque white base with smeared green and blue lines. Nice marble. Possibly Germany. 3/4". Mint (9.9). $12. (Auction #64, Lot 30.20).

NON-GLASS HANDMADE. Pottery. Glazed lined pottery. Opaque white base with smeared green and blue lines. Nice marble. Possibly Germany. 3/4". Mint (9.9). $12. (Auction #71, Lot 7.50).

NON-GLASS HANDMADE. Pottery. Glazed lined pottery. Opaque white base with smeared green and blue lines. Nice marble. Possibly Germany. 3/4". Mint (9.9). $12. (Auction #64, Lot 30).

NON-GLASS HANDMADE. Pottery. Glazed lined pottery. Opaque white base with smeared green and blue lines. Nice marble. Possibly Germany. 3/4". Mint (9.9). $12. (Auction #71, Lot 7.40).

NON-GLASS HANDMADE. Pottery. Glazed lined pottery. Opaque white base with smeared green and blue lines. Nice marble. Possibly Germany. 3/4". Mint (9.9). $12. (Auction #71, Lot 7.30).

NON-GLASS HANDMADE. Pottery. Glazed lined pottery. Opaque white base with smeared green and blue lines. Nice marble. Possibly Germany. 3/4". Mint (9.9). $10. (Auction #64, Lot 30.40).

NON-GLASS HANDMADE. Pottery. Glazed lined pottery. Opaque white base with smeared green and blue lines. Nice marble. Possibly Germany. 3/4". Mint (9.9). $10. (Auction #64, Lot 30.30).

NON-GLASS HANDMADE. Pottery. Handpainted pottery. Red bands on one axis, lavender bands on another, light green on a third. 31/32". Mint (9.9). $7. (Auction #165, Lot 3).

NON-GLASS HANDMADE. Scenic china. Extremely rare glazed handpainted china. Superb marble. This is the china that I acquired on eBay. 1-1/4". Mint (9.4). $6925. (Auction #131, Lot 50).

NON-GLASS HANDMADE. Steelie. Nice, large handmade steelie. Hollow. Nice "X". Great example. Origin unknown, probably American. 1". Mint (9.7). $55. (Auction #56, Lot 26).

NON-GLASS HANDMADE. Steelie. Hollow steelie. Nice "X" on it. Some light corrosion. Probably American, probably pre-1930. 5/8". Mint (9.3). $15. (Auction #80, Lot 28).

NON-GLASS HANDMADE. Stoneware. Very nice stoneware with blue spatter splotches. Salt-glazed. In great shape. Origin unknown. 1-1/2". Mint (9.9). $65. (Auction #138, Lot 23).

NON-GLASS HANDMADE. Stoneware. Salt glazed stoneware. Blue band around equator. In excellent shape. These are hard to find. 7/8". Mint (9.8). $40. (Auction #147, Lot 31).

NON-GLASS HANDMADE. Stoneware. Salt glazed stoneware. Blue band around equator. In excellent shape. These are hard to find. 11/16". Mint (9.8). $35. (Auction #77, Lot 3).

NON-GLASS HANDMADE. Stoneware. Salt glazed stoneware. Blue splatter around equator. One small chip. In excellent shape. 1-1/2". Near Mint(+) (8.7). $32. (Auction #133, Lot 23).

NON-GLASS HANDMADE. Stoneware. Salt glazed stoneware. Blue circle at each pole. In excellent shape. These are hard to find. 23/32". Mint (9.8). $25. (Auction #182, Lot 18).

NON-GLASS HANDMADE. Stoneware. Opaque gray base with two large spots of spatter light blue on it. Salt glazed. Super example. German. 7/8". Mint (9.9). $24. (Auction #109, Lot 49).

NON-GLASS HANDMADE. Stoneware. Very nice stoneware with blue splotches. Salt-glazed. In great shape. Origin unknown, circa 1850-1920s. 7/8". Mint (9.9). $23. (Auction #109, Lot 14).

OTHER HANDMADE. Alley Agate. Superb example of an Alley Agate flame swirl. Translucent lavender and dark purple. Excellent swirling. 21/32". Mint (9.9). $47. (Auction #85, Lot 26).

OTHER HANDMADE. Alley Agate. Nice Alley Agate swirl. Transparent olive/brown with translucent light blue swirls. Some minor flame. 11/16". Mint(-) (9). $27. (Auction #71, Lot 1).

OTHER HANDMADE. Alley Agate. Light green flame swirls on opaque white. Nice pattern. West Virginia, circa 1935-1945. 5/8". Mint (9.8).

$14. (Auction #158, Lot 1).

OTHER HANDMADE. Alley Agate. Lot of two marbles. Both are swirls. Transparent green and opaque white. Each has a thin swirl of oxblood. $11. (Auction #76, Lot 33).

OTHER HANDMADE. Alley Agate. Lot of three marbles. All are swirls with some minor flame tips. Green on white, black on white, red. $10. (Auction #95, Lot 7).

OTHER HANDMADE. Aventurine. Stunning and superior example of an aventurine swirl. 29/32". Mint (9.6). $95. (Auction #181, Lot 43).

OTHER HANDMADE. Aventurine. Semi-opaque white base with green aventurine swirls. Probably Alley Agate. American, circa 1935-1950. 9/16". Mint (9.9). $28. (Auction #167, Lot 7).

OTHER HANDMADE. Banded opaque. Superb example. Opaque white base. Two bands covering about ninety percent of the surface. 21/32". Mint (9.4). $525. (Auction #98, Lot 49).

OTHER HANDMADE. Banded opaque. Opaque light green base. About seventy percent covered by wispy red and white. 21/32". Mint(-) (9.1). $140. (Auction #87, Lot 43).

OTHER HANDMADE. Banded opaque. Opaque white base. Two bands covering about half the surface. One is pink, the other is blue. 21/32". Mint (9.8). $140. (Auction #101, Lot 5).

OTHER HANDMADE. Banded opaque. A beauty. Opaque white base. Two bands covering about forty percent of the surface. One is blue. 11/16". Mint (9.9). $130. (Auction #101, Lot 52).

OTHER HANDMADE. Banded opaque. Opaque light green base. Two bands covering about half the surface. Both are wispy white. 11/16". Mint (9.6). $130. (Auction #181, Lot 44).

OTHER HANDMADE. Banded opaque. Nice banded opaque. Another hard to find marble. Opaque blue base. 21/32". Near Mint(+) (8.9). $125. (Auction #80, Lot 39).

OTHER HANDMADE. Banded opaque. Gorgeous marble. Opaque white base. Two bands covering about seventy percent of the surface. 21/32". Near Mint (8.8). $120. (Auction #56, Lot 40).

OTHER HANDMADE. Banded opaque. Opaque white base. Two bands covering about half the surface. One is pink and one is blue. 23/32". Mint(-) (9). $120. (Auction #101, Lot 10).

OTHER HANDMADE. Banded opaque. Outstanding example. Opaque white base. Completely covered by translucent yellow and transparent pink. 21/32". Mint(-) (9). $110. (Auction #168, Lot 47).

OTHER HANDMADE. Banded opaque. Opaque white base. Pink band covering about twenty percent of the surface. There is one wisp of blue. 21/32". Mint (9.8). $110. (Auction #101, Lot 17).

OTHER HANDMADE. Banded opaque. Light green opaque base. Two narrow bands of dark red. Possibly from near an end of the cane. 21/32". Near Mint(+) (8.8). $80. (Auction #144, Lot 45).

OTHER HANDMADE. Banded opaque. Semi-opaque white base. Two blue bands and one white band on the surface. Shooter. Interesting design. 27/32". Near Mint(+) (8.7). $80. (Auction #185, Lot 41).

OTHER HANDMADE. Banded opaque. Opaque white base with translucent pink bands. Large marble, but it has been re-melted and polished. $75. (Auction #118, Lot 29).

OTHER HANDMADE. Banded opaque. Very nice banded opaque. Translucent white base. Two bands of pink strands covering about forty percent. 11/16". Near Mint(+) (8.8). $75. (Auction #158, Lot 40).

OTHER HANDMADE. Banded opaque. Semi-opaque white base. Two bands covering about forty percent of the surface. Both are pastel light. 25/32". Near Mint (8.6). $70. (Auction #173, Lot 14).

OTHER HANDMADE. Banded opaque. Opaque white base. Almost completely covered by pink. One subsurface moon. One flake. 5/8". Near Mint (8.3). $50. (Auction #147, Lot 18).

OTHER HANDMADE. Banded opaque. Opaque white base. Two bands covering about half the marble. One band is pink with some yellow. 9/16". Near Mint(-) (8.2). $47. (Auction #74, Lot 9).

OTHER HANDMADE. Banded opaque. Opaque white base. Two bands covering about half the marble. One band is pink with some yellow. 9/16". Near Mint(-) (8.2). $42. (Auction #104, Lot 11).

OTHER HANDMADE. Banded opaque. Rare satin glass banded opaque. Base is translucent very light green satin glass. 23/32". Near Mint(-) (8). $40. (Auction #123, Lot 8).

OTHER HANDMADE. Banded opaque. Opaque white base. Two bands covering about sixty percent of the surface. Dark blue bands. 11/16". Near Mint (8.6). $40. (Auction #76, Lot 6).

OTHER HANDMADE. Banded opaque. From near the end of a cane. Semi-opaque white base. One narrow band of bright yellow. 23/32". Near Mint(-) (8.1). $15. (Auction #147, Lot 8).

OTHER HANDMADE. Banded Opaque. Superb banded opaque. Opaque white base. Two bands covering about sixty percent of the marble. 21/32". Mint (9.9). $390. (Auction #94, Lot 48).

OTHER HANDMADE. Banded Opaque. Very rare banded opaque. Translucent light blue base. Almost completely covered by stretched bands. 21/32". Good(+) (7.80). $180. (Auction #118, Lot 44).

OTHER HANDMADE. Banded Opaque. Super example. Opaque white base. Two bands covering about thirty percent of the surface. 21/32". Mint (9.5). $150. (Auction #94, Lot 24).

OTHER HANDMADE. Banded Opaque. A beauty. Opaque white base. Two bands covering about fifty percent of the surface. 21/32". Mint (9.8). $110. (Auction #160, Lot 42).

OTHER HANDMADE. Banded Opaque. Semi-opaque white base. Two bands of blue covering about forty percent of the surface. Very pretty. 19/32". Near Mint(+) (8.9). $110. (Auction #162, Lot 38).

OTHER HANDMADE. Banded Opaque. Opaque white base. One band covering about fifteen percent of the surface. Green, blue and yellow. 11/16". Mint (9.5). $100. (Auction #94, Lot 16).

OTHER HANDMADE. Banded Opaque. Translucent white base. Completely covered by transparent bands and looping of pink. Has a few chips. 1-1/16". Good(+) (7.90). $60. (Auction #163, Lot 38).

OTHER HANDMADE. Banded Opaque. Semi-opaque white base with pink bands covering about three quarters of the marble. Two tiny pits. 23/32". Near Mint(+) (8.8). $55. (Auction #66, Lot 10).

OTHER HANDMADE. Banded Opaque. Blue base. Two narrow bands covering about fifteen percent of the surface. Both are red and white. 5/8". Good(+) (7.90). $44. (Auction #166, Lot 15).

OTHER HANDMADE. Banded Opaque. Semi-opaque white base with two bands of translucent pink bands. The two bands cover about forty percent. 11/16". Near Mint(-) (8). $30. (Auction #176, Lot 6).

OTHER HANDMADE. Banded Opaque. Semi-opaque white base with pink bands. A couple of chips and haziness. German or American. 23/32". Good(+) (7.80). $25. (Auction #67, Lot 2).

OTHER HANDMADE. Banded translucent. Rare variant of a banded opaque. Translucent milky base with two bands covering about sixty percent. 23/32". Near Mint (8.6). $85. (Auction #102, Lot 42).

OTHER HANDMADE. Banded Translucent. Rare marble. Translucent white base. Filament core. Outer surface is covered by bands and loops. 23/32". Mint (9.9). $300. (Auction #164, Lot 46).

OTHER HANDMADE. Banded transparent. Superior single pontil start-of-cane banded transparent. Transparent clear base. Overall very light. 11/16". Near Mint(+) (8.9). $120. (Auction #131, Lot 13).

OTHER HANDMADE. Banded transparent. Very odd marble. Defies categorization. Transparent green base. Opaque white loops. 17/32". Mint (9.7). $90. (Auction #77, Lot 9).

OTHER HANDMADE. Banded transparent. Very odd marble. Transparent clear base. Stretched splotches of white, brown, blue and olive green. 23/32". Good(+) (7.90). $25. (Auction #123, Lot 10).

OTHER HANDMADE. Banded Transparent. Very rare end of cane banded transparent. Trasnparent blue base. Small partially stretched splotches. 25/32". Near Mint(-) (8.2). $100. (Auction #160, Lot 16).

OTHER HANDMADE. Bullet mold. The type of glass marble found in Codd bottles. Transparent clear marble with very light green/blue. 23/32". Near Mint(+) (8.8). $5. (Auction #90, Lot 19).

OTHER HANDMADE. Cairo Novelty. Lot of two marbles. I believe that these are Cairo Novelty company swirls, based on the lavender. $30. (Auction #90, Lot 36).

OTHER HANDMADE. Cased clambroth. Popularly referred to as a "cased clambroth" by collectors. 9/16". Mint (9.7). $320. (Auction #83, Lot 45).

OTHER HANDMADE. Cased Clambroth. These are referred to by collectors as 'cased clambroths", although the construction is not clambroth. 19/32". Mint(-) (9.2). $190. (Auction #159, Lot 49).

OTHER HANDMADE. Cased Clambroth. These are referred to by collectors as 'cased clambroths", although the construction is not clambroth. 11/16". Mint(-) (9.2). $150. (Auction #168, Lot 18).

OTHER HANDMADE. Catseye. Another unbelievable marble. This is a shooter size nine-vane catseye. I have never seen one this large. 15/16". Mint(-) (9.2). $110. (Auction #116, Lot 49).

OTHER HANDMADE. Catseye. An eight vane catseye. Not quite as hard to find as a nine vane. But still, very hard to find. 19/32". Mint (9.9). $12. (Auction #57, Lot 3).

OTHER HANDMADE. Catseye. Lot of two marbles. Both are nine vane catseyes. Each has very light pitting. Origin and age unknown. 5/8". Near Mint (8.6). $9. (Auction #76, Lot 15).

OTHER HANDMADE. Catseye. Foreign shooter size catseye. Transparent clear base. Core of white, yellow, orange, blue. 1-1/8". Mint (9.5). $8. (Auction #90, Lot 32).

OTHER HANDMADE. Catseye. Lot of two marbles. First is a nine vane catseye. Second is a four vane, same manufacturer. 5/8". Near Mint (8.6). $3. (Auction #77, Lot 8).

OTHER HANDMADE. Champion Agate. Lot of five items. All are poly bags. Each has a cardboard header label that indicates 20 Champion Agate. $17. (Auction #174, Lot 16.20).

OTHER HANDMADE. Champion Agate. Lot of five items. All are poly bags. Each has a cardboard header label that indicates 20 Champion Agate. $17. (Auction #174, Lot 16).

OTHER HANDMADE. Champion Agate. Lot of five items. All are poly bags. Each has a cardboard header label that indicates 20 Champion Agate. $15. (Auction #174, Lot 16.40).

OTHER HANDMADE. Champion Agate. Lot of five items. All are poly bags. Each has a cardboard header label that indicates 20 Champion Agate. $15. (Auction #174, Lot 16.30).

OTHER HANDMADE. Champion Agate Company. Lot of nin marbles. Assortment of transparent swirls in various colors. Ten different colors. $10. (Auction #163, Lot 30).

OTHER HANDMADE. Champion Agate Company. Lot of ten marbles. Assortment of swirls in various colors. Ten different colors. Excellent sampler. $10. (Auction #163, Lot 23).

OTHER HANDMADE. Champion Agate Company. Lot of nin marbles. Assortment of transparent swirls in various colors. Ten different colors. $10. (Auction #163, Lot 30.20).

OTHER HANDMADE. Champion Agate Company. Lot of ten marbles. Assortment of swirls in various colors. Ten different colors. Excellent sampler. $10. (Auction #163, Lot 23.30).

OTHER HANDMADE. Champion Agate Company. Lot of ten marbles. Assortment of swirls in various colors. Ten different colors. Excellent sampler. $10. (Auction #163, Lot 23.20).

OTHER HANDMADE. Champion Agate Company. Lot of nin marbles. Assortment of transparent swirls in various colors. Ten different colors. $10. (Auction #163, Lot 30.30).

OTHER HANDMADE. Champion Agate Company. Lot of ten marbles. Assortment of swirls in various colors. Ten different colors. Excellent sampler. $8. (Auction #163, Lot 23.50).

OTHER HANDMADE. Champion Agate Company. Lot of nin marbles. Assortment of transparent swirls in various colors. Ten different colors. $8. (Auction #163, Lot 30.50).

OTHER HANDMADE. Champion Agate Company. Lot of nin marbles. Assortment of transparent swirls in various colors. Ten different colors. $8. (Auction #163, Lot 30.40).

OTHER HANDMADE. Champion Agate Company. Lot of ten marbles. Assortment of swirls in various colors. Ten different colors. Excellent sampler. $8. (Auction #163, Lot 23.40).

OTHER HANDMADE. Champion Agate Company. Original poly bag. Thin poly. Red header label. Reads "60 CHAMPION AGATES". $5. (Auction #163, Lot 24).

OTHER HANDMADE. Clambroth. Opaque white base with pink strands. One small very shallow flake (not as deep as the pink strand). 1-7/8". Good(+) (7.90). $725. (Auction #166, Lot 50).

OTHER HANDMADE. Clambroth. Unbelievable marble. Very rare coloring. Opaque black base. Thirteen light red bands. Very rare color. 23/32". Mint (9.9). $700. (Auction #113, Lot 46).

OTHER HANDMADE. Clambroth. Rare clambroth. Opaque white base. Band pattern on the surface is: Pink band, yellow strand, green band. 21/32". Mint (9.8). $385. (Auction #179, Lot 47).

OTHER HANDMADE. Clambroth. Opaque black base. Seventeen white strands. Very nicely made. Has a couple of tiny manufacturing mark. 11/16". Mint (9.6). $220. (Auction #68, Lot 39).

OTHER HANDMADE. Clambroth. Black base with fifteen white bands. Some surface wear but no chips, flakes, hits or damage. Germany. 21/32". Mint(-) (9.1). $200. (Auction #94, Lot 45).

OTHER HANDMADE. Clambroth. Unbelievable marble. Very rare coloring. Opaque black base. Eight light red bands. Very rare coloring. 19/32". Near Mint(+) (8.9). $200. (Auction #156, Lot 48).

OTHER HANDMADE. Clambroth. Semi-opaque white base with ten pink strands on it. Stunning marble. "Wet" mint. 3/4". Mint (9.5). $200. (Auction #145, Lot 49).

OTHER HANDMADE. Clambroth. Translucent white base. Eleven blue bands. Well-spaced. Super looking marble!!! Has one small moon. 25/32". Near Mint(+) (8.9). $200. (Auction #97, Lot 43).

OTHER HANDMADE. Clambroth. Semi opaque white base with thirteen green narrow bands on it. Surface is pristine. 5/8". Mint (9.9). $180. (Auction #116, Lot 48).

OTHER HANDMADE. Clambroth. Opaque black base with eighteen white bands. The surface is wet, shiny. 17/32". Mint(-) (9.2). $175. (Auction #57, Lot 44).

OTHER HANDMADE. Clambroth. Really nice clambroth. Semi-opaque white base. Six pink stripes and five blue stripes. 11/16". Near Mint(+) (8.9). $170. (Auction #80, Lot 42).

OTHER HANDMADE. Clambroth. Superb and beautiful clambroth. Semi-opaque white base. Opalescent! Seventeen transparent pink bands. 19/32". Mint(-) (9.1). $160. (Auction #69, Lot 45).

OTHER HANDMADE. Clambroth. Opaque black base with fourteen white bands. Flake on one side and a small chip. Some very minor wear. 11/16". Near Mint (8.5). $150. (Auction #137, Lot 39).

OTHER HANDMADE. Clambroth. Opaque white base with fourteen green strands. In super shape. Nice marble. Germany, circa 1870-1915. 11/16". Mint (9.7). $140. (Auction #121, Lot 44).

OTHER HANDMADE. Clambroth. Opaque black base with sixteen white strands. Has overall haziness, but no chips, flakes or moons. 21/32". Near Mint(+) (8.2). $130. (Auction #63, Lot 32).

OTHER HANDMADE. Clambroth. Opaque white base. Thirteen lime green strands and two blue strands. 11/16". Mint(-) (9). $125. (Auction #148, Lot 46).

OTHER HANDMADE. Clambroth. Opaque white base. Eight blue lines alternating with eight pink lines. One tiny subsurface moon. 5/8". Near Mint(+) (8.8). $125. (Auction #70, Lot 45).

OTHER HANDMADE. Clambroth. Translucent white base with fifteen dark purple narrow bands. Unusual to find translucent base. 21/32". Near Mint (8.5). $120. (Auction #123, Lot 20).

OTHER HANDMADE. Clambroth. Opaque black base with seventeen white strands. Some shallow flakes and some haziness. Germany. 5/8". Near Mint(-) (8.2). $120. (Auction #125, Lot 35).

OTHER HANDMADE. Clambroth. Opaque white base. Five bands of blue and five of pink. Excellent design and super execution. 3/4". Near Mint(+) (8.8). $110. (Auction #150, Lot 43).

OTHER HANDMADE. Clambroth. Very rare color for a clambroth. Opaque light blue with eighteen white strands. 23/32". Good (7.50). $110. (Auction #77, Lot 38).

OTHER HANDMADE. Clambroth. Opaque white base with fourteen translucent green bands. Pinprick and a sparkle. 5/8". Mint(-) (9). $100. (Auction #134, Lot 48).

OTHER HANDMADE. Clambroth. Nice black clambroth. Opaque black base. Eighteen white strands, evenly spaced. 17/32". Mint(-) (9). $100. (Auction #102, Lot 19).

OTHER HANDMADE. Clambroth. Opaque white base. Nine blue strands and nine pink strands. Surface has some tiny chips and pits. 3/4". Good(+) (7.80). $100. (Auction #87, Lot 31).

OTHER HANDMADE. Clambroth. Very odd clambroth. Opaque white base. Possibly from near the end of the cane. Twelve blue bands. 11/16". Near Mint (8.6). $95. (Auction #67, Lot 10).

OTHER HANDMADE. Clambroth. Very odd marble. These have been around for a while, although no one is certain of their age or origins. $95. (Auction #113, Lot 26).

OTHER HANDMADE. Clambroth. Opaque white base with four blue strands, three green strands and eight pink strands. 17/32". Near Mint (8.6). $85. (Auction #142, Lot 43).

OTHER HANDMADE. Clambroth. Opaque white base. Surface is about seventy percent covered by blue bands. Two areas are missing. 19/32". Mint (9.6). $85. (Auction #153, Lot 27).

OTHER HANDMADE. Clambroth. Opaque white with twelve lime green strands. Tiny subsurface moon and a couple couple of sparkles. 11/16". Near Mint(+) (8.9). $85. (Auction #109, Lot 45).

OTHER HANDMADE. Clambroth. Semi-opaque white base, with pink lines. Small flake and several tiny subsurface moons. Germany. 19/32". Near Mint (8.6). $80. (Auction #175, Lot 48).

OTHER HANDMADE. Clambroth. Very nice coloring. Semi-opaque white base. Seven narrow bands of light blue. 11/16". Near Mint (8.4). $80. (Auction #123, Lot 4).

OTHER HANDMADE. Clambroth. Semi-opaque white base. Fourteen blue bands. Has a small chip and some haziness. 21/32". Near Mint (8.6). $80. (Auction #55, Lot 41).

OTHER HANDMADE. Clambroth. Semi-opaque white base with fifteen transparent pink strands. One manufacturing dimple. 19/32". Near Mint (8.6). $80. (Auction #163, Lot 10).

OTHER HANDMADE. Clambroth. Nice example from near the end of the cane. Opaque white base. Five blue strands and five pink strands. 19/32". Mint(-) (9.3). $75. (Auction #141, Lot 50).

OTHER HANDMADE. Clambroth. Semi-opaque white base. Eight blue lines alternating with eight pink lines. Overall hit marks. Germany. 5/8". Mint(-) (8). $75. (Auction #75, Lot 39).

OTHER HANDMADE. Clambroth. Semi-opaque white base. Eight blue bands alternating with nine pink bands. Has a small subsurface moon. 21/32". Near Mint (8.5). $70. (Auction #94, Lot 21).

OTHER HANDMADE. Clambroth. Translucent white base. Fourteen translucent pink bands. Several tiny pits and chips. 11/16". Near Mint (8.6). $65. (Auction #101, Lot 13).

OTHER HANDMADE. Clambroth. Semi-opaque white base. Nineteen pink strands. Looks like there are two missing. One small flake. 11/16". Near Mint(+) (8.8). $65. (Auction #104, Lot 4).

OTHER HANDMADE. Clambroth. Semi-opaque white base. Nineteen pink strands. Looks like there are two missing. One small flake. 11/16". Near Mint(+) (8.8). $65. (Auction #81, Lot 32).

OTHER HANDMADE. Clambroth. Semi-opaque white base with twenty two bands. Eleven pink and eleven blue. Overall subsurface moons. 29/32". Good (7.40). $65. (Auction #57, Lot 21).

OTHER HANDMADE. Clambroth. Semi-opaque white base with twenty two bands. Eleven pink and eleven blue. Overall subsurface moons. 29/32". Good (7.40). $60. (Auction #104, Lot 18).

OTHER HANDMADE. Clambroth. Huge clambroth, but damaged. Still, size is hard to find. Semi-opaque white base. Ten blue bands. 1-11/16". Collectible . $40. (Auction #82, Lot 24).

OTHER HANDMADE. Clearie. Superb marble. From near the end of the cane, but it is a two pontil. Transparent clear base. 1-5/16". Mint(-) (9). $100. (Auction #137, Lot 49).

OTHER HANDMADE. Clearie. Lot of three marbles. Matched set of three two-pontil handmade clearies, all off of the same cane. $90. (Auction #150, Lot 34).

OTHER HANDMADE. Clearie. Transparent clear base. Just a small area of cloudiness at the bottom near the pontil. 1-3/4". Near Mint(+) (8.8). $75. (Auction #170, Lot 28).

OTHER HANDMADE. Clearie. Hard to find two pontil handmade clearie. Transparent clear glass. Inner air bubbles. 1-1/16". Near Mint(+) (8.9). $55. (Auction #61, Lot 42).

OTHER HANDMADE. Clearie. Superb two pontil clearie. Transparent clear. Surface in great shape. Hard to find these this large. 1". Mint (9.8). $55. (Auction #56, Lot 41).

OTHER HANDMADE. Clearie. Single pontil clear. Rare. Very light blue glass. Two very tiny subsurface moons. 11/16". Near Mint(+) (8.9). $55. (Auction #182, Lot 43).

OTHER HANDMADE. Clearie. Superb two pontil clearie. Transparent clear. Ghost core. Surface in great shape. Hard to find these. 1-1/16". Mint (9.9). $50. (Auction #184, Lot 43).

OTHER HANDMADE. Clearie. Large clearie with a large air bubble in it. Single gathered and hand-blown, not rod-cut. 1-5/8". Near Mint (8.5). $50. (Auction #154, Lot 27).

OTHER HANDMADE. Clearie. Semi-transparent clear with a ghost core and two ghost veils. Great example. Probably German. 1-1/16". Mint (9.7). $39. (Auction #166, Lot 44).

OTHER HANDMADE. Clearie. Transparent very dark green. Lots of stretched air bubbles. Unusual example. 11/16". Mint(-) (9). $29. (Auction #93, Lot 39).

OTHER HANDMADE. Clearie. Two pontil brown clearie. Hard to find handmade marble. One tiny chip, one tiny subsurface moon. Germany. 19/32". Near Mint(+) (8.9). $20. (Auction #162, Lot 19).

OTHER HANDMADE. Cloisonne. Cloisonne sphere. Hollow sphere. Probably copper base. Copper wire patterns with colored enamel. 2". Mint (9.9). $55. (Auction #154, Lot 31).

OTHER HANDMADE. Handmade. I believe that this marble is cane cut, and not single-gather. Rare marble anyway. Transparent clear. 1-1/16". Mint (9.9). $65. (Auction #65, Lot 11).

OTHER HANDMADE. Handmade corkscrew. The only way to describe this is as a handmade corkscrew. One side of the marble is transparent aqua. 11/16". Near Mint(+) (8.7). $65. (Auction #71, Lot 30).

OTHER HANDMADE. Heaton Agate Company. Original poly bag of twenty two catseyes. Cardboard label reads "Big Shot". Nice original bag. Mint. $13. (Auction #118, Lot 22).

OTHER HANDMADE. Indian. Superb and very rare four-panel three hundred and sixty degree Indian. Opaque black base. Four panel. 19/32". Mint (9.8). $625. (Auction #88, Lot 13).

OTHER HANDMADE. Indian. Astounding three hundred sixty degree Indian! Opaque black base. 23/32". Mint (9.9). $420. (Auction #64, Lot 36).

OTHER HANDMADE. Indian. Hard to find three hundred and sixty degree Indian. 11/16". Mint (9.9). $420. (Auction #81, Lot 38).

OTHER HANDMADE. Indian. Three hundred and sixty degree Indian. Superb marble. Opaque black base. 11/16". Near Mint(+) (8.9). $310. (Auction #74, Lot 43).

OTHER HANDMADE. Indian. Superior shooter size Indian. Opaque black base. Two bands covering about seventy five percent. 7/8". Mint (9.7). $310. (Auction #160, Lot 36).

OTHER HANDMADE. Indian. Three hundred sixty degree Indian. Super marble. Opaque black base. Completely covered by white. 23/32". Mint(-) (9.2). $290. (Auction #78, Lot 39).

OTHER HANDMADE. Indian. What can I say but Wow! Shooter size Indian. Very hard to find these this large. 29/32". Mint(-) (9.2). $265. (Auction #60, Lot 45).

OTHER HANDMADE. Indian. Opaque black base. Two bands covering about forty percent of the marble. The bands are end of day. 7/8". Mint(-) (9.1). $250. (Auction #76, Lot 42).

OTHER HANDMADE. Indian. Super shooter. Opaque black base. Stretched white, green and yellow covering about ninety percent of the surface. 3/4". Mint (9.5). $220. (Auction #82, Lot 41).

OTHER HANDMADE. Indian. Large shooter Indian. Opaque black base. Two bands covering over seventy five percent of the surface. 15/16". Near Mint(+) (8.8). $200. (Auction #101, Lot 50).

OTHER HANDMADE. Indian. Extremely rare end of cane (first off cane) Indian. Opaque black base with wide white splotches. 11/16". Near Mint (8.6). $190. (Auction #93, Lot 44).

OTHER HANDMADE. Indian. Superb and very rare Indian. Transparent cobalt blue base. Two bands covering about half the surface. 11/16". Mint (9.9). $190. (Auction #61, Lot 32).

OTHER HANDMADE. Indian. Rare end of cane (first-off-cane)indian. Opaque black base. White band running from the bottom pontil. 3/4". Near Mint(+) (8.9). $180. (Auction #179, Lot 45).

OTHER HANDMADE. Indian. Opaque black base. Two bands covering about sixty percent of the surface. Both are pink and mustard. 23/32". Mint (9.9). $170. (Auction #105, Lot 46).

OTHER HANDMADE. Indian. Beautiful marble. Opaque black base. White bands covering most of the marble. Surface in great shape. 11/16". Mint (9.9). $170. (Auction #77, Lot 18).

OTHER HANDMADE. Indian. Superior Indian. Almost a three hundred sixty degree Indian. Opaque black base. 21/32". Mint (9.8). $170. (Auction #80, Lot 44).

OTHER HANDMADE. Indian. Nice marble. Opaque black base. Colored bands covering about ninety percent of the surface. 19/32". Mint (9.9). $170. (Auction #74, Lot 33).

OTHER HANDMADE. Indian. Opaque black base with two bands covering about thirty percent of the surface. 3/4". Mint (9.9). $155. (Auction #109, Lot 50).

OTHER HANDMADE. Indian. Superb shooter Indian. Opaque black base. Two bands covering about eighty percent of the surface. 3/4". Mint (9.7). $150. (Auction #78, Lot 34).

OTHER HANDMADE. Indian. Big Indian. Opaque black base. Two bands covering aobut eighty percent of the surface. One is light. 29/32". Near Mint(+) (8.7). $150. (Auction #67, Lot 30).

OTHER HANDMADE. Indian. Transparent Indian. Almost completely covered by color. Transparent clear base. 11/16". Mint (9.4). $140. (Auction #182, Lot 42).

OTHER HANDMADE. Indian. A real beauty. Opaque black base. Two bands covering about forty percent of the surface. 21/32". Mint (9.5). $130. (Auction #71, Lot 19).

OTHER HANDMADE. Indian. Peewee Indian. Opaque black base. Two bands covering about sixty percent of the surface. 15/32". Mint (9.9). $130. (Auction #76, Lot 13).

OTHER HANDMADE. Indian. Superb Indian. Opaque black base. Two bands of stretched translucent white covering seventy percent of the surface. 19/32". Mint (9.9). $120. (Auction #57, Lot 38).

OTHER HANDMADE. Indian. Large Indian. Opaque black base. About eighty percent covered by two bands. One is yellow and pink. 1-1/16". Near Mint(+) (8). $120. (Auction #185, Lot 16).

OTHER HANDMADE. Indian. Superb shooter Indian. This is the last one from the Indian collection that was consigned. Opaque blue. 25/32". Near Mint(+) (8.9). $110. (Auction #95, Lot 43).

OTHER HANDMADE. Indian. Large shooter Indian. Opaque white base. Two bands covering about twenty percent of the surface. 1-1/16". Near Mint (8.3). $110. (Auction #168, Lot 3).

OTHER HANDMADE. Indian. Transparent Indian. Transparent gooseberry honey brown base. Two bands of stretched opaque yellow. 21/32". Near Mint(+) (8.9). $110. (Auction #173, Lot 38).

OTHER HANDMADE. Indian. Opaque black base. Two bands covering seventy percent of the surfae. Each band is stretched white. 23/32". Mint(-) (9). $100. (Auction #59, Lot 35).

OTHER HANDMADE. Indian. Superior Indian from near the end of the cane. Opaque black base. Two bands covering about forty percent of the surface. 21/32". Mint(-) (9.3). $100. (Auction #68, Lot 41).

OTHER HANDMADE. Indian. Opaque black base. Two bands covering about twenty percent of the surface. One band is opaque white. 17/32". Mint (9.8). $100. (Auction #74, Lot 22).

OTHER HANDMADE. Indian. Rare Indian. Dark transparent amethyst base. One band covering about twenty percent of the surface. 21/32". Mint (9.9). $95. (Auction #69, Lot 5).

OTHER HANDMADE. Indian. Lot of two marbles. Both are very nice Indians. First is a nice shooter. Two color bands. $95. (Auction #155, Lot 6).

OTHER HANDMADE. Indian. Opaque black base. Two bands covering about forty percent of the surface. Both are opaque white strands. 9/16". Mint (9.9). $90. (Auction #71, Lot 5).

OTHER HANDMADE. Indian. Very interesting Indian. Opaque black base. Two very thin bands. Almost non-existent. Both are red. 23/32". Mint (9.9). $90. (Auction #63, Lot 28).

OTHER HANDMADE. Indian. Shooter. Opaque black base. Three bands covering over eighty percent of the surface. 13/16". Near Mint(+) (8.7). $90. (Auction #110, Lot 19).

OTHER HANDMADE. Indian. Superb Indian. Opaque black base. Two bands covering about sixty percent of the surface. 11/16". Mint (9.9). $90. (Auction #65, Lot 16).

OTHER HANDMADE. Indian. Opaque black base with about seventy percent coverage by two bands. One band is light blue and white. 25/32". Mint (9.8). $90. (Auction #154, Lot 3).

OTHER HANDMADE. Indian. Rare transparent Indian. Super example. Transparent amethyst base. Two bands covering about ninety percent of the surface. 11/16". Mint(-) (9). $90. (Auction #159, Lot 42).

OTHER HANDMADE. Indian. Opaque black base. Covered about ninety percent by two bands. One band is pink and mustard. 21/32". Mint (9.9). $90. (Auction #95, Lot 35).

OTHER HANDMADE. Indian. Opaque black base. Two bands covering about fifty percent of the surface. Both are subsurface white. 21/32". Mint (9.9). $85. (Auction #65, Lot 29).

OTHER HANDMADE. Indian. Superb Indian. Opaque black base with two bands covering almost ninety percent of the surface. 23/32". Near Mint(+) (8.9). $85. (Auction #70, Lot 17).

OTHER HANDMADE. Indian. Super swirl-type Indian. Opaque black base. Two bands covering about thirty percent of the marble. 11/16". Mint(-) (9.2). $85. (Auction #57, Lot 42).

OTHER HANDMADE. Indian. Super Indian! Opaque black base. Two bands covering about forty percent of the surface. One is blue. 11/16". Mint (9.9). $85. (Auction #62, Lot 43).

OTHER HANDMADE. Indian. Opaque black base. Two bands covering about thirty percent of the surface. The bands are both stretched. 23/32". Mint(-) (9.2). $85. (Auction #77, Lot 34).

OTHER HANDMADE. Indian. Interesting Indian. Opaque black base. One band covering about twenty percent of the surface. 21/32". Mint(-) (9). $85. (Auction #140, Lot 22).

OTHER HANDMADE. Indian. Opaque black base. Covered about eighty percent by two bands. One is pink and white, one is light blue. 11/16". Near Mint(+) (8.9). $85. (Auction #130, Lot 39).

OTHER HANDMADE. Indian. Very hard to find peewee Indian. Opaque black base. Two bands covering about thirty percent of the surface. 15/32". Mint (9.9). $80. (Auction #73, Lot 45).

OTHER HANDMADE. Indian. Opaque black base with two bands covering about seventy percent of the surface. 9/16". Near Mint(+) (8.9). $80. (Auction #63, Lot 42).

OTHER HANDMADE. Indian. Super shooter size Indian. Very unusual. Opaque black base. Three bands covering about ninety percent of the surface. 13/16". Near Mint (8.6). $80. (Auction #70, Lot 20).

OTHER HANDMADE. Indian. Opaque black base. Two bands covering about eighty percent of the surface. 11/16". Mint(-) (9). $80. (Auction #172, Lot 32).

OTHER HANDMADE. Indian. Opaque black base. Two bands covering about seventy percent of the surface. 19/32". Near Mint(+) (8.9). $80. (Auction #97, Lot 33).

OTHER HANDMADE. Indian. Opaque black base. Two bands covering about forty percent of the surface. One is light blue and white. 5/8". Mint (9.9). $80. (Auction #130, Lot 44).

OTHER HANDMADE. Indian. Very nice peewee Indian. Opaque black base. Two bands covering almost the entire surface. 15/32". Mint (9.9). $75. (Auction #116, Lot 42).

OTHER HANDMADE. Indian. I've classified this as an Indian, although technically I suppose it is a black base banded opaque. 21/32". Mint (9.5). $75. (Auction #81, Lot 15).

OTHER HANDMADE. Indian. Hard to find type of Indian. Opaque black base. Three bands covering about twenty percent of the surface. 11/16". Near Mint(+) (8.7). $75. (Auction #69, Lot 38).

OTHER HANDMADE. Indian. Very nice shooter Indian. Opaque black base. Two outer bands of transparent blue covering opaque white. 25/32". Mint(-) (9). $75. (Auction #90, Lot 42).

OTHER HANDMADE. Indian. This is categorized as an Indian by collectors, although technically it is an opaque banded swirl. 11/16". Mint (9.9). $75. (Auction #167, Lot 17).

OTHER HANDMADE. Indian. Opaque black base. Two bands covering about sixty percent of the surface. One band is light blue. 21/32". Mint (9.9). $75. (Auction #69, Lot 9).

OTHER HANDMADE. Indian. Nice Indian. Opaque black base. Two bands covering about twenty percent of the surface. 11/16". Near Mint(+) (8.9). $75. (Auction #88, Lot 39).

OTHER HANDMADE. Indian. Opaque black base. Two bands covering about twenty percent of the surface. 21/32". Mint (9.9). $70. (Auction #100, Lot 42).

OTHER HANDMADE. Indian. Opaque black base. Two bands covering about fifty percent of the surface. One is transparent green. 21/32". Mint (9.9). $70. (Auction #91, Lot 36).

OTHER HANDMADE. Indian. Opaque black base. Two bands covering about eighty five percent of the surface. 11/16". Near Mint(+) (8.9). $70. (Auction #163, Lot 42).

OTHER HANDMADE. Indian. Opaque black base. Two bands covering about half the marble. Both are light blue and white. 11/16". Mint(-) (9). $70. (Auction #55, Lot 35).

OTHER HANDMADE. Indian. Opaque black base. Two bands covering about sixty five percent of the surface. 11/16". Mint (9.9). $70. (Auction #69, Lot 7).

OTHER HANDMADE. Indian. Opaque black base. Two bands covering about sixty percent of the surface. 21/32". Mint(-) (9). $70. (Auction #73, Lot 39).

OTHER HANDMADE. Indian. Stunning marble. Opaque black base. Two bands cover about forty percent of the surface. 21/32". Mint(-) (9). $70. (Auction #55, Lot 16).

OTHER HANDMADE. Indian. Opaque black base. Two bands covering about seventy percent of the surface. This is a very odd marble. 21/32". Near Mint (8.6). $70. (Auction #74, Lot 3).

OTHER HANDMADE. Indian. Opaque black base. About seventy percent coverage. One band is light blue and white. Other is mustard. 11/16". Mint (9.2). $70. (Auction #136, Lot 9).

OTHER HANDMADE. Indian. Very nice Indian. Two bands covering about forty percent of the surface. Both are wide red bands. 5/8". Near Mint(+) (8.8). $67. (Auction #147, Lot 34).

OTHER HANDMADE. Indian. Opaque black base with two bands covering about eighty five percent of the surface. One band is mustard. 19/32". Mint (9.9). $67. (Auction #68, Lot 8).

OTHER HANDMADE. Indian. Opaque black base. Two bands covering sixty percent of the surface. Both bands are wispy white. Peewee. 15/32". Mint (9.9). $65. (Auction #98, Lot 41).

OTHER HANDMADE. Indian. Opaque black base covered about sixty percent by two bands. One is white, one is mustard. 21/32". Mint (9.5). $65. (Auction #97, Lot 27).

OTHER HANDMADE. Indian. Lot of two marbles. I have classified these as transparent Indians. $65. (Auction #139, Lot 36).

OTHER HANDMADE. Indian. Transparent Indian. Transparent brown base. Two bands covering about twenty percent of the surface. 11/16". Near Mint(+) (8.8). $65. (Auction #94, Lot 3).

OTHER HANDMADE. Indian. Opaque black base. Two bands covering about seventy percent of the surface. One band is blue and white. 21/32". Mint(-) (9.2). $65. (Auction #150, Lot 9).

OTHER HANDMADE. Indian. Opaque black base with two bands covering about ninety percent of the surface. One band is opaque white. 19/32". Mint (9.9). $65. (Auction #112, Lot 43).

OTHER HANDMADE. Indian. Opaque black base. Two bands of color covering almost the entire surface. One band is wispy white. 21/32". Mint(-) (9.2). $65. (Auction #159, Lot 34).

OTHER HANDMADE. Indian. Opaque black base. One wide red band, edged by white. No second band. A couple of small chips. 25/32". Good(+) (7.90). $65. (Auction #54, Lot 31).

OTHER HANDMADE. Indian. Another transparent Indian. Nice marble. Transparent clear base. Two bands covering about twenty percent of the surface. 11/16". Mint(-) (9.2). $60. (Auction #94, Lot 7).

OTHER HANDMADE. Indian. Lot of two marbles. Both are Indians. 21/32" & Near Mint (8.6). 11/16" & Near Mint (8.6). $60. (Auction #112, Lot 5).

OTHER HANDMADE. Indian. Opaque black base. Two bands covering about sixty percent of the surface. One is white and pink. 21/32". Mint(-) (9.1). $60. (Auction #105, Lot 38).

OTHER HANDMADE. Indian. Very nice transparent Indian. Transparent clear blue base. Two bands of red on the surface. 21/32". Near Mint (8.6). $60. (Auction #182, Lot 45).

OTHER HANDMADE. Indian. Opaque black base. Two bands covering about seventy percent of the marble. 11/16". Mint (9.5). $60. (Auction #102, Lot 9).

OTHER HANDMADE. Indian. Opaque black base. Two bands covering about seventy five percent of the surface. 11/16". Mint (9.5). $60. (Auction #56, Lot 38).

OTHER HANDMADE. Indian. Opaque black base. Two bands covering about thirty percent of the surface. 5/8". Mint(-) (9.1). $60. (Auction #100, Lot 47).

OTHER HANDMADE. Indian. Opaque black base. About eighty five percent coverage. Two wide color bands. 25/32". Near Mint (8.4). $55. (Auction #185, Lot 4).

OTHER HANDMADE. Indian. Opaque black base. Two bands covering about twenty percent of the surface. 7/8". Good(+) (7.90). $55. (Auction #106, Lot 2).

OTHER HANDMADE. Indian. Shooter. Opaque black base. Two bands covering over seventy percent of the surface. One is a red band. 25/32". Near Mint (8.5). $55. (Auction #107, Lot 38).

OTHER HANDMADE. Indian. I've been calling this type transparent Indian. 19/32". Mint (9.9). $55. (Auction #183, Lot 4).

OTHER HANDMADE. Indian. Nice Indian. Opaque black base. Two bands covering about twenty percent of the surface. 11/16". Near Mint(+) (8.9). $55. (Auction #64, Lot 34).

OTHER HANDMADE. Indian. Opaque black base. Two bands covering about sixty percent of the surface. One is blue and white. 21/32". Mint(-) (9). $55. (Auction #65, Lot 36).

OTHER HANDMADE. Indian. Opaque black base. Two bands covering about thirty percent of the surface. 21/32". Mint (9.7). $50. (Auction #136, Lot 38).

OTHER HANDMADE. Indian. Opaque black base. Two bands covering about seventy five percent of the surface. 9/16". Mint(-) (9). $50. (Auction #156, Lot 13).

OTHER HANDMADE. Indian. Opaque black base. Two bands covering about forty percent of the marble. 11/16". Mint(-) (9). $50. (Auction #67, Lot 16).

OTHER HANDMADE. Indian. Transparent "currant purple" base. Has two bands covering about thirty percent of the surface. 21/32". Mint(-) (9.2). $50. (Auction #56, Lot 34).

OTHER HANDMADE. Indian. Opaque black base. Two narrow bands covering about twenty percent of the surface. One is transparent. 21/32". Near Mint(+) (8.9). $50. (Auction #176, Lot 34).

OTHER HANDMADE. Indian. Nice Indian. Opaque black base. Two bands covering about seventy percent of the surface. 23/32". Near Mint(+) (8.7). $50. (Auction #66, Lot 44).

OTHER HANDMADE. Indian. Very hard to find peewee Indian. Opaque black base. Two white bands covering ten percent of the surface. 15/32". Mint (9.9). $50. (Auction #66, Lot 45).

OTHER HANDMADE. Indian. Opaque black base. Two bands coveirng about seventy percent of the marble. Bands are opaque and wispy. 11/16". Mint (9.9). $50. (Auction #152, Lot 47).

OTHER HANDMADE. Indian. Exceptional Indian. Opaque black base. Two bands covering about forty percent of the surface. 11/16". Near Mint(+) (8.7). $50. (Auction #174, Lot 38).

OTHER HANDMADE. Indian. Rare transparent three-band shooter Indian. Base glass is very dark transparent purple. 3/4". Near Mint(-) (8.2). $50. (Auction #94, Lot 19).

OTHER HANDMADE. Indian. Nice peewee Indian. Opaque black base. Three evenly space white strands as the outer layer. 1/2". Mint (9.9). $50. (Auction #91, Lot 27).

OTHER HANDMADE. Indian. Opaque black base. Two bands covering about seventy percent of the surface. The bands are wispy white. 9/16". Mint (9.9). $49. (Auction #102, Lot 44).

OTHER HANDMADE. Indian. Shooter Indian. A beauty, even though it has haziness. Opaque black. Two bands covering fifty percent of the surface. 25/32". Near Mint (8.5). $49. (Auction #128, Lot 39).

OTHER HANDMADE. Indian. Lot of two marbles. Both are Indians. First is black base with two bands covering about thirty percent of the surface. $48. (Auction #163, Lot 3).

OTHER HANDMADE. Indian. Transparent Indian in a very rare color! Transparent amethyst glass. Two bands covering about thirty percent of the surface. 19/32". Near Mint(+) (8.7). $47. (Auction #185, Lot 12).

OTHER HANDMADE. Indian. Transparent Indian. Transparent blue base. Two bands covering about seventy five percent of the surface. 9/16". Near Mint(+) (8.9). $46. (Auction #164, Lot 18).

OTHER HANDMADE. Indian. Nice Indian. Opaque black base. Two bands covering about eighty five percent of the surface. 21/32". Near Mint(+) (8.9). $46. (Auction #63, Lot 10).

OTHER HANDMADE. Indian. Black base. One band covering about one-quarter of the surface. The other band is missing. 3/4". Near Mint(+) (8.9). $46. (Auction #66, Lot 8).

OTHER HANDMADE. Indian. Opaque black base. Two bands covering about seventy five percent of the surface. 21/32". Near Mint(+) (8.9). $46. (Auction #76, Lot 25).

OTHER HANDMADE. Indian. Opaque black base. Two bands covering about forty percent of the surface. 11/16". Near Mint(+) (8.7). $45. (Auction #154, Lot 44).

OTHER HANDMADE. Indian. Transparent Indian. Transparent olive green base. Two bands covering over half the surface. One band. 11/16". Near Mint(-) (8.2). $45. (Auction #101, Lot 15).

OTHER HANDMADE. Indian. Opaque black base. One band covering about thirty percent of the surface. It is mustard and white. 5/8". Mint (9.9). $45. (Auction #97, Lot 30).

OTHER HANDMADE. Indian. Opaque black base. Two bands covering about thirty percent of the marble. 3/4". Near Mint(-) (8.2). $45. (Auction #134, Lot 25).

OTHER HANDMADE. Indian. Opaque black base. Two bands covering about thirty percent of the surface. 23/32". Near Mint(+) (8.7). $45. (Auction #110, Lot 15).

OTHER HANDMADE. Indian. Opaque black base with two bands covering about twenty percent of the surface. 11/16". Mint (9.9). $45. (Auction #66, Lot 35).

OTHER HANDMADE. Indian. A hard to find end of cane Indian. Opaque black base. One band, covering about ten percent of the surface. 5/8". Near Mint(+) (8.9). $45. (Auction #55, Lot 2).

OTHER HANDMADE. Indian. Opaque black base. Two bands covering about seventy percent of the marble. 5/8". Near Mint (8.6). $44. (Auction #144, Lot 41).

OTHER HANDMADE. Indian. Large Indian. Opaque black base. About eighty percent covered by two bands. Both are yellow and pink. 31/32". Good(+) (7.90). $43. (Auction #185, Lot 35).

OTHER HANDMADE. Indian. Opaque black base. Two bands covering about thirty percent of the surface. 21/32". Near Mint (8.5). $42. (Auction #133, Lot 6).

OTHER HANDMADE. Indian. Interesting Indian. Opaque black base with a number of translucent white bands on the surface. 11/16". Near Mint(+) (8.9). $42. (Auction #85, Lot 2).

OTHER HANDMADE. Indian. Opaque black base with two thin white bands. A peewee. Hard to find. One very tiny pinprick. Germany. 1/2". Mint(-) (9.1). $42. (Auction #113, Lot 13).

OTHER HANDMADE. Indian. Black base. Two bands covering about fifteen percent of the surface. One is blue, green and mustard . 23/32". Mint (9.6). $42. (Auction #167, Lot 35).

OTHER HANDMADE. Indian. Opaque black base. Two bands covering about thirty five percent of the surface. One is transparent pink. 11/16". Near Mint(+) (8.9). $40. (Auction #110, Lot 13).

OTHER HANDMADE. Indian. Opaque black base. Two bands covering about thirty percent of the surface. 11/16". Mint(-) (9). $40. (Auction #85, Lot 39).

OTHER HANDMADE. Indian. Opaque black base. Two bands covering about forty percent of the surface. 21/32". Near Mint(+) (8.9). $40. (Auction #166, Lot 40).

OTHER HANDMADE. Indian. Interesting end of cane Indian. Opaque black base. One side of has a wide white and transparent red . 21/32". Good(+) (7.90). $39. (Auction #56, Lot 18).

OTHER HANDMADE. Indian. Beautiful coloring. Opaque black base. Two bands covering about sixty percent of the surface. 23/32". Near Mint(+) (8.9). $39. (Auction #161, Lot 44).

OTHER HANDMADE. Indian. Opaque black base. One band covering about twenty percent and one thin band on the other side. 21/32". Mint (9.4). $37. (Auction #68, Lot 35).

OTHER HANDMADE. Indian. Shooter size Indian. Odd design. Opaque black base. Two bands covering about sixty percent of the surface. 27/32". Near Mint(-) (8.1). $37. (Auction #169, Lot 6).

OTHER HANDMADE. Indian. Opaque black base. Two bands covering about seventy five percent of the surface. 21/32". Near Mint(+) (8.8). $37. (Auction #158, Lot 3).

OTHER HANDMADE. Indian. Opaque black base. Two bands covering about half the marble. 21/32". Near Mint (8.6). $35. (Auction #149, Lot 9).

OTHER HANDMADE. Indian. Opaque black base. Two bands covering about twenty five percent of the surface. 23/32". Near Mint (8.4). $34. (Auction #185, Lot 24).

OTHER HANDMADE. Indian. Opaque black base. Covered about sixy percent by two bands. One is white and one is mustard yellow. 11/16". Near Mint (8.6). $33. (Auction #73, Lot 15).

OTHER HANDMADE. Indian. Opaque black base. About sixty percent coverage by two bands of stretched semi-opaque white. 11/16". Near Mint(+) (8.7). $30. (Auction #117, Lot 8).

OTHER HANDMADE. Indian. Opaque black base. Two bands covering about forty percent of the marble. One is red and yellow. 21/32". Near Mint(+) (8.2). $29. (Auction #103, Lot 33).

OTHER HANDMADE. Indian. Opaque black base covered about thirty percent by two bands. 21/23". Near Mint (8.6). $27. (Auction #115, Lot 38).

OTHER HANDMADE. Indian. Opaque black base. Almost completely covered by bands of yellow, blue, white. $25. (Auction #168, Lot 14).

OTHER HANDMADE. Indian. Opaque black base with two bands. Two bands covering about thirty percent of the surface. 21/32". Near Mint (8.5). $24. (Auction #82, Lot 4).

OTHER HANDMADE. Indian. Lot of two marbles. Both are opaque black with very light wispy white bands. Both have damage. 5/8". $5. (Auction #152, Lot 8).

OTHER HANDMADE. Lightning Strike. Very rare marble. I've seen maybe a dozen of these in over ten years. And this one is exceptional. 1-5/8". Mint(-) (9). $2625. (Auction #154, Lot 50).

OTHER HANDMADE. Metallic. Metallic swirl. Probably Champion Agate Company. Transparent green marble with silver metallic swirl. 5/8". Near Mint(+) (8.8). $16. (Auction #87, Lot 11).

OTHER HANDMADE. Metallic. Unknown manufacturer. My guess is probably Alley Agate or Champion Agate. Unusual three color swirl. 5/8". Mint (9.9). $13. (Auction #82, Lot 7).

OTHER HANDMADE. Mica. Very large mica!!!! Transparent green with a superior subsurface layer of mica. Four shallow lobes. 1-7/8". Near Mint (8.5). $575. (Auction #121, Lot 50).

OTHER HANDMADE. Mica. Exceptional large mica. Just over an inch. Green mica. Core of mica and a subsurface layer of mica. 1-1/16". Mint (9.9). $160. (Auction #84, Lot 34).

OTHER HANDMADE. Mica. Exceptional large mica. Just over an inch. Green mica. Core of mica and a subsurface layer of mica. 1-1/16". Mint (9.9). $150. (Auction #96, Lot 30).

OTHER HANDMADE. Mica. Very hard to find yellow mica. Outstanding example of this type! Filament core with mica around it. 21/32". Mint (9.9). $150. (Auction #154, Lot 6).

OTHER HANDMADE. Mica. Shooter green mica. Nice subsurface layer of mica and a core of mica. Super ground pontil. 1-1/16". Mint (9.8). $140. (Auction #107, Lot 50).

OTHER HANDMADE. Mica. Superb marble!!! Transparent green mica. Super layer of mica. Excellent surface. 1-1/16". Mint (9.4). $130. (Auction #64, Lot 41).

OTHER HANDMADE. Mica. Hard color to find. Very dark transparent purple/red mica. The color of black currants. 25/32". Mint (9.8). $125. (Auction #175, Lot 32).

OTHER HANDMADE. Mica. Shooter green mica. Double ghost core. Super subsurface layer of mica. Excellent ground pontil. 1-1/16". Mint (9.9). $110. (Auction #150, Lot 41).

OTHER HANDMADE. Mica. Shooter green mica. Nice subsurface layer of mica. Ghost core. Super ground pontil. 1-1/16". Mint(-) (9.2). $110. (Auction #173, Lot 42).

OTHER HANDMADE. Mica. Shooter green mica. Nice subsurface layer of mica and mica core. Super ground pontil. Pinprick. 1". Near Mint(+) (8.8). $90. (Auction #166, Lot 48).

OTHER HANDMADE. Mica. Very hard to find amethyst mica. Transparent light amethyst glass. Superb layer of finely ground mica. 27/32". Mint (9.4). $85. (Auction #96, Lot 35).

OTHER HANDMADE. Mica. Lot of two marbles. One is a blue mica. The other is an aqua. Both are superb marbles. Excellent mica. 19/32". Mint (9.9). $80. (Auction #78, Lot 11).

OTHER HANDMADE. Mica. Superb example of a large green mica. Transparent green. Core of mica and a subsurface layer of mica. 1". Mint (9.5). $80. (Auction #81, Lot 40).

OTHER HANDMADE. Mica. Shooter green mica. Air bubble ghost core. Nice subsurface layer of mica. Super ground pontil. Germany. 1". Mint (9.9). $75. (Auction #88, Lot 35).

OTHER HANDMADE. Mica. Superb example of a large green mica. Transparent green. Core of mica and a subsurface layer of mica. 1". Mint (9). $70. (Auction #136, Lot 46).

OTHER HANDMADE. Mica. Larger green mica. Filament core. Subsurface layer of finely ground mica. 7/8". Mint (9.7). $70. (Auction #118, Lot 46).

OTHER HANDMADE. Mica. Peewee amethyst mica. Excellent amethyst color. Big flakes of mica. Excellent marble. Germany. 15/32". Mint (9.9). $70. (Auction #162, Lot 42).

OTHER HANDMADE. Mica. Rare single-pontil cloud mica. Transparent very dark blue glass. Mica cloud in the marble. One pontil. 3/4". Mint (9.7). $65. (Auction #150, Lot 36).

OTHER HANDMADE. Mica. Rare mica with oxblood. Aqua mica. Has a mica core encrusting an oxblood band. 15/16". Good(+) (7.90). $60. (Auction #173, Lot 13).

OTHER HANDMADE. Mica. Aqua mica. Three layers of mica. One of those is on the surface (a few pieces). Filament core. 21/32". Mint (9.9). $60. (Auction #76, Lot 22).

OTHER HANDMADE. Mica. Transparent emerald green mica. Superior example. Germany, circa 1880-1915. 25/32". Mint (9.9). $60. (Auction #57, Lot 40).

OTHER HANDMADE. Mica. Lot of two marbles. Both are large shooter green micas. Excellent mica in the marbles. $60. (Auction #104, Lot 37).

OTHER HANDMADE. Mica. Shooter size. Light olive yellow/green marble. Very odd color. Ghost core. Nice layer of mica. 25/32". Near Mint(+) (8.9). $55. (Auction #115, Lot 41).

OTHER HANDMADE. Mica. Green mica. Subsurface layer containing an incredible amount of finely ground mica. 13/16". Mint (9.7). $55. (Auction #93, Lot 17).

OTHER HANDMADE. Mica. Yellow mica. Not the bright yellow color, but the honey amber color. Not quite brown though. 5/8". Mint (9.7). $55. (Auction #162, Lot 31).

OTHER HANDMADE. Mica. Blue mica. Dark blue. Nice layer of mica. Surface in great shape. Germany, circa 1870-1915. 25/32". Mint (9.9). $55. (Auction #109, Lot 32).

OTHER HANDMADE. Mica. Lot of two marbles. Both are large shooter green micas. Excellent mica in the marbles. $55. (Auction #66, Lot 13).

OTHER HANDMADE. Mica. Transparent dark brown base with a nice mica layer. Surface in great shape. Shooter size marble. Germany. 29/32". Mint (9.8). $50. (Auction #67, Lot 41).

OTHER HANDMADE. Mica. Clear mica. Very light green tint to it. In great shape. Shooter. Germany, circa 1870-1915. 7/8". Mint (9.9). $50. (Auction #165, Lot 44).

OTHER HANDMADE. Mica. Lot of two marbles. Both are beauties. First is an aqua mica. Filament core with mica. $46. (Auction #150, Lot 15).

OTHER HANDMADE. Mica. Lot of two micas. Both are blue. Smaller has a mica core. Germany, circa 1870-1915. 9/16" & 21/32". $46. (Auction #59, Lot 8).

OTHER HANDMADE. Mica. Lot of three marbles. Nice group of micas. All are pristine!!!! Clear mica, 19/32", Mint (9.9). Blue. $46. (Auction #103, Lot 11).

OTHER HANDMADE. Mica. Nice shooter size green mica. Two layers of finely ground mica. A melt spot near the bottom pontil. 7/8". Mint(-) (9.2). $45. (Auction #142, Lot 33).

OTHER HANDMADE. Mica. Blue mica. Shooter. Excellent subsurface layer of mica. Loads of tiny air bubbles in the marble. 13/16". Mint (9.9). $45. (Auction #165, Lot 9).

OTHER HANDMADE. Mica. Aqua mica. Super subsurface layer of mica in the marble. One tiny manufacturing mark on the surface. 25/32". Mint (9.6). $45. (Auction #162, Lot 16).

OTHER HANDMADE. Mica. Blue mica. Exceptional marble, in great shape. Germany, circa 1870-1915. 25/32". Mint (9.9). $45. (Auction #56, Lot 9).

OTHER HANDMADE. Mica. Peewee amethyst mica. Super coloring. Very hard color to find. Germany, circa 1870-1915. 1/2". Mint (9.9). $45. (Auction #140, Lot 29).

OTHER HANDMADE. Mica. Emerald green mica. Superb subsurface layer of mica. This one is an absolute beauty! Germany. 11/16". Mint (9.9). $45. (Auction #136, Lot 40).

OTHER HANDMADE. Mica. Lot of four marbles. Blue, aqua, green, brown. All have some minor damage. Germany, circa 1870-1915. $44. (Auction #136, Lot 11).

OTHER HANDMADE. Mica. Dark blue mica. Nice shooter. Excellent core of mica. Minor lobes. Germany, circa 1870-1915. 25/32". Mint (9.9). $42. (Auction #105, Lot 35).

OTHER HANDMADE. Mica. Green mica. Cloud type. Cloud of large mica flakes filling two-thirds of the marble. 21/32". Mint (9.9). $42. (Auction #147, Lot 35).

OTHER HANDMADE. Mica. Blue mica. Nice subsurface layer of mica. Germany, circa 1870-1915. 3/4". Mint (9.7). $42. (Auction #127, Lot 30).

OTHER HANDMADE. Mica. Lot of five marbles. One clear, two blue, two green. 21/32" to 27/32". Near Mint(+) (8.7) to Near Mint. $41. (Auction #115, Lot 8).

OTHER HANDMADE. Mica. Very light green mica. Subsurface layer of excellent mica. Surface is in great shape. Nice example. 25/32". Mint (9.9). $40. (Auction #61, Lot 36).

OTHER HANDMADE. Mica. Lot of four marbles. All are Mint micas. Nice set. Clear, 19/32", Mint (9.9). Green, 5/8", Mint (9.9). $40. (Auction #54, Lot 15).

OTHER HANDMADE. Mica. Shooter green mica. Nice subsurface layer of mica. Super ground pontil. Two small subsurface moons. 1". Near Mint (8.6). $40. (Auction #77, Lot 11).

OTHER HANDMADE. Mica. Green mica. Exceptional subsurface layer of mica. In super shape. Excellent example. Germany. 21/32". Mint (9.9). $39. (Auction #160, Lot 27).

OTHER HANDMADE. Mica. Gorgeous green mica. Core of mica and an outstanding subsurface layer of mica. Surface is pristine. 5/8". Mint (9.9). $39. (Auction #113, Lot 18).

OTHER HANDMADE. Mica. Lot of six marbles. All are Micas. One clear, one very light blue, one aqua, one blue, two green. 5/8". $38. (Auction #139, Lot 15).

OTHER HANDMADE. Mica. Aqua mica. Excellent subsurface layer of finely ground mica. Filament core. Germany, circa 1870-1915. 3/4". Mint (9.7). $37. (Auction #168, Lot 7).

OTHER HANDMADE. Mica. Filament core. Two layers of lots of mica! Stunning marble! Germany, circa 1870-1915. 25/32". Mint (9.9). $37. (Auction #55, Lot 32).

OTHER HANDMADE. Mica. Superb ice blue mica. Nice mica in the marble. Excellent color. In great shape. Germany, circa 1870. 21/32". Mint (9.9). $36. (Auction #60, Lot 31).

OTHER HANDMADE. Mica. Light blue mica. Excellent layer of mica. Nice marble. Germany, circa 1870-1915. 25/32". Mint (9.8). $36. (Auction #62, Lot 32).

OTHER HANDMADE. Mica. Dark blue mica. Nice subsurface layer of mica. Surface in great shape. Germany, circa 1870-1915. 3/4". Mint (9.9). $35. (Auction #100, Lot 5).

OTHER HANDMADE. Mica. Brown mica. Super subsurface layer of mica. There is a huge air bubble in the core. Germany. 23/32". Mint (9.9). $35. (Auction #124, Lot 36).

OTHER HANDMADE. Mica. Green mica. Excellent subsurface layer of mica. Superb marble. Germany, circa 1870-1915. 21/32". Mint (9.9). $35. (Auction #83, Lot 10).

OTHER HANDMADE. Mica. Peewee amethyst mica. Light amethyst color. Big flakes of mica. Excellent marble. Germany. 1/2". Mint (9.9). $35. (Auction #59, Lot 3).

OTHER HANDMADE. Mica. Light brown mica. Core of mica and a nice mica subsurface layer. Slight lobe in the subsurface layer. 5/8". Mint (9.9). $35. (Auction #59, Lot 29).

OTHER HANDMADE. Mica. Blue mica. Beautiful subsurface layer of mica, heavy in some spots. Germany, circa 1870-1915. 11/16". Mint (9.9). $35. (Auction #110, Lot 20).

OTHER HANDMADE. Mica. Green mica. Super subsurface mica layer and some mica in the core. Surface in great shape. Germany. 25/32". Mint (9.9). $35. (Auction #110, Lot 40).

OTHER HANDMADE. Mica. Blue mica. Nice subsurface layer of large mica flakes. Beauty. Germany, circa 1870-1915. 23/32". Mint (9.9). $35. (Auction #176, Lot 19).

OTHER HANDMADE. Mica. Transparent very light smokey gray base. Filament core. Two layers of mica. Surface in great shape. 13/16". Mint (9.5). $34. (Auction #66, Lot 34).

OTHER HANDMADE. Mica. Superior "cloud" mica from near the end of the cane. Transparent dark blue base. Shrunken core. 3/4". Near Mint(+) (8.9). $34. (Auction #76, Lot 35).

OTHER HANDMADE. Mica. Emerald green mica. Ghost core. Subsurface layer of mica flakes. A beauty. Germany, circa 1870-1915. 19/32". Mint (9.9). $34. (Auction #163, Lot 36).

OTHER HANDMADE. Mica. Transparent cobalt blue glass with a fat ribbon of mica inside. Glass is very dark. 13/16". Near Mint (8.6). $34. (Auction #133, Lot 36).

OTHER HANDMADE. Mica. Clear mica. Super subsurface layer of mica. Surface is in great shape. Excellent marble. Germany. 27/32". Mint (9.9). $33. (Auction #58, Lot 39).

OTHER HANDMADE. Mica. Clear mica. Superb "tornado" air bubble core. The core is actually one large air bubble. Excellent. 25/32". Mint (9.8). $33. (Auction #183, Lot 36).

OTHER HANDMADE. Mica. Green mica. Nice flakes in it. Germany, circa 1870-1915. 21/32". Mint (9.9). $32. (Auction #117, Lot 20).

OTHER HANDMADE. Mica. Light green, almost turquoise. Nice layer of mica. Germany, circa 1870-1915. 19/32." Mint (9.9). $32. (Auction #83, Lot 33).

OTHER HANDMADE. Mica. Peewee amethyst mica. Hard marble to find. In great shape. Germany, circa 1870-1915. 1/2". Mint (9.9). $32. (Auction #66, Lot 4).

OTHER HANDMADE. Mica. Lot of six marbles. All are Micas. Two brown and four blue. Nice mica. Each has some damage. 9/16". $32. (Auction #123, Lot 35).

OTHER HANDMADE. Mica. Peewee amethyst mica. Light amethyst color. Big flakes of mica. Tiny subsurface moon near the bottom. 1/2". Near Mint(+) (8.9). $31. (Auction #173, Lot 24).

OTHER HANDMADE. Mica. Lot of two marbles. Both are blue micas. Appear to be same cane based on amount of mica. $30. (Auction #168, Lot 17).

OTHER HANDMADE. Mica. Blue mica. Mica core and nice subsurface layer. Two melt spots. Germany, circa 1870-1915. 19/32". Mint(-) (9). $30. (Auction #83, Lot 30).

OTHER HANDMADE. Mica. Transparent green mica. Core of mica and a subsurface layer of mica. Nice marble. 7/8". Near Mint(+) (8.9). $30. (Auction #122, Lot 49).

OTHER HANDMADE. Mica. Clear Mica. Subsurface layer of mica. Nice twist to the layer and has a fold in it. 11/16". Near Mint(+) (8.9). $30. (Auction #162, Lot 36).

OTHER HANDMADE. Mica. Brown mica. Shooter. Ghost core with mica on it and then a nice subsurface layer of mica. Germany. 13/16". Mint (9.5). $30. (Auction #112, Lot 41).

OTHER HANDMADE. Mica. Blue mica. Gorgeous shade of blue. Nice mica flakes in it. One tiny melt spot. Germany, circa 1870. 21/32". Mint(-) (9.2). $30. (Auction #75, Lot 35).

OTHER HANDMADE. Mica. Light blue mica. Core is mica, no subsurface layer. Very unusual. Germany, circa 1870-1915. 21/32". Mint (9.9). $30. (Auction #87, Lot 28).

OTHER HANDMADE. Mica. Lot of two marbles. Both are shooter micas. Clear, 13/16", Near Mint (8.6). Blue, shrunken mica layer. $30. (Auction #165, Lot 19).

OTHER HANDMADE. Mica. Green mica. Super subsurface layer of mica. Surface in great shape. Germany, circa 1870-1915. 11/16". Mint (9.9). $30. (Auction #77, Lot 26).

OTHER HANDMADE. Mica. Very odd color. Very light olive green. Has an inner with finely ground mica. 11/16". Mint(-) (9.3). $30. (Auction #55, Lot 9).

OTHER HANDMADE. Mica. Yellow mica. Nice coloring. A number of small and tiny moons, with two tiny subsurface moons. Germany. 3/4". Good(+) (7.80). $29. (Auction #175, Lot 37).

OTHER HANDMADE. Mica. Green mica. Two subsurface layers of mica. In great shape. Germany, circa 1870-1915. 19/32". Mint (9.9). $29. (Auction #165, Lot 38).

OTHER HANDMADE. Mica. Lot of two marbles. Both are micas. One is light blue, the other is turquoise. Both have great mica. $28. (Auction #116, Lot 24).

OTHER HANDMADE. Mica. Green mica. In nice shape. 9/16". Mint (9.9). $28. (Auction #175, Lot 11).

OTHER HANDMADE. Mica. Green mica. Ghost core. Subsurface layer of large mica flakes. Small airhole at the top pontil. 5/8". Mint (9.5). $28. (Auction #183, Lot 16).

OTHER HANDMADE. Mica. Outstanding example of a green mica. Core is a ghost core of air bubbles with some mica on it. 19/32". Mint (9.9). $28. (Auction #118, Lot 37).

OTHER HANDMADE. Mica. Lot of two marbles. Both are beauties. First is a clear mica. Mica core and a mica subsurface layer. $28. (Auction #142, Lot 8).

OTHER HANDMADE. Mica. Gorgeous green mica. Two layers of mica in the marble. Superb example and in pristine shape. Germany. 11/16". Mint (9.9). $28. (Auction #70, Lot 32).

OTHER HANDMADE. Mica. Lot of two marbles. Both are beauties. First is a clear mica. Mica core and a mica subsurface layer. $28. (Auction #140, Lot 35).

OTHER HANDMADE. Mica. This is an absolutely beautiful mica. Light blue glass. Has an inner mica core. 27/32". Near Mint(+) (8.9). $27. (Auction #58, Lot 10).

OTHER HANDMADE. Mica. Blue mica. Light blue. Filament core. Two layers of mica. A beauty. Germany, circa 1870-1915. 11/16". Mint (9.9). $27. (Auction #120, Lot 15).

OTHER HANDMADE. Mica. Very unusual peewee. Green core!! Subsurface layer of mica flakes and stretched air bubbles. 1/2". Mint (9.9). $27. (Auction #169, Lot 12).

OTHER HANDMADE. Mica. Transparent aqua mica. Mica core and a super subsurface layer of mica. One extremely tiny pit. 11/16". Mint(-) (9). $27. (Auction #97, Lot 37).

OTHER HANDMADE. Mica. Lot of two marbles. Blue mica and a green mica. Both are outstanding. Both about 5/8" and Mint (9.9). $27. (Auction #95, Lot 13).

OTHER HANDMADE. Mica. Blue mica. Shooter. Wispy white core. Subsurface layer of finely ground mica. A couple of tiny pinpricks. 3/4". Mint(-) (9). $27. (Auction #165, Lot 4).

OTHER HANDMADE. Mica. Very hard to find type of mica. Transparent aqua glass. 21/32". Mint(-) (9). $26. (Auction #130, Lot 13).

OTHER HANDMADE. Mica. Nice green mica. Mica core as well as a mica subsurface layer. Several small manufacturing melt spot. 3/4". Mint(-) (9.1). $26. (Auction #63, Lot 34).

OTHER HANDMADE. Mica. Blue mica. Dark blue. Nice layer of mica. One tiny flat spot and one tiny pinprick on it. Germany. 11/16". Mint(-) (9.2). $26. (Auction #88, Lot 32).

OTHER HANDMADE. Mica. Blue mica. Gorgeous color. Nice layer of mica, shrunken. One tiny rough spot on the surface. Germany. 13/16". Mint(-) (9.2). $26. (Auction #62, Lot 19).

OTHER HANDMADE. Mica. Transparent ice blue. Loads of very tiny air bubbles in the marble. Two layers of mica. 19/32". Mint (9.9). $26. (Auction #96, Lot 16).

OTHER HANDMADE. Mica. Brown mica. Tiny marble. Super mica flakes in the marble. Outstanding example. Germany, circa 1870. 17/32". Mint (9.9). $26. (Auction #65, Lot 25).

OTHER HANDMADE. Mica. Light turquoise color. Gorgeous sprinkling of finely ground mica and loads of very tiny air bubbles. 5/8". Mint (9.9). $25. (Auction #84, Lot 29).

OTHER HANDMADE. Mica. Lot of two marbles. Both are green micas. Shooters. Each has a couple of tiny pits or tiny moons. Germany. $25. (Auction #73, Lot 31).

OTHER HANDMADE. Mica. Shrunken core cloud mica. Transparent green base with a rectangular shaped mica core. Subsurface moons. 13/16". Good(+) (7.70). $25. (Auction #89, Lot 36).

OTHER HANDMADE. Mica. Clear mica. Nice subsurface layer of mica. Two small manufacturing melt spots. Germany, circa 1870. 21/32". Mint (9.5). $25. (Auction #62, Lot 35).

OTHER HANDMADE. Mica. Clear mica. Air bubble core. Subsurface layer of mica and stretched tiny air bubbles. In great shape. 11/16". Mint (9.9). $25. (Auction #184, Lot 23).

OTHER HANDMADE. Mica. Lot of two marbles. Green mica, great mica flakes, 21/32", Mint (9.9). Brown mica, light wear, 9/16". $25. (Auction #60, Lot 10).

OTHER HANDMADE. Mica. Dark brown mica. Core of mica and a subsurface layer of mica. Very nice. In great shape. Germany. 23/32". Mint (9.8). $25. (Auction #168, Lot 1).

OTHER HANDMADE. Mica. Peewee mica. Transparent teal marble. Light subsurface layer of mica. Surface in great shape. Germany. 15/32". Mint (9.9). $25. (Auction #126, Lot 6).

OTHER HANDMADE. Mica. Peewee. Green mica. Very nice mica in the marble. Germany, circa 1870-1915. 15/32". Mint (9.9). $25. (Auction #81, Lot 1).

OTHER HANDMADE. Mica. Brown mica. Small melt spot on one side and slightly flattened on that side too. Surface has no damage. 25/32". Mint (9.5). $24. (Auction #113, Lot 10).

OTHER HANDMADE. Mica. Nice shooter blue mica. Ghost core. Excellent subsurface layer of mica. Some surface wear. Germany. 13/16". Mint(-) (9). $24. (Auction #95, Lot 34).

OTHER HANDMADE. Mica. Green mica. Mica core and a subsurface layer of mica. One small melt pit. Nice looking marble. Germany. 11/16". Mint(-) (9.1). $24. (Auction #182, Lot 37).

OTHER HANDMADE. Mica. Lot of two marbles. A green mica and a clear mica. 21/32" & Near Mint(+) (8.9), 23/32" & Near Mint(+) (8.9). $24. (Auction #144, Lot 7).

OTHER HANDMADE. Mica. Rare pale amethyst mica. This color is very hard to find. Light amethyst! Nice mica. Some haziness. 17/32". Near Mint (8.6). $23. (Auction #71, Lot 35).

OTHER HANDMADE. Mica. Lot of two marbles. Both are beauties. First is a clear mica. Mica core and a mica subsurface layer. $23. (Auction #145, Lot 3).

OTHER HANDMADE. Mica. Yellow mica. Hard to find this color. Excellent subsurface layer of mica. One large chip. 21/32". Good(+) (7.90). $23. (Auction #131, Lot 11).

OTHER HANDMADE. Mica. Gorgeous green mica. Nice subsurface layer with excellent mica. A couple of very tiny pits. Germany. 11/16". Mint(-) (9). $23. (Auction #98, Lot 17).

OTHER HANDMADE. Mica. Blue mica. Peewee. Good mica flakes. Nice marble, in great shape. Germany, circa 1870-1915. 1/2". Mint (9.9). $22. (Auction #66, Lot 38).

OTHER HANDMADE. Mica. Lot of four marbles. All are clear micas. One has a ghost core. Each has tiny moons or hits on them. $22. (Auction #73, Lot 10).

OTHER HANDMADE. Mica. Very dark transparent cobalt blue. Super subsurface layer of mica. Surface in excellent shape. Germany. 3/4". Mint (9.9). $22. (Auction #85, Lot 38).

OTHER HANDMADE. Mica. Very light green. Peewee. Nice subsurface layer of mica. One tiny melt spot. Germany, circa 1870. 1/2". Mint (9.5). $22. (Auction #130, Lot 37).

OTHER HANDMADE. Mica. Yellow mica. Hard to find this color. Excellent subsurface layer of mica. One large chip. 3/4". Good(+) (7.90). $22. (Auction #129, Lot 6).

OTHER HANDMADE. Mica. Blue mica. Two layers of mica. In great shape. Germany, circa 1870-1915. 21/32". Mint (9.9). $22. (Auction #100, Lot 19).

OTHER HANDMADE. Mica. Clear mica. Ghost core. Almost all the mica is on side. Nice big flakes on that side though. 5/8". Mint(-) (9.1). $22. (Auction #78, Lot 9).

OTHER HANDMADE. Mica. Dark blue glass. Finely ground mica just below the surface and lots of stretched air bubbles. 25/32". Mint(-) (9.2). $21. (Auction #120, Lot 10).

OTHER HANDMADE. Mica. Green mica. Some large flakes just below the surface and some flakes forming around the core. Germany. 11/16". Mint (9.4). $21. (Auction #110, Lot 11).

OTHER HANDMADE. Mica. Green mica. Small marble and a beauty. Germany, circa 1870-1915. 17/32". Mint (9.9). $21. (Auction #69, Lot 32).

OTHER HANDMADE. Mica. Green mica. Excellent subsurface layer of mica. There is one very tiny, barely visible surface flake. 25/32". Near Mint(+) (8.9). $21. (Auction #185, Lot 26).

OTHER HANDMADE. Mica. Lot of two marbles. Both are brown mica. Neither is Mint. 9/16". Near Mint(+) (8.8) and Near Mint. $21. (Auction #117, Lot 4).

OTHER HANDMADE. Mica. Lot of two marbles. Blue mica, several manufacturing pits, 19/32", Mint(-) (9.0). The other is clear. $21. (Auction #63, Lot 12).

OTHER HANDMADE. Mica. Very nice amethyst mica. This color is hard to find. Inner core of tiny air bubbles. Subsurface layer. 21/32". Near Mint(+) (8.9). $21. (Auction #61, Lot 24).

OTHER HANDMADE. Mica. Lot of two marbles. First is green. Two layers of mica. 17/32". Mint (9.9). The other is clear. $20. (Auction #166, Lot 10).

OTHER HANDMADE. Mica. Lot of two marbles. Both are blue micas. One has a lot of finely ground mica. $20. (Auction #128, Lot 9).

OTHER HANDMADE. Mica. Transparent clear base. Thin green core. Ghost core surrounding that with some mica on it. 9/16". Mint (9.9). $20. (Auction #90, Lot 12).

OTHER HANDMADE. Mica. Green mica. Subsurface layer of large flakes of mica. A beauty. Germany, circa 1870-1915. 5/8". Mint (9.9). $20. (Auction #164, Lot 6).

OTHER HANDMADE. Mica. Clear mica. Superb subsurface layer of mica. One side is shrunken. This is a stunning marble! Germany. 19/32". Mint (9.9). $20. (Auction #85, Lot 7).

OTHER HANDMADE. Mica. Clear mica. Nice flakes in the mica layer. Germany, circa 1880-1915. 5/8". Mint (9.9). $20. (Auction #64, Lot 31).

OTHER HANDMADE. Mica. Lot of three marbles. Clear mica, 19/32", Near Mint(+) (8.9). Aqua mica, 9/16", Near Mint(+) (8.7). $20. (Auction #82, Lot 6).

OTHER HANDMADE. Mica. Green mica. Filament core. Deep subsurface layer of mica. A beauty. Germany, circa 1870-1915. 11/16". Mint (9.9). $19. (Auction #124, Lot 2).

OTHER HANDMADE. Mica. Green mica. Nice layer of mica. One rough spot. Germany, circa 1870-1915. 5/8". Near Mint(+) (8.9). $19. (Auction #125, Lot 41).

OTHER HANDMADE. Mica. Lot of three marbles. Green (8.9), blue (9.1), clear (9.9). All 5/8". $19. (Auction #106, Lot 4).

OTHER HANDMADE. Mica. Clear mica. Excellent subsurface layer of mica. No twist. Interesting effect. Germany, circa 1870-1915. 21/32". Mint (9.8). $19. (Auction #167, Lot 15).

OTHER HANDMADE. Mica. Clear mica. Nice mica in it. Germany, circa 1870-1915. 11/16". Mint (9.9). $18. (Auction #119, Lot 43).

OTHER HANDMADE. Mica. Lot of three marbles. Aqua, two blue. The aqua has some chips. The blues have some rough spots. 1/2". $18. (Auction #145, Lot 20).

OTHER HANDMADE. Mica. Transparent clear mica. Filament green core. Surrounded by a white "ghost" core. 9/16". Mint(-) (9.2). $18. (Auction #129, Lot 10).

OTHER HANDMADE. Mica. Aqua shooter. Large subsurface pieces of mica. Several small chips. Germany, circa 1870-1915. 13/16". Near Mint(-) (8). $18. (Auction #137, Lot 32).

OTHER HANDMADE. Mica. Transparent teal blue mica. Nice subsurface layer of mica. Two thin bands in the core. 19/32". Mint (9.9). $18. (Auction #153, Lot 2).

OTHER HANDMADE. Mica. Peewee aqua mica. Two rough spots. Very pretty. Germany, circa 1870-1915. 15/32". Near Mint(+) (8.9). $17. (Auction #138, Lot 2).

OTHER HANDMADE. Mica. Clear mica. Nice subsurface layer of mica. A beauty. Germany, circa 1870-1915. 17/32". Mint (9.9). $17. (Auction #168, Lot 11).

OTHER HANDMADE. Mica. Lot of four marbles. Green, blue, brown. Also, one banded swirl (no mica). All have damage. 5/8". $17. (Auction #166, Lot 13).

OTHER HANDMADE. Mica. Clear mica shooter. Interesting. Ghost core surrounded by small air bubbles. Subsurface layer of mica. 27/32". Near Mint (8.5). $17. (Auction #168, Lot 37).

OTHER HANDMADE. Mica. Lot of three marbles. All three are minutes. Two are transparent clear and one is transparent green. $17. (Auction #87, Lot 12).

OTHER HANDMADE. Mica. Beautiful green mica. Nice mica in it. A beauty. Germany, circa 1870-1915. 17/32". Mint (9.7). $17. (Auction #168, Lot 19).

OTHER HANDMADE. Mica. Brown mica. Nice layer of mica. Smaller marble. One pit. Germany, circa 1870-1915. 9/16". Near Mint(+) (8.9). $16. (Auction #63, Lot 26).

OTHER HANDMADE. Mica. Blue mica. Nice subsurface layer of mica. Germany, circa 1870-1915. 19/32." Mint (9.9). $16. (Auction #116, Lot 32).

OTHER HANDMADE. Mica. Lot of two marbles. Both are green micas. Light dusting of mica in each. One has a tiny fracture. $16. (Auction #104, Lot 10).

OTHER HANDMADE. Mica. Lot of two marbles. Green, 5/8", Near Mint (8.5). Clear, 9/16", Mint (9.9). $16. (Auction #97, Lot 11).

OTHER HANDMADE. Mica. Lot of four marbles. Light brown, two blue, green. All have been used. 9/16" to 13/16". Near Mint. $16. (Auction #171, Lot 13).

OTHER HANDMADE. Mica. Green mica. Excellent subsurface layer of mica, shrunken on one side. One tiny subsurface moon. Germany. 11/16". Near Mint(+) (8.9). $16. (Auction #184, Lot 19).

OTHER HANDMADE. Mica. Clear mica. Peewee. In great shape. Germany, circa 1870-1915. 1/2". Mint (9.9). 1/2". Mint (9.9). $16. (Auction #93, Lot 34).

OTHER HANDMADE. Mica. Lot of two marbles. Blue mica, 5/8", Near Mint (8.5). Green mica, 25/32", Good (7.6). $16. (Auction #89, Lot 31).

OTHER HANDMADE. Mica. Blue mica. Small manufacturing melt spot on it. Germany, circa 1870-1915. 21/32". Mint(-) (9.2). $15. (Auction #118, Lot 9).

OTHER HANDMADE. Mica. Blue mica. Subsurface moon and some pitting. 5/8". Near Mint(+) (8.7). $15. (Auction #174, Lot 35).

OTHER HANDMADE. Mica. Blue mica. In nice shape. One tiny pit. Germany, circa 1870-1915. 3/4". Near Mint(+) (8.9). $15. (Auction #60, Lot 17).

OTHER HANDMADE. Mica. Transparent clear base. Very slightly smoky. Shooter. Nice mica. Some very tiny flaking and pitting. 29/32". Near Mint (8.5). $15. (Auction #61, Lot 2).

OTHER HANDMADE. Mica. Nice blue mica. Small marble. Nice mica. One very tiny pinprick. Peewee, just barely fitting through. 1/2". Mint(-) (9.3). $15. (Auction #71, Lot 13).

OTHER HANDMADE. Mica. Small marble. Blue mica. Nice mica in it. Surface in great shape. Germany, circa 1870-1915. 17/32". Mint (9.9). $14. (Auction #67, Lot 12).

OTHER HANDMADE. Mica. Peewee clear mica. Filament core with mica around it too. Germany, circa 1870-1915. 1/2". Mint (9.9). $14. (Auction #128, Lot 19).

OTHER HANDMADE. Mica. Clear mica. Nice subsurface mica. In great shape. Germany, circa 1870-1915. 9/16". Mint (9.9). $14. (Auction #165, Lot 30).

OTHER HANDMADE. Mica. Brown mica. Nice sprinkling of mica. Slightly flattened. A couple of tiny pinpricks. Germany. 11/16". Mint(-) (9.1). $13. (Auction #171, Lot 8).

OTHER HANDMADE. Mica. Blue mica. One tiny subsurface moon. Germany, circa 1870-1915. 21/32". Near Mint(+) (8.9). $12. (Auction #177, Lot 35).

OTHER HANDMADE. Mica. Green core. Subsurface layer of mica flakes and stretched air bubbles. In great shape. Germany. 1/2". Mint (9.9). $12. (Auction #145, Lot 16).

OTHER HANDMADE. Mica. Turquoise mica. One flake and some pits. Germany, circa 1870-1915. 11/16". Near Mint (8.6). $12. (Auction #118, Lot 2).

OTHER HANDMADE. Mica. Blue mica. Very dark blue. Shrunken layer of mica. One small manufacturing chip. Germany, circa 1870. 21/32". Mint(-) (9). $12. (Auction #62, Lot 3).

OTHER HANDMADE. Mica. Transparent clear mica. One tiny manufacturing pit. Nice mica. Germany, circa 1870-1915. 17/32". Mint (9.6). $11. (Auction #92, Lot 7).

OTHER HANDMADE. Mica. Lot of two marbles. Both are blue micas. 23/32" & Near Mint (8.6). 7/8" & poorly buffed. $11. (Auction #184, Lot 8).

OTHER HANDMADE. Mica. Lot of two marbles. Both are micas. Both have been polished. One is brown, 25/32". The other is clear. $10. (Auction #63, Lot 8).

OTHER HANDMADE. Mica. Small clear mica. Very nice marble. Germany, circa 1870-1915. 17/32". Mint (9.9). $10. (Auction #105, Lot 2).

OTHER HANDMADE. Mica. Blue mica. Almost translucent. Nice cloud of mica in the marble. There are tiny pits on the surface. 25/32". Near Mint(+) (8.7). $10. (Auction #69, Lot 28).

OTHER HANDMADE. Mica. Brown mica. Three small chips. 19/32". Germany, circa 1870-1915. 19/32". Near Mint (8.5). $10. (Auction #97, Lot 8).

OTHER HANDMADE. Mica. Light green mica. One small moon, severa tinier moons. Germany, circa 1870-1915. 21/32". Near Mint (8.4). $10. (Auction #107, Lot 33).

OTHER HANDMADE. Mica. Very, very dark transparent green base. Has mica in it. Some pitting and hits on the surface. 11/16". Near Mint (8.6). $9. (Auction #69, Lot 13).

OTHER HANDMADE. Mica. Transparent clear mica. Very nice, smaller marble. Germany, circa 1870-1915. 1/2". Mint (9.9). $9. (Auction #154, Lot 11).

OTHER HANDMADE. Mica. Peewee clear mica. Nice mica flakes. Two pits and a small moon. Germany, circa 1870-1915. 1/2". Near Mint (8.6). $9. (Auction #122, Lot 30).

OTHER HANDMADE. Mica. Clear mica. One tiny subsurface moon. Germany, circa 1870-1915. 17/32". Near Mint(+) (8.8). $4. (Auction #109, Lot 5).

OTHER HANDMADE. Mist. Superb marble! Three panel Mist. Subsurface panels of transparent pink, transparent blue. 21/32". Mint(-) (9.2). $200. (Auction #164, Lot 44).

OTHER HANDMADE. Mist. Very hard to find Mist. Transparent clear base. Subsurface layer of transparent pink bands. 11/16". Mint (9.9). $120. (Auction #150, Lot 38).

OTHER HANDMADE. Mist. Mist marble. Superior example. Transparent clear glass with lots of stretched tiny air bubbles in it. 11/16". Mint (9.9). $110. (Auction #140, Lot 48).

OTHER HANDMADE. Mist. Absolutely outstanding example of a mist. And large, you hardly ever see them this large. 1". Near Mint(+) (9.7). $100. (Auction #181, Lot 38).

OTHER HANDMADE. Mist. Outstanding mist with mica. Very hard color combination to find. Transparent clear base. 9/16". Mint (9.9). $90. (Auction #80, Lot 38).

OTHER HANDMADE. Mist. Super end of cane mist. Transparent clear base. Green filament core. One subsurface band of blue. 7/8". Near Mint(+) (8.9). $90. (Auction #128, Lot 49).

OTHER HANDMADE. Mist. I can't really think of what else to call this except that it is a banded swirl/mist hybrid. 15/32". Mint (9.9). $85. (Auction #148, Lot 48).

OTHER HANDMADE. Mist. Superb mist with mica. Transparent clear base. Subsurface layer of transparent blue bands. Nice coat. 11/16". Near Mint(+) (8.8). $70. (Auction #170, Lot 43).

OTHER HANDMADE. Mist. Transparent clear base. Subsurface layer of transparent blue bands and one transparent green band. 21/32". Near Mint(+) (8.9). $70. (Auction #93, Lot 2).

OTHER HANDMADE. Mist. Looks like a blue mica at first glance, but is actually a mist with mica. Transparent clear base. 21/32". Mint (9.9). $70. (Auction #77, Lot 32).

OTHER HANDMADE. Mist. Very unusual marble. At first glance, it appears to be a banded swirl in transparent smoky gray glass. 5/8". Mint(-) (9.2). $60. (Auction #74, Lot 6).

OTHER HANDMADE. Mist. Beautiful mist. Four panel marble. Transparent clear base. Two panels of transparent blue. 11/16". Mint (9.7). $60. (Auction #71, Lot 15).

OTHER HANDMADE. Mist. Transparent light aqua blue base. Outer surface is covered by stretched opaque yellow strands. 19/32". Mint (9.2). $56. (Auction #57, Lot 31).

OTHER HANDMADE. Mist. Very nice marble. Transparent clear base. Two subsurface panels of opaque white and transparent blue. 3/4". Mint(-) (9). $55. (Auction #89, Lot 40).

OTHER HANDMADE. Mist. Super Mist! Transparent clear base. Filament core. Subsurface layer of transparent green. 21/32". Mint(-) (9.2). $55. (Auction #62, Lot 37).

OTHER HANDMADE. Mist. Very unusual marble. At first I thought it was an odd Indian, until I took a maglite to it. 5/8". Mint (9.9). $55. (Auction #149, Lot 46).

OTHER HANDMADE. Mist. Transparent clear base. Subsurface layer of transparent blue with mica. Two tiny manufacturing melt . 21/32". Mint(-) (9). $55. (Auction #162, Lot 46).

OTHER HANDMADE. Mist. Nice mist!!!! Transparent clear base. Subsurface layer of translucent blue bands. 11/16". Near Mint(+) (8.7). $50. (Auction #81, Lot 27).

OTHER HANDMADE. Mist. Very nice, and hard to find, mist with mica. Transparent clear mica. Core of transparent green bands. 13/16". Near Mint (8.4). $42. (Auction #92, Lot 9).

OTHER HANDMADE. Mist. Peewee mist. Transparent clear base. Subsurface layer of translucent light blue and white bands. 15/32". Mint (9.9). $42. (Auction #74, Lot 10).

OTHER HANDMADE. Mist. Very nice Mist with mica. Transparent clear base. Subsurface layer of transparent blue and green band. 5/8". Near Mint(+) (8.9). $38. (Auction #154, Lot 8).

OTHER HANDMADE. Mist. From near the end of the cane. Transparent clear base. $36. (Auction #56, Lot 36).

OTHER HANDMADE. Mist. End of cane mist marble. Transparent aqua base. There are some wispy white bands. 15/16". Near Mint(-) (8.1). $32. (Auction #104, Lot 6).

OTHER HANDMADE. Mist. Rare colors. Transparent clear base. Subsurface layer of transparent yellow with loads of mica. $30. (Auction #91, Lot 2).

OTHER HANDMADE. Mist. Transparent clear base. Subsurface layer of transparent green with some translucent orange bands. 5/8". Near Mint (8.6). $24. (Auction #161, Lot 37).

OTHER HANDMADE. Mist. Transparent clear base. Subsurface layer of transparent blue with mica. A chip, subsurface moon. 25/32". Near Mint(-) (8). $16. (Auction #123, Lot 2).

OTHER HANDMADE. Opaque. This has to be one of the finest examples of a pink opaque I have ever seen. Actually, semi-opaque. 25/32". Near Mint(+) (8.9). $150. (Auction #92, Lot 42).

OTHER HANDMADE. Opaque. Lot of six marbles. Smaller opaques. Several hard colors to find. Olive green, salmon pink, light blue. $55. (Auction #177, Lot 32).

OTHER HANDMADE. Opaque. Semi-opaque opalescent white handmade two-pontil marble. A handmade moonie! Surface is pristine. 25/32". Mint (9.9). $55. (Auction #110, Lot 29).

OTHER HANDMADE. Opaque. Semi-opaque white two-pontil handmade. A couple of small subsurface moons and some sparkles. 1-1/8". Near Mint(+) (8.7). $45. (Auction #168, Lot 5).

OTHER HANDMADE. Opaque. Semi-opaque light blue marble. Two pontils. Nice shade of blue. One very tiny flake. Surface is great. 13/16". Near Mint(+) (8.9). $42. (Auction #147, Lot 4).

OTHER HANDMADE. Opaque. Lot of five marbles. All are harder to find colors, but all have some minor damage. $40. (Auction #121, Lot 38).

OTHER HANDMADE. Opaque. Semi-opaque blue. Gorgeous color. Several small and tiny sparkles. Two pontil. German or American. 3/4". Mint(-) (9). $40. (Auction #168, Lot 42).

OTHER HANDMADE. Opaque. Opaque rose-pink marble. Nice coloring. Has a discoloration spot on one side, typical of this type. 11/16". Mint(-) (9). $38. (Auction #160, Lot 2).

OTHER HANDMADE. Opaque. Lot of two marbles. First is a semi-opaque white. Several very tiny chips and some tiny subsurface moons. $32. (Auction #160, Lot 8).

OTHER HANDMADE. Opaque. Lot of two marbles. Semi-opaque white, 11/16", Near Mint(+) (8.7). Other is opaque green, 3/4", Near Mint. $28. (Auction #56, Lot 6).

OTHER HANDMADE. Opaque. Two pontil blue opaque. Shooter. Cold roll line near top. One small moon. A couple of tiny pits. Germany. 29/32". Near Mint(+) (8.8). $27. (Auction #172, Lot 42).

OTHER HANDMADE. Opaque. Rose pink two-pontil opaque. Very nice color. Three tiny moons and some tiny pinpricking. Hard color. 13/16". Near Mint (8.5). $27. (Auction #185, Lot 10).

OTHER HANDMADE. Opaque. Two pontil opaque. Semi-opaque white. Lots of tiny stretched air bubbles. Tiny annealing fracture. 7/8". Near Mint(+) (8.9). $26. (Auction #147, Lot 45).

OTHER HANDMADE. Opaque. Green opaque. Two pontil. Very nice. One sparkle, but an excellent example. German or American. 23/32". Mint(-) (9.2). $26. (Auction #154, Lot 1).

OTHER HANDMADE. Opaque. Translucent opalescent white opaque. Two pontils. Ghost core. Slightly opalescent. 25/32". Near Mint(+) (8.7). $26. (Auction #147, Lot 17).

OTHER HANDMADE. Opaque. Lot of eight marbles. All are two pontil handmade marbles. Three are black opaques. 19/32". Mint. $25. (Auction #145, Lot 7).

OTHER HANDMADE. Opaque. Two pontil green opaque. Actually, semi-opaque. Probably German, possibly American, circa 1880-1920. 9/16". Mint (9.7). $24. (Auction #162, Lot 9).

OTHER HANDMADE. Opaque. Lot of six marbles. All are two pontil handmade ballot box marbles. All about 17/32". Mint to Near Mint. $22. (Auction #95, Lot 27).

OTHER HANDMADE. Opaque. Lot of five marbles. All are white opaque two pontil. Ballot box marbles. German, possibly American. $21. (Auction #136, Lot 6).

OTHER HANDMADE. Opaque. Semi-opaque green. Two pontils. Germany or United States, circa 1880-1920. 5/8". Mint (9.8). $20. (Auction #97, Lot 10).

OTHER HANDMADE. Opaque. Lot of three marbles. Two are white glazed china. No decoration. 1/2". Mint (9.9). The other is a blue. $19. (Auction #83, Lot 11).

OTHER HANDMADE. Opaque. Lot of three marbles. Two white opaques and one black. All are two pontil ballot box marbles. 9/16". Mint (9.9). $17. (Auction #116, Lot 5).

OTHER HANDMADE. Opaque. Two pontil black ballot box marble. Two pontil opaque. Germany or American, circa 1880-1920. 9/16". Mint (9.5). $16. (Auction #59, Lot 37).

OTHER HANDMADE. Opaque. Lot of four marbles. White, light green, green, blue. All have some damage. 5/8" to 3/4". Near Mint. $16. (Auction #165, Lot 17).

OTHER HANDMADE. Opaque. Lot of four ballot box marbles. Two are black two pontil handmade glass, one is a white china. $14. (Auction #102, Lot 6).

OTHER HANDMADE. Opaque. Opaque white two-pontil. Very, very light aqua tint to it. One small flake and some sparkles. German. 25/32". Near Mint (8.6). $14. (Auction #154, Lot 36).

OTHER HANDMADE. Opaque. Opaque blue two-pontil marble. One flake and a couple of areas of very light roughness. German or American. 19/32". Near Mint (8.4). $14. (Auction #118, Lot 13).

OTHER HANDMADE. Opaque. Lot of two marbles. Both are two pontil handmade opaques. Green, 25/32", Good (7.6). White. 13/16". $14. (Auction #80, Lot 7).

OTHER HANDMADE. Opaque. Lot of three marbles. All are white opaques. Each is two pontil. $12. (Auction #148, Lot 4).

OTHER HANDMADE. Opaque. Lot of three marbles. White opaque ballot box marbles. Two pontil each. Either American or German. $11. (Auction #162, Lot 3).

OTHER HANDMADE. Opaque. Lot of three marbles. Nice assortment. Black ballot box marble, 17/32", Mint (9.7). $11. (Auction #97, Lot 13).

OTHER HANDMADE. Original box. An original "Big Dime Special" cardboard box. Distributed by J. Pressman & Co., Inc. New York. $70. (Auction #93, Lot 21).

OTHER HANDMADE. Paperweight. Rare paperweight or confetti marble. Transparent clear base. Chunks of white, yellow and red glass. 21/32". Mint (9.8). $160. (Auction #173, Lot 48).

OTHER HANDMADE. Patch. Lot of three marbles. All peewees. Nice set of patches. I am not sure who the manufacturer is. $6. (Auction #73, Lot 8).

OTHER HANDMADE. Premium. Lot of three items. Poly tubes filled with five 5/8" catseyes. The marbles are probably Heaton Agate. $15. (Auction #138, Lot 46).

OTHER HANDMADE. Premium. Poly tube filled with five 5/8" catseyes. The marbles are probably Heaton Agate Company. $7. (Auction #118, Lot 26.40).

OTHER HANDMADE. Premium. Poly tube filled with five 5/8" catseyes. The marbles are probably Heaton Agate Company. $7. (Auction #118, Lot 26).

OTHER HANDMADE. Premium. Poly tube filled with five 5/8" catseyes. The marbles are probably Heaton Agate Company. $7. (Auction #118, Lot 26.20).

OTHER HANDMADE. Premium. Poly tube filled with five 5/8" catseyes. The marbles are probably Heaton Agate Company. $7. (Auction #118, Lot 26.30).

OTHER HANDMADE. Slag. Superior two pontil handmade slag. Very hard to find. Very dark purple glass with white and swirls. 13/16". Mint (9.9). $140. (Auction #103, Lot 26).

OTHER HANDMADE. Slag. Very hard to find handmade slag. This one is transparent dark purple with lots of white. Two pontils. $95. (Auction #148, Lot 38).

OTHER HANDMADE. Slag. Handmade two-pontil slag. Opaque black with bands of white. One small air hole. Nice marble! German. 21/32". Mint (9.5). $55. (Auction #66, Lot 29).

OTHER HANDMADE. Slag. Two pontil, handmade slag. Opaque black with wispy white blankets. In pristine shape. Possibly German. 5/8". Mint (9.9). $47. (Auction #115, Lot 43).

OTHER HANDMADE. Slag. Opaque black base with blankets of white on the surface. Lots of black showing through. 21/32". Near Mint (8.6). $27. (Auction #73, Lot 7).

OTHER HANDMADE. Slag. Two-pontil slag. Semi-opaque dark purple base with opaque white swirls in it. Usually these are black. 3/4". Near Mint(+) (8.7). $17. (Auction #154, Lot 28).

OTHER HANDMADE. Submarine. Transparent light green base. Two subsurface bands of opaque white. 23/32". Mint (9.9). $160. (Auction #116, Lot 50).

OTHER HANDMADE. Submarine. Lot of two marbles. Matched pair off the same cane. Very rare! I've classified these as submarine. Near Mint(-) . $145. (Auction #160, Lot 10).

OTHER HANDMADE. Submarine. Very interesting submarine. Transparent aquamarine base glass. There is an outer layer of two bands. 5/8". Mint (9.9). $100. (Auction #59, Lot 43).

OTHER HANDMADE. Submarine. Hard marble to find. Opaque blue base. Two surface bands covering about sixty five percent of the marble. $70. (Auction #55, Lot 43).

OTHER HANDMADE. Swirl. Lot of about sixty marbles. Assortment of transparent swirls. Predominately Champion Agate. $15. (Auction #109, Lot 27).

OTHER HANDMADE. Translucent. Two pontil translucent. Translucent blue. A beauty and hard to find. A couple of very tiny pits. 11/16". Near Mint(+) (8.9). $36. (Auction #87, Lot 2).

OTHER HANDMADE. Translucent. Two pontil handmade translucent white. Possibly German or American, circa 1870-1920. 19/32". Mint (9.5). $13. (Auction #85, Lot 4.20).

OTHER HANDMADE. Translucent. Two pontil handmade translucent white. Possibly German or American, circa 1870-1920. 19/32". Mint (9.5). $13. (Auction #85, Lot 4.30).

OTHER HANDMADE. Translucent. Two pontil handmade translucent white. Possibly German or American, circa 1870-1920. 19/32". Mint (9.5). $13. (Auction #85, Lot 4).

OTHER HANDMADE. Translucent. Two pontil translucent. Light green. Some overall light wear and a subsurface moon. German or American. 19/32". Near Mint(+) (8.9). $12. (Auction #103, Lot 28).

OTHER HANDMADE. Wire pull. Transparent clear base. "Lumpy" orange wire with translucent white next to it. In great shape. German. 29/32". Mint (9.9). $26. (Auction #76, Lot 27).

OTHER MACHINE MADE. Lot of approximately one hundred marbles. All are fluorescent. Assortment of swirls, patches, Rainbo. $60. (Auction #132, Lot 25).

OTHER MACHINE MADE. Lot of six marbles. Christensen Agate swirl, 5/8", Near Mint(+) (8.8). Peltier Glass Wasp, 19/32". $34. (Auction #175, Lot 6).

OTHER MACHINE MADE. Lot of three marbles. These are referred to as corals. They are not Christensen Agate. $31. (Auction #171, Lot 20).

OTHER MACHINE MADE. Unknown manufacturer. Alley has been suggested by some, but the pattern does not look like any other. 9/16". Mint(-) (9.1). $20. (Auction #96, Lot 19).

OTHER MACHINE MADE. Lot of two marbles. My guess is that they are Champion Agate. Transparent clear base with pink blank. $17. (Auction #73, Lot 16).

OTHER MACHINE MADE. Lot of two items. Both are the red ten cent Marbles jobber boxes. One is filled with chinese checker. $15. (Auction #143, Lot 34).

OTHER MACHINE MADE. Lot of approximately eighty marbles. All are Japanese chinese checker marbles. Transparent clear base. $15. (Auction #177, Lot 11).

OTHER MACHINE MADE. Lot of two marbles. Unknown manufacturer, but probably Champion Agate. First is a wire pull. $14. (Auction #69, Lot 12).

OTHER MACHINE MADE. Lot of two marbles. First is a Champion Agate transparent red with bright yellow swirl New Old Fashion. $12. (Auction #69, Lot 8).

OTHER MACHINE MADE. I am not completely certain as to the manufacturer of this marble, but I think it is Champion Agate . 17/32". Mint (9.9). $10. (Auction #61, Lot 31).

OTHER MACHINE MADE. Modern comic marble. Modern Marble King patch marble with a multicolor silk screen of Sambo on it. 27/32". Mint (9.9). $9. (Auction #92, Lot 3).

OTHER MACHINE MADE. Either Alley Agate or Ravenswood Novelty. Shooter. Opaque white base. Lavender swirls. 29/32". Mint(-) (9). $6. (Auction #101, Lot 14).

OTHER MACHINE MADE. Lot of twelve marbles. Six are opalescent yellow and six are semi-opaque pink. About 9/16". $4. (Auction #55, Lot 33).

OTHER MACHINE MADE. Poly bag. Red label reading "60 Champion Agates". Contains predominately Marble King and Vitro. Mint. $4. (Auction #178, Lot 20).

OTHER MACHINE MADE. Advertising bag. Yellow mesh bag. Orange header label reading "Drink Klicker Everybody's Favorite" on one side. $27. (Auction #121, Lot 26).

OTHER MACHINE MADE. Advertising Marbles. Lot of fou marbles. All made by Qualatex/Lucky Dog. All are white base. The Green Hornet Adventure. $16. (Auction #55, Lot 25).

OTHER MACHINE MADE. Alley Agate. Lot of three marbles. All are common flames. Nice set in assorted colors. 5/8" to 21/32". Mint (9.9). $59. (Auction #54, Lot 13).

OTHER MACHINE MADE. Alley Agate. This is one of the tiny Alley Agate swirls that popped up a few years ago in Columbus. 3/8". Mint (9.9). $50. (Auction #184, Lot 40).

OTHER MACHINE MADE. Alley Agate. Superior Alley Agate flame swirl with Alley Agate oxblood. Exceptional example. 21/32". Mint (9.7). $44. (Auction #113, Lot 35).

OTHER MACHINE MADE. Alley Agate. Stunning example of an Alley Agate calligraphy swirl. Opaque purple and transparent clear base. 21/32". Mint (9.9). $32. (Auction #82, Lot 38).

OTHER MACHINE MADE. Alley Agate. Lot of four marbles. All are Alley Agate common swirl flames. Two green on white, a yellow on white. $32. (Auction #54, Lot 19).

OTHER MACHINE MADE. Alley Agate. Superior Alley Agate flame swirl. Opaque white and translucent bright red. Looks almost like a Christensen. 5/8". Mint (9.9). $32. (Auction #124, Lot 22).

OTHER MACHINE MADE. Alley Agate. Blue swirl flame on white and clear. Excellent example. West Virginia, circa 1935-1945. 19/32". Mint (9.9). $31. (Auction #58, Lot 41).

OTHER MACHINE MADE. Alley Agate. Lot of four marbles. Assortment of Alley Agate common flames. One is just a swirl, not a flame. $29. (Auction #65, Lot 17).

OTHER MACHINE MADE. Alley Agate. White base with brown swirls. Numerous flame tips. Super example. West Virginia, circa 1935-1950. 5/8". Mint (9.9). $27. (Auction #73, Lot 35).

OTHER MACHINE MADE. Alley Agate. Lot of four marbles. All are Alley Agate. Nice set of swirls with some flame tips. One each of green. 5/8". Mint (9.9). $26. (Auction #90, Lot 27).

OTHER MACHINE MADE. Alley Agate. Very nice Alley Agate swirl. Transparent red on mustard yellow. Super example. A few flame tips. 21/32". Mint (9.9). $25. (Auction #98, Lot 12).

OTHER MACHINE MADE. Alley Agate. Lot of four marbles. Four Alley Agate swirls. Several have flames. Two have sparkles. 19/32" to 5/8". $24. (Auction #83, Lot 15).

OTHER MACHINE MADE. Alley Agate. Lot of nine marbles. Eight are Alley Agate calligraphy swirls. Brown/red (almost oxblood). $22. (Auction #69, Lot 21).

OTHER MACHINE MADE. Alley Agate. Lot of seven marbles. All are Alley Agate swirls with some flame tips. Four red on white, three green. $20. (Auction #93, Lot 16).

OTHER MACHINE MADE. Alley Agate. Very nice example of an Alley Agate swirl. Opaque white base. Swirls of two different shades of green. 19/32". Mint (9.9). $18. (Auction #134, Lot 14).

OTHER MACHINE MADE. Alley Agate. Lot of eight marbles. Opaque white base with green and "oxblood" swirls. West Virginia, circa 1935. $16. (Auction #54, Lot 18).

OTHER MACHINE MADE. Alley Agate. Lot of five marbles. All are Alley Agate two color swirls. Four have some wide flame tips. $15. (Auction #68, Lot 11).

OTHER MACHINE MADE. Alley Agate. White swirl on light blue. Very pretty marble. Shooter. Some minor flame tips. Some minor sparkles. 13/16". Mint(-) (9). $13. (Auction #136, Lot 31).

OTHER MACHINE MADE. Alley Agate. Lot of five marbles. All are two-color swirls. Two are green on white, two are orange on white. $13. (Auction #136, Lot 16).

OTHER MACHINE MADE. Alley Agate. Lot of five marbles. All are Alley Agate swirls with some flame tips. Three red on white, one green. $12. (Auction #91, Lot 20).

OTHER MACHINE MADE. Alley Agate. Alley flame-type swirl. Opaque off-white, transparent brown and transparent clear. A couple of sparkles. 21/32". Near Mint(+) (8.7). $10. (Auction #185, Lot 27).

OTHER MACHINE MADE. Alley Agate. Lot of eight marbles. All are two-color swirls. Three are green on white, five are orange on white. $10. (Auction #145, Lot 9).

OTHER MACHINE MADE. Alley Agate. Lot of four marbles. All are Alley Agate two color swirls. All are shooters. 27/32" to 15/16". Mint. $10. (Auction #97, Lot 21).

OTHER MACHINE MADE. Alley Agate. Lot of four marbles. All are Alley Agate swirls. Green swirls on white. Nice set. West Virginia. $10. (Auction #70, Lot 2).

OTHER MACHINE MADE. Alley Agate. Lot of seven marbles. All are swirls. Three are white and green (unusual), rest are assorted white. $9. (Auction #102, Lot 4).

OTHER MACHINE MADE. Alley Agate. Lot of two marbles. Both are white swirl on very light blue. Very nice looking. $8. (Auction #115, Lot 32).

OTHER MACHINE MADE. Alley Agate. Lot of five marbles. All are Alley Agate swirls. Four are orange on white, one is green on white. $8. (Auction #110, Lot 35).

OTHER MACHINE MADE. Alley Agate. Lot of five marbles. All are two color swirls. Orange, green or black swirls on white. Some flame tips. $7. (Auction #139, Lot 14).

OTHER MACHINE MADE. Alley Agate. Lot of three marbles. Three swirls, two have wispy oxblood on them. All about 5/8" and Mint (9.9). $7. (Auction #82, Lot 12).

OTHER MACHINE MADE. Alley Agate. Lot of four marbles. All are two-color swirls. Two are green on white, two are orange on white. Nice. $7. (Auction #123, Lot 9).

OTHER MACHINE MADE. Alley Agate. Opaque light blue base with white swirls. Has a few tiny pits on it. West Virginia, circa 1935-1945. 27/32". Near Mint(+) (8.7). $2. (Auction #60, Lot 35).

OTHER MACHINE MADE. Alox Agate. Original yellow mesh bag. Red on white header label. Genuine. Contains Alox transparent swirls. $32. (Auction #132, Lot 35).

OTHER MACHINE MADE. Assorted. Lot of three marbles. First is Champion Agate Company. Semi-opaque and transparent green swirl. Near Mint . $12. (Auction #149, Lot 17).

OTHER MACHINE MADE. Aventurine. Translucent aventurine green shooter with translucent white swirls. In great shape. 29/32". Mint (9.9). $50. (Auction #96, Lot 37).

OTHER MACHINE MADE. Aventurine. Solid opaque green aventurine. Super fire. The manufacturer, age and origin of these is unknown. 11/16". Mint (9.9). $40. (Auction #109, Lot 12).

OTHER MACHINE MADE. Aventurine. Opaque solid aventurine green marble. Nice fire. Unknown maker and age. 5/8". Mint (9.9). $37. (Auction #69, Lot 15).

OTHER MACHINE MADE. Aventurine. Opaque solid aventurine green marble. Nice fire. Unknown maker and age. 5/8". Mint (9.9). $35. (Auction #69, Lot 15.20).

OTHER MACHINE MADE. Aventurine. Solid opaque aventurine green marble. Lots of fire. Manufacturer and age are unknown. 5/8". Mint (9.9). $32. (Auction #75, Lot 5).

OTHER MACHINE MADE. Aventurine. I am not sure who made these, my guess is Vitro. They are hard to find. Semi-transparent amber glass. 15/16". Near Mint(+) (8.7). $25. (Auction #116, Lot 2).

OTHER MACHINE MADE. Aventurine. Opaque white base with aventurine green swirls. Unidentified manufacturer, my guess is Champion. 5/8". Mint (9.9). $25. (Auction #176, Lot 3).

OTHER MACHINE MADE. Aventurine. I am not sure who made these, my guess is Vitro. They are hard to find. Semi-transparent amber glass. 15/16". Near Mint(+) (8.7). $22. (Auction #116, Lot 2.20).

OTHER MACHINE MADE. Aventurine. Opaque white base with aventurine green swirls. Unidentified manufacturer, my guess is Champion. 5/8". Mint (9.9). $21. (Auction #182, Lot 38).

OTHER MACHINE MADE. Aventurine. Solid aventurine green marble. Very fiery. Manufacturer and date of manufacture unknown. 5/8". Mint (9.9). $19. (Auction #182, Lot 30).

OTHER MACHINE MADE. Aventurine. Solid aventurine green marble. Very fiery. Manufacturer and date of manufacture unknown. 5/8". Mint (9.9). $15. (Auction #63, Lot 15.30).

OTHER MACHINE MADE. Aventurine. Solid aventurine green marble. Very fiery. Manufacturer and date of manufacture unknown. 5/8". Mint (9.9). $15. (Auction #63, Lot 15.50).

OTHER MACHINE MADE. Aventurine. Solid aventurine green marble. Very fiery. Manufacturer and date of manufacture unknown. 5/8". Mint (9.9). $15. (Auction #63, Lot 15.20).

OTHER MACHINE MADE. Aventurine. Solid aventurine green marble. Very fiery. Manufacturer and date of manufacture unknown. 5/8". Mint (9.9). $15. (Auction #63, Lot 15.40).

OTHER MACHINE MADE. Aventurine. Solid aventurine green marble. Very fiery. Manufacturer and date of manufacture unknown. 5/8". Mint (9.9). $15. (Auction #63, Lot 15).

OTHER MACHINE MADE. Aventurine. Solid aventurine green marble. Very fiery. Manufacturer and date of manufacture unknown. 5/8". Mint (9.9). $14. (Auction #153, Lot 1).

OTHER MACHINE MADE. Aventurine swirl. Light green aventurine swirled on opaque white. Nice fire in the aventurine. It is not known who made it. 19/32". Mint (9.9). $20. (Auction #151, Lot 34).

OTHER MACHINE MADE. Bottle hangers. Lot of four items. All are poly bags with cardboard advertising bottle hangers. $38. (Auction #79, Lot 15).

OTHER MACHINE MADE. C.E. Bogard & Sons Agate Company. "Mountaineer Shooters". Cardboard backed blister pack of fifteen catseyes. Nice. Some creasing. Mint. $25. (Auction #175, Lot 29).

OTHER MACHINE MADE. C.E. Bogard and Sons. Poly bag of fifty catseyes. White label with purple printing. "Cat Eyes" with cat head on label. $20. (Auction #179, Lot 25).

OTHER MACHINE MADE. Cairo Novelty Company. Lot of two marbles. Excellent examples of Cairo marbles. One is light blue base with the Cairo lavender. $26. (Auction #59, Lot 11).

OTHER MACHINE MADE. Cairo Novelty Company. Baby blue and white swirl. Gorgeous. Cairo WV, circa 1940-1950. 11/16". Mint (9.9). $11. (Auction #150, Lot 3).

OTHER MACHINE MADE. Cairo Novelty. Opaque white and translucent light blue swirl. A beauty. Cairo WV, circa 1945-1955. 5/8". Mint (9.9). $5. (Auction #90, Lot 2).

OTHER MACHINE MADE. Catseye. Lot of ten marbles. Excellent group of harder to find catseyes. Two Marble King St. Mary's, 19/32". $65. (Auction #173, Lot 10).

OTHER MACHINE MADE. Catseye. A hard to find nine vane catseye. Transparent clear base. Three yellow, three blue. 19/32". Mint (9.9). $50. (Auction #139, Lot 44.20).

OTHER MACHINE MADE. Catseye. A hard to find nine vane catseye. Transparent clear base. Three yellow, three blue and three white. 19/32". Mint (9.9). $50. (Auction #139, Lot 44).

OTHER MACHINE MADE. Catseye. Excellent nine-vane catseye. Transparent clear base. Four white vanes in an "X", three red. 5/8". Mint (9.9). $49. (Auction #102, Lot 49).

OTHER MACHINE MADE. Catseye. Lot of approximately four hundred marbles. Assortment of catseyes. Various types, colors and sizes. $42. (Auction #144, Lot 26).

OTHER MACHINE MADE. Catseye. Nine vane catseye. Transparent clear base. Three bands each of yellow, red and white. 19/32". Mint(-) (9). $37. (Auction #117, Lot 41).

OTHER MACHINE MADE. Catseye. A hard to find nine vane catseye. Transparent clear base. Three yellow, three blue and three white. 19/32". Mint (9.9). $35. (Auction #57, Lot 33).

OTHER MACHINE MADE. Catseye. Nine vane catseye. Transparent clear base. Three yellow, three green and three red bands in the core. 19/32". Mint (9.9). $31. (Auction #161, Lot 14).

OTHER MACHINE MADE. Catseye. Lot of approximately three hundred marbles. Assortment of catseyes and clearies. About half catseye. $30. (Auction #108, Lot 23).

OTHER MACHINE MADE. Catseye. Nine vane catseye. Transparent clear base. Three yellow, three green and three red bands in the core. 19/32". Mint (9.9). $29. (Auction #161, Lot 14.30).

OTHER MACHINE MADE. Catseye. Nine vane catseye. Transparent clear base. Three yellow, three green and three red bands in the core. 19/32". Mint (9.9). $29. (Auction #153, Lot 38.20).

OTHER MACHINE MADE. Catseye. Nine vane catseye. Transparent clear base. Three yellow, three green and three red bands in the core. 19/32". Mint (9.9). $29. (Auction #153, Lot 38).

OTHER MACHINE MADE. Catseye. Nine vane catseye. Transparent clear base. Three yellow, three green and three red bands in the core. 19/32". Mint (9.9). $27. (Auction #153, Lot 38.30).

OTHER MACHINE MADE. Catseye. Lot of two marbles. Nine vane catseye. Transparent clear base. Three bands each of yellow, red and white. 19/32". Mint(-) (9). $25. (Auction #120, Lot 9).

OTHER MACHINE MADE. Catseye. Nine vane catseye. Transparent clear base. Three yellow, three green and three red bands in the core. 19/32". Mint (9.9). $25. (Auction #161, Lot 14.20).

OTHER MACHINE MADE. Catseye. Lot of four marbles. All are nine vane catseyes. But all have some blended or mis-formed vanes. Nice. $22. (Auction #125, Lot 15).

OTHER MACHINE MADE. Catseye. Nine vane catseye. Very nice marble. Three vanes each of three different colors. In great shape. 19/32". Mint (9.9). $19. (Auction #125, Lot 39.20).

OTHER MACHINE MADE. Catseye. Nine vane catseye. Very nice marble. Three vanes each of three different colors. In great shape. 19/32". Mint (9.9). $19. (Auction #125, Lot 39.30).

OTHER MACHINE MADE. Catseye. Nine vane catseye. Very nice marble. Three vanes each of three different colors. In great shape. 19/32". Mint (9.9). $19. (Auction #125, Lot 39).

OTHER MACHINE MADE. Catseye. Nine vane catseye. Transparent clear base. Three yellow, three green and three red bands in the core. 19/32". Mint (9.9). $18. (Auction #179, Lot 31.20).

OTHER MACHINE MADE. Catseye. Nine vane catseye. Transparent clear base. Three yellow, three green and three red bands in the core. 19/32". Mint (9.9). $18. (Auction #179, Lot 31).

OTHER MACHINE MADE. Catseye. Lot of two marbles. First is a Marble King St. Mary's catseye. One yellow plane and one blue plane. $17. (Auction #74, Lot 13.10).

OTHER MACHINE MADE. Catseye. Lot of two marbles. First is a Marble King St. Mary's catseye. One yellow plane and one blue plane. $17. (Auction #74, Lot 13).

OTHER MACHINE MADE. Catseye. Nine vane catseye. Very nice marble. Three vanes each of three different colors. In great shape. 19/32". Mint (9.9). $17. (Auction #125, Lot 39.40).

OTHER MACHINE MADE. Catseye. Lot of approximately sixty marbles. Assortment of catseyes. Includes hybrids. Nice set. Some damaged. $16. (Auction #127, Lot 15).

OTHER MACHINE MADE. Catseye. Nine vane catseye. Transparent clear base. Three yellow, three green and three red bands in the core. 19/32". Mint (9.9). $15. (Auction #158, Lot 33).

OTHER MACHINE MADE. Catseye. Nine vane catseye. Transparent clear base. Three yellow, three green and three red bands in the core. 19/32". Mint (9.9). $15. (Auction #158, Lot 33.20).

OTHER MACHINE MADE. Catseye. Nine vane catseye. Transparent clear base. Three yellow, three green and three red bands in the core. 19/32". Mint (9.9). $15. (Auction #152, Lot 18.20).

OTHER MACHINE MADE. Catseye. Nine vane catseye. Very nice marble. Three vanes each of three different colors. In great shape. 19/32". Mint (9.9). $15. (Auction #125, Lot 39.50).

OTHER MACHINE MADE. Catseye. Nine vane catseye. Transparent clear base. Three yellow, three green and three red bands in the core. 19/32". Mint (9.9). $15. (Auction #152, Lot 18).

OTHER MACHINE MADE. Catseye. Nine vane catseye. Transparent clear base. Three yellow, three green and three red bands in the core. 19/32". Mint (9.9). $13. (Auction #148, Lot 35.20).

OTHER MACHINE MADE. Catseye. Nine vane catseye. Transparent clear base. Three yellow, three green and three red bands in the core. 19/32". Mint (9.9). $13. (Auction #148, Lot 35).

OTHER MACHINE MADE. Catseye. Nine vane catseye. Transparent clear base. Three yellow, three green and three red bands in the core. 19/32". Mint (9.9). $13. (Auction #173, Lot 3).

OTHER MACHINE MADE. Catseye. Lot of twelve marbles. All are peewee catseyes. Assortment of American and foreign. Assorted colors. $13. (Auction #184, Lot 30).

OTHER MACHINE MADE. Catseye. Odd catseye type. Seven bands of white on one side of the marble. Five bands of transparent blue. 19/32". Mint (9.9). $12. (Auction #147, Lot 5).

OTHER MACHINE MADE. Catseye. Transparent very light blue glass. Six vane opaque white catseye. Unknown manufacturer. 1-3/8". Near Mint(+) (8.9). $12. (Auction #143, Lot 8).

OTHER MACHINE MADE. Catseye. Nine vane catseye. Transparent clear base. Three yellow, three green and three red bands in the core. 19/32". Mint (9.9). $11. (Auction #173, Lot 3.20).

OTHER MACHINE MADE. Catseye. Lot of eleven marbles. Shooter catseyes. Six vane. Vanes are a combination of yellow, blue, orange. $10. (Auction #82, Lot 21).

OTHER MACHINE MADE. Catseye. Lot of eight marbles. All are large catseyes. Vacor de Mexico. 1-3/8". Mint (9.9) to Near Mint(+). $10. (Auction #177, Lot 18).

OTHER MACHINE MADE. Catseye. Lot of three marbles. All are the same. Japanese catseyes. Six vane. Two vanes are lumpy green aventurine. $7. (Auction #101, Lot 38).

OTHER MACHINE MADE. Catseye. Lot of twelve marbles. Ten are Vitro Agate hybrid, two are Peltier Bananas. All about 5/8". $6. (Auction #136, Lot 5).

OTHER MACHINE MADE. Catseye. Lot of fourteen marbles. Includes Bananas, Vitro Hybrids and a few six vane foreigns. 19/32". $1. (Auction #109, Lot 21).

OTHER MACHINE MADE. Catseyes. Lot of approximately one hundred twenty five marbles. All catseyes, including a group in a poly pack. $11. (Auction #175, Lot 28).

OTHER MACHINE MADE. Catseyes. Lot of fifty marbles. Twenty foreign catseyes. Thirty Vitro hybrid and Gladding-Vitro catseyes. 9/16". $10. (Auction #68, Lot 13).

OTHER MACHINE MADE. Champion Agate Company. Lot of thirteen marbles. All are New Old Fashioneds. Bright yellow swirl on red. Nice set. Pennsboro. $42. (Auction #78, Lot 26).

OTHER MACHINE MADE. Champion Agate. "Furnace scraping" marble. Limited run about ten years ago. Opaque yellow and transparent brown swirl. 5/8". Mint (9.9). $40. (Auction #160, Lot 31).

OTHER MACHINE MADE. Champion Agate. "Furnace scraping" marble. Limited run about ten years ago. Opaque yellow and transparent brown swirl. 5/8". Mint (9.9). $38. (Auction #160, Lot 31.20).

OTHER MACHINE MADE. Champion Agate Company. "Furnace scraping" marble. Swirl of opaque yellow and transparent light brown. Bright. Pennsboro, WV. 19/32". Mint (9.9). $24. (Auction #172, Lot 35.20).

OTHER MACHINE MADE. Champion Agate. I've classified this as a Champion, possibly it is an Alley or Heaton. White base with blue swirls. 19/32". Mint (9.9). $21. (Auction #126, Lot 29).

OTHER MACHINE MADE. Champion Agate Company. Lot of two marbles. Two "New Old Fashioneds". Electric yellow on bright orange/red. West Virginia. 19/32". Mint (9.9). $20. (Auction #64, Lot 6).

OTHER MACHINE MADE. Champion Agate Company. "Furnace scraping" marble. Swirl of opaque yellow & transparent light brown. Bright. Pennsboro, WV. 19/32". Mint (9.9). $20. (Auction #172, Lot 35).

OTHER MACHINE MADE. Champion Agate. Lot of twenty marbles. All are peewee opalescent white. Pennsboro WV, circa 1985-1995. 3/8". Mint (9.9). $14. (Auction #87, Lot 17).

OTHER MACHINE MADE. Champion Agate. Lot of thirty five marbles. All Champion Agate transparent swirls in assorted colors. 19/32" to 5/8". $13. (Auction #106, Lot 29).

OTHER MACHINE MADE. Champion Agate Company. Three color swirl. White, yellow and red. Flame-type patterns. Some cold roll creasing. Pennsboro, WV. 25/32". Mint (9.7). $12. (Auction #185, Lot 1).

OTHER MACHINE MADE. Champion Agate Company. Lot of two marbles. Both are bright red and yellow swirl. "New Old Fashioned". Pennsboro, WV. $12. (Auction #113, Lot 5).

OTHER MACHINE MADE. Champion Agate Company. Lot of five marbles. All are New Old Fashioneds. They are all the bright yellow swirl on bright red. $11. (Auction #170, Lot 1).

OTHER MACHINE MADE. Champion Agate Company. New Old-Fashioned. Bright red and electric yellow swirl. Pennsboro WV, circa 1980-1990. 5/8". Mint (. 5/8". Mint (9.9). $8. (Auction #140, Lot 31).

OTHER MACHINE MADE. Champion Agate. Original poly bag. Contains twenty one 9/16" chinese checkers, swirls, catseyes and clearies. Paper. $7. (Auction #106, Lot 19).

OTHER MACHINE MADE. Champion Agate Company. Transparent light green bubble filled base with a swirl of oxblood-looking red with some gray on it. 23/32". Near Mint(+) (8.8). $5. (Auction #181, Lot 5).

OTHER MACHINE MADE. Champion Agate. Original poly bag. Contains twenty one 9/16" chinese checkers, swirls, catseyes and clearies. Paper. $5. (Auction #90, Lot 24).

OTHER MACHINE MADE. Champion Agate. Transparent green with lots of wispy white swirls in it. Also, some salmon-red swirls. 9/16". Mint (9.9). $5. (Auction #110, Lot 14).

OTHER MACHINE MADE. Champion Agate. Original poly bag. Contains twenty one 9/16" chinese checkers, swirls, catseyes and clearies. Paper. $5. (Auction #90, Lot 24.20).

OTHER MACHINE MADE. Character. Lot of nine marbles The first group has four marbles. All of those are opaque white with a decal. $38. (Auction #149, Lot 36).

OTHER MACHINE MADE. Character. Lot of two marbles. One is printed "Perot 96". The other is for the "National Rolley Hole Marble Tournament". $24. (Auction #117, Lot 31).

OTHER MACHINE MADE. Character. Lot of three marbles. Modern character marbles. Opaque white marble. $22. (Auction #116, Lot 16).

OTHER MACHINE MADE. Character. Modern character marble. Logo of the Michigan State Police on a modern Marble King two-patch. Image. 31/32". Mint (9.9). $14. (Auction #158, Lot 9).

OTHER MACHINE MADE. Character. Lot of seven marbles. All are plastic Rad Rollors. Major League Baseball series. Each is different. $7. (Auction #141, Lot 23).

OTHER MACHINE MADE. Character. Lot of seven marbles. All are plastic Rad Rollors. Major League Baseball series. Each is different. $7. (Auction #141, Lot 23.20).

OTHER MACHINE MADE. Character. Reproduction of the Tom Mix design on a modern two-patch Marble King. Transfer in black. 23/32". Mint (9.9). $7. (Auction #158, Lot 16).

OTHER MACHINE MADE. Character. Reproduction of the Cote's Master Loaf design on a modern two-patch Marble King. Transfer in brown. 23/32". Mint (9.9). $5. (Auction #158, Lot 5).

OTHER MACHINE MADE. Character marble. Lot of three marbles. All are modern character marbles. Marilyn Monroe, Betty Boop, Hoppy. $20. (Auction #127, Lot 29).

OTHER MACHINE MADE. Character marble. Modern character marble. Multicolor Betty Boop transfer on a new Marble King. American, circa 1975. 1-3/16". Mint (9.9). $17. (Auction #123, Lot 34).

OTHER MACHINE MADE. Character marble. Modern Marble King marble with a silkscreen of Sambo on it. In nice shape. American, circa 1980-1998. 7/8. Mint (9.9). $5. (Auction #146, Lot 36).

OTHER MACHINE MADE. Character marble. Transfer of "Topsy" on a Marble King shooter. Signed "Bennett". Presumably made by Harold Bennett. C. 7/8". Mint (9.9). $5. (Auction #109, Lot 33).

OTHER MACHINE MADE. Character marble. Transparent clear marble with "There's a Ford in your future" silkscreened on it in red. 31/32". Near Mint (8.5). $5. (Auction #138, Lot 11).

OTHER MACHINE MADE. Character marble. Large Marble King catseye with green eye. Printed on it in red is "Coca-Cola". Modern. 1-3/16". Mint(-) (9). $5. (Auction #151, Lot 3).

OTHER MACHINE MADE. Character marbles. Lot of four marbles. Hoppy on black, Mickey Mouse on white, computer airplane on white, horse and rider. $12. (Auction #119, Lot 26).

OTHER MACHINE MADE. Chinese Checker. Lot of about forty five marbles. Assortment of opaque chinese checker marbles. Assorted colors. $5. (Auction #180, Lot 36).

OTHER MACHINE MADE. Foreign sparkler. "Bright" European type. These are fairly hard to find. Transparent clear base. Core of yellow, red. 3/4". Mint (9.7). $37. (Auction #183, Lot 22).

OTHER MACHINE MADE. Foreign sparkler. A nice example of the "bright" type of foreign sparkler. Probably German. Very nice example. 23/32". Mint (9.9). $20. (Auction #70, Lot 26.40).

OTHER MACHINE MADE. Foreign sparkler. Excellent example of a foreign sparkler. In super shape, with really nice colors. The "bright" type. 21/32". Mint (9.9). $18. (Auction #121, Lot 15).

OTHER MACHINE MADE. Foreign sparkler. A nice example of the "bright" type of foreign sparkler. Probably German. Very nice example. 23/32". Mint (9.9). $17. (Auction #70, Lot 26).

OTHER MACHINE MADE. Foreign sparkler. A nice example of the "bright" type of foreign sparkler. Probably German. Very nice example. 23/32". Mint (9.9). $17. (Auction #70, Lot 26.20).

OTHER MACHINE MADE. Foreign sparkler. A nice example of the "bright" type of foreign sparkler. Probably German. Very nice example. 23/32". Mint (9.9). $17. (Auction #70, Lot 26.30).

OTHER MACHINE MADE. Foreign sparkler. Foreign sparkler. Transparent clear base. Interior bands of assorted colors. Large marble. 1-1/16". Near Mint(+) (8.9). $16. (Auction #56, Lot 17).

OTHER MACHINE MADE. Foreign sparkler. "Bright type" foreign sparkler. Transparent clear base with a ribbon of yellow, green, blue and white. 3/4". Mint (9.9). $13. (Auction #91, Lot 3).

OTHER MACHINE MADE. Foreign Sparkler. Pastel-type foreign sparkler. Transparent clear base with a wide ribbon vane of white, orange and blue. 1-1/16". Mint (9.9). $17. (Auction #60, Lot 5).

OTHER MACHINE MADE. Foreign Sparkler. Transparent clear base with a flat ribbon in the core. Opaque white ribbon. 19/32". Mint (9.9). $9. (Auction #103, Lot 38).

OTHER MACHINE MADE. German. Lot of six marbles. Assortment of German striped transparents. All are two seams. $95. (Auction #176, Lot 13).

OTHER MACHINE MADE. German. Striped transparent. Opaque white and clear base. Bands of opaque light blue on one side and opaque. 15/16". Mint (9.9). $70. (Auction #89, Lot 49).

OTHER MACHINE MADE. German. Striped transparent. Transparent peach base with bands of opaque white striped on the surface on one. 5/8". Mint (9.9). $45. (Auction #89, Lot 37).

OTHER MACHINE MADE. German. Lot of twelve marbles. Excellent assortment of ten striped transparents and two striped opaques. $40. (Auction #89, Lot 28).

OTHER MACHINE MADE. German. Clear striped transparent. Transparent clear base with bands of opaque white striped on the surface. 27/32". Mint (9.9). $37. (Auction #89, Lot 4).

OTHER MACHINE MADE. German. Striped transparent. Transparent peach base with bands of opaque white striped on the surface on one. 5/8". Mint (9.9). $30. (Auction #90, Lot 37).

OTHER MACHINE MADE. German. Lot of three marbles. German striped transparents. Each is a different color base: green, brown. $27. (Auction #112, Lot 44).

OTHER MACHINE MADE. German. Lot of eighteen marbles. All are Wire Pulls. All have some damage. Assortment of colors. 11/16" to 7. $20. (Auction #89, Lot 25).

OTHER MACHINE MADE. German. Striped opaque. Opaque white with transparent light blue and transparent lavender. 15/16". Near Mint(-) (8.2). $19. (Auction #90, Lot 13).

OTHER MACHINE MADE. German. Lot of two marbles. Both are clear striped transparent. Transparent clear base with opaque bands. Near Mint(-) (9.9). $15. (Auction #90, Lot 34).

OTHER MACHINE MADE. German. Lot of nine marbles. All are Wire Pulls. All have some damage. Assortment of colors. 11/16" to 7/8". $15. (Auction #104, Lot 30.20).

OTHER MACHINE MADE. German. Lot of nine marbles. All are Wire Pulls. All have some damage. Assortment of colors. 11/16" to 7/8". $15. (Auction #104, Lot 30).

OTHER MACHINE MADE. German. Lot of two marbles. Both are Wire Pulls. One is transparent clear base with transparent green and white. $14. (Auction #89, Lot 35).

OTHER MACHINE MADE. German. Lot of five marbles. All are Wire Pulls. $12. (Auction #90, Lot 7).

OTHER MACHINE MADE. German. Lot of two marbles. Both are wire pulls. One is transparent clear with translucent blue and white. $8. (Auction #89, Lot 15).

OTHER MACHINE MADE. German. A German "slag". Two seam (like Christensen Agates). The seams have "U"s like Masters. 7/8". Mint(-) (9.1). $3. (Auction #139, Lot 18).

OTHER MACHINE MADE. Golden Rule. A Golden Rule marble. Translucent white plastic marble with an equatorial band bearing the Golden Rule. 13/16". Mint (9.9). $25. (Auction #183, Lot 28).

OTHER MACHINE MADE. Golden Rule. A Golden Rule marble. Translucent white plastic marble with an equatorial band bearing the Golden Rule 13/16". Mint (9.9). $10. (Auction #116, Lot 38).

OTHER MACHINE MADE. Golden Rule. A Golden Rule marble. Translucent blue plastic marble with an equatorial band bearing the Golden Rule. 13/16". Mint (9.9). $3. (Auction #154, Lot 2).

OTHER MACHINE MADE. Heaton Agate Company. Probably Heaton Agate. Opaque white and transparent green swirl. Oxblood like color edging the green. 5/8". Mint (9.9). $32. (Auction #165, Lot 39).

OTHER MACHINE MADE. Heaton Agate Company. Original poly bag. I have never seen this bag, or the one in Lot #34 before. Very hard to find. $28. (Auction #152, Lot 35.20).

OTHER MACHINE MADE. Heaton Agate Company. Original poly bag. I have never seen this bag, or the one in Lot #34 before. Very hard to find. $28. (Auction #152, Lot 35).

OTHER MACHINE MADE. Heaton Agate Company. Original poly bag. Very hard to find. Cardboard label. Front reads "30 BIG SHOT 10 cents". $25. (Auction #178, Lot 24).

OTHER MACHINE MADE. Heaton Agate Company. Original poly bag. Very hard to find. Cardboard label. Front reads "30 BIG SHOT 10 cents". $23. (Auction #178, Lot 24.20).

OTHER MACHINE MADE. Heaton Agate Company. Original poly bag. I have never seen this bag, or the one in Lot #35 before. Very hard to find. Card. $21. (Auction #152, Lot 34).

OTHER MACHINE MADE. Heaton Agate Company. Original poly bag. I have never seen this bag, or the one in Lot #35 before. Very hard to find. Card. $21. (Auction #152, Lot 34.20).

OTHER MACHINE MADE. Heaton Agate Company. Original poly bag. Very hard to find. Cardboard label. Front reads "14 BIG SHOT 5 cents". $20. (Auction #178, Lot 25).

OTHER MACHINE MADE. Heaton Agate Company. Original poly bag. I have never seen this bag, or the one in Lot #35 before. Very hard to find. Card. $19. (Auction #152, Lot 34.30).

OTHER MACHINE MADE. Heaton Agate Company. Original poly bag. Very hard to find. Cardboard label. Front reads "30 BIG SHOT 10 cents". $19. (Auction #178, Lot 24.30).

OTHER MACHINE MADE. Heaton Agate Company. Original poly bag. Very hard to find. Cardboard label. Front reads "30 BIG SHOT 10 cents". $19. (Auction #178, Lot 24.40).

OTHER MACHINE MADE. Heaton Agate Company. Original poly bag. Very hard to find. Cardboard label. Front reads "14 BIG SHOT 5 cents". $18. (Auction #178, Lot 25.40).

OTHER MACHINE MADE. Heaton Agate Company. Original poly bag. Very hard to find. Cardboard label. Front reads "14 BIG SHOT 5 cents". $18. (Auction #178, Lot 25.30).

OTHER MACHINE MADE. Heaton Agate Company. Baby blue and white swirl. A beauty. West Virgina, circa 1945-1955. 5/8". Mint (9.9). $17. (Auction #161, Lot 36.20).

OTHER MACHINE MADE. Heaton Agate Company. Baby blue and white swirl. A beauty. West Virgina, circa 1945-1955. 5/8". Mint (9.9). $17. (Auction #161, Lot 36).

OTHER MACHINE MADE. Heaton Agate Company. Original poly bag. Cardboard label. Front reads "BIG SHOT". Back reads "CAT EYES / Heaton Agate Co. $16. (Auction #172, Lot 27).

OTHER MACHINE MADE. Heaton Agate Company. Original poly bag. Very hard to find. Cardboard label. Front reads "14 BIG SHOT 5 cents". $15. (Auction #178, Lot 25.20).

OTHER MACHINE MADE. Heaton Agate Company. Baby blue and white swirl. A beauty. West Virginia, circa 1945-1955. 5/8". Mint (9.9). $11. (Auction #166, Lot 33).

OTHER MACHINE MADE. Heaton Agate Company. Baby blue and white swirl. A beauty. West Virginia, circa 1945-1955. 5/8". Mint (9.9). $9. (Auction #166, Lot 33.20).

OTHER MACHINE MADE. Heaton Agate Company. Baby blue and white swirl. A beauty. West Virginia, circa 1945-1955. 5/8". Mint (9.9). $7. (Auction #166, Lot 33.40).

OTHER MACHINE MADE. Heaton Agate Company. Baby blue and white swirl. A beauty. West Virginia, circa 1945-1955. 5/8". Mint (9.9). $7. (Auction #166, Lot 33.30).

OTHER MACHINE MADE. J. Pressman Bag. Hard to find cloth J. Pressman "Marble Champ" bag. "King size super assortment contains jumbo shooter. $32. (Auction #79, Lot 19).

OTHER MACHINE MADE. Jabo-Vitro Agate. Lot of approximately one hundred marbles. All are recent Jabo-Vitro Agate swirls and patches. $10. (Auction #102, Lot 31).

OTHER MACHINE MADE. JABO, Inc. Lot of two marbles. I believe that these are JABO swirls. Green and white. Minor flame pattern. $8. (Auction #66, Lot 7).

OTHER MACHINE MADE. JABO, Inc. Lot of three marbles. All are JABO swirls. Light green transparent with wispy white. Swirled. $7. (Auction #142, Lot 20).

OTHER MACHINE MADE. Jobber box. Square orange jobber box. Small puncture in the top. About 3-1/4" x 3-1/4". Near Mint(+) (8.9). $40. (Auction #119, Lot 40).

OTHER MACHINE MADE. Jobber box. Blue and white "30 Marbles" jobber box. Contains Champion Agate transparent swirls. Box is Mint. $19. (Auction #119, Lot 37).

OTHER MACHINE MADE. Metallic. Interesting patch with metallic stripes. Opaque white base. Yellow patch. 19/32". Mint (9.6). $18. (Auction #170, Lot 35).

OTHER MACHINE MADE. Metallic. Lot of three marbles. All are pee-wee opaque with a metallic stripe. One white, two blue. $17. (Auction #156, Lot 12).

OTHER MACHINE MADE. Metallic. Very nice opaque white, transparent orange and clear swirl. Some flame patterning. Silver/black metallic. 11/16". Mint (9.7). $17. (Auction #153, Lot 26).

OTHER MACHINE MADE. Metallic. Transparent olive green and opaque white swirl. My guess is that it is either Heaton Agate or Champion Agate. 21/32". Mint (9.9). $15. (Auction #149, Lot 7).

OTHER MACHINE MADE. Metallic. Opaque white base swirl with blue swirls and silver metallic swirls. Unknown maker. My guess is Champion Agate. 19/32". Mint (9.9). $14. (Auction #96, Lot 2).

OTHER MACHINE MADE. Metallic. Blue on white swirl with silver metallic on it. Probably Champion Agate. 5/8". Mint (9.9). $12. (Auction #130, Lot 18).

OTHER MACHINE MADE. Metallic. Lot of two marbles. First is opaque light blue with metallic swirls. 9/16".Mint (9.9). $5. (Auction #60, Lot 18).

OTHER MACHINE MADE. Opaque aventurine. Opaque aventurine green marble. Origin and age unknown. 21/32". Mint (9.9). $14. (Auction #76, Lot 36).

OTHER MACHINE MADE. Original bag. Original poly bag of "Uncle Jack's Genuine Cat's Eye Glass Marbles". J. Pressman bag. $35. (Auction #79, Lot 9).

OTHER MACHINE MADE. Original bag. Red mesh bag. "30 Playtime Marbles 30". Red cardboard label. Label is ripped. $33. (Auction #156, Lot 26.20).

OTHER MACHINE MADE. Original bag. Red mesh bag. "30 Playtime Marbles 30". Red cardboard label. Label is ripped. $33. (Auction #156, Lot 26).

OTHER MACHINE MADE. Original bag. Original yellow mesh advertising bag. Cardboard label advertises Drake's Cakes. Contains Alley Agate. $28. (Auction #79, Lot 5).

OTHER MACHINE MADE. Original bag. These bags turned up at Brimfield. I have never seen them before. J Pressman mesh bags. Yellow mesh. $27. (Auction #126, Lot 23).

OTHER MACHINE MADE. Original bag. These bags turned up at Brimfield. I have never seen them before. J Pressman mesh bags. Yellow mesh. $25. (Auction #126, Lot 23.20).

OTHER MACHINE MADE. Original bag. Original poly bag of catseyes. Cardboard header. Red on white. Reads on one side "GLASS MARBLE". $22. (Auction #162, Lot 26).

OTHER MACHINE MADE. Original bag. These bags turned up at Brimfield. I have never seen them before. J Pressman mesh bags. Yellow mesh. $22. (Auction #126, Lot 23.30).

OTHER MACHINE MADE. Original bag. Original poly bag of catseyes. Cardboard header. Red on white. Reads on one side "GLASS MARBLE". $22. (Auction #162, Lot 26.20).

OTHER MACHINE MADE. Original bag. Lot of four items. All are foreign catseye poly bags. First is "Cat's Eye Glass Marbles", Japanese. $21. (Auction #79, Lot 13).

OTHER MACHINE MADE. Original bag. Original poly bag. Cardboard label reads "20 - Penny King - 20, Pittsburgh 3 PA". This is a Champion. $14. (Auction #79, Lot 6).

OTHER MACHINE MADE. Original bag. Lot of two items. The first is a Heaton Agate Big Shot poly bag. Contains five shooter catseyes. $12. (Auction #79, Lot 11).

OTHER MACHINE MADE. Original bag. Original poly bag. "20 Winners / Nationwide". Contains twenty two Champion Agate swirls. $7. (Auction #79, Lot 10).

OTHER MACHINE MADE. Original bag. Original mesh bag. Cardboard label reads "Genuine 16 Old Fashion 16 Marbles". Contains Champion Agate. $4. (Auction #79, Lot 2).

OTHER MACHINE MADE. Original box. Hard to find original jobber box. "Tournament Glass Marbles" "The Rosenthal Co. New York City". $160. (Auction #106, Lot 50).

OTHER MACHINE MADE. Original box. Yellow cardboard sleeve advertising Red Goose Shoes. Two oval cutouts. Same basic size as an Akro. $100. (Auction #124, Lot 41).

OTHER MACHINE MADE. Original box. Yellow cardboard sleeve advertising Red Goose Shoes. Two oval cutouts. Same basic size as an Akro. $100. (Auction #79, Lot 22).

OTHER MACHINE MADE. Original box. Four ten cent jobber boxes. These are the red ones with the oval cutouts. The boxes are 5-3/4". $28. (Auction #79, Lot 21).

OTHER MACHINE MADE. Original box. Original box of marbles. Bell brand marbles. Yellow box with child shooting marbles on the front. $19. (Auction #68, Lot 14).

OTHER MACHINE MADE. Original box. Original advertising sleeve for Weather Bird Shoes. Sleeve is missing an end tab and has a large tap. $15. (Auction #94, Lot 35).

OTHER MACHINE MADE. Original package. Very unusual and hard to find item. This is an original cardboard shipping box with ten original. $75. (Auction #150, Lot 28).

OTHER MACHINE MADE. Original package. Bottle hanger. Poly bag with a white bottle hanger. Coca Cola hanger. Contains fourteen Marble King. $50. (Auction #133, Lot 35).

OTHER MACHINE MADE. Original package. Green and white jobber marble box. Two oval cutouts. Star pattern. $38. (Auction #158, Lot 23).

OTHER MACHINE MADE. Original package. Rare package. Poly bag of twenty catseyes. Contains Heaton Agate catseyes. Label on the bag is a Heaton. $27. (Auction #178, Lot 23).

OTHER MACHINE MADE. Original package. Poly bag. "This is Your Bag of Marbles", Chemtoy Corporation, Cicero IL. Copyright 1973. Cardboard. $26. (Auction #178, Lot 26).

OTHER MACHINE MADE. Original package. Bottle hanger. Poly bag with a red bottle hanger. Hanger reads "HAVE FUN / Compliments of TOWER ROOT. $25. (Auction #133, Lot 28).

OTHER MACHINE MADE. Original package. Lot of three items. Two red jobber boxes, two oval, white stars. Both of those are damaged. Near Mint. $17. (Auction #178, Lot 28).

OTHER MACHINE MADE. Original package. Poly bag of five Japanese shooter catseyes. Header label reads "Sun Brand Genuine Cat's Eye Marbles". $7. (Auction #117, Lot 30).

OTHER MACHINE MADE. Original packages. Lot of three marbles. All three are unused jobber boxes. Two are the red ten cents Marbles boxes. $15. (Auction #143, Lot 33).

OTHER MACHINE MADE. Original packages. Lot of two items. First is a poly bag of 25 count of catseyes. Red, black and white label. $15. (Auction #143, Lot 32).

OTHER MACHINE MADE. **Packages.** Lot of five items. All are fairly recent packages. One Playtime catseyes, four Bell packages. $19. (Auction #106, Lot 24).

OTHER MACHINE MADE. **Packages.** Lot of six items. All are fairly recent packages. One Marble King catseyes, one Playtime catseyes. $16. (Auction #102, Lot 32).

OTHER MACHINE MADE. **Patch.** Lot of eight marbles. Nice assortment of smaller patches. Includes Akro, Master and Vitro. All peewees. $15. (Auction #117, Lot 11).

OTHER MACHINE MADE. **Patch.** Lot of two marbles. Both are shooter patches. One is blue on milky white. The other is orange on milky white. $14. (Auction #87, Lot 20).

OTHER MACHINE MADE. **Patch.** Lot of thirteen marbles. Assortment of Master and Akro patches. Nice group. 19/32" to 21/32". Mint. $12. (Auction #123, Lot 36).

OTHER MACHINE MADE. **Patch.** Lot of two marbles. Both are shooter patches. One is blue on milky white. The other is orange on milky white. $12. (Auction #87, Lot 20.20).

OTHER MACHINE MADE. **Patch.** Lot of nine marbles. Assortment of Master Marble and Vitro Agate patches. Nice assortment. 1/2" to 5/8". $11. (Auction #180, Lot 12).

OTHER MACHINE MADE. **Patch.** I think that this marble is probably Vacor de Mexico, although there is a possibility that it is Vitro. 1". Mint (9.7). $7. (Auction #58, Lot 13).

OTHER MACHINE MADE. **Plastic.** Original blister card of five "Star Trek The Next Generation" marbles. Plastic marbles. $9. (Auction #119, Lot 35).

OTHER MACHINE MADE. **Ravenswood Novelty Works.** Four page catalogue from Ravenswood. Circa 1940s. Features pictures of the various marble boxes. $55. (Auction #149, Lot 24.20).

OTHER MACHINE MADE. **Ravenswood Novelty Works.** Four page catalogue from Ravenswood. Circa 1940s. Features pictures of the various marble boxes. $55. (Auction #149, Lot 24).

OTHER MACHINE MADE. **Ravenswood Novelty Company.** Lot of two marbles. Both are two-color shooter Ravenswood swirls (Big Boy). One is orange on white. $41. (Auction #158, Lot 15).

OTHER MACHINE MADE. **Ravenswood Novelty Works.** Four page catalogue from Ravenswood. Circa 1940s. Features pictures of the various marble boxes. $40. (Auction #112, Lot 21).

OTHER MACHINE MADE. **Ravenswood Novelty Works.** Nice shooter. White, gray and green. Several sparkles. Ravenswood, WV, circa 1930-1945. 1-1/16". Near Mint(+) (8.9). $23. (Auction #102, Lot 15).

OTHER MACHINE MADE. **Ravenswood Novelty Works.** Lot of two marbles. One is white base with green swirls. One is white base with yellow swirls. "Big . $22. (Auction #170, Lot 20).

OTHER MACHINE MADE. **Ravenswood Novelty Works.** Lot of fifteen marbles. Assortment of two and three color swirls. Nice group. All about 5/8". Most Mint. $22. (Auction #123, Lot 1).

OTHER MACHINE MADE. **Ravenswood Novelty Works.** Lot of seven marbles. All are three color. They are all red and blue on white. Nice assortment. $20. (Auction #56, Lot 1).

OTHER MACHINE MADE. **Ravenswood Novelty Works.** Lot of five marbles. All are large two-color swirls. Three green on white, one blue on white. $17. (Auction #180, Lot 34).

OTHER MACHINE MADE. **Ravenswood Novelty Works.** Two color swirl shooter. Orange swirl on white. One tiny subsurface moon. Ravenswood, WV, circa 1940. 1". Near Mint(+) (8.9). $16. (Auction #172, Lot 31).

OTHER MACHINE MADE. **Ravenswood Novelty Works.** Lot of five marbles. All are two color Buddy shooters. Nice swirls. 1". Mint(-) (9.0) to Near Mint(+). $16. (Auction #112, Lot 28).

OTHER MACHINE MADE. **Ravenswood Novelty Works.** Lot of three marbles. All are large Buddy shooters. Assorted colors. Each has minor damage. 1". $14. (Auction #122, Lot 42).

OTHER MACHINE MADE. **Ravenswood Novelty Works.** Lot of three marbles. All are shooter Buddy marbles. One is green swirl on white, one blue on white. $14. (Auction #181, Lot 23).

OTHER MACHINE MADE. **Ravenswood Novelty Works.** Lot of two marbles. Two shooter Buddy marbles. One is green swirl on white. $12. (Auction #120, Lot 13).

OTHER MACHINE MADE. **Slag.** Lot of twenty two marbles. All shooters. Assorment of M.F. Christensen and Akro. Ten green. $150. (Auction #75, Lot 23).

OTHER MACHINE MADE. **Slag.** Lot of approximately seventy five marbles. Excellent assormtent of Akro slags, with some M.F. Christensen. $110. (Auction #177, Lot 22).

OTHER MACHINE MADE. **Slag.** Lot of approximately one hundred marbles. Assorment of slags. Includes most companies and colors. $90. (Auction #95, Lot 25).

OTHER MACHINE MADE. **Slag.** Lot of ten marbles. Assortment of M.F. Christensen and Akro slags. Six brown, two blue, two green. $60. (Auction #70, Lot 21).

OTHER MACHINE MADE. **Slag.** Lot of approximately eighty marbles. Most are Akro slags. Some common machine mades tow. Assortment. $46. (Auction #95, Lot 14).

OTHER MACHINE MADE. **Slag.** Lot of four marbles. Blue, Akro, 1-3/16", buffed. Brown, MFC, 1-1/16", buffed. Brown, MFC, 1", Near Mint. $42. (Auction #97, Lot 22).

OTHER MACHINE MADE. **Slag.** Lot of twenty eight marbles. All are brown slags. A few M.F. Christensen, but mostly Akro Agate. $40. (Auction #130, Lot 28).

OTHER MACHINE MADE. **Slag.** Lot of four marbles. Three are two-seam Christensen Agate. Those are red, green and aqua. 19/32". $39. (Auction #178, Lot 6).

OTHER MACHINE MADE. **Slag.** Lot of five marbles. All are shooter slags. A green M.F. Christensen. The other four are Akro Agate. $33. (Auction #73, Lot 20).

OTHER MACHINE MADE. **Slag.** Lot of approximately one hundred marbles. All are slags. Mostly Akro with some M.F. Christensen mixed in. $28. (Auction #127, Lot 16).

OTHER MACHINE MADE. **Slag.** Lot of forty nine marbles. All are slags. All have some damage. Assortment of Akro and M.F. Christensen. $25. (Auction #102, Lot 26).

OTHER MACHINE MADE. **Slag.** Lot of twelve marbles. All are Akro. Four blue, four brown, three green, one clear. All have some damage. $21. (Auction #122, Lot 15).

OTHER MACHINE MADE. **Slag.** Lot of five marbles. All brown slags. Four Akros. One crease pontil, unknown manufacturer. 9/16". $16. (Auction #75, Lot 19).

OTHER MACHINE MADE. **Slag.** Lot of seventeen marbles. Mostly Akro, with some M.F. Christensen. Five brown, three blue, two aqua. $15. (Auction #122, Lot 20).

OTHER MACHINE MADE. **Swirl.** Lot of approximately forty five marbles. Assortment of Alley, Ravenswood, Heaton and Champion swirls. $30. (Auction #180, Lot 35).

OTHER MACHINE MADE. **Swirl.** Lot of four marbles. All are foreign swirls. Made in West Germany, circa 1960s. Nice patterns. $25. (Auction #55, Lot 22).

OTHER MACHINE MADE. **Swirl.** Lot of about sixty marbles. Assortment of transparent swirls. Predominately Champion Agate. $23. (Auction #180, Lot 24).

OTHER MACHINE MADE. **Swirl.** Lot of six marbles. Assortment of Alley Agate, Ravenswood, and one Heaton. All are two color swirls. $22. (Auction #178, Lot 5).

OTHER MACHINE MADE. **Swirl.** Lot of four marbles. All are foreign swirls. Made in West Germany, circa 1960's. Nice patterns. $20. (Auction #54, Lot 16).

OTHER MACHINE MADE. **Swirl.** Lot of nineteen marbles. All are two-color white base swirl. Assortment of Heaton and Ravenswood. Al. $19. (Auction #180, Lot 28).

OTHER MACHINE MADE. **Swirl.** Lot of forty five marbles. All are two-color white base swirl. Assortment of Heaton and Ravenswood. $19. (Auction #180, Lot 37).

OTHER MACHINE MADE. **Swirl.** Lot of fourteen marbles. Assortment of swirls. Nice group of Alley, Heaton and Champion. 19/32". $16. (Auction #115, Lot 21).

OTHER MACHINE MADE. **Swirl.** Lot of seventeen marbles. All are two-color white base swirl. Assortment of Alley and Ravenswood. $16. (Auction #180, Lot 40).

OTHER MACHINE MADE. **Swirl.** Probably Alley Agate. Nice flame! Translucent light blue swirl in translucent white and clear. 5/8". Near Mint(+) (8.9). $15. (Auction #180, Lot 48).

OTHER MACHINE MADE. **Swirl.** Lot of nine marbles. Assortment of two color swirl. White base, transparent color swirl. Some Ravenswood. $13. (Auction #180, Lot 11).

OTHER MACHINE MADE. **Swirl.** Very nice three color swirl. My guess is that it is Cairo Novelty, based on the base color. 5/8". Mint (9.9). $12. (Auction #107, Lot 23).

OTHER MACHINE MADE. **Swirl.** Gorgeous swirl, although I am not sure of the manufacturer. Probably Alley Agate, possibly Heaton. 29/32". Near Mint(+) (8.9). $12. (Auction #68, Lot 40).

OTHER MACHINE MADE. **Swirl.** Three color swirl. Opaque white with red and blue swirls. This is not a Ravenswood. 19/32". Mint (9.9). $11. (Auction #152, Lot 15).

OTHER MACHINE MADE. **Swirl.** Lot of twenty seven marbles. Assortment of common swirls, predominately Heaton with some Alley. $10. (Auction #109, Lot 24).

OTHER MACHINE MADE. Swirl. Lot of four marbles. All are swirl. Three are transparent orange in translucent white. $9. (Auction #180, Lot 8).

OTHER MACHINE MADE. Swirl. I do not know who made this marble. I lean towards Cairo Novelty because of the odd colors. 21/32". Mint (9.9). $7. (Auction #103, Lot 30).

OTHER MACHINE MADE. Swirl. Lot of approximately sixty marbles. All are two color swirls. Red/brown on blue or red/brown on white. $7. (Auction #132, Lot 23).

OTHER MACHINE MADE. Swirl. Unusual swirl. I am not sure who the maker is, but is American and I feel it is 1955-1965. Opaque white. 19/32". Near Mint(+) (8.9). $5. (Auction #60, Lot 29).

OTHER MACHINE MADE. Swirl. My guess is that it is Cairo Novelty, based on the colors and design. You decide. Opaque white. 19/32". Mint (9.9). $2. (Auction #102, Lot 43).

OTHER MACHINE MADE. Swirl. Lot of three marbles. An Alley and two Champion. 19/32" to 21/32". Mint (9.9-9.5). $2. (Auction #102, Lot 8).

OTHER MACHINE MADE. Tournament marble. This is a marble used in the 1998 National Marbles Tournament in Wildwood New Jersey in June 1998. 5/8". Mint (9.9). $11. (Auction #147, Lot 19).

OTHER MACHINE MADE. Tournament marble. This is a marble used in the 1998 National Marbles Tournament in Wildwood New Jersey in June 1998. 5/8". Mint (9.9). $9. (Auction #147, Lot 19.10).

OTHER MACHINE MADE. Vacor de Mexico. Lot of thirty marbles. All are Vacor de Mexico patches. Shooters. All about 1". Almost all Mint. $20. (Auction #177, Lot 19).

OTHER MACHINE MADE. Vacor de Mexico. Lot of twenty four marbles. All are Vacor de Mexico Shooters. About 1". Most Mint. $14. (Auction #125, Lot 21).

OTHER MACHINE MADE. Vacor de Mexico. Lot of ten marbles. Assortment of modern Mexican marbles. 19/32" to 15/16". Mint (9.9-9.7). $4. (Auction #171, Lot 12).

OTHER MACHINE MADE. Vacor de Mexico. Lot of three marbles. All are shooter patches. 15/16" to 31/32". Mint (9.9). $4. (Auction #94, Lot 23).

OTHER MACHINE MADE. Vacor de Mexico. Modern Wasp. Black base, two red patches. 5/8". Mint (9.9). $3. (Auction #185, Lot 15).

OTHER MACHINE MADE. Vacor de Mexico. Lot of four marbles. All are two-color swirls, mimicking Christensen Agate swirls. 19/32". Mint (9.9). $2. (Auction #102, Lot 18).

OTHER MACHINE MADE. Wire pull. Lot of two marbles. One orange, one blue. Probably German, probably 1960s. 31/32". Mint(-) (9.1-9.0). $32. (Auction #185, Lot 30).

OTHER MACHINE MADE. Wire pull. Lot of two marbles. One green, one blue. Probably German, probably 1960s. 25/32". Mint (9.9). $22. (Auction #155, Lot 2).

OTHER MACHINE MADE. Wire pull. Lot of five marbles. Two clear, one green, one brown, one orange. Probably German, probably 1960s. $20. (Auction #127, Lot 2).

OTHER MACHINE MADE. Wire pull. Transparent clear base with translucent lime green wire edged by translucent white wire. 7/8". Mint (9.9). $17. (Auction #69, Lot 29).

OTHER MACHINE MADE. Wire pull. Nice wire pull. Transparent clear base. Opaque wire with transparent yellow wire next to it. 29/32". Mint (9.9). $15. (Auction #120, Lot 39).

OTHER MACHINE MADE. Wire pull. Lot of three marbles. All are transparent clear. Each has opaque white wire. $12. (Auction #167, Lot 1).

OTHER MACHINE MADE. Wire Pull. Lot of ten marbles. Nice assortment of colors. Clear base with white wire (2), blue base with white. $60. (Auction #55, Lot 26.20).

OTHER MACHINE MADE. Wire Pull. Lot of eleven marbles. Nice assortment of colors. Clear base with white wire (2), clear base with green. $60. (Auction #54, Lot 24).

OTHER MACHINE MADE. Wire Pull. Lot of ten marbles. Nice assortment of colors. Clear base with white wire (2), blue base with white. $60. (Auction #55, Lot 26).

OTHER MACHINE MADE. Wire Pull. Lot of ten marbles. Nice assortment of colors. Clear base with white wire (2), blue base with white. $60. (Auction #55, Lot 26.30).

OTHER MACHINE MADE. Wire Pull. Lot of eleven marbles. Nice assortment of colors. Clear base with white wire (2), clear base with green. $60. (Auction #54, Lot 24.30).

OTHER MACHINE MADE. Wire Pull. Lot of eleven marbles. Nice assortment of colors. Clear base with white wire (2), clear base with green. $60. (Auction #54, Lot 24.20).

OTHER MACHINE MADE. Wire Pull. One of the nicest wire pulls that I have ever seen. Transparent clear base. Superb wire of opaque white. 7/8". Mint (9.7). $55. (Auction #183, Lot 40).

OTHER MACHINE MADE. Wire Pull. Lot of two marbles. Both are wire pulls. First is transparent light green base with blue and white. $30. (Auction #54, Lot 12).

OTHER MACHINE MADE. Wire Pull. Transparent clear base. Translucent orange wire with translucent white wire next to it. 29/32". Mint (9.9). $30. (Auction #78, Lot 28).

OTHER MACHINE MADE. Wire Pull. Lot of five marbles. Assortment of wire pulls. White in blue, white in clear, white in blue. $27. (Auction #106, Lot 34).

OTHER MACHINE MADE. Wire Pull. Lot of four marbles. All clear base. All white wire with a second color. One is clear, one blue. $17. (Auction #127, Lot 14).

OTHER MACHINE MADE. Wire Pull. Lot of two marbles. Both are wire pulls. First is transparent light green base with white wire. 31/32". $15. (Auction #55, Lot 13).

OTHER MACHINE MADE. Wire Pull. Lot of four marbles. All clear base. All white wire with a second color. One is clear, one blue. $15. (Auction #127, Lot 14.20).

OTHER MACHINE MADE. Wire Pull. Transparent clear base. Translucent green wire edged by translucent white. Lots of unmelted sand. 7/8". Mint (9.9). $7. (Auction #68, Lot 9).

OTHER MACHINE MADE. Wire Pull. Transparent clear base with opaque white wire. Some small air bubbles. Surface in great shape. 7/8". Mint (9.9). $5. (Auction #62, Lot 11).

PELTIER GLASS COMPANY. Remnants of a mesh bag of Peltier Rainbos. Approximately thirty Rainbos. Mesh bag is missing. $21. (Auction #120, Lot 25).

PELTIER GLASS COMPANY. Acme Realer. Transparent dark blue base with four orange ribbons. Nice marble. Odder color for this type. Ottawa. 9/16". Mint (9.9). $14. (Auction #64, Lot 15).

PELTIER GLASS COMPANY. Assorted. Lot of approximately one hundred marbles. Assortment of Rainbo, Acme Realer, tri-color, multicolor. $85. (Auction #180, Lot 22).

PELTIER GLASS COMPANY. Assorted. Lot of seven marbles. Includes a Bumblebee, Christmas Tree, two slags multicolor, Bloodie and a Heaton. $65. (Auction #166, Lot 7).

PELTIER GLASS COMPANY. Assorted. Lot of approximately one hundred sixty marbles. Excellent assorment of Rainbos, Acme Realers. $60. (Auction #117, Lot 25).

PELTIER GLASS COMPANY. Assorted. Lot of twenty three marbles. Two Peerless Patch. Remainder are multicolor. 19/32" to 11/16". Mint. $55. (Auction #68, Lot 19).

PELTIER GLASS COMPANY. Assorted. Lot of seven marbles. Rebel, 3/4", Good(+) (7.9). Bumblebee, 21/32", Good(+) (7.9). National Line Rainbos. $50. (Auction #163, Lot 9).

PELTIER GLASS COMPANY. Assorted. Lot of four marbles. Three National Line Rainbos and one Bloodie. $50. (Auction #166, Lot 35).

PELTIER GLASS COMPANY. Assorted. Lot of approximately sixty marbles. Assortment of Sunsets and Acme Realers. Nice group. All about 5/8". $49. (Auction #163, Lot 25).

PELTIER GLASS COMPANY. Assorted. Lot of approximately forty five marbles. All are Peltier. Predominately Rainbo. Includes six-ribbons. $48. (Auction #180, Lot 33).

PELTIER GLASS COMPANY. Assorted. Lot of seven marbles. Includes three National Line Rainbo (two color) and four Peerless Patch. $46. (Auction #139, Lot 33).

PELTIER GLASS COMPANY. Assorted. Lot of sixteen marbles. Incudes four Bloodies, three Sunsets and nine multicolors. $42. (Auction #106, Lot 27).

PELTIER GLASS COMPANY. Assorted. Lot of six marbles. Includes a National Line Rainbo Tiger (Near Mint(+)), two Peerless Patch. $38. (Auction #75, Lot 17).

PELTIER GLASS COMPANY. Assorted. Lot of twenty nine marbles. All are tri-color or Rainbo. 19/32" to 5/8". Mint (9.9-9.5). $35. (Auction #171, Lot 27).

PELTIER GLASS COMPANY. Assorted. Lot of approximately forty marbles. Assortment of multicolor, Champion Jr., Rainbo and tri-color. $34. (Auction #146, Lot 18).

PELTIER GLASS COMPANY. Assorted. Lot of thirty marbles. Ten are yellow ribbon on white Rainbos. Ten are red or orange ribbon. $34. (Auction #159, Lot 20).

PELTIER GLASS COMPANY. Assorted. Lot of approximately forty five marbles. All are Peltier. Predominately Rainbo. Includes six-ribbons. $32. (Auction #180, Lot 31).

PELTIER GLASS COMPANY. Assorted. Lot of seventeen marbles. Two National Line Rainbo, two slags, one Peerless Patch, two tri-color. $32. (Auction #122, Lot 11).

PELTIER GLASS COMPANY. Assorted. Lot of forty five marbles. Forty four Rainbos, one slag. 5/8". Almost all are Mint. Mint (9.9) to Near Mint. $29. (Auction #172, Lot 28).

PELTIER GLASS COMPANY. Assorted. Lot of seventeen marbles. Two bloodies, one six-ribbon Rainbo, seven Sunsets, one Champion Jr. $27. (Auction #58, Lot 31).

PELTIER GLASS COMPANY. Assorted. Lot of seven marbles. Nice assortment. Includes a hard to find four color multicolor ribbon (Mint). $26. (Auction #112, Lot 13).

PELTIER GLASS COMPANY. Assorted. Lot of twenty marbles. Three Peerless Patch, seven Sunsets, ten tri-color. Almost all Mint. 19/32". $25. (Auction #132, Lot 20).

PELTIER GLASS COMPANY. Assorted. Lot of four marbles. A clear Rainbo, green slag, red slag, and two-color National Line Rainbo Zebra. $22. (Auction #175, Lot 38).

PELTIER GLASS COMPANY. Assorted. Lot of seventeen marbles. Fifteen are Peltier. Mostly Rainbos and tricolors, with a Peerless Patch. $21. (Auction #125, Lot 38).

PELTIER GLASS COMPANY. Assorted. Lot of thirteen marbles. Five Champion Jr, eight tri-color. 19/32" to 21/32". Mint (9.9) to Mint(-). $18. (Auction #171, Lot 15).

PELTIER GLASS COMPANY. Assorted. Lot of two marbles. First is a multicolor. Gorgeous. 11/16". Mint (9.9). The other is Champion Jr. $16. (Auction #173, Lot 5).

PELTIER GLASS COMPANY. Assorted. Lot of two marbles. One is a multicolor.Yellow, light blue and white on transparent light green. 5/8. $12. (Auction #172, Lot 33).

PELTIER GLASS COMPANY. Assorted. Lot of eleven marbles. Assortment of multicolors, Rainbos and a slag. Everything has some damage. 5/8". $9. (Auction #109, Lot 18).

PELTIER GLASS COMPANY. Assorted. Lot of three marbles. Two are Sunsets. Both are yellow, orange and white in transparent. 5/8" & 21/3. $7. (Auction #139, Lot 16).

PELTIER GLASS COMPANY. Banana. Rare Banana. Opaque white banana in transparent ruby red glass. Ottawa, IL, circa 1930-1945. 17/32". Mint (9.9). $50. (Auction #77, Lot 44).

PELTIER GLASS COMPANY. Banana. Lot of nine marbles. All are shooters. Assortment of color cores. 29/32" to 15/16". Mint (9.9-9.1). $24. (Auction #171, Lot 26).

PELTIER GLASS COMPANY. Bloodie. Lot of twenty five marbles. All are Bloodies. Excellent group. 5/8" to 11/16". Mint (9.9-9.7). $50. (Auction #139, Lot 26).

PELTIER GLASS COMPANY. Bloodie. Super example of a shooter Bloodie. Opalescent white base. Four ribbons of semi-opaque red and orange. 15/16". Mint (9.9). $44. (Auction #150, Lot 35).

PELTIER GLASS COMPANY. Bloodie. Shooter size Bloodie. One sparkle. Great example. Ottawa, IL, circa 1930-1940. 31/32". Mint(-) (9.2). $34. (Auction #120, Lot 4).

PELTIER GLASS COMPANY. Bloodie. Lot of seven marbles. All are Bloodies. Opalescent white base with transparent red ribbons. $30. (Auction #64, Lot 18).

PELTIER GLASS COMPANY. Bloodie. Super example of a Type I Bloodie shooter. Translucent milky white base. Translucent red band. 25/32". Mint (9.9). $28. (Auction #129, Lot 13).

PELTIER GLASS COMPANY. Bloodie. Lot of seven marbles. All are Peltier Bloodie Rainbos. Nice assortment of excellent design. Ottawa, IL. $27. (Auction #128, Lot 6).

PELTIER GLASS COMPANY. Bloodie. Shooter size Bloodie. One rough spot. Great example. Ottawa, IL, circa 1930-1940. 31/32". Mint(-) (9.0). 31/32". Mint(-) (9). $26. (Auction #138, Lot 20).

PELTIER GLASS COMPANY. Bloodie. Lot of eight marbles. All are Bloodies. Excellent group. 5/8" to 11/16". Mint (9.9-9.7). $25. (Auction #145, Lot 23.30).

PELTIER GLASS COMPANY. Bloodie. Lot of eight marbles. All are Bloodies. Excellent group. 5/8" to 11/16". Mint (9.9-9.7). $25. (Auction #145, Lot 23).

PELTIER GLASS COMPANY. Bloodie. Lot of eight marbles. All are Bloodies. Excellent group. 5/8" to 11/16". Mint (9.9-9.7). $25. (Auction #145, Lot 23.20).

PELTIER GLASS COMPANY. Champion Jr. Lot of ten marbles. All are Champion Jr. Transparent dark green base with stretched white and yellow. $22. (Auction #142, Lot 12).

PELTIER GLASS COMPANY. Champion Jr. Very nice and hard to find color combination for a Champion Jr. Opaque gray base. 11/16". Mint (9.9). $18. (Auction #116, Lot 36).

PELTIER GLASS COMPANY. Clear Rainbo. Hard to find five color Rainbo. Transparent clear glass. One ribbon each of opaque white, red. 9/16". Mint (9.9). $80. (Auction #150, Lot 42).

PELTIER GLASS COMPANY. Clear Rainbo. Hard to find five color Clear Rainbo. Transparent clear glass. One ribbon each of opaque white, red. 9/16". Mint(-) (9). $60. (Auction #71, Lot 8).

PELTIER GLASS COMPANY. Clear Rainbo. Beautiful example of this type. Transparent clear base. One ribbon each of opaque red, opaque white. 21/32". Mint (9.9). $55. (Auction #126, Lot 31).

PELTIER GLASS COMPANY. Clear Rainbo. Hard to find five color Clear Rainbo. Transparent clear glass. One ribbon each of opaque white, red. 9/16". Mint(-) (9). $38. (Auction #160, Lot 43).

PELTIER GLASS COMPANY. Clear Rainbo. Hard to find Clear Rainbo. Transparent clear base. Opaque white ribbon, opaque yellow ribbon. 5/8". Mint(-) (9). $35. (Auction #80, Lot 40).

PELTIER GLASS COMPANY. Clear Rainbo. Four color National Line Rainbo. Transparent clear base. Two red ribbons, one yellow, one white. 5/8". Mint (9.9). $24. (Auction #56, Lot 39).

PELTIER GLASS COMPANY. Clear Rainbo. Transparent clear base. Two green ribbons, two red ribbons and two white ribbons. 21/32". Near Mint(+) (8.9). $20. (Auction #55, Lot 38).

PELTIER GLASS COMPANY. Clear Rainbo. Transparent clear base. Two green ribbons, two red ribbons and two white ribbons. 21/32". Near Mint(+) (8.9). $20. (Auction #104, Lot 46).

PELTIER GLASS COMPANY. Craft nuggets. Lot of forty one items. Assortment of flattened Bananas and clearies. Used in craft projects. $7. (Auction #138, Lot 19).

PELTIER GLASS COMPANY. Jobber box. Original rectangular jobber box. The box is pink leather-grained paper on cardboard. These are usual. $60. (Auction #107, Lot 28).

PELTIER GLASS COMPANY. Miller machine. This is a great Miller machine swirl. Super example. Semi-opaque blue base with dark red swirls cover. 21/32". Mint(-) (9.3). $150. (Auction #121, Lot 34).

PELTIER GLASS COMPANY. Miller swirl. Superb example of a two color Miller swirl Zebra. One of the finest I have ever seen!! Opaque white. 21/32". Mint (9.9). $220. (Auction #65, Lot 41).

PELTIER GLASS COMPANY. Miller swirl. Exceptional two color Miller Swirl Ketchup and Mustard. Opaque white base. Almost completely covered. 11/16". Mint(-) (9). $170. (Auction #100, Lot 41).

PELTIER GLASS COMPANY. Miller swirl. Three color Miller Swirl Christmas Tree. Outstanding example!!!. Opaque white. Almost completely covered. 5/8". Mint (9.9). $170. (Auction #121, Lot 10).

PELTIER GLASS COMPANY. Miller swirl. Miller swirl Wasp. Opaque red with black swirling. One small seam. One tiny air hole. 5/8". Mint (9.7). $130. (Auction #75, Lot 30).

PELTIER GLASS COMPANY. Miller swirl. Super example of a Miller Swirl. Opaque light blue base. Six brown/red ribbons on it. One seam. Nice. 21/32". Mint (9.9). $120. (Auction #118, Lot 49).

PELTIER GLASS COMPANY. Miller swirl. Shooter size two color Miller Zebra. Opaque white base with eight black ribbons. Has a small chip. 25/32". Mint (8.7). $30. (Auction #113, Lot 12).

PELTIER GLASS COMPANY. Miller swirl. Three color Miller swirl Superman. Light blue base with opaque red and yellow swirls. One seam. 11/16". Good(+) (7.80). $17. (Auction #76, Lot 10).

PELTIER GLASS COMPANY. Multicolor. Lot of thirty seven marbles. All are multicolors. Excellent assortment of colors and designs. $100. (Auction #155, Lot 21).

PELTIER GLASS COMPANY. Multicolor. Superior marble. Swirl type. Light transparent green base with swirls of yellow, light blue and white. 21/32". Mint (9.9). $75. (Auction #182, Lot 5).

PELTIER GLASS COMPANY. Multicolor. Lot of approximately thirty five marbles. Almost all are Peltier multicolors. Also, a Rainbo. $75. (Auction #151, Lot 15).

PELTIER GLASS COMPANY. Multicolor. Superb multicolor swirl. Transparent light green base. Opaque yellow, light blue and light yellow swirl. 5/8". Mint (9.9). $65. (Auction #71, Lot 6).

PELTIER GLASS COMPANY. Multicolor. Lot of twenty three marbles. All are multicolor. Excellent assortment of types, patterns and colors. $60. (Auction #163, Lot 28).

PELTIER GLASS COMPANY. Multicolor. Shooter size multicolor. Hard to find these larger sizes. Transparent dark green base. Two ribbons. 1-1/16". Near Mint(+) (8.9). $60. (Auction #142, Lot 7).

PELTIER GLASS COMPANY. Multicolor. Lot of four marbles. Assortment of colors and designs. Some real beauties here. 21/32" to 11/16". Near Mint (8.6). $50. (Auction #185, Lot 11).

PELTIER GLASS COMPANY. Multicolor. Lot of five marbles. Assortment of styles and colors. Two are Mint, others have tiny hit marks. Ottawa. $47. (Auction #60, Lot 39).

PELTIER GLASS COMPANY. Multicolor. Lot of eight marbles. Excellent assortment of patterns and colors. Very nice group! All about 5/8". $46. (Auction #139, Lot 24).

PELTIER GLASS COMPANY. **Multicolor.** Outstanding pattern. Transparent dark green base. Two ribbons each of white, yellow and light blue. 21/32". Near Mint(+) (8.9). $44. (Auction #181, Lot 35).

PELTIER GLASS COMPANY. **Multicolor.** Lot of five marbles. All are multicolors. Excellent variety of colors and patterns. Super set. 19/32". $42. (Auction #170, Lot 21).

PELTIER GLASS COMPANY. **Multicolor.** Lot of five marbles. All are multicolor. Six ribbons in three colors on transparent green. Assorted. $41. (Auction #159, Lot 11).

PELTIER GLASS COMPANY. **Multicolor.** Very nice design. Transparent green base with orange, blue and white ribbons. Looks great. Ottawa, IL. 5/8". Mint (9.9). $40. (Auction #185, Lot 3).

PELTIER GLASS COMPANY. **Multicolor.** Lot of five marbles. Each a different color pattern, including a rare six ribbon salmon, white. $38. (Auction #184, Lot 9).

PELTIER GLASS COMPANY. **Multicolor.** Gorgeous multicolor swirl. Super marble. Transparent light green base. Swirls of light blue, orange. 5/8". Mint (9.9). $37. (Auction #152, Lot 38).

PELTIER GLASS COMPANY. **Multicolor.** Lot of approximately sixty marbles. Assortment of colors. All are about 5/8". Almost all are Mint. $37. (Auction #138, Lot 26).

PELTIER GLASS COMPANY. **Multicolor.** Lot of six marbles. All are multicolor. Transparent dark green base with assorted color ribbons. $36. (Auction #101, Lot 42).

PELTIER GLASS COMPANY. **Multicolor.** Nice multicolor. Very light transparent green base. Two ribbons each of red, white and green brushed. 11/16". Mint (9.9). $35. (Auction #140, Lot 20).

PELTIER GLASS COMPANY. **Multicolor.** Lot of thirteen marbles. All are basically the same color. Transparent green base with ribbons. $31. (Auction #171, Lot 14).

PELTIER GLASS COMPANY. **Multicolor.** Transparent very light green base with opaque white, opaque green and opaque orange/red swirls. 11/16". Mint (9.5). $30. (Auction #83, Lot 6).

PELTIER GLASS COMPANY. **Multicolor.** Lot of two marbles. Both are multicolors. First is transparent dark green base with two ribbons each. $30. (Auction #88, Lot 29).

PELTIER GLASS COMPANY. **Multicolor.** Super example of this type. Light transparent green base. Ribbons of ruddy orange, white and blue. 5/8". Mint (9.9). $29. (Auction #70, Lot 35).

PELTIER GLASS COMPANY. **Multicolor.** Beautiful example. Light transparent green base. Swirls of light green, red, white. 5/8". Mint (9.7). $27. (Auction #156, Lot 11).

PELTIER GLASS COMPANY. **Multicolor.** Super example of this type. Light transparent green base. Ribbons of ruddy orange, white and blue. 5/8". Mint (9.9). $27. (Auction #70, Lot 35.20).

PELTIER GLASS COMPANY. **Multicolor.** Super example of this type. Light transparent green base. Ribbons of ruddy orange, white and blue. 5/8". Mint (9.9). $27. (Auction #70, Lot 35.30).

PELTIER GLASS COMPANY. **Multicolor.** Lot of four marbles. Assortment of multicolors. Two are yellow, light blue and white on transparent. $26. (Auction #58, Lot 32).

PELTIER GLASS COMPANY. **Multicolor.** Super multicolor. Very light transparent green base. Bands of light blue, white and orange on one side. 5/8". Mint (9.9). $26. (Auction #121, Lot 17).

PELTIER GLASS COMPANY. **Multicolor.** Transparent green base. Two ribbons each of red, light blue and white. One sparkle. Nice example. 21/32". Mint(-) (9.1). $25. (Auction #162, Lot 18).

PELTIER GLASS COMPANY. **Multicolor.** Transparent dark green base with two ribbons each of white, light blue and yellow. Nice marble. Ottawa. 5/8". Mint (9.7). $25. (Auction #87, Lot 38).

PELTIER GLASS COMPANY. **Multicolor.** Light transparent green base. Light blue, yellow and white swirls. Two seam. Nice pattern. 23/32". Near Mint(+) (8.9). $24. (Auction #65, Lot 31).

PELTIER GLASS COMPANY. **Multicolor.** Transparent dark green base with red and light blue ribbons. Excellent swirling pattern. 21/32". Mint(-) (9.1). $22. (Auction #77, Lot 31).

PELTIER GLASS COMPANY. **Multicolor.** Transparent green base. Ribbons of green, red and white. Nice pattern. Two seams. Ottawa, IL. 21/32". Mint (9.7). $22. (Auction #65, Lot 26).

PELTIER GLASS COMPANY. **Multicolor.** Super example of this type. Light transparent green base. Ribbons of ruddy orange, white and blue. 5/8". Mint (9.9). $21. (Auction #70, Lot 35.40).

PELTIER GLASS COMPANY. **Multicolor.** Super multicolor swirl. Transparent green base. Swirls of orange, blue and white. One tiny melt spot. 23/32". Mint(-) (9). $21. (Auction #150, Lot 1).

PELTIER GLASS COMPANY. **Multicolor.** Superb example. Very light transparent green base. Four light blue ribbons, two white ribbons. 5/8". Mint (9.9). $21. (Auction #56, Lot 11).

PELTIER GLASS COMPANY. **Multicolor.** Superb multicolor. Very light transparent green base glass. Two seams. Swirls of orange, light blue. 23/32". Mint (9.7). $20. (Auction #65, Lot 1).

PELTIER GLASS COMPANY. **Multicolor.** Nice multicolor. Transparent green base. Swirls of red, light blue and white. Nice design. Ottawa, IL. 21/32". Mint (9.8). $20. (Auction #158, Lot 31).

PELTIER GLASS COMPANY. **Multicolor.** Lots of swirl, but still a two seam type. White, light blue, light orange and transparent light red. 5/8". Near Mint (8.4). $20. (Auction #60, Lot 34).

PELTIER GLASS COMPANY. **Multicolor.** Transparent light green base. Swirls of blue, white and orange. One sparkle. Ottawa, IL, circa 1930. 21/32". Mint(-) (9.1). $20. (Auction #153, Lot 3).

PELTIER GLASS COMPANY. **Multicolor.** Transparent dark green base with orange, blue and white swirls. Two seam. Nice design. One small melt spot. 3/4". Mint (9.3). $17. (Auction #65, Lot 12).

PELTIER GLASS COMPANY. **Multicolor.** Transparent green base. Wide ribbons of white, light blue and yellow. A real beauty. 11/16". Mint(-) (9.1). $16. (Auction #126, Lot 25).

PELTIER GLASS COMPANY. **Multicolor.** Very pretty multicolor. Transparent dark green base. Band of light blue and band of dark red. 21/32". Mint (9.9). $14. (Auction #129, Lot 5).

PELTIER GLASS COMPANY. **Multicolor.** Lot of nine marbles. Assortment of multicolors in various styles and colors. All about 5/8". $11. (Auction #122, Lot 33).

PELTIER GLASS COMPANY. **Multicolor.** Transparent green base with two ribbons each of light blue, white and yellow. One subsurface moon. 3/4". Near Mint(+) (8.7). $10. (Auction #131, Lot 6).

PELTIER GLASS COMPANY. **Multicolor.** Transparent dark green base. Ribbons of white, light blue and red. One tiny pit. Ottawa, IL. 11/16". Near Mint(+) (8.9). $6. (Auction #143, Lot 6).

PELTIER GLASS COMPANY. **Multicolor ribbon.** Lot of eight marbles. All are transparent green base with yellow, light blue and white ribbons. $35. (Auction #54, Lot 29).

PELTIER GLASS COMPANY. **Multicolor swirl.** Excellent example of a multicolor swirl. Transparent light green base. Mostly opaque orange. 5/8". Mint(-) (9). $25. (Auction #61, Lot 3).

PELTIER GLASS COMPANY. **National Line Rainbo.** Shooter size three color National Line Rainbo Golden Rebel. Very difficult size to find. 25/32". Near Mint(-) (8.2). $485. (Auction #71, Lot 41).

PELTIER GLASS COMPANY. **National Line Rainbo.** This is barely a Superman. Large shooter though and in great shape! Opaque light blue base. 27/32". Mint (9.9). $400. (Auction #103, Lot 47).

PELTIER GLASS COMPANY. **National Line Rainbo.** Harder to find shooter three color National Line Rainbo Christmas Tree. Reverse design. Opaque white. 13/16". Mint (9.9). $325. (Auction #65, Lot 44).

PELTIER GLASS COMPANY. **National Line Rainbo.** What else can I say, but Wow!! A very rare three color National Line Rainbo Superman. 25/32". Near Mint(+) (8.8). $310. (Auction #58, Lot 45).

PELTIER GLASS COMPANY. **National Line Rainbo.** Three-color National Line Rainbo Superman. An exceptional example, a Type II National Line. 11/16". Mint (9.9). $310. (Auction #110, Lot 48).

PELTIER GLASS COMPANY. **National Line Rainbo.** Three color National Line Rainbo Superman. Light blue base. Three red ribbons, three yellow ribbons. 5/8". Mint (9.9). $305. (Auction #55, Lot 40).

PELTIER GLASS COMPANY. **National Line Rainbo.** Unusual four color National Line Rainbo Superman. Opaque light blue base. Six opaque red ribbons. 5/8". Mint (9.8). $290. (Auction #71, Lot 43).

PELTIER GLASS COMPANY. **National Line Rainbo.** Three color shooter National Line Rainbo Liberty. Opaque white base. Six translucent red/orange ribbons. 25/32". Mint(-) (9.2). $270. (Auction #184, Lot 49).

PELTIER GLASS COMPANY. **National Line Rainbo.** Shooter size three color National Line Rainbo Superman. Opaque light blue base with two yellow ribbons. 27/32". Near Mint(+) (8.7). $260. (Auction #94, Lot 49).

PELTIER GLASS COMPANY. **National Line Rainbo.** Three color National Line Rainbo Superman. Opaque light blue base with four red ribbons and two yellow. 21/32". Mint (9.9). $235. (Auction #81, Lot 43).

PELTIER GLASS COMPANY. **National Line Rainbo.** Three color National Line Rainbo Superman. Very unusual example. Opaque light blue base. Six ribbons. 21/32". Near Mint(+) (8.9). $230. (Auction #96, Lot 44).

PELTIER GLASS COMPANY. **National Line Rainbo.** Shooter three color National Line Rainbo Christmas Tree. Opaque white base. Four transparent red ribbons. 3/4". Mint (9.5). $220. (Auction #131, Lot 20).

PELTIER GLASS COMPANY. **National Line Rainbo.** Three color National Line Rainbo Superman. Light blue base. Three red ribbons and three yellow ribbons. 5/8". Near Mint(-) (8.2). $220. (Auction #54, Lot 45).

PELTIER GLASS COMPANY. National Line Rainbo. Very hard to find four color National Line Rainbo. This is a type of Blue Galaxy. Opaque light blue. 21/32". Near Mint(+) (8.8). $220. (Auction #63, Lot 45).

PELTIER GLASS COMPANY. National Line Rainbo. Three color National Line Rainbo Christmas Tree. Outstanding example. Opaque white base. 19/32". Mint (9.9). $215. (Auction #129, Lot 44).

PELTIER GLASS COMPANY. National Line Rainbo. Three color National Line Rainbo Superman. Opaque light blue base, three red ribbons and three yellow. 19/32". Mint (9.9). $210. (Auction #91, Lot 43).

PELTIER GLASS COMPANY. National Line Rainbo. Three-color National Line Rainbo Graycoat. Opaque white base. Four thin ribbons of translucent red. 21/32". Mint(-) (9). $210. (Auction #151, Lot 47).

PELTIER GLASS COMPANY. National Line Rainbo. Three color National Line Rainbo Superman. Opaque light blue base. Four ribbons of red. 11/16". Mint (9.9). $200. (Auction #121, Lot 45).

PELTIER GLASS COMPANY. National Line Rainbo. Three color National Line Rainbo Liberty. Shooter size. Superior example. Opaque white base. 23/32". Mint (9.6). $200. (Auction #147, Lot 47).

PELTIER GLASS COMPANY. National Line Rainbo. Three color National Line Rainbo Superman. Very unusual example. Opaque light blue base. 5/8". Mint (9.9). $200. (Auction #130, Lot 49).

PELTIER GLASS COMPANY. National Line Rainbo. Shooter three-color National Line Rainbo Christmas Tree. Opaque white base. Four transparent red ribbons. 25/32". Mint(-) (9). $200. (Auction #183, Lot 47).

PELTIER GLASS COMPANY. National Line Rainbo. Three color National Line Rainbo Ketchup and Mustard. Shooter size. Exceptional marble. Opaque white. 25/32". Near Mint(+) (8.9). $180. (Auction #125, Lot 47).

PELTIER GLASS COMPANY. National Line Rainbo. Two color National Line Rainbo Blue Zebra. Opaque white base. Four ribbons of blue/black. 5/8". Mint (9.9). $175. (Auction #134, Lot 33).

PELTIER GLASS COMPANY. National Line Rainbo. Three color National Line Rainbo Superman. Light blue base. Six ribbons of red and three of yellow. 5/8". Near Mint(+) (8.8). $170. (Auction #164, Lot 45).

PELTIER GLASS COMPANY. National Line Rainbo. Two color National Line Rainbo Chocolate Cow. Aventurine black ribbons on opaque cocoa brown. 19/32". Mint (9.9). $170. (Auction #162, Lot 47).

PELTIER GLASS COMPANY. National Line Rainbo. Two color National Line Rainbo Chocolate Cow. Aventurine black ribbons on opaque cocoa brown. 19/32". Mint (9.9). $160. (Auction #175, Lot 49).

PELTIER GLASS COMPANY. National Line Rainbo. Three color National Line Rainbo Ketchup and Mustard. Opaque white base. Three ribbons of orange/red. 3/4". Mint(-) (9). $155. (Auction #148, Lot 49).

PELTIER GLASS COMPANY. National Line Rainbo. Three color National Line Rainbo Liberty. Outstanding example!!! Opaque white base. 21/32". Mint (9.9). $150. (Auction #124, Lot 49).

PELTIER GLASS COMPANY. National Line Rainbo. Very rare four color National Line Rainbo Hybrid. Christmas Tree/Ketchup and Mustard. 5/8". Near Mint(+) (8.9). $145. (Auction #136, Lot 33).

PELTIER GLASS COMPANY. National Line Rainbo. Three color National Line Rainbo Ketchup and Mustard. Shooter size. Opaque white base. 23/32". Mint (9.9). $135. (Auction #112, Lot 42).

PELTIER GLASS COMPANY. National Line Rainbo. Lot of eight marbles. Nice assortment, but all have some damage. Includes a Superman, Liberty, Rebel. $130. (Auction #97, Lot 16).

PELTIER GLASS COMPANY. National Line Rainbo. Lot of two marbles. First is a three color Superman. Shooter size!! Excellent coloring and design. $130. (Auction #136, Lot 20).

PELTIER GLASS COMPANY. National Line Rainbo. Four color National Line Rainbo Liberty/Gray Coat hybrid. Opaque white base. Four translucent red ribbons. 21/32". Mint (9.9). $130. (Auction #64, Lot 27).

PELTIER GLASS COMPANY. National Line Rainbo. Three color National Line Rainbo Christmas Tree. Opaque white base. Four ribbons of red. 5/8". Near Mint(+) (8.9). $120. (Auction #172, Lot 41).

PELTIER GLASS COMPANY. National Line Rainbo. Three color National Line Rainbo Rebel. Opaque white base. Two ribbons of transparent red. 19/32". Mint(-) (9.2). $120. (Auction #136, Lot 45).

PELTIER GLASS COMPANY. National Line Rainbo. Two color National Line Rainbo Tiger. Four aventurine black ribbons on bright orange. Superior shape. 21/32". Mint (9.9). $120. (Auction #164, Lot 41).

PELTIER GLASS COMPANY. National Line Rainbo. Three color National Line Rainbo Ketchup and Mustard shooter. Opaque white base with four red ribbons. 23/32". Mint (9.9). $120. (Auction #81, Lot 39).

PELTIER GLASS COMPANY. National Line Rainbo. Three color National Line Rainbo Superman. Shooter size. Opaque light blue base

with four red ribbons. $110. (Auction #122, Lot 39).

PELTIER GLASS COMPANY. National Line Rainbo. Three color National Line Rainbo Liberty. Opaque white base with four transparent red ribbons. 5/8". Mint (9.8). $101. (Auction #59, Lot 33).

PELTIER GLASS COMPANY. National Line Rainbo. Three color National Line Rainbo Christmas Tree. Opaque white base. Four ribbons of red. 5/8". Near Mint(+) (8.9). $100. (Auction #134, Lot 8).

PELTIER GLASS COMPANY. National Line Rainbo. Shooter size three color National Line Rainbo Ketchup and Mustard. Opaque white base. 3/4". Near Mint(+) (8.8). $99. (Auction #60, Lot 44).

PELTIER GLASS COMPANY. National Line Rainbo. Three color National Line Rainbo Rebel. Opaque white base. Four translucent red ribbons. 23/32". Mint (9.9). $95. (Auction #65, Lot 40).

PELTIER GLASS COMPANY. National Line Rainbo. Beautiful three color National Line Rainbo Ketchup and Mustard. Opaque white base. Four red ribbons. 5/8". Mint (9.9). $95. (Auction #71, Lot 12).

PELTIER GLASS COMPANY. National Line Rainbo. Three-color National Line Rainbo Superman. Light blue base. Four red on yellow ribbons, two yellow ribbons. $95. (Auction #170, Lot 5).

PELTIER GLASS COMPANY. National Line Rainbo. Three color National Line Rainbo Rebel. Type II National Line Rainbo. Opaque white base. Three bands. 17/32". Mint (9.9). $95. (Auction #129, Lot 42).

PELTIER GLASS COMPANY. National Line Rainbo. Three color National Line Rainbo Rebel. Opaque white base. Four ribbons of red, two of black. 5/8". Mint(-) (9). $92. (Auction #171, Lot 47).

PELTIER GLASS COMPANY. National Line Rainbo. Harder to find type. Opaque white base. Six ribbons of transparent red/brown on green. Some aventurine. 23/32". Near Mint(+) (8.9). $90. (Auction #131, Lot 16).

PELTIER GLASS COMPANY. National Line Rainbo. Three color National Line Rainbo Ketchup and Mustard. Opaque white base. Four red ribbons, two yellow. 9/16". Mint (9.9). $90. (Auction #133, Lot 37).

PELTIER GLASS COMPANY. National Line Rainbo. Three color National Line Rainbo Liberty. Opaque white base. Four transparent orange/red ribbons. 5/8". Mint (9.9). $90. (Auction #88, Lot 34).

PELTIER GLASS COMPANY. National Line Rainbo. Two color National Line Rainbo Graycoat. Opaque white base. Four wide transparent red ribbons. 5/8". Mint (9.9). $90. (Auction #65, Lot 15).

PELTIER GLASS COMPANY. National Line Rainbo. Three color National Line Rainbo Liberty. Opaque white base. Four wide ribbons of transparent red. 13/16". Near Mint(-) (8). $90. (Auction #170, Lot 32).

PELTIER GLASS COMPANY. National Line Rainbo. Three color National Line Rainbo Liberty. Opaque white base. Four orange/red ribbons. Two blue ribbons. 5/8". Mint (9.9). $85. (Auction #105, Lot 8).

PELTIER GLASS COMPANY. National Line Rainbo. A very rare marble. A peewee size two color National Line Rainbo Chocolate Cow. 1/2". Near Mint(+) (8.9). $85. (Auction #70, Lot 40).

PELTIER GLASS COMPANY. National Line Rainbo. Very unusual three color National Line Rainbo Liberty. Opaque white base. Four wide translucent red ribbons. 5/8". Mint(-) (9.2). $85. (Auction #92, Lot 43).

PELTIER GLASS COMPANY. National Line Rainbo. Three color National Lien Rainbo Superman. Opaque light blue base. Four wide red ribbons. 21/32". Near Mint(+) (8.2). $80. (Auction #109, Lot 38).

PELTIER GLASS COMPANY. National Line Rainbo. Superb two color National Line Rainbo Tiger. Opaque orange base with four aventurine black ribbons. 19/32". Mint (9.9). $80. (Auction #91, Lot 17).

PELTIER GLASS COMPANY. National Line Rainbo. Lot of two marbles. Both are three color National Line Rainbo. First is a Christmas Tree, 19/32". $80. (Auction #94, Lot 39).

PELTIER GLASS COMPANY. National Line Rainbo. Three color National Line Rainbo Superman. Polished. 19/32". $80. (Auction #125, Lot 11).

PELTIER GLASS COMPANY. National Line Rainbo. Three color National Line Rainbo Liberty. Opaque white base. Three ribbons of transparent red. 21/32". Mint (9.9). $80. (Auction #116, Lot 44).

PELTIER GLASS COMPANY. National Line Rainbo. Three color National Line Rainbo Christmas Tree. Opaque white base. Four red ribbons and two green. 21/32". Mint(-) (9.1). $75. (Auction #164, Lot 39).

PELTIER GLASS COMPANY. National Line Rainbo. Three color National Line Rainbo Liberty. Semi-opaque milky white glass. Four transparent red ribbon. 5/8". Mint (9.9). $75. (Auction #149, Lot 47).

PELTIER GLASS COMPANY. National Line Rainbo. Two color National Line Rainbo Tiger. Superb example. Aventurine black ribbons on opaque orange. 5/8". Mint (9.9). $75. (Auction #131, Lot 40).

PELTIER GLASS COMPANY. National Line Rainbo. Three color National Line Rainbo Christmas Tree. Opaque white base. Four brown/red ribbons. 5/8". Mint (9.9). $75. (Auction #105, Lot 34).

PELTIER GLASS COMPANY. National Line Rainbo. Three color National Line Rainbo Rebel. Opaque white base. Three transparent orange/red ribbons. 21/32". Near Mint(+) (8.9). $75. (Auction #93, Lot 10).

PELTIER GLASS COMPANY. National Line Rainbo. Beautiful two color National Line Rainbo Tiger. Four aventurine black ribbon on opaque orange. 5/8". Mint (9.9). $75. (Auction #80, Lot 43).

PELTIER GLASS COMPANY. National Line Rainbo. Shooter size two color National Line Rainbo. Light blue base with yellow ribbons. In great shape. 27/32". Mint (9.9). $75. (Auction #59, Lot 16).

PELTIER GLASS COMPANY. National Line Rainbo. Three color National Line Rainbo Christmas Tree. Opaque white base with three transparent ribbons. 5/8". Mint (9.8). $73. (Auction #158, Lot 47).

PELTIER GLASS COMPANY. National Line Rainbo. Lot of two marbles. First is a three color National Line Rainbo Superman. 19/32". Polished. $70. (Auction #115, Lot 16).

PELTIER GLASS COMPANY. National Line Rainbo. Shooter size three color National Line Rainbo Superman. Opaque light blue base, four red ribbons. 25/32". Good(-) (7.10). $70. (Auction #104, Lot 12).

PELTIER GLASS COMPANY. National Line Rainbo. A beautiful three color National Line Rainbo Ketchup and Mustard. White base. Four red ribbons. 19/32". Mint (9.9). $70. (Auction #58, Lot 34).

PELTIER GLASS COMPANY. National Line Rainbo. Three color National Line Rainbo Rebel. Opaque white base with three red ribbons and three black ribbons. 21/32". Mint(-) (9.1). $70. (Auction #115, Lot 42).

PELTIER GLASS COMPANY. National Line Rainbo. Three color National Line Rainbo Liberty/Christmas Tree hybrid. Opaque white base. 5/8". Near Mint(+) (8.9). $70. (Auction #185, Lot 40).

PELTIER GLASS COMPANY. National Line Rainbo. Two color National Line Rainbo Ketchup and Mustard. Opaque white base. Four transparent orange/red ribbons. 5/8". Mint (9.9). $65. (Auction #64, Lot 42).

PELTIER GLASS COMPANY. National Line Rainbo. Three color National Line Rainbo Liberty. Outstanding example. Opaque white base. 5/8". Near Mint(+) (8.9). $65. (Auction #172, Lot 45).

PELTIER GLASS COMPANY. National Line Rainbo. Shooter. Two color National Line Rainbo. Opaque green base with six red ribbons. 13/16". Near Mint(+) (8.9). $65. (Auction #103, Lot 36).

PELTIER GLASS COMPANY. National Line Rainbo. Two color National Line Rainbo Bumblebee. Opaque yellow base with aventurine black ribbons. 9/16". Mint (9.9). $65. (Auction #93, Lot 4).

PELTIER GLASS COMPANY. National Line Rainbo. Lot of two marbles. Both are three color National Line Rainbo. Christmas Tree, 5/8", Near Mint(+). $65. (Auction #101, Lot 40).

PELTIER GLASS COMPANY. National Line Rainbo. Shooter two-color National Line Rainbo Zebra. Opaque white base with aventurine black ribbons. 13/16". Mint (9). $65. (Auction #173, Lot 35).

PELTIER GLASS COMPANY. National Line Rainbo. Three color National Line Rainbo Ketchup and Mustard. Opaque white base. Four transparent ribbons. 21/32". Mint (9.9). $65. (Auction #175, Lot 41).

PELTIER GLASS COMPANY. National Line Rainbo. Lot of four marbles. Set of two-color National Line Rainbo "animals". Zebra, black on white, 5/8", $60. (Auction #92, Lot 14).

PELTIER GLASS COMPANY. National Line Rainbo. Three color National Line Rainbo Ketchup and Mustard. Semi-opaque white base. Four wide ribbons. 19/32". Mint (9.9). $60. (Auction #164, Lot 30).

PELTIER GLASS COMPANY. National Line Rainbo. Three color National Line Rainbo Christmas Tree. Opaque white base. Four thin transparent swirls. 23/32". Near Mint (8.4). $60. (Auction #172, Lot 10).

PELTIER GLASS COMPANY. National Line Rainbo. Two color National Line Rainbo. Four brown/red ribbons on semi-opaque blue. Hard to find coloring. 9/16". Mint (9.9). $60. (Auction #180, Lot 49).

PELTIER GLASS COMPANY. National Line Rainbo. This is another very rare marrble. Two color National Line Rainbo Tiger. 21/32". Mint(-) (9). $60. (Auction #61, Lot 35).

PELTIER GLASS COMPANY. National Line Rainbo. Two color National Line Rainbo. Six ribbons of yellow on opaque light blue. Usually, four. 15/16". Near Mint(+) (8.9). $60. (Auction #158, Lot 43).

PELTIER GLASS COMPANY. National Line Rainbo. Yellow ribbons on green. Very heavy twist. Some very minor aventurine next to some of the yellow. 23/32". Mint (9.9). $55. (Auction #136, Lot 10).

PELTIER GLASS COMPANY. National Line Rainbo. Two color National Line Rainbo Tiger. Opaque orange base with aventurine black ribbons. 5/8". Mint (9.9). $55. (Auction #121, Lot 49).

PELTIER GLASS COMPANY. National Line Rainbo. Two color National Line Rainbo Wasp. Opaque bright red base with aventurine black ribbons. Excellent. 19/32". Mint(-) (9.2). $55. (Auction #105, Lot 42).

PELTIER GLASS COMPANY. National Line Rainbo. Interesting three color, four ribbon, National Line Rainbo. Light blue base. Four orange ribbons. 5/8". Mint (9.9). $55. (Auction #103, Lot 6).

PELTIER GLASS COMPANY. National Line Rainbo. Very unusual three color National Line Rainbo Rebel. Opaque white base. Six wide transparent red ribbons. 5/8". Near Mint (8.6). $55. (Auction #70, Lot 16).

PELTIER GLASS COMPANY. National Line Rainbo. Exceptional two color National Line Rainbo Bumblebee. Aventurine black ribbons on pale yellow. 19/32". Mint (9.9). $55. (Auction #56, Lot 44).

PELTIER GLASS COMPANY. National Line Rainbo. Very odd three color National Line Rainbo Rebel. Opaque white base. Two transparent red ribbons. 5/8". Mint (9.9). $55. (Auction #54, Lot 6).

PELTIER GLASS COMPANY. National Line Rainbo. Oddly colored three color National Line Rainbo. Opaque light blue base. Five ribbons of yellow cover. 5/8". Mint (9.9). $55. (Auction #105, Lot 21).

PELTIER GLASS COMPANY. National Line Rainbo. Three color National Line Rainbo Ketchup and Mustard. Opaque white base. Four translucent ribbons. 21/32". Mint(-) (9). $55. (Auction #163, Lot 32).

PELTIER GLASS COMPANY. National Line Rainbo. Three color National Line Rainbo Rebel. Opaque white base. Three orange/red ribbons and three black. 21/32". Mint(-) (9). $55. (Auction #173, Lot 47).

PELTIER GLASS COMPANY. National Line Rainbo. Three color National Line Rainbo Liberty. Opaque white base. Three red ribbons and three blue bands. 5/8". Mint (9.5). $55. (Auction #163, Lot 46).

PELTIER GLASS COMPANY. National Line Rainbo. Opaque light blue base with six red ribbons. Nice swirling pattern. A shooter, which is hard to find. 7/8". Near Mint (8.6). $55. (Auction #77, Lot 20).

PELTIER GLASS COMPANY. National Line Rainbo. Opaque creamy white base with transparent green and transparent red ribbons. Excellent swirling. 11/16". Near Mint(+) (8.9). $55. (Auction #97, Lot 6).

PELTIER GLASS COMPANY. National Line Rainbo. Three color National Line Rainbo Ketchup and Mustard. Opaque white base with four transparent red ribbons. 5/8". Mint (9.9). $55. (Auction #167, Lot 36).

PELTIER GLASS COMPANY. National Line Rainbo. Three color National Line Rainbo Rebel. Opaque white base. Three ribbons of transparent red. 5/8". Mint(-) (9). $50. (Auction #164, Lot 33).

PELTIER GLASS COMPANY. National Line Rainbo. Nice two color shooter size National Line Rainbo. Red ribbons on blue. In exceptional shape. 23/32". Mint (9.9). $50. (Auction #56, Lot 33).

PELTIER GLASS COMPANY. National Line Rainbo. Two color National Line Rainbo Zebra. Opaque white base with four aventurine black ribbons. 5/8". Mint (9.9). $50. (Auction #81, Lot 37).

PELTIER GLASS COMPANY. National Line Rainbo. Three color National Line Rainbo Christmas Tree. Translucent milky white base. 19/32". Mint (9.7). $50. (Auction #173, Lot 37).

PELTIER GLASS COMPANY. National Line Rainbo. Two color National Line Rainbo. Four yellow ribbons on opaque blue. Some darker blue. 23/32". Mint (9.9). $50. (Auction #150, Lot 16).

PELTIER GLASS COMPANY. National Line Rainbo. Two color National Line Rainbo Tiger. Opaque orange base with four aventurine black ribbons. Ottawa, IL. 5/8". Mint (9.9). $50. (Auction #118, Lot 3).

PELTIER GLASS COMPANY. National Line Rainbo. Two color National Line Rainbo Tiger. Aventurine black ribbons on opaque orange base. Broken corkscrew. 5/8". Mint (9.9). $50. (Auction #63, Lot 37).

PELTIER GLASS COMPANY. National Line Rainbo. Three color National Line Rainbo Liberty. Opaque white base. Two wide transparent blue ribbons. 11/16". Near Mint(+) (8.8). $49. (Auction #158, Lot 45).

PELTIER GLASS COMPANY. National Line Rainbo. Very unusual. Opaque orange base. Four ribbons of aventurine black. 5/8". Mint (9). $49. (Auction #144, Lot 49).

PELTIER GLASS COMPANY. National Line Rainbo. Four red ribbons on light blue. The ribbons are edged by dark brown. 21/32". Mint (9.9). $48. (Auction #130, Lot 40).

PELTIER GLASS COMPANY. National Line Rainbo. Two color National Line Rainbo Bumblebee. Four aventurine black ribbons on opaque yellow. 5/8". Mint (9.9). $47. (Auction #124, Lot 47).

PELTIER GLASS COMPANY. National Line Rainbo. Two color National Line Rainbo Wasp. Aventurine black ribbons in a broken corkscrew pattern. 5/8". Mint(-) (9). $47. (Auction #153, Lot 43).

PELTIER GLASS COMPANY. National Line Rainbo. Two color National Line Rainbo Zebra. Four black ribbons on white. Some aventurine. Excellent swirling. 11/16". Mint (9.7). $46. (Auction #91, Lot 39).

PELTIER GLASS COMPANY. National Line Rainbo. Three color National Line Rainbo Ketchup and Mustard. Nice example. Three wide red bands, three thin. 5/8". Mint(-) (9.2). $45. (Auction #54, Lot 8).

PELTIER GLASS COMPANY. National Line Rainbo. Translucent red ribbons on yellow. Super marble. Ottawa, IL, circa 1928-1935. 9/16". Mint (9.9). $45. (Auction #125, Lot 42).

PELTIER GLASS COMPANY. National Line Rainbo. Two color National Line Rainbo Bumblebee. Opaque yellow base with four aventurine black ribbons. 5/8". Mint (9.9). $44. (Auction #134, Lot 35).

PELTIER GLASS COMPANY. National Line Rainbo. Two color National Line Rainbo Bumblebee. Opaque yellow core with four wide black ribbons. No aventurine. 11/16". Mint (9.7). $42. (Auction #181, Lot 46).

PELTIER GLASS COMPANY. National Line Rainbo. Three color National Line Rainbo Ketchup and Mustard. Unusual. Opaque white base. Two red ribbons. 21/32". Near Mint(+) (8.9). $42. (Auction #96, Lot 34).

PELTIER GLASS COMPANY. National Line Rainbo. Two color National Line Rainbo Tiger. Orange base with aventurine black bands. Beautiful marble. Ottawa, IL. 21/32". Mint (9.7). $42. (Auction #126, Lot 40).

PELTIER GLASS COMPANY. National Line Rainbo. Shooter size two color National Line Rainbo. Yellow ribbons on green. Some pits. 3/4". Near Mint (8.6). $42. (Auction #60, Lot 1).

PELTIER GLASS COMPANY. National Line Rainbo. Two color National Line Rainbo shooter. Opaque light blue base with four orangish-yellow ribbons. 27/32". Mint (9.8). $42. (Auction #81, Lot 2).

PELTIER GLASS COMPANY. National Line Rainbo. Two color National Line Rainbo. Opaque light blue base with four red/orange ribbons. 5/8". Mint (9.9). $42. (Auction #110, Lot 22).

PELTIER GLASS COMPANY. National Line Rainbo. Three color National Line Rainbo Rebel. Opaque white base. Four translucent orange/red ribbons. 5/8". Near Mint(+) (8.8). $42. (Auction #64, Lot 35).

PELTIER GLASS COMPANY. National Line Rainbo. Two color National Line Rainbo Bumblebee. Opaque yellow base. Four ribbons of aventurine black. 9/16". Mint (9.9). $41. (Auction #129, Lot 34).

PELTIER GLASS COMPANY. National Line Rainbo. Lot of four marbles. All are two color. Yellow on blue, red on blue, yellow on green, red on green. $40. (Auction #127, Lot 38).

PELTIER GLASS COMPANY. National Line Rainbo. Very unusual three color National Line Rainbo. Opaque whtie base. Four transparent red ribbons. $40. (Auction #117, Lot 19).

PELTIER GLASS COMPANY. National Line Rainbo. Two color National Line Rainbo Bumblebee. Opaque yellow base with four aventurine black ribbons. 5/8". Mint (9.9). $40. (Auction #105, Lot 32).

PELTIER GLASS COMPANY. National Line Rainbo. Mustard yellow base with orange/red ribbons. In great shape. Super example. Ottawa, IL, circa 1928. 11/16". Mint (9.9). $40. (Auction #139, Lot 42).

PELTIER GLASS COMPANY. National Line Rainbo. Super two color National Line Rainbo. Four wide red ribbons on light blue. Ribbons are edged in brown. 23/32". Mint(-) (9). $40. (Auction #123, Lot 43).

PELTIER GLASS COMPANY. National Line Rainbo. Lot of three marbles. First is a three-color National Line Rainbo Liberty. Annealing fracture. 5/8". $40. (Auction #152, Lot 6).

PELTIER GLASS COMPANY. National Line Rainbo. Lot of four marbles. First is a Christmas Tree, 19/32", Good(+) (7.9). Two are Tigers, 19/32" & 5/8". $40. (Auction #163, Lot 16).

PELTIER GLASS COMPANY. National Line Rainbo. Two color National Line Rainbo Zebra. Black ribbons on opaque white. 23/32". Mint (9.9). $40. (Auction #61, Lot 38).

PELTIER GLASS COMPANY. National Line Rainbo. A beauty. Light blue base. Four wide dark red ribbons and one wide wispy black band. 21/32". Mint (9.9). $39. (Auction #109, Lot 10).

PELTIER GLASS COMPANY. National Line Rainbo. Shooter two color National Line Rainbo Zebra. Opaque white base with black ribbons. 29/32". Near Mint (8.6). $39. (Auction #76, Lot 29).

PELTIER GLASS COMPANY. National Line Rainbo. Two color National Line Rainbo Zebra. Opaque white base with aventurine black ribbons. 5/8". Mint (9.9). $39. (Auction #138, Lot 30).

PELTIER GLASS COMPANY. National Line Rainbo. Two color National Line Rainbo Bumblebee. Opaque yellow base with aventurine black ribbons. 21/32". Mint(-) (9.2). $37. (Auction #144, Lot 42).

PELTIER GLASS COMPANY. National Line Rainbo. Very interesting two color National Line Rainbo Chocolate Cow. Aventurine black ribbons. 5/8". Near Mint(+) (8.9). $37. (Auction #61, Lot 21).

PELTIER GLASS COMPANY. National Line Rainbo. Two color National Line Rainbo Zebra. Aventurine black ribbon on opaque white. Beautiful! 21/32". Mint (9.9). $36. (Auction #127, Lot 27).

PELTIER GLASS COMPANY. National Line Rainbo. Beautiful two color National Line Rainbo shooter. Thin yellow ribbons on opaque light blue. 27/32". Mint (9.9). $36. (Auction #129, Lot 20).

PELTIER GLASS COMPANY. National Line Rainbo. Two color National Line Rainbo Bumblebee. Opaque yellow base with aventurine black ribbons. 19/32". Mint (9.6). $35. (Auction #170, Lot 41).

PELTIER GLASS COMPANY. National Line Rainbo. Two color National Line Rainbo. Translucent red ribbons on opaque white. Four ribbons. 5/8". Mint (9.9). $35. (Auction #121, Lot 40).

PELTIER GLASS COMPANY. National Line Rainbo. Lot of two marbles. First is a two color National Line Rainbo Tiger. Aventurine black ribbons. $35. (Auction #54, Lot 14).

PELTIER GLASS COMPANY. National Line Rainbo. Two color National Line Rainbo Bumblebee. Super example. Opaque black ribbons on opaque yellow. 21/32". Mint (9.9). $35. (Auction #131, Lot 36).

PELTIER GLASS COMPANY. National Line Rainbo. Two color National Line Rainbo Zebra. Opaque white base with four aventurine black ribbons. Nice. 17/32". Mint (9.7). $35. (Auction #115, Lot 46).

PELTIER GLASS COMPANY. National Line Rainbo. Lot of two marbles. Both are two color National Line Rainbos. Light red on yellow. 5/8", Mint (9.9). $35. (Auction #62, Lot 26).

PELTIER GLASS COMPANY. National Line Rainbo. Shooter size two color National Line Rainbo. Four red ribbons on green base. Has a small flake. 25/32". Near Mint(+) (8.9). $35. (Auction #55, Lot 42).

PELTIER GLASS COMPANY. National Line Rainbo. Three color shooter National Line Rainbo. 3/4". Near Mint(-) (8.1). $34. (Auction #184, Lot 32).

PELTIER GLASS COMPANY. National Line Rainbo. Two color National Line Rainbo Zebra. Four aventurine black ribbons on white. A beauty, in great shape. 5/8". Mint (9.9). $34. (Auction #124, Lot 31).

PELTIER GLASS COMPANY. National Line Rainbo. Opaque light blue base with four red ribbons. An extremely narrow black ribbon at each pole. 19/32". Mint (9.8). $34. (Auction #127, Lot 34).

PELTIER GLASS COMPANY. National Line Rainbo. Two color Nationa Line Rainbo. Translucent red ribbons on opaque yellow. 11/16". Near Mint(+) (8.9). $34. (Auction #63, Lot 35).

PELTIER GLASS COMPANY. National Line Rainbo. Two color National Line Rainbo Wasp. Red base with aventurine black bands. Nice marble. Ottawa, IL. 21/32". Mint (9.7). $34. (Auction #112, Lot 2).

PELTIER GLASS COMPANY. National Line Rainbo. Two color National Line Rainbo Zebra. Opaque white base with black ribbons. Fiery aventurine. 19/32". Mint (9.9). $34. (Auction #182, Lot 26).

PELTIER GLASS COMPANY. National Line Rainbo. Very nice two color National Line Rainbo Zebra. Aventurine black ribbons on white. Beautiful example. 5/8". Mint (9.9). $33. (Auction #105, Lot 17).

PELTIER GLASS COMPANY. National Line Rainbo. Two color National Line Rainbo Wasp. Aventurine black ribbons on red base. A couple of tiny rough spots. 19/32". Mint(-) (9). $33. (Auction #165, Lot 45).

PELTIER GLASS COMPANY. National Line Rainbo. Two color National Line Rainbo Bumblebee. Light yellow base with aventurine black ribbons. 5/8". Near Mint(+) (8.8). $32. (Auction #55, Lot 17).

PELTIER GLASS COMPANY. National Line Rainbo. Lot of two marbles. Nice pair of National Line Rainbo. Four orange/red ribbons on mustard yellow base. $32. (Auction #80, Lot 32).

PELTIER GLASS COMPANY. National Line Rainbo. Two color National Line Rainbo. Yellow ribbons on light blue. Five ribbons. In great shape. Ottawa, IL. 21/32". Mint (9.9). $32. (Auction #121, Lot 29).

PELTIER GLASS COMPANY. National Line Rainbo. Two color National Line Rainbo Wasp. Aventurine black bands on opaque red. Nice marble. 19/32. Near Mint (8.6). $32. (Auction #62, Lot 31).

PELTIER GLASS COMPANY. National Line Rainbo. Three color National Line Rainbo Ketchup and Mustard. Opaque white base with four transparent red. 5/8". Near Mint (8.6). $32. (Auction #60, Lot 16).

PELTIER GLASS COMPANY. National Line Rainbo. Opaque white base with light red ribbons. Very heavily swirled. Almost looks like a Miller. 21/32". Mint (9.9). $31. (Auction #126, Lot 28).

PELTIER GLASS COMPANY. National Line Rainbo. Two color National Line Rainbo Wasp. Aventurine black ribbons on opaque red. Interesting pattern. 19/32". Near Mint(+) (8.9). $30. (Auction #57, Lot 16).

PELTIER GLASS COMPANY. National Line Rainbo. Shooter size two color National Line Rainbo Zebra. Aventurine black ribbons on white. Nice, large example. 25/32". Near Mint(+) (8.7). $30. (Auction #54, Lot 36).

PELTIER GLASS COMPANY. National Line Rainbo. Two color National Line Rainbo Wasp. Aventurine black ribbons on opaque red. Broken corkscrew design. 5/8". Near Mint(+) (8.8). $30. (Auction #64, Lot 11).

PELTIER GLASS COMPANY. National Line Rainbo. Rare marble. Opaque yellow base. Four wide ribbons of transparent slate green brushed on the surface. 21/32". Mint (9.7). $30. (Auction #113, Lot 49).

PELTIER GLASS COMPANY. National Line Rainbo. Lot of two marbles. Both are the same. Four transparent red ribbons on opaque creamy white. $30. (Auction #127, Lot 35).

PELTIER GLASS COMPANY. National Line Rainbo. Two color National Line Rainbo. Four ribbons of yellow on light blue. Ottawa, IL, circa 1930-1935. 11/16". Mint (9.9). $30. (Auction #127, Lot 36).

PELTIER GLASS COMPANY. National Line Rainbo. Two color National Line Rainbo Zebra. Aventurine black ribbons on opaque white. Type 5 design. Super. 5/8". Mint (9.9). $30. (Auction #123, Lot 11).

PELTIER GLASS COMPANY. National Line Rainbo. Creamy white base with six brown/red ribbons. Swirled pattern, but two seams. Nice example. Ottawa, IL. 5/8". Mint (9.9). $30. (Auction #77, Lot 12).

PELTIER GLASS COMPANY. National Line Rainbo. Lot of three marbles. Two Zebras with aventurine, and a red on yellow. All have some damage. 19/32". $29. (Auction #161, Lot 12).

PELTIER GLASS COMPANY. National Line Rainbo. Two color National Line Rainbo. Four brown/red ribbons on dark blue. In great shape. Ottawa, IL. 11/16". Mint (9.9). $29. (Auction #131, Lot 8).

PELTIER GLASS COMPANY. National Line Rainbo. Two color National Line Rainbo Zebra. Opaque white base with four ribbons of aventurine black. 21/32". Mint (9.7). $29. (Auction #159, Lot 35).

PELTIER GLASS COMPANY. National Line Rainbo. Two color National Line Rainbo. Thin yellow ribbons on light blue. A beauty! Ottawa, IL, circa 1930. 11/16". Mint (9.9). $29. (Auction #152, Lot 5).

PELTIER GLASS COMPANY. National Line Rainbo. Two color National Line Rainbo Zebra. Aventurine black ribbons on white. Excellent fire in the aventurine. 9/1". Mint (9.9). $29. (Auction #179, Lot 39).

PELTIER GLASS COMPANY. National Line Rainbo. Two color National Line Rainbo Bumblebee. Opaque yellow base with four aventurine black ribbons. 19/32". Mint(-) (9). $29. (Auction #104, Lot 16).

PELTIER GLASS COMPANY. National Line Rainbo. Two color National Line Rainbo. Four red ribbons on green. Some orange in with the red. Ottawa, IL. 5/8". Mint (9.8). $28. (Auction #175, Lot 39).

PELTIER GLASS COMPANY. National Line Rainbo. Two color National Line Rainbo Bumblebee. Opaque yellow and black with some very minor aventurine. 19/32". Mint (9.9). $28. (Auction #107, Lot 11).

PELTIER GLASS COMPANY. National Line Rainbo. Two color National Line Rainbo Zebra. Aventurine black ribbons on opaque white. Excellent aventurine. 21/32". Mint (9.9). $28. (Auction #61, Lot 14).

PELTIER GLASS COMPANY. National Line Rainbo. Two color National Line Rainbo Zebra. Aventurine black ribbons on white. Surface in great shape. Ottawa, IL. 21/32". Mint (9.9). $28. (Auction #56, Lot 37).

PELTIER GLASS COMPANY. National Line Rainbo. Two color National Line Rainbo. Transparent green ribbons on pale yellow. Some aventurine. 21/32". Near Mint(+) (8.7). $27. (Auction #133, Lot 41).

PELTIER GLASS COMPANY. National Line Rainbo. Lot of four marbles. Three are two color Naitional Line Rainbo. Red ribbon on mustard. 19/32". Mint . $27. (Auction #115, Lot 35).

PELTIER GLASS COMPANY. National Line Rainbo. Two color National Line Rainbo. Opaque light blue base with four red/brown ribbons in a broken corks. 5/8". Mint (9.9). $27. (Auction #116, Lot 27).

PELTIER GLASS COMPANY. National Line Rainbo. Three color National Line Rainbo Christmas Tree. Opaque white base. Six transparent red bands. 5/8". Near Mint (8.4). $27. (Auction #181, Lot 7).

PELTIER GLASS COMPANY. National Line Rainbo. Two color National Line Rainbo Wasp. Opaque red with aventurine black ribbons. 19/32". Near Mint(+) (8.8). $27. (Auction #139, Lot 20).

PELTIER GLASS COMPANY. National Line Rainbo. Two color National Line Rainbo Zebra. Aventurine black bands on opaque white. Gorgeous marble. 21/32". Mint (9.9). $26. (Auction #60, Lot 3).

PELTIER GLASS COMPANY. National Line Rainbo. Shooter three color National Line Rainbo Superman. One large chip, two blown out air holes. 3/4". Good(-) (7). $26. (Auction #108, Lot 5).

PELTIER GLASS COMPANY. National Line Rainbo. Two color National Line Rainbo Bumblebee. Black ribbons on yellow. No aventurine. Several tiny sparkles. 21/32". Mint(-) (9). $26. (Auction #138, Lot 15).

PELTIER GLASS COMPANY. National Line Rainbo. Two color National Line Rainbo. Four transparent green ribbons on yellow. In great shape. Ottawa, IL. 5/8". Mint (9.9). $25. (Auction #117, Lot 3).

PELTIER GLASS COMPANY. National Line Rainbo. Two color National Line Rainbo. Yellow ribbons on light blue. Light pink stripe in one of the yellow. 21/32". Mint (9.7). $25. (Auction #138, Lot 16).

PELTIER GLASS COMPANY. National Line Rainbo. Two color National Line Rainbo. Opaque blue base with four red ribbons. Nice marble. Air hole. 11/16". Near Mint(+) (8.9). $25. (Auction #113, Lot 29).

PELTIER GLASS COMPANY. National Line Rainbo. Two color National Line Rainbo. Transparent green ribbons on opaque yellow. One tiny pit. Ottawa, IL. 5/8". Mint(-) (9). $25. (Auction #145, Lot 29).

PELTIER GLASS COMPANY. National Line Rainbo. Two color National Line Rainbo. Four mustard yellow ribbons on light blue. Red highlights on the yellow. 21/32". Mint (9.9). $24. (Auction #87, Lot 3).

PELTIER GLASS COMPANY. National Line Rainbo. Two color National Line Rainbo. Red on blue. Ottawa, IL, circa 1928-1935. 5/8". Mint (9.9). $24. (Auction #119, Lot 41).

PELTIER GLASS COMPANY. National Line Rainbo. Lot of two marbles. Ketchup and Mustard. 11/16". Near Mint(-) (8.0). Christmas Tree. 21/32". Near Mint. $22. (Auction #113, Lot 17).

PELTIER GLASS COMPANY. National Line Rainbo. Nice two color National Line Rainbo Zebra. Aventurine black ribbons on white. Broken corkscrew design. 5/8". Mint (9.7). $22. (Auction #63, Lot 27).

PELTIER GLASS COMPANY. National Line Rainbo. Lot of two marbles. First is four red/orange ribbons on green. A couple more red than orange. $22. (Auction #163, Lot 6).

PELTIER GLASS COMPANY. National Line Rainbo. Two color National Line Rainbo. Six ribbons of yellow on opaque light blue. Some are thin. A beauty. 23/32". Mint (9.9). $22. (Auction #155, Lot 44).

PELTIER GLASS COMPANY. National Line Rainbo. Two color National Line Rainbo Bumblebee. Four aventurine black ribbons on opaque yellow. 5/8". Near Mint(+) (8.9). $22. (Auction #156, Lot 4).

PELTIER GLASS COMPANY. National Line Rainbo. Two color National Line Rainbo Zebra. Nice Type V example. Ottawa, IL, circa 1928-1935. 9/16". Mint (9.9). $22. (Auction #121, Lot 6).

PELTIER GLASS COMPANY. National Line Rainbo. Opaque light blue base with four red ribbons. An extremely narrow black ribbon at each pole. 19/32". Near Mint(+) (8.9). $21. (Auction #126, Lot 5).

PELTIER GLASS COMPANY. National Line Rainbo. Lot of two marbles. Both are two color National Line Rainbo. A Bumblebee, yellow base with aventurine. $21. (Auction #76, Lot 1).

PELTIER GLASS COMPANY. National Line Rainbo. Rare coloring. Opaque blue base with four transparent brown ribbons. Several air holes. 11/16". Near Mint(+) (8.8). $20. (Auction #176, Lot 1).

PELTIER GLASS COMPANY. National Line Rainbo. Two color National Line Rainbo Zebra. Four black ribbons on white. Some very minor aventurine. 21/32". Mint (9.7). $20. (Auction #163, Lot 37).

PELTIER GLASS COMPANY. National Line Rainbo. Lot of two marbles. Nice pair of harder to find two color National Line Rainbos. $20. (Auction #54, Lot 5).

PELTIER GLASS COMPANY. National Line Rainbo. Two color National Line Rainbo Zebra. Opaque white base with aventurine black ribbons. Light aventurine. 5/8". Mint(-) (9). $20. (Auction #95, Lot 12).

PELTIER GLASS COMPANY. National Line Rainbo. Two color National Line Rainbo. Ruddy red on light blue. Ottawa, IL, circa 1928-1935. Hit marks. 11/16". Near Mint(+) (8.7). $20. (Auction #127, Lot 28).

PELTIER GLASS COMPANY. National Line Rainbo. Lot of three marbles. All are two-color National Line Rainbo. Orange on white, red on green, orange. $20. (Auction #119, Lot 3).

PELTIER GLASS COMPANY. National Line Rainbo. Opaque light blue base. Six ribbons of red, edged by brown. Very nice design. Has some roughness. 19/32". Near Mint (8.3). $20. (Auction #185, Lot 29).

PELTIER GLASS COMPANY. National Line Rainbo. Lot of three marbles. All are two-color National Line Rainbos. Zebra, 5/8", Near Mint (8.6). Bumblebee. $20. (Auction #171, Lot 4).

PELTIER GLASS COMPANY. National Line Rainbo. Two color National Line Rainbo Zebra. Aventurine black ribbons on opaque white. Type 5 design. Super. 5/8". Mint (9.9). $20. (Auction #169, Lot 15).

PELTIER GLASS COMPANY. National Line Rainbo. Two color National Line Rainbo. Yellow on blue. Lots of yellow. A beauty. One sparkle. Ottawa, IL. 21/32". Mint(-) (9.1). $19. (Auction #138, Lot 1).

PELTIER GLASS COMPANY. National Line Rainbo. Two color National Line Rainbo Bumblebee. Black ribbons on yellow. Thin ribbons. 5/8". Mint(-) (9). $19. (Auction #156, Lot 31).

PELTIER GLASS COMPANY. National Line Rainbo. Hard to find two-color six-ribbon National Line Rainbo. Opaque white base. Six translucent red ribbons. 27/32". Near Mint (8.3). $19. (Auction #161, Lot 49).

PELTIER GLASS COMPANY. National Line Rainbo. Two color National Line Rainbo. Light green base with six ribbons of translucent red on light yellow. 21/32". Near Mint (8.6). $19. (Auction #66, Lot 17).

PELTIER GLASS COMPANY. National Line Rainbo. Light blue base with four red ribbons. A couple of the ribbons have thin translucent black/gray next. 19/32". Mint (9.9). $19. (Auction #82, Lot 40).

PELTIER GLASS COMPANY. National Line Rainbo. Two color National Line Rainbo Zebra. Opaque white base with aventurine black ribbons. Some pitting. 11/16". Near Mint (8.6). $18. (Auction #161, Lot 41).

PELTIER GLASS COMPANY. National Line Rainbo. Lot of three marbles. All are two color National Line Rainbo. All are red ribbons on white. $17. (Auction #143, Lot 12).

PELTIER GLASS COMPANY. National Line Rainbo. Two color National Line Rainbo Zebra. Opaque white base with four aventurine black ribbons. Some pitting. 19/32". Near Mint (8.6). $17. (Auction #143, Lot 4).

PELTIER GLASS COMPANY. National Line Rainbo. Lot of three marbles. All are Type 5 National Line Rainbos (equatorial ribbon, pole patches). Green . $17. (Auction #119, Lot 24).

PELTIER GLASS COMPANY. National Line Rainbo. Three color National Line Rainbo Rebel. Opaque white base. Red and aventurine black ribbons. 5/8". Near Mint (8.4). $17. (Auction #57, Lot 5).

PELTIER GLASS COMPANY. National Line Rainbo. Two color National Line Rainbo Zebra. Four aventurine black ribbons on opaque white. In nice shape. 21/32". Mint (9.9). $17. (Auction #55, Lot 3).

PELTIER GLASS COMPANY. National Line Rainbo. Two color National Line Rainbo Zebra. Opaque white base iwth aventurine black ribbons. Ottawa, IL. 19/32". Mint (9.7). $17. (Auction #166, Lot 9).

PELTIER GLASS COMPANY. National Line Rainbo. Two color National Line Rainbo. Green ribbons on pale yellow. A subsurface moon and a few pinpricks. 19/32". Near Mint(+) (8.7). $16. (Auction #137, Lot 7).

PELTIER GLASS COMPANY. National Line Rainbo. Opaque white base with seven semi-opaque red ribbons. Ottawa, IL, circa 1925-1935. 21/32". Mint (9.7). $15. (Auction #85, Lot 40).

PELTIER GLASS COMPANY. National Line Rainbo. Two color National Line Rainbo Zebra. Aventurine black ribbons on opaque white. Two air holes. 5/8". Mint(-) (9). $15. (Auction #60, Lot 9).

PELTIER GLASS COMPANY. National Line Rainbo. Two color National Line Rainbo Zebra. Opaque white base with four ribbons of aventurine black. 11/16". Near Mint(+) (8.9). $15. (Auction #153, Lot 17).

PELTIER GLASS COMPANY. National Line Rainbo. Three color National Line Rainbo Liberty. Translucent white base. Two ribbons of transparent blue. $15. (Auction #162, Lot 35).

PELTIER GLASS COMPANY. National Line Rainbo. Two color National Line Rainbo. Opaque green base. Six ribbons of red and red/orange. Two small chips. 25/32". Near Mint(+) (8.7). $14. (Auction #134, Lot 23).

PELTIER GLASS COMPANY. National Line Rainbo. Opaque green base with four red ribbons. Some cold roll creasing and one tiny sparkle. Ottawa, IL. 21/32". Mint(-) (9.2). $13. (Auction #105, Lot 3).

PELTIER GLASS COMPANY. National Line Rainbo. Very unusual two color National Line Rainbo. Transparent brown base with four opaque yellow ribbons. 19/32". Mint(-) (9). $12. (Auction #90, Lot 10).

PELTIER GLASS COMPANY. National Line Rainbo. Two color National Line Rainbo Zebra. Black on white. No aventurine. Nice marble. Ottawa, IL. 5/8". Mint (9.9). $12. (Auction #95, Lot 29).

PELTIER GLASS COMPANY. National Line Rainbo. Two color National Line Rainbo Zebra. Aventurine black on white. Broken corkscrew design. 21/32". Mint(-) (9.1). $12. (Auction #171, Lot 34).

PELTIER GLASS COMPANY. National Line Rainbo. Two color National Line Rainbo. Red ribbons on mustard yellow. One pinprick. Smaller than normal size. 17/32". Mint(-) (9.1). $10. (Auction #123, Lot 15).

PELTIER GLASS COMPANY. National Line Rainbo. Two color, four band, National Line Rainbo Zebra. Opaque white base with four aventurine black ribbons. 21/32". Near Mint(+) (8.7). $10. (Auction #103, Lot 8).

PELTIER GLASS COMPANY. National Line Rainbo. Two color National Line Rainbo. Light blue base. Four red ribbons. Several have some light gray next. 21/32". Near Mint(+) (8.8). $8. (Auction #139, Lot 31).

PELTIER GLASS COMPANY. National Line Rainbo. Very nice two color National Line Rainbo. Opaque yellow base with six transparent cherry red ribbons. 5/8". Near Mint (8.3). $8. (Auction #57, Lot 8).

PELTIER GLASS COMPANY. Original bag. Original advertising bag for Morton's Salt. Red mesh bag. Contains sixteen Peltier Rainbos. $37. (Auction #79, Lot 3).

PELTIER GLASS COMPANY. Original bag. Original mesh bag with a header reading "Champion" on one side and "Glass Marbles" on the other. $21. (Auction #108, Lot 12).

PELTIER GLASS COMPANY. Original box. Hard to find, original, No. 28 Lucky Boy Champion Marble Set. Blue damasked cover with gold imprinting. $625. (Auction #119, Lot 50).

PELTIER GLASS COMPANY. Original box. Nice "Big Value Marble Assortment" cube. Cardboard box. "Approximatley 100 Marbles". Blue graphics. $185. (Auction #136, Lot 22).

PELTIER GLASS COMPANY. Original box. Original cardboard cube. "Big Value Marble Marble Assortment". "Contains approximately 100 marbles". $170. (Auction #79, Lot 32).

PELTIER GLASS COMPANY. Original box. Hard to find original "No. 5 National Rainbo Marbles Assorted Colors" box. M. Gropper & Sons. $120. (Auction #163, Lot 48).

PELTIER GLASS COMPANY. Original package. Poly bag. "19 Champion Jr." Orange label. 6" x 3-1/2" (sight). Mint (9.5). $28. (Auction #132, Lot 34).

PELTIER GLASS COMPANY. Original package. Poly bag of twenty two Bananas. No header label. Printed on the bag "Peltier Glass Marbles".

$24. (Auction #178, Lot 27).

PELTIER GLASS COMPANY. Original package. Poly bag "Cat's Eye Champion". Green printing on white. Contains fourteen 5/8" Bananas. 5" x 4". $20. (Auction #133, Lot 24).

PELTIER GLASS COMPANY. Original package. Very hard to find original poly bag. This is an original "Cat's Eye Champion" bag. Green header label. $16. (Auction #105, Lot 25).

PELTIER GLASS COMPANY. Pearlized Peerless Patch. Perhaps the rarest Peltier marble!!! Super example; it has as-made defects that are typical. 5/8". Near Mint(+) (8.9). $110. (Auction #139, Lot 50).

PELTIER GLASS COMPANY. Peerless Patch. Very hard to find opalescent base Peerless Patch. Aventurine black patch. Very hard to find. 5/8". Mint (9.9). $55. (Auction #126, Lot 32).

PELTIER GLASS COMPANY. Peerless Patch. Lot of nine marbles. Two each of yellow on olive, red on white, yellow on aqua, black on white. $47. (Auction #66, Lot 28).

PELTIER GLASS COMPANY. Peerless Patch. Lot of six marbles. All are Peerless Patch. Two are yellow on aqua, two are yellow on green, one red. $42. (Auction #83, Lot 17).

PELTIER GLASS COMPANY. Peerless Patch. Lot of nine marbles. Red on orange (1) (rare), black on white (2), yellow on aqua (2), red on white. $42. (Auction #54, Lot 28).

PELTIER GLASS COMPANY. Peerless Patch. Lot of four marbles. All are Peerless patch. Aventurine black on white, yellow on olive green, yellow. $40. (Auction #64, Lot 23).

PELTIER GLASS COMPANY. Peerless Patch. Lot of nine marbles. All are Peerless Patch. Four are red on aqua, two are yellow on aqua, two yellow. $38. (Auction #55, Lot 21).

PELTIER GLASS COMPANY. Peerless Patch. Lot of four marbles. All are Peerless patch. Aventurine black on white, yellow on olive green, yellow. $37. (Auction #64, Lot 23.40).

PELTIER GLASS COMPANY. Peerless Patch. Lot of four marbles. All are Peerless patch. Aventurine black on white, yellow on olive green, yellow. $37. (Auction #64, Lot 23.50).

PELTIER GLASS COMPANY. Peerless Patch. Lot of four marbles. All are Peerless patch. Aventurine black on white, yellow on olive green, yellow. $37. (Auction #64, Lot 23.30).

PELTIER GLASS COMPANY. Peerless Patch. Nice three-color Peerless Patch. Hard to find, these are usually two-color. Probably a hybrid. 19/32". Mint(-) (9). $37. (Auction #142, Lot 9).

PELTIER GLASS COMPANY. Peerless Patch. Lot of four marbles. All are Peerless patch. Aventurine black on white, yellow on olive green, yellow. $37. (Auction #64, Lot 23.20).

PELTIER GLASS COMPANY. Peerless Patch. Super Peerless Patch. Semi-opaque white base with an opaque black patch covering almost half the marble. 21/32". Mint (9.5). $34. (Auction #57, Lot 12).

PELTIER GLASS COMPANY. Peerless Patch. Lot of four marbles. Four are red on aqua. One is red on opalescent white. That one is rare. $32. (Auction #180, Lot 43).

PELTIER GLASS COMPANY. Peerless Patch. Lot of four marbles. Yellow on aqua, yellow on olive green, black on white, red on orange (rare). $28. (Auction #65, Lot 20.30).

PELTIER GLASS COMPANY. Peerless Patch. Lot of four marbles. Yellow on aqua, yellow on olive green, black on white, red on orange (rare). $28. (Auction #65, Lot 20).

PELTIER GLASS COMPANY. Peerless Patch. Lot of four marbles. Yellow on aqua, yellow on olive green, black on white, red on orange (rare). $28. (Auction #65, Lot 20.50).

PELTIER GLASS COMPANY. Peerless Patch. Lot of four marbles. Yellow on aqua, yellow on olive green, black on white, red on orange (rare). $28. (Auction #65, Lot 20.20).

PELTIER GLASS COMPANY. Peerless Patch. Lot of four marbles. Yellow on aqua, yellow on olive green, black on white, red on orange (rare). $28. (Auction #65, Lot 20.40).

PELTIER GLASS COMPANY. Peerless Patch. Lot of five marbles. All are Peerless Patch. Two red on blue, two yellow on blue, one yellow on green. $27. (Auction #73, Lot 24.20).

PELTIER GLASS COMPANY. Peerless Patch. Lot of five marbles. All are Peerless Patch. Two red on blue, two yellow on blue, one yellow on green. $27. (Auction #73, Lot 24).

PELTIER GLASS COMPANY. Peerless Patch. Lot of four marbles. All are Peerless patch. Aventurine black on white, yellow on olive green, yellow. $26. (Auction #64, Lot 23.60).

PELTIER GLASS COMPANY. Peerless Patch. Lot of four marbles. Yellow on aqua, yellow on olive green, black on white, red on orange (rare). $26. (Auction #65, Lot 20.60).

PELTIER GLASS COMPANY. Peerless Patch. Lot of seventeen marbles. Fifteen are Peerless Patch. One is a corkscrew and one is Vitro patch.

$26. (Auction #113, Lot 33).

PELTIER GLASS COMPANY. Peerless Patch. Lot of five marbles. All are Peerless Patch. Two red on blue, two yellow on blue, one yellow on green. $25. (Auction #73, Lot 24.30).

PELTIER GLASS COMPANY. Peerless Patch. Lot of two marbles. Both are Peerless Patch. Aventurine black on white. 19/32". Mint (9.5 & 9.3). $22. (Auction #102, Lot 39).

PELTIER GLASS COMPANY. Peerless Patch. Lot of four marbles. One each of yellow on olive, black on white, yellow on aqua, red on aqua. $22. (Auction #70, Lot 23.20).

PELTIER GLASS COMPANY. Peerless Patch. Lot of four marbles. One each of yellow on olive, black on white, yellow on aqua, red on aqua. $22. (Auction #70, Lot 23).

PELTIER GLASS COMPANY. Peerless Patch. Lot of four marbles. One each of yellow on olive, black on white, yellow on aqua, red on aqua. $22. (Auction #70, Lot 23.30).

PELTIER GLASS COMPANY. Peerless Patch. Lot of two marbles. One is red patch on salmon pink. Rare. 5/8". Mint(-) (9.0) (sparkles). $21. (Auction #169, Lot 40).

PELTIER GLASS COMPANY. Peerless Patch. Very unusual Peerless Patch. Base glass is opalescent milky white. Black patch, no aventurine. Nice. 19/32". Mint (9.9). $20. (Auction #58, Lot 4).

PELTIER GLASS COMPANY. Peerless Patch. Lot of seven marbles. Assortment of colors. Four red on blue, two yellow on blue, one black on white. $19. (Auction #117, Lot 40).

PELTIER GLASS COMPANY. Peerless Patch. Orange patch on olive green base. Unusual coloring for a Peerless Patch. Ottawa, IL, 1928-1935. 21/32". Mint (9.9). $15. (Auction #109, Lot 6).

PELTIER GLASS COMPANY. Peerless Patch. Opalescent translucent white base. Black patch. Tiny rough area on the patch. 19/32". Mint(-) (9). $15. (Auction #68, Lot 33).

PELTIER GLASS COMPANY. Peerless Patch. Lot of two marbles. Both are red patch on yellow. Ottawa, IL, circa 1925-1935. 19/32" & 21/32". Mint. $14. (Auction #76, Lot 5).

PELTIER GLASS COMPANY. Peerless Patch. Lot of seven marbles. Each is a different color Peerless Patch. Three are Mint. 19/32" to 5/8". Mint. $14. (Auction #164, Lot 7).

PELTIER GLASS COMPANY. Picture marble - comic. Black transfer of Annie on a white base/red patch marble. Nice, dark transfer. Well centered. 21/32". Mint (9.9). $160. (Auction #71, Lot 21).

PELTIER GLASS COMPANY. Picture marble - comic. Black transfer of Annie on a white base/red patch marble. Nice, dark transfer. Well centered. 21/32". Mint (9.9). $145. (Auction #109, Lot 44).

PELTIER GLASS COMPANY. Picture marble - comic. Black transfer of Sandy, on a white base/light blue patch marble. Average transfer, well centered. 11/16". Mint (9.9). $130. (Auction #97, Lot 42).

PELTIER GLASS COMPANY. Picture marble - comic. A gorgeous example of a Bimbo comic marble. The marble is a Peerless Patch. Mustard base with red patch. 21/32". Mint (9.9). $120. (Auction #104, Lot 43).

PELTIER GLASS COMPANY. Picture marble - comic. Black transfer of Skeezix. Excellent, dark transfer. Blue patch/white base marble. Large blue patch. 21/32". Mint (9.9). $100. (Auction #57, Lot 29).

PELTIER GLASS COMPANY. Picture marble - comic. Black transfer of Sandy, on a white base/light blue patch marble. Average transfer, well centered. 11/16". Mint (9.9). $95. (Auction #113, Lot 41).

PELTIER GLASS COMPANY. Picture marble - comic. Black transfer of Koko on a white base, transparent green patch marble. Nice transfer, well centered. 21/32". Mint (9.9). $80. (Auction #133, Lot 7).

PELTIER GLASS COMPANY. Picture marble - comic. Black transfer of Koko on a white base, transparent green patch marble. Nice transfer, well centered. 21/32". Mint (9.9). $80. (Auction #133, Lot 7.20).

PELTIER GLASS COMPANY. Picture marble - comic. Black transfer of Koko on a white base, transparent green patch marble. Nice transfer, well centered. 21/32". Mint (9.9). $75. (Auction #124, Lot 18.30).

PELTIER GLASS COMPANY. Picture marble - comic. Black transfer of Bimbo on a white base/transparent green patch marble. The figure is a dark strike. 5/8". Mint (9.9). $75. (Auction #73, Lot 38).

PELTIER GLASS COMPANY. Picture marble - comic. Black transfer of Koko on a white base, transparent green patch marble. Nice transfer, well centered. 21/32". Mint (9.9). $75. (Auction #124, Lot 18.40).

PELTIER GLASS COMPANY. Picture marble - comic. Black transfer of Betty. Mustard base, red patch marble. The transfer is very light, but is well-centered. 21/32". Near Mint(+) (8.7). $75. (Auction #146, Lot 49).

PELTIER GLASS COMPANY. Picture marble - comic. Black transfer of Bimbo. Mustard base, red patch marble. Slightly light transfer. Well centered. 21/32". Mint (9.9). $75. (Auction #146, Lot 37).

PELTIER GLASS COMPANY. Picture marble - comic. Black transfer of Emma on a white base/light blue patch. Dark transfer. Well centered. Ottawa, IL. 21/32". Mint (9.9). $71. (Auction #65, Lot 30).

PELTIER GLASS COMPANY. Picture marble - comic. Black transfer of Koko on a white base, transparent green patch marble. Nice transfer, well centered. 21/32". Mint (9.9). $70. (Auction #124, Lot 18.50).

PELTIER GLASS COMPANY. Picture marble - comic. Black transfer of Koko on a white base, transparent green patch marble. Nice transfer, well centered. 21/32". Mint (9.9). $65. (Auction #124, Lot 18).

PELTIER GLASS COMPANY. Picture marble - comic. Black transfer of Koko. White base, transparent green patch marble. Above average transfer. Well centered. 21/32". Mint (9.9). $61. (Auction #146, Lot 40).

PELTIER GLASS COMPANY. Picture marble - Comic. Black transfer of Emma on a white base/light blue patch marble. Average transfer. Well centered. 21/32". Mint (9.9). $61. (Auction #76, Lot 40).

PELTIER GLASS COMPANY. Picture marble - Comic. Black transfer of Koko on a white base, transparent green patch marble. Nice transfer, well centered. 21/32". Mint (9.9). $60. (Auction #124, Lot 18.20).

PELTIER GLASS COMPANY. Picture marble - Comic. Black transfer of Emma on a white base/light blue patch marble. Average transfer. Well centered. 21/32". Mint (9.9). $56. (Auction #76, Lot 40.10).

PELTIER GLASS COMPANY. Picture marble - comic. Black transfer of Skeezix on a blue patch/white base marble. Dark transfer. 11/16". Mint (9.9). $55. (Auction #81, Lot 10).

PELTIER GLASS COMPANY. Picture marble - Comic. Black transfer of Emma on a white base/light blue patch marble. Average transfer. Well centered. 21/32". Mint (9.9). $51. (Auction #76, Lot 40.20).

PELTIER GLASS COMPANY. Picture marble - comic. Black transfer of Koko on a white base, transparent green patch marble. Nice transfer, well centered. 21/32". Mint (9.9). $50. (Auction #127, Lot 4).

PELTIER GLASS COMPANY. Picture marble - comic. Black transfer of Emma on a white base/light blue patch. Dark transfer. Extraneous graphite. Well centered. 21/32". Mint (9.9). $50. (Auction #119, Lot 45).

PELTIER GLASS COMPANY. Picture marble - Comic. Black transfer of Emma on a white base/light blue patch marble. Average transfer. Well centered. 21/32". Mint (9.9). $49. (Auction #76, Lot 40.30).

PELTIER GLASS COMPANY. Picture marble - comic. Black transfer of Skeezix on a white base, light blue patch marble. Good transfer, well centered. 5/8". Mint(-) (9). $46. (Auction #115, Lot 44).

PELTIER GLASS COMPANY. Picture marble - comic. Black transfer of Koko on a transparent green patch/opaque white base marble. Excellent transfer. 21/32". Mint (9.8). $42. (Auction #60, Lot 15).

PELTIER GLASS COMPANY. Picture marble - comic. Black transfer of Emma on a white base/light blue patch. Average transfer. Well centered. 21/32". Mint (9.7). $40. (Auction #182, Lot 32).

PELTIER GLASS COMPANY. Picture marble - comic. Black transfer of Smitty. Mustard base, green patch marble. The transfer is very light, but is well centered. 21/32". Near Mint (8.4). $38. (Auction #146, Lot 45).

PELTIER GLASS COMPANY. Picture Marble - comic. Black transfer of Betty (Boop) on a mustard base, red patch marble. Average strike, a little light. 21/32". Mint (9.9). $410. (Auction #117, Lot 49).

PELTIER GLASS COMPANY. Picture Marble - comic. Black transfer of Betty on a white base/aventurine black patch marble. Excellent, very dark transfer. 11/16". Mint (9.9). $250. (Auction #134, Lot 47).

PELTIER GLASS COMPANY. Picture Marble - comic. Black transfer of Moon. Mustard yellow, light green patch. Light transfer. The "N" in Moon just visible. 21/32". Mint (9.4). $200. (Auction #168, Lot 45).

PELTIER GLASS COMPANY. Picture Marble - comic. Black transfer of Betty (Boop) on a mustard base, red patch marble. Average strike. Very well centered. 11/16". Mint(-) (9). $200. (Auction #162, Lot 39).

PELTIER GLASS COMPANY. Picture Marble - comic. Black transfer of Moon. Mustard base, light green patch marble. Figure is a little light on the left. 21/32". Near Mint(+) (8.9). $150. (Auction #150, Lot 46).

PELTIER GLASS COMPANY. Picture Marble - comic. Black transfer of Herbie on a white base, aventurine black patch marble. Dark transfer. well centered. 21/32". Mint (9.9). $130. (Auction #118, Lot 35).

PELTIER GLASS COMPANY. Picture Marble - Comic. Black transfer of Annie. White base, orange/red patch. Patch is a little lighter than usual. 21/32". Mint (9.3). $120. (Auction #154, Lot 42).

PELTIER GLASS COMPANY. Picture Marble - comic. Black transfer of Andy on a mustard base/light green patch marble. Excellent dark transfer. Very well centered. 11/16". Mint (9.7). $110. (Auction #105, Lot 19).

PELTIER GLASS COMPANY. Picture Marble - comic. Black transfer of Sandy. On a white base, light blue patch marble. Dark transfer. Well centered. 21/32". Mint (9.3). $110. (Auction #165, Lot 49).

PELTIER GLASS COMPANY. Picture Marble - comic. Black transfer of Annie. Opaque white, red patch marble. Transfer is average. Well centered. 11/16". Mint (9.9). $100. (Auction #160, Lot 41).

PELTIER GLASS COMPANY. Picture Marble - comic. Black transfer of Andy on a mustard base/light green patch marble. Excellent dark transfer. Very well centered. 11/16". Mint (9.7). $100. (Auction #105, Lot 19.10).

PELTIER GLASS COMPANY. Picture Marble - comic. Black transfer of Skeezix on a white base/light blue patch marbles. Excellent transfer. Well centered. 21/32". Mint (9.9). $95. (Auction #66, Lot 12).

PELTIER GLASS COMPANY. Picture Marble - comic. Black transfer of Annie on a white base/red patch marble. Nice transfer. 21/32". Mint (9.9). $85. (Auction #101, Lot 49).

PELTIER GLASS COMPANY. Picture Marble - comic. Black transfer of Herbie. Opaque white base, black patch. Transfer is average. Well centered. 21/32". Mint (9.8). $80. (Auction #151, Lot 45).

PELTIER GLASS COMPANY. Picture Marble - comic. Black transfer of Andy on a mustard yellow base/light green patch marble. Nice transfer. Well centered. 21/32". Mint (9.9). $75. (Auction #74, Lot 34).

PELTIER GLASS COMPANY. Picture Marble - comic. Black transfer of Kayo. Opaque white base, black patch. The figure is well centered on the white. 21/32". Near Mint (8.6). $75. (Auction #147, Lot 30).

PELTIER GLASS COMPANY. Picture Marble - comic. Black transfer of Skeezix on a white base, blue patch marble. Average transfer. Set slightly off-center. 11/16". Mint (9.9). $75. (Auction #100, Lot 35).

PELTIER GLASS COMPANY. Picture Marble - comic. Black transfer of Emma on a white base, light blue patch marble. Dark transfer, part missing. 11/16". Mint (9.9). $70. (Auction #118, Lot 41).

PELTIER GLASS COMPANY. Picture Marble - comic. Black transfer of Koko on a transparent green patch/white base marble. Transfer is a little light. 21/32". Mint (9.9). $70. (Auction #88, Lot 33).

PELTIER GLASS COMPANY. Picture Marble - comic. Black transfer of Smitty on a mustard base, light green patch marble. Transfer is dark and well centered. 21/32". Mint (9.7). $70. (Auction #112, Lot 48).

PELTIER GLASS COMPANY. Picture Marble - comic. Black transfer of Smitty on a mustard base, light green patch marble. Transfer is dark and well centered. 21/32". Mint (9.7). $67. (Auction #112, Lot 48.10).

PELTIER GLASS COMPANY. Picture Marble - comic. Black transfer of Bimbo. Mustard yellow base with red patch. Dark transfer. Slightly off-center. 21/32". Near Mint(+) (8.9). $66. (Auction #156, Lot 33).

PELTIER GLASS COMPANY. Picture Marble - comic. Black transfer of Bimbo on a white base/transparent green patch marble. Excellent transfer, well centered. 21/32". Mint (9.8). $65. (Auction #94, Lot 25).

PELTIER GLASS COMPANY. Picture Marble - comic. Black transfer of Emma on a white base, light blue patch marble. Transfer is very dark. 21/32". Mint (9.9). $60. (Auction #110, Lot 39).

PELTIER GLASS COMPANY. Picture Marble - comic. Black transfer of Bimbo. Mustard yellow base with red patch. Dark transfer, well-centered. Excellent. 11/16". Near Mint(+) (8.7). $60. (Auction #185, Lot 32).

PELTIER GLASS COMPANY. Picture Marble - comic. Black transfer of Koko. White base, thin transparent green patch. Dark transfer, well centered. Nice. 11/16". Mint (9.8). $55. (Auction #150, Lot 12).

PELTIER GLASS COMPANY. Picture Marble - comic. Black transfer of Sandy. White base, red patch marble. Light transfer. Unusual marble color. 11/16". Near Mint(+) (8.9). $55. (Auction #154, Lot 16).

PELTIER GLASS COMPANY. Picture Marble - comic. Black transfer of Emma on a white base, light blue patch marble. Transfer is very dark. 21/32". Mint (9.9). $55. (Auction #110, Lot 39.10).

PELTIER GLASS COMPANY. Picture Marble - comic. Black transfer of Skeezix. White base, light blue patch marble. Light transfer. Well-centered. Ottawa, IL. 21/32". Mint (9.5). $55. (Auction #151, Lot 40).

PELTIER GLASS COMPANY. Picture Marble - comic. Black transfer of Emma. White base, light blue patch marble. Dark transfer. Fairly well-centered. 11/16". Mint(-) (9.1). $50. (Auction #152, Lot 40).

PELTIER GLASS COMPANY. Picture Marble - comic. Black transfer of Bimbo. Mustard base, red patch marble. Light transfer. Slightly off-center. 5/8". Mint (9.5). $46. (Auction #151, Lot 30).

PELTIER GLASS COMPANY. Picture Marble - comic. Black transfer of Herbie. Opaque white base, aventurine black patch. Very large patch. 21/32". Mint(-) (9). $45. (Auction #168, Lot 4).

PELTIER GLASS COMPANY. Picture Marble - comic. Black transfer of Koko. White base, transparent green patch marble. Dark transfer, well centered. 21/32". Mint (9.8). $42. (Auction #160, Lot 15).

PELTIER GLASS COMPANY. Picture Marble - comic. Black transfer of Herbie on a white base/black patch marble. Light transfer. Small air hole. 21/32". Mint (9.6). $40. (Auction #92, Lot 10).

PELTIER GLASS COMPANY. Picture Marble - comic. Black transfer of Koko on a transparent green patch/white base marble. Transfer is a little light. 21/32". Mint (9.9). $40. (Auction #54, Lot 41).

PELTIER GLASS COMPANY. Picture Marble - comic. Lot of two marbles. First is Koko on a white base, blue patch marble. Part of transfer missing. $36. (Auction #94, Lot 46).

PELTIER GLASS COMPANY. Picture Marble - comic. Black transfer of Koko. White base, transparent green patch. Dark transfer, well centered. 5/8". Near Mint(+) (8.7). $35. (Auction #155, Lot 34).

PELTIER GLASS COMPANY. Picture Marble - comic. Black transfer of Skeezix. White base, light blue patch marble. Light transfer. Well centered. Ottawa, IL. 21/32". Mint (9.5). $29. (Auction #178, Lot 40).

PELTIER GLASS COMPANY. Picture Marble - comic. Black transfer of Emma. Opaque white, light blue patch. Light transfer. Well-centered. Small flake. 21/32". Near Mint(+) (8.9). $24. (Auction #151, Lot 35).

PELTIER GLASS COMPANY. Rainbo. Rare Rainbo, and this is an exceptional example. Bifurcated Rainbo. 21/32". Mint (9.9). $310. (Auction #92, Lot 30).

PELTIER GLASS COMPANY. Rainbo. One of the most unusual Rainbos I have ever seen. I guess you would call it a four color Rainbo. 9/16". Mint (9.9). $70. (Auction #176, Lot 43).

PELTIER GLASS COMPANY. Rainbo. Lot of approximately seventy marbles. Assortment of Rainbos. Nice set of colors. $55. (Auction #132, Lot 24).

PELTIER GLASS COMPANY. Rainbo. Lot of five marbles. All are shooters. Four are Peltier, appears to be Ravenswood. $55. (Auction #62, Lot 17).

PELTIER GLASS COMPANY. Rainbo. Lot of forty two marbles. Nice assortment of Bloodies, Rainbos, Acme Realers, Sunset, Tri-color. $55. (Auction #57, Lot 25).

PELTIER GLASS COMPANY. Rainbo. Very interesting and hard to find three color Rainbo Christmas Tree. Opalescent white base. 15/32". Mint (9.7). $50. (Auction #57, Lot 32).

PELTIER GLASS COMPANY. Rainbo. Lot of approximately one hundred twenty five marbles. Excellent assortment of Rainbows, Acme Realers. $40. (Auction #177, Lot 25).

PELTIER GLASS COMPANY. Rainbo. Hard to find Rainbo. Transparent green base. Two ribbons of red and two ribbons of yellow. A beauty. 19/32". Mint (9.9). $38. (Auction #119, Lot 46).

PELTIER GLASS COMPANY. Rainbo. Lot of approximately seventy five marbles. Assortment of Peltier Rainbos. A few are fluorescent. $38. (Auction #102, Lot 25).

PELTIER GLASS COMPANY. Rainbo. This is a very rare experimental four color Rainbo. Opaque white base. One hemisphere is a two opaque. 5/8". Mint (9.5). $35. (Auction #63, Lot 6).

PELTIER GLASS COMPANY. Rainbo. Very nice two color Rainbo. Almost qualifies as a bifurcated example. 11/16". Mint (9.9). $30. (Auction #105, Lot 15).

PELTIER GLASS COMPANY. Rainbo. Lot of approximately forty five marbles. All are Rainbos. Assorted colors. Nice group. 5/8". Mint (9. $27. (Auction #179, Lot 28).

PELTIER GLASS COMPANY. Rainbo. Three color Rainbo Ketchup and Mustard. Semi-opaque white base. Four ribbons of yellow, two of red. 5/8". Mint(-) (9). $26. (Auction #182, Lot 41).

PELTIER GLASS COMPANY. Rainbo. Lot of five marbles. All are shooters. White on blue Acme Realer, 3/4", Mint (9.9). Sunset, 13/16". $25. (Auction #73, Lot 23).

PELTIER GLASS COMPANY. Rainbo. Transparent Rainbo. Transparent clear base with unmelted sand. Two ribbons of opaque green. 11/16". Mint (9.9). $23. (Auction #185, Lot 25).

PELTIER GLASS COMPANY. Rainbo. Lot of three marbles. All are shooter Rainbos. One Bloodie, one red on white, one blue on white. $22. (Auction #103, Lot 15).

PELTIER GLASS COMPANY. Rainbo. Lot of thirteen marbles. All are the same. Semi-opaque lemonade yellow/green base. $22. (Auction #178, Lot 10).

PELTIER GLASS COMPANY. Rainbo. Lot of five marbles. All are shooter Rainbos! Assorted color ribbons on white. 13/16" to 15/16". Mint. $22. (Auction #180, Lot 44).

PELTIER GLASS COMPANY. Rainbo. Two color Rainbo. Odd coloring and design. Four opaque white ribbons in opaque slate gray/blue. 5/8". Mint (9.9). $20. (Auction #153, Lot 7).

PELTIER GLASS COMPANY. Rainbo. Lot of seven marbles. Opaque to translucent white base. Green, blue or green & blue ribbons. $20. (Auction #70, Lot 6).

PELTIER GLASS COMPANY. Rainbo. Harder to find six-ribbon Rainbo. Transparent olive green base. Six semi-opaque white ribbons. 19/32". Mint (9.9). $20. (Auction #117, Lot 7).

PELTIER GLASS COMPANY. Rainbo. Lot of five marbles. All are shooters. Two Bloodies, two blue on white, one green on white. $17. (Auction #81, Lot 21).

PELTIER GLASS COMPANY. Rainbo. Very unusual six ribbon Rainbo Christmas Tree. Alternating bands of translucent red, transparent blue. 9/16". Near Mint (8.6). $17. (Auction #62, Lot 2).

PELTIER GLASS COMPANY. Rainbo. Lot of four marbles. All are peewee Peltier Rainbos. Hard to find. White base. Two are green ribbons. $17. (Auction #68, Lot 23).

PELTIER GLASS COMPANY. Rainbo. Lot of two marbles. Harder to find six ribbon Rainbo. Translucent blue ribbons on white. $17. (Auction #55, Lot 10).

PELTIER GLASS COMPANY. Rainbo. Lot of five marbles. Assortment of five shootes. 7/8" to 31/32". Mint (9.9) to Near Mint (8.6). $15. (Auction #112, Lot 22).

PELTIER GLASS COMPANY. Rainbo. Nice three color Rainbo. Ketchup and Mustard coloring. Opaque white base. Two ribbons of transparent. 5/8". Mint (9.9). $15. (Auction #153, Lot 12).

PELTIER GLASS COMPANY. Rainbo. Shooter Rainbo. Nice example. Actually, an Acme Realer. Transparent dark green base. 7/8". Mint (9.9). $14. (Auction #100, Lot 38).

PELTIER GLASS COMPANY. Rainbo. Interesting coloring. Translucent slate gray/blue with opaque white ribbons. In great shape. Ottawa, IL. 5/8". Mint (9.8). $13. (Auction #128, Lot 14).

PELTIER GLASS COMPANY. Rainbo. Lot of three marbles. All are Rainbos. Transparent green ribbons on opaque white. $12. (Auction #76, Lot 21).

PELTIER GLASS COMPANY. Rainbo. Lot of three marbles. All are Rainbo shooters. Same color scheme. Blue on white. All about 15/16". $12. (Auction #132, Lot 5).

PELTIER GLASS COMPANY. Rainbo. Six ribbon rainbo. Transparent green base with six wide opaque white ribbons. Some sparkles. Ottawa, IL. 23/32". Near Mint(+) (8.8). $12. (Auction #161, Lot 39).

PELTIER GLASS COMPANY. Rainbo. Lot of three marbles. Two are shooter Peltier Rainbos. The other is a shooter common swirl. $11. (Auction #108, Lot 1).

PELTIER GLASS COMPANY. Rainbo. Lot of nine marbles. All are Rainbos. Nice assortment of colors. 19/32" to 5/8". Mint (9.9-9.3). $10. (Auction #143, Lot 14).

PELTIER GLASS COMPANY. Rainbo. Lot of four marbles. All are tiny Rainbos. White base with blue or green ribbons. Ottawa, IL. $10. (Auction #78, Lot 2).

PELTIER GLASS COMPANY. Rainbo. Interesting color. Red ribbons on mustard/orange. Ottawa, IL, circa 1930-1950. 19/32". Mint (9.9). $9. (Auction #166, Lot 12).

PELTIER GLASS COMPANY. Rainbo. Interesting color. Red ribbons on mustard/orange. Ottawa, IL, circa 1930-1950. 19/32". Mint (9.9). $9. (Auction #166, Lot 12.20).

PELTIER GLASS COMPANY. Rainbo. Lot of thirteen marbles. All are Rainbos, the same color. Off-white base with red ribbons. 19/32". $8. (Auction #180, Lot 5).

PELTIER GLASS COMPANY. Rainbo. Harder to find six-ribbon Rainbo. Transparent olive green base. Six semi-opaque white ribbons. 19/32". Mint (9.9). $8. (Auction #124, Lot 16).

PELTIER GLASS COMPANY. Rainbo. Lot of two Rainbos. One is opaque white base with four thin transparent yellow ribbons. One is opaque. $5. (Auction #110, Lot 30).

PELTIER GLASS COMPANY. Rainbo. Interesting Rainbo. Combination of semi-opaque white, transparent clear and transparent blue bands. 9/16". Mint (9.9). $5. (Auction #181, Lot 31).

PELTIER GLASS COMPANY. Rainbo. Lot of four marbles. All are shooter Rainbos. Blue on white, blue on gray, green on white, red on white. $2. (Auction #102, Lot 1).

PELTIER GLASS COMPANY. Rainbo/Bloodie. Experimental Rainbo/Bloodie. Rare shooter. Translucent opalescent white base. A Rainbo Type I. 29/32". Near Mint(+) (8.9). $37. (Auction #81, Lot 16).

PELTIER GLASS COMPANY. Reproduction box. Reproduction red box for 12 Picture Marbles. Yellow bottom (all the repros are yellow bottoms), red . $85. (Auction #183, Lot 30).

PELTIER GLASS COMPANY. Reproduction box. Reproduction red box for 12 Picture Marbles. Yellow bottom (all the repros are yellow bottoms), red . $70. (Auction #88, Lot 22).

PELTIER GLASS COMPANY. Root Bear Float. Transparent root beer brown base glass with an opaque white ribbon in the core. Shooter size. Harder. 29/32". Mint (9.9). $85. (Auction #59, Lot 24).

PELTIER GLASS COMPANY. Root Bear Float. Transparent root beer brown base glass with an opaque white ribbon in the core. Shooter size. Harder. 29/32". Mint (9.9). $80. (Auction #59, Lot 24.20).

PELTIER GLASS COMPANY. Root Bear Float. Transparent root beer brown base glass with an opaque white ribbon in the core. Shooter size. Harder. 29/32". Mint (9.9). $75. (Auction #59, Lot 24.40).

PELTIER GLASS COMPANY. Root Bear Float. Transparent root beer brown base glass with an opaque white ribbon in the core. Shooter size. Harder. 29/32". Mint (9.9). $70. (Auction #59, Lot 24.30).

PELTIER GLASS COMPANY. Root Beer Float. Transparent brown base with a flat opaque white ribbon inside. Surface in great shape. Ottawa, IL, da. 15/16". Mint (9.9). $55. (Auction #136, Lot 37).

PELTIER GLASS COMPANY. Root Beer Float. Shooter marble. Transparent root beer brown base with an opaque white ribbon in it. 29/32". Mint (9.7). $50. (Auction #98, Lot 46).

PELTIER GLASS COMPANY. Root Beer Float. Shooter marble. Transparent root beer brown base with an opaque white ribbon in it. 29/32". Mint (9.7). $48. (Auction #98, Lot 46.20).

PELTIER GLASS COMPANY. Root Beer Float. Transparent brown base with a flat opaque white ribbon inside. Surface in great shape. 31/32". Near Mint(+) (9.9). $47. (Auction #128, Lot 17).

PELTIER GLASS COMPANY. Root Beer Float. Transparent brown base with a flat opaque white ribbon inside. Surface in great shape. Ottawa, IL. 15/16". Mint (9.9). $45. (Auction #176, Lot 41).

PELTIER GLASS COMPANY. Root Beer Float. Transparent brown base with a flat opaque white ribbon inside. Surface in great shape. Ottawa, IL. 15/16". Mint (9.9). $43. (Auction #161, Lot 21.40).

PELTIER GLASS COMPANY. Root Beer Float. Transparent brown base with a flat opaque white ribbon inside. Surface in great shape. Ottawa, IL. 15/16". Mint (9.9). $43. (Auction #161, Lot 21.30).

PELTIER GLASS COMPANY. Root Beer Float. Transparent brown base with a flat opaque white ribbon inside. Surface in great shape. Ottawa, IL. 15/16". Mint (9.9). $42. (Auction #150, Lot 25.30).

PELTIER GLASS COMPANY. Root Beer Float. Transparent brown base with a flat opaque white ribbon inside. Surface in great shape. Ottawa, IL. 15/16". Mint (9.9). $42. (Auction #150, Lot 25.20).

PELTIER GLASS COMPANY. Root Beer Float. Transparent brown base with a flat opaque white ribbon inside. Surface in great shape. Ottawa, IL. 15/16". Mint (9.9). $42. (Auction #150, Lot 25).

PELTIER GLASS COMPANY. Root Beer Float. Shooter marble. Transparent root beer brown base with an opaque white ribbon in it. 29/32". Mint (9.7). $40. (Auction #98, Lot 46.30).

PELTIER GLASS COMPANY. Root Beer Float. Transparent brown base with a flat opaque white ribbon inside. Surface in great shape. Ottawa, IL. 15/16". Mint (9.9). $40. (Auction #161, Lot 21).

PELTIER GLASS COMPANY. Root Beer Float. Shooter marble. Transparent root beer brown base with an opaque white ribbon in it. 29/32". Mint (9.7). $38. (Auction #91, Lot 22).

PELTIER GLASS COMPANY. Root Beer Float. Transparent brown base with a flat opaque white ribbon inside. Surface has a few very tiny pits. Ottawa, IL. 15/16". Mint(-) (9). $36. (Auction #140, Lot 19).

PELTIER GLASS COMPANY. Root Beer Float. Shooter marble. Transparent root beer brown base with an opaque white ribbon in it. 29/32". Mint (9.7). $36. (Auction #91, Lot 22.20).

PELTIER GLASS COMPANY. Root Beer Float. Transparent brown base with a flat opaque white ribbon inside. Surface has a few very tiny pits. Ottawa, IL. 15/16". Mint(-) (9). $36. (Auction #140, Lot 19.20).

PELTIER GLASS COMPANY. Root Beer Float. Shooter marble. Transparent root beer brown base with an opaque white ribbon in it. 29/32". Mint (9.7). $36. (Auction #100, Lot 18).

PELTIER GLASS COMPANY. Root Beer Float. Shooter marble. Transparent root beer brown base with an opaque white ribbon in it. 29/32". Mint (9.7). $35. (Auction #91, Lot 22.30).

PELTIER GLASS COMPANY. Root Beer Float. Shooter marble. Transparent root beer brown base with an opaque white ribbon in it. 29/32". Mint (9.7). $34. (Auction #100, Lot 18.10).

PELTIER GLASS COMPANY. Root Beer Float. Transparent brown base with a flat opaque white ribbon inside. Surface in great shape. Ottawa, IL. 15/16". Mint (9.9). $32. (Auction #74, Lot 4).

PELTIER GLASS COMPANY. Root Beer Float. Transparent brown base with a flat opaque white ribbon inside. Surface in great shape. Ottawa, IL. 15/16". Mint (9.9). $30. (Auction #161, Lot 21.20).

PELTIER GLASS COMPANY. Root Beer Float. Transparent brown base with a flat opaque white ribbon inside. Surface has some scratching. 15/16". Mint(-) (9). $28. (Auction #172, Lot 15).

PELTIER GLASS COMPANY. Root Beer Float. Shooter marble. Transparent root beer brown base with an opaque white ribbon in it. 29/32". Mint (9.7). $20. (Auction #115, Lot 39).

PELTIER GLASS COMPANY. Root Beer Float. Shooter marble. Transparent root beer brown base with an opaque white ribbon in it. 29/32". Mint (9.7). $20. (Auction #115, Lot 39.20).

PELTIER GLASS COMPANY. Root Beer Float. Lot of two marbles. Transparent brown base with a flat opaque white ribbon inside. One has tiny pits. Mint. $17. (Auction #121, Lot 35).

PELTIER GLASS COMPANY. Slag. Lot of six marbles. All are red slags. Two are Mint. 19/32" to 5/8". Mint (9.9) to Near Mint (8.5). $44. (Auction #125, Lot 18).

PELTIER GLASS COMPANY. Slag. Purple slag. Superior pattern to the white. Larger than typical size. Cold roll mark and a sparkle. 23/32". Mint(-) (9.1). $37. (Auction #123, Lot 49).

PELTIER GLASS COMPANY. Slag. Lot of three marbles. All are slags. Aqua (two airholes), brown (chips), green (chips). Ottawa, IL. $33. (Auction #117, Lot 33).

PELTIER GLASS COMPANY. Slag. Hard to find yellow Peltier slag. Great feathering. And in great shape. The hardest Peltier slag. 19/32". Mint (9.9). $32. (Auction #58, Lot 6).

PELTIER GLASS COMPANY. Slag. Red slag. Nice feathering of the white. No airholes. A beauty. Ottawa, IL, circa 1925-1935. 5/8". Mint (9.9). $28. (Auction #164, Lot 5).

PELTIER GLASS COMPANY. Slag. Lot of two marbles. One yellow (rare) and one green. 9/16" & 19/32". Near Mint(+) (8.9) and Mint(-). $25. (Auction #180, Lot 45).

PELTIER GLASS COMPANY. Slag. Lot of two marbles. Both are green slags. Excellent pair. Ottawa, IL, circa 1925-1935. 19/32". Mint. $24. (Auction #56, Lot 2).

PELTIER GLASS COMPANY. Slag. Lot of two marbles. Both are slags with nice white feathering. Red slag, a couple of airholes, 9/16". $23. (Auction #67, Lot 1).

PELTIER GLASS COMPANY. Slag. Lot of five marbles. Two green, two brown, one blue. 9/16" to 5/8". Mint(-) (9.0) to Near Mint (8.6). $23. (Auction #75, Lot 21).

PELTIER GLASS COMPANY. Slag. Blue slag. Smaller marble. Excellent white pattern. One very tiny pinprick. Ottawa, IL, circa 1925. 9/16". Mint(-) (9.2). $23. (Auction #73, Lot 6).

PELTIER GLASS COMPANY. Slag. Lot of two marbles. Both are red slags. One has a manufacturing deep scratch. Nice ones. Ottawa, IL. $22. (Auction #125, Lot 44).

PELTIER GLASS COMPANY. Slag. Lot of two marbles. Both are Peltier slags. Green, 5/8", Mint (9.9). Red, 5/8", Near Mint(+) (8.7). $20. (Auction #54, Lot 11).

PELTIER GLASS COMPANY. Slag. Aqua slag. Nice white feathering. Several air holes. Ottawa, IL, circa 1925-1935. 5/8". Mint (9.5). $19. (Auction #85, Lot 29).

PELTIER GLASS COMPANY. Slag. Lot of two marbles. Red slag, 9/16", buffed. Aqua slag, 19/32", Near Mint(+) (8.9). $18. (Auction #75, Lot 36).

PELTIER GLASS COMPANY. Slag. Green slag. Nice feathering. In great shape. Ottawa, IL, circa 1925-1935. 5/8". Mint (9.9). $18. (Auction #176, Lot 31).

PELTIER GLASS COMPANY. Slag. Brown slag. Very nice feathering of the white. One tiny airhole. Ottawa, IL, circa 1925-1935. 5/8". Mint (9.4). $14. (Auction #161, Lot 5).

PELTIER GLASS COMPANY. Slag. Lot of two marbles. Both are slags. One is aqua, one is brown. Aqua has some flakes. $12. (Auction #179, Lot 1).

PELTIER GLASS COMPANY. Slag. Purple slag. Nice feathering of the white. A couple of blown-out airholes, typical of this type. Ottawa, IL. 21/32". Mint (9.5). $12. (Auction #140, Lot 15).

PELTIER GLASS COMPANY. Slag. Blue slag. Excellent pattern to the white. A couple of sparkles. Ottawa, IL, circa 1925-1935. 5/8". Mint(-) (9). $11. (Auction #82, Lot 5).

PELTIER GLASS COMPANY. Slag. Brown slag. Nice white feathering. Two pinpricks on it. Ottawa, IL, circa 1925-1935. 5/8". Mint(-) (9). $9. (Auction #75, Lot 10).

PELTIER GLASS COMPANY. Slag. Green slag. Nice feathering. One sparkle. Ottawa, IL, circa 1925-1935. 5/8". Near Mint(+) (8.9). $4. (Auction #97, Lot 4).

PELTIER GLASS COMPANY. Sunset. Very hard to find hybrid Sunset. Transparent bubble filled base. Three yellow ribbons, two white ribbons. 19/32". Mint (9.9). $40. (Auction #121, Lot 33).

PELTIER GLASS COMPANY. Sunset. Shooter orange Sunset. Very hard to find. Transparent bubble-filled clear base with ribbons of orange. 15/16". Mint (9.9). $39. (Auction #134, Lot 6).

PELTIER GLASS COMPANY. Sunset. Shooter orange Sunset. Very hard to find. Transparent bubble-filled clear base with ribbons of orange. 29/32". Mint (9.9). $30. (Auction #171, Lot 45).

PELTIER GLASS COMPANY. Sunset. Lot of eighteen marbles. All are red Sunsets. Great group. Ottawa, IL, circa 1930-1940. 19/32" to 5/8". $27. (Auction #63, Lot 22).

PELTIER GLASS COMPANY. Sunset. Shooter size marble. Red and white ribbons in a bubble filled transparent base. 15/16". Mint (9.9). $26. (Auction #56, Lot 27).

PELTIER GLASS COMPANY. Sunset. Shooter red Sunset. Transparent bubble-filled clear base with ribbons of red and white. 31/32". Near Mint(+) (8.7). $25. (Auction #137, Lot 40).

PELTIER GLASS COMPANY. Sunset. Shooter Sunset. Orange and white ribbons. A real beauty. Has one tiny sparkle and one tiny annealing. 29/32". Mint(-) (9). $25. (Auction #78, Lot 13).

PELTIER GLASS COMPANY. Sunset. Lot of eleven marbles. All are Sunsets. All about 5/8". Almost all Mint. $15. (Auction #122, Lot 9).

PELTIER GLASS COMPANY. Sunset. Hard to find peewee yellow and white Sunset. Ottawa, IL, circa 1930-1940. 1/2". Mint (9.9). $12. (Auction #119, Lot 9).

PELTIER GLASS COMPANY. Sunset. Lot of ten marbles. All are Sunsets. All about 5/8". Almost all Mint. $9. (Auction #159, Lot 30).

PELTIER GLASS COMPANY. Tri-color. Very hard to find shooter transparent tri-color. Transparent very dark green base. 31/32". Mint (9.9). $70. (Auction #173, Lot 9).

PELTIER GLASS COMPANY. Tricolor. Lot of ten marbles. Assortment of ribbons and swirls on opaque green or brown base. All are red. $22. (Auction #60, Lot 22).

RAVENSWOOD NOVELTY WORKS. Big Boy. Lot of ten marbles. Assortment of Big Boy swirls. All about 1". A few are Mint. Mint (9.9) to Near Mint. $41. (Auction #75, Lot 27).

RAVENSWOOD NOVELTY WORKS. Big Boy. Lot of two marbles. Both are Ravenswood Big Boys. Yellow on blue and brown on white. 31/32" & Near Mint. $18. (Auction #60, Lot 14).

RAVENSWOOD NOVELTY WORKS. Catalogue. Four page catalogue from Ravenswood. Circa 1940s. Features pictures of the various marble boxes. $44. (Auction #137, Lot 28).

RAVENSWOOD NOVELTY WORKS. Catalogue. Four page catalogue from Ravenswood. Circa 1940s. Features pictures of the various marble boxes. $42. (Auction #137, Lot 28.20).

RAVENSWOOD NOVELTY WORKS. Original box. Original tan cardboard box. Diagonal oval cutout on the front. "MARBLES" printed twice in red. $70. (Auction #137, Lot 30).

RAVENSWOOD NOVELTY WORKS. Original box. Original tan cardboard box. Diagonal oval cutout on the front. "MARBLES" printed twice in red. $65. (Auction #137, Lot 30.20).

RAVENSWOOD NOVELTY WORKS. Original box. Original tan cardboard box. Diagonal oval cutout on the front. "MARBLES" printed twice in red. $55. (Auction #175, Lot 30).

RAVENSWOOD NOVELTY WORKS. Original box. Original tan cardboard box. Diagonal oval cutout on the front. "MARBLES" printed twice in red. $55. (Auction #175, Lot 30.20).

RAVENSWOOD NOVELTY WORKS. Original box. Original cardboard "Buddy Marbles" box. Oval cutout. Red checkerboard. Larger box. 4" x 3-1/4". $47. (Auction #138, Lot 47).

RAVENSWOOD NOVELTY WORKS. Original box. Original cardboard "Buddy Marbles" box. Oval cutout. Red checkerboard. Larger box. 4" x 3-1/4". $45. (Auction #138, Lot 47.20).

RAVENSWOOD NOVELTY WORKS. Original box. Original tan cardboard box. Diagonal oval cutout on the front. "MARBLES" printed twice in red. $40. (Auction #155, Lot 30.30).

RAVENSWOOD NOVELTY WORKS. Original box. Original tan cardboard box. Diagonal oval cutout on the front. "MARBLES" printed twice in red. $40. (Auction #155, Lot 30.20).

RAVENSWOOD NOVELTY WORKS. Original box. Original tan cardboard box. Diagonal oval cutout on the front. "MARBLES" printed twice in red. $40. (Auction #155, Lot 30.40).

RAVENSWOOD NOVELTY WORKS. Original box. Original tan cardboard box. Diagonal oval cutout on the front. "MARBLES" printed twice in red. $40. (Auction #155, Lot 30).

RAVENSWOOD NOVELTY WORKS. Original box. Original tan cardboard box. Diagonal oval cutout on the front. "MARBLES" printed twice in red. $37. (Auction #145, Lot 24).

RAVENSWOOD NOVELTY WORKS. Original box. Original tan cardboard box. Diagonal oval cutout on the front. "MARBLES" printed twice in red. $37. (Auction #145, Lot 24.20).

RAVENSWOOD NOVELTY WORKS. Original box. Original tan cardboard box. Diagonal oval cutout on the front. "MARBLES" printed twice in red. $37. (Auction #145, Lot 24.30).

RAVENSWOOD NOVELTY WORKS. Original box. Original tan cardboard box. Diagonal oval cutout on the front. "MARBLES" printed twice in red. $37. (Auction #155, Lot 30.50).

RAVENSWOOD NOVELTY WORKS. Swirl. Three color swirl. Red and blue on white. Some sparkles. Ravenswood, WV, circa 1940-1955. 19/32". Mint(-) (9). $8. (Auction #163, Lot 2).

SULPHIDE. Very rare figure in colored glass. This figure has been called a leprachaun seated on a chair. 1-7/16". Near Mint(+) (8.8). $4300.

(Auction #168, Lot 50).

SULPHIDE. Rare handpainted sulphide. Transparent clear glass. The figure is handpainted. Standing male lion. 1-3/8". Near Mint (8.6). $2125. (Auction #147, Lot 50).

SULPHIDE. Extremely rare sulphide. Disk with image of a lauging boy on both sides. 1-3/8". Mint(-) (9). $1775. (Auction #160, Lot 50).

SULPHIDE. Handpainted sulphide. Figure of a reclining ram. Black horns, eyes, eyebrows, nostril and mouth. 1-1/4". Near Mint(-) (8.1). $1085. (Auction #179, Lot 50).

SULPHIDE. One of the finest sulphides that I have seen. 1-5/8". Mint (9.8). $550. (Auction #59, Lot 45).

SULPHIDE. Superior, very large sulphide. Figure of a grazing sheep. Exceptional detail to the figure. 2-1/8". Mint(-) (9.2). $355. (Auction #160, Lot 22).

SULPHIDE. Figure of Kate Greenaway. Nice detail to the figure. This is the type with her arms at her side. 1-3/8". Near Mint(+) (8.9). $350. (Auction #74, Lot 38).

SULPHIDE. Huge marble. Figure is usually called a standing doe or deer. Exceptional detail to the figure. 2-5/16". Near Mint(+) (8.9). $340. (Auction #150, Lot 48).

SULPHIDE. Figure of a floating angel. Male figure. Figure is floating, with slightly bended knees. $330. (Auction #58, Lot 44).

SULPHIDE. Very nice sulphide in great shape. Figure is a seated dog, head cocked to one side. Excellent detail. 1-1/4". Mint(-) (9.1). $310. (Auction #96, Lot 43).

SULPHIDE. Figure of a standing horse, head turned slightly to one side, with a English saddle. $295. (Auction #77, Lot 45).

SULPHIDE. Very rare figure. Demonic figure seated on a rock. Naked. Crossed legs. 1-1/4". Good (7.50). $280. (Auction #65, Lot 42).

SULPHIDE. Superb figure of a crouched rabbit with its head turned to one side. Excellent three-dimensional figure. 1-1/2". Near Mint(+) (8.7). $270. (Auction #121, Lot 46).

SULPHIDE. Very rare figure. Standing angel. Clothed figure, wearing a robe similar to a shepherd. Hands clasped. 1-3/8". Near Mint(+) (8.1). $260. (Auction #173, Lot 46).

SULPHIDE. Numeral #5. Numerals are hard to find. This one is well centered. Small air bubble on the front. 1-5/8". Near Mint (8.3). $250. (Auction #76, Lot 44).

SULPHIDE. Figure of a floating angel. Male angel. Hands clasped over his groin. Two outspread wings. $240. (Auction #104, Lot 47).

SULPHIDE. Rare type of sulphide. Roaring male lion with a "doughnut hole" between the body and the ground. 1-11/16". Near Mint (8.6). $235. (Auction #147, Lot 38).

SULPHIDE. One of the largest sulphides I have ever seen. Figure is a feeding cow, with it's ribs showing. 2-1/8". Near Mint(+) (8.9). $235. (Auction #126, Lot 48).

SULPHIDE. Outstanding figure. Razorback. Exceptional detail to the figure. Nice silvering. 1-11/16". Mint (9.3). $220. (Auction #65, Lot 19).

SULPHIDE. Exceptional figure of a billy goat. Excellent detail. You can even see the beard under his chin. 1-7/16". Mint (9.4). $215. (Auction #71, Lot 42).

SULPHIDE. Very nice sulphide. Figure of a standing donkey. Hard figure to find. Excellent detail. Very well centered. 2". Near Mint(+) (8.9). $213. (Auction #154, Lot 32).

SULPHIDE. Figure of a floating angel. Male angel. Hands clasped over his groin. Two outspread wings. $200. (Auction #85, Lot 32).

SULPHIDE. Hard to find figure. Three dimensional spreadwinged owl. Exceptional detail to the figure. 1-7/16". Near Mint(-) (8.2). $170. (Auction #78, Lot 41).

SULPHIDE. Hard to find figure of bathing girl. Nice sized figure, well-centered. 1-11/16". Near Mint (8.3). $160. (Auction #81, Lot 36).

SULPHIDE. Figure of a crowing rooster. Excellent detail to the figure. It is set slightly back in the marble. 1-1/2". Mint (9.7). $140. (Auction #83, Lot 25).

SULPHIDE. Large figure of a songbird. Exceptional detail to the figure. Large for the marble. Well centered. 1-7/8". Mint(-) (9.2). $130. (Auction #174, Lot 50).

SULPHIDE. Lot of three marbles. All have been buffed and are very hazy. A sheep, a songbird, a bear. 1-1/4" to. $130. (Auction #101, Lot 23).

SULPHIDE. Figure of a standing horse. The figure has average detail. It cracked during insertion. 1-9/16". Mint(-) (9). $130. (Auction #183, Lot 48).

SULPHIDE. Figure of a standing sheep. Very shallow air bubble on back side. Slightly off center. 2-1/8". Near Mint (8.3). $120. (Auction #108, Lot 19).

SULPHIDE. Superb marble. This is a small sulphide marble. This one has a figure of a razorback in it. 1-3/16". Mint (9.7). $120. (Auction #124, Lot 46).

SULPHIDE. Figure of a seated rabbit. Slightly above average detail to the figure. Nice silvering. 1-11/16". Near Mint(+) (8.9). $120. (Auction #71, Lot 29).

SULPHIDE. This marble has some serious condition problems. 2-1/4". Good(-) (7.20). $120. (Auction #94, Lot 34).

SULPHIDE. Very nice sulphide. Figure is a standing rooster. Average detail to the figure. Minor air bubble. 1-1/4". Mint(-) (9). $120. (Auction #63, Lot 39).

SULPHIDE. Seated figure of a frog. Slightly above average detail. The figure is large and well centered. $120. (Auction #55, Lot 29).

SULPHIDE. Figure of a standing dog. Excellent detail to the figure. Slightly off-center. Small air bubble. $120. (Auction #181, Lot 22).

SULPHIDE. Figure of a reclining cow. Average detail to the figure. Very slight air bubbling on it. Well center. 1-3/4". Near Mint(+) (8.8). $110. (Auction #82, Lot 22).

SULPHIDE. Figure of a standing rooster. Outstanding figure. Large, with excellent detail. Slightly off center. $110. (Auction #103, Lot 21).

SULPHIDE. Figure of Kate Greenaway, holding the purse in front of her. Exceptional detail to the figure. Set high. 1-13/16". Good(-) (7.30). $110. (Auction #122, Lot 21).

SULPHIDE. The marble was polished, but the figure is beautiful. $110. (Auction #91, Lot 28).

SULPHIDE. Large marble. Figure of a standing sheep. Excellent detail to the figure. Set slightly back in the marble. 1-15/16". Near Mint(+) (8.8). $110. (Auction #139, Lot 49).

SULPHIDE. Figure of a cat seated on it's hind legs. Excellent detail to the figure. Small air bubble. 1-3/8". Near Mint(+) (8.9). $110. (Auction #176, Lot 38).

SULPHIDE. Figure of a rooster. Large figure. Exceptional detail to the figure. Well-centered. No air bubbles. $110. (Auction #134, Lot 29).

SULPHIDE. Figure of a male lion seated on its rear haunches, and roaring. Slightly above average detail. $110. (Auction #110, Lot 27).

SULPHIDE. Figure of a seated lamb. Average detail. Air bubble on the figure, although you can see it. Set back. $105. (Auction #172, Lot 25).

SULPHIDE. Superb marble. This is a small sulphide marble. This one has a figure of a rabbit in it. Above average. 1-3/16". Near Mint(+) (8.9). $100. (Auction #134, Lot 40).

SULPHIDE. Superb marble. This is a small sulphide marble. This one has a figure of a squirrel in it. 1-3/16". Mint (9.7). $100. (Auction #126, Lot 35).

SULPHIDE. Figure of a passenger pigeon seated on a tree stump. Excellent detail to the figure. No air bubbles. $100. (Auction #98, Lot 25).

SULPHIDE. Interesting small figure. Nice detail. My guess is that it is a rat. Shallow air bubbling. 1-3/8". Mint(-) (9.1). $100. (Auction #159, Lot 47).

SULPHIDE. Figure of a seated dove. Nice figure. Above average detail. Well centered with no air bubbles. 1-5/16". Near Mint(+) (8). $100. (Auction #56, Lot 30).

SULPHIDE. Figure of a dog standing on all fours and howling. Average detail to figure. Small air bubble on one. 1-1/4". Mint (9.5). $100. (Auction #129, Lot 45).

SULPHIDE. Figure of a male lion. Figure is a little small for the marble. Very minor air bubble on the figure,. 1-7/16". Near Mint(+) (8.7). $95. (Auction #142, Lot 40).

SULPHIDE. Lot of two marbles. Running rabbit, 1-1/2", Near Mint (8.6). Standing song bird, 1-5/8", Good (7.4). $95. (Auction #94, Lot 12).

SULPHIDE. Reclining male lion. Excellent detail to the figure. Very small air bubble on one side. $95. (Auction #181, Lot 29).

SULPHIDE. Figure of a standing elephant. Excellent detail to the figure, right down to the tusks!! Large figure. $90. (Auction #67, Lot 21).

SULPHIDE. Figure of a numeral #2. Numerals are hard to find. Nice figure, but some chips, subsurface moon. 1-5/8". Good (7.40). $90. (Auction #122, Lot 14).

SULPHIDE. Large marble. Figure of a standing sheep. Excellent detail to the figure. Set slightly back in the marble. 1-15/16". Near Mint(+) (8.8). $85. (Auction #69, Lot 25).

SULPHIDE. Figure of a bear walking on all fours. Excellent detail to the figure. Well-centered. No air bubbles. $85. (Auction #180, Lot 30).

SULPHIDE. Figure of a seated dog. Nice figure with good detail. No air bubbles. Well centered. 1-5/16". Near Mint (8.6). $85. (Auction #67, Lot 33).

SULPHIDE. Figure of baby chick, pecking, in very light pink glass. Very rare figure. Excellent detail to the figure. 1-7/16". Near Mint(-) (8.1). $85. (Auction #163, Lot 49).

SULPHIDE. Figure of a dog seated on his rear haunches. Average detail to dog. Well centered. $85. (Auction #105, Lot 28).

SULPHIDE. Figure of a squirrel eating a nut. Large figure for the marble. Excellent detail. Very well centered. 1-9/16". Near Mint(-) (8.2). $85. (Auction #177, Lot 14).

SULPHIDE. Lot of two marbles. Lion, 1-5/16", Polished. Squirrel eating nut, deep chip, 1-7/16". Good (7.5). $80. (Auction #94, Lot 33).

SULPHIDE. Hard to find figure. Lizard sunning itself on a rock. Poor detail (but, they usually are). Air bubble. 1-3/16". Near Mint (8.5). $80. (Auction #80, Lot 35).

SULPHIDE. Lot of two marbles. First is a figure of standing bear. One chip on the bottom. Some pinpricking. $80. (Auction #89, Lot 27).

SULPHIDE. Figure of a seated lamb. Figure is small for the marble. Average detail. Well centered. Small air bubble. 1-1/2". Near Mint (8.6). $80. (Auction #85, Lot 21).

SULPHIDE. Figure of a seated lamb. Figure is small for the marble. Average detail. Well centered. Small air bubble. 1-1/2". Near Mint (8.6). $80. (Auction #104, Lot 29).

SULPHIDE. Figure of a chicken bending down to peck at seed. Average detail to the figure, which is large. 1-9/16". Near Mint (8.6). $75. (Auction #70, Lot 22).

SULPHIDE. Exceptional figure of a pointer-type dog. Excellent detail. No air bubbles, figure slightly off center. 1-11/16". Near Mint(-) (8.2). $75. (Auction #125, Lot 40).

SULPHIDE. Figure of a standing elephant. Figure is average detail. Set back in the marble. Air bubble on each . 1-7/16". Near Mint(+) (8.9). $75. (Auction #89, Lot 23).

SULPHIDE. Figure of a razorback. Small figure. Excellent detail. Slightly off to one side. No air bubbles. $75. (Auction #74, Lot 24).

SULPHIDE. Tiny sulphide. Figure is a bushy tail dog. I am not a dog expert, so I can't name the breed. $70. (Auction #64, Lot 37).

SULPHIDE. Figure of a standing cow. Not well-fed, it's ribs show. Fills almost the whole marble. Slightly off-center. 1-7/16". Good(+) (7.80). $70. (Auction #117, Lot 22).

SULPHIDE. Standing figure of a goat. Average detail. No air bubbles. Slightly off-center. Polished surface. $70. (Auction #174, Lot 2).

SULPHIDE. Figure of a seated cat. Average detail to the figure. No air bubbles. Slightly off-center. 1-3/16". Near Mint(+) (8.7). $70. (Auction #179, Lot 22).

SULPHIDE. Figure of a standing duck. Nice detail. The very front of the beak broke off during manufacture. 1-5/8". Good(+) (7.80). $70. (Auction #180, Lot 41).

SULPHIDE. Figure of a standing rooster. Excellent detail to figure. Figure is large for the marble. 1-1/2". Near Mint (8.3). $70. (Auction #161, Lot 42).

SULPHIDE. Figure of a male lion. Above average detail to the figure. Small air bubble on one side of the chest. 1-13/16". Near Mint(-) (8.2). $70. (Auction #141, Lot 30).

SULPHIDE. Standing male lion. Exceptional detail to the figure. Well centered. No air bubbles. Overall pitting. 1-11/16". Good(+) (7.80). $70. (Auction #125, Lot 32).

SULPHIDE. Figure of a standing chicken. Average detail. No air bubbles. Set slightly high. Overall scratching. 1-7/16". Near Mint(+) (8.8). $65. (Auction #101, Lot 20).

SULPHIDE. Figure of an elephant. Superior figure. Excellent detail. Well centered. Very small bubble on one side. 1-7/8". Good(+) (7.70). $65. (Auction #143, Lot 36).

SULPHIDE. Figure of an unidentified animal. Small head, furry body, bushy tail. Figure is exceptionally well done. 1-5/16". Near Mint (8.6). $65. (Auction #57, Lot 28).

SULPHIDE. Lot of two collectible marbles. Chicken, 1-7/8". Sheep, 2". $60. (Auction #101, Lot 34).

SULPHIDE. Figure of a begging dog. Average detail. Set a little high. No air bubbles. Polished surface. German. $60. (Auction #174, Lot 36).

SULPHIDE. Figure of a running rabbit. Well centered. Average detail. Several small chips and subsurface moons. 1-9/16". Near Mint(+) (8.2). $60. (Auction #75, Lot 29).

SULPHIDE. Very unusual fish. Very large dorsal and ventral fins on it. Excellent detail, well-centered. $60. (Auction #101, Lot 19).

SULPHIDE. Even though this has damage, I've separated it because the figure is unusual. Crouching bunny. 1-5/8". Good(+) (7.80). $60. (Auction #94, Lot 15).

SULPHIDE. Figure of a reclining lamb. Slightly below average detail to figure. Small air bubble on one side. 1-3/4". Near Mint (8.4). $60. (Auction #89, Lot 21).

SULPHIDE. Figure of an apeman, seated on a stump. One hand on his chest, one at his side. Excellent detail. 1-11/16". Good(-) (7.10). $55. (Auction #84, Lot 13).

SULPHIDE. Figure of what appears to be a donkey. Not well-fed, it's ribs are showing. Average detail. Well centered. 1-7/16". Good(+) (7.80). $55. (Auction #130, Lot 31).

SULPHIDE. Figure is a bear seated on an overturned drum. Small air bubble on one side. Well-centered. 1-15/16". Good(+) (7.80). $55. (Auction #108, Lot 9).

SULPHIDE. Figure of standing donkey. Ribs showing. Average detail. No air bubbles. Well centered. 1-5/8". Near Mint(-) (8.2). $50. (Auction #158, Lot 30).

SULPHIDE. Small sulphide. The figure is a begging dog. Poor detail to the figure. No air bubbles. $50. (Auction #116, Lot 22).

SULPHIDE. Figure of a running rabbit. Excellent detail to the figure. Shallow air bubble on one side. 1-13/16". Good(+) (7.70). $50. (Auction #143, Lot 38).

SULPHIDE. Figure of a standing male lion. Average detail to figure. No air bubbles. Set slightly off-center. $50. (Auction #109, Lot 11).

SULPHIDE. Figure of a hungry cow (his ribs are showing). Slightly off-center. Very minor air bubbling. 1-1/2". Good(+) (7.90). $50. (Auction #133, Lot 17).

SULPHIDE. Figure of a grazing sheep. Average detail. Well centered. No air bubbles. Overall chips. $50. (Auction #101, Lot 21).

SULPHIDE. Figure of a running dog. Average detail of to the figure. Some minor shallow air bubbling on the figure. 1-7/16". Near Mint (8.4). $48. (Auction #177, Lot 40).

SULPHIDE. Figure of an unknown animal. Perhaps a badger or some small mammal like that. Excellent detail. 1-5/16". Good(+) (7.80). $47. (Auction #181, Lot 6).

SULPHIDE. Figure of a donkey. Excellent detail, no air bubbling. Set off to one side. 1-3/4". Good(+) (7.90). $45. (Auction #94, Lot 36).

SULPHIDE. Assorted core. Lot of fifteen marbles. Assortment of cores. Nice variety of colors and designs. 1/2" to 13/16". Min. $80. (Auction #108, Lot 13).

SULPHIDE. Latticinio core. White latticinio core swirl. Outer layer is three blue bands and three pink on white bands. $60. (Auction #166, Lot 28).

SULPHIDE. Latticinio core. Orange latticinio core. Hard color to find. Outer layer is three orange bands. 11/16". Mint (9.7). $27. (Auction #93, Lot 1).

SWIRL. Lot of eleven marbles. Five are latticinio core (including an orange), four are divided core. $120. (Auction #166, Lot 26).

SWIRL. Hard one to categorize. I suspect that it is a divided core from near the end of the cane. 19/32". Mint(-) (9). $14. (Auction #92, Lot 29).

SWIRL. Assorted. Lot of thirteen marbles. Eight latticinio core (including several yellow), three divided core. $150. (Auction #84, Lot 14).

SWIRL. Assorted. Lot of eleven marbles. Five latticinio core (including several yellow) (also a white in blue glass). $100. (Auction #169, Lot 27).

SWIRL. Assorted. Lot of six marbles. Orange latticinio core, 1-3/16", Good (7.5). Double ribbon core, 1-1/16", Near Mint. $65. (Auction #177, Lot 10).

SWIRL. Assorted. Lot of nine marbles. Includes a peppermint, four latticinio core, four divided core. $60. (Auction #174, Lot 37).

SWIRL. Assorted. Lot of two marbles. First is a divided core. English colors. Only one outer band. Almost naked. 21/3. $40. (Auction #84, Lot 10).

SWIRL. Assorted. Lot of two marbles. White latticinio core, 3/4", Mint (9.9). Solid core, 3/4", Near Mint(+) (8.7). $29. (Auction #158, Lot 17).

SWIRL. Assorted core. Lot of thirty two marbles, with a solitaire board. The board is an English wood, probably poplar. $470. (Auction #126, Lot 21).

SWIRL. Assorted core. Lot of forty nine marbles. All are handmade swirls. Assortment of cores including latticinio core. $315. (Auction #94, Lot 26).

SWIRL. Assorted core. Lot of five marbles. All are large swirls. Three divided core, a solid core and a lobed solid core. $210. (Auction #101, Lot 35).

SWIRL. Assorted core. Lot of thirty four swirls. Includes latticinio core, divided core, solid core and banded. $210. (Auction #157, Lot 11).

SWIRL. Assorted core. Lot of twenty four marbles. Mostly latticinio core with some divided and solid cores. $160. (Auction #174, Lot 7).

SWIRL. Assorted core. Lot of twenty five marbles. Assortment, including latticinio core, divided core, solid core, ribbon. $155. (Auction #128, Lot 27).

SWIRL. Assorted core. Lot of thirty six marbles. Assortment of latticinio core, divided core and solid core. 1/2" to 13/16. $150. (Auction #101, Lot 36).

SWIRL. Assorted core. Lot of ten marbles. All are large. All have damage. Five latticinio core, three divided core. $130. (Auction #94, Lot 29).

SWIRL. Assorted core. Lot of eight marbles. All are large swirls. All have damage. Six latticino core, a solid core. $100. (Auction #94, Lot 28).

SWIRL. Assorted core. Lot of ten marbles. All have very minor damage. Four latticinio core, three divided core. $95. (Auction #97, Lot 19).

SWIRL. Assorted core. Lot of eleven marbles. Includes five divided core and six solid core. $90. (Auction #89, Lot 17).

SWIRL. Assorted core. Lot of five marbles. Matched pair of yellow latticino core, 3/4". White latticinio core, 3/4". Solid. $90. (Auction #157, Lot 15).

SWIRL. Assorted core. Lot of six marbles. All are peewee. Three divided core and three solid core (one lobed). $90. (Auction #157, Lot 39).

SWIRL. Assorted core. Lot of seven marbles. Assortment of six damaged swirls and one damaged onionskin. Excellent assortment. $85. (Auction #174, Lot 13).

SWIRL. Assorted core. Lot of seven marbles. Four divided core, two latticinio core (one yellow), one translucent solid core. $85. (Auction #144, Lot 17).

SWIRL. Assorted core. Lot of three marbles. Divided core, tight twist, overall haziness, 15/16", Near Mint(-) (8.1). White. $85. (Auction #175, Lot 1).

SWIRL. Assorted core. Lot of nine marbles. Three latticinio core, two divided core, four solid core. Excellent assortment. $85. (Auction #106, Lot 1).

SWIRL. Assorted core. Lot of five marbles. Two latticinio core, one divided core, two solid core. Excellent group. 17/32". $80. (Auction #158, Lot 14).

SWIRL. Assorted core. Lot of two larger marbles. First is a white latticinio core. 1-1/2". Good(+) (7.9). $80. (Auction #95, Lot 15).

SWIRL. Assorted core. Lot of seven marbles. Three white latticinio core, three divided core, one solid core. $80. (Auction #161, Lot 1).

SWIRL. Assorted core. Lot of six marble. Four are latticinio core, two are solid core. All have some damage. $70. (Auction #155, Lot 18).

SWIRL. Assorted core. Lot of two marbles. Both have been polished. One solid core. One divided core. 1-3/4" & 1-7/8". $70. (Auction #174, Lot 14).

SWIRL. Assorted core. Lot of ten marbles. Assortment of latticinio core, divided core and solid core. $70. (Auction #127, Lot 3).

SWIRL. Assorted core. Lot of nine marbles. Three white latticinio core, three divided core, three solid core. $70. (Auction #57, Lot 27).

SWIRL. Assorted core. Lot of eight marbles. All are shooter marbles. Includes four latticinio core, two divided core. $70. (Auction #94, Lot 11).

SWIRL. Assorted core. Lot of three marbles. The first is a start-of-cane solid core. The inner core comes out one side. $65. (Auction #83, Lot 13).

SWIRL. Assorted core. Lot of ten marbles. Assortment of latticinio core, divided core and solid core. All have some damage. $65. (Auction #174, Lot 28).

SWIRL. Assorted core. Lot of eleven marbles. Two latticinio, four divided core, four solid core, a Joseph Coat. $65. (Auction #89, Lot 32).

SWIRL. Assorted core. Lot of nine marbles. One latticinio core, eight divided core. 5/8" to 1-1/16". Near Mint(+) (8.9). $65. (Auction #175, Lot 15).

SWIRL. Assorted core. Lot of nine marbles. All are swirls. Five latticinio core, three divided core, one solid core. $65. (Auction #143, Lot 22).

SWIRL. Assorted core. Lot of three marbles. Very nice group of shooters. First is a divided core in light blue glass. $63. (Auction #80, Lot 1).

SWIRL. Assorted core. Lot of four marbles. Orange latticinio core, yellow latticinio core and two solid cores. $60. (Auction #168, Lot 10).

SWIRL. Assorted core. Lot of five marbles. Four are swirls. One is a black ballot box handmade. 19/32". Mint (9.2). Yellow. $55. (Auction #102, Lot 22).

SWIRL. Assorted core. Lot of two marbles. Divided core. Multiple colored bands. Outer layer is several yellow strands. $55. (Auction #89, Lot 33).

SWIRL. Assorted core. Lot of four marbles. Super set of swirls. Each has just a minor defect. Caged solid core, two white. $55. (Auction #161, Lot 6).

SWIRL. Assorted core. Lot of five marbles. Three white latticinio core and two divided core. 21/32" to 15/16". Near Mint(+). $55. (Auction #175, Lot 10).

SWIRL. Assorted core. Lot of five marbles. A latticinio core, divided core, three solid core. Four are Mint. 9/16" to 5/8". $55. (Auction #157,

SWIRL. Assorted core. Lot of three marbles. Orange latticinio core, 27/32", Near Mint (8.6). Divided core, 25/32", Near Mint. $55. (Auction #134, Lot 1).

SWIRL. Assorted core. Lot of five marbles. Three are latticinio core, two are divided core. $55. (Auction #155, Lot 33).

SWIRL. Assorted core. Lot of five marbles. Three solid core and two divided core. One solid core is naked. $50. (Auction #174, Lot 21).

SWIRL. Assorted core. Lot of four marbles. All are peewees. One white latticinio core, three divided cores. Nice variety. $50. (Auction #168, Lot 8).

SWIRL. Assorted core. Lot of seven marbles. One latticinio, three divided core, two solid core (one lobed) and one double. $50. (Auction #92, Lot 18).

SWIRL. Assorted core. Lot of four marbles. Single ribbon core, 1", Collectible. Divided core, 1-1/16", Near Mint (8.6). $50. (Auction #101, Lot 25).

SWIRL. Assorted core. Lot of six marbles. Two latticinio core, one divided core, three solid core. Each has a tiny pit. $50. (Auction #74, Lot 26).

SWIRL. Assorted core. Lot of seven marbles. Two latticinio core, a solid core and four banded swirls. All have minor damage. $50. (Auction #70, Lot 27).

SWIRL. Assorted core. Lot of four marbles. Two white latticinio core, two divided core. Two marbles have very minor imperfections. $45. (Auction #117, Lot 2).

SWIRL. Assorted core. Lot of six marbles. One latticinio core, four divided core, one solid core. All have been polished. $44. (Auction #164, Lot 20).

SWIRL. Assorted core. Lot of four marbles. Yellow latticinio core, white latticinio core, divided core, solid core. $42. (Auction #155, Lot 36).

SWIRL. Assorted core . Lot of two marbles. First is a superb divided core swirl. Three thin bands of transparent light green. $42. (Auction #90, Lot 30).

SWIRL. Assorted core. Lot of five marbles. Three are latticinio core. Two are solid core. Nice group. 25/32" to 27/32". $42. (Auction #180, Lot 13).

SWIRL. Assorted core. Lot of four marbles. Green glass latticinio swirl. 21/32". Collectible. Divided core swirl. 1-3/8". $40. (Auction #104, Lot 19).

SWIRL. Assorted core. Lot of two marbles. Both are unusual swirls. First is a single ribbon. Overall haziness. $40. (Auction #108, Lot 3).

SWIRL. Assorted core. Lot of two marbles. Both are peewee swirls. One is a white latticinio core. 15/32". Mint (9.9). $40. (Auction #176, Lot 18).

SWIRL. Assorted core. Lot of seven marbles. Three latticinio core (including one three layer, one divided core). $37. (Auction #141, Lot 25).

SWIRL. Assorted core. Lot of fifteen marbles. Assortment of cores, patterns and colors. All have damage. 11/16" to 1-3/16". $37. (Auction #89, Lot 30).

SWIRL. Assorted core. Lot of two marbles. The first is a double ribbon core. The faces are yellow and white latticinio. $37. (Auction #75, Lot 15).

SWIRL. Assorted core. Lot of four marbles. Three latticino core and a divided core. 17/32" to 3/4". Mint(-) (9.0) to Near Mint. $36. (Auction #112, Lot 15).

SWIRL. Assorted core. Lot of nine marbles. Four latticinio core, three divided core, one solid core, one coreless. $35. (Auction #180, Lot 6).

SWIRL. Assorted core. Lot of five marbles. Four solid core, one latticinio core. 19/32" to 11/16". Near Mint (8.4) to Near Mint. $35. (Auction #175, Lot 3).

SWIRL. Assorted core. Lot of four marbles. All shooters that have seen some use. Three are solid core with white cores. $34. (Auction #144, Lot 12).

SWIRL. Assorted core. Lot of two marbles. Both are peewee swirls. One is a white latticinio core. From near an end of the cane. $34. (Auction #173, Lot 8).

SWIRL. Assorted core. Lot of nine marbles. Seven white latticinio core, one solid core, one coreless. All have some damage. $32. (Auction #180, Lot 1).

SWIRL. Assorted core. Lot of nine marbles. Assorted cores, designs and colors. All have haziness and damage. 19/32" to 13/32". $32. (Auction #108, Lot 15).

SWIRL. Assorted core. Lot of five marbles. Two latticinio core, one divided core, two solid core (one is caged). $32. (Auction #130, Lot 4).

SWIRL. Assorted core. Lot of four marbles. One banded, two latticinio core (including a peewee), one divided core. $32. (Auction #166, Lot

4).

SWIRL. Assorted core. Lot of three marbles. White latticinio core, 1-15/16", badly buffed with damage remaining. $30. (Auction #177, Lot 12).

SWIRL. Assorted core. Lot of two marbles. Both are naked cores. One is a rare naked divided core. 9/16" & Mint(-) (9.3). $30. (Auction #112, Lot 12).

SWIRL. Assorted core. Lot of three marbles. A yellow latticinio core and two divided core. Excellent group. 15/32", 1/2". $30. (Auction #106, Lot 38).

SWIRL. Assorted core. Lot of two marbles. Both are peewees. One is a solid core, one is a latticinio core. 15/32". Mint. $28. (Auction #157, Lot 48).

SWIRL. Assorted core. Lot of nine marbles. Includes two latticinio, three divided core, two banded, one cornhusk. $28. (Auction #172, Lot 20).

SWIRL. Assorted core. Lot of two marbles. First is wispy white latticinio core with English red and yellow outer bands. $25. (Auction #139, Lot 3).

SWIRL. Assorted core. Lot of two marbles. Single ribbon core swirl. Peewee. Nice core. 1/2". Near Mint (8.5). English type. $25. (Auction #73, Lot 13).

SWIRL. Assorted core. Lot of six marbles. Assorted cores and colors. All have been used. 1/2" to 13/16". Near Mint (8.6). $25. (Auction #171, Lot 17).

SWIRL. Assorted core. Lot of four marbles. Two solid core, one divided core, one coreless. All have some damage. 1/2". $24. (Auction #55, Lot 12).

SWIRL. Assorted core. Lot of five marbles. Three banded swirls. All are subsurface white and red strands. $24. (Auction #106, Lot 8).

SWIRL. Assorted core. Lot of two marbles. First is a peewee divided core. 15/32". Mint (9.9). Second is a white latticinio. $22. (Auction #144, Lot 19).

SWIRL. Assorted core. Lot of three marbles. Assortment of English colors. A white latticinio core and two divided cores. $22. (Auction #175, Lot 9).

SWIRL. Assorted core. Lot of three marbles. All are peewee. White latticinio core, 15/32", Mint (9.5). Solid core, 15/32". $21. (Auction #101, Lot 7).

SWIRL. Assorted core. Lot of four marbles. Two divided core and two solid core (one is naked). All have damage. 5/8". $21. (Auction #94, Lot 44).

SWIRL. Assorted core. Lot of two marbles. First is a divided core. Four very wide bands in two different odd color schemes. $20. (Auction #120, Lot 2).

SWIRL. Assorted core. Lot of three marbles. White latticinio core. Divided core, part of core missing. Solid core. $20. (Auction #157, Lot 4).

SWIRL. Assorted core. Lot of two marbles. Yellow latticinio core, 25/32", Good(+) (7.9). Divided core, 25/32", Near Mint(-). $16. (Auction #178, Lot 1).

SWIRL. Assorted core. Lot of two marbles. Both have damage. First is a white latticinio core. 1-3/4". Collectible. $12. (Auction #108, Lot 11).

SWIRL. Banded. Very odd, large, banded swirl. Probably from near the end of the cane. Transparent green base. 1-1/8". Mint(-) (9.3). $150. (Auction #54, Lot 44).

SWIRL. Banded. Very unusual banded swirl. Transparent blue base. Two stretched white bands on one side of the marble. 23/32". Mint (9.9). $140. (Auction #61, Lot 40).

SWIRL. Banded. Very unusual and rare swirl. In superb condition. Base glass is transparent cobalt blue. 11/16". Mint (9.9). $95. (Auction #84, Lot 2).

SWIRL. Banded . Very unusual marble. Superb! Transparent clear base. There is a very thin green strand in the center. 31/32". Mint (9.9). $80. (Auction #147, Lot 41).

SWIRL. Banded. Superb larger banded swirl. Transparent blue base. Three opaque white bands of varying widths. 15/16". Near Mint(+) (8.9). $65. (Auction #85, Lot 30).

SWIRL. Banded. One of the most unusual banded swirls I have seen. Transparent clear base. Two narrow opaque yellow. 11/16". Mint (9.9). $60. (Auction #105, Lot 23).

SWIRL. Banded. Nice two-band banded swirl. Technically, this is a transparent Indian. Transparent clear base. 7/16". Mint (9.9). $60. (Auction #117, Lot 32).

SWIRL. Banded. Could be a banded swirl or a transparent Indian. 1/2". Mint (9.6). $55. (Auction #156, Lot 5).

SWIRL. Banded. Very interesting banded swirl, almost a Joseph's Coat. Core is translucent white bands and yellow bands. 11/16". Mint (9.9). $55. (Auction #98, Lot 37).

SWIRL. Banded. You could look at this as a transparent Indian or as a banded swirl. Transparent clear base. 5/8". Mint (9.9). $55. (Auction #91, Lot 7).

SWIRL. Banded. Excellent large banded swirl. Transparent dark blue base. Four bands of white strands edged by blue. 29/32". Near Mint(+) (8.9). $55. (Auction #58, Lot 42).

SWIRL. Banded. Looks opaque, but is actually transparent very dark brown. Ghost core. Three opaque white strands. 13/16". Mint(-) (9.1). $50. (Auction #184, Lot 48).

SWIRL. Banded. Nice marble. Transparent clear base. Two bands covering about seventy five percent of the surface. 9/16". Mint (9.9). $49. (Auction #76, Lot 16).

SWIRL. Banded. Lot of two marbles. Both are shooter size banded swirls. First is transparent green glass. $47. (Auction #115, Lot 5).

SWIRL. Banded. Very unusual marble. Transparent bubble filled clear base. Ghost core. Two bands of bright yellow. 13/16". Near Mint(+) (8.8). $46. (Auction #159, Lot 12).

SWIRL. Banded. Lot of three marbles. I don't know whether to call these banded swirls or mists. $45. (Auction #56, Lot 12).

SWIRL. Banded. Lot of three marbles. All are small banded swirls. Transparent clear base with assorted colored surfaces. $44. (Auction #123, Lot 16).

SWIRL. Banded. Transparent green base. Three outer bands of yellow and white strands. In great shape. Germany. 11/16". Mint (9.9). $42. (Auction #87, Lot 19).

SWIRL. Banded. Peewee banded swirl. Transparent clear base. Surface is almost completely covered by translucent white. 15/32". Mint (9.9). $42. (Auction #88, Lot 30).

SWIRL. Banded. Rare color. Transparent red base with opaque white subsurface bands. One side of the marble is rough. 21/32". Near Mint (8.5). $41. (Auction #69, Lot 34).

SWIRL. Banded. Lot of three marbles. All are peewee banded swirls. Transparent clear base with assorted subsurface colors. $39. (Auction #103, Lot 14).

SWIRL. Banded. Lot of six marbles. Assortment of banded swirls. All transparent clear base. Assortment of outer bands. $37. (Auction #166, Lot 2).

SWIRL. Banded. Super example. Very light green base. Ghost core. Surface has two white bands, one yellow band. 25/32". Mint (9.7). $36. (Auction #183, Lot 32).

SWIRL. Banded. Exceptional banded swirl. Transparent clear base. Three wide bands of white, green and a little red. 17/32". Mint (9.9). $35. (Auction #109, Lot 30).

SWIRL. Banded. Peewee. Transparent clear base with two wide bands covering almost the entire surface. 15/32". Mint (9.9). $34. (Auction #81, Lot 30).

SWIRL. Banded. Transparent light green base. Two bands of white and orange strands. One thinner band of white. 9/16". Mint (9.9). $34. (Auction #74, Lot 18).

SWIRL. Banded. Peewee. Unusual marble. Translucent light brown/green base. 15/32". Mint (9.9). $34. (Auction #82, Lot 37).

SWIRL. Banded. Superior example. Transparent light blue base. Surface is covered by bands of opaque white. 5/8". Mint (9.9). $34. (Auction #167, Lot 42).

SWIRL. Banded. Transparent clear base. Translucent stretched yellow covering almost the entire surface. 15/32". Mint (9.9). $32. (Auction #77, Lot 17).

SWIRL. Banded. Lot of two marbles. Matched pair of banded swirl. Transparent clear base. Four surface bands. $32. (Auction #101, Lot 46).

SWIRL. Banded. Lot of two marbles. Both are peewee banded swirls. Both are transparent blue base. $32. (Auction #104, Lot 25).

SWIRL. Banded. Transparent light blue base. Two wide panels consisting of transparent white strands and some opaque. 21/32". Mint (9.9). $31. (Auction #85, Lot 27).

SWIRL. Banded. Possibly a Joseph Coat from near the end of the cane. Ghost core with green filament. 11/16". Mint (9.9). $30. (Auction #162, Lot 5).

SWIRL. Banded. I've been calling these banded swirls, although technically it would be a transparent Indian. 15/32". Mint (9.9). $29. (Auction #113, Lot 4).

SWIRL. Banded. Transparent light olive green base. Four bands of green, white and blue. One sparkle. Nice marble. 21/32". Mint(-) (9). $27. (Auction #94, Lot 9).

SWIRL. Banded. I've classified this as a banded swirl, although you could call it a divided core swirl in blue glass. 9/16". Mint(-) (9.2). $26. (Auction #70, Lot 11).

SWIRL. Banded. Transparent very light green base. Three outer bands. Each consists of translucent white strands. 11/16". Mint (9.9). $26. (Auction #82, Lot 32).

SWIRL. Banded. Very colorful banded swirl from near an end of the cane. Transparent clear base with bands of brown. 11/16". Near Mint(+) (8.8). $25. (Auction #128, Lot 15).

SWIRL. Banded. Peewee. Unusual coloring. Base is transparent light olive green. There are transparent green and white. 15/32". Mint (9.9). $25. (Auction #82, Lot 18).

SWIRL. Banded. Transparent clear bubble filled base. Two bands. One is bands of blue, yellow and white. 9/16". Mint (9.9). $25. (Auction #74, Lot 32).

SWIRL. Banded. This was probably meant to be a Joseph's Coat. Transparent clear base. Two subsurface bands. 5/8". Good(+) (7.80). $25. (Auction #80, Lot 17).

SWIRL. Banded. Lot of two marbles. Both are banded swirls. Both transparent clear base with assorted lightly colored. $25. (Auction #121, Lot 1).

SWIRL. Banded. Transparent white base. Two bands covering about sixty percent of the surface. Stretched translucent. 9/16". Mint (9.9). $25. (Auction #97, Lot 29).

SWIRL. Banded. Transparent clear base. Some wispy white strands inside the marble. Three outer bands of white, orange. 11/16". Mint (9.9). $24. (Auction #70, Lot 19).

SWIRL. Banded. Peewee banded swirl. Transparent clear base. Surface almost completely covered by stretched bands. 15/32". Mint (9.9). $24. (Auction #112, Lot 36).

SWIRL. Banded. Peewee banded swirl. Transparent clear base. Three bands on the surface. Not evenly spaced. 15/32". Mint (9.9). $23. (Auction #80, Lot 29).

SWIRL. Banded. Transparent olive green base. Three subsurface bands of red/orange and white. Very lightly buffed. $23. (Auction #185, Lot 22).

SWIRL. Banded. Transparent base tinted light blue. Two surface bands covering about half the surface. Both are white. 15/32". Mint (9.9). $22. (Auction #75, Lot 12).

SWIRL. Banded. Interesting marble, probably from near an end of the cane. Transparent bubble filled green glass. 19/32". Mint(-) (9). $22. (Auction #183, Lot 2).

SWIRL. Banded. English type. Nice banded swirl. Four subsurface bands (one is near the core). Each band is translucent. 11/16". Mint(-) (9.1). $21. (Auction #64, Lot 9).

SWIRL. Banded. Transparent clear base. Two bands of light blue and white and two bands of light blue, white and orange. 21/32". Mint(-) (9). $20. (Auction #113, Lot 3).

SWIRL. Banded. Very nice small banded swirl. Transparent clear base with three orange and gray subsurface bands. 1/2". Mint (9.9). $20. (Auction #116, Lot 8).

SWIRL. Banded. Transparent clear base. Three outer bands consisting of translucent white and translucent yellow/orange. 11/16". Mint (9.9). $20. (Auction #70, Lot 5).

SWIRL. Banded. Transparent clear base. Two wide bands covering about seventy five percent of the surface. 15/32". Mint (9.9). $19. (Auction #98, Lot 34).

SWIRL. Banded. Transparent clear base. Three bands of green, white and blue. 21/32". Mint(-) (9.1). $19. (Auction #57, Lot 13).

SWIRL. Banded. Transparent light blue base. Two bands covering about twenty percent of the surface. 9/16". Mint(-) (9.2). $19. (Auction #77, Lot 6).

SWIRL. Banded. Nice one. Transparent clear base. One subsurface band of red, yellow, green and blue. 21/32". Mint(-) (9). $19. (Auction #96, Lot 8).

SWIRL. Banded. Transparent clear base with two bands of translucent white and green. Germany, circa 1870-1915. 17/32". Mint (9.9). $18. (Auction #84, Lot 4).

SWIRL. Banded. Very odd banded swirl, probably near the end of the cane. Transparent slightly smoky base. 11/16". Near Mint(+) (8.9). $18. (Auction #85, Lot 11).

SWIRL. Banded. Slightly cloudy transparent clear base. Two opaque white surface strands, as well as an opaque yellow. 21/32". Near Mint(+) (8.9). $17. (Auction #117, Lot 6).

SWIRL. Banded. Super banded swirl. Transparent very slight blue base with loads of elongated tiny air bubbles. 19/32". Mint (9.9). $17. (Auction #100, Lot 23).

SWIRL. Banded. Lot of two items. Nice set. Each has different colored outer bands. Both have a few hits. 11/16" & 3. $17. (Auction #161, Lot 9).

SWIRL. Banded. Light transparent aqua base with four opaque white narrow bands on the surface. Very nice marble. 17/32". Mint (9.7). $17. (Auction #142, Lot 29).

SWIRL. Banded. Transparent green base. Core is transparent dark green. Several bands of green and white on the surface. 11/16". Mint (9.9). $17. (Auction #101, Lot 9).

SWIRL. Banded. Very light olive green base. Four equidistantly space subsurface white thin bands. 23/32". Near Mint(+) (8.8). $16. (Auction #66, Lot 19).

SWIRL. Banded. Opaque white base. Two subsurface bands of translucent white, with a little red. Germany, circa 1870. 17/32". Mint (9.9). $16. (Auction #159, Lot 28).

SWIRL. Banded. Peewee. Beautiful banded swirl. Transparent clear base with two bands covering about fifty percent. 15/32". Mint (9.9). $16. (Auction #82, Lot 2).

SWIRL. Banded. Transparent clear base. Three outer bands consisting of red, yellow and blue. One manufacturing spot. 11/16". Near Mint(+) (8.9). $15. (Auction #70, Lot 9).

SWIRL. Banded. Transparent light green base filled with tiny air bubbles. Has two bands of stretched glass covering. 19/32". Near Mint (8.6). $14. (Auction #77, Lot 5).

SWIRL. Banded. Transparent clear base. Four bands of opaque white, opaque blue, and opaque light green. 21/32". Mint(-) (9). $14. (Auction #101, Lot 3).

SWIRL. Banded. Transparent clear base with three sets of subsurface bands. Each is translucent white. 9/16". Mint (9.1). $14. (Auction #83, Lot 1).

SWIRL. Banded. Transparent clear base. Six band outer layer. Three are orange and three are white. Tiny chip. Germany. 9/16". Near Mint(+) (8.9). $13. (Auction #169, Lot 39).

SWIRL. Banded. Transparent clear base. Two bands of white and blue. A strand of red and a strand of green on one side. 9/16". Mint (9.8). $13. (Auction #159, Lot 3).

SWIRL. Banded. Transparent clear base. Subsurface layer of bands and strands of blue, white and yellow. $12. (Auction #167, Lot 4).

SWIRL. Banded. Transparent clear base. Subsurface bands of white and transparent blue. In great shape. Germany. 9/16". Mint (9.9). $12. (Auction #164, Lot 32).

SWIRL. Banded. Shooter. Very light blue base. Subsurface layer of five narrow white and yellow bands. Lightly buffed. $12. (Auction #179, Lot 5).

SWIRL. Banded. Transparent very lightly blue tinted base with four subsurface white bands. Several tiny flakes. 21/32". Near Mint(+) (8.7). $11. (Auction #87, Lot 4).

SWIRL. Banded . Transparent clear base. Surface is completely covered by transparent white with a couple of opaque white. 1/2". Near Mint(+) (8.8). $7. (Auction #90, Lot 9).

SWIRL. Banded. From very near the end of the cane. Transparent very light blue base. Two thin white strands on it. 11/16". Mint(-) (9). $7. (Auction #160, Lot 1).

SWIRL. Banded. Transparent clear base. One subsurface red band and two subsurface white bands. 11/16". Near Mint(+) (8.9). $5. (Auction #122, Lot 10).

SWIRL. Banded. Transparent clear base. Several outer bands of blue and white. Two of the bands are near the center. 11/16". Near Mint(+) (8.9). $4. (Auction #171, Lot 7).

SWIRL. Banded swirl. Beautiful peewee banded swirl. Transparent cobalt blue base. Subsurface layer is three sets of white. 15/32". Mint (9.9). $24. (Auction #93, Lot 9).

SWIRL. Butterscotch. Stunning translucent butterscotch swirl. Translucent butterscotch brown base. 11/16". Mint (9.9). $100. (Auction #160, Lot 45).

SWIRL. Butterscotch. Semi-opaque butterscotch brown base with surface transparent pink bands. One tiny pit and a few pinpricks. 3/4". Near Mint(+) (8.9). $65. (Auction #168, Lot 40).

SWIRL. Butterscotch. Nice butterscotch swirl. Translucent light brown base with transparent pink/brown bands on the surface. 11/16". Near Mint(+) (8.7). $60. (Auction #149, Lot 18).

SWIRL. Butterscotch. Semi-opaque butterscotch brown base with surface transparent pink bands. 23/32". Near Mint (8.3). $27. (Auction #160, Lot 4).

SWIRL. Caramel. Superior example of this type. Translucent caramel brown base. Bands of transparent red. 21/32". Mint (9.5). $185. (Auction #147, Lot 46).

SWIRL. Caramel. Transparent dark brown glass. Subsurface bands and loops of opaque white. Shooter. Some small chips. 1-1/2". Near Mint(-) (8.2). $75. (Auction #168, Lot 29).

SWIRL. Caramel. Very hard to find caramel swirl with mica. Transparent dark brown base. Core has two wide bands. 21/32". Near Mint(-) (8.1). $70. (Auction #181, Lot 19).

SWIRL. Caramel. Transparent dark caramel brown base with subsurface opaque white bands. 27/32". Near Mint (8.4). $55. (Auction #80, Lot 13).

SWIRL. Caramel. Nice caramel swirl. Transparent dark brown base. Opaque bands of white inside the marble. 1". Near Mint (8.3). $45. (Auction #140, Lot 40).

SWIRL. Caramel. Very nice caramel swirl. Transparent dark brown base. Opaque bands and swirls of white inside the marble. 21/32". Near Mint(+) (8.8). $43. (Auction #92, Lot 4).

SWIRL. Caramel. Very nice caramel swirl. Transparent dark brown base. Opaque bands and swirls of white inside the marble. 11/16". Near Mint (8.6). $42. (Auction #182, Lot 24).

SWIRL. Caramel. Nice caramel swirl. Transparent dark brown base. Opaque bands and swirls of white inside the marble. 19/32". Near Mint (8.6). $37. (Auction #152, Lot 13).

SWIRL. Caramel. Transparent caramel brown base with subsurface bands of opaque white. A number of small and tiny moons. 21/32". Near Mint(+) (8.2). $34. (Auction #118, Lot 19).

SWIRL. Coreless. Lot of four marbles. Very rare matched set of four coreless swirls, off the same cane. $170. (Auction #113, Lot 40).

SWIRL. Coreless. Super example. Transparent clear base. Outer layer is two bands that are white strands and two bands. 7/8". Mint (9.9). $75. (Auction #137, Lot 45).

SWIRL. Coreless. Superb example. Transparent very light blue/green base. Four wide subsurface bands of opaque white. 11/16". Mint (9.9). $60. (Auction #91, Lot 30).

SWIRL. Coreless. I am not sure what to classify this marble as. It is very, very unusual. Transparent clear base. 21/32". Near Mint(+) (8.9). $60. (Auction #80, Lot 19).

SWIRL. Coreless. Terrific coreless swirl. Transparent clear base. One subsurface band of orange edged by white strand. 15/32". Mint (9.9). $55. (Auction #76, Lot 19).

SWIRL. Coreless. Superior coreless swirl in colored glass. Transparent emerald green base. Three subsurface wide bands. 11/16". Near Mint(+) (8.8). $55. (Auction #160, Lot 47).

SWIRL. Coreless. Excellent example of this type. Transparent very slightly tinted green base. Four subsurface bands. 21/32". Mint (9.9). $55. (Auction #61, Lot 26).

SWIRL. Coreless. Another nice coreless swirl. Transparent clear base. No core. Outer layer is two blue on white band. 25/32". Mint (9.7). $42. (Auction #58, Lot 20).

SWIRL. Coreless. Transparent clear base. Four bands of white, green and blue strands, in assorted configurations. 27/32". Mint (9.9). $42. (Auction #113, Lot 16).

SWIRL. Coreless. Transparent teal base. Three subsurface bands of opaque yellow with red strands. Some light haziness. 19/32". Near Mint(+) (8.9). $40. (Auction #129, Lot 39).

SWIRL. Coreless. Lot of two marbles. Matched pair of coreless swirls, off the same cane. Interesting pair. $39. (Auction #158, Lot 38).

SWIRL. Coreless. Nice coreless swirl, in colored glass. Transparent gooseberry brown base with three wide bands of red. 9/16". Near Mint (8.9). $35. (Auction #124, Lot 4).

SWIRL. Coreless. Transparent clear base. Three bands of yellow and two of white. Overall haziness. 1-5/16". Near Mint(-) (8). $34. (Auction #125, Lot 33).

SWIRL. Coreless. Super example. Transparent very lightly tinted blue base. Subsurface layer of four bands. 21/32". Mint(-) (9.2). $32. (Auction #153, Lot 16).

SWIRL. Coreless. Exceptional example. Transparent clear base. Two subsurface bands of blue and white. 1". Near Mint(+) (8.9). $32. (Auction #139, Lot 38).

SWIRL. Coreless. Transparent clear base. No inner core. Outer layer of three red and white bands. Very hard to find. 21/32". Mint (9.8). $30. (Auction #150, Lot 11).

SWIRL. Coreless. Transparent clear base. Four subsurface bands. Each is transparent blue edged by white and yellow. 25/32". Mint (9.9). $30. (Auction #164, Lot 26).

SWIRL. Coreless. From near the end of the cane. Transparent clear base. Air bubbles in the center. Two subsurface bands. 13/16". Mint (9.9). $29. (Auction #71, Lot 11).

SWIRL. Coreless. Super coreless swirl. Outer layer is three bands. Each is edged by a yellow strand and a white strand. 19/32". Mint (9.9). $28. (Auction #75, Lot 8).

SWIRL. Coreless. Transparent, bubble suffused, clear base. Three subsurface blue bands and three subsurface white bands. 7/8". Near Mint(+)

SWIRL. Coreless. (8.7). $27. (Auction #66, Lot 32).

SWIRL. Coreless. A true coreless swirl. No core. Subsurface layer consists of three orange bands. 17/32". Mint (9.9). $27. (Auction #117, Lot 39).

SWIRL. Coreless. Lot of two marbles. Matched pair, likely off the same cane. Transparent clear base. $27. (Auction #161, Lot 40).

SWIRL. Coreless. Transparent clear base. Three subsurface bands of the same design of white, yellow and red. Peewee. 15/32". Mint (9.9). $25. (Auction #91, Lot 13).

SWIRL. Coreless. Transparent clear base. Three outer bands. Two are white and red, one is just white with a little red. 11/16". Mint (9.9). $24. (Auction #70, Lot 1).

SWIRL. Coreless. Transparent clear marble. Three blue subsurface strands and two yellow. Several thin strands of yellow. 15/32". Mint (9.9). $24. (Auction #80, Lot 27).

SWIRL. Coreless. Rather interesting coreless swirl. Subsurface layer of three bands. Each is a combination of white. 25/32". Mint(-) (9.2). $24. (Auction #158, Lot 12).

SWIRL. Coreless. Very nice example. Transparent clear base. Three subsurface bands of red, three of blue and yellow. 19/32". Near Mint (8.6). $22. (Auction #161, Lot 32).

SWIRL. Coreless. Peewee. From near an end of the cane. Transparent clear with one thin subsurface band of white. 15/32". Mint (9.9). $22. (Auction #84, Lot 8).

SWIRL. Coreless. Peewee. Transparent clear base. Subsurface layer of three bands. Bands are translucent yellow and red. 1/2". Mint (9.9). $20. (Auction #84, Lot 31).

SWIRL. Coreless. Interesting marble. No core. Outer layer is five bands. Three are red, white and green. Two are red. 11/16". Near Mint(+) (8.9). $20. (Auction #58, Lot 3).

SWIRL. Coreless. Transparent clear base. Three subsurface bands consisting of white, yellow and blue. 1/2". Mint (9.9). $20. (Auction #83, Lot 39).

SWIRL. Coreless. Transparent clear base with four subsurface bands of assorted color schemes. 9/16". Mint (9.9). $17. (Auction #131, Lot 17).

SWIRL. Coreless. Transparent clear base. Outer layer of three opaque yellow bands and two opaque light blue bands. 19/32". Mint(-) (9.1). $17. (Auction #64, Lot 1).

SWIRL. Coreless. Transparent clear base. Three subsurface bands, all the same color scheme. Each is light blue strand. 11/16". Near Mint(+) (8.8). $16. (Auction #87, Lot 39).

SWIRL. Coreless. Well, technically, not a coreless, but close. Transparent clear base. 9/16". Mint(-) (9). $15. (Auction #169, Lot 8).

SWIRL. Coreless. Very lightly tinted green glass. Four subsurface bands. Two are yellow, two are white. 23/32". Near Mint(+) (8.7). $15. (Auction #167, Lot 8).

SWIRL. Coreless. Transparent clear base. No core. Four subsurface bands. Two are dark red and green. 9/16". Mint(-) (9.1). $15. (Auction #182, Lot 2).

SWIRL. Coreless. Transparent clear base. Two subsurface bands. One is blue, pink and white. The other is pink, yellow. 15/32". Mint(-) (9.2). $14. (Auction #89, Lot 10).

SWIRL. Coreless. Tranparent clear base. Three bands. Two are orange next to white. One is orange next to yellow. Nice. 21/32". Near Mint (8.6). $14. (Auction #136, Lot 17).

SWIRL. Coreless. Transparent clear base. Two subsurface bands of two white strands. 5/8". Mint (9.7). $10. (Auction #173, Lot 6).

SWIRL. Cornhusk. Cornhusk variety of a banded swirl. Transparent amber base with a wide subsurface opaque white band. 7/8". Mint (9.9). $160. (Auction #145, Lot 42).

SWIRL. Cornhusk. Very unusual cornhusk. The base glass is a very dark transparent brown. 11/16". Mint (9.9). $110. (Auction #148, Lot 36).

SWIRL. Cornhusk. Cornhusk variety of a banded swirl. Peewee! Transparent amber base. 17/32". Mint (9.9). $95. (Auction #67, Lot 8).

SWIRL. Cornhusk. Cornhusk variety of a banded swirl. Transparent amber base with a wide subsurface opaque white band. 17/32". Mint (9.9). $85. (Auction #91, Lot 4).

SWIRL. Cornhusk. Cornhusk variety of a banded swirl. Transparent amber base with a wide subsurface opaque white band. 17/32". Mint(-) (9.2). $80. (Auction #153, Lot 13).

SWIRL. Cornhusk. Peewee. Tranparent honey amber base. One subsurface opaque white band. A wispy band opposite it. 1/2". Mint (9.9). $75. (Auction #81, Lot 20).

SWIRL. Cornhusk. Large cornhusk. Hard to find. Transparent dark amber brown base with a subsurface band of opaque white. 7/8". Near Mint (8.5). $70. (Auction #181, Lot 13).

SWIRL. Cornhusk. Cornhusk variety of a banded swirl. Transparent amber base with a wide subsurface opaque white band. 17/32". Mint (9.9).

$65. (Auction #66, Lot 14).

SWIRL. Cornhusk. Cornhusk variety of a banded swirl. Transparent amber base with a wide subsurface opaque white band. 17/32". Mint (9.9). $65. (Auction #139, Lot 48).

SWIRL. Cornhusk. Cornhusk variety of a banded swirl. Transparent amber base with two wide subsurface opaque white band. 17/32". Mint (9.9). $55. (Auction #103, Lot 9).

SWIRL. Cornhusk. Cornhusk variety of a banded swirl. Transparent amber base with a wide subsurface opaque white band. 17/32". Mint (9.9). $55. (Auction #74, Lot 35).

SWIRL. Cornhusk. Cornhusk variety of a banded swirl. Transparent amber base with a wide subsurface opaque white band. 17/32". Mint (9.9). $50. (Auction #83, Lot 5).

SWIRL. Cornhusk. Cornhusk variety of a banded swirl. Transparent amber base with a wide subsurface opaque white band. 17/32". Mint (9.9). $44. (Auction #113, Lot 44).

SWIRL. Custard. Hard to find custard swirl. Semi-opaque yellow/brown base. Surface is covered by transparent pink band. 21/32". Near Mint(+) (8.9). $50. (Auction #170, Lot 6).

SWIRL. Custard. Semi-opaque yellow/brown base with translucent pink bands. One very tiny chip and one sparkle. 11/16. 11/16". Near Mint(+) (8.9). $50. (Auction #175, Lot 36).

SWIRL. Divided. Super naked divided core swirl. Each band is an assortment of white strands with pink, blue, yellow. 17/32". Mint (9.8). $44. (Auction #179, Lot 38).

SWIRL. Divided core. Superior colored glass divided core swirl in English colors from near an end of the cane. 1-3/8". Mint (9.8). $650. (Auction #89, Lot 50).

SWIRL. Divided core. Outstanding example of a large swirl. Core is three bands, very closely space. Almost a solid core. 1-23/32". Mint (9.7). $250. (Auction #167, Lot 44).

SWIRL. Divided core. Superb divided core swirl. Three band core. Each band is the same color scheme. 1-9/16". Mint (9.4). $210. (Auction #82, Lot 45).

SWIRL. Divided core. Super divided core swirl. Core is four bands. Two each of two different complex color scheme. 1-11/16". Mint (9.1). $200. (Auction #164, Lot 40).

SWIRL. Divided core. Rare marble. Three band, caged divided core, in transparent teal glass. Rare coloring. 1-3/4". Near Mint (8.6). $190. (Auction #155, Lot 43).

SWIRL. Divided core. Core is four very wide bands. Two are pink, yellow and blue on white. Two are pink, green and yellow. 1-5/8". Near Mint(+) (8.9). $160. (Auction #169, Lot 48).

SWIRL. Divided core. Outstanding example of a large swirl. Four band core. Two bands are pink and green on yellow. 1-7/8". Near Mint(+) (8.9). $155. (Auction #183, Lot 21).

SWIRL. Divided core. Lot of nine marbles. Matched set, probably off the same cane. Three band divided core swirl. Mint . $150. (Auction #182, Lot 46).

SWIRL. Divided core. Nice larger divided core swirl. Four band core. Two are pink, blue and white, two are green, pink. 1-1/4". Mint (9.7). $145. (Auction #150, Lot 33).

SWIRL. Divided core. Superb marble. Four band core. Two bands are pink and green on yellow. Two are pink and blue on white. 1-1/2". Mint(-) (9). $140. (Auction #173, Lot 27).

SWIRL. Divided core. Huge marble, approaching the technical limits for an antique handmade. Four band core. 2-7/16". Good(+) (7.80). $135. (Auction #183, Lot 29).

SWIRL. Divided core. Very rare broken cane example. Three band core. Each band is the same color scheme of pink on yellow. $130. (Auction #122, Lot 26).

SWIRL. Divided core. Large divided core from very close to the end of the cane. Core is supposed to be six bands. 1-13/16". Near Mint (8.3). $125. (Auction #122, Lot 22).

SWIRL. Divided core. This one is a beauty!!! Three band core. Each band is the same, transparent blue on opaque white. 1-1/16". Mint (9.7). $120. (Auction #117, Lot 14).

SWIRL. Divided core. "Flower"-type first-off-cane divided core swirl. Four band core. Two bands are blue on white. 11/16". Mint (9.7). $120. (Auction #147, Lot 43).

SWIRL. Divided core. Harder to find six band divided core. The core consists of narrow bands. Three are transparent pink . 1-13/16". Near Mint (8.6). $110. (Auction #59, Lot 21).

SWIRL. Divided core. Rare type. Latticinio in divided core form. Four bands. Each consists of four strands. Two are white. 2". Good(+) (7.90). $110. (Auction #171, Lot 22).

SWIRL. Divided core. Superior divided core swirl. Three band core. Each is bright orange and bright green bands on opaque. 1-5/16". Near

Mint(+) (8.7). $110. (Auction #124, Lot 32).

SWIRL. Divided core. Four band core. Narrow. Two are green on pink and white. One is blue on pink. One is blue and white. 1-3/4". Near Mint(+) (8.8). $110. (Auction #157, Lot 50).

SWIRL. Divided core. Four band core. Two are pink and green on white, two are pink and green on yellow. 1-3/8". Near Mint(+) (8.8). $110. (Auction #108, Lot 40).

SWIRL. Divided core. Three band core. Each band is red, orange, yellow, green, blue and white. 1-1/16". Mint(-) (9). $95. (Auction #164, Lot 21).

SWIRL. Divided core. Rare four layer divided core swirl. Inner core is three narrow bands of green on yellow. 1-11/16". Near Mint(-) (8). $95. (Auction #157, Lot 3).

SWIRL. Divided core. Very subtle divided core. Almost looks like a solid core!! Three layer marble. $95. (Auction #146, Lot 15).

SWIRL. Divided core. Four band divided core from near an end of the cane. Larger marble. Two panels of pink, yellow. 1-1/2". Near Mint(+) (8.9). $95. (Auction #156, Lot 41).

SWIRL. Divided core. Larger swirl. Three band core. Each is the same complex color scheme. Outer layer is a cage of eleven. 1-11/16". Near Mint (8.6). $91. (Auction #134, Lot 27).

SWIRL. Divided core. Large divided core swirl from near an end of the cane. Four band core. Two are pink, yellow and white. 1-1/2". Near Mint(+) (8.9). $90. (Auction #175, Lot 46).

SWIRL. Divided core. Very rare marble. Divided core swirl in transparent cherry red glass. Four white bands in the core. 21/32". Near Mint (8.3). $90. (Auction #182, Lot 10).

SWIRL. Divided core. Rare marble. Six band divided core with an outer cage of strands that are reverse twisted at the top. 1-1/2". Near Mint(-) (8.1). $90. (Auction #152, Lot 25).

SWIRL. Divided core. Three band core. Very wide bands. Each is the same color scheme of white, yellow, blue, pink and green. 1-13/16". Near Mint(-) (8). $85. (Auction #149, Lot 33).

SWIRL. Divided core. Large divided core from very close to the end of the cane. Core is supposed to be six bands. 1-13/16". Near Mint (8.3). $85. (Auction #157, Lot 10).

SWIRL. Divided core. Three band divided core. Each band is the same. Blue, white, yellow, red. Nice bright colors. 1-1/4". Mint(-) (9.2). $85. (Auction #160, Lot 49).

SWIRL. Divided core. Core is four wide bands. Each is the same complex color scheme. 1-15/16". Near Mint (8.3). $85. (Auction #126, Lot 24).

SWIRL. Divided core. Outstanding caged divided core swirl. Three band core. Each band is about the same width. 1-11/16". Near Mint (8.6). $85. (Auction #176, Lot 42).

SWIRL. Divided core. Interesting color scheme. Three band divided core. Each band is opaque white. Covered by transparent. 1-1/4". Mint(-) (9.1). $85. (Auction #104, Lot 39).

SWIRL. Divided core. Lot of four marbles. All are divided core and about the same size. Nice assortment of colors. $80. (Auction #97, Lot 17).

SWIRL. Divided core. Lot of three marbles. Matched set of swirls. Three band core. One green and white, one red and white. $80. (Auction #169, Lot 44).

SWIRL. Divided core. Caged divided core swirl. Three band core. All three bands are the same color scheme. 1-11/16". Near Mint(-) (8.2). $80. (Auction #128, Lot 29).

SWIRL. Divided core. Three band divided core. Each band is wide and is blue and pink on white. 1-7/16". Near Mint(+) (8.7). $80. (Auction #184, Lot 41).

SWIRL. Divided core. English type colors. Inner core is three bands of different coloring. 1". Mint (9.8). $80. (Auction #89, Lot 7).

SWIRL. Divided core. Super end-of-cane (last off cane) swirl. Transparent clear base. A narrow band of pink. 13/16". Mint (9.6). $80. (Auction #122, Lot 6).

SWIRL. Divided core. Three band core. All are the same color scheme. They are all wide, leaving very little space between. 1-11/16". Near Mint(-) (8.2). $80. (Auction #152, Lot 39).

SWIRL. Divided core. Four band core. Two bands of blue and pink on white, two of green and yellow on white. 1-5/8". Near Mint(+) (8.9). $75. (Auction #165, Lot 50).

SWIRL. Divided core. Lot of three marbles. Matched set of divided core swirls. Each core is four bands. $75. (Auction #55, Lot 30).

SWIRL. Divided core. Lot of four marbles. Nice assortment of colors and designs. All are Mint! All are peewees!! Germany,. $75. (Auction #116, Lot 30).

SWIRL. Divided core. Quite frankly, I'm only guessing at what type of core this was meant to be. From near the end of the cane. 27/32". Near

Mint(+) (8.9). $75. (Auction #183, Lot 39).

SWIRL. Divided core. Interesting color scheme. Three band divided core. Each band is opaque white. 1-1/4". Mint(-) (9.1). $75. (Auction #80, Lot 36).

SWIRL. Divided core. Nice, larger marble. Three band core. Each is the same complex color scheme. 1-5/16". Near Mint(+) (8.9). $75. (Auction #134, Lot 19).

SWIRL. Divided core. Superior end-of-cane cage style divided core swirl. Three band core. 21/32". Mint (9.9). $70. (Auction #129, Lot 12).

SWIRL. Divided core. Very hard to find marble. Naked divided core in red glass. Transparent cherry red base. 21/32". Good (7.40). $70. (Auction #173, Lot 32).

SWIRL. Divided core. Lot of three marbles. Matched set off the same cane. Superior set. Each is four band core. $70. (Auction #170, Lot 40).

SWIRL. Divided core. Lot of four marbles. Nice assortment of divided cores. All are Mint!! Three are peewees. 15/32" to 9. $70. (Auction #116, Lot 3).

SWIRL. Divided core. Four band core. Two bands each in two different color schemes. 1-11/16". Near Mint (8.3). $66. (Auction #180, Lot 38).

SWIRL. Divided core. Lot of three marbles. Matched set of swirls. Three band core. One green and white, one red and white. $66. (Auction #176, Lot 16).

SWIRL. Divided core. Lot of two marbles. Matched pair, off the same cane. Each is a three band divided core. $65. (Auction #54, Lot 42).

SWIRL. Divided core. Nice divided core swirl. Four band core. Two each of two different color schemes. 1-1/2". Near Mint(+) (8.9). $65. (Auction #103, Lot 23).

SWIRL. Divided core. Lot of four marbles. Nice assortment of divided core swirls. 3/4". Mint (9.9-9.6). $65. (Auction #174, Lot 41).

SWIRL. Divided core. Naked divided core swirl. I've called this a divided core, although you could also call it a double. $65. (Auction #165, Lot 27).

SWIRL. Divided core. Superior English color swirl. Three band core. Each is the same complex pattern of bright colors. 5/8". Mint (9.9). $60. (Auction #123, Lot 48).

SWIRL. Divided core. Three band divided core swirl. Each band is wide and the same color scheme of blue, white, pink, yellow. 1-11/16". Good(+) (7.90). $60. (Auction #155, Lot 3).

SWIRL. Divided core. Four band core. All are wide. Two are pink, green, yellow and white. Two are pink, blue, yellow. $60. (Auction #157, Lot 45).

SWIRL. Divided core. Lot of three marbles. First is four band core. Two bands are white, red and blue. Two are "lumpy" yellow. Good(+) . $60. (Auction #143, Lot 39).

SWIRL. Divided core. English type swirl. Four band divided core. Two bands are white and two are yellow. Bright colors. 27/32". Mint (9.9). $60. (Auction #71, Lot 40).

SWIRL. Divided core. Lot of two marbles. Super matched set of divided core swirls. Each has a six-band core. $60. (Auction #153, Lot 4).

SWIRL. Divided core. Outstanding three layer divided core swirl. Three band core. Each band is very wide and is opaque white. 21/32". Mint (9.9). $60. (Auction #116, Lot 43).

SWIRL. Divided core. Three band core. Each is the same color scheme. Outer layer of three sets of yellow and white strand. 27/32". Mint (9.9). $60. (Auction #118, Lot 6).

SWIRL. Divided core. Lot of three marbles. All off the same cane. Super group. Each is four band divided core. $60. (Auction #138, Lot 18).

SWIRL. Divided core. Superior divided core swirl. Exceptional design. The core is three wide bands, all the same color scheme. 9/16". Mint (9.9). $56. (Auction #148, Lot 33).

SWIRL. Divided core. Base glass is tinted very lightly blue. Three band core. Each band is wide. Two are the same colors. 1-11/16". Near Mint(-) (8). $55. (Auction #152, Lot 28).

SWIRL. Divided core. Lot of three marbles. All are divided core. Nice set of colors and designs. $55. (Auction #128, Lot 32).

SWIRL. Divided core. Three band core. One is green on white, one blue on white, one red on white. $55. (Auction #104, Lot 22).

SWIRL. Divided core. Nice swirl. Four bands. Two are transparent blue on white, two are transparent red on yellow. 15/16". Near Mint(+) (8.9). $55. (Auction #96, Lot 26).

SWIRL. Divided core. Four band core. Two are white with pink and blue. Two are yellow with pink and green. 1-7/16". Good(+) (7.90). $55. (Auction #122, Lot 41).

SWIRL. Divided core. Four band core. Two are red on yellow, one is green on white, one is blue on white. 29/32". Mint (9.8). $55. (Auction #84, Lot 7).

SWIRL. Divided core. Nice divided core swirl. Four band core. Two are pink and yellow, one is blue and white, one is green. 1-1/16". Mint (9.5). $55. (Auction #126, Lot 26).

SWIRL. Divided core. Three band divided core. Two bands one color scheme, one band a different color scheme. 1-3/4". Good(+) (7.90). $55. (Auction #157, Lot 34).

SWIRL. Divided core. Lot of two marbles. Matched pair off the same cane. Four band core. Two are red on white, one is blue. 1". Near Mint(+) (8.8). $51. (Auction #159, Lot 45).

SWIRL. Divided core. Base glass is very lightly tinted blue. Core is four bands, all the same color combination of pink. 11/16". Mint(-) (9.3). $50. (Auction #96, Lot 36).

SWIRL. Divided core. Lot of six marbles. All are divided cores. Assorted styles and colors. All have some damage. 5/8". $50. (Auction #165, Lot 12).

SWIRL. Divided core. Four band core. Pink on yellow, pink on white, blue on white, green on yellow. $50. (Auction #165, Lot 25).

SWIRL. Divided core. Three band core. One is white with blue bands, one is white with green bands. 1". Near Mint(+) (8.7). $50. (Auction #84, Lot 40).

SWIRL. Divided core swirl. Lot of two marbles. Matched pair, possibly off the same cane. Each is a three band core. $50. (Auction #93, Lot 8).

SWIRL. Divided core. Four band core. Two are pink on white, two are blue on whie. 15/16". Mint (9.8). $50. (Auction #129, Lot 18).

SWIRL. Divided core. Four band core. Super example. Two bands are bright white with red bands. 3/4". Mint (9.9). $50. (Auction #141, Lot 13).

SWIRL. Divided core. Lot of two marbles. Matched pair of divided core swirls. Four band core. Two are English style yellow. $50. (Auction #147, Lot 32).

SWIRL. Divided core. Four band core. Two bands of pink on white, one of blue on white, one of green on yellow. $50. (Auction #157, Lot 38).

SWIRL. Divided core. Lot of two marbles. Matched pair of divided core swirls off the same cane. Three band core. $50. (Auction #59, Lot 25).

SWIRL. Divided core. Nice divided core swirl. Three band core. All are an assortment of transparent blue, transparent pink. 1-1/16". Mint(-) (9.2). $50. (Auction #70, Lot 30).

SWIRL. Divided core. Four band core. Two bands each of two different sets of alternating colors. Outer layer is a cage. $48. (Auction #157, Lot 47).

SWIRL. Divided core. Very interesting marble. Core is three thin bands, all the same color scheme. Opaque white. 21/32". Mint (9.7). $46. (Auction #104, Lot 35).

SWIRL. Divided core. Three band core. Each band is the same color scheme. Outer layer is three sets of white strands. 1-5/8". Near Mint(-) (8.2). $46. (Auction #151, Lot 22).

SWIRL. Divided core. Four band core. Two bands each in two different complementary color schemes. Outer layer is a cage. 7/8". Mint (9.3). $45. (Auction #110, Lot 21).

SWIRL. Divided core. Thin core. Three bands. One is red on white, one is blue on one, one is green on yellow. 1-3/16". Near Mint(+) (8.7). $45. (Auction #159, Lot 40).

SWIRL. Divided core. Lot of four marbles. Nice assortment of designs and colors. 21/32" to 13/16". One Mint. Mint(-) (9.1). $44. (Auction #157, Lot 35).

SWIRL. Divided core. Lot of two marbles. Both are divided core. Different colors and patterns. Nice pair. 29/32" & Near Mint. $44. (Auction #144, Lot 2).

SWIRL. Divided core. Lot of two marbles. Matched pair off the same cane. Three band core. Each band is blue, white and orange. $44. (Auction #173, Lot 40).

SWIRL. Divided core. Nice divided core swirl. Four band core. Two are green, pink and yellow, two are blue, pink and white. 1-3/16". Near Mint(+) (8.8). $44. (Auction #172, Lot 38).

SWIRL. Divided core. From near an end of the cane. Only two narrow bands remain of the core. 1-9/16". Near Mint(+) (8). $44. (Auction #128, Lot 22).

SWIRL. Divided core. Unusual divided core swirl. Three bands. Each band is opaque white with three red bands on it. 29/32". Near Mint(+) (8.9). $43. (Auction #60, Lot 28).

SWIRL. Divided core. Three band divided core swirl. Two bands are pink and green on white. One is pink and blue on white. 1-1/16". Near Mint(+) (8.9). $42. (Auction #164, Lot 13).

SWIRL. Divided core. Four band core. Two bands are blue and pink on white. Two are green and pink on yellow. Odd core. $42. (Auction #157, Lot 41).

SWIRL. Divided core. Excellent example. Tight core. Four bands in two alternating color schemes. Outer layer is a cage. 3/4". Mint (9). $42. (Auction #67, Lot 26).

SWIRL. Divided core. Very hard to find naked divided core swirl. Core is three bands. Each consists of three white strand. 21/32". Mint (9.9). $42. (Auction #77, Lot 39).

SWIRL. Divided core. Four band core. All four bands are the same color scheme. Outer layer is four sets of yellow and white. $42. (Auction #157, Lot 17).

SWIRL. Divided core. Four band core. Two different complex patterns. Outer layer is four bands. Two are white latticinio. $41. (Auction #146, Lot 25).

SWIRL. Divided core. Four band core. Very nice marble. Each band is different: transparent blue on opaque white. 13/16". Mint (9.9). $41. (Auction #183, Lot 7).

SWIRL. Divided core. English type divided core swirl. Three thin bands, all the same color scheme. 19/32". Mint (9.9). $40. (Auction #73, Lot 33).

SWIRL. Divided core. Four band core. Each band is the same color scheme of white, yellow, blue and pink. 1-11/16". Good(+) (7.70). $40. (Auction #143, Lot 24).

SWIRL. Divided core. Four band core. Two are pink on white, two are blue on white. 3/4". Mint (9.7). $40. (Auction #88, Lot 4).

SWIRL. Divided core. Super three layer swirl. Core is three bands, opaque white with pink strands. 23/32". Near Mint(+) (8.9). $40. (Auction #109, Lot 47).

SWIRL. Divided core. This is a superb divided core swirl. Four band core. Two pink on white, one blue on white, one green. 19/32". Mint (9.9). $40. (Auction #80, Lot 11).

SWIRL. Divided core. Four band core. Two pink on yellow, one blue on white, one green on white. 21/32". Mint (9.9). $40. (Auction #159, Lot 5).

SWIRL. Divided core. English type colors. Three band core. Each is the same pattern of green and red on white. 5/8". Mint (9.9). $40. (Auction #91, Lot 18).

SWIRL. Divided core. Three band core. Wide bands. Each is the same pattern of pink, blue and yellow on white. 1-9/16". Near Mint (8.4). $40. (Auction #174, Lot 4).

SWIRL. Divided core. Outstanding divided core swirl. Four band core. Two are yellow and two are white. 7/8". Mint(-) (9.1). $40. (Auction #105, Lot 41).

SWIRL. Divided core. Divided core swirl from near an end of the cane. Four bands. Two are blue on white. 11/16". Mint (9.9). $40. (Auction #98, Lot 9).

SWIRL. Divided core. Lot of two marbles. Both are divided core swirls. Both are peewees. Two different designs. 1/2". Mint. $40. (Auction #107, Lot 31).

SWIRL. Divided core. Beautiful three band core. Each is orange, blue, white and yellow. Outer layer is a cage of six yellow. 9/16". Mint (9.3). $39. (Auction #166, Lot 34).

SWIRL. Divided core. Nice shooter swirl. Four band divided core. Two bands of one color scheme and two of another. 7/8". Mint (9.4). $39. (Auction #134, Lot 12).

SWIRL. Divided core. Four band core. Very odd core. Each band is a different color scheme. Transparent pink on opaque white. 23/32". Mint (9.8). $39. (Auction #81, Lot 5).

SWIRL. Divided core. Lot of three marbles. All are divided core. Assorted patterns and colors. All in excellent shape. $39. (Auction #107, Lot 3).

SWIRL. Divided core. Unusual divided core swirl. Three bands. Each band is opaque white with three red bands on it. 29/32". Near Mint(+) (8.9). $38. (Auction #112, Lot 1).

SWIRL. Divided core. Three band core. Each is white with transparent pink and transparent blue. Outer layer is three sets. $38. (Auction #130, Lot 29).

SWIRL. Divided core. Superior English color swirl. Three band core. Each is the same complex pattern of bright colors. 5/8". Mint(-) (9.2). $38. (Auction #123, Lot 42).

SWIRL. Divided core. Another unusual divided core swirl. Four band core. Outer layer is four bands also. 13/16". Mint (9.9). $37. (Auction #182, Lot 35).

SWIRL. Divided core. Beautiful marble. Four band core. Two are red, green and yellow. Two are red, white and blue. 25/32". Near Mint(+) (8.9). $37. (Auction #176, Lot 46).

SWIRL. Divided core. English colors. Three band core. Each is the same color scheme of mostly bright orange with some blue. 25/32". Mint (9.9). $37. (Auction #158, Lot 42).

SWIRL. Divided core. Very unusual divided core. Three bands. All the same complex color scheme. 21/32". Mint (9.9). $37. (Auction #113, Lot 30).

SWIRL. Divided core. Beautiful divided core in English colors from near the end of the cane. Three band core. 21/32". Mint (9.9). $37. (Auction #107, Lot 20).

SWIRL. Divided core. Superior marble. Very odd coloring. Probably English. Three band core. 11/16". Near Mint(+) (8.9). $36. (Auction #156, Lot 3).

SWIRL. Divided core. Three band divided core swirl. Each band is one half orange and one half light yellow. 19/32". Mint (9.9). $36. (Auction #182, Lot 14).

SWIRL. Divided core. Beautiful English type divided core swirl. Three band core. Each band is the same width and color scheme. 5/8". Mint (9.9). $36. (Auction #71, Lot 32).

SWIRL. Divided core. Four band divided core swirl. Two bands are pink and blue on white, two are pink and green on white. 3/4". Mint (9.7). $36. (Auction #159, Lot 38).

SWIRL. Divided core. Nice English divided core. Core is three bands in the same color scheme of white, red, blue and yellow. 21/32". Mint (9.7). $35. (Auction #62, Lot 25).

SWIRL. Divided core. English type divided core swirl Four bands. Two are red, edged by blue. The other two are yellow. 21/32". Mint(-) (9). $35. (Auction #77, Lot 19).

SWIRL. Divided core. Four band core. Two are pink on yellow, one is blue on white, one is green on white. 7/8". Mint(-) (9). $35. (Auction #126, Lot 2).

SWIRL. Divided core. Three band core. All bands wide, all the same color pattern. $35. (Auction #157, Lot 13).

SWIRL. Divided core. Superb marble. Three band core. Each band is opaque white with transparent green on it, edged by red. 9/16". Mint (9.9). $35. (Auction #103, Lot 43).

SWIRL. Divided core. Very pretty and exceptionally well designed marble. Core is four bands. 9/16". Mint (9.9). $35. (Auction #125, Lot 19).

SWIRL. Divided core. Very unusual divided core swirl. Core is six narrow bands. One transparent pink, one transparent pink. 27/32". Mint (9.6). $35. (Auction #110, Lot 17).

SWIRL. Divided core. Orange latticinio strands in divided form. Three bands. Outer layer is three bands, one each of pink. 15/32". Mint (9.9). $34. (Auction #92, Lot 33).

SWIRL. Divided core. Three band core. One band is green on white, one is blue on white, one is pink on white. 1-1/16". Near Mint(+) (8.9). $34. (Auction #143, Lot 46).

SWIRL. Divided core. Superb solid core swirl. Exceptionally well made. Three band core of pink on white. Well-formed. 11/16". Mint (9.7). $34. (Auction #93, Lot 26).

SWIRL. Divided core. Naked divided core swirl. Hard to find. Three band core. Each is latticinio strands edged by red. 9/16". Mint (9.8). $34. (Auction #131, Lot 41).

SWIRL. Divided core. Lot of three marbles. Very similar to each other, but not matched. One is three band core. $34. (Auction #179, Lot 12).

SWIRL. Divided core. Beautiful English type swirl. Three band core. Each is orange, blue, white and yellow. 9/16". Mint (9.5). $32. (Auction #129, Lot 37).

SWIRL. Divided core. Nice swirl. Four band core. Two pink on white, one blue on white, one green on white. 7/8". Mint (9.5). $32. (Auction #105, Lot 1).

SWIRL. Divided core. Four band core. Each band is wide. Two are orange with a little yellow. 31/32". Near Mint(+) (8.8). $32. (Auction #148, Lot 31).

SWIRL. Divided core. Superior English type three band divided core. Almost looks like a ribbon. Very colorful bands. 19/32". Mint (9.6). $32. (Auction #73, Lot 21).

SWIRL. Divided core. Three band core. Each band is wide and the same color combination: red, white, green, yellow and blue. 5/8". Mint (9.9). $32. (Auction #126, Lot 8).

SWIRL. Divided core. Four band divided core swirl. Two bands each of two different complex color schemes. 1-15/16". Good (7.40). $32. (Auction #180, Lot 27).

SWIRL. Divided core. Four band divided core. Two bands each of two different color schemes. 11/16". Mint(-) (9). $32. (Auction #134, Lot 9).

SWIRL. Divided core. Four band core. Three bands are the same pattern of pink and blue on white. 5/8". Near Mint(+) (8.9). $32. (Auction #183, Lot 10).

SWIRL. Divided core. Lot of eight marbles. All are solid core swirls. Nice assortment of styles and color. $32. (Auction #177, Lot 4).

SWIRL. Divided core. Lot of two marbles. Almost matched pair. Each is four band divided core. $32. (Auction #141, Lot 32).

SWIRL. Divided core. Four band core. Exceptional design to the bands. 27/32". Near Mint(+) (8.8). $31. (Auction #61, Lot 15).

SWIRL. Divided core. Three band core. Each band is the same complex color scheme. Three outer bands. 11/16". Near Mint(+) (8.8). $31. (Auction #141, Lot 47).

SWIRL. Divided core. Three band core. Outer layer is three sets of two strands. Base glass is a milky color. Very odd. 21/32". Mint (9.9). $30. (Auction #106, Lot 31).

SWIRL. Divided core. English type divided core swirl. Super three band core. Nice coloring. Surface is in great shape. 19/32". Mint (9.9). $30. (Auction #73, Lot 4).

SWIRL. Divided core. Fantastic little divided core. Three band core. Each is transparent pink bands on opaque white. 15/32". Mint (9.9). $30. (Auction #115, Lot 13).

SWIRL. Divided core. Naked divided core from near the end of the cane. Was a three band core. Two bands remain. 21/32". Mint (9.9). $30. (Auction #87, Lot 37).

SWIRL. Divided core. Peewee divided core. Four band core. Outer layer is four sets of white or yellow strands. 7/16". Mint (9.9). $30. (Auction #128, Lot 5).

SWIRL. Divided core. Three band divided core. Each band is the same pattern of green, yellow, red, white and blue. 1-3/16". Near Mint (8.4). $30. (Auction #109, Lot 3).

SWIRL. Divided core. Four band core. Two different color schemes. Outer layer is a cage of yellow strands. A beauty. Germany. 9/16". Mint (9.9). $30. (Auction #144, Lot 46).

SWIRL. Divided core. Exceptional small divided core swirl. Four bands. Each is white. Two have pink bands and two have black. 11/16". Near Mint(+) (8.9). $30. (Auction #156, Lot 19).

SWIRL. Divided core. Core is four bands. Odd design. Two are opaque white center, edged by transparent blue. 21/32". Mint (9.9). $30. (Auction #93, Lot 35).

SWIRL. Divided core. Four band core. Two different color designs. Outer layer is two sets of white strands and two of yellow. 1-3/16". Near Mint(+) (8.9). $29. (Auction #108, Lot 38).

SWIRL. Divided core. Three band core. Blue on white, green on white, pink on white. Outer layer is a cage of seventeen. 23/32". Mint(-) (9.3). $28. (Auction #58, Lot 5).

SWIRL. Divided core. Thin divided core. Three bands. Each the same scheme of white, yellow, pink and green. 29/32". Mint(-) (9). $28. (Auction #164, Lot 8).

SWIRL. Divided core. Three band core. Each band is the same color scheme: predominately orange on white with some blue. 1". Near Mint (8.3). $28. (Auction #130, Lot 6).

SWIRL. Divided core. Three band core. One green on white, one blue on white, one orange on clear. 1". Near Mint (8.5). $28. (Auction #128, Lot 46).

SWIRL. Divided core. English type. Three band core. Each band is wide and the same color scheme of red, green and yellow. 19/32". Mint (9.9). $28. (Auction #171, Lot 46).

SWIRL. Divided core. Four band core. Two each of two different color schemes. One is white pink and blue. 27/32". Mint(-) (9.2). $27. (Auction #140, Lot 33).

SWIRL. Divided core. Peewee divided core. Transparent clear base. Three bands of white, pink, green and blue. 7/16". Mint (9.9). $27. (Auction #133, Lot 14).

SWIRL. Divided core. Nice divided core. Thick casing of outer glass. Four thin bands for the core. 3/4". Mint (9.7). $27. (Auction #107, Lot 16).

SWIRL. Divided core. Peewee divided core swirl. Four band core. Two are pink on white, two are blue on white. 15/32". Mint (9.9). $27. (Auction #147, Lot 29).

SWIRL. Divided core. Three band divided core. Each band is the same color scheme of white, pink, blue and yellow. 27/32". Mint (9.9). $27. (Auction #110, Lot 5).

SWIRL. Divided core. Three band core. Very thin core. Each band is an assortment of white, blue, yellow and/or pink. 13/16". Mint (9.7). $27. (Auction #124, Lot 11).

SWIRL. Divided core. Really pretty solid core swirl. The core is five panels of opaque orange on opaque white. 9/16". Mint (9.9). $27. (Auction #89, Lot 1).

SWIRL. Divided core. Four band core. Two pink on white, two blue on white. Outer layer is four sets of four white strands. 3/4". Mint(-) (9.1). $27. (Auction #105, Lot 33).

SWIRL. Divided core. Lot of five marbles. All are divided cores. Assorted colors and styles. All have some damage. 23/32". $27. (Auction #104, Lot 24).

SWIRL. Divided core. Four band core, in four different color schemes, which is kind of odd. Tranparent pink strands on white. 23/32". Mint(-) (9.1). $27. (Auction #60, Lot 19).

SWIRL. Divided core. Another simplistic, but exceptional divided core swirl. Core is three bands of green on yellow. 5/8". Mint (9.9). $27. (Auction #165, Lot 41).

SWIRL. Divided core . Lot of three marbles. All are divided core shooters. All have damage. 7/8" to 31/32". Near Mint(-) (. $27. (Auction #144, Lot 36).

SWIRL. Divided core. Interesting small divided core. From near the end of the cane. Several bands in yellow, pink, white. 17/32". Mint (9.9). $27. (Auction #154, Lot 14).

SWIRL. Divided core. Four band core. Two are green on white, two are blue on yellow. Outer layer is a cage of white strands. 27/32". Mint(-) (9.1). $26. (Auction #184, Lot 29).

SWIRL. Divided core. Four band core. Two are pink, green, yellow and white. One is pink, blue and white. 25/32". Near Mint(+) (8.7). $26. (Auction #183, Lot 14).

SWIRL. Divided core. Yellow latticinio strands creating three bands. Super core. Outer layer is three bands of pink on white. 19/32". Mint (9.9). $26. (Auction #145, Lot 8).

SWIRL. Divided core. Very odd swirl. One band is opaque orange edged by white. Thinner band of transparent green. 1/2". Mint (9.9). $26. (Auction #74, Lot 15).

SWIRL. Divided core. Outstanding divided core. English type colors. Three band core. Each band is a band of yellow. 5/8". Mint (9.5). $26. (Auction #96, Lot 18).

SWIRL. Divided core. Four band core. Each is opaque white with pink and blue bands. 1/2". Mint (9.9). $26. (Auction #122, Lot 8).

SWIRL. Divided core. Four band core. Two bands each of two different color schemes. 7/8". Near Mint (8.6). $26. (Auction #74, Lot 12).

SWIRL. Divided core. Four band core. Two each of two similar color schemes. Bands are very close together. 11/16". Mint (9.8). $25. (Auction #162, Lot 34).

SWIRL. Divided core. Superior example. Exceptional design and execution. Three band core. Each is opaque white with blue. 23/32". Mint (9.5). $25. (Auction #169, Lot 20).

SWIRL. Divided core. Four band core. Two bands each of two different multi-color schemes. Outer layer is four sets of yellow. 21/32". Mint (9.9). $25. (Auction #107, Lot 7).

SWIRL. Divided core. Three band core. All are pink and blue bands on white. Outer layer is three bands of three yellow strands. 23/32". Mint(-) (9.2). $25. (Auction #157, Lot 8).

SWIRL. Divided core. Very interesting marble. Nice peewee. Three band core. Each band is the same complex color scheme. 1/2". Mint (9.9). $25. (Auction #80, Lot 3).

SWIRL. Divided core. Outstanding divided core swirl. Three band core. One is transparent blue with opaque white strands. 11/16". Mint (9.9). $24. (Auction #96, Lot 20).

SWIRL. Divided core. Naked divided core swirl. Hard to find. Three band core. White bands with blue. 9/16". Mint(-) (9). $23. (Auction #124, Lot 17).

SWIRL. Divided core. Four band core. Each band is the same color scheme of blue and red on white. 7/8". Near Mint(+) (8.7). $23. (Auction #174, Lot 39).

SWIRL. Divided core. Simplistic design, but stunning. Core is four bands. Two are teal on white, two are blue on white. 21/32". Near Mint(+) (8.9). $23. (Auction #165, Lot 32).

SWIRL. Divided core. Four band core. Very wide bands, almost no space between them. Two are pink, blue, yellow and white. 9/16". Mint (9.9). $22. (Auction #183, Lot 12).

SWIRL. Divided core. Lot of two marbles. Nice pair in two different color schemes. Each has a tiny defect. 9/16". Near Mint. $22. (Auction #125, Lot 1).

SWIRL. Divided core. Three band core. Outer layer is three sets of yellow strands mirroring the core bands. 7/8". Mint(-) (9.1). $22. (Auction #108, Lot 4).

SWIRL. Divided core. Nice divided core swirl. Core is four bands. Two of pink on white, one of green on white. 11/16". Mint(-) (9). $22. (Auction #91, Lot 25).

SWIRL. Divided core. Four band core. Two bands are blue and red on white. One is red and green on yellow. The last is red. 5/8". Mint(-) (9.1). $21. (Auction #142, Lot 19).

SWIRL. Divided core. Nice three band peewee divided core. Three thin bands. Each is transparent blue and yellow on white. 15/32". Mint (9.9). $21. (Auction #103, Lot 37).

SWIRL. Divided core. Very interesting marble. Almost no twist. Four band core. Each band is a white center with pink. 5/8". Mint(-) (9.1). $21. (Auction #182, Lot 4).

SWIRL. Divided core. Four band core. Thin core. Two are blue on white, two are red on white. 1-3/8". Good(+) (7.70). $20. (Auction #171, Lot 3).

SWIRL. Divided core. Super divided core swirl. Three band core. Each is a wide band of transparent pink on yellow. 17/32". Mint(-) (9.1). $20. (Auction #145, Lot 1).

SWIRL. Divided core. Four band narrow core. Two bands each of two different color schemes. Outer layer is two sets of two. 3/4". Near Mint(+) (8.9). $20. (Auction #177, Lot 39).

SWIRL. Divided core. Peewee. Three band core. One green, one blue, one orange. Three sets of yellow outer strands. 1/2". Mint(-) (9.1). $20. (Auction #78, Lot 29).

SWIRL. Divided core. Four band core. Two are pink on yellow, one is blue on white, one is green on white. 27/32". Mint (9.8). $20. (Auction #165, Lot 15).

SWIRL. Divided core. Three band core. Each band is white, green, blue and pink. Three sets of yellow strands as the outer layer. 25/32". Near Mint(+) (8.9). $20. (Auction #120, Lot 20).

SWIRL. Divided core. Four band core. Two are transparent pink on white, one is transparent blue on white. 27/32". Near Mint(+) (8.9). $20. (Auction #97, Lot 40).

SWIRL. Divided core. Three band core. Transparent pink on opaque white. Outer layer is three sets of blue on white bands. 17/32". Mint (9.8). $20. (Auction #136, Lot 13).

SWIRL. Divided core. Four band core. Two are blue, pink and white, two are green, pink and white. 19/32". Mint (9.7). $20. (Auction #87, Lot 16).

SWIRL. Divided core. Latticinio strands in divided form. Core is three bands of alternating white and yellow. 19/32". Mint (9.6). $20. (Auction #124, Lot 9).

SWIRL. Divided core. Three band core. Each is a different color scheme. Outer layer is three sets of yellow strands. 17/32". Mint (9.9). $20. (Auction #89, Lot 44).

SWIRL. Divided core. Very unusual end of cane divided core swirl. Core is mis-shapen and partial bands of red, white. 19/32". Mint(-) (9.2). $19. (Auction #182, Lot 31).

SWIRL. Divided core. Peewee. Three band core. Each band is very thin and a different color scheme. 15/32". Mint (9.9). $19. (Auction #142, Lot 15).

SWIRL. Divided core. Lot of two marbles. Matched pair of three-band divided cores. Each is blue and pink on white inner band. $18. (Auction #144, Lot 15).

SWIRL. Divided core. Four band core. Each is pink and blue on white. 25/32". Mint(-) (9.2). $18. (Auction #179, Lot 36).

SWIRL. Divided core. Lot of two marbles. Both are divided core swirls. Two different colors and patterns. Both 5/8". Near Mint. $18. (Auction #166, Lot 17).

SWIRL. Divided core. Nice marble. Four band core. Two bands each of two different color schemes. Wide core. 19/32". Near Mint(+) (8.9). $18. (Auction #126, Lot 19).

SWIRL. Divided core. Four band core. Each band is same color scheme. Outer layer is four sets of yellow strands. $18. (Auction #171, Lot 24).

SWIRL. Divided core. Three narrow bands form the core. Outer layer is three sets of white strands. Double twisted. Nice. 9/16". Mint (9.9). $18. (Auction #115, Lot 33).

SWIRL. Divided core. Peewee. Four band core. Two bands are white, pink and blue. Two bands are white, pink and purple. 15/32". Mint (9.9). $17. (Auction #100, Lot 30).

SWIRL. Divided core. Lot of two marbles. Matched pair of swirls off the same cane. The inner core is thin bands. $17. (Auction #144, Lot 10).

SWIRL. Divided core. From near the end of a the cane. Four band core. Multicolor bands. Outer layer is two sets of white. 29/32". Near Mint(+) (8.9). $17. (Auction #105, Lot 7).

SWIRL. Divided core. Three band core. Each band is the same combination of opaque white, pink and blue. 25/32". Mint(-) (9). $16. (Auction #102, Lot 11).

SWIRL. Divided core. Four band core. Wide bands, very little space between. Cage of white outer strands. Almost no twist. 5/8". Mint(-) (9). $16. (Auction #162, Lot 1).

SWIRL. Divided core. Three band core. Each is the same combination of red, blue, yellow and green on white. 19/32". Mint(-) (9). $16. (Auction #159, Lot 32).

SWIRL. Divided core. Very unusual swirl. Core has one complete band, one partial band, and is missing one or two bands. 21/32". Mint(-) (9).

$16. (Auction #65, Lot 6).

SWIRL. Divided core. Three band core. Each band is narrow. One is green on white, one pink on white, one blue on white. 11/16". Mint (9.8). $16. (Auction #121, Lot 3).

SWIRL. Divided core. Nice small divided core swirl. Four band core. Two patterns of yellow. Four sets of white outer strands. 21/32". Mint(-) (9.3). $15. (Auction #57, Lot 15).

SWIRL. Divided core. Three band divided core. Each band is pink and blue on white. Thin bands. 21/32". Mint (9.9). $15. (Auction #158, Lot 34).

SWIRL. Divided core. Lot of two marbles. Both are odd divided cores. $15. (Auction #144, Lot 38).

SWIRL. Divided core. Nice divided core swirl. Two bands are pink and blue on white, two are green on yellow. 23/32". Mint (9.4). $14. (Auction #98, Lot 13).

SWIRL. Divided core. Three band core. Bands are blue on white. Outer layer is a cage of white strands. The core is shoved. 9/16". Mint (9.7). $14. (Auction #142, Lot 27).

SWIRL. Divided core. Three band core. Each the same design of four colors. Outer layer is three sets of yellow strands. 23/32". Mint(-) (9). $14. (Auction #141, Lot 2).

SWIRL. Divided core. Interesting error. Three band core, but one band is missing. Outer layer is three sets of pale orange. 5/8". Mint (9.9). $14. (Auction #113, Lot 28).

SWIRL. Divided core. Four band core in two different, alternating color schemes. Outer layer is two sets of white strands. 5/8". Mint (9.9). $14. (Auction #94, Lot 43).

SWIRL. Divided core. Unusual divided core swirl. Three bands that consist of white latticinio strands alternating with yellow. 21/32". Near Mint(+) (8.7). $13. (Auction #64, Lot 16).

SWIRL. Divided core. Four band core. Two different complementary color schemes. 21/32". Near Mint(+) (8.9). $13. (Auction #62, Lot 6).

SWIRL. Divided core. Four band core. Multicolor bands. Outer layer is four sets of strands. Two are four yellow strands. 9/16". Mint(-) (9). $12. (Auction #105, Lot 36).

SWIRL. Divided core. Three band divided core. Each is white, blue and pink. Outer layer is three sets of yellow strands. 19/32". Mint(-) (9.2). $10. (Auction #165, Lot 36).

SWIRL. Divided core. Three band core. Fat core, bands packed close together. One pink on white, blue on white. 5/8". Mint(-) (9). $10. (Auction #136, Lot 2).

SWIRL. Divided core. Three band core. Each band is white base with a green center. Red around the center and blue edging. 19/32". Near Mint(+) (8.7). $8. (Auction #173, Lot 34).

SWIRL. Divided core. Four band core. Two pink on white, one blue on white, one green on white. 21/32". Mint (9.6). $8. (Auction #140, Lot 6).

SWIRL. End of cane. Superior and very rare looped first-off-cane swirl. This was solid core swirl with a white core. 7/8". Near Mint (8.6). $260. (Auction #85, Lot 15).

SWIRL. Gooseberry. I have categorized this as a gooseberry swirl, although it could be called a caged latticinio core. 11/16". Near Mint(-) (8). $85. (Auction #58, Lot 17).

SWIRL. Gooseberry. Transparent dark brown gooseberry base. Eighteen subsurface white strands, fairly evenly space. 21/32". Mint(-) (9.2). $85. (Auction #112, Lot 45).

SWIRL. Gooseberry. Light green/brown transparent base. Nineteen translucent white strands subsurface. One open panel. 11/16". Near Mint (8.5). $60. (Auction #77, Lot 13).

SWIRL. Gooseberry. I have categorized this as a gooseberry swirl, although it could be called a caged latticinio core. 11/16". Near Mint(-) (8). $55. (Auction #104, Lot 13).

SWIRL. Gooseberry. Nice marble, but it is damaged. Transparent honey brown base. 19/32". Near Mint (8.6). $47. (Auction #91, Lot 16).

SWIRL. Gooseberry. Transparent amber brown base with subsurface layer of white strands. Two tiny subsurface moons. 9/16". Near Mint (8.6). $37. (Auction #158, Lot 6).

SWIRL. Gooseberry. You decide, this is either a two-layer gooseberry or a white latticinio swirl in gooseberry base. 23/32". Good (7.60). $36. (Auction #65, Lot 23).

SWIRL. Joseph Coat. Stunning example. Transparent clear base. Subsurface layer of strands of white, green. 1". Mint (9.9). $445. (Auction #184, Lot 50).

SWIRL. Joseph Coat. Wow!!! Looks just like a Wald Beach Ball, but it's an antique handmade. Transparent clear base. 11/16". Mint(-) (9.2). $230. (Auction #85, Lot 12).

SWIRL. Joseph Coat. Superior example. One of the finest that I have ever seen!!! Transparent light blue base. 21/32". Mint (9.9). $205. (Auction #93, Lot 41).

SWIRL. Joseph Coat. Lot of six marbles. All are Joseph Coats in very dark colors. $190. (Auction #128, Lot 7).

SWIRL. Joseph Coat. Excellent Joseph Coat. Subsurface layer of tightly packed strands of color. Predominately earth tone. 3/4". Mint (9.7). $180. (Auction #112, Lot 47).

SWIRL. Joseph Coat. Very colorful Joseph Coat with a thin lutz band. Transparent clear base. Thin strands of orange, red. 9/16". Near Mint (8.6). $180. (Auction #89, Lot 9).

SWIRL. Joseph Coat. Superb Joseph Coat. Excellent marble. Transparent clear base. Subsurface layer of colored strands. 11/16". Mint (9.7). $160. (Auction #87, Lot 45).

SWIRL. Joseph Coat. Bright example. Subsurface bands of whites, oranges, green, blues, blacks and reds. Excellent coloring. 11/16". Mint (9.8). $155. (Auction #185, Lot 45).

SWIRL. Joseph Coat. Superb English Joseph Coat swirl. Transparent clear base. Colorful subsurface bands. 9/16". Mint (9). $140. (Auction #75, Lot 45).

SWIRL. Joseph Coat. Transparent clear base. Subsurface layer of tightly packed narrow bands of white, yellow, orange, blue. 7/8". Near Mint (8.4). $135. (Auction #121, Lot 30).

SWIRL. Joseph Coat. Transparent clear base. Subsurface bands of orange, yellow, blue, light green, white. 19/32". Mint (9.9). $130. (Auction #85, Lot 35).

SWIRL. Joseph Coat. Transparent clear base with a subsurface layer of yellow and orange strands. Very pretty marble. 11/16". Mint (9.9). $120. (Auction #126, Lot 44).

SWIRL. Joseph Coat. Superior example!!!. Transparent light blue base glass. Subsurface layer of red, yellow, white, green. 25/32". Near Mint (8.6). $110. (Auction #170, Lot 47).

SWIRL. Joseph Coat. Super marble. Transparent clear base. Subsurface layer of white, blue, yellow and orange strands. 21/32". Mint (9.6). $110. (Auction #145, Lot 38).

SWIRL. Joseph Coat. Nice Joseph Coat. Transparent clear base. Subsurface layer of orange, yellow, lavender, green, red. 5/8". Mint (9.9). $95. (Auction #77, Lot 43).

SWIRL. Joseph Coat. Super marble. Transparent clear base. Subsurface layer of colored strands. 19/32". Near Mint(+) (8.8). $91. (Auction #145, Lot 32).

SWIRL. Joseph Coat. Gorgeous large Joseph Coat swirl. Fat core of strands of assorted colors. Includes white, green, blue. 7/8". Near Mint (8.6). $90. (Auction #152, Lot 49).

SWIRL. Joseph Coat. Transparent clear base. Subsurface layer of tightly packed narrow bands of whtie, yellow, orange, blue. 7/8". Near Mint (8.4). $86. (Auction #148, Lot 8).

SWIRL. Joseph Coat. Very unusual. Full inner core of white strands and bands, as well as a few green bands. 23/32". Mint(-) (9.1). $85. (Auction #147, Lot 6).

SWIRL. Joseph Coat. Transparent clear base. Bands of yellow, light blue, white and lavender. Some clear spaces. 19/32". Mint (9.5). $85. (Auction #105, Lot 44).

SWIRL. Joseph Coat. Transparent clear base. Subsurface layer of colored bands, including blue, white, green, yellow, orange. 9/16". Mint (9.9). $80. (Auction #84, Lot 35).

SWIRL. Joseph Coat. Transparent light blue base. Subsurface layer of red, orange, yellow, blue and white strands. 21/32". Near Mint(+) (8.9). $80. (Auction #60, Lot 6).

SWIRL. Joseph Coat. Transparent clear base. Subsurface bands of orange, yellow, blue, green, red and white. 3/4". Near Mint(+) (8.9). $75. (Auction #131, Lot 43).

SWIRL. Joseph Coat. Dark example. Predominately transparent green and blue bands. Also, red, orange and white. 25/32". Near Mint (8.6). $70. (Auction #128, Lot 42).

SWIRL. Joseph Coat. Bright example. Subsurface bands of whites, oranges, green, blues, blacks and reds. Excellent coloring. 11/16". Near Mint (8.6). $70. (Auction #128, Lot 45).

SWIRL. Joseph Coat. Stunning example. Subsurface layer, close to the core, of very bright yellow and red strands. 7/8". Near Mint(-) (8.2). $70. (Auction #168, Lot 33).

SWIRL. Joseph Coat. Transparent clear marble with a subsurface layer of red, orange, yellow, blue and green bands. 9/16". Mint(-) (9). $70. (Auction #160, Lot 32).

SWIRL. Joseph Coat. Transparent clear base. Subsurface layer of thin strands, tightly packed. Predominately ruddy reds. 3/4". Near Mint (8.6). $65. (Auction #129, Lot 41).

SWIRL. Joseph Coat. Very pretty paneled Joseph's Coat. Transparent clear base. Four panels, all the same size. 11/16". Near Mint (8.6). $60. (Auction #107, Lot 48).

SWIRL. Joseph Coat. Was supposed to be a Joseph Coat, but has as much clear space as it does color. 9/16". Mint (9.9). $60. (Auction #81, Lot 7).

SWIRL. Joseph Coat. Very nice Joseph Coat in earthy tones. Transparent clear base. Subsurface layer of orange, blue. 23/32". Near Mint(+) (8.8). $60. (Auction #70, Lot 14).

SWIRL. Joseph Coat. Transparent clear base. Lots of clear spaces. Outer bands are white, light red, light green, orange. 17/32". Mint (9.9). $55. (Auction #133, Lot 20).

SWIRL. Joseph Coat. Very nice Joseph Coat swirl. Transparent clear glass with a subsurface layer of yellow, white. 9/16". Mint(-) (9). $55. (Auction #107, Lot 25).

SWIRL. Joseph Coat. A beauty. Subsurface layer of colored strands. Predominately greens with red, white, blue, lavender. 19/32". Near Mint (8.6). $50. (Auction #144, Lot 48).

SWIRL. Joseph Coat. Transparent clear base. Subsurface layer of bands of yellow, brown, white, gray, blue, green and orange. 9/16". Mint (9.9). $50. (Auction #116, Lot 13).

SWIRL. Joseph Coat. Banded swirl Joseph Coat with lots of clear bands. Subsurface layer of red, blue, white, yellow, green. 9/16". Mint (9.9). $50. (Auction #136, Lot 7).

SWIRL. Joseph Coat. Transparent clear base. Ghost core. Subsurface layer of strands and bands of red, yellow, light green. 17/32". Mint (9.9). $48. (Auction #183, Lot 5).

SWIRL. Joseph Coat. Banded swirl Joseph Coat with lots of clear bands. Subsurface layer of red, blue, white, yellow, green. 17/32". Near Mint(+) (8.9). $47. (Auction #154, Lot 17).

SWIRL. Joseph Coat. Transparent clear base with lots of air bubbles. Subsurface layer of yellow, blue, orange and white. 19/32". Mint(-) (9). $42. (Auction #123, Lot 18).

SWIRL. Joseph Coat. Lot of two marbles. Both are Joseph Coat. Very nice color. Both have lots of damage. 3/4" & 25/32". $40. (Auction #101, Lot 43).

SWIRL. Joseph Coat. Nice Joseph Coat. Transparent clear base. Predominately orange subsurface bands, with some white, blue. 3/4". Near Mint (8.3). $40. (Auction #125, Lot 3).

SWIRL. Joseph Coat. I've called this one a Joseph Coat, although techinically it is a paneled Joseph Coat. Transparent . 25/32". Near Mint (8.3). $38. (Auction #104, Lot 32).

SWIRL. Joseph Coat. Banded swirl Joseph Coat. Subsurface layer of red, blue, white, yellow, green and light blue. 9/16". Near Mint(+) (8.7). $35. (Auction #168, Lot 31).

SWIRL. Joseph Coat. Transparent clear base with lots of air bubbles. Subsurface layer of yellow, blue, orange and white. 19/32". Mint(-) (9). $35. (Auction #169, Lot 2).

SWIRL. Joseph Coat. Super subsurface layer of packed strands of bright red, green, yellow, blue, purple, black, white. 9/16". Near Mint(-) (8). $32. (Auction #118, Lot 25).

SWIRL. Joseph Coat. Banded swirl Joseph Coat with lots of clear bands. Subsurface layer of red, blue, white, yellow, green. 9/16". Near Mint(+) (8.9). $29. (Auction #84, Lot 1).

SWIRL. Joseph Coat. Transparent clear base. Subsurface layer of mostly orange and white tightly pack strands. 19/32". Near Mint (8.3). $27. (Auction #137, Lot 36).

SWIRL. Joseph Coat. Transparent clear base. Subsurface bands of yellow, white and aqua blue. Some clear spaces. Overall . 9/16". Near Mint(-) (8.1). $27. (Auction #122, Lot 43).

SWIRL. Joseph Coat. I've called this one a Joseph Coat, although techinically it is a paneled Joseph Coat. Transparent . 25/32". Near Mint (8.3). $20. (Auction #62, Lot 16).

SWIRL. Joseph's Coat. Rare shrunken core Joseph's Coat swirl in superior shape. Nice core of orange, red, green, white. 11/16". Mint (9.9). $185. (Auction #97, Lot 44).

SWIRL. Joseph's Coat. Gorgeous marble. Transparent clear base. Subsurface layer of translucent bands. Mostly bright orange. 21/32". Near Mint(+) (8.9). $75. (Auction #73, Lot 7.80).

SWIRL. Joseph's Coat. Very odd Joseph's Coat. Almost looks like an onionskin. Transparent clear glass. 9/16". Mint (9.6). $65. (Auction #98, Lot 15).

SWIRL. Joseph's Coat. Gorgeous marble. Transparent clear base. Subsurface layer of translucent bands. Mostly bright orange. 21/32". Near Mint(+) (8.9). $60. (Auction #83, Lot 7).

SWIRL. Joseph's Coat. Very nice marble. Transparent clear base. Subsurface layer of stretched bands. Green, white, red. 11/16". Near Mint (8.4). $45. (Auction #54, Lot 35).

SWIRL. Joseph's Coat. Two layer Joseph's Coat. Transparent clear base. Subsurface layer of thin bands, predominately red. 5/8". Near Mint (8.6). $36. (Auction #68, Lot 26).

SWIRL. Latticinio core. Superior marble!! Yellow latticinio core swirl. Six outer bands of transparent red and opaque white. 1-3/4". Mint (9.9). $400. (Auction #76, Lot 45).

SWIRL. Latticinio core. Huge first-off-cane white latticinio core swirl in superior condition. Teardrop air bubble inside. 2-1/8". Mint (9.7). $300. (Auction #150, Lot 45).

SWIRL. Latticinio core. Very interesting swirl, in remarkably Mint condition given the condition of almost every other big example. 2-1/16". Mint(-) (9.1). $290. (Auction #94, Lot 51).

SWIRL. Latticinio core. Very rare, larger latticinio core swirl in emerald green glass. 31/32". Near Mint(-) (8.2). $290. (Auction #160, Lot 24).

SWIRL. Latticinio core. Very rare core. Core consists of eighteen strands. Four sets of four white and one bright red. 1-5/8". Near Mint (8.5). $270. (Auction #100, Lot 45).

SWIRL. Latticinio core. Very rare swirl. White latticinio core is olive yellow base glass. Yellow glass with a slight green. 25/32". Mint(-) (9.1). $220. (Auction #154, Lot 18).

SWIRL. Latticinio core. Extremely rare latticino core swirl. Unbelievable alternating white, yellow and blue latticino core! 9/16". Mint (9.9). $200. (Auction #116, Lot 34).

SWIRL. Latticinio core. Superior large white latticinio core. Exceptional example. Transparent clear base (very slight green). 1-9/16". Mint(-) (9.2). $190. (Auction #93, Lot 22).

SWIRL. Latticinio core. White latticinio core. Outer layer is three bands of red, green and white. 1-3/8". Mint (9.7). $180. (Auction #89, Lot 38).

SWIRL. Latticinio core. White latticinio core. Fat core. Outer layer is three narrow yellow bands, altenating with three wide. 1-7/16". Mint (9.9). $160. (Auction #119, Lot 49).

SWIRL. Latticinio core. Outstanding example of a large latticinio core. White core. Outer layer is four bands. 1-3/4". Near Mint(+) (8.9). $160. (Auction #96, Lot 22).

SWIRL. Latticinio core. Wow! Super yellow latticinio core swirl. Nice coloring. Perfectly formed core. 1-5/8". Near Mint(+) (8.9). $160. (Auction #91, Lot 42).

SWIRL. Latticinio core. Rare core!! Alternating white and red. Very hard to find. Super core. 29/32". Near Mint(+) (8.9). $150. (Auction #69, Lot 40).

SWIRL. Latticinio core. Very nice, large latticinio core. Core is white strands. Outer layer is four sets of bands. 1-15/16". Near Mint (8.5). $150. (Auction #107, Lot 30).

SWIRL. Latticinio core. White latticinio core swirl. Outer layer is two red edged by white bands, alternating with two blue. 1-5/16". Mint(-) (9.1). $150. (Auction #78, Lot 44).

SWIRL. Latticinio core. White latticino core. Core surrounds a trapped air bubble. Outer layer is four yellow strands. 1-7/8". Near Mint (8.6). $150. (Auction #179, Lot 44).

SWIRL. Latticinio core. Nice, large, white latticinio core. Outer layer is four blue on white band alternating with four orange. 1-13/16". Near Mint(+) (8.7). $140. (Auction #88, Lot 25).

SWIRL. Latticinio core. Rare colored glass white latticinio core swirl. Base glass is greenish/blue. Core is white strands. 23/32". Mint (9.9). $140. (Auction #65, Lot 32).

SWIRL. Latticinio core. Very rare core colors. Alternating red and white latticinio strands. Excellent red color!!! 25/32". Mint(-) (9). $140. (Auction #140, Lot 42).

SWIRL. Latticinio core. Very nice, larger, white latticinio core swirl. Outer layer is two bands of pink on white. 1-11/16". Near Mint(+) (8.9). $135. (Auction #123, Lot 50).

SWIRL. Latticinio core. Three layer swirl. Huge. White latticinio core swirl. Middle layer is eight transparent bands. $130. (Auction #171, Lot 28).

SWIRL. Latticinio core. Very nice larger swirl. White latticinio core. Very well formed core. Outer layer is four bands. 1-7/8". Near Mint(+) (8.8). $130. (Auction #137, Lot 24).

SWIRL. Latticinio core. Super example. Exceptional workmanship and design. Yellow latticinio core. Excellent spacing. 1-9/16". Near Mint(+) (8.9). $120. (Auction #162, Lot 49).

SWIRL. Latticinio core. Lot of two marbles. Exceptional matched pair of white latticinio core swirls off the same cane. $120. (Auction #156, Lot 37).

SWIRL. Latticinio core. Lot of five marbles. A matched set of five marbles, all off the same cane. Yellow core latticinio. $120. (Auction #151, Lot 44).

SWIRL. Latticinio core. Rare caged white latticinio core. Superior marble. White latticinio core. 1". Near Mint(+) (8.9). $110. (Auction #96, Lot 40).

SWIRL. Latticinio core. Yellow latticinio core swirl. Fat core. Outer layer is three fat opaque white bands. 1-3/16". Mint (9.8). $110. (Auction #161, Lot 47).

SWIRL. Latticinio core. White latticinio core. Nice core. Outer layer is four bands. Two are pink and yellow, two are blue. 1-5/8". Mint (9.1). $110. (Auction #105, Lot 30).

SWIRL. Latticinio core. Orange latticinio core. Hard to find color. Outer layer is four bands. Each is transparent pink on white. 27/32". Mint (9.7). $110. (Auction #91, Lot 40).

SWIRL. Latticinio core. Lot of three marbles. Super set of matched latticinio swirls off the same cane. White latticinio core. $110. (Auction #148, Lot 40).

SWIRL. Latticinio core. Lot of two marbles. Matched pair of shooter latticinio core swirls in very unusual colors. $100. (Auction #134, Lot 36).

SWIRL. Latticinio core. White latticinio core. Outer layer is a cage of eight bands in three different color schemes. 1-5/8". Near Mint(+) (8.9). $100. (Auction #98, Lot 23).

SWIRL. Latticinio core. Outstanding example of a large latticinio core. White core. Outer layer is four bands. 1-3/4". Near Mint(+) (8.9). $100. (Auction #169, Lot 46).

SWIRL. Latticinio core. White core swirl. Outer layer is four bands of pink on white alternating with two bands of blue on white. 1-11/16". Near Mint(+) (8.8). $100. (Auction #134, Lot 30).

SWIRL. Latticinio core. Lot of three marbles. Matched set of three off the same cane. White latticinio core. $100. (Auction #163, Lot 44).

SWIRL. Latticinio core. Superb tornado core swirl. White latticinio wound tight with a double twist. Outer layer is one band. 1-1/16". Near Mint(+) (8.9). $100. (Auction #181, Lot 45).

SWIRL. Latticinio core. Stunning and superior swirl in excellent condition. White latticinio core swirl. 27/32". Mint (9.9). $100. (Auction #139, Lot 40).

SWIRL. Latticinio core. White latticinio core swirl. Outer layer is three pink on yellow bands alternating with three green. 1-15/16". Near Mint(+) (8.2). $95. (Auction #149, Lot 39).

SWIRL. Latticinio core. White latticinio core swirl. Outer layer is four bands. Two are blue with yellow in the center. 1-15/16". Near Mint(-) (8.1). $95. (Auction #149, Lot 29).

SWIRL. Latticinio core. Lot of seven marbles. Four white latticinio core, three yellow latticinio core. Four are peewees. $95. (Auction #157, Lot 33).

SWIRL. Latticinio core. Yellow latticinio core swirl. Nice marble. Bright yellow core. 1-3/8". Near Mint(+) (8.7). $90. (Auction #151, Lot 5).

SWIRL. Latticinio core. White latticinio core swirl. Outer layer is four bands in two different color schemes. Nicely made. 1-13/16". Near Mint(-) (8). $90. (Auction #155, Lot 37).

SWIRL. Latticinio core. White latticinio core swirl. Outer layer is three bands of pink on white. 1-7/16". Near Mint(+) (8.9). $90. (Auction #92, Lot 44).

SWIRL. Latticinio core. White latticino core swirl. Probably from near the end of the cane. Outer layer is two sets of bands. 1". Mint (9.9). $90. (Auction #145, Lot 43).

SWIRL. Latticinio core. End of cane yellow latticinio core swirl. Outer layer was supposed to be four bands of assorted colors. 11/16". Near Mint(+) (8.7). $90. (Auction #103, Lot 48).

SWIRL. Latticinio core. White latticinio core swirl. Bubble filled transparent clear glass with a sligh smokey tint to it. 1-5/8". Near Mint(+) (8.8). $85. (Auction #124, Lot 24).

SWIRL. Latticinio core. Broken cane, end of cane marble. Yellow latticinio core swirl. Four outer bands in two color schemes. 13/16". Mint(-) (9.1). $85. (Auction #74, Lot 41).

SWIRL. Latticinio core. White latticinio core swirl. Four outer bands. Two each of two different color schemes. Well-made. 2". Near Mint(+) (8). $85. (Auction #155, Lot 32).

SWIRL. Latticinio core. Hard to find orange latticinio core. Nice orange core. Outer layer is two sets of pink on yellow bands. 7/8". Mint(-) (9.2). $85. (Auction #162, Lot 37).

SWIRL. Latticinio core. Rare orange latticinio core swirl. Superb marble. Gorgeous orange core. 21/32". Mint (9.9). $80. (Auction #78, Lot 33).

SWIRL. Latticinio core. Lot of two marbles. Matched set of white latticinio core swirls off the same cane. $80. (Auction #133, Lot 44).

SWIRL. Latticinio core. Orange latticinio core swirl. Outer layer is four bands. Each has a white strand in the center. $80. (Auction #146, Lot 13).

SWIRL. Latticinio core. Lot of two marbles. Matched pair of white latticinio core, off the same cane. $80. (Auction #103, Lot 45).

SWIRL. Latticinio core. Lot of three marbles. Matched set of swirls. Odd latticinio core. Four equal-size panels. $80. (Auction #176, Lot

SWIRL. Latticinio core. Lot of two marbles. Matched pair of yellow latticinio swirl shooters. One is the last marble off the cane. $80. (Auction #168, Lot 30).

SWIRL. Latticinio core. Very hard to find white latticinio core swirl in transparent cobalt blue glass. 9/16". Near Mint(+) (8.8). $80. (Auction #160, Lot 12).

SWIRL. Latticinio core. Lot of two marbles. Matched pair of white latticinio core swirls. Nice pair of larger marbles. $75. (Auction #118, Lot 27).

SWIRL. Latticinio core. Larger yellow and white alternating core swirl. Outer layer is three bands of white, yellow, pink. 1-3/16". Near Mint(+) (8.8). $75. (Auction #145, Lot 35).

SWIRL. Latticinio core. Orangish/yellow latticinio core. Outer layer is four bands. Two are pink on white, two are blue on white. $75. (Auction #149, Lot 37).

SWIRL. Latticinio core. Pale yellow latticinio core. The outer layer is only two bands. One is red, white and blue. 7/8". Mint (9.9). $73. (Auction #148, Lot 19).

SWIRL. Latticinio core. Lot of eleven marbles. Nice assortment of colors and styles. 9/16" to 5/8". Mint(-) (9.0) to Near Mint. $71. (Auction #175, Lot 7).

SWIRL. Latticinio core. Alternating white and yellow core. Light blue base glass. Four outer bands. Two pink and white. $70. (Auction #157, Lot 31).

SWIRL. Latticinio core. White latticinio core. Outer layer is eight bands. Four each of two different color schemes. 1-7/8". Near Mint(-) (8.1). $70. (Auction #157, Lot 1).

SWIRL. Latticinio core. Lot of four marbles. Nice assortment of white latticinio core. One has a melt spot. 3/4". Mint (9.9). $70. (Auction #174, Lot 43).

SWIRL. Latticinio core. Very nice latticinio core end of cane (last off cane) swirl. The upper two thirds is a yellow latticino. 21/32". Near Mint (8.6). $70. (Auction #109, Lot 43).

SWIRL. Latticinio core. Yellow latticinio core swirl. Two pink on yellow outer bands, one green on white, one blue on white. 1-5/16". Near Mint(+) (8.9). $70. (Auction #125, Lot 48).

SWIRL. Latticinio core. Lot of three marbles. All are latticinio core, one is yellow. All are polished. 1-1/8", 1-3/8", 1-7/8". $70. (Auction #174, Lot 24).

SWIRL. Latticinio core. Lot of two marbles. Matched pair of white latticinio core. Outer layer is four bands. $70. (Auction #62, Lot 22).

SWIRL. Latticinio core. White latticinio core swirl. Outer layer is two pink on white bands, one blue on white band, one green. 1-5/16". Mint(-) (9.1). $66. (Auction #165, Lot 6).

SWIRL. Latticinio core. Lot of sixteen marbles. All are latticinio core swirls. Variety of colors and styles. $65. (Auction #177, Lot 8).

SWIRL. Latticinio core. Large yellow latticinio core swirl. Outer layer is three transparent red bands, three transparent blue. $65. (Auction #151, Lot 19).

SWIRL. Latticinio core. Lot of five marbles. All are white latticinio core peewees. All are Mint. Great group. 15/32" to 1/2". $65. (Auction #97, Lot 15).

SWIRL. Latticinio core. Lot of four marbles. Matched set, all off the same cane. Very hard to find this many. White latticino. $65. (Auction #105, Lot 20).

SWIRL. Latticinio core. Three-layer white latticinio core swirl. Middle layer is two pink on white bands. 13/16". Mint (9.7). $65. (Auction #164, Lot 38).

SWIRL. Latticinio core. Lot of four marbles. Two yellow latticinio core and two white latticinio core. $65. (Auction #118, Lot 15).

SWIRL. Latticinio core. Lot of four marbles. Three white latticinio core and one yellow latticinio core. One is a peewee. 15. $61. (Auction #116, Lot 45).

SWIRL. Latticinio core. Alternating white and yellow latticinio core. The yellow is a slightly orange.yellow. 1-1/16". Near Mint(+) (8.9). $61. (Auction #164, Lot 2).

SWIRL. Latticinio core. White latticinio core swirl. Outer layer is four bands. Pink on yellow, pink on white, blue on white. 1-1/2". Near Mint (8.3). $60. (Auction #146, Lot 30).

SWIRL. Latticinio core. Lot of two marbles. Matched pair of white latticinio core swirls. Nice pair of larger marbles. $60. (Auction #145, Lot 13).

SWIRL. Latticinio core. Lot of four marbles. All are white latticinio core. Nice set. Assorted outer layer designs and color. $60. (Auction #140, Lot 27).

SWIRL. Latticinio core. Rare red latticinio core. Two outer bands are red and white, one is blue and white. 9/16". Near Mint (8.6). $60.

(Auction #104, Lot 42).

SWIRL. Latticinio core. Yellow latticinio core swirl. Outer layer is two red bands edged by yellow and two green bands edged. 1-1/2". Near Mint(+) (8.8). $60. (Auction #153, Lot 31).

SWIRL. Latticinio core. Very unusual core. An alternating opaque orange and translucent white core. 25/32". Near Mint(+) (8.9). $60. (Auction #63, Lot 36).

SWIRL. Latticinio core. Left-hand twist yellow latticinio core swirl. Outer layer is three bands of opaque orange. 11/16". Mint (9.9). $60. (Auction #159, Lot 14).

SWIRL. Latticinio core. Red latticinio core swirl. The core is the light red color, not the dark or bright red. 3/4". Near Mint (8.6). $60. (Auction #148, Lot 9).

SWIRL. Latticinio core. Gorgeous yellow latticinio core swirl. Two orange on yellow and two green on yellow bands. 21/32". Mint (9.9). $60. (Auction #65, Lot 34).

SWIRL. Latticinio core. Lot of eleven marbles. Nice assortment of colors and types. 19/32" to 3/4". Near Mint(+) (8.9) to Good. $60. (Auction #175, Lot 5).

SWIRL. Latticinio core. Very rare orange and white alternating latticinio core swirl. This was Lot #36 in CyberAuction #63. 25/32". Near Mint(+) (8.9). $56. (Auction #81, Lot 13).

SWIRL. Latticinio core. Yellow latticino core. Three bands of green on yellow, alternating with three bands of red on white. 13/16". Mint (9.7). $55. (Auction #134, Lot 46).

SWIRL. Latticinio core. White latticinio core swirl. Outer layer is three red, white and blue bands. 1-3/4". Near Mint(-) (8.1). $55. (Auction #133, Lot 31).

SWIRL. Latticinio core. Lot of four marbles. All are white latticinio core. All have some minor damage. 9/16" to 3/4". Mint. $55. (Auction #152, Lot 21).

SWIRL. Latticinio core. Yellow latticinio core. Outer layer is three red and white bands, a blue and white band, a blue, green. 13/16". Mint(-) (9.3). $55. (Auction #118, Lot 36).

SWIRL. Latticinio core. Superior latticinio core swirl. Translucent yellow filigree latticinio core. Outer layer is four bands. 21/32". Mint (9.9). $55. (Auction #100, Lot 9).

SWIRL. Latticinio core. Very hard to find left-hand twist swirl!! Pristine! Translucent white latticinio core. 9/16". Mint (9.8). $55. (Auction #117, Lot 18).

SWIRL. Latticinio core. Lot of two marbles. A matched pair of yellow latticinio core swirls. $55. (Auction #55, Lot 15).

SWIRL. Latticinio core. Transparent clear base. White latticinio core. Outer layer is three transparent red bands. 1-3/16". Near Mint(+) (8.9). $55. (Auction #158, Lot 46).

SWIRL. Latticinio core. Orange latticinio core swirl. Outer layer is two dark purple on white bands. 7/8". Mint (9.9). $52. (Auction #165, Lot 46).

SWIRL. Latticinio core. Alternating white and yellow latticinio core. Six outer bands in two different color schemes. $51. (Auction #157, Lot 37).

SWIRL. Latticinio core. Lot of six marbles. All are white latticinio core swirls. Nice assortment of outer bands. 5/8". $50. (Auction #165, Lot 16).

SWIRL. Latticinio core. Stunning example. White latticinio core. Outer layer is three blue and white bands. 25/32". Mint (9.9). $50. (Auction #179, Lot 10).

SWIRL. Latticinio core. White latticinio core swirl in light blue base glass. Outer layer is four bands. 15/16". Near Mint (8.6). $50. (Auction #185, Lot 6).

SWIRL. Latticinio core. White latticinio core. Outer layer is three transparent green on yellow bands. 1-3/16". Near Mint(+) (8.9). $50. (Auction #110, Lot 42).

SWIRL. Latticinio core. Bright yellow core. Outer layer is four opaque white bands alternating with two opaque blue bands. 1-1/16". Near Mint (8.6). $50. (Auction #89, Lot 11).

SWIRL. Latticinio core. Left-hand twist yellow latticinio core swirl in the form of a bead. Very rare!!!! 21/32". Near Mint(+) (8.9). $50. (Auction #160, Lot 28).

SWIRL. Latticinio core. Odd core. Translucent white strands, with one orange strand. Outer layer is three orange bands. 7/8". Mint (9.8). $50. (Auction #182, Lot 33).

SWIRL. Latticinio core . White latticinio core swirl. Outer layer is four opaque yellow bands, two opaque orange bands. 1-3/16". Near Mint(-) (8.2). $50. (Auction #89, Lot 46).

SWIRL. Latticinio core. Superior example of a peewee latticinio core swirl. White core. Three orange bands. 15/32". Mint (9.6). $50. (Auction #70, Lot 29).

SWIRL. Latticinio core. Nice white latticinio core swirl. Outer layer is two bands of transparent pink on white. 1-1/16". Mint (9.5). $50. (Auction #130, Lot 17).

SWIRL. Latticinio core. White latticinio core. Outer layer is eight bands. Four red on white, two blue on white. 1-7/16". Near Mint(-) (8). $50. (Auction #130, Lot 33).

SWIRL. Latticinio core. Large white latticinio core swirl. Six outer bands. Three pink on orange and three black on white. P. $50. (Auction #109, Lot 22).

SWIRL. Latticinio core. White latticinio core swirl. Very light bottle glass tint to the marble. 1-7/16". Near Mint(-) (8). $50. (Auction #146, Lot 4).

SWIRL. Latticinio core. Very hard to find alternating green and white latticinio core (very light green). 9/16". Mint (9.9). $50. (Auction #122, Lot 35).

SWIRL. Latticinio core. Lot of four marbles. Two white core, one yellow core, one alternating white and yellow. 19/32". $50. (Auction #122, Lot 12).

SWIRL. Latticinio core. White latticinio core swirl. Outer layer is three narrow blue bands and three narrow white bands. So. 1-3/8". Near Mint(+) (8.9). $50. (Auction #165, Lot 29).

SWIRL. Latticinio core. Lot of two marbles. Matched pair, off the same cane. White latticinio core. Outer layer is three blue. $50. (Auction #167, Lot 37).

SWIRL. Latticinio core. White latticinio core. Outer layer is three blue and white bands, alternating with three pink and yellow. $49. (Auction #133, Lot 33).

SWIRL. Latticinio core. Superb white latticinio core swirl. Superior example. Outer layer is six bands. 3/4". Mint (9.9). $49. (Auction #96, Lot 32).

SWIRL. Latticinio core. Lot of four marbles. All are white latticinio core. Assortment of outer bands. One is Mint. $48. (Auction #68, Lot 10).

SWIRL. Latticinio core. Lot of two marbles. Both are white latticinio core swirls. 1-9/16 & Good (7.4). 1-5/8" & Near Mint(-). $47. (Auction #89, Lot 29).

SWIRL. Latticinio core. A yellow and white alternating latticinio core. Outer layer is three blue on white bands. 13/16". Mint (9.9). $47. (Auction #58, Lot 33).

SWIRL. Latticinio core. Outstanding marble. Probably English. Bright white latticinio core. Outer layer is three bands. 21/32". Mint (9.9). $47. (Auction #165, Lot 8).

SWIRL. Latticinio core. Orange latticinio core swirl. Hard to find. Bright orange core. Outer layer is three bright red band. 19/32". Near Mint(+) (8.8). $47. (Auction #183, Lot 25).

SWIRL. Latticinio core. Very hard to find red latticinio core swirl. Nice red core (duller red, not the English bright type). 21/32". Near Mint(-) (8.1). $46. (Auction #141, Lot 17).

SWIRL. Latticinio core. Three layer swirl. White latticinio core. Middle layer is four bands. Two are pink on white. 5/8". Mint (9.9). $45. (Auction #165, Lot 31).

SWIRL. Latticinio core. White latticinio core swirl. Large. Outer layer is three pink on yellow bands. 1-7/8". Good(+) (7.70). $45. (Auction #166, Lot 23).

SWIRL. Latticinio core. White latticinio core swirl. Bright colors, probably English. Outer layer is two blue bands edged. 23/32". Mint (9.9). $45. (Auction #153, Lot 33).

SWIRL. Latticinio core. Lot of three marbles. Matched set of three marbles, off the same cane. Yellow latticinio core. $45. (Auction #179, Lot 20).

SWIRL. Latticinio core. Superb end of cane three layer latticinio core swirl. Orange latticinio core swirl. 15/32". Mint (9.9). $45. (Auction #120, Lot 48).

SWIRL. Latticinio core. Orange latticinio core swirl. Beautiful orange core. Outer layer of four transparent green bands. 9/16". Mint (9.9). $44. (Auction #95, Lot 39).

SWIRL. Latticinio core. Orange latticinio core. A beauty. Four outer bands in two different color schemes. Germany. 17/32". Mint (9.9). $44. (Auction #102, Lot 40).

SWIRL. Latticinio core. Lot of two marbles. Both are white latticinio core. 9/16" & Mint (9.9). 11/16" & Mint (9.5). $43. (Auction #84, Lot 30).

SWIRL. Latticinio core. Lot of two marbles. Matched pair, off the same cane. White latticinio core. $42. (Auction #176, Lot 14).

SWIRL. Latticinio core. Lot of two marbles. Both are yellow latticinio core swirls. 1-9/16 & Near Mint(-) (8.0). 1-11/16". $42. (Auction #89, Lot 24).

SWIRL. Latticinio core. Lot of three marbles. All are white latticinio core. Assorted outer layers. All in great shape. 7/16". $42. (Auction #107, Lot 36).

SWIRL. Latticinio core. Very rare naked latticinio core. Much less common than the naked divided, solid or ribbon cores. Yellow. 3/4". Near Mint (8.3). $41. (Auction #109, Lot 7).

SWIRL. Latticinio core. Interesting yellow latticinio core. Outer layer is four multicolor bands alternating with four bands. 1-9/16". Good(+) (7.80). $40. (Auction #115, Lot 22).

SWIRL. Latticinio core. Lot of three marbles. Two white latticino core and one yellow latticinio core. All are peewees. $40. (Auction #116, Lot 37).

SWIRL. Latticinio core. Superb yellow latticinio core swirl. Outer layer is four bands, all the same color scheme. 25/32". Mint(-) (9.1). $40. (Auction #71, Lot 17).

SWIRL. Latticinio core. Lot of three marbles. All are peewees. Two white core and one yellow core. 15/32" to 1/2". Mint (9.9). $40. (Auction #102, Lot 38).

SWIRL. Latticinio core. Yellow latticinio core. Outer layer is two pink bands edged by white, one green band edged by white. 1-1/16". Near Mint(-) (8.2). $40. (Auction #122, Lot 4).

SWIRL. Latticinio core. White latticinio core swirl. Six outer bands. Three are translucent yellow, one orange. 7/8". Mint (9.4). $40. (Auction #131, Lot 37).

SWIRL. Latticinio core. White and yellow alternating latticinio core. Outer layer is three red bands. 21/32". Mint(-) (9.2). $40. (Auction #88, Lot 19).

SWIRL. Latticinio core. Rare red latticinio core. Two outer bands are red and white, one is blue and white. 9/16". Near Mint (8.6). $40. (Auction #62, Lot 41).

SWIRL. Latticinio core. Lot of two marbles. Bright colors. Probably English. Similar marbles. Bright white latticinio core. $40. (Auction #169, Lot 14).

SWIRL. Latticinio core. Orange latticinio core swirl. Super orange color. Outer layer is four bands. Two purple with white. 1-5/16". Near Mint(-) (8.1). $40. (Auction #166, Lot 8).

SWIRL. Latticinio core. Lot of two marbles. Matched pair of white latticinio core, off the same cane. $40. (Auction #157, Lot 18).

SWIRL. Latticinio core. Superb white latticinio core swirl. Shooter. Outer layer is three transparent pink on opaque yellow. 7/8". Mint (9.9). $40. (Auction #97, Lot 32).

SWIRL. Latticinio core. Yellow latticinio core swirl. Wide yellow core. Outer lyaer is six bands. Four are green and white. 11/16". Mint (9.9). $39. (Auction #155, Lot 15).

SWIRL. Latticinio core. English type. Translucent orange latticinio core. Outer layer is three orange bands. 9/16". Mint (9.7). $39. (Auction #64, Lot 12).

SWIRL. Latticinio core. Pale yellow latticinio core. Three outer bands. Each is edged by a yellow strand and a white strand. 11/16". Mint (9.9). $38. (Auction #57, Lot 17).

SWIRL. Latticinio core. White latticinio core swirl. Outer layer is three transparent red bands. 1-5/8". Good(+) (7.90). $38. (Auction #146, Lot 11).

SWIRL. Latticinio core. Hard to find orange latticinio core swirl. Outer layer is three orange strands. 11/16". Near Mint (8.5). $38. (Auction #88, Lot 2).

SWIRL. Latticinio core . From near the end of a cane. White latticinio core (only two strands remain). There is a faint ghost. 27/32". Mint (9.7). $37. (Auction #139, Lot 32).

SWIRL. Latticinio core. Lot of three marbles. All are peewees. All white latticinio core. Assorted outer layers. All are Mint. $37. (Auction #106, Lot 35).

SWIRL. Latticinio core. Superior latticinio core swirl. White core. Outer layer is a cage of eight bands. 29/32". Mint(-) (9.1). $37. (Auction #123, Lot 44).

SWIRL. Latticinio core. White latticinio core swirl. Outer layer is two bands of transparent black with a yellow edge. 1-7/16". Good(+) (7.90). $37. (Auction #161, Lot 17).

SWIRL. Latticinio core. Excellent end of cane swirl. White latticinio core swirl. Outer layer is three transparent blue band. 3/4". Mint(-) (9.1). $37. (Auction #101, Lot 1).

SWIRL. Latticinio core. White latticinio core swirl. Outer layer is four bands. Two are pink, white and blue. Two are pink. 1-7/8". Good(-) (7.10). $37. (Auction #143, Lot 37).

SWIRL. Latticinio core. White latticinio core swirl. Nice core. Outer layer is four bands. Two orange with white, one green . 21/32". Mint (9.9). $37. (Auction #169, Lot 18).

SWIRL. Latticinio core. Yellow latticinio core swirl. Outer layer is three transparent light blue bands. 21/32". Mint (9.9). $37. (Auction #116, Lot 28).

SWIRL. Latticinio core. Super English colors. Yellow latticinio core. Outer layer is a subsurface layer of bright blue bands. 9/16". Mint (9.8). $36. (Auction #160, Lot 39).

SWIRL. Latticinio core. Lot of three marbles. Two white latticinio core and one yellow. Assorted outer bands. All are Mint! $36. (Auction #106, Lot 33).

SWIRL. Latticinio core. Three layer yellow latticinio core swirl. Middle layer is three wide bands of transparent red. 11/16". Mint (9.9). $36. (Auction #164, Lot 34).

SWIRL. Latticinio core. Lot of two marbles. First is a yellow core. 1-9/16". Good(+) (7.8). The other is a white core. 1-3/16". $35. (Auction #108, Lot 17).

SWIRL. Latticinio core. Excellent example. Light yellow latticinio core with a tear drop center. 23/32". Mint (9.9). $35. (Auction #55, Lot 39).

SWIRL. Latticinio core. White latticinio core. Base glass is transparent very light pink. Germany, circa 1870-1915. 19/32." Mint (9.9). $35. (Auction #125, Lot 37).

SWIRL. Latticinio core. Orange latticinio core. Outer layer is three transparent blue bands and three opaque white. 9/16". Mint (9.9). $35. (Auction #84, Lot 32).

SWIRL. Latticinio core. White latticinio core. Outer layer is six bands. Three opaque white bands. 1-9/16". Good(+) (7.70). $35. (Auction #149, Lot 26).

SWIRL. Latticinio core. Yellow latticinio core. Outer layer is three red/orange bands alternating with three white bands. 7/8". Mint(-) (9.2). $35. (Auction #98, Lot 27).

SWIRL. Latticinio core. Harder to find alternating white and yellow latticinio core. Super core. 11/16". Mint (9.9). $35. (Auction #128, Lot 35).

SWIRL. Latticinio core. White latticinio core swirl. Core not completely closed. Outer layer is two bands of pink on yellow. 1". Mint(-) (9.2). $34. (Auction #164, Lot 29).

SWIRL. Latticinio core. White latticinio core swirl in light blue glass. Outer layer is three narrow orange bands. 11/16". Mint (9.6). $34. (Auction #124, Lot 13).

SWIRL. Latticinio core. Lot of two marbles. Both are peewee latticinio cores. One is white and the other is yellow. $34. (Auction #74, Lot 8).

SWIRL. Latticinio core. Lot of two marbles. Matched pair of white latticinio core swirls. Odd outer layer. $34. (Auction #68, Lot 37).

SWIRL. Latticinio core. Transparent lightly tinted blue glass. Yellow latticinio core. Tint in the glass makes it appear lighter. 5/8". Mint (9.3). $33. (Auction #98, Lot 29).

SWIRL. Latticinio core. About as close to a coreless as you can get. Two thin yellow latticinio strands in the marble. 25/32". Mint(-) (9.2). $32. (Auction #181, Lot 8).

SWIRL. Latticinio core. Yellow latticinio core. Core has a slight green tint. Outer layer is three blue and white bands. 25/32". Mint (9.9). $32. (Auction #128, Lot 37).

SWIRL. Latticinio core. White latticinio core swirl. Outer layer is two bands of blue and white. 23/32". Mint (9.9). $32. (Auction #113, Lot 34).

SWIRL. Latticinio core. A yellow and white alternating latticinio core. Outer layer is three blue on white bands. 13/16". Mint (9.9). $32. (Auction #104, Lot 8).

SWIRL. Latticinio core. Peewee pale orange latticinio core swirl. Outer layer is two red bands and two transparent dark purple. 1/2". Mint (9.9). $32. (Auction #153, Lot 6).

SWIRL. Latticinio core. Yellow core. Outer layer is six narrow bands. Three are opaque white. Alternating with a red, a blue. 3/4". Mint (9.7). $32. (Auction #167, Lot 24).

SWIRL. Latticinio core. Beautiful yellow latticinio core swirl. Outer layer is three narrow opaque blue bands. 23/32". Mint (9.7). $32. (Auction #167, Lot 2).

SWIRL. Latticinio core. Shooter white latticinio core swirl. Outer layer is four bands. Two pink on white, one blue on white. 1". Near Mint(+) (8.9). $32. (Auction #110, Lot 3).

SWIRL. Latticinio core. Yellow latticinio core. Outer layer is two sets of transparent pink and opaque white. 25/32". Mint(-) (9.2). $32 (Auction #77, Lot 36).

SWIRL. Latticinio core. Lot of four marbles. All are latticinio core, three white, one yellow. All shooters, but with damage. $32. (Auction #144, Lot 35).

SWIRL. Latticinio core. White latticinio core swirl. Outer layer is three transparent red bands. 21/32". Mint (9.9). $32. (Auction #69, Lot 16).

SWIRL. Latticinio core. Alternating white and yellow latticinio core swirl. One tiny flake and a couple of tiny pits. 25/32". Near Mint(+) (8.9). $31. (Auction #133, Lot 42).

SWIRL. Latticinio core. English colors. Yellow latticinio core. Outer layer is four white bands, two orange bands, a green band. 19/32". Mint (9.9). $31. (Auction #100, Lot 17).

SWIRL. Latticinio core. Excellent start-of-cane latticino core swirl. White latticinio core. Outer layer is three sets of blue. 19/32". Mint (9.5). $30. (Auction #61, Lot 13).

SWIRL. Latticinio core. White latticinio core swirl. Outer layer is four bands in two different complex color patterns. Germany. 19/32". Mint (9.9). $30. (Auction #177, Lot 33).

SWIRL. Latticinio core. White latticinio core. Outer layer is six bands. Three each of two different color schemes. 1-7/16". Good(+) (7.90). $30. (Auction #152, Lot 23).

SWIRL. Latticinio core. White latticinio core swirl. Six outer bands. Three are translucent yellow, one orange. 7/8". Mint (9.4). $30. (Auction #100, Lot 2).

SWIRL. Latticinio core. Yellow latticinio core swirl. Two outer bands. Appears to be one band missing. The bands are opaque. 7/8". Mint(-) (9). $30. (Auction #74, Lot 20).

SWIRL. Latticinio core. Alternating yellow and white latticinio core. Very hard to find. 9/16". Mint (9.9). $30. (Auction #82, Lot 17).

SWIRL. Latticinio core. Another beauty. Yellow latticinio core. Outer layer is three opaque white strands. 13/16". Mint (9.9). $30. (Auction #129, Lot 14).

SWIRL. Latticinio core. End of cane (first-off-cane) latticinio core swirl. White core. Outer layer is a band of white. 23/32". Near Mint(+) (8.9). $30. (Auction #154, Lot 5).

SWIRL. Latticinio core. Unusual latticinio core swirl from near an end of the cane. 23/32". Near Mint(+) (8.9). $30. (Auction #175, Lot 42).

SWIRL. Latticinio core. Peewee white latticinio core swirl. Six bands for the outer layer. Three are white. 15/32". Mint (9.9). $30. (Auction #126, Lot 38).

SWIRL. Latticinio core. Translucent yellow latticinio core. From near the end of the cane. Outer layer has three white strands. 9/16". Mint (9.7). $30. (Auction #121, Lot 36).

SWIRL. Latticinio core. White latticinio core swirl. Outer layer is three pale blue on white bands. 7/8". Mint (9). $29. (Auction #150, Lot 24).

SWIRL. Latticinio core. White latticinio core swirl. Outer layer is three bands of mustard yellow and orange. 29/32". Mint(-) (9.3). $29. (Auction #129, Lot 4).

SWIRL. Latticinio core. Peewee. Wispy tranlucent white latticinio core. Outer layer is six bands. A combination of ruddy red. 15/32". Mint (9.9). $28. (Auction #81, Lot 18).

SWIRL. Latticinio core. White latticinio core swirl. Outer layer is a three red bands alternating with three light orange strands. 1". Near Mint (8.6). $28. (Auction #122, Lot 47).

SWIRL. Latticinio core. White latticinio core swirl. Outer layer is three blue on white bands, alternating with three red. 15/16". Mint(-) (9). $28. (Auction #163, Lot 8).

SWIRL. Latticinio core. English style. White latticinio core. Outer layer is three orange strands alternating with three yellow. 9/16". Mint (9.7). $28. (Auction #64, Lot 7).

SWIRL. Latticinio core. Peewee. Yellow latticinio core swirl. Outer layer is three orange and white bands. 15/32". Mint(-) (9). $27. (Auction #81, Lot 11).

SWIRL. Latticinio core. Orange latticinio core. Outer layer is three wide orange bands alternating with three wide white bands. 23/32". Mint (9.7). $27. (Auction #184, Lot 2).

SWIRL. Latticinio core. Lot of three marbles. All are yellow latticinio core. Three different sizes, shades and designs. $27. (Auction #130, Lot 15).

SWIRL. Latticinio core. Alternating white and pale yellow latticinio core swirl. Outer layer is three transparent colored bands. 11/16". Mint (9.7). $27. (Auction #118, Lot 32).

SWIRL. Latticinio core. White latticinio core swirl. Outer layer is six bands. Three are orange, one black, one blue, one green. 11/16". Mint(-) (9). $27. (Auction #162, Lot 13).

SWIRL. Latticinio core. White and yellow alternating latticinio core. Outer layer is six sets of bands in two different colors. 31/32". Near Mint(-) (8). $27. (Auction #127, Lot 33).

SWIRL. Latticinio core. Translucent white latticinio core. Three outer bands of translucent dark purple and opaque yellow. 9/16". Mint (9). $27. (Auction #80, Lot 9).

SWIRL. Latticinio core. White latticinio core. Six outer bands. Three are red and yellow, three are yellow. 1-1/8". Near Mint(-) (8.2). $26. (Auction #171, Lot 31).

SWIRL. Latticinio core. White latticinio core swirl. Outer layer is two red/yellow/green bands alternating with two red/white. 19/32". Mint (9.9). $26. (Auction #70, Lot 7).

SWIRL. Latticinio core. Beautiful yellow latticinio core. Outer layer is four bands. Two are pink on white, one is blue on white. 21/32". Mint (9.9). $26. (Auction #153, Lot 18).

SWIRL. Latticinio core. Translucent white core. Outer layer is two narrow red on white strands and two black bands. 19/32". Mint (9.9). $25. (Auction #124, Lot 40).

SWIRL. Latticinio core. Super yellow latticinio core swirl. Outer layer is six opaque white bands covered by transparent green. 5/8". Mint (9.7). $25. (Auction #96, Lot 28).

SWIRL. Latticinio core. Beautiful yellow latticinio core. Outer layer is three bands. Each a different transparent color. 11/16". Mint (9.9). $25. (Auction #110, Lot 31).

SWIRL. Latticinio core. Lot of two marbles. Matched pair, perhaps off the same cane. White latticinio core. $25. (Auction #179, Lot 13).

SWIRL. Latticinio core. Yellow core. Outer layer is three transparent pink bands on white. 15/32". Mint (9.9). $25. (Auction #82, Lot 28).

SWIRL. Latticinio core . Lot of two marbles. Both are peewees. White latticinio core. Two different styles of outer bands. 1/2". Mint (9.9). $25. (Auction #179, Lot 18).

SWIRL. Latticinio core. White latticinio core swirl. Outer layer is three narrow red bands and three narrow orange bands. 25/32". Mint (9.9). $25. (Auction #97, Lot 5).

SWIRL. Latticinio core. Superb swirl. Translucent white/gray latticinio core. Outer layer is six red narrow bands. 21/32". Mint (9.9). $25. (Auction #110, Lot 1).

SWIRL. Latticinio core. Lot of three marbles. Nice group. One is latticinio in divided core form. All have some damage. 7/8". $25. (Auction #174, Lot 34).

SWIRL. Latticinio core. English type. White latticinio core. Three outer bands. Each consists of bright red, green and yellow. 19/32". Near Mint(+) (8.9). $25. (Auction #71, Lot 9).

SWIRL. Latticinio core. Peewee Yellow latticinio core. Outer layer is four bands in assorted color schemes. Nice marble. Germany. 1/2". Mint (9.9). $25. (Auction #146, Lot 44).

SWIRL. Latticinio core. White latticinio core swirl. Outer layer is four bands. Two red and white, one blue and white, one green. 3/4". Mint (9.3). $25. (Auction #177, Lot 37).

SWIRL. Latticinio core. White latticinio core. English type swirl Three red outer bands alternating with three yellow. 5/8". Mint (9.9). $24. (Auction #78, Lot 17).

SWIRL. Latticinio core. White latticinio core. Three light red bands alternating with three light blue bands. Surface in nice shape. 11/16". Mint (9.9). $24. (Auction #60, Lot 38).

SWIRL. Latticinio core. White and yellow alternating latticinio core. Outer layer is four bands of pink, white and blue. 19/32". Mint (9.9). $24. (Auction #129, Lot 2).

SWIRL. Latticinio core. White latticinio core swirl. Nice core. Outer layer is four bands. Two orange with white, one green. 21/32". Mint (9.9). $24. (Auction #105, Lot 4).

SWIRL. Latticinio core. Outstanding, hard to find, alternating core. White and yellow latticinio core. 11/16". Mint(-) (9.2). $24. (Auction #105, Lot 9).

SWIRL. Latticinio core. Nice peewee white latticinio core swirl in light blue tinted glass. Three outer bands. Colored glass. 15/32". Mint(-) (9.1). $24. (Auction #112, Lot 32).

SWIRL. Latticinio core. Yellow latticinio mist core. OUter layer is four light blue bands alternaitng with four white bands. 7/8". Near Mint(+) (8.7). $24. (Auction #63, Lot 30).

SWIRL. Latticinio core. Peewee yellow latticinio core. Great marble. Outer layer is two transparent dark blue bands. 7/16". Mint (9.9). $23. (Auction #65, Lot 14).

SWIRL. Latticinio core. White latticino core. Outer layer is three bands of transparent dark purple and white. A few pits. 25/32". Near Mint(+) (8.9). $23. (Auction #157, Lot 6).

SWIRL. Latticinio core. Yellow latticinio core swirl. Four outer bands in two different color schemes. A beauty. Germany. 9/16". Mint (9.9). $23. (Auction #131, Lot 5).

SWIRL. Latticinio core. Yellow latticinio core. Four outer bands. Two are transparent blue. The other two are transparent red. 19/32". Mint (9.9). $22. (Auction #85, Lot 41).

SWIRL. Latticinio core. White latticinio core swirl. Unusual yellow and white alternating core. 13/16". Near Mint(+) (8.8). $22. (Auction #110, Lot 38).

SWIRL. Latticinio core. White latticinio core swirl. Outer layer is three red on white bands. 25/32". Near Mint(+) (8.9). $22. (Auction #182, Lot 39).

SWIRL. Latticinio core. Yellow latticinio core swirl. Outer layer is four bands. Two are red, white, blue. 9/16". Mint (9.7). $22. (Auction #166, Lot 32).

SWIRL. Latticinio core. White latticino core swirl. Outer layer is two bands of orange with yellow, and two of transparent blue. 21/32". Mint (9.9). $22. (Auction #137, Lot 3).

SWIRL. Latticinio core. Yellow latticinio core. Outer layer is three red on white bands, alternating with three blue on white. 1-1/16". Near Mint(-) (8.2). $22. (Auction #130, Lot 2).

SWIRL. Latticinio core. Gorgeou white latticinio core swirl. The outer layer is two transparent pink bands (one on white). 11/16". Mint (9.5). $22. (Auction #115, Lot 1).

SWIRL. Latticinio core. Peewee. White latticinio core. Three outer bands in the same complex color scheme. In great shape. 1/2". Mint (9.9). $22. (Auction #131, Lot 35).

SWIRL. Latticinio core. Peewee. Yellow latticinio core. Outer layer is three white bands, alternating with two blue. 1/2". Mint (9.7). $22. (Auction #82, Lot 13).

SWIRL. Latticinio core. Yellow core. Outer layer is three bands of pink on white and three of green on white. 21/32". Mint(-) (9). $21. (Auction #95, Lot 2).

SWIRL. Latticinio core. From near an end of the core. Yellow latticinio core. Outer layer is six transparent pink on white bands. 19/32". Mint (9.9). $21. (Auction #116, Lot 19).

SWIRL. Latticinio core. Bright yellow core. Outer layer is two pink on white bands, one green on white band, one blue on white. 21/32". Mint (9.9). $21. (Auction #146, Lot 6).

SWIRL. Latticinio core. Yellow latticinio core swirl. Outer layer is four double bands. Each set is the same transparent color. 17/32". Mint (9.9). $21. (Auction #146, Lot 33).

SWIRL. Latticinio core. White latticinio core swirl. Outer layer is three transparent blue bands alternating with three opaque. 5/8". Mint (9.9). $21. (Auction #78, Lot 3).

SWIRL. Latticinio core. White latticinio core. Outer layer consists of four sets of two bands each. Two sets are pink, one blue. 29/32". Near Mint(+) (8.1). $21. (Auction #128, Lot 4).

SWIRL. Latticinio core. White latticinio core swirl. Outer layer is two transparent blue bands (one has a white band). 29/32". Near Mint(+) (8.8). $20. (Auction #137, Lot 21).

SWIRL. Latticinio core. White core. Outer layer is three opaque yellow bands alternating with three transparent black bands. 9/16". Mint (9.9). $20. (Auction #74, Lot 14).

SWIRL. Latticinio core. Yellow latticinio core. Four outer bands. Two are white, red and blue. Two are white, red and green. 9/16". Mint (9.9). $20. (Auction #84, Lot 5).

SWIRL. Latticinio core. English colors. White latticinio core swirl. Outer layer is three sets of bands. Each is a narrow band. 5/8". Near Mint(+) (8.9). $20. (Auction #96, Lot 6).

SWIRL. Latticinio core. Yellow latticino core swirl. Outer layer is six bands in two alternating colors. Has a tiny pit. Germany. 9/16". Mint(-) (9.1). $20. (Auction #177, Lot 45).

SWIRL. Latticinio core. Harder to find alternating white and yellow latticinio core. Outer layer is four multicolor bands. 11/16". Near Mint(+) (8.9). $20. (Auction #67, Lot 6).

SWIRL. Latticinio core. White latticinio core swirl. Outer layer is three narrow yellow bands. 7/8". Mint (9.9). $20. (Auction #165, Lot 2).

SWIRL. Latticinio core. Lot of two marbles. Both have similar outer bands. One is yellow core and one is white core. 19/32" . $20. (Auction #108, Lot 6).

SWIRL. Latticinio core. Yellow latticinio core. Outer layer is two blue and red bands alternating with two green and red bands. 23/32". Mint (9.9). $19. (Auction #170, Lot 15).

SWIRL. Latticinio core. White latticinio core. Four outer bands in two different color schemes. Some cold roll lines. Germany. 21/32". Mint (9.6). $19. (Auction #184, Lot 10).

SWIRL. Latticinio core. Bright colors, probably English. White latticinio core. Outer layer is three bright red strands. 1/2". Mint (9.9). $19. (Auction #155, Lot 17).

SWIRL. Latticinio core. Peewee. White latticinio core. Outer layer is three thin bands of blue and three thin bands of orange. 1/2". Mint (9.9). $19. (Auction #85, Lot 33).

SWIRL. Latticinio core. Core is greenish yellow strands. Outer layer is three white strands alternating with three blue on white. 9/16". Mint (9.9). $19. (Auction #124, Lot 28).

SWIRL. Latticinio core. White latticinio core. The outer layer is three bands in a complex set of colors. 17/32". Mint (9.9). $19. (Auction #78, Lot 14).

SWIRL. Latticinio core. White latticinio core. Interesting outer layer. Three bands of white, pink and green. 21/32". Mint (9.9). $18. (Auction #105, Lot 11).

SWIRL. Latticinio core. Unusual swirl, probably from near an end of the cane. Alternating white and yellow latticinio core. 19/32". Mint(-) (9.1). $18. (Auction #107, Lot 9).

SWIRL. Latticinio core. Nice white latticinio core, probably from near the end of the cane. Outer layer is one red and one yellow. 11/16". Mint (9.7). $18. (Auction #139, Lot 43).

SWIRL. Latticinio core. White latticino core. Outer layer is three bands. Each is white band edged on one side by green. 21/32". Mint (9.9). $18. (Auction #170, Lot 8).

SWIRL. Latticinio core. From near the end of a cane. Core is alternating yellow and white latticinio. Not completely closed. 9/16". Mint (9.7). $18. (Auction #64, Lot 28).

SWIRL. Latticinio core. Peewee. Very odd core. Wispy white. Outer layer is one light blue band and one wispy white band. 7/16". Mint (9.9). $18. (Auction #78, Lot 31).

SWIRL. Latticinio core. Alternating orange and white core. Three outer bands of blue and thin white. Two melt spots on one side. 21/32". Near Mint(+) (8.9). $18. (Auction #144, Lot 6).

SWIRL. Latticinio core. Peewee yellow latticinio core. Outer layer is four bands in two different color schemes. 1/2". Near Mint(+) (8.9). $18. (Auction #151, Lot 33).

SWIRL. Latticinio core. White latticinio core swirl. Outer layer is three transparent blue, white and pink bands. 11/16". Mint(-) (9.2). $18. (Auction #87, Lot 8).

SWIRL. Latticinio core. Yellow latticinio core. Greenish tint to the yellow. Four outer bands. Nice marble. Germany. 19/32'. Mint (9.9). $17. (Auction #128, Lot 2).

SWIRL. Latticinio core. Lot of two marbles. Both are latticinio core. One white, one yellow. Both 15/32". White is Mint (9.9). $17. (Auction #184, Lot 6).

SWIRL. Latticinio core. White core. Four outer bands. Two are pink on white, one green on white, one blue on white. Germany,. 21/32". Mint (9.8). $17. (Auction #108, Lot 7).

SWIRL. Latticinio core. Peewee white latticinio core swirl. Outer layer is four bands of two different color schemes. Germany. 1/2". Mint (9.8). $17. (Auction #160, Lot 7).

SWIRL. Latticinio core. White latticinio core swirl. Outer layer is two different color schemes. Two bands of each. 11/16". Mint (9.9). $17. (Auction #102, Lot 14).

SWIRL. Latticinio core. Yellow latticinio core. Outer layer is three bands of transparent green on opaque white. 11/16". Mint(-) (9.2). $17. (Auction #88, Lot 37).

SWIRL. Latticinio core. Yellow latticinio core. Outer layer is two bands of transparent light green edged by yellow and white. 9/16". Mint (9.9). $17. (Auction #90, Lot 28).

SWIRL. Latticinio core. Yellow latticinio core. Six outer bands in two different color schemes. A moon and a rough spot. Germany. 3/4". Near Mint (8.5). $16. (Auction #57, Lot 10).

SWIRL. Latticinio core. Transparent clear with a very light blue tint. White core. Four outer bands. Two are pink on yellow. 7/8". Near Mint(+) (8.8). $16. (Auction #137, Lot 8).

SWIRL. Latticinio core. Translucent white latticinio core swirl. Outer layer is three translucent purple bands. 9/16". Mint(-) (9.1). $16. (Auction #169, Lot 4).

SWIRL. Latticinio core. Translucent white latticinio core. Two outer bands of lavender and white. 19/32". Mint(-) (9.2). $16. (Auction #92, Lot 31).

SWIRL. Latticinio core. White latticinio core swirl. Outer layer is four bands. One blue on white, one pink on yellow, one green. 3/4". Mint (9.9). $16. (Auction #98, Lot 1).

SWIRL. Latticinio core. Yellow latticinio core swirl. Outer layer is three very narrow white bands. 11/16". Mint (9.9). $16. (Auction #165, Lot 35).

SWIRL. Latticinio core. White latticinio core peewee. Two pink on white and two green on white outer bands. Small airhole. 1/2". Mint(-) (9.2). $16. (Auction #75, Lot 4).

SWIRL. Latticinio core. White latticinio core. Four outer bands. Two orange edged by white, two green edged by yellow. Germany. 3/4". Mint (9.9). $15. (Auction #106, Lot 6).

SWIRL. Latticinio core. White latticinio core swirl. Translucent white core. Outer layer is transparent blue bands edged. 21/32". Mint (9.7). $15. (Auction #98, Lot 39).

SWIRL. Latticinio core. White latticinio core. Outer layer is three sub-surface bands. One is pink, white and blue. One is pink. 19/32". Mint (9.9). $15. (Auction #124, Lot 7).

SWIRL. Latticinio core. A beautiful peewee. White latticinio core. Outer layer is three orange bands. 1/2". Mint (9.9). $15. (Auction #130, Lot 19).

SWIRL. Latticinio core . White latticincio core. Outer layer is four opaque white bands with pink strands. Two are edged by blue. 21/32". Near Mint (8.6). $15. (Auction #133, Lot 18).

SWIRL. Latticinio core. From near the end of the cane. White latticinio core. Not closed. Four outer bands. Two are orange. 9/16". Mint (9.7). $15. (Auction #64, Lot 32).

SWIRL. Latticinio core. White latticinio core. Four transparent green outer band. One tiny manufacturing pit. Nice looking marble. 21/32". Mint(-) (9.1). $15. (Auction #85, Lot 1).

SWIRL. Latticinio core. White latticinio core. Outer layer is four bands. Two are red and yellow, one is blue and white. 9/16". Mint (9.9). $14. (Auction #64, Lot 14).

SWIRL. Latticinio core. White latticinio core swirl. Six outer bands in two color schemes. Some cold roll creasing on the surface. 9/16". Mint (9.5). $14. (Auction #71, Lot 2).

SWIRL. Latticinio core. Very interesting yellow latticinio core swirl. Nice core. Only one outer band, transparent blue on white. 11/16". Mint (9.7). $14. (Auction #57, Lot 1).

SWIRL. Latticinio core. White latticinio core swirl. Beautiful filligree core. Outer layer is three opaque yellow bands. 23/32". Mint(-) (9.1). $14. (Auction #93, Lot 29).

SWIRL. Latticinio core. Yellow latticinio core. Outer layer is three pink, white, green and blue bands. In great shape. Germany. 21/32". Mint (9.9). $14. (Auction #150, Lot 8).

SWIRL. Latticinio core. Transparent yellow core. Very tight and thin. Outer layer is two pink on yellow strands and two blue. 21/32". Mint (9.8). $14. (Auction #87, Lot 33).

SWIRL. Latticinio core. White latticinio core swirl. Core is slightly flat on one side. Outer layer is three narrow green. 5/8". Mint (9.8). $14. (Auction #173, Lot 4).

SWIRL. Latticinio core. White latticinio core. Four bands, two each in two different color schemes. Nice marble. Germany. 21/32". Mint (9.9). $14. (Auction #94, Lot 18).

SWIRL. Latticinio core. White latticinio core swirl. Outer layer is three bands, all the same color scheme. Yellow, pink, green. 21/32". Mint(-) (9). $13. (Auction #160, Lot 18).

SWIRL. Latticinio core. Yellow latticinio core swirl. Four band outer layer. One small flake. Germany, circa 1870-1915. 9/16". Near Mint(+) (8.7). $13. (Auction #152, Lot 27).

SWIRL. Latticinio core. Yellow latticinio core swirl. Outer layer is four sets of orange and blue bands. Some flakes and pit. 25/32". Near Mint(+) (8.1). $13. (Auction #87, Lot 13).

SWIRL. Latticinio core. White latticinio core swirl. Six bands as the outer layer. Three are pink on white, three are green . 25/32". Mint(-) (9). $13. (Auction #169, Lot 41).

SWIRL. Latticinio core. Fat translucent white latticinio core. Outer layer is two bands of transparent blue and white. 9/16". Mint (9.9). $12. (Auction #100, Lot 11).

SWIRL. Latticinio core. White latticinio core. Four outer bands in two color schemes. One tiny manufacturing flat spot. Germany. 17/32". Mint(-) (9.1). $12. (Auction #61, Lot 23).

SWIRL. Latticinio core. White latticinio core swirl. Outer layer is three opaque red and opaque white bands. 23/32". Near Mint(+) (8.8). $12. (Auction #176, Lot 10).

SWIRL. Latticinio core. Peewee white latticinio core. Outer layer is three bands. A transparent blue, a transparent pink. 15/32". Mint (9.9). $12. (Auction #110, Lot 23).

SWIRL. Latticinio core. Translucent white latticinio core. Three outer bands of green on yellow. Surface in great shape. Germany. 17/32". Mint (9.9). $12. (Auction #122, Lot 40).

SWIRL. Latticinio core. White latticinio core swirl. Four outer bands. One melt spot. Germany, circa 1870-1915. 19/32". Mint (9.5). $11. (Auction #177, Lot 48).

SWIRL. Latticinio core. White latticinio core swirl. Outer layer is four bands. Two are orange on white, two are blue on white. 21/32". Mint (9.9). $10. (Auction #106, Lot 12).

SWIRL. Latticinio core. White latticinio core. Three outer bands, all same color scheme. Two tiny pinpricks. Germany. 9/16". Near Mint(+) (8.9). $10. (Auction #94, Lot 40).

SWIRL. Latticinio core. Peewee. Translucent white latticinio core. Two outer bands of transparent green edged by yellow. 1/2". Mint (9.9). $10. (Auction #84, Lot 38).

SWIRL. Latticinio core. Yellow latticinio core swirl. Four outer bands, all the same multicolor scheme. Two large melt spots. 25/32". Mint(-) (9). $10. (Auction #171, Lot 43).

SWIRL. Latticinio core. White latticinio core swirl. Three light blue outer bands alternating with three yellow outer bands. 9/16". Mint(-) (9). $9. (Auction #70, Lot 3).

SWIRL. Latticinio core. Lot of two marbles. Both are white latticinio cores. Both are hazy, with some tiny flakes. 1/2" & 9/16". $8. (Auction #54, Lot 2).

SWIRL. Latticinio core. English-type swirl. White latticinio core. The outer layer is on one side of the marble only. 5/8". Near Mint(+) (8.9). $8. (Auction #56, Lot 3).

SWIRL. Latticinio core. White latticinio core swirl. Outer layer is three transparent blue on whie bands and two orange ones. 21/32". Mint(-) (9.1). $7. (Auction #90, Lot 15).

SWIRL. Latticinio core. Peewee white latticinio core swirl. The core is shoved to one side of the marble. 15/32". Near Mint(+) (8.9). $5. (Auction #146, Lot 48).

SWIRL. Latticinio core. Pale yellow latticinio core. Four outer bands in two color schemes. Surface has several tiny pits. 21/32". Near Mint (8.6). $5. (Auction #90, Lot 3).

SWIRL. Latticino core. Superior marble. Latticinio core of alternating white and yellow strands. There is an elongated tear. 2". Mint (9.4). $420. (Auction #71, Lot 27).

SWIRL. Latticino core. Superb larger latticinio core swirl. Three-layer. Transparent, slightly smoky glass. 1-13/16". Mint (9.7). $260. (Auction #131, Lot 26).

SWIRL. Latticino core. Lot of six marbles. Four white latticinio core, two yellow. One is in light green glass. $95. (Auction #157, Lot 32).

SWIRL. Latticino core. Super white latticinio core shooter. Two pink outer bands, a green one and a blue one. 7/8". Mint (9.7). $56. (Auction #140, Lot 44).

SWIRL. Latticino core. Lot of two marbles. Matched pair of white latticino core swirls. Outer layer is three orange bands. $30. (Auction #157, Lot 9).

SWIRL. Latticino core. White latticinio core. Outer layer is three bands of light olive green and three bands of orange. 19/32". Mint (9.9). $24. (Auction #170, Lot 10).

SWIRL. Latticino core. Yellow latticinio core swirl. Outer layer is four blue on white bands alternating with four pink. 13/16". Near Mint(+) (8.8). $22. (Auction #172, Lot 47).

SWIRL. Latticino core. White core. Outer layer is three strands of orange, alternating with three strands of yellow. 9/16". Mint(-) (9.2). $17. (Auction #167, Lot 26).

SWIRL. Mist. I have to call this a mist swirl, for lack of a better categorization. Very unusual. Transparent clear. 23/32". Near Mint(+) (8.9). $65. (Auction #181, Lot 11).

SWIRL. Mist core. Another very rare marble. The core is a mist of stretched transparent blue bands. Very unusual. 13/16". Mint(-) (9). $45. (Auction #61, Lot 37).

SWIRL. Peppermint. Outstanding example of a peppermint swirl. Transparent clear base. Subsurface layer of opaque white. 25/32". Mint (9.8). $180. (Auction #96, Lot 41).

SWIRL. Peppermint. Superior example. Shooter size. One of the nicest I have seen a long time. Opaque white subsurface. 3/4". Near Mint(+) (8.9). $147. (Auction #147, Lot 37).

SWIRL. Peppermint. Beach ball type. Opaque white layer with two transparent blue bands and two transparent pink bands. 3/4". Near Mint(+) (8.9). $90. (Auction #77, Lot 25).

SWIRL. Peppermint. Very hard to find, end of cane peppermint swirl. Transparent clear base. One white panel. 21/32". Near Mint(+) (8.7). $80. (Auction #104, Lot 45).

SWIRL. Peppermint. Nice peppermint swirl. Harder marble to find. Opaque white subsurface layer. 21/32". Near Mint(+) (8.7). $75. (Auction #183, Lot 18).

SWIRL. Peppermint. End of cane peppermint swirl. Hard to find. Subsurface white layer. Two wide transparent blue bands. 21/32". Near Mint(+) (8). $65. (Auction #70, Lot 37).

SWIRL. Peppermint. Nice peppermint swirl. Harder marble to find. Opaque white subsurface layer. 21/32". Mint (9.4). $65. (Auction #65, Lot 3).

SWIRL. Peppermint. Nice example. Transparent clear base. Opaque white subsurface layer. Two bands of wide light blue. 9/16". Near Mint(+) (8.7). $55. (Auction #103, Lot 29).

SWIRL. Peppermint. Transparent base. Subsurface layer of opaque white. Two transparent blue bands and four narrow pink. 21/32". Near Mint(+) (8.7). $50. (Auction #120, Lot 17).

SWIRL. Peppermint. Nice peppermint swirl. Harder marble to find. Opaque white subsurface layer. Two transparent blue bands. 19/32". Near Mint(+) (8.9). $49. (Auction #98, Lot 36).

SWIRL. Peppermint. Beach ball type. Opaque white subsurface layer. Two bands of transparent blue. 25/32". Near Mint(+) (8.9). $48. (Auction #133, Lot 49).

SWIRL. Peppermint. Nice, smaller peppermint swirl. Two wide blue bands and four thin pink bands, on white. 9/16". Near Mint(+) (8.9). $45. (Auction #58, Lot 7).

SWIRL. Peppermint. Very nice peppermint swirl. Transparent clear base. Opaque white subsurface layer. 5/8". Near Mint(+) (8.9). $44. (Auction #112, Lot 34).

SWIRL. Peppermint. From near the end of the cane. Opaque white subsurface layer. One blue band, three pink bands on one. 7/8". Good(+) (7.70). $39. (Auction #185, Lot 37).

SWIRL. Peppermint. Opaque white subsurface layer. Two wide bands of transparent blue. 9/16". Near Mint(-) (8.1). $30. (Auction #133, Lot 2).

SWIRL. Peppermint. Nice peppermint swirl. Opaque white subsurface layer. Two dark transparent blue bands. Three pink bands. 9/16". Near Mint (8.5). $28. (Auction #177, Lot 43).

SWIRL. Peppermint. Transparent clear base. Opaque white subsurface layer. Two wide bands of transparent blue. 9/16". Near Mint (8.5). $27. (Auction #118, Lot 8).

SWIRL. Peppermint. Transparent clear base. Opaque white subsurface layer. Two wide bands of transparent blue. 5/8". Near Mint (8.6). $23. (Auction #115, Lot 15).

SWIRL. Peppermint. Subsurface layer of opaque white. Two wide blue bands, six narrow pink bands. 11/16". Collectible . $20. (Auction #128, Lot 16).

SWIRL. Peppermint with mica. Very rare peppermint swirl with mica. Transparent clear base. Subsurface layer of opaque white. 9/16". Near Mint(+) (8.8). $270. (Auction #85, Lot 43).

SWIRL. Ribbon. Superior, very hard to find, naked razor thin single ribbon core swirl. Outstanding marble. 27/32". Mint(-) (9). $160. (Auction #93, Lot 14).

SWIRL. Ribbon. Razor thin, naked single ribbon core swirl. Core is an opaque white center, with orange on one half. 19/32". Mint (9.6). $50. (Auction #154, Lot 10).

SWIRL. Ribbon. Single ribbon core swirl. Opaque white ribbon. Transparent pink band in the center of each face. 5/8". Mint(-) (9). $25. (Auction #112, Lot 38).

SWIRL. Ribbon core. Naked single ribbon core swirl. Outstanding design. Ribbon is thin. Opaque white, opaque yellow. 1-5/16". Near Mint (8.4). $310. (Auction #150, Lot 40).

SWIRL. Ribbon core. Outstanding example. Single ribbon. Razor thin. Wide. Transparent clear base. Ribbon is white, pink. 13/16". Mint(-) (9). $260. (Auction #167, Lot 48).

SWIRL. Ribbon core. Very hard to find large razor thin single ribbon core. This is a superior example. 1-3/4". Near Mint (8.6). $230. (Auction #102, Lot 50).

SWIRL. Ribbon core. Outstanding end of cane (first off cane) single ribbon core swirl. Transparent clear base. Opaque white. 13/16". Near Mint(+) (8.7). $175. (Auction #81, Lot 44).

SWIRL. Ribbon core. One of the rarest swirls I have ever seen. Naked single ribbon. The ribbon is triple twisted. 21/32". Near Mint (8.6). $170. (Auction #85, Lot 8).

SWIRL. Ribbon core. Rare, super end of cane (last-off-cane) three-layer caged single ribbon core swirl. 25/32". Mint (9.8). $160. (Auction #133, Lot 4).

SWIRL. Ribbon core. Rare double ribbon core swirl in transparent aqua green glass. Very difficult to find large swirls. 1-5/8". Near Mint(+) (8.1). $160. (Auction #101, Lot 18).

SWIRL. Ribbon core. Latticino in double ribbon core form. Two ribbons each consisting of white latticinio strands. 1-1/16". Near Mint(+) (8.9). $146. (Auction #162, Lot 40).

SWIRL. Ribbon core. Large single ribbon core swirl. Opaque white ribbon. Wide pink band one each face, green band on each. $140. (Auction #181, Lot 27).

SWIRL. Ribbon core. Hard to find large double ribbon core swirl. Exceptional design and workmanship. 1-15/16". Near Mint(-) (8). $130. (Auction #122, Lot 16).

SWIRL. Ribbon core. Hard to find large double ribbon core swirl. Exceptional design and workmanship. 1-15/16". Near Mint(-) (8). $110. (Auction #157, Lot 16).

SWIRL. Ribbon core. Stunning start of cane ribbon core. This marble is from near the beginning of the cane. 27/32". Mint (9.4). $100. (Auction #82, Lot 25).

SWIRL. Ribbon core. Single ribbon core swirl. Very unusual. Opaque white core. Flat core. 21/32". Mint (9.9). $95. (Auction #160, Lot 30).

SWIRL. Ribbon core. Gorgeous naked ribbon core swirl. 9/16". Mint (9.9). $95. (Auction #70, Lot 39).

SWIRL. Ribbon core. Stunning start of cane ribbon core. This marble is from near the beginning of the cane. 27/32". Mint (9.4). $95. (Auction

#59, Lot 41).

SWIRL. Ribbon core. Superior razor-thin naked single ribbon core swirl. Opaque white ribbon. Yellow in the center of each. 13/16". Near Mint(+) (8.9). $95. (Auction #131, Lot 49).

SWIRL. Ribbon core. Outstanding naked ribbon core swirl. Transparent clear base. Fat ribbon. 11/16". Mint (9.9). $80. (Auction #136, Lot 44).

SWIRL. Ribbon core. Gorgeous ribbon core swirl. Polished marble. Double ribbon core. One is green on yellow, other is blue. $80. (Auction #152, Lot 41).

SWIRL. Ribbon core. Very hard to find first-off-cane ribbon core swirl. Transparent very lightly tinted blue base. 21/32". Mint(-) (9). $76. (Auction #134, Lot 32).

SWIRL. Ribbon core. Very odd double ribbon core swirl. Probably from near the end of the cane. The core is brightly colored. 1-7/16". Near Mint(+) (8.1). $75. (Auction #63, Lot 19).

SWIRL. Ribbon core. Super example. Double ribbon core swirl. One ribbon is yellow with a band of bright orange on half. 7/8". Mint (9.3). $75. (Auction #153, Lot 46).

SWIRL. Ribbon core. Single ribbon core. Center is a blue band. Edged by white bands. The outer edge is very interesting. 25/32". Near Mint(-) (8.1). $65. (Auction #168, Lot 34).

SWIRL. Ribbon core. Caged single ribbon core. Core is opaque white. Green band on one face, blue band on the other. $55. (Auction #183, Lot 46).

SWIRL. Ribbon core. Naked single ribbon core. Opaque white ribbon. Each side has two bands of transparent pink. 11/16". Mint(-) (9.1). $55. (Auction #116, Lot 26).

SWIRL. Ribbon core. Naked razor thin ribbon core swirl. Core is opaque white, yellow, pink and green. Super core. 11/16". Near Mint(+) (8.8). $50. (Auction #133, Lot 47).

SWIRL. Ribbon core. Double ribbon core swirl. One ribbon is yellow with green and pink. The other is white with blue. 13/16". Near Mint(+) (8.9). $50. (Auction #92, Lot 37).

SWIRL. Ribbon core. Razor thin, single ribbon core. Ribbon is a combination of transparent pink, transparent blue. 13/16". Near Mint(+) (8.9). $50. (Auction #183, Lot 41).

SWIRL. Ribbon core. Lot of three swirls. All are ribbon core. Single ribbon, polished, chips remain, 1-1/4". Single ribbon. $50. (Auction #101, Lot 22).

SWIRL. Ribbon core. Hard to find naked single ribbon core swirl. Razor think ribbon. White center, with red on one edge. 25/32". Near Mint(+) (8.7). $50. (Auction #88, Lot 40).

SWIRL. Ribbon core. Super razor thin naked ribbon core swirl. Transparent clear base. Single ribbon of transparent blue. 11/16". Mint(-) (9.1). $48. (Auction #98, Lot 45).

SWIRL. Ribbon core. One of the most unusual ribbon cores I have ever seen. Inner core is a single ribbon. 25/32". Near Mint (8.3). $48. (Auction #84, Lot 43).

SWIRL. Ribbon core. Peewee double ribbon core swirl. Two opaque white ribbons. One has pink at either edge. 15/32". Mint (9.9). $46. (Auction #137, Lot 11).

SWIRL. Ribbon core. Naked double ribbon core swirl. Both ribbons are the same pattern of yellow, green, red and blue. 5/8". Mint (9.7). $44. (Auction #185, Lot 43).

SWIRL. Ribbon core. Beautiful double ribbon core swirl. Each ribbon consists of a white band, orange band and yellow band. 5/8". Mint (9.9). $42. (Auction #103, Lot 25).

SWIRL. Ribbon core. Lot of four marbles. All are ribbon cores. Shooter size. Assorted colors and designs. All have damage. $42. (Auction #144, Lot 39).

SWIRL. Ribbon core. Fat single ribbon core. Opaque yellow ribbon. Transparent pink band in the center. 3/4". Near Mint(+) (8.9). $42. (Auction #75, Lot 43).

SWIRL. Ribbon core. Super small ribbon core. Single ribbon. Yellow ribbon with pink and green bands. Caged outer layer. 9/16". Mint (9.9). $42. (Auction #145, Lot 11).

SWIRL. Ribbon core. Fat single ribbon core. Opaque yellow with two green bands on each face and a pink band on each edge. 13/16". Near Mint(+) (8.9). $42. (Auction #158, Lot 36).

SWIRL. Ribbon core. Naked single ribbon core. Fat opaque white core with two transparent pink bands. 23/32". Near Mint(+) (8.9). $41. (Auction #142, Lot 39).

SWIRL. Ribbon core. Double ribbon core swirl. Two ribbons. One is yellow with pink and green. $40. (Auction #137, Lot 17).

SWIRL. Ribbon core. Excellent example. Single ribbon core. Opaque yellow core. A pink bnad on either face. 11/16". Mint(-) (9.1). $40. (Auction #160, Lot 33).

SWIRL. Ribbon core. Double ribbon core swirl with a caged outer layer. One ribbon is opaque white with a wide band of blue. 13/16". Near Mint (8.6). $37. (Auction #142, Lot 10).

SWIRL. Ribbon core. Single narrow ribbon core. Core is pink on white. Outer layer is three narrow yellow bands. 11/16". Mint (9.9). $37. (Auction #165, Lot 48).

SWIRL. Ribbon core. Double ribbon core swirl. Each ribbon is semi-opaque white with a transparent blue band. 15/16". Near Mint(+) (8.9). $37. (Auction #116, Lot 10).

SWIRL. Ribbon core. Three layer single ribbon core. Opaque core, although the ribbon is open on one side. Strands of blue. 9/16". Mint (9.7). $35. (Auction #119, Lot 5).

SWIRL. Ribbon core. Rare latticinio in double ribbon form. Ribbons are white latticinio strands. 17/32". Mint (9.8). $35. (Auction #170, Lot 33).

SWIRL. Ribbon core. Very nice ribbon core. Single ribbon. Opaque white with pink edges and a blue band in the center. 3/4'. Near Mint(+) (8.7). $35. (Auction #56, Lot 32).

SWIRL. Ribbon core. Hard to find naked single ribbon core swirl. Razor think ribbon. White center, with red on one edge. 25/32". Near Mint(+) (8.7). $35. (Auction #60, Lot 40).

SWIRL. Ribbon core. Stunning English-style double ribbon core swirl. The core has two ribbons. One is one-half yellow. 5/8". Near Mint(+) (8.9). $35. (Auction #59, Lot 9).

SWIRL. Ribbon core. Outstanding double ribbon core. One ribbon is pink on white, the other is green on white. Wide space. 21/32". Mint (9.7). $30. (Auction #173, Lot 21).

SWIRL. Ribbon core. Single ribbon core swirl Opaque white ribbon. Transparent pink band in the center, transparent green. 5/8". Near Mint(+) (8.8). $30. (Auction #75, Lot 41).

SWIRL. Ribbon core. From near the end of the cane, possibly first-off-cane. Thin opaque white single ribbon. $30. (Auction #176, Lot 8).

SWIRL. Ribbon core. Naked double ribbon core. From near an end of the cane. Transparent clear base. Two ribbons. 1/2". Mint (9.9). $29. (Auction #80, Lot 31). ·

SWIRL. Ribbon core. Double ribbon core swirl. From near an end of the cane. Each ribbon is opaque white. 9/16". Mint (9.9). $28. (Auction #167, Lot 19).

SWIRL. Ribbon core. Naked single ribbon core. Fat opaque white core with two transparent pink bands. 25/32". Near Mint (8.5). $28. (Auction #141, Lot 11).

SWIRL. Ribbon core. Fat single ribbon core. Opaque white core. Two blue bands on each face, pink band on each edge. 5/8". Mint(-) (9.2). $27. (Auction #157, Lot 20).

SWIRL. Ribbon core. Single ribbon core swirl. Core is opaque white with pink strands on the faces. 13/16". Mint (9.9). $25. (Auction #128, Lot 11).

SWIRL. Ribbon core. Nice smaller single ribbon core swirl. Opaque fat single white ribbon. One edge has a pink band. 9/16". Mint (9.4). $15. (Auction #112, Lot 9).

SWIRL. Ribbon core. Peewee. Possibly a solid core missing a panel or else a double ribbon core. 1/2". Mint (9.9). $15. (Auction #82, Lot 11).

SWIRL. Ribbon core. Lot of two marbles. Matched pair of naked single ribbon core swirl shooters. Hard pair to find. $14. (Auction #94, Lot 5).

SWIRL. Solid core. Superior first-off-cane "flower-type" end of cane solid core. Stunning marble. 3/4". Mint (9.4). $400. (Auction #91, Lot 38).

SWIRL. Solid core. A superb three layer caged solid core swirl. Very large marble. Opaque white solid core. 2-1/8". Near Mint(+) (8.9). $380. (Auction #147, Lot 39).

SWIRL. Solid core. Lot of ten marbles. An unbelievable set of ten matched solid core swirls, all off the same cane. $350. (Auction #178, Lot 50).

SWIRL. Solid core. Very unusual marble. Transparent green/blue glass. Solid core of four panels, two different color schemes. 2-7/16". Good (7.50). $295. (Auction #165, Lot 21).

SWIRL. Solid core. Extremely rare, huge, three layer, solid core, from near the end of the cane. 2-1/16". Near Mint(+) (8.9). $275. (Auction #100, Lot 49).

SWIRL. Solid core. Superior three layer solid core swirl. Outstanding example. Opaque white core. 1-5/8". Mint(-) (9.2). $250. (Auction #172, Lot 50).

SWIRL. Solid core. Superior example of an end-of-cane (last-off-cane) swirl. Opaque white core with two bands of blue. 11/16". Mint (9.9). $210. (Auction #168, Lot 9).

SWIRL. Solid core. Super cage style larger swirl. Opaque yellow core. Outer layer is eight orange bands. 1-1/8". Mint (9.8). $190. (Auction

#126, Lot 49).

SWIRL. Solid core. Huge three-layer solid core. Fat opaque white core. Middle layer is four bands of translucent colors. $180. (Auction #115, Lot 19).

SWIRL. Solid core. Superb end of cane (last off cane) solid core swirl. Opaque white core. Two panels of transparent red. 1-3/8". Near Mint(+) (8.9). $175. (Auction #148, Lot 42).

SWIRL. Solid core. Very unusual swirl, from near the start of the cane. Four panel core. Two are pink on white. 2-1/16". Near Mint (8.4). $160. (Auction #121, Lot 48).

SWIRL. Solid core. This is an extremely rare marble. Not only is it a left hand twist swirl (!!), but it is in light blue. 23/32". Mint(-) (9.1). $160. (Auction #61, Lot 45).

SWIRL. Solid core. Lot of seven marbles. Outstanding matched set of seven marbles, probably same cane. Opaque white core. $150. (Auction #170, Lot 44).

SWIRL. Solid core. Very rare marble. Naked solid core in colored glass. Transparent aquamarine blue/green base. 25/32". Mint (9.5). $150. (Auction #69, Lot 44).

SWIRL. Solid core. Yet another three layer solid core swirl. And this one is large! Opaque yellow core. 1-11/16". Near Mint(+) (8.8). $150. (Auction #117, Lot 21).

SWIRL. Solid core. Large solid core swirl, from near an end of the cane. Opaque white core with alternating pink and blue. 2". Near Mint (8.4). $110. (Auction #182, Lot 29).

SWIRL. Solid core. Outstanding looking marble. Rare design. Fat opaque white core. Three deep lobes. 1-7/16". Near Mint(-) (8.1). $110. (Auction #181, Lot 24).

SWIRL. Solid core. End of cane (first-off-cane) solid core swirl. Opaque yellow and white core. Two bands of pink. 13/16". Mint(-) (9.2). $110. (Auction #168, Lot 44).

SWIRL. Solid core. Subtle five-layer solid core swirl. Opaque white core. Floating above that are opaque red bands. 1-9/16". Near Mint (8.3). $110. (Auction #151, Lot 28).

SWIRL. Solid core. Superb solid core swirl. One of the nicest around this size that I have seen in a long time. 15/16". Mint (9.8). $110. (Auction #67, Lot 42).

SWIRL. Solid core. Opaque white four-panel core. Two panels are opaque orange, one transparent blue, one transparent green. 1-9/16". Near Mint (8.6). $100. (Auction #117, Lot 24).

SWIRL. Solid core. Superior design and execution. Needs a very light buff. Opaque white core covered with transparent pink. 1-5/8". Near Mint(+) (8.7). $100. (Auction #95, Lot 17).

SWIRL. Solid core. Three layer solid core swirl. Opaque white core. Middle layer is two transparent bands. 1-7/8". Good(+) (7.90). $100. (Auction #165, Lot 26).

SWIRL. Solid core. Lot of three marbles. Matched set off the same cane. Translucent white core. $100. (Auction #173, Lot 19).

SWIRL. Solid core. Superior solid core swirl. Three panels, each the same color scheme. Each panel is alternating lavender. 13/16". Mint (9.6). $100. (Auction #184, Lot 13).

SWIRL. Solid core. Superior solid core swirl. Core is three panels of the same width. One is white, one is orange. 13/16". Mint(-) (9.1). $95. (Auction #124, Lot 44).

SWIRL. Solid core. Solid core swirl. Core consists of four panels in two different color schemes. Some clear spaces. 1-3/8". Mint(-) (9). $95. (Auction #89, Lot 19).

SWIRL. Solid core. Superior end of cane swirl. Last off cane. Opaque white core with complex bands of green/pink and blue. 13/16". Mint (9.6). $95. (Auction #160, Lot 35).

SWIRL. Solid core. Very pretty solid core swirl. Opaque white core with four transparent pink bands. 7/8". Mint (9.9). $90. (Auction #110, Lot 45).

SWIRL. Solid core. A beauty. Thin three-lobe solid core. Opaque white core. Blue in each trough, pink on each peak. $90. (Auction #157, Lot 21).

SWIRL. Solid core. Nice solid core. Opaque white core. Four panels. Two are pink bands, two are blue bands. 1-7/16". Near Mint(+) (8.9). $85. (Auction #137, Lot 41).

SWIRL. Solid core. Very pretty naked solid core, in a larger size for this type. Opaque white core with light blue strands. 1-1/16". Mint(-) (9.2). $85. (Auction #109, Lot 17).

SWIRL. Solid core. Super end-of-cane (last off cane) solid core swirl. Yellow core with two pink bands and two blue. 3/4". Near Mint(+) (8.9). $85. (Auction #92, Lot 27).

SWIRL. Solid core. Lot of two marbles. Matched pair off the same cane. Rare set. Nice caged solid core swirl. Opaque white. Near Mint(+) . $80. (Auction #160, Lot 14).

SWIRL. Solid core. Unusual. These colored types are hard to find. Was meant to be a solid core. 1-5/16". Near Mint (8.4). $75. (Auction #181, Lot 4).

SWIRL. Solid core. Beautiful solid core swirl. Opaque yellow core. Three transparent pink bands and three transparent green. 25/32". Mint(-) (9). $75. (Auction #118, Lot 23).

SWIRL. Solid core. Three layer solid core swirl. Opaque white core. Middle layer is four bands. 1-1/2". Near Mint(-) (8.2). $75. (Auction #146, Lot 21).

SWIRL. Solid core. A very nice lobed solid core. Opaque white core. Three lobes. Pink on the peak of each lobe. 1-1/16". Near Mint(+) (8.8). $70. (Auction #58, Lot 11).

SWIRL. Solid core. Rare solid core swirl in colored glass. Base glass is transparent teal. Core is translucent yellow. 1/2". Mint (9.7). $70. (Auction #106, Lot 40).

SWIRL. Solid core. Lot of two marbles. Match pair of latticinio core swirls, off the same cane. Both are white core. $70. (Auction #126, Lot 17).

SWIRL. Solid core. Outstanding three-layer solid core swirl. Opaque white core with four blue bands on it. 29/32". Mint(-) (9.1). $67. (Auction #167, Lot 39).

SWIRL. Solid core. Very nice solid core swirl. Core is opaque yellow. Two bands of green and two of red. 1-1/16". Near Mint(+) (8.8). $66. (Auction #104, Lot 15).

SWIRL. Solid core. Interesting. May be English. Transparent very light green base. Semi-opaque narrow white core. 29/32". Mint(-) (9.1). $65. (Auction #181, Lot 15).

SWIRL. Solid core. Nice caged solid core swirl. Core is opaque white with three bands each of transparent pink. 1-5/8". Near Mint(-) (8.2). $65. (Auction #151, Lot 13).

SWIRL. Solid core. Three-lobe solid core swirl. Shallow lobes. Pink and green band on each peak (one is missing the pink). 1". Mint (9.8). $65. (Auction #159, Lot 16).

SWIRL. Solid core. Nice solid core swirl. Opaque white core with bands of blue on it. Cage of white strands. 1-3/16". Near Mint(+) (8.7). $65. (Auction #92, Lot 5).

SWIRL. Solid core. Opaque white core with red bands. Outer layer is a cage of yellow strands. Surface has been polished. $65. (Auction #157, Lot 24).

SWIRL. Solid core. Lot of two marbles. Matched pair off the same cane. Opaque white core. Four outer bands. Two are red. $65. (Auction #169, Lot 37).

SWIRL. Solid core. English type. Thin core consisting of three panels of the same color scheme. 19/32". Mint (9.9). $65. (Auction #83, Lot 34).

SWIRL. Solid core. Lot of two marbles. Very hard to find pair of matched English type naked solid core swirls. $65. (Auction #58, Lot 35).

SWIRL. Solid core. Hard to find lobed solid core. Opaque white core. Four lobes. Two lobe troughs have transparent pink. 23/32". Mint(-) (9). $65. (Auction #66, Lot 42).

SWIRL. Solid core. English type. Translucent white core. Outer layer is eight equidistantly spaced bands. 21/32". Mint (9.9). $65. (Auction #85, Lot 5).

SWIRL. Solid core. Lot of two marbles. Matched pair off the same cane. Both are lobed solid core swirls. $61. (Auction #172, Lot 36).

SWIRL. Solid core. Superb lobed solid core. Translucent white core. Four lobes. 23/32". Mint (9.9). $60. (Auction #93, Lot 5).

SWIRL. Solid core. Outstanding marble!! Solid core swirl with three very deep lobes, creating razor thin peaks. 11/16". Near Mint(+) (8.9). $60. (Auction #102, Lot 17).

SWIRL. Solid core. Peewee. Opaque white core with two bands of pink and two of blue. Outer layer is sets of white strands. 15/32". Mint (9.9). $60. (Auction #84, Lot 28).

SWIRL. Solid core. Stunning English type solid core. Core is three panels. Very subtle combination. 5/8". Mint (9.9). $60. (Auction #118, Lot 17).

SWIRL. Solid core. Lot of two marbles. Excellent matched pair of English swirls. Translucent white core. $60. (Auction #123, Lot 14).

SWIRL. Solid core. A very pretty solid core swirl. Opaque white core with seven blue strands and seven pink strands. $60. (Auction #155, Lot 9).

SWIRL. Solid core. Complex three-layer solid core swirl. Opaque white core. Middle layer is four bands. 1-5/8". Good(+) (7.90). $55. (Auction #155, Lot 20).

SWIRL. Solid core. English style colors. Three panel core. Each panel is orange, blue, white and green. 21/32". Mint (9.9). $55. (Auction #84, Lot 36).

SWIRL. Solid core. Superior three layer solid core. Simplistic colors and designs, but it creates an outstanding marble. 25/32". Mint (9.8).

$55. (Auction #136, Lot 19).

SWIRL. Solid core. Solid core swirl. Core is four panels two are opaque red on opaque yellow and two are opaque light blue. 1-3/8". Near Mint (8.5). $55. (Auction #89, Lot 13).

SWIRL. Solid core. Really nice naked solid core swirl. Interesting core of peach, orange, yellow and transparent lavender. 9/16". Mint (9.9). $55. (Auction #63, Lot 3).

SWIRL. Solid core. Unusual solid core swirl, very well designed. Opaque yellow core. There are three bands on the core. 31/32". Mint(-) (9.1). $55. (Auction #168, Lot 46).

SWIRL. Solid core. Lot of two marbles. A very hard to find matched pair of lobed solid core swirls, off the same cane. $55. (Auction #60, Lot 42).

SWIRL. Solid core. Naked solid core swirl. Opaque white base. Thin bands of trasparent light blue. 21/32". Mint (9.9). $55. (Auction #59, Lot 2).

SWIRL. Solid core. Very unusual coloring to this one. Opaque white core. Two strands of yellow on the core and two of blue. 7/8". Near Mint(+) (8.8). $55. (Auction #173, Lot 36).

SWIRL. Solid core. Super caged marble. Core is opaque white with two bands of transparent light blue. 11/16". Mint(-) (9). $55. (Auction #103, Lot 27).

SWIRL. Solid core. Lobed solid core swirl. Opaque white core. Three deep lobes. Pink strand floating above each lobe. 31/32". Near Mint(+) (8.8). $55. (Auction #163, Lot 34).

SWIRL. Solid core. Lot of two marbles. Both are solid core swirls. One is a thin core and caged. $55. (Auction #152, Lot 9).

SWIRL. Solid core. Superior end of cane solid core swirl. Fat core. Translucent white with two panels of transparent blue. 7/8". Near Mint(+) (8.9). $55. (Auction #156, Lot 43).

SWIRL. Solid core. Lot of three marbles. Nice assortment. All are pretty. Each has some damage. 5/8" to 3/4". Near Mint. $51. (Auction #152, Lot 30).

SWIRL. Solid core. Exceptional three-layer solid core swirl. I would have to say that this is a definitive example!! 3/4". Mint(-) (9.2). $51. (Auction #117, Lot 10).

SWIRL. Solid core. Very nice solid core swirl. Core is opaque yellow. Two bands of green and two of red. 1-1/16". Near Mint(+) (8.8). $51. (Auction #58, Lot 14).

SWIRL. Solid core. Very unusual marble. Technically a three layer. Core is opaque white and very fat, almost subsurface. 27/32". Mint(-) (9.3). $51. (Auction #100, Lot 40).

SWIRL. Solid core. Super English type solid core swirl. Opaque white core. Outer layer is four orange strands. 11/16". Mint (9.9). $50. (Auction #91, Lot 11).

SWIRL. Solid core. Gorgeous marble. Opaque white core. Shallow lobing. Four lobes. Two have transparent pink in the troughs. 23/32". Mint (9.9). $50. (Auction #142, Lot 25).

SWIRL. Solid core. Hard to find four-layer solid core swirl. Opaque yellow core. Six tranparent pink narrow bands. 19/32". Mint (9.5). $50. (Auction #137, Lot 19).

SWIRL. Solid core. Nice, slightly lobed, solid core swirl. Opaque white base. Four very shallow lobes. 29/32". Mint(-) (9). $50. (Auction #96, Lot 15).

SWIRL. Solid core. Lot of three marbles. All are solid core. Each is a white core with two pink bands and a blue. $50. (Auction #174, Lot 32).

SWIRL. Solid core. Rare four layer solid core swirl. Opaque yellow core. Next layer is four transparent pink bands. 19/32". Mint (9.5). $50. (Auction #88, Lot 17).

SWIRL. Solid core. Super three layer solid core swirl. Opaque white base. The middle layer is four bands. 21/32". Mint (9.7). $50. (Auction #113, Lot 48).

SWIRL. Solid core. Lot of two marbles. Both are solid core. Different colors. 1-1/4" & Near Mint(-). 1-1/4" & Good(+). $50. (Auction #108, Lot 34).

SWIRL. Solid core. Very narrow core. White core with pink bands. Outer layer is six bands in two color schemes. $50. (Auction #157, Lot 27).

SWIRL. Solid core. Opaque yellow core. Outer layer is two bands of white strands edged by pink. 3/4". Near Mint(+) (8.9). $50. (Auction #124, Lot 34).

SWIRL. Solid core. Peewee naked solid core swirl. Opaque white core. Two blue bands, two black bands. Odd. Germany. 15/32". Mint (9.9). $50. (Auction #157, Lot 28).

SWIRL. Solid core. Stunning smaller marble. Opaque white core. Cage of transparent green strands on it. 17/32". Mint (9.9). $50. (Auction #136, Lot 42).

SWIRL. Solid core. Three-layer lobed solid core swirl. Rare marble. Core is opaque yellow. Four deep lobes. 11/16". Near Mint(+) (8.8). $49. (Auction #134, Lot 7).

SWIRL. Solid core. Lot of two marbles. Nice pair of matched solid core swirls. Both are translucent white cores. $49. (Auction #107, Lot 12).

SWIRL. Solid core. Gorgeous naked solid core swirl. Core is alternating panels of opaque baby blue and transparent green. 21/32". Mint (9.9). $49. (Auction #82, Lot 39).

SWIRL. Solid core. Very interesting marble. Opaque white core. Two bands of transparent blue and two of transparent green. 13/16". Near Mint(+) (8.9). $48. (Auction #145, Lot 14).

SWIRL. Solid core. Excellent marble. Opaque white core. Pink strands on the core. Outer layer is five bright yellow strands. 25/32". Near Mint(+) (8.9). $48. (Auction #147, Lot 10).

SWIRL. Solid core. Lot of four marbles. Two matched sets. Translucent white core. $47. (Auction #178, Lot 42).

SWIRL. Solid core. Super cage-style, three-layer solid core swirl. Opaque white core. 5/8". Mint (9.9). $46. (Auction #105, Lot 39).

SWIRL. Solid core. Very nice solid core. Core is four-lobed. Opaque white. Transparent pink strand on each lobe peak. 21/32". Mint(-) (9). $46. (Auction #126, Lot 12).

SWIRL. Solid core. Very nice naked solid core swirl. Fat core. Four transparent cobalt blue panels. 9/16". Mint (9.9). $45. (Auction #113, Lot 14).

SWIRL. Solid core. Super three layer solid core swirl. Opaque white core. Middle layer is four transparent pink bands. 21/32". Mint (9.8). $45. (Auction #91, Lot 35).

SWIRL. Solid core. Lot of two marbles. Matched set of solid core swirls, off the same cane. Opaque yellow core. $45. (Auction #146, Lot 41).

SWIRL. Solid core. Core is transparent pink on opaque white. Outer layer is two bands of transparent blue on white. 11/16". (9.6). $45. (Auction #93, Lot 32).

SWIRL. Solid core. Translucent yellow core. Subsurface outer layer of three bands of transparent blue and white. 7/8". Mint (9.5). $45. (Auction #117, Lot 47).

SWIRL. Solid core. A real beauty. Opaque yellow core covered by transparent pink strands. Outer layer is a cage of yellow. 17/32". Mint (9.7). $44. (Auction #91, Lot 33).

SWIRL. Solid core. Three layer solid core swirl. Opaque white core. Middle layer is six pink strands. $44. (Auction #67, Lot 35).

SWIRL. Solid core. Lot of three marbles. All are peewee solid core. Nice assortment. 15/32" to 1/2". Mint (9.9). $44. (Auction #115, Lot 36).

SWIRL. Solid core. Very nice naked solid core swirl. Core consists of panels of transparent blue, opaque yellow. 9/16". Mint (9.9). $43. (Auction #103, Lot 2).

SWIRL. Solid core. Naked solid core swirl. Core is panels of opaque white, opaque yellow, transparent blue. 21/32". Mint (9.9). $42. (Auction #95, Lot 30).

SWIRL. Solid core. Super looking solid core. Core consists of transparent dark blue panels alternating with opaque white. 3/4". Mint (9.9). $42. (Auction #100, Lot 36).

SWIRL. Solid core. Lot of two marbles. Both are peewee solid core. Nice pair in great shape. Germany, circa 1870-1915. $42. (Auction #95, Lot 32).

SWIRL. Solid core. Interesting solid core. Opaque yellow core. Outer layer is three bands of red, with one blue edge. 1-7/16". Good(+) (7.70). $42. (Auction #161, Lot 13).

SWIRL. Solid core. Naked solid core swirl. Excellent core. Five bands of transparent blue. 9/16". Mint (9.9). $40. (Auction #77, Lot 30).

SWIRL. Solid core. Nice end of cane (last-off-cane) swirl. Core is four panels in two different color schemes. 13/16". Near Mint (8.3). $40. (Auction #107, Lot 41).

SWIRL. Solid core. Nice example of a three-layer. Semi-opaque white core. 3/4". Mint(-) (9.1). $40. (Auction #181, Lot 32).

SWIRL. Solid core. End of cane solid core. Very nice marble. Core is opaque white with pink and blue bands. 29/32". Near Mint(+) (8.7). $40. (Auction #56, Lot 28).

SWIRL. Solid core. Very nice naked solid core swirl. Core is four yellow/orange bands, alternating with four white bands. 11/16". Mint (9.7). $39. (Auction #149, Lot 3).

SWIRL. Solid core. Beautiful naked solid core swirl. Opaque white core with two opaque orange bands, one transparent green. 25/32". Mint (9.9). $39. (Auction #98, Lot 7).

SWIRL. Solid core. Translucent yellow core. Outer layer is two pink bands edged by white, one blue band edged by white. 9/16". Mint (9.9). $39. (Auction #120, Lot 12).

SWIRL. Solid core. English type. Opaque red core. Outer layer is three blue bands alternating with three white bands. 21/32". Near Mint (8.3). $39. (Auction #185, Lot 31).

SWIRL. Solid core. Core is four panels, two of two different color schemes. Outer layer is two sets of white strands. 1-7/8". Good (7.40). $38. (Auction #161, Lot 28).

SWIRL. Solid core. Beautiful solid core swirl. Core is bands of white, orange, light blue, yellow and light green. 23/32". Mint (9.5). $38. (Auction #185, Lot 20).

SWIRL. Solid core. Narrow opaque yellow core with transparent pink bands. Outer layer is four sets of white strands. 27/32". Mint (9.9). $38. (Auction #128, Lot 41).

SWIRL. Solid core. Super solid core swirl. Core is opaque white. 23/32". Mint (9.9). $37. (Auction #116, Lot 39).

SWIRL. Solid core. Lobed solid core swirl. Opaque white core. Four deep lobes. Transparent pink band on each lobe peak. 23/32". Near Mint(+) (8.9). $37. (Auction #154, Lot 39).

SWIRL. Solid core. Lot of two marbles. Matched pair, off the same cane. Opaque white core. Two bands of pink. $37. (Auction #181, Lot 36).

SWIRL. Solid core. Three layer solid core swirl. Opaque white core. Middle layer is four pink strands. 9/16". Mint (9.9). $37. (Auction #88, Lot 9).

SWIRL. Solid core. Outstanding solid core swirl. Swirl consists of twenty bands of color. 13/16". Mint (9.5). $37. (Auction #110, Lot 34).

SWIRL. Solid core. I've classified this as a solid core, but it is highly unusual. Transparent clear base. 11/16". Near Mint(+) (8.8). $37. (Auction #118, Lot 48).

SWIRL. Solid core. Three layer solid core swirl. Fat opaque white core. Middle layer is three bands of transparent blue. 3/4". Mint (9.9). $36. (Auction #184, Lot 21).

SWIRL. Solid core. Solid core swirl. Core is opaque white and transparent blue. Outer layer is six bands of red. 19/32". Near Mint(+) (8.9). $36. (Auction #93, Lot 38).

SWIRL. Solid core. English colors. Opaque yellow core. Outer layer is three bands of white. 21/32". Mint (9.9). $36. (Auction #146, Lot 35).

SWIRL. Solid core. Opaque yellow core with pink strands on it. Outer layer is a cage of white strands. A beauty. Germany. 9/16". Mint (9.9). $36. (Auction #185, Lot 28).

SWIRL. Solid core. Interesting core. Three wide panels, each bordered by a yellow strands. Each panel is opaque white. 3/4". Mint(-) (9). $35. (Auction #129, Lot 28).

SWIRL. Solid core. Interesting solid core swirl. Opaque white core. Four lobes. Transparent pink band in two lobes. 27/32". Mint (9.8). $35. (Auction #167, Lot 31).

SWIRL. Solid core. Nice peewee solid core swirl. Core is assorted bands and strands. Some of the bands are transparent. 15/32". Mint (9.8). $34. (Auction #184, Lot 33).

SWIRL. Solid core. Three layer solid core. Opaque white core. Middle layer is three transparent pink bands. 5/8". Mint (9.9). $34. (Auction #106, Lot 42).

SWIRL. Solid core. Translucent yellow core. Outer layer is six bands: three each of two different color schemes. 3/4". Mint (9.5). $34. (Auction #126, Lot 14).

SWIRL. Solid core. Opaque white core. Two transparent pink bands and two transparent dark blue bands on it. 21/32". Mint (9.9). $34. (Auction #64, Lot 3).

SWIRL. Solid core. Naked solid core swirl. Core is four wide panels of opaque orange. 21/32". Mint (9.8). $33. (Auction #142, Lot 31).

SWIRL. Solid core. Narrow core. Solid white. Four shallow lobes. Two are pink, one green, one blue. 25/32". Mint (9.5). $33. (Auction #137, Lot 23).

SWIRL. Solid core. Naked solid core swirl. Opaque white core. Two bands of opaque orange on it, two of transparent green. 11/16". Mint(-) (9.2). $33. (Auction #162, Lot 30).

SWIRL. Solid core. Superior lobed solid core swirl. Opaque white core. Three very deep lobes. Pink band at the peak. 9/16". Mint (9.9). $33. (Auction #145, Lot 28).

SWIRL. Solid core. Lot of two marbles. Both are English type solid core. Each has an opaque white core. $33. (Auction #144, Lot 11).

SWIRL. Solid core. From near the end of the cane. Thin core. White base with green, pink and blue bands. 13/16". Mint (9.6). $33. (Auction #74, Lot 31).

SWIRL. Solid core. Nice swirl with a fat solid core. Core is opaque white with three pink bands. 21/32". Mint (9.9). $33. (Auction #89, Lot 2).

SWIRL. Solid core. Core is opaque white with alternating bands of transparent purple and pink. 11/16". Mint (9.9). $32. (Auction #139, Lot 7).

SWIRL. Solid core. Lobed solid core swirl. Opaque white core. Three lobes. Each lobe trough has a transparent pink band. 21/32". Mint(-) (9). $32. (Auction #140, Lot 10).

SWIRL. Solid core. Opaque white core. Outer layer is a cage of three transparent blue bands. 29/32". Mint(-) (9.1). $32. (Auction #119, Lot 47).

SWIRL. Solid core. Interesting solid core. End of cane. Transparent green core with four opaque white strands on it. 25/32". Near Mint (8.6). $32. (Auction #160, Lot 5).

SWIRL. Solid core. Opaque white core. Outer layer is four bands. Two are blue with white, two are pink with yellow. 7/8". Mint(-) (9.2). $32. (Auction #131, Lot 19).

SWIRL. Solid core. Caged solid core. Opaque white core. Three blue strands on it and one pale green band. 7/8". Near Mint(+) (8.7). $32. (Auction #153, Lot 35).

SWIRL. Solid core. Opaque white core. Two bands of orange on it, and two of transparent blue. 11/16". Mint (9.7). $32. (Auction #149, Lot 42).

SWIRL. Solid core. Opaque yellow core with two pink bands and two green bands on it. Outer layer is four yellow strands. 7/8". Mint(-) (9). $31. (Auction #57, Lot 36).

SWIRL. Solid core. Nice English solid core. Core is only half closed. Yellow, light blue, white and orange. 9/16". Mint (9.9). $31. (Auction #64, Lot 5).

SWIRL. Solid core. English type solid core swirl. Orange core. Six outer bands in two color schemes. 9/16". Mint (9.9). $31. (Auction #76, Lot 32).

SWIRL. Solid core. Three layer solid core swirl. Opaque white core. Cage of blue and light green bands floating above. 29/32". Near Mint(+) (8.7). $31. (Auction #139, Lot 45).

SWIRL. Solid core. Very nice naked solid core. Core is supposed to be two transparent blue bands and two opaque yellow. 19/32". Mint (9.4). $31. (Auction #120, Lot 19).

SWIRL. Solid core. Lot of two marbles. First is opaque white core with transparent pink strands on it. $30. (Auction #133, Lot 10).

SWIRL. Solid core. Naked solid core swirl. Core includes opaque white, translucent baby blue/gray, transparent light green. 21/32". Mint(-) (9.2). $30. (Auction #167, Lot 11).

SWIRL. Solid core. Nice three layer solid core swirl. Opaque white base. Middle layer is four panels of colored strands. 11/16". Mint (9.9). $30. (Auction #121, Lot 11).

SWIRL. Solid core. Lot of two marbles. One is a lobed solid core, the other is a caged solid core. Nice pair. $30. (Auction #130, Lot 35).

SWIRL. Solid core. English-type solid core. Opaque red core. A cage of alternating white and light blue strands. 3/4". Near Mint(+) (8.9). $30. (Auction #59, Lot 39).

SWIRL. Solid core. Opaque white core. Two narrow bands of transparent pink on it, one narrow band of transparent blue. $30. (Auction #125, Lot 16).

SWIRL. Solid core. Superior three layer solid core swirl. Opaque white core. Middle layer is yellow latticinio. 25/32". Near Mint(+) (8.9). $30. (Auction #98, Lot 3).

SWIRL. Solid core. Opaque white core. Two pink bands on the core and two blue bands. 21/32". Mint (9.9). $29. (Auction #67, Lot 32).

SWIRL. Solid core. Three layer marble. Yellow solid core. Four transparent green strands and four transparent pink strands. 11/16". Mint (9.9). $29. (Auction #179, Lot 16).

SWIRL. Solid core. Caged solid core. Opaque white core. Bands of transparent pink and dark blue on the core. 25/32". Mint (9.7). $29. (Auction #183, Lot 23).

SWIRL. Solid core. Another nice three-layer solid core. This one is smaller, but the coloring is rarer. 17/32". Near Mint(+) (8.8). $29. (Auction #117, Lot 12).

SWIRL. Solid core. Lot of two marbles. Both are peewees. Both are solid cores, in two different color schemes. $29. (Auction #113, Lot 8).

SWIRL. Solid core. Core is three panels of yellow alternating with three panels of white with transparent blue. 25/32". Mint (9.7). $29. (Auction #103, Lot 41).

SWIRL. Solid core. Peewee solid core. Core is pink (2), blue and green bands on white. 15/32". Mint (9.9). $29. (Auction #113, Lot 24).

SWIRL. Solid core. Small naked solid core swirl. Core is eight light green bands. 9/16". Mint (9.9). $29. (Auction #62, Lot 13).

SWIRL. Solid core. Very nice solid core swirl. Core is predominately orange with some transparent blue, transparent yellow. 11/16". Near Mint(+) (8.9). $28. (Auction #81, Lot 28).

SWIRL. Solid core. Fat opaque white core. There are six pink bands on the core, alternating with three blue bands. 27/32". Near Mint(+) (8.9). $28. (Auction #70, Lot 15).

SWIRL. Solid core. Nice solid core swirl. Opaque white core with two transparent pink and two transparent blue bands. 3/4". Mint (9.5). $28. (Auction #65, Lot 9).

SWIRL. Solid core. Opaque white base with translucent blue bands. Outer layer is a cage of sixteen white strands. 25/32". Near Mint (8.8). $28. (Auction #62, Lot 34).

SWIRL. Solid core. Outstanding English solid core swirl. Translucent white core. Three bands of orange. 11/16". Mint(-) (9.2). $27. (Auction #118, Lot 42).

SWIRL. Solid core. Very nice lobed solid core swirl. Transparent clear base. Opaque white core with three slight lobes. 25/32". Mint (9.7). $27. (Auction #90, Lot 41).

SWIRL. Solid core. Core is transparent dark blue panels separated by thin translucent white and opaque red bands. 11/16". Mint (9.5). $27. (Auction #71, Lot 3).

SWIRL. Solid core. Three-layer peewee solid core. Opaque white base, slightly flattened on one side. Four bands floating. 15/32". Mint (9.9). $27. (Auction #140, Lot 18).

SWIRL. Solid core. Naked solid core swirl. Core includes opaque white, translucent baby blue/gray, transparent light green. 21/32". Mint(-) (9.2). $26. (Auction #141, Lot 43).

SWIRL. Solid core. Interesting core. The core consists of four panels. Two are orange on white, one is transparent blue. 11/16". Mint (9.8). $26. (Auction #81, Lot 17).

SWIRL. Solid core. Four lobed solid core swirl. The lobes are very deep. 17/32". Mint (9.9). $26. (Auction #74, Lot 2).

SWIRL. Solid core. Three layer solid core swirl. Opaque white core. Open panel in the core. 23/32". Mint (9.6). $26. (Auction #62, Lot 10).

SWIRL. Solid core. Superb three layer solid core swirl. Opaque yellow core. Middle layer is six bands. 21/32". Near Mint(+) (8.7). $26. (Auction #57, Lot 41).

SWIRL. Solid core. Pretty solid core. Nice core of multiple colored bands. Outer layer is two sets of white strands. 3/4". Mint(-) (9). $26. (Auction #175, Lot 44).

SWIRL. Solid core. Pretty marble. Opaque white solid core swirl. Outer layer is two red on white bands, one blue on white. 21/32". Mint (9.9). $26. (Auction #176, Lot 2).

SWIRL. Solid core. Rather odd design. Opaque white core. Outer layer is eight bands. Four are pink on white. 13/16". Near Mint (8.6). $26. (Auction #136, Lot 32).

SWIRL. Solid core. Nice caged solid core swirl. Opaque white core with pink bands on it. Outer layer is a cage of yellow. 25/32". Near Mint(+) (8.9). $26. (Auction #137, Lot 13).

SWIRL. Solid core. Yellow core. Eight outer bands. Four are white. Two are pink on white. One is blue on white. 9/16". Mint (9.9). $26. (Auction #82, Lot 30).

SWIRL. Solid core swirl. Very nice three layer solid core swirl. Opaque white core. Middle layer is three transparent red bands. 11/16". Mint (9.9). $26. (Auction #81, Lot 3).

SWIRL. Solid core. Naked solid core swirl. Excellent core. Three bands of transparent blue on one side. 11/16". Mint (9.4). $25. (Auction #91, Lot 5).

SWIRL. Solid core. Lot of thirteen marbles. All are solid core swirls. Nice assortment of styles and color. $25. (Auction #177, Lot 2).

SWIRL. Solid core. Peewee solid core swirl. Opaque white core with pink and blue bands. 7/16". Mint (9.9). $25. (Auction #89, Lot 39).

SWIRL. Solid core . Naked solid core swirl. A band of orange, band of blue and band of green, separated by narrower band. 9/16". Mint (9.9). $25. (Auction #185, Lot 33).

SWIRL. Solid core. Very nicely designed and very well made. Opaque thin white core. Two bands of transparent blue. 1-1/16". Near Mint (8.5). $24. (Auction #73, Lot 6.80).

SWIRL. Solid core. Nice caged solid core. Opaque white core with pink bands on it. Outer layer is a cage of twelve white. 21/32". Mint(-) (9.2). $24. (Auction #153, Lot 25).

SWIRL. Solid core. Opaque white core with transparent pink strands. Outer layer is a cage of eight yellow strands. 3/4". Near Mint(+) (8.9). $24. (Auction #56, Lot 15).

SWIRL. Solid core. Opaque white core. Outer layer is three bands of transparent green on white. 23/32". Mint (9.8). $24. (Auction #59, Lot 17).

SWIRL. Solid core. Opaque white core with three very slight lobes. There is a band of transparent pink in each trough. 5/8". Mint(-) (9.3). $24. (Auction #57, Lot 19).

SWIRL. Solid core. Nice three-layer solid core swirl. Opaque white core. Middle layer is three transparent blue bands. 11/16". Mint (9.9). $24. (Auction #107, Lot 2).

SWIRL. Solid core. Transparent clear base. Opaque white core. Outer layer is two bands of red, one of blue and one of green. 21/32". Mint (9.9). $24. (Auction #84, Lot 37).

SWIRL. Solid core. Opaque white core. Core has several narrow pale yellow bands on it. Outer layer is two blue bands. 13/16". Near Mint(+) (8.9). $24. (Auction #162, Lot 17).

SWIRL. Solid core. Interesting solid core. Core is three panels of yellow and three of white. 21/32". Mint (9.5). $24. (Auction #113, Lot 21).

SWIRL. Solid core. Nice fat core. Three panels of transparent green on opaque white. 11/16". Mint (9.9). $24. (Auction #105, Lot 18).

SWIRL. Solid core. Naked solid core swirl. Thin core. Opaque white with bands of opaque orange and transparent dark green. 11/16". Near Mint(+) (8.9). $24. (Auction #148, Lot 13).

SWIRL. Solid core. Interesting peewee solid core. Opaque white core. One band each of transparent red, blue, green. 1/2". Mint (9.7). $24. (Auction #68, Lot 24).

SWIRL. Solid core. Core is opaque red, transparent blue, opaque yellow and transparent green. 11/16". Mint (9.9). $24. (Auction #96, Lot 9).

SWIRL. Solid core. English type swirl. Translucent yellow core. Outer layer is three blue bands and three narrow white bands. 11/16". Mint(-) (9.1). $24. (Auction #151, Lot 48).

SWIRL. Solid core. Very nicely designed and very well made. Opaque thin white core. Two bands of transparent blue. 1-1/16". Near Mint (8.5). $24. (Auction #68, Lot 6).

SWIRL. Solid core. Solid core swirl from near the end of the cane. Core is yellow with red and green on it. 5/8". Near Mint(+) (8.7). $23. (Auction #160, Lot 11).

SWIRL. Solid core. Superb small solid core swirl. Core is alternating panels of transparent pink and green edged. 9/16". Mint (9.9). $23. (Auction #75, Lot 31).

SWIRL. Solid core. Translucent white core. Outer layer is three orange and three blue on white bands. Odd marble. 9/16". Mint (9.9). $22. (Auction #55, Lot 37).

SWIRL. Solid core. Super solid core swirl. Three panels of transparent pink, alternating with three narrow opaque panels. 9/16". Mint (9.4). $22. (Auction #159, Lot 36).

SWIRL. Solid core. Peewee solid core swirl. White core with four lobes. In each lobe trough is either a pink (2), blue. 1/2". Mint (9.7). $22. (Auction #179, Lot 14).

SWIRL. Solid core. Tiny solid core swirl. Opaque yellow core with two bands of green and two of pink. 17/32". Mint (9.9). $22. (Auction #164, Lot 10).

SWIRL. Solid core. Peewee solid core. Opaque white core. Two bands of transparent pink on it. $22. (Auction #141, Lot 6).

SWIRL. Solid core. Another fantastic small swirl. Opaque white core. Fat core. Three equidistantly space narrow bands. 15/32". Mint (9.9). $22. (Auction #115, Lot 17).

SWIRL. Solid core. Opaque white core. Two bands of transparent salmon, one of transparent green, one of transparent blue. 25/32". Near Mint(+) (8.8). $22. (Auction #141, Lot 15).

SWIRL. Solid core. Interesting error swirl. Core is three wide translucent white panels. 21/32". Mint (9.9). $22. (Auction #93, Lot 36).

SWIRL. Solid core. Naked solid core swirl. Super marble. Core is two transparent green bands. 21/32". Near Mint(+) (8.8). $22. (Auction #63, Lot 14).

SWIRL. Solid core. Very interesting core. Six panels, all about the same size. Three are transparent blue on white strands. 19/32". Mint (9.9). $21. (Auction #69, Lot 3).

SWIRL. Solid core. Core is semi-opaque yellow core with a light green tint. Outer layer is two white bands, one blue band. 11/16". Mint(-) (9). $21. (Auction #96, Lot 11).

SWIRL. Solid core. Naked solid core. Core is thin. Opaque yellow with two red bands and two dark green bands. 9/16". Mint(-) (9). $20. (Auction #70, Lot 34).

SWIRL. Solid core. Very nice caged solid core swirl. Opaque yellow core. Two bands of transparent pink. 21/32". Mint (9.9). $20. (Auction #112, Lot 3).

SWIRL. Solid core. Lot of three marbles. Assortment of colors and designs. Two are Mint, one Near Mint. 17/32" to 9/16". $20. (Auction #128, Lot 1).

SWIRL. Solid core. Naked solid core swirl. Core is alternating white bands and transparent green bands. 9/16". Mint (9.6). $20. (Auction #177, Lot 42).

SWIRL. Solid core. Very odd swirl. The core is misshapen. Opaque white and yellow bands, with lots of space in between. 19/32". Near Mint (8.6). $20. (Auction #54, Lot 38).

SWIRL. Solid core. Very interesting and subtlely colored marble. Translucent white core. Middle layer is yellow latticino. 9/16". Near Mint(+) (8.9). $20. (Auction #118, Lot 11).

SWIRL. Solid core. Translucent yellow core. Outer layer is four bands in two different color schemes. One melt flat spot. 15/16". Near Mint(+) (8.9). $20. (Auction #102, Lot 3).

SWIRL. Solid core. Translucent yellow and white core. Outer layer is four transparent blue strands. 9/16". Mint(-) (9.2). $20. (Auction #150, Lot 4).

SWIRL. Solid core. Opaque white core with salmon bands on it. Four sets of four yellow strands. Almost no twist. 21/23". Mint(-) (9). $20. (Auction #131, Lot 9).

SWIRL. Solid core. Beautiful solid core swirl. The core is very unusual. Four panels. Two panels are white strands. 9/16". Mint (9.9). $20. (Auction #77, Lot 15).

SWIRL. Solid core. Pretty solid core swirl. Opaque white core. Two panels of transparent pink, one of transparent green. 11/16". Mint (9.9). $19. (Auction #116, Lot 1).

SWIRL. Solid core. Very nice marble. Fat core. Opaque white, with two transparent pink bands. 25/32". Near Mint (8.6). $19. (Auction #54, Lot 40).

SWIRL. Solid core. English colors. Pale blue core. Outer layer is three narrow white bands. 5/8". Mint(-) (9.2). $19. (Auction #165, Lot 40).

SWIRL. Solid core. Opaque white core. Two bands of transparent blue and two of transparent pink. Double twisted. 5/8". Mint(-) (9). $18. (Auction #97, Lot 3).

SWIRL. Solid core. Super three-layer solid core swirl. Translucent yellow core. Middle layer is a cage of white strands. 21/32". Near Mint(+) (8.9). $18. (Auction #110, Lot 10).

SWIRL. Solid core. Opaque white core. Alternating strands of pink and blue on it. Core has one clear band. 3/4". Near Mint(+) (8.9). $18. (Auction #134, Lot 38).

SWIRL. Solid core. Yellow solid core swirl. Outer layer is three transparent blue bands alternating with three orange. 17/32". Mint (9.9). $18. (Auction #179, Lot 3).

SWIRL. Solid core. Opaque white core. Three pink bands and three turquoise bands on it. Flattened on one side. 19/32". Mint(-) (9). $17. (Auction #176, Lot 32).

SWIRL. Solid core. Super naked solid core. Core consists of five panels: white, blue, yellow, orange and transparent green. 9/16". Mint (9.9). $17. (Auction #83, Lot 38).

SWIRL. Solid core. Nice, small solid core swirl. Core is opaque white with several blue bands on it. 17/32". Mint (9.6). $17. (Auction #155, Lot 13).

SWIRL. Solid core. Very lightly tinted blue base. Four panel core. Yellow core with two pink panels and two green panels. 21/32". Near Mint(+) (8.8). $17. (Auction #120, Lot 38).

SWIRL. Solid core. Very pretty marble. Opaque white core. Alternating bands on the core of blue and pink. 21/32". Near Mint(+) (8.8). $16. (Auction #142, Lot 37).

SWIRL. Solid core. Opaque white core with two bands of yellow on it. Outer layer is two bands of transparent pink on white. 21/32". Mint (9.9). $16. (Auction #103, Lot 4).

SWIRL. Solid core. Caged solid core. Opaque white base with two pink bands and two blue bands on it. 3/4". Near Mint (8.6). $16. (Auction #103, Lot 39).

SWIRL. Solid core. Translucent misty yellow core. Outer layer is three opaque white bands. 9/16". Near Mint(+) (8.9). $15. (Auction #68, Lot 30).

SWIRL. Solid core. Yellow core. Bands of green and pink on it. Outer layer is four sets of white strands. Cold roll. 23/32". Mint(-) (9). $14. (Auction #170, Lot 2).

SWIRL. Solid core. Really pretty solid core. Core is thin and opaque white. Two panels of two pink strands each. 9/16". Mint (9.7). $14. (Auction #115, Lot 7).

SWIRL. Solid core. Opaque white core. Four pink strands, two blue strands and two green strands on the core. 11/16". Mint(-) (9.2). $14. (Auction #179, Lot 7).

SWIRL. Solid core. Three layer marble. Translucent yellow core. Four bands floating above it. 5/8". Mint (9.9). $14. (Auction #182, Lot 9).

SWIRL. Solid core. Solid core swirl from somewhere near an end of the cane. Core is multicolor. Clear spaces in it. 19/32". Near Mint(+) (8.8). $14. (Auction #151, Lot 37).

SWIRL. Solid core. Very nice naked solid core swirl. Unusual core. Three opaque yellow bands. 11/16". Mint(-) (9). $14. (Auction #54, Lot 4).

SWIRL. Solid core. Nice solid core swirl. Opaque white core. Two bands of transparent green and two of transparent pink. 17/32". Mint (9.9).

$14. (Auction #110, Lot 36).

SWIRL. Solid core. Nice colorful core. Outer layer is three sets of yellow strands. Germany, circa 1870-1915. 17/32". Mint (9.7). $13. (Auction #184, Lot 4).

SWIRL. Solid core. English type colors. Opaque white core. Two bands of red and yellow, two bands of blue and yellow. 11/16". Near Mint(+) (8.7). $13. (Auction #104, Lot 2).

SWIRL. Solid core. Opaque yellow solid core, shoved to one side. Outer layer is four sets of bands in the same color scheme. 27/32". Near Mint(+) (8.9). $12. (Auction #128, Lot 12).

SWIRL. Solid core. Nice three layer solid core swirl. Opaque white core. Middle layer is two sets of two transparent pink. 5/8". Near Mint(+) (8.8). $12. (Auction #61, Lot 30).

SWIRL. Solid core. English style colors. Opaque white core. Outer layer is three red on white. 9/16". Near Mint(+) (8.7). $11. (Auction #107, Lot 14).

SWIRL. Solid core. Opaque yellow core. Outer layer is three orange bands alternating with three light blue bands. English. 11/16". Near Mint (8.4). $11. (Auction #139, Lot 19).

SWIRL. Solid core. Three layer solid core in very light blue glass. Opaque yellow core. Cage of white strands floating. 21/32". Near Mint(+) (8.9). $9. (Auction #172, Lot 3).

SWIRL. Solid core. Opaque white core. Outer layer is two bands of transparent pink, one of transparent blue. 11/16". Mint (9.6). $9. (Auction #165, Lot 10).

SWIRL. Solid core. Translucent white core. Six outer bands. Three are transparent blue on a red strand. 9/16". Near Mint (8.4). $7. (Auction #69, Lot 1).

SWIRL. Solid core. Nice smaller marble. Core is thin. Alternating bands of transparent blue and opaque white strands. 9/16". Near Mint(+) (8.9). $7. (Auction #61, Lot 7).

TRANSITIONAL. Assorted. Lot of two marbles. First is a pinch pontil. Opaque white and electric red swirl. Looks like an American. $27. (Auction #172, Lot 2).

TRANSITIONAL. Assorted. Lot of two marbles. First is a ground pontil. Purple slag. One small flake. 11/16". Near Mint(+). $19. (Auction #115, Lot 34).

TRANSITIONAL. Assorted. Lot of two marbles. Both are brown slag type. One is a pinch pontil, 11/16", Mint(-) (9.1). $9. (Auction #146, Lot 3).

TRANSITIONAL. Assorted pontil. Lot of six marbles. Assortment of crease and pinch pontil. Translucent color swirled on opaque white. $21. (Auction #120, Lot 11).

TRANSITIONAL. Bullet mold. Transparent red/brown marble. Ground flat-spot pontil on one side. Mold line running around the marble. 23/32". Near Mint(+) (8.8). $15. (Auction #142, Lot 5).

TRANSITIONAL. Bullet mold. Transparent red/brown marble. Ground flat-spot pontil on one side. Mold line running around the marble. 23/32". Near Mint(+) (8.8). $14. (Auction #162, Lot 41).

TRANSITIONAL. Crease pontil. Rare example of a crease pontil. Opaque white base with bright yellow/orange swirls. 1-1/16". Near Mint(+) (8.7). $100. (Auction #83, Lot 2).

TRANSITIONAL. Crease pontil. Lot of five marbles. Each is opaque white with a colored swirl. Colors are blue, red, orange, aventu. $75. (Auction #100, Lot 39).

TRANSITIONAL. Crease pontil. Lot of eight marbles. Assortment of colors including aqua, blue, greens and browns. Nice group. $70. (Auction #137, Lot 18).

TRANSITIONAL. Crease pontil. Opaque white base with a swirl of aventurine (!!) green. 11/16". Mint (9.9). $50. (Auction #120, Lot 36).

TRANSITIONAL. Crease pontil. Lot of six marbles. All are crease pontil transitional. Two blue slag, two aqua slag, one brown slag. $43. (Auction #67, Lot 20.20).

TRANSITIONAL. Crease pontil. Lot of six marbles. All are crease pontil transitional. Two blue slag, two aqua slag, one brown slag. $43. (Auction #67, Lot 20).

TRANSITIONAL. Crease pontil. Lot of six marbles. All are crease pontil transitional. Two blue slag, two aqua slag, one brown slag. $41. (Auction #67, Lot 20.40).

TRANSITIONAL. Crease pontil. Lot of six marbles. All are crease pontil transitional. Two blue slag, two aqua slag, one brown slag. $41. (Auction #67, Lot 20.50).

TRANSITIONAL. Crease pontil. Lot of six marbles. All are crease pontil transitional. Two blue slag, two aqua slag, one brown slag. $41. (Auction #67, Lot 20.30).

TRANSITIONAL. Crease pontil. Lot of four marbles. All are crease pontil. Three blue, one purple. Three are Mint. $30. (Auction #176, Lot 7).

TRANSITIONAL. Crease pontil. Lot of five marbles. Nice assortment of crease pontil transitionals. Three are blue slags. $27. (Auction #75, Lot 7).

TRANSITIONAL. Crease pontil. A beauty. Transparent lavender base with opaque white swirl. Nice crease pontil on bottom. Origin unknown. 19/32". Mint (9.9). $27. (Auction #115, Lot 31).

TRANSITIONAL. Crease pontil. Nice example. Electric red swirls on white. Barely visible crease pontil. Coloring would indicate 25/32". Mint (9.7). $26. (Auction #134, Lot 31).

TRANSITIONAL. Crease pontil. Lot of six marbles. All are crease pontil. Nice assortment of colors. 9/16" to 5/8". Mint (9.9) & Near Mint. $25. (Auction #132, Lot 6).

TRANSITIONAL. Crease pontil. Lot of five marbles. Three brown, one green, one blue. 5/8" to 11/16". Mint (9.9) to Near Mint(+). $24. (Auction #132, Lot 8).

TRANSITIONAL. Crease pontil. Lot of four marbles. All are crease pontil. Two blue, one green, one brown. All in nice shape. $22. (Auction #162, Lot 6).

TRANSITIONAL. Crease pontil. Beautiful shooter crease pontil transitional. Aqua slag. 27/32". Mint (9.7). $22. (Auction #67, Lot 38).

TRANSITIONAL. Crease pontil. Lot of three marbles. All are crease pontil. One blue, one green, one brown. All in nice shape. $21. (Auction #148, Lot 1).

TRANSITIONAL. Crease pontil. Lot of two marbles. One is transparent brown with opaque white. The other is opaque white. $20. (Auction #57, Lot 39).

TRANSITIONAL. Crease pontil. Lot of two marbles. Both are blue slag crease pontils. Unknown maker. Could be American or Japanese. 11/16". Mint (9.9). $20. (Auction #66, Lot 20).

TRANSITIONAL. Crease pontil. Lot of two marbles. Both are crease pontil. One blue slag and one green slag. Origin and age unknown. $18. (Auction #78, Lot 24.20).

TRANSITIONAL. Crease pontil. Aqua slag. Nice white swirl. Large crease pontil. Origin unknown. 1910-1930. 21/32". Mint (9.9). $18. (Auction #115, Lot 4).

TRANSITIONAL. Crease pontil. Lot of two marbles. Each is a light green slag. Crease pontil on the bottom of each. It is unknown. $17. (Auction #74, Lot 30).

TRANSITIONAL. Crease pontil. Blue opaque slag. Nice crease pontil. Very unusual. 11/16". Mint (9.9). $17. (Auction #128, Lot 36).

TRANSITIONAL. Crease pontil. Crease pontil transitional. Opaque white with an aventurine green spiral. Nice crease pontil. 11/16". Mint (9.9). $17. (Auction #110, Lot 32).

TRANSITIONAL. Crease pontil. Lot of two marbles. Both are crease pontil. One blue slag and one green slag. Origin and age unknown. $16. (Auction #78, Lot 24).

TRANSITIONAL. Crease pontil. Lot of two marbles. One is a brown slag, the other is a gree slag. Both are in nice shape. Origin unknown. $15. (Auction #62, Lot 4).

TRANSITIONAL. Crease pontil. Lot of four marbles. Two are blue slags, one is aqua and one is light green. All are crease pontil. $15. (Auction #70, Lot 28).

TRANSITIONAL. Crease pontil. Exceptional example. Electric red swirls on white. Nice crease pontil. 5/8". Mint (9.7). $15. (Auction #120, Lot 3).

TRANSITIONAL. Crease pontil. Blue slag. Nice crease pontil. Origin unconfirmed, either American or Japanese, circa 1910-1930. 11/16". Mint (9.7). $14. (Auction #172, Lot 12).

TRANSITIONAL. Crease pontil. Crease pontil transitional. Opaque white with an orange spiraling. Nice crease pontil. 11/16". Mint(-) (9). $13. (Auction #163, Lot 5).

TRANSITIONAL. Crease pontil. Two blue slags. Nice crease pontil on each. In great shape. It is unknown if these are American or Japanese. 9/16". Mint (9.9). $13. (Auction #62, Lot 30).

TRANSITIONAL. Crease pontil. Transparent light green with opaque white swirling. Origin and age unknown, probably 1910-1930. 19/32". Mint (9.9). $12. (Auction #139, Lot 4).

TRANSITIONAL. Crease pontil. Transparent dark blue base with opaque white spiral. Long, thin crease pontil on the bottom. 11/16". Mint (9.9). $10. (Auction #110, Lot 37).

TRANSITIONAL. Crease pontil. Brown slag. Nice crease pontil. Origin unconfirmed, either American or Japanese, circa 1910-1930. 9/16". Mint (9.9). $8. (Auction #121, Lot 37).

TRANSITIONAL. Crease pontil. Blue slag. Nice crease pontil. Origin unconfirmed, either American or Japanese, circa 1910-1930. 9/16". Mint(-) (9). $5. (Auction #161, Lot 7).

TRANSITIONAL. Crease pontil. Blue slag. Nice crease pontil. Origin unconfirmed, either American or Japanese, circa 1910-1930. 9/16". Mint(-) (9). $3. (Auction #95, Lot 1).

TRANSITIONAL. Crease pontil. Green slag. Nice crease pontil. Origin unconfirmed, either American or Japanese, circa 1910-1930. 9/16". Mint(-) (9). $2. (Auction #95, Lot 4.20).

TRANSITIONAL. Crease pontil. Green slag. Nice crease pontil. Origin unconfirmed, either American or Japanese, circa 1910-1930. 9/16". Mint(-) (9). $2. (Auction #95, Lot 4).

TRANSITIONAL. Fold pontil. Excellent hand gathered blue slag. Nice "9" on top. Exceptional fold pontil on the bottom. American. 27/32". Mint (9.9). $75. (Auction #116, Lot 40).

TRANSITIONAL. Fold pontil. Beautiful example of a fold pontil. Gray/brown slag. Nice looping. Very nice pontil. American. 23/32". Mint (9.9). $50. (Auction #117, Lot 36).

TRANSITIONAL. Fold pontil. Very early Akro Agate red slag. The glass was too cool when made, so there is a fold pontil. 11/16". Mint(-) (9.1). $45. (Auction #78, Lot 5).

TRANSITIONAL. Fold pontil. Purple slag. Very little white. Excellent fold pontil. Super marble. American, circa 1905-1920. 21/32". Mint (9.9). $30. (Auction #127, Lot 6).

TRANSITIONAL. Fold pontil. Akro Agate red slag. Nice example of an early Akro slag. Glass was too cool when the marble was made. 21/32". Mint (9.9). $25. (Auction #55, Lot 5).

TRANSITIONAL. Fold pontil. Nice fold pontil transitional. Very dark purple base with a blanket white spiral. Nice fold pontil. 11/16". Near Mint (8.5). $20. (Auction #130, Lot 7).

TRANSITIONAL. Fold pontil. Dark purple slag. Nice "9" pattern on the top. Very nice fold pontil on the bottom. 11/16". Near Mint(+) (8.9). $14. (Auction #145, Lot 6).

TRANSITIONAL. Ground pontil. Stunning example!!!!! Transparent blue base with wispy white swirling. Opaque white "9". 25/32". Mint (9.9). $220. (Auction #183, Lot 35).

TRANSITIONAL. Ground pontil. Very rare ground pontil transitional with oxblood. Transparent green base with opaque white. 21/32". Near Mint(+) (8.8). $185. (Auction #88, Lot 44).

TRANSITIONAL. Ground pontil. Exceptional example. Light green slag. Superior "9" and excellent ground pontil. Surface is pristine. 13/16". Mint (9.9). $145. (Auction #110, Lot 47).

TRANSITIONAL. Ground pontil. Green slag. Gorgeous "9". Surface in great shape. Superb ground pontil on the bottom. Exceptional. 21/32". Mint (9.9). $140. (Auction #75, Lot 42).

TRANSITIONAL. Ground pontil. Superb example. Blue and white slag. Excellent "9" on the top. Great pontil on the bottom. 25/32". Mint (9.4). $135. (Auction #104, Lot 44).

TRANSITIONAL. Ground pontil. Green slag. Super "9" on the top and an excellent ground pontil on the bottom. Surface in superb shape. 13/16". Mint (9.9). $95. (Auction #76, Lot 34).

TRANSITIONAL. Ground pontil. Very unusual transitional. Light lavender slag. Thin white swirling. Interesting reverse "9" on it. 1/2". Mint (9). $75. (Auction #170, Lot 36).

TRANSITIONAL. Ground pontil. White and blue swirled marble. Excellent pattern. Great ground pontil. Super example. 13/16". Mint(-) (9.2). $75. (Auction #147, Lot 36).

TRANSITIONAL. Ground pontil. Transparent blue glass with spirals of white. Excellent "9" on the top. Super ground pontil. 13/16". Mint (9.1). $75. (Auction #168, Lot 43).

TRANSITIONAL. Ground pontil. Gorgeous ground pontil transitional. Transparent green base with swirls of semi-opaque white. Superb. 13/16". Mint(-) (9). $70. (Auction #160, Lot 40).

TRANSITIONAL. Ground pontil. Transparent purple base with a translucent white spiral. Excellent ground pontil. One airhole. American. 25/32". Mint (9.5). $65. (Auction #117, Lot 34).

TRANSITIONAL. Ground pontil. Superb example in a harder to find color. Translucent very light vaseline-type yellow (not fluorescent). 21/32". Mint (9.9). $65. (Auction #82, Lot 29).

TRANSITIONAL. Ground pontil. This is a Leighton type transitional, even though it has no yellow, oxblood or lavender. Transparent. 13/16". Near Mint(+) (8.9). $65. (Auction #176, Lot 47).

TRANSITIONAL. Ground pontil. Excellent marble. Transparent aqua blue glass with a light white swirl inside it. Exceptionally well. 27/32". Mint(-) (9). $60. (Auction #182, Lot 47).

TRANSITIONAL. Ground pontil. Beautiful ground pontil transitional. Transparent green glass with some interior white near the bottom. 3/4". Mint (9.7). $60. (Auction #131, Lot 4).

TRANSITIONAL. Ground pontil. A rare transparent transitional. Transparent bubble filled aqua with just a few white swirls in it. 25/32". Mint(-) (9). $55. (Auction #91, Lot 24).

TRANSITIONAL. Ground pontil. Very hard to find transitional with loads of oxblood on the surface. Transparent smokey base. $50. (Auction #84,

Lot 9).

TRANSITIONAL. Ground pontil. Aqua base with thin translucent white swirl. Several subsurface moons. Excellent ground pontil. 27/32". Near Mint (8.4). $41. (Auction #173, Lot 23).

TRANSITIONAL. Ground pontil. This is very similar to the pinch pontil transitionals in Lot #20 (same consignor). 11/16". Mint(-) (9). $40. (Auction #82, Lot 44).

TRANSITIONAL. Ground pontil. Transparent very dark purple base with a swirl of "lumpy" white. Nice ground pontil. Subsurface moon. 27/32". Near Mint (8.5). $32. (Auction #120, Lot 33).

TRANSITIONAL. Ground pontil. Dark purple base with a super spiral of opaque white on it, forming a super "9". 5/8". Near Mint(-) (8.2). $30. (Auction #142, Lot 26).

TRANSITIONAL. Ground pontil. Superior example of a transparent transitional. Transparent dull purple/brown glass. 21/32". Mint(-) (9.1). $30. (Auction #90, Lot 6).

TRANSITIONAL. Ground pontil. Transparent aqua glass with a little opaque white in it and on it. Very nicely faceted ground pontil. 25/32". Near Mint (8.3). $22. (Auction #130, Lot 9).

TRANSITIONAL. Leighton. Outstanding and very rare ground pontil transitional. Transparent clear base. Perfect spiral. 13/16". Mint(-) (9.1). $825. (Auction #156, Lot 49).

TRANSITIONAL. Leighton. Rare Leighton ground pontil transitional. Transparent olive green base swirled with opaque lavender . $230. (Auction #129, Lot 33).

TRANSITIONAL. Leighton. A beauty. Transparent green base with lots of unmelted sand in it. Swirl of translucent yellow in it. 13/16". Near Mint(+) (8.9). $160. (Auction #172, Lot 46).

TRANSITIONAL. Leighton. Rare marble. Transparent clear base. Swirled with opaque white, opaque yellow and oxblood. 13/16". Good(+) (7.80). $150. (Auction #179, Lot 17).

TRANSITIONAL. Leighton. Very hard to find Leighton transitional. Translucent white and milky base with a slight green cast. 11/16". Near Mint(+) (8.7). $150. (Auction #154, Lot 48).

TRANSITIONAL. Leighton. Nice Leighton transitional. Ground pontil. Swirled transparent teal, bright yellow and wispy white. 7/8". Near Mint (8.4). $120. (Auction #181, Lot 47).

TRANSITIONAL. Leighton. Super example. Transparent smoky gray base with a wispy white swirl in it. "9" on the top. Excellent. 13/16". Mint (9.8). $110. (Auction #142, Lot 44).

TRANSITIONAL. Leighton. Very hard to find Leighton transitional. Predominately bright yellow, with some aqua. Nice ground pontil. 27/32". Near Mint (8.5). $95. (Auction #120, Lot 49).

TRANSITIONAL. Leighton. Transparent clear base. Spiral of translucent yellow starting at the top and spiraling about halfway. 11/16". Near Mint(+) (8.4). $60. (Auction #167, Lot 43).

TRANSITIONAL. Leighton. Very hard to find Leighton regular pontil transitional with oxblood. Transparent clear base. 13/16". Good(-) (7.10). $25. (Auction #89, Lot 8).

TRANSITIONAL. Leighton ground pontil. Extremely rare marble. This is a Leighton ground pontil transitional with an incredible amount of oxblood. 27/32". Mint (9.5). $130. (Auction #63, Lot 43).

TRANSITIONAL. Melted pontil. Nice, large melted pontil transitional. Transparent birch beer brown base with opaque white swirls. 1-5/16". Near Mint(+) (8.9). $95. (Auction #162, Lot 50).

TRANSITIONAL. Melted pontil. Excellent example. M.F. Christensen. Purple slag. Excellent "9" on the top. Superb melted pontil. 21/32". Mint(-) (9.2). $70. (Auction #74, Lot 42).

TRANSITIONAL. Melted pontil. Super example. Exceptional design. Very dark transparent purple with a white swirl. Excellent "9". 27/32". Near Mint(+) (8.9). $61. (Auction #172, Lot 37).

TRANSITIONAL. Melted pontil. Very nice green and white slag. Lots of white. Excellent melted pontil. Very nice looking marble. 31/32". Near Mint(+) (8.9). $50. (Auction #159, Lot 46).

TRANSITIONAL. Melted pontil. Superb Navarre transitional. Transparent slate gray base with white loopings. Excellent pontil. Superb. 11/16". Mint (9.9). $45. (Auction #109, Lot 42).

TRANSITIONAL. Melted pontil. A beauty. Very dark brown slag with just one white spiral. Excellent melted pontil on the bottom. 27/32". Mint (9.9). $45. (Auction #116, Lot 11).

TRANSITIONAL. Melted pontil. Green and white slag. Exceptional small melted pontil. Great pattern. Super marble. 21/32". Near Mint(+) (8.9). $44. (Auction #163, Lot 45).

TRANSITIONAL. Melted pontil. Excellent example. Very dark purple base. White loops on it. Super melted pontil. One tiny air hole. 21/32". Mint(-) (9:2). $42. (Auction #131, Lot 29).

TRANSITIONAL. Melted pontil. Brown slag. Beautiful melted pontil. Probably Navarre Glass. Navarre OH, circa 1905-1912. 21/32". Mint

(9.9). $32. (Auction #76, Lot 30).

TRANSITIONAL. Melted pontil. Transparent dark emerald green base with an excellent spiral of white and yellow. 31/32". Near Mint(-) (8). $31. (Auction #168, Lot 15).

TRANSITIONAL. Melted pontil. Lot of three marbles. All are melted pontils. Nice set of brown slag marble. $30. (Auction #152, Lot 12).

TRANSITIONAL. Melted pontil. Very dark purple slag with translucent white blankets and loops. Probably Navarre. Nice pontil. 23/32". Near Mint(+) (8.8). $30. (Auction #69, Lot 33).

TRANSITIONAL. Melted pontil. Dark olive green base with white swirling. Nice wide "9" on top. Excellent melted pontil on bottom. 21/32". Mint (9.8). $28. (Auction #170, Lot 7).

TRANSITIONAL. Melted pontil. Lot of two marbles. One is a brown slag with lots of wispy white. Has a large melt spot on it. $27. (Auction #137, Lot 14).

TRANSITIONAL. Melted pontil. Lot of two marbles. Both are dark purple with white swirls. One is 21/32" and Mint(-) (9.2). $27. (Auction #56, Lot 16).

TRANSITIONAL. Melted pontil. Green slag. Lots of white on the marble. Looping pattern. Super pontil. Two sparkles. 5/8". Mint(-) (9). $23. (Auction #164, Lot 35).

TRANSITIONAL. Melted pontil. Brown slag with lots of white opaque looping. Probably Navarre. Nice melted pontil on it. 21/32". Near Mint (8.6). $22. (Auction #70, Lot 10).

TRANSITIONAL. Melted pontil. This type is referred to by collectors as a "horizontal slag". Transparent smokey gray/brown base. 15/16". Good(-) (7). $22. (Auction #169, Lot 7).

TRANSITIONAL. Melted pontil. Dark green slag with a beautiful melted pontil. Nice hand gather melted in the surface, but no white. 5/8". Mint(-) (9). $22. (Auction #131, Lot 14).

TRANSITIONAL. Melted pontil. Lot of three marbles. All are melted pontil transitionals. Two are purple and one is green. $20. (Auction #155, Lot 1).

TRANSITIONAL. Melted pontil. Transparent brown single pontil marble, with a little white inside. Nice melted pontil. One melt spot. 21/32". Near Mint(+) (8.9). $19. (Auction #130, Lot 3).

TRANSITIONAL. Melted pontil. Very light brown slag. Excellent melted pontil. 23/32". Mint (9.9). There are three identical marbles. 5/8". Mint (9.9). $18. (Auction #177, Lot 46.20).

TRANSITIONAL. Melted pontil. Very light brown slag. Excellent melted pontil. 23/32". Mint (9.9). There are three identical marbles. 5/8". Mint (9.9). $18. (Auction #177, Lot 46).

TRANSITIONAL. Melted pontil. Very light brown slag. Excellent melted pontil. 23/32". Mint (9.9). There are three identical marbles. 5/8". Mint (9.9). $16. (Auction #177, Lot 46.30).

TRANSITIONAL. Melted pontil. Lot of two marbles. One has a great "9" on it. Larger is damaged. $15. (Auction #143, Lot 2).

TRANSITIONAL. Melted pontil. Lot of two marbles. Both are melted pontil transitionals. One is a brown slag, the other a dark purple. $14. (Auction #177, Lot 3).

TRANSITIONAL. Melted Pontil. An exceptional example of a melted pontil transitional. Transparent light olive green base. 27/32". Mint(-) (9). $110. (Auction #64, Lot 38).

TRANSITIONAL. Pinch pontil. Rare coloring. Opaque white and transparent orange swirl. Nice pinch pontil. Excellent example. Unknnown. 21/32". Mint (9.9). $44. (Auction #178, Lot 45).

TRANSITIONAL. Pinch pontil. Lot of two marbles. Nice pair of pinch pontil transitionals. Unknown manufacturer. Probably M.F. Christensen. $40. (Auction #96, Lot 23).

TRANSITIONAL. Pinch pontil. Lot of six marbles. Three blue, two aqua, one purple. All have small pinch pontils. Probably America. $37. (Auction #166, Lot 5).

TRANSITIONAL. Pinch pontil. White and blue swirled marble. Excellent pattern. Great pinch pontil. Super example. Origin and age unknown. 13/16". Mint (9.9). $37. (Auction #120, Lot 47).

TRANSITIONAL. Pinch pontil. Lot of two marbles. Both are pinch pontil transitionals. One is green, one is blue. $32. (Auction #159, Lot 25).

TRANSITIONAL. Pinch pontil. M.F. Christensen and Son Company marble. Superior example of a pinch pontil transitional. Blue slag. 27/32". Mint (9.9). $32. (Auction #67, Lot 5).

TRANSITIONAL. Pinch pontil. Translucent bright red on white. Superb "9" on the top pole, probably the best I've seen on this type. 11/16". Mint (9.7). $29. (Auction #118, Lot 16).

TRANSITIONAL. Pinch pontil. Shooter size. Light green slag. Lots of white. Faint "9" on top, nice pinch pontil. 27/32". Near Mint(+) (8.9). $29. (Auction #158, Lot 2).

TRANSITIONAL. Pinch pontil. Lot of two marbles. One opaque white and transparent light red spiral. $27. (Auction #107, Lot 15).

TRANSITIONAL. Pinch pontil. Lot of two marbles. Both are almost the same exact pontil. Two different colors. One is translucent. $26. (Auction #117, Lot 15).

TRANSITIONAL. Pinch pontil. Outstanding example. Brown and white slag. Excellent "9" on the top. Super pinch pontil. American. 9/16". Mint (9.9). $25. (Auction #124, Lot 20).

TRANSITIONAL. Pinch pontil. Opaque white and translucent electric red swirl. Long pinch line, looking like a typical M.F. Christensen. 5/8". Mint (9.9). $25. (Auction #165, Lot 28).

TRANSITIONAL. Pinch pontil. A beauty. Tiny pontil, almost looks like a pinpoint. Transparent aqua blue with nice translucent white. 21/32". Mint (9.9). $23. (Auction #158, Lot 37).

TRANSITIONAL. Pinch pontil. Nice example of a pinch pontil. Transparent red and opaque white swirl. Nice pontil. 21/32". Near Mint(+) (8.9). $22. (Auction #55, Lot 36).

TRANSITIONAL. Pinch pontil. Translucent red spiral on opaque white. Excellent pinch pontil on the bottom. In great shape. American. 11/16". Mint (9.9). $20. (Auction #62, Lot 12).

TRANSITIONAL. Pinch pontil. Opaque white and translucent bright red swirls. Thin pinch pontil on the bottom. Unidentified maker. 21/32". Mint (9.9). $19. (Auction #150, Lot 6).

TRANSITIONAL. Pinch pontil. Lot of three marbles. Two blue slags and one brown one. Nice pinch pontil on all three. $19. (Auction #149, Lot 13).

TRANSITIONAL. Pinch pontil. Blue slag. Nice pinch pontil on the bottom. In great shape. Ohio, circa 1910-1920. 11/16". Mint (9.9). $19. (Auction #77, Lot 21).

TRANSITIONAL. Pinch pontil. Opaque white and translucent electric red swirl. Long pinch line, looking like a typical M.F. Christensen. 5/8". Mint(-) (9.2). $17. (Auction #160, Lot 17).

TRANSITIONAL. Pinch pontil. Opaque white and transparent light red spiral. Nice pinch pontil on the bottom. In nice shape. 9/16". Mint (9.9). $14. (Auction #107, Lot 10).

TRANSITIONAL. Pinch pontil. Opaque white and transparent light red spiral. Nice pinch pontil on the bottom. In nice shape. $14. (Auction #116, Lot 23).

TRANSITIONAL. Pinch pontil. Lot of three marbles. All are pinch pontil. One transparent blue and white, one transparent green. $13. (Auction #161, Lot 33).

TRANSITIONAL. Pinch pontil. Opaque white and translucent bright red swirls. Thin pinch pontil on the bottom. Unidentified maker. 21/32". Mint (9.9). $12. (Auction #103, Lot 34).

TRANSITIONAL. Pinch pontil. Opaque white and translucent bright red swirls. Thin pinch pontil on the bottom. One tiny flake. 21/32". Near Mint(+) (8.9). $11. (Auction #154, Lot 9).

TRANSITIONAL. Pinch pontil. Opaque white and translucent bright red swirls. Thin pinch pontil on the bottom. One very tiny rough spot. 21/32". Mint(-) (9). $11. (Auction #168, Lot 6).

TRANSITIONAL. Pinch pontil. Lot of two marbles. Both are brown slags. Both have a small pinch pontil. $10. (Auction #112, Lot 10).

TRANSITIONAL. Pinch pontil. Brown slag. Nice open "9". Excellent pinch pontil. Two blown out airholes and two pits. Origin unknown. 25/23". Near Mint(+) (8.7). $8. (Auction #117, Lot 45).

TRANSITIONAL. Pinch Pontil. Superb example of a pinch pontil transitional. Blue slag. M.F. Christensen. Superior "9" on one end. 21/32". Mint (9.9). $50. (Auction #73, Lot 2).

TRANSITIONAL. Pinpoint pontil. Stunning example of this rare type. Aqua slag with a nice white "9" on one end. 3/4". Mint (9.9). $170. (Auction #110, Lot 50).

TRANSITIONAL. Pinpoint pontil. Super example of this rare type. Aqua slag with a nice white "9" on one end and a small pinpoint pontil. 25/32". Mint (9.9). $140. (Auction #134, Lot 42).

TRANSITIONAL. Pinpoint pontil. Very hard to find marble. Opaque white base with transparent orange swirl. 11/16". Mint(-) (9). $66. (Auction #93, Lot 3).

TRANSITIONAL. Pinpoint pontil. Transparent green marble with some wispy white and loads of tiny air bubbles. Very rare pinpoint pontil. 7/8". Near Mint(+) (8.8). $55. (Auction #73, Lot 41).

TRANSITIONAL. Pinpoint pontil. Brown slag. Lots of white. Tiny pinpoint pontil on it. A couple of tiny pits on the surface too. 11/16". Near Mint(+) (8.9). $20. (Auction #126, Lot 15).

TRANSITIONAL. Regular pontil. This is a single-pontil hand-gathered slag. Very early American marble. 1-5/16". Near Mint(+) (8.9). $200. (Auction #150, Lot 30).

TRANSITIONAL. Regular pontil. Outstanding example of this type. I believe that this marble is Navarre. Very dark purple with white. 15/16". Mint(-) (9.1). $140. (Auction #179, Lot 48).

TRANSITIONAL. Regular pontil. 29/32". Good(+) (7.90). $85. (Auction #168, Lot 13).

TRANSITIONAL. Regular pontil. Opaque purple base with some with swirls. Nice regular pontil. One tiny pit. Nice marble. American. 19/32". Mint(-) (9). $37. (Auction #115, Lot 45).

TRANSITIONAL. Regular pontil. Beautiful regular pontil transitional. Purple slag, lots of white. Excellent pontil. 21/32". Mint(-) (9.2). $35. (Auction #158, Lot 41).

TRANSITIONAL. Regular pontil. Very odd slag. Early manufacturer. Out of round. Light blue slag. "9" pattern on the top. 5/8". Mint(-) (9). $28. (Auction #67, Lot 28).

VITRO AGATE COMPANY. Lot of twenty marbles. All are the same color JABO-Vitro Agate swirl. Semi-opaque lavender swirled. $20. (Auction #151, Lot 17).

VITRO AGATE COMPANY. Lot of twenty five marbles. Assortment of patch type. Assorted types. 19/32" to 5/8". Mint (9.9-9.7). $15. (Auction #152, Lot 19).

VITRO AGATE COMPANY. Advertising bags. Lot of two items. Both are poly advertising bags. Both have cardboard labels. $36. (Auction #79, Lot 16).

VITRO AGATE COMPANY. All-Red. Lot of approximately two hundred marbles. Almost all are Vitro All-Reds. Assorted types and colors. $38. (Auction #177, Lot 26).

VITRO AGATE COMPANY. All-Red. Lot of about seventy marbles. All are All-Reds. Nice assortment of colors. All about 5/8". $24. (Auction #108, Lot 35).

VITRO AGATE COMPANY. All-Red. Lot of eleven marbles. Two-patch, black-line variety. Assortment of colored patches. 19/32". Mint. $16. (Auction #171, Lot 25).

VITRO AGATE COMPANY. All-Red. Lot of eleven marbles. Two-patch, black-line variety. Assortment of colored patches. 19/32". Mint. $16. (Auction #171, Lot 25.20).

VITRO AGATE COMPANY. All-Red. Four-color All-Red with a great swirl pattern and "V" to it. Opaque white base. Red, blue and green. 7/8". Mint(-) (9.1). $15. (Auction #141, Lot 40).

VITRO AGATE COMPANY. All-Red. Lot of eleven marbles. Two-patch, black-line variety. Assortment of colored patches. 19/32". Mint. $14. (Auction #171, Lot 25.30).

VITRO AGATE COMPANY. All-Red. Lot of eight marbles. Six are shooter All-Reds. One is a shooter Peltier Rainbo. One is a shooter. $14. (Auction #115, Lot 20).

VITRO AGATE COMPANY. All-Red. Lot of eleven marbles. Two-patch, black-line variety. Assortment of colored patches. 19/32". Mint. $12. (Auction #171, Lot 25.40).

VITRO AGATE COMPANY. All-Red. Lot of eleven marbles. Two-patch, black-line variety. Assortment of colored patches. 19/32". Mint. $12. (Auction #171, Lot 25.50).

VITRO AGATE COMPANY. All-Red. Lot of thirty five marbles. An assortment of All-Reds. No black line. 5/8". Mint (9.9-9.5). $12. (Auction #119, Lot 12).

VITRO AGATE COMPANY. All-Red. Lot of three marbles. Two-patch All-Reds. On white base. Shooters. 7/8". Mint (9.9-9.7). $8. (Auction #171, Lot 23).

VITRO AGATE COMPANY. All-Red. Lot of three marbles. Two-patch All-Reds. On white base. Shooters. 7/8". Mint (9.9-9.7). $6. (Auction #171, Lot 23.20).

VITRO AGATE COMPANY. All-Red. Lot of fifty eight marbles. Two-patch All-Reds. On white base. One shooter. Rest are 5/8". Mint (9.9). $5. (Auction #171, Lot 29).

VITRO AGATE COMPANY. Assorted. Lot of eight marbles. Five shooter Parrots, one shooter tri-color, one shooter All-Red. $80. (Auction #132, Lot 16).

VITRO AGATE COMPANY. Assorted. Lot of thirty five marbles. Assortment of brushed and of Conquerors. 19/32" to 15/16". Mint (9.9) to. $28. (Auction #77, Lot 22).

VITRO AGATE COMPANY. Assorted. Lot of five marbles. All are shooters. All are modern Parrots. Nice set of colors. $24. (Auction #92, Lot 21).

VITRO AGATE COMPANY. Assorted. Lot of nine marbles. Assortment. Includes Victory, Tri-color patch, All-Red and some assorted patches. $9. (Auction #132, Lot 1).

VITRO AGATE COMPANY. Assorted. Lot of sixteen marbles. Assortment of brushed, patch, All-Red and modern Parrot. Nice group. 5/8". $9. (Auction #163, Lot 26).

VITRO AGATE COMPANY. Assorted. Lot of four marbles. Assorted group of swirl and ribbon. 19/32" to 23/32". Mint (9.9). $7. (Auction #133, Lot 15).

VITRO AGATE COMPANY. Assorted. Lot of eleven marbles. Assortment of patch type. Two are Victory. 19/32" to 1". Mint (9.9-9.0). $5. (Auction #143, Lot 16).

VITRO AGATE COMPANY. Aventurine. Interesting marble with loads of aventurine on it. Opaque white base with a layer of green and turquoise. 11/16". Mint (9.9). $23. (Auction #173, Lot 31).

VITRO AGATE COMPANY. Blackie. Nice example of a shooter Blackie. Brushed black equatorial ribbon. Red poles. In great shape. 7/8". Mint (9.9). $28. (Auction #66, Lot 1).

VITRO AGATE COMPANY. Brushed. Very interesting marble. My best guess is that it is Vitro Agate Company. Opaque white base. 7/8". Mint (9.9). $20. (Auction #148, Lot 20).

VITRO AGATE COMPANY. Brushed. Very interesting marble. My best guess is that it is Vitro Agate Company. Opaque white base. 7/8". Mint (9.9). $20. (Auction #148, Lot 20.20).

VITRO AGATE COMPANY. Brushed. Very interesting marble. My best guess is that it is Vitro Agate Company. Opaque white base. 7/8". Mint (9.9). $18. (Auction #148, Lot 20.30).

VITRO AGATE COMPANY. Brushed oxblood. Early Vitro Agate. Transparent green base. Surface is three brushed patches: white, orange and oxblood. 23/32". Mint (9.9). $21. (Auction #127, Lot 1).

VITRO AGATE COMPANY. Brushed patch. Early Vitro. This is a Parrot on transparent clear. An earlier example of the much more common Parrot. 31/32". Near Mint(+) (8.9). $47. (Auction #73, Lot 14).

VITRO AGATE COMPANY. Brushed patch. Lot of two marbles. Early Vitro Brushed Patch marbles. Both clear base with white and orange brushed. $22. (Auction #119, Lot 42).

VITRO AGATE COMPANY. Catseye. Lot of sixty one marbles. This is an assortment of Vitro hybrid catseyes. Excellent assortment. $38. (Auction #57, Lot 24).

VITRO AGATE COMPANY. Catseye. Shooter hybrid catseye. Yellow vanes edged by baby blue. A real beauty. Five vanes, which is odd. 7/8". Mint (9.9). $15. (Auction #78, Lot 27).

VITRO AGATE COMPANY. Catseye. Superb example of a hybrid catseye shooter. Transparent clear base. Five semi-opaque yellow vanes. 7/8". Mint(-) (9). $5. (Auction #65, Lot 2).

VITRO AGATE COMPANY. Catseye. Lot of three marbles. All are hybrid catseyes. Two are blue and white vane, edged slightly in brown. $3. (Auction #61, Lot 1).

VITRO AGATE COMPANY. Catseye. Lot of four marbles. Three are hybrid catseyes. Nice variety of colors. Other is probably a foreign . $2. (Auction #69, Lot 27).

VITRO AGATE COMPANY. Clear oxblood. Transparent clear base. Wispy white in the center. Band of transparent yellow on one side. 19/32". Mint (9.9). $30. (Auction #113, Lot 43).

VITRO AGATE COMPANY. Hybrid catseye. Hybrid catseye shooter. Brown/red vanes, edged by blue. Some roller marks on the surface. In nice shape. 29/32". Mint (9.5). $40. (Auction #68, Lot 29).

VITRO AGATE COMPANY. Hybrid catseye. Oddly colored hybrid catseye. Red/purple vanes edged by yellow. Parkersburg WV, circa 1948-1955. 5/8". Mint (9.9). $10. (Auction #83, Lot 29).

VITRO AGATE COMPANY. Jabo-Vitro Agate. Lot of two marbles. Both are Jabo-Vitro Agate swirls. White, translucent dark green and lavender. $22. (Auction #84, Lot 22).

VITRO AGATE COMPANY. Metallic. Nice, smaller metallic stripe. Semi-opaque opalescent white base. One band of metallic silver on it. 15/32". Mint (9.9). $25. (Auction #134, Lot 20).

VITRO AGATE COMPANY. Opaque. Opaque marble of solid aventurine green. Nice marble. Two seams. Parkerburg WV, circa 1950-1965. 17/32". Mint (9.9). $30. (Auction #87, Lot 1).

VITRO AGATE COMPANY. Original bag. Hard bag to find. About a half dozen of these showed up recently at an East Coast antique show. $80. (Auction #96, Lot 25).

VITRO AGATE COMPANY. Original bag. Original yellow mesh bag of Conquerors. Contains about forty or so Conquerors. In great shape. $50. (Auction #100, Lot 24).

VITRO AGATE COMPANY. Original bag. Original yellow mesh bag of Conquerors. Contains about forty or so Conquerors. In great shape. $46. (Auction #83, Lot 24).

VITRO AGATE COMPANY. Original bag. Original yellow mesh bag of Conquerors. Contains about forty or so Conquerors. In great shape. $37. (Auction #79, Lot 4).

VITRO AGATE COMPANY. Original bag. Original poly bag of "VITRO CAT EYES" "40 - Made in U.S.A - 40". $36. (Auction #129, Lot 21).

VITRO AGATE COMPANY. Original bag. Original Conquerors mesh bag. Pale yellow mesh bag. Cardboard label (piece torn from one side). $28. (Auction #79, Lot 8).

VITRO AGATE COMPANY. Original bag. Original poly bag of "Vitro Cat Eyes 40 count Five Star Brand 10cents". Forty 5/8" catseyes. $21. (Auction #162, Lot 27).

VITRO AGATE COMPANY. Original bag. Original poly bag of "Vitro All Reds 30 count Five Star Brand". Thirty 5/8" All Reds. $20. (Auction #69, Lot 24).

VITRO AGATE COMPANY. Original bag. Original yellow mesh bag of Conquerors. Contains about forty or so Conquerors. Bag has some dry rot. $18. (Auction #104, Lot 26).

VITRO AGATE COMPANY. Original bags. Lot of three items. All are poly bags. Red and black label, Five Star Brand. Circa 1960s. $34. (Auction #79, Lot 12).

VITRO AGATE COMPANY. Original bags. Lot of two items. Both are older "Five Star Brand" bags. One has 12 7/8" All-Reds. Sold for 19 cents. $26. (Auction #56, Lot 23).

VITRO AGATE COMPANY. Original bags. Lot of four items. All are poly bags. All are Vitro Agate Company, Subsidiary of Paris Manufacturing. $22. (Auction #56, Lot 22).

VITRO AGATE COMPANY. Original bags. Lot of four items. All are poly bags. All are Vitro Agate Company, Subsidiary of Paris Manufacturing. $22. (Auction #56, Lot 22.20).

VITRO AGATE COMPANY. Original box. Original "Circle-X" game. Cardboard box containing a cardboard tic-tac-toe game with four white opaque. $36. (Auction #127, Lot 48).

VITRO AGATE COMPANY. Original box. Original cardboard box of "60 GAME MARBLES NO. 00". Tan box. One split corner. Minor stains. $35. (Auction #61, Lot 39).

VITRO AGATE COMPANY. Original box. Original box of "60 Game Marbles No. 00". Tan box. Vitro logo on the top. Punctures at one corner. $32. (Auction #145, Lot 25).

VITRO AGATE COMPANY. Original package. Very hard to find original Blackies poly bag. Label is white cardboard. Red background. $60. (Auction #176, Lot 24).

VITRO AGATE COMPANY. Original package. Very hard to find original Shooters poly bag. Label is white cardboard. Red background. $55. (Auction #176, Lot 26).

VITRO AGATE COMPANY. Original package. Very hard to find original Tiger Eyes poly bag. Label is white cardboard. Red background. $42. (Auction #176, Lot 25).

VITRO AGATE COMPANY. Original package. Original poly bag of "Vitro All Reds / 70 count Five Star Brand". White label. Contains seventy 5/8". $37. (Auction #107, Lot 27).

VITRO AGATE COMPANY. Original package. Original poly bag of "Vitro All Reds / 70 count Five Star Brand". White label. Contains seventy 5/8". $35. (Auction #80, Lot 20).

VITRO AGATE COMPANY. Original package. Vitro Agate 60 Game Marbles box. Tan cardboard box. Old Vitro logo on it. Has full complement of marbles. $32. (Auction #178, Lot 29).

VITRO AGATE COMPANY. Original package. Vitro Agate 60 Game Marbles box. Tan cardboard box. Old Vitro logo on it. Has full complement of marbles. $30. (Auction #178, Lot 29.20).

VITRO AGATE COMPANY. Original package. Original poly bag of forty Cat Eyes. Black and yellow printing on white label. $30. (Auction #118, Lot 28).

VITRO AGATE COMPANY. Original package. Early poly bag. Red on white header label. "14 VITRO-AGATES". Continues three color brushed patch. $29. (Auction #158, Lot 26).

VITRO AGATE COMPANY. Original package. Lot of five items. All are original poly bags. Three are 14 Count Five Star Brand Cat Eyes. $28. (Auction #127, Lot 44).

VITRO AGATE COMPANY. Original package. Poly bag with eight shooter "white parrots". Vitro Agate Company, Subsidiary of Paris Manufacturing. $23. (Auction #140, Lot 24).

VITRO AGATE COMPANY. Original package. Early poly bag. Red on white header label. "14 VITRO-AGATES". Contains three color brushed patch. $22. (Auction #161, Lot 27.30).

VITRO AGATE COMPANY. Original package. Poly bag. Label reads "FREE MARBLES When You Buy This Package". Contains fourteen tri-color patches. $20. (Auction #133, Lot 26).

VITRO AGATE COMPANY. Original package. Early poly bag. Red on white header label. "14 VITRO-AGATES". Contains three color brushed patch. $20. (Auction #161, Lot 27.40).

VITRO AGATE COMPANY. Original package. Early poly bag. Red on white header label. "14 VITRO-AGATES". Continues three color brushed patch. $20. (Auction #170, Lot 25).

VITRO AGATE COMPANY. Original package. Early poly bag. Red on white header label. "14 VITRO-AGATES". Continues three color brushed patch. $18. (Auction #170, Lot 25.20).

VITRO AGATE COMPANY. Original package. Poly bag of forty six marbles. This is the last packaging made by Vitro Agate before they were acquired. $17. (Auction #117, Lot 26).

VITRO AGATE COMPANY. Original package. Early poly bag. Red on white header label. "14 VITRO-AGATES". Contains three-color brushed patch. $17. (Auction #161, Lot 27).

VITRO AGATE COMPANY. Original package. Early poly bag. Red on white header label. "14 VITRO-AGATES". Contains three color brushed patch. $15. (Auction #161, Lot 27.20).

VITRO AGATE COMPANY. Original packages. Lot of two items. Both are poly bags. One is "Vitro AQUA JEWELS / 12 Count Five Star Brand. 19cents. $22. (Auction #152, Lot 32).

VITRO AGATE COMPANY. Oxblood. Outstanding example of a Vitro oxblood. Semi-opaque white base. Band of wispy Vitro oxblood. 9/16". Mint (9.9). $70. (Auction #98, Lot 40).

VITRO AGATE COMPANY. Oxblood. Very hard to find Vitro Agate oxblood patch. Almost transparent milky white base. 19/32". Mint(-) (9). $37. (Auction #107, Lot 8).

VITRO AGATE COMPANY. Oxblood. Excellent example. This is a patch marble with oxblood on it. White patch on transparent clear. 21/32". Mint(-) (9.1). $35. (Auction #167, Lot 32).

VITRO AGATE COMPANY. Oxblood. Early Vitro Agate marble. Brushed Conqueror style with oxblood. Transparent clear base. 19/32". Mint (9.9). $21. (Auction #122, Lot 46).

VITRO AGATE COMPANY. Oxblood. Early Vitro Agate marble. Brushed Conqueror style with oxblood. Transparent clear base. 19/32". Mint (9.9). $19. (Auction #122, Lot 46.20).

VITRO AGATE COMPANY. Oxblood. Early Vitro Agate marble. Brushed Conqueror style with oxblood. Transparent clear base. 19/32". Mint (9.9). $17. (Auction #122, Lot 46.30).

VITRO AGATE COMPANY. Oxblood. Semi-opaque white base. Patch of light blue surrounded by a patch of oxblood. One sparkle. $10. (Auction #166, Lot 37).

VITRO AGATE COMPANY. Oxblood patch. Translucent white base with and "oxblood" patch on the top. This is a "Phantom Conqueror" with an oxblood. 9/16". Mint(-) (9). $25. (Auction #134, Lot 18).

VITRO AGATE COMPANY. Parrot. Exceptional and definitive example of this type!! Opaque white base. Patches of black, aventurine green. 29/32". Mint(-) (9). $75. (Auction #59, Lot 19).

VITRO AGATE COMPANY. Parrot. Superb Parrot. Opaque white base. Black patch, yellow patch and aventurine green patch in between. 29/32". Mint (9.9). $65. (Auction #78, Lot 32).

VITRO AGATE COMPANY. Parrot. Nice Parrot. Opaque white base. Aventurine green, yellow, orange and black. Excellent white "V". 29/32". Mint (9.9). $65. (Auction #126, Lot 9).

VITRO AGATE COMPANY. Parrot. Superb example. Opaque white base. Patches of light blue, blue, lavender and yellow. Stylized "V". 15/16". Mint (9.9). $65. (Auction #167, Lot 38).

VITRO AGATE COMPANY. Parrot. Five color Parrot. Opaque white base. Patches of yellow, blue, red and aventurine green. Poor "V". 15/16". Mint (9.9). $61. (Auction #88, Lot 26.20).

VITRO AGATE COMPANY. Parrot. Five color Parrot. Opaque white base. Patches of yellow, blue, red and aventurine green. Poor "V". 15/16". Mint (9.9). $61. (Auction #88, Lot 26).

VITRO AGATE COMPANY. Parrot. Five color Parrot. Opaque white base. Patches of yellow, blue, red and aventurine green. Poor "V". 15/16". Mint (9.9). $56. (Auction #88, Lot 26.30).

VITRO AGATE COMPANY. Parrot. Five color Parrot. Opaque white base. Patches of yellow, blue, red and aventurine green. Poor "V". 15/16". Mint (9.9). $56. (Auction #88, Lot 26.40).

VITRO AGATE COMPANY. Parrot. Nice Parrot. Opaque white base. Aventurine green, blue, lavender, red and yellow. Some minor "V"s. 15/16". Mint (9.9). $55. (Auction #134, Lot 45).

VITRO AGATE COMPANY. Parrot. Nice Parrot. Opaque white base. Aventurine green, blue and red. Poor "V". Surface in great shape. 29/32". Mint (9.9). $50. (Auction #56, Lot 13).

VITRO AGATE COMPANY. Parrot. Opaque white base. Patches of green and lavender. Thin patch of blue. Some white shows through. 29/32". Mint (9.9). $50. (Auction #77, Lot 40).

VITRO AGATE COMPANY. Parrot. Super example. Opaque white core. Brushed patches of yellow, light orange, green and lavender. 7/8". Mint (9.9). $40. (Auction #60, Lot 41).

VITRO AGATE COMPANY. Parrot. Lot of two marbles. Anemic Parrots. Opaque white base. One patch of aventurine green and one of yellow. $37. (Auction #88, Lot 12).

VITRO AGATE COMPANY. Parrot. Super Parrot. Opaque white base. Patches of aventurine green, blue, lavender and yellow. 15/16". Mint (9.9). $35. (Auction #92, Lot 40).

VITRO AGATE COMPANY. Parrot. Opaque white base. Patches of aventurine green, yellow and black. A nice "V" in the black and an orange. 29/32". Mint (9.9). $35. (Auction #66, Lot 41).

VITRO AGATE COMPANY. Parrot. Opaque white base. Patches of light blue, yellow, red and aventurine green. Small subsurface moon. 15/16". Near Mint(+) (8.9). $33. (Auction #116, Lot 20).

VITRO AGATE COMPANY. Parrot. White base with blue, lavender, orange and yellow patches. The orange forms an excellent "9". 7/8". Mint (9.9). $30. (Auction #113, Lot 25).

VITRO AGATE COMPANY. Parrot. Excellent coloring on this marble. Opaque white base with patches of blue, red, aventurine green. 27/32". Near Mint(+) (8.9). $30. (Auction #161, Lot 43).

VITRO AGATE COMPANY. Parrot. Lot of three marbles. All are newer white Parrots. Opaque white base. One has blue patch. $28. (Auction #88, Lot 23).

VITRO AGATE COMPANY. Parrot. Excellent coloring on this marble. Opaque white base with patches of light blue, green, lavender. 29/32". Near Mint(+) (8.7). $26. (Auction #171, Lot 48).

VITRO AGATE COMPANY. Parrot. Newer white Parrot. Opaque white base. Light blue, yellow and orange patches. Lots of white showing. 15/16". Mint (9.7). $19. (Auction #162, Lot 12.20).

VITRO AGATE COMPANY. Parrot. Newer white Parrot. Opaque white base. Light blue, yellow and orange patches. Lots of white showing. 15/16". Mint (9.7). $19. (Auction #162, Lot 12).

VITRO AGATE COMPANY. Parrot. Lot of five marbles. The later white Parrot type. Lots of white. None with any "V"s. Parkersburg WV. $18. (Auction #60, Lot 23).

VITRO AGATE COMPANY. Parrot. Excellent coloring on this marble. Opaque white base with patches of blue, green (no aventurine). 29/32". Mint (9.9). $15. (Auction #62, Lot 9).

VITRO AGATE COMPANY. Parrot. Transparent clear base. About one half brushed light green and one half brushed white. 31/32". Mint (9.9). $10. (Auction #76, Lot 41).

VITRO AGATE COMPANY. Patch. I have only seen about a dozen of these in the past five years. Opaque white base. 29/32". Mint (9.9). $30. (Auction #87, Lot 5).

VITRO AGATE COMPANY. Patch. Superior early patch. Opaque white base of varying degrees of white. Transparent navy blue patch. 15/16". Mint (9.7). $27. (Auction #156, Lot 36).

VITRO AGATE COMPANY. Patch. Superior early patch. Opaque white base of varying degrees of white. Transparent cranberry red patch. 15/16". Near Mint(+) (8.9). $26. (Auction #148, Lot 43).

VITRO AGATE COMPANY. Patch. I have only seen about a dozen of these in the past five years. Opaque white base. 31/32". Near Mint(+) (8.9). $24. (Auction #85, Lot 31).

VITRO AGATE COMPANY. Patch. Lot of approximately one hundred twenty five marbles. Almost all are Vitro Agate patches. 19/32". $22. (Auction #177, Lot 23).

VITRO AGATE COMPANY. Patch. Lot of thirty one marbles. Includes a nice variety of patches, including Conqueror, Phantom Conqueror. $21. (Auction #108, Lot 33).

VITRO AGATE COMPANY. Patch. Opaque green base. Yellow and red patch forming a very nice "V". Parkersburg WV, circa 1970-1985. 5/8". Mint (9.8). $18. (Auction #161, Lot 18).

VITRO AGATE COMPANY. Patch. Lot of twelve marbles. All are the same color scheme. Older ones. Nice group. 5/8". Mint (9.9). $17. (Auction #140, Lot 26).

VITRO AGATE COMPANY. Patch. Nice shooter Vitro patch. Opalescent translucent white base White orange patch, edged by green. 29/32". Mint (9.9). $16. (Auction #108, Lot 8).

VITRO AGATE COMPANY. Patch. Early Vitro brushed patch. Conqueror-type. Transparent clear base. White, blue and orange brushed on. 5/8". Mint (9.6). $15. (Auction #184, Lot 18).

VITRO AGATE COMPANY. Patch. Lot of approximately forty marbles. All are blue patch on white. All about 5/8". Almost all Mint. $15. (Auction #146, Lot 12).

VITRO AGATE COMPANY. Patch. Lot of twenty seven marbles. Mostly Conquerors, with a couple of "TigerEyes". All about 5/8". $15. (Auction #180, Lot 25).

VITRO AGATE COMPANY. Patch. Lot of two marbles. Both are white base with several different color patches on them. $15. (Auction #136, Lot 1).

VITRO AGATE COMPANY. Patch. Lot of thirteen marbles. Assortment of four-color brushed patches. Nice group. About half are Mint. $15. (Auction #104, Lot 20).

VITRO AGATE COMPANY. Patch. Lot of five marbles. All are Vitro opaque patches. Very fluorescent vaseline green base. $14. (Auction #109, Lot 4).

VITRO AGATE COMPANY. Patch. Vitro Agate patch that looks just like an Akro Popeye Patch. Transparent clear with wispy white. 19/32". Mint (9.9). $13. (Auction #179, Lot 4).

VITRO AGATE COMPANY. Patch. Lot of seven marbles. Assortment of Vitro patches. All about 5/8". All Mint. $13. (Auction #102, Lot 12).

VITRO AGATE COMPANY. Patch. Lot of fourteen marbles. Assortment of patches, including five Victory. 19/32" to 5/8". Mint (9.9). $12. (Auction #102, Lot 37).

VITRO AGATE COMPANY. Patch. A Sparkler look-a-like. Colored core on one side of a transparent clear marble. Core is green, orange. 5/8". Mint (9.9). $12. (Auction #56, Lot 19).

VITRO AGATE COMPANY. Patch. Nice shooter patch. Translucent orange, opaque yellow and wispy white in clear. Parkersburg WV. 7/8". Mint (9.8). $11. (Auction #77, Lot 16).

VITRO AGATE COMPANY. Patch. Lot of four marbles. Assorment of patches. Nice, older assortment, probably 1950s. $9. (Auction #97, Lot 14).

VITRO AGATE COMPANY. Patch. Lot of two marbles. Both are four color patch on white. One has a "V". 27/32" & Mint (9.5). 29/32". $9. (Auction #180, Lot 10).

VITRO AGATE COMPANY. Patch. Lot of three marbles. All are the same basic Vitro patch. Translucent light green with wispy white. 27/32". Mint (9.9). $8. (Auction #103, Lot 12).

VITRO AGATE COMPANY. Patch. Lot of two marbles. First is a Vitro Popeye Patch. Yellow, blue, white and clear. 5/8". Mint. $7. (Auction #152, Lot 2).

VITRO AGATE COMPANY. Patch. Lot of two marbles. Both the same. Opaque white and light gray with a black patch and a red patch. $7. (Auction #180, Lot 3).

VITRO AGATE COMPANY. Patch. Transparent clear, translucent orange, translucent white, translucent green. A "V" on either side. 5/8". Mint (9.9). $7. (Auction #185, Lot 23).

VITRO AGATE COMPANY. Patch. Lot of approximately forty marbles. All are patch. Opaque type with wispy white. All about 5/8". $7. (Auction #158, Lot 27).

VITRO AGATE COMPANY. Patch. Very interesting Vitro. Two seam. Opaque white on one hemisphere, light blue on the other. 25/32". Mint (9.9). $6. (Auction #103, Lot 3).

VITRO AGATE COMPANY. Patch. Lot of eleven marbles. All are the same. Transparent light yellow bubble filled base with opaque yellow. $5. (Auction #145, Lot 21).

VITRO AGATE COMPANY. Patch. A Vitro Agate patch that resembles an Akro Agate Popeye Patch. Transparent clear base with wispy white. 5/8". Near Mint(+) (8.9). $5. (Auction #181, Lot 3).

VITRO AGATE COMPANY. Patch. Lot of two marbles. Jabo-Vitro Agate patch. Transparent clear base with one patch of yellow bands. $5. (Auction #180, Lot 14).

VITRO AGATE COMPANY. Patch. Nice, small Vitro patch. Transparent clear and wispy white base with a transparent dark green patch. 1/2". Mint (9.9). $1. (Auction #63, Lot 1).

VITRO AGATE COMPANY. Patch oxblood. A shooter Vitro patch oxblood with very minor aventurine. Semi-opaque white base. 3/4". Mint (9.9). $43. (Auction #176, Lot 35).

VITRO AGATE COMPANY. Patch oxblood. It is my opinion that this marble is a Vitro Agate. One half clear and one half opaque yellow. 5/8". Near Mint(+) (8.9). $17. (Auction #119, Lot 7).

VITRO AGATE COMPANY. Ribbon. Transparent yellow base with eight white ribbons. Two seams. One is "U" shape, the other is straight. 9/16". Mint (9.9). $22. (Auction #113, Lot 37).

VITRO AGATE COMPANY. Tri-color patch. Lot of ten marbles. All are tri-color brushed patches, in assorted colors. Parkersburg, WV. $17. (Auction #60, Lot 25.20).

VITRO AGATE COMPANY. Tri-color patch. Lot of ten marbles. All are tri-color brushed patches, in assorted colors. Parkersburg, WV. $17. (Auction #60, Lot 25).

VITRO AGATE COMPANY. Tri-color patch. Lot of ten marbles. All are tri-color brushed patches, in assorted colors. Parkersburg, WV. $15. (Auction #60, Lot 25.30).

VITRO AGATE COMPANY. Tri-color patch. Lot of ten marbles. All are tri-color brushed patches, in assorted colors. Parkersburg, WV. $12. (Auction #60, Lot 25.40).

VITRO AGATE COMPANY. Tri-color patch. Lot of ten marbles. All are tri-color brushed patches, in assorted colors. Parkersburg, WV. $12. (Auction #60, Lot 25.50).

VITRO AGATE COMPANY. Tri-color patch. Lot of ten marbles. Assortment of tri-color patch. Transparent clear base with white. $10. (Auction #119, Lot 14).

VITRO AGATE COMPANY. Tri-color patch. Lot of ten marbles. Assortment of tri-color patch. Transparent clear base with white. $10. (Auction #127, Lot 11).

VITRO AGATE COMPANY. Tri-color patch. Lot of ten marbles. Assortment of tri-color patch. Transparent clear base with white. $9. (Auction #119, Lot 14.30).

VITRO AGATE COMPANY. Tri-color patch. Lot of ten marbles. Assortment of tri-color patch. Transparent clear base with white. $9. (Auction #119, Lot 14.20).

VITRO AGATE COMPANY. Tri-color patch. Lot of ten marbles. Assortment of tri-color patch. Transparent clear base with white. $8. (Auction #127, Lot 11.20).

VITRO AGATE COMPANY. Tri-color patch. Lot of ten marbles. Assortment of tri-color patch. Transparent clear base with white. $6. (Auction #127, Lot 11.30).

VITRO AGATE COMPANY. Whitie. Lot of three marbles. One is aventurine green ribbon, the other two are aventurine aqua and green ribbons. $22. (Auction #62, Lot 21).

VITRO AGATE COMPANY. Whitie. Lot of six marbles. All are Whities, with various colored ribbons. Yellow, light blue, green (aventurine). $14. (Auction #85, Lot 20).

VITRO AGATE COMPANY. Whitie. Lot of two marbles. Both are Whities. One is an aventurine green equatorial ribbon on white. 5/8". Mint (9.9). $13. (Auction #58, Lot 21).

VITRO AGATE COMPANY. Whitie. Opaque white base with an equatorial ribbon of aventurine green (almost pearlized. Parkersburg, WV. 19/32". Mint (9.9). $3. (Auction #146, Lot 2.20).

VITRO AGATE COMPANY. Whitie. Opaque white base with an equatorial ribbon of aventurine green (almost pearlized. Parkersburg, WV. 19/32". Mint (9.9). $3. (Auction #146, Lot 2).

VITRO AGATE COMPANY. Whitie. Opaque white base. Equator is encircled by light green. Parkersburg, WV, circa 1960-1980. 5/8". Mint (9.9). $3. (Auction #105, Lot 6).

VITRO AGATE COMPANY. Whitie. Opaque white base. Equator is encircled by light green. Parkersburg, WV, circa 1960-1980. 5/8". Mint (9.9). $3. (Auction #105, Lot 6.10).